Lost
Sounds

Music in American Life

A list of books in the series
appears at the end of this book.

Lost Sounds

BLACKS AND THE BIRTH OF
THE RECORDING INDUSTRY,
1890–1919

Tim Brooks

Appendix of Caribbean and
South American Recordings
by Dick Spottswood

UNIVERSITY OF ILLINOIS PRESS
URBANA AND CHICAGO

Publication of this book was supported by grants from the
H. Earle Johnson Fund of the Society for American Music
and from the Henry and Edna Binkele Classical Music Fund.

⊚ This book is printed on acid-free paper.

Library of Congress Cataloging-in-Publication Data
Brooks, Tim.
Lost sounds: blacks and the birth of the recording industry,
1890–1919 / Tim Brooks ; appendix of Caribbean and South
American recordings by Dick Spottswood.
p.   cm. — (Music in American life)
Includes bibliographical references (p.), discography (p.)
and index.
ISBN 0-252-02850-3 (cloth : alk. paper)
1. African Americans—Music—History and criticism.
2. Sound recording industry—History.
3. Music—United States—History and criticism.
I. Spottswood, Dick (Richard Keith)
II. Title.
III. Series.
ML3479.B76   2004
781.64'149'08996073—dc21   2003001102

CONTENTS

PREFACE

George W. Johnson has always seemed to me an intriguing character. The first black recording "star," he is almost completely forgotten today. Colorful stories swirled around his life. Had he been born a slave? Was he really discovered panhandling on the streets of Washington, D.C.? When did he begin recording, and how popular were his records? Was he really hanged for murdering his wife?

In the late 1980s I began doing research to try to learn more about this elusive character. There were no books about him, and the only serious articles, written by pioneering researcher Jim Walsh in 1944 and 1971, left many questions unanswered. What followed was a long odyssey through census records, slave registers, dusty legal archives, early newspapers and catalogs, as well as trips to the beautiful old towns of Virginia's Loudoun County (where he was born), New York's Hell's Kitchen (whose streets he walked), and a New York area cemetery (where he came to rest). Finding copies of his records was a challenge, since most had been out of print for more than eighty years.

As the story of America's first black recording artist slowly came into focus, it became apparent that there were other black artists at the time, equally unrecognized, whose stories needed to be preserved. I kept running into their names in my research. So I decided to expand the study to cover all African Americans who recorded commercially in the United States prior to the explosion of interest in black music in 1920. This time period has received little attention, with some writers even denying that there *were* any recordings by blacks in the earliest days. Eventually I identified nearly forty black artists and groups who had recorded during this period. Remarkably, they represented nearly every type of black artistic expression, from a street performance like that of Johnson, to minstrelsy, vaudeville, theater, spirituals, jazz, poetry, speech, even the concert hall—a veritable cross-section of black art and culture.

My original intent was to add brief biographical sketches of these other artists, drawn from previously published work. How naive I was! There *was* nothing published about most of them, and their biographies had to be painstakingly reconstructed from original sources, just like that of Johnson. Back to the archives and microfilms, and the search for original cylinders and 78s. Many of these people were minor names in the entertainment world, so little had been written about them when they were alive. Of course their race was another reason they were ignored in "official" records and the media. Even when biographies existed (like those for boxing champ Jack Johnson), they disagreed on so many details that original research was required, especially regarding the recordings.

I hope that the reader will excuse the preliminary nature of much that appears in these pages and that others will take up the crusade and uncover more about the pioneers who introduced America to a wide range of African American culture before it became economically rewarding to do so. This book merely opens the door on a world we need to celebrate and learn more about.

These biographies are as complete as the author could make them, but there are doubtless errors as well as additional recordings and artists yet to be discovered. Additions and corrections from readers are enthusiastically welcomed; send these to me at P.O. Box 31041, Glenville Station, Greenwich CT 06831.

Tim Brooks

ACKNOWLEDGMENTS

Nobody does it alone. Like the artists profiled here, I have been helped by many hands along the way. Whether it was checking their local libraries, raiding their own files (or, in one case, giving me their files), making copies of articles or tapes of otherwise unobtainable recordings, taking pictures of important sites, or simply providing leads, researchers in the United States and around the world have responded to my inquiries during the long years this book was being researched. Some of them probably wondered if "the book" would ever actually be published. My debt, and yours, to them is immense.

Among those contributing information and advice were Lynn Abbott, George Adams (a member of the Fisk Jubilee Singers in the 1950s), Barry Ashpole, Dr. Lawrence Auspos, Arthur Badrock, Mark Berresford, Carol Blais, William Bryant, Sam Brylawski, Peter Burgis, Brigitte Burkett, Paul Charosh, Norm Cohen, Frederick Crane, John S. Dales, Prof. Allen Debus, John Devine, Sherwin Dunner, Bevis Faversham, Patrick Feaster, Harold Flakser, Ray Funk, David Giovannoni, David Goldenberg, Tim Gracyk, John Graziano, Dr. Lawrence Gushee, Lawrence Holdridge, Rick Huff, Eliott Hurwitt, Asa M. Janney, David Jasen, Bill Klinger, Allen Koenigsberg, Len Kunstadt, Gary Le Gallant, Dr. Rainer E. Lotz, Richard I. Markow, Michael Montgomery, William Moran, Kurtz Myers, Dr. Charles Poland, Steven Ramm, Quentin Riggs, Prof. Thomas Riis, Brian Rust, Howard Rye, Doug Seroff, William Shaman, Peter Shambarger, Steve Smolian, Jean Snyder, Bronwen C. Sounders, Dick Spottswood, Linda Stevens, Paul W. Stewart, Patricia Turner, Steve Walker, and Prof. Raymond Wile.

Institutions from which I drew information included the Center for Black Music Research at Columbia College, Chicago (Suzanne Flandreau, Dr. Sam Floyd); Detroit Public Library (Agatha Kalkanis); Edison National Historic Site (Jerry Fabris, George Tselos, Doug Tarr); Emerson College Archives (Robert Fleming); Greenwich Public Library; Hogan Jazz Archive at Tulane University (Dr. Bruce Boyd Raeburn); John Jay College of Criminal Justice, City University of New York (Eileen Rowland); Library of Congress (Sam Brylawski); New York City Municipal Archives (Kenneth R. Cobb); New York Public Library Theater Collection and Rodgers and Hammerstein Archive of Recorded Sound (Don McCormick); Ohio Historical Society (Thomas J. Rieder); Schomburg Center for Research in Black Culture; Sony/Columbia

Records Archives (Martine McCarthy, Nathaniel Brewster); Thomas Balch Library, Leesburg, Virginia (Jane Sullivan); U.S. Department of Veterans Affairs, Hartford, Connecticut, office; and the Historical Sound Recordings Archive at Yale University (Richard Warren).

Special thanks to the most supportive editor an obsessed author could wish for, Judith McCulloh, and to Therese Boyd for her painstaking work compiling the index.

Some of the recordings discussed here are finally being reissued on CD (see discography), but for this study I have relied primarily on original 78s and cylinders due to their superior sonic quality and the clues they reveal regarding original issue and marketing practices. For example, the form of artist credit, characterization of the musical genre, and approximate year of manufacture can all be gleaned from inspection of the original discs but not from modern reissues. Manufacturing codes in the shellac can also be revealing, at least to experts. Biographical details are in many cases drawn from original sources, due to the lack of reliable modern sources.

Early versions of some chapters appeared in *American Music, ARSC Journal, The New Amberola Graphic,* and *Storyville.* Dick Spottswood, a preeminent authority on early ethnic recording, contributed the appendix on black recording in Latin America prior to 1920 and graciously helped proof the entire manuscript.

To all those who have helped make this work possible, my sincere appreciation. Errors and omissions—and there must be many—are my responsibility.

Lost
Sounds

INTRODUCTION:
LOST, STOLEN, OR STRAYED?

One of the most honored television documentaries of the late 1960s was a *CBS News Hour* written by Andy Rooney and Perry Wolff called "Black History: Lost, Stolen, or Strayed?" That title kept coming back to me during the years in which this book was being researched. African Americans made significant contributions to the recording industry in its formative years, from 1890 to 1919, and their recordings reveal much about evolving African American culture during that period. Yet little of that aural history is now available, and less has been written about it. Is this another piece of black history that is lost, stolen, or strayed?

The stories of the first black recording artists turned out to be fascinating on several levels. It would be easy to write a book about the injustices done to African Americans over the course of the nation's history. From the cold shackles of slavery to the more subtle discrimination of modern times, America's attitude toward its black citizens has always been a stain on the national character and a source of embarrassment. The examples are many and obvious. As tempting as it might be to focus solely on the racial injustices of early twentieth-century America, it is arguably more productive—and helpful to our own time—to examine the ways in which those injustices were gradually ameliorated. How did change come about?

The stories of the first black recording artists are stories not only of barriers, but of how some of those barriers were reduced. Progress—slow and halting, to be sure—was won not so much by changes in the law, or by dramatic confrontations between "good" and "evil," as by the actions of ordinary people who when faced with instances of unfairness quietly and without fanfare "did the right thing." Through their actions they acknowledged that the "color line" was fundamentally wrong. We still have a considerable distance to travel in ensuring equal rights for all. The lessons of those times can help guide us today.

One agent of change that has been little recognized was the early recording industry.

The First Modern Mass Medium

Before television, before radio, before even motion pictures, an earlier mass medium began paving the way for the shared social experience that has so profoundly changed modern society. It startled and amazed the citizens of the late nineteenth century. Who could ever have imagined an entertainer, orator, or famous person being "bottled up," only to spring to life, as if by magic, simultaneously in hundreds of remote locations? Nothing in five thousand years of human history anticipated such a possibility. And yet here it was—recorded sound.

The public was first teased with the possibility of "bottling sound" in 1878 when thirty-one-year-old inventor Thomas A. Edison demonstrated his new tinfoil phonograph. At first it was only a laboratory curiosity. Not until a decade or so later did more or less permanent wax cylinder recordings of singers, orators, and jokesmiths begin to be heard in hamlets across America. Eventually even presidential candidates sent out prerecorded speeches on cylinders and discs in which they personally explained the issues and exhorted voters. The idea that a singer or speaker could be heard across the land, and that a person could be heard after death, was nothing short of a miracle, even to citizens in the Age of Wonders.

Generally overlooked has been the effect this revolution had on the integration of minorities into the social mainstream. Jews, Italians, and others who would hardly have been welcomed into the neighborhood in person carried their cultural values into many a genteel Victorian parlor through the medium of recordings. Once there, it can be argued, they gradually became less threatening. Blacks faced the most difficult challenge of all. Considered no more than animal chattel in the days of slavery, barely thirty years earlier, they lived in a rigidly segregated, inferior world. Entertainment was one of the few fields in which they could achieve some prominence, but until the advent of mass media this was largely a localized phenomenon. It was one thing for a black man named Bert Williams to become a stage star in liberal New York, but once his recordings began to be bought and played in homes and neighborhood entertainment establishments everywhere, at least a small step had been taken toward the acceptance of his race.

Blacks' entry into the recording studio was not easily accomplished, but it took place much earlier than most historians acknowledge. Our focus will be on the first thirty years of the industry, from 1890 to 1919, prior to the explosion in black recording in the 1920s. These are the stories of the very first black recording artists.

Mass Media and the Integration of Minorities into the Mainstream

Several overarching themes emerge from these performers' biographies. The first is the way in which a new technology provided opportunities for a minority that was excluded from other fields of endeavor. Then, as now, technology tended to gradually break down social barriers. The white, and mostly young, entrepreneurs who were struggling to build the new recording industry did not set out to change the social order. They simply did not have the luxury of enforcing irrational social conventions like "the color line." Looked down upon themselves by more established interests, such as banking and commerce, the "talking machine men" recruited any performer who could induce people to buy their records and drop nickels into their automatic music machines. If that was a black man singing "The Whistling Coon" or a black quartet singing "Swing Low, Sweet Chariot," so be it.

In the same way that media such as movies, radio, and television would later open doors to previously excluded minorities, the new medium of recording offered blacks an opportunity to be heard across America precisely because it was *not* run by the old-line, white establishment.[1]

Despite the relative openness of the recording industry, any path was rarely easy for blacks during this era. Considering what these pioneers had to overcome, their stories resemble a kind of "profiles in black courage." George W. Johnson, an ex-slave, could gain employment only by singing songs mocking his own race; likewise, Williams and Walker had to begin as "Two Real Coons" before stardom allowed them to soften their material. Even then they were boycotted by bigoted white performers like Walter C. Kelly, who would not appear on the same stage with them. In 1910 Williams was almost prevented from joining the Ziegfeld Follies due to the protests of white cast members. To placate them, Florenz Ziegfeld promised that Williams would not appear on stage with any white females.

Conservatory-trained baritone Carroll Clark chafed at being allowed to sing only sentimental songs about the Old South, while his picture was never published and his label concealed his race. Charley Case, a very popular stage humorist, lived with an even greater frustration, the persistent rumor that he was "passing for white." He eventually shot himself. On the other side of the racial divide, Polk Miller, a wealthy white Southerner and apologist for slavery, toured American with a black quartet illustrating the black music he had grown up with on his father's Virginia plantation. His 1909 Edison recordings are perhaps the most direct musical link we have to black music in the pre–Civil War South. Ironically, he was forced to quit touring by the same prejudice he had encouraged when audiences refused to accept a white man on stage with blacks.

Others tackled barriers no less formidable. Jim Europe fought successfully to establish high musical standards and improved working conditions for black musicians in New York, despite opposition from white unions. He pioneered in bringing syncopated black music to a white audience through his records. He faced down racists in the South during his Army days and became a war hero in France before being stabbed to death by one of his own musicians in 1919. His protege, Dan Kildare, was on the path to a brilliant career as a bandleader and composer when he apparently fell under the influence of drugs and died in a triple homicide in London in 1920.

Crusty composer Will Marion Cook fought other types of battles. After paying his dues in early black theater, he began to insist on artistic integrity and music that reflected his black heritage in the face of commercial pressures to do otherwise. The team of Sissle and Blake, on the other hand, largely "sold out" and gave the white folks what they wanted.[2] They nevertheless achieved unparalleled success, and reopened the Broadway stage to black musicals in the early 1920s.

Roland Hayes overcame incredible odds to make the first records of black concert music. W. C. Handy showed that a black man could extract himself from the clutches of white publishers and successfully own and publish his own music. It wasn't easy, and he almost lost everything in the early 1920s. Almost every story told here contains examples of the struggle to bring black musical culture to America.

A second major theme that emerges from these stories concerns how whites interacted with these early black artists. Race relations in the United States were not a simple matter of black versus white. To be sure there were extremists, dyed-in-the-wool racists who fought fiercely to maintain the status quo, and reformers who fought just as strongly for equality. Most whites were somewhere in the middle. Many accepted the prevailing assumption that blacks were an inferior class (e.g., ethnomusicologist Natalie Curtis Burlin's patronizing characterization of them as "a child-race") but nevertheless provided a helping hand. Sometimes they even defied the law, as in the case of the Moore family of pre–Civil War Virginia when they took George W. Johnson into their home and taught him to read and write. Later the son of Johnson's one-time owner came to his defense in a questionable murder trial, as did numerous other whites who knew him. White boxing authorities and some politicians intervened on behalf of Jack Johnson when racists were trying to run him out of the sport, and even biased newspapers had to admit that he had won his title fairly. Vernon and Irene Castle enthusiastically promoted the career of black bandleader Jim Europe, as did Joan Sawyer that of Dan Kildare (Sawyer was a suffragist, which may have given her some perspective on what it meant to be denied one's rights). Showman Flo Ziegfeld was color-blind in promoting Bert Williams and bandleader Ford Dabney, and many white hands helped Sissle and Blake, W. C. Handy, Roland Hayes, and Harry T. Burleigh further their careers.

On a human level segregation and "the color line" collided with a basic American value—that of fairness. This was perhaps most blindingly clear in the case of Jack Johnson. Eventually, something had to give.

How It All Began: The Birth of the Recording Industry

The phonograph was invented, as most schoolchildren know, by Thomas A. Edison in 1877. It was first demonstrated to the public the following year. Edison's original invention was a clumsy affair that recorded indentations on a strip of tinfoil wrapped around a revolving drum. It was barely audible, and a few playings of a newly recorded piece of tinfoil quickly obliterated it. Moreover, the tinfoil could not be removed from the drum without destroying it—hence, there were no permanent recordings. The fact that sound had been reproduced at all was a miracle, but clearly the equipment needed a lot of work. Unfortunately, after several months of demonstrating the device to an easily-awed public, Edison was compelled to put it aside in order to concentrate on his rapidly developing (and more lucrative) electric light.

For nearly ten years the phonograph lay fallow, a laboratory curiosity. Other inventors puttered with it and gradually improved it enough to arouse Edison's jealousy and anger. It had been, after all, *his* invention. In 1886, with characteristic energy, he plunged back into the field and within a year produced an improved machine, recording on more or less "permanent," removable, wax cylinders. At first both Edison and his competitors believed the phonograph's principal use would be for business dictation and for household appliances such as talking clocks. What may be the oldest playable recording now in existence (from c. 1878) is in fact the voice of a man slowly reciting "one o'clock, two o'clock, three o'clock . . . ."[3]

The production of entertainment records began on a small scale in 1888 by Edison and a few local companies, but it remained for a group of entrepreneurs in Washington, D.C., to become the principal promoters of recordings as an entertainment medium. Their enterprise was incorporated in 1889 as the Columbia Phonograph Company and is the lineal ancestor of today's Sony/CBS Records.[4] At first their products were sold not to individuals but to exhibitors who demonstrated them at fairs and in other public places. Automatic music machines (much later dubbed "jukeboxes") were set up where curious patrons could drop a coin in the slot and hear the latest popular song. The first commercial phonographs were large, expensive, battery-driven units. By the late 1890s smaller and less expensive spring-driven models had been developed and were being sold to the public at large. Records, both cylinders and the newer discs, began to find their way into the home.

During the 1890s few established performers deigned to record for the fledgling phonograph companies, which probably could not have afforded them anyway. For an established star, stage work was far more lucrative, and the primitive, squawking phonograph was a novelty item some felt was "beneath" them. In addition, recording required a special kind of voice, one that penetrated through the still-severe limitations of the technology and could at least be understood. Clarity and articulation were greatly valued (how times have changed!). Women generally did not record well, nor did softer instruments such as the piano or ensemble strings. As a result, most recordings were made by the same small group of performers, little known in the larger world of entertainment and located mostly in the recording centers of the Northeast. Virtually all of them were white, as were the businessmen who ran the industry. The phonograph was a white middle-class toy, and in the rigidly segregated America of the 1890s the idea that this "mass" medium might reach into other strata of society scarcely occurred to most people. Anyone, that is, except the hard-pressed recording companies struggling to survive. A dollar is a dollar, and several of the early entrepreneurs recognized that their white customers would pay to hear blacks entertain them on those coin-in-the-slot juke boxes, and at least some blacks would pay to hear "their own." And so the stage was set.

Who Was First?

The first black to make records for commercial sale appears to have been a middle-aged panhandler from the streets of New York City. Jovial street musician George W. Johnson became one of the best-known and most successful recording artists of his time, producing two of the biggest selling records of the entire decade of the 1890s. While many aspects of this era are shrouded in obscurity, Johnson's first recordings can be dated with some precision. Entries in the ledgers of the Metropolitan Phonograph Company of New York document that his cylinders were being sold by them in May 1890. They do not appear in a c. January 1890 catalog issued by the company, so he presumably began recording between January and May. By the summer of 1890 his cylinders were already quite popular, leading to a long and successful career in front of the recording horn. It is possible that someone obscure and unknown preceded him, but for now we will assume he was the first.

If the definition is expanded to "first to record" (not necessarily for commercial sale), there are a number of candidates. Several companies made cylinders for their own use in exhibitions in 1888 and 1889, and some of them recruited blacks to perform. A newspaper account of a phonograph exhibition given by a Mr. Wicks on January 7, 1889, at a Kansas City hotel, reported, "Then came the reproduction of a song rendered about one week ago by one of the colored waiters of the hotel. It was 'Dixie,' and the rich music peculiar to the darkey seemed admirably adapted to the phonograph. Mr. Wicks says that when the darkey first heard his song reproduced he was frightened half out of his wits. He thought he was 'hoodooed.'" An Albany, New York, exhibition in July 1889 included a cylinder by "a negro street quartet." One account said, "Negro street singers, whose melodies were caught from the office windows in New York, gave 'The Magnolia Tree,' with banjo accompaniment, in true darkey style."[5] So from the very beginning black Americans whistled "Dixie" and offered up streetcorner quartets to sing for the phonograph.

In the fall of 1889 the Missouri Phonograph Company exhibited at an exposition in St. Louis, where it made demonstration recordings by, among others, "the best colored quartettes [in the city]."[6] Other early examples of black exhibition recordings include those of the Bohee Brothers (James and George), Afro-Canadian song-and-dance men of the 1880s and 1890s whose specialty was playing dual banjos while dancing. In 1890 they were living and performing in England. The evidence that they recorded that early is a November 1890 advertisement placed by Douglas Archibald, a showman traveling in Australia, who included in his phonograph exhibition a cylinder recorded by them. Since Archibald left England for Australia around March 1890 and "likely" brought the Bohee cylinder with him, they may have recorded in 1889 or early 1890.[7] Among the other custom-made cylinders exhibited by Archibald were spirituals by "the Jubilee Coloured Concert Company of New York," possibly made during Archibald's stop in New York in April 1890 on his way to Australia.

However, the honor of "first black to record" might well belong to the aforementioned George W. Johnson. In later years a publicity item mentioned that he had recorded for Edison's original tinfoil phonograph, presumably during the tinfoil exhibition period in 1879 and 1880.

Entry of Blacks into the Record Industry

Once the commercial record industry got underway in the early 1890s other blacks followed Johnson into the studio. The first wave included performers from the black vaudeville and tent-show circuits who, though not headliners, were reasonably well known at the time. They included the Unique Quartette, which toured widely in the Northeast, and the Standard Quartette, a featured act in the touring spectacle *South before the War*. Louis "Bebe" Vasnier was a popular local minstrel performer in his hometown of New Orleans when the Louisiana Phonograph Company made him one of its star attractions. Blacks and whites alike listened to his "Brudder Rasmus" sermons on coin-slot phonographs in the city's public venues and summer resorts.

By the early 1900s more famous black performers were being engaged to record.

Bert Williams and George Walker were already stars on Broadway when the fledgling Victor Talking Machine Company persuaded them to make a few discs in 1901. Victor said that it had paid handsomely for the privilege. The Fisk University Jubilee Singers were world famous when they began recording for Victor in 1909, and Polk Miller and his Old South Quartette were nationally known at the time of their Edison sessions in that year.

Additional well-known blacks stepped in front of the recording horn during the second decade of the century. James Reese Europe was the "hot" bandleader for dancers Vernon and Irene Castle when he made the first black orchestra recordings in the United States in 1913. Following him into the studio was Dan Kildare, bandleader for Castle rival Joan Sawyer. The eminent composer Will Marion Cook led his Afro-American Folk Song Singers in a 1914 recording, and the Tuskegee Institute Singers (a chorus) also began recording in that year.

When America was swept up in the jazz craze in 1917, black artists were, appropriately, among the first to record the new music or variations on it. Wilbur C. Sweatman, Ford T. Dabney's Broadway orchestra, and W. C. Handy's Memphis musicians (most of them actually from Chicago) all made numerous discs. Noble Sissle and Eubie Blake brought ragtime and show music to record buyers, while the lively Right Quintette and the elegant Four Harmony Kings reproduced their cabaret acts. Black concert music finally began to be heard with tenor Roland Hayes's privately produced recordings in 1918 and the founding of the black-owned Broome Special Phonograph label in 1919. Broome issued historic and little-known recordings by such prominent artists as Harry T. Burleigh, Florence Cole-Talbert, R. Nathaniel Dett, and Clarence Cameron White. Public figures on record included educator Booker T. Washington and controversial boxing champ Jack Johnson.

A few black Americans recorded in Europe but not in the United States prior to 1920, among them Pete Hampton and Belle Davis. These expatriates will not be dealt with here; for more information on them the reader is urged to seek out the excellent but unfortunately little-known book *Black People: Entertainers of African Descent in Europe and Germany* by Rainer Lotz.

While white record companies were willing to record blacks, they wanted those who would appeal to white customers. Curiously, the prevailing thinking was that blacks themselves were not a market worth pursuing, so certain types of music, presumed not of interest to the white majority, were ignored. Some interesting documents have surfaced that directly address this situation. In 1915 violinist Clarence Cameron White wrote to Victor urging that it record black concert artists. The company declined, saying that blacks would not support their own and that whites cared only about excellence (implying that black artists weren't good enough). The following year the *Chicago Defender,* a black newspaper, started a campaign to find out how many blacks had phonographs, so that the information could be used to persuade the record companies to relent. Nothing came of this. (See the chapters on White and Roland Hayes for more.)

Also ignored, to the great dismay of modern collectors were folk blues and other "roots" music. The companies were probably correct in assuming that such unfamiliar sounds would find little favor with white consumers. It is notable that there were no black executives making recording decisions prior to the World War I era, when Roland Hayes and entrepreneur George W. Broome decided to market records themselves. Until then, patent laws gave effective control of the industry to three large companies, Victor, Columbia, and Edison, which ensured that there would be no smaller operators to explore peripheral genres.

Comparison of White versus Black Recordings

A question debated among record researchers is how well early recordings actually reflect the musical culture of their time. It is true that recordings are sometimes not representative of public performance styles. Record companies employed a small group of regular singers whose voices recorded well and who were available to work cheaply and for long hours. Most specialized in recording and were seldom heard by a live audience. Their "audience" was a tin recording horn, and they adapted their styles to its requirements with strong projection, exaggerated articulation, and very even modulation (the acoustic recording process was not very good at capturing soft and loud passages). Performances were generally strict readings of published music with minimal improvisation. This is why so many early recordings sound "stiff" to today's ears.

Instrumentation was also modified for recording. Orchestras were replaced by brass bands, which were in turn cut down for the cramped recording studio (only about a dozen men from Sousa's fifty-man Marine Band actually recorded as "Sousa's Band"). Vocal accompaniments were tampered with, as illustrated by the treatment of songs from the hit Broadway musical *Florodora*.[8] At least fifty-eight recordings of songs from the show were made during its original run in 1901–2. On stage these songs were performed by both female and male cast members, often as production numbers with choruses and accompaniment by the house orchestra. The showstopper, "Tell Me, Pretty Maiden," was sung by a double sextet of men and women. However nearly every vocal recording of songs from the show was by a male vocalist with piano accompaniment. Anything more than that was too complicated to record. Instrumental versions were by clarinets, banjos, zithers, and brass bands, instrumentation never heard in the theater.

Some white entertainers did preserve their public performance style on record (Al Jolson, Enrico Caruso), but they were the exception. In the main the song, not the performer, sold the record.

In contrast, black recordings appear to be relatively accurate representations of black performance style in this period. After all, the purpose of recording black artists was to offer a novelty, "Negro music" as it was heard in theaters and on the streets. While few white recording artists had outside performing careers, nearly all of the blacks who recorded did so. Most of them were not professional recording artists, but rather professional artists who were asked to record. George W. Johnson probably slurred "The Laughing Song" (for effect) much the same on the streets of New York as he did in the recording studio; the Unique and Standard quartets in the 1890s and the Fisk Jubilee Singers in the 1910s sang their fervent spirituals much the same on record as on tour; and Jim Europe's Clef Club orchestra, with its unusually large mandolin section and shouted interjections, sounded the same on record as in descriptions of its concerts. Reverend J. A. Myers and Edward Sterling Wright read poetry, Bert Williams delivered his half-spoken songs, and the Right Quintette performed their talking/singing cabaret act much as they did in public. All of these sound quite different from white recording artists of the period, and most are anything but stiff.

Even more remarkably, the personalities profiled here represent an exceptionally wide range of black music and culture, including popular and concert songs, band music, spirituals, monologues, speeches, even poetry readings. It is an aural portrait of black musical culture at the turn of the twentieth century, in considerable diversity.

Where Are These Records Today? A Plea for Preservation and Dissemination

Records by most of these artists still exist. The advent of the CD has brought a boom in the field of reissues, and while most of it focuses on rock, big bands, and jazz of the 1920s—saleable product that can bring quick profits—specialist labels such as Europe's Document label have reissued discs and even cylinders from the late nineteenth and early twentieth centuries.

Just in time, I might add. Recordings from a hundred years ago are in dire need of preservation. This is especially true of the soft wax cylinders made in the 1890s, which are highly vulnerable to deterioration and breakage. The vast majority of copies are already lost, and many of the remainder have deteriorated beyond repair, with the recorded sound barely audible under a sea of surface noise. A few examples can still be found in good condition, for example, the remarkably clear 1893 Edison cylinder described in the chapter on the Unique Quartette.

They probably won't survive much longer. It is not too late to save what is left; however, record companies and even public archives have shown little interest in preserving commercial recordings of this early era, presumably because they are not as trendy as jazz of the 1920s.[9] While record companies might be excused for focusing on profits, there is no excuse for the scandalous neglect of this earliest sound heritage by publicly funded archives. A survey by this author of the five largest public sound archives in the United States revealed that they hold only a few hundred commercial cylinder recordings from the 1890s between them; most surviving examples are in private hands. There is no organized program of preservation of publicly and privately held early recordings by transfer to modern media. Unlike flammable nitrate motion-picture film, wax cylinders do not threaten to burn down the building, so funding for their preservation has been given secondary priority. In a few more decades, the problem will in a sense be solved, as there may be nothing left to preserve.

Private collectors have been chiefly responsible for saving most of what now exists; however, they are not trained or equipped for professional preservation work,

and much has been lost through simple ignorance (see the sad story of the one surviving cylinder by early black minstrel Louis Vasnier). Moreover, when collectors
die their collections are usually broken up and sold, or sometimes simply discarded
by uncaring heirs.

Using Copyright Law to Suppress Black History

Preservation is of little value if these historic sound documents are kept inaccessible
to students and scholars. Most people are not aware that this inaccessibility is not
due to a lack of parties willing to reissue them but rather to extremely onerous copyright laws in the United States that have the effect of actively suppressing the circulation of historic recordings. Not only can present-day record companies decline
to reissue this material themselves, but they can—and do—prevent others from
doing so by legal action or by demanding exorbitant fees.

Some early recordings made by now-defunct companies have entered the public domain, but many are under the control of modern successor corporations such
as BMG (successor to Berliner and Victor) and Sony Music (Columbia). With the
cooperation of a compliant U.S. Congress, the principle of copyright as a reward for
creativity has been perverted into a tool to ensure the more or less permanent control of creative works by these huge multinational corporations. The number of
years historic recordings are owned by them, not us, has been steadily lengthened,
most recently by the quaintly named "Sonny Bono Copyright Term Extension Act"
of 1998. Under current U.S. law the earliest black recordings covered in this book
(from about 1890) will be under the control of modern corporations until 2067, that
is, for more than 170 years. Until, of course, the next "copyright term extension act."

Based on my research I estimate that approximately eight hundred commercial
recordings were made by African Americans prior to 1920.[10] The majority still exist
in some form, but about half are controlled by successor corporations that will neither release them nor allow others to do so. Of the four hundred still under copyright I know of only two that have been reissued by the copyright holders in the CD
era (see the discography). There is a demand for such recordings, as demonstrated
by the fact that more than one hundred have been reissued by overseas labels who
are not subject to U.S. law or illegally by small operators in the United States. These
are often hard to find. For legal reasons few established labels, associations, or archives are willing to risk publishing such reissues.

European countries, which seem to care more about their cultural heritage than
does the United States, generally have fifty-year copyright terms for recordings. That
is why so many reissues of early American material emanate from abroad. U.S. companies have attempted to deny those reissues to American citizens through laws
forbidding "parallel imports" of recordings they control, though these laws are often not enforced. The bottom line is that early black recorded history—indeed, all
early recorded history—is being held hostage by ill-advised laws that serve no one's
interests, except perhaps those of the lawyers who are kept employed enforcing
them. Modern record companies and artists have a right to have exclusive control
of their creations for a reasonable period (the U.S. Constitution speaks of copyright

for "limited times") and to secure effective protection against infringement during that period. But 170 years is clearly not "limited times."

I hope that our scholarly, archival, and political communities will wake up to the outrageous suppression and in some cases actual destruction of our earliest sound heritage. I have made that appeal before, and I will make it again.[11] We must act before it is too late.

Organization of This Book

Part 1 traces the life and career of George W. Johnson, the first successful black recording artist. Because so little has been written about him, and because his story is so interesting, he is treated at some length. Parts 2–5 look at black artists who followed Johnson on record in the United States. Part 6 consists of a chapter about miscellaneous, unissued, and unconfirmed recordings by blacks prior to 1920, and a few mysteries. An appendix by Dick Spottswood on pre-1920 recordings by blacks in the Caribbean and South America is followed by the endnotes, a select discography of CD reissues, a bibliography, and an index.

PART ONE
George W. Johnson,
the First Black Recording Artist

1 The Early Years

Prologue

The New York City courtroom is packed and buzzing with anticipation. Finally the judge gavels for order. He nods at the bailiff who begins to read, "the State of New York versus George W. Johnson . . . the charge, murder in the first . . ."

Suddenly the room erupts, and the judge gavels repeatedly. "Order, order! Order, or I'll clear this courtroom." He glares down at the prosecutor, a small inept-looking man, who looks back and shrugs as if to say, "Don't ask *me* what's going on."

The judge has never seen such a turnout for a case like this. There must be one hundred people in the noisy courtroom. Rows of black men and women from the defendant's neighborhood pack the seats on one side of the aisle, there to lend support and show how beloved he is in their marginal world. Opposite them, incredibly, are rows of white people, prosperous-looking citizens, businessmen in their suits and vests, even a corporate attorney who has worked to ensure that this "itinerant Negro" gets the best defense the white legal system can provide. At the defense table sit two of the leading criminal lawyers in the city, both white.

Seated between them is the defendant, a burly black man with a very dark complexion and in his early fifties, dressed for the occasion but obviously not wealthy. His well-worn face bespeaks a long life of hardship, but his expression is serene. He has been charged with beating his mulatto mistress to death while drunk. Judge Newburger has seen cases like his many times before. The city's teeming slums are filled with violence, committed by poor blacks and immigrants whom decent citizens have never heard of and certainly don't care about. This ought to be an open-and-shut case.

Rumors abound. White people have collected a substantial defense fund for him; the son of the slave master who owned him fifty years ago has come from hundreds of miles away to speak on his behalf; the white company he works for has volunteered to defend him against this murder charge. Sensing a juicy story, reporters from all the major city newspapers crowd the back of the courtroom. The judge, a politically ambitious man, knows he had better be careful.

While he continues to gavel forcefully, the judge leans over to the court clerk and whispers, "Who *is* he, anyway?" The answer, if any, is lost in the din. Finally the room quiets and the bailiff tries again, this time louder, "THE CHARGE, MURDER IN THE FIRST DEGREE."

It is Wednesday morning, December 20, 1899, New York Criminal Court.[1]

"Who Is He?"

For years the life of the first black man to record, and the first to gain a degree of fame through recordings, has been shrouded in mystery. His music survives on antique

Leesburg, Virginia, around the time George W. Johnson was born. (Woodcut in H. Howe, *Virginia,* c. 1845)

cylinders and discs, as do many references to him in early catalogs. But when and where was he born? What sort of life did he live? When did he die? And most of all, what happened at that fabled trial? We might well wonder, as the judge no doubt did, who exactly *is* this man?

The most familiar story about him originated in the 1942 book *The Music Goes Round,* the reminiscences of pioneer phonograph executive Fred Gaisberg. An important figure in the early days of the industry, Gaisberg presumably knew what he was talking about when he mentioned, in passing, "the tragic Negro George W. Johnson. . . . George achieved fame and riches with just two titles. His whistle was low-pitched and fruity, like a contralto voice. His laugh was deep-bellied, lazy like a carefree darky. His life ended in tragedy . . . [he] was hanged for throwing his wife out of a window when in a drunken frenzy."[2]

The story is false on nearly all key points. Johnson never achieved riches, he wasn't hanged, and he didn't throw his wife out a window. Since the Johnsons lived in a basement apartment, that would have been difficult. Nevertheless, Gaisberg's colorful anecdote has frequently been repeated, first by researcher Jim Walsh in a 1944 article that recounted what little was known then of Johnson's life.[3]

Walsh tried to set the record straight in a 1971 update entitled "In Justice to George W. Johnson," after he found the recollections of another industry pioneer who said that Johnson had been acquitted.[4] As with many other pioneer artists, Walsh's work was seminal, but unfortunately he had to leave a great many questions about Johnson unanswered, including when he was born, when he died, and what exactly *did* happen at the trial (the transcript could not be located).

Despite Walsh's efforts, justice continues to elude poor George W. Johnson. Erroneous stories about him—particularly about his having been hanged—continued to be printed.[5] This author is indebted to Walsh's pioneering work, and with extensive research and some extraordinary luck I have been able to fill in most of the missing pieces. The life of the first black recording artist turns out to be a more fascinating saga than anyone imagined.

George W. Johnson began making records in 1890, just a few months after commercial recording began and thirty years before blacks became prominent in the medium. He was for years the only African American whose recordings achieved wide circulation. Those recordings were extremely popular, and in fact, his "Laughing Song" was probably the best-selling record of the 1890s. Although the infant phonograph industry and its customers were nearly all white, and prejudice was strong in those days, his race was not concealed. His picture was often published in catalogs, and he was promoted as a "star" of the new medium. From all evidence he was extremely well liked within the industry, and was paid and treated as well as any white artist of the time. Yet, perhaps because of the almost total lack of information about him, Johnson is today virtually unknown to writers on black history.[6]

George W. Johnson was a New York City "street artist" when he began recording, a poor black man who whistled and sang jaunty tunes for the coins of passersby and a well-known character in the city's tenement-filled lower West Side. His life—spanning some of the most significant eras in American history, the Antebellum South, the Civil War and Reconstruction, and the inception of the age of modern mass media—began in a social order far removed from anything we can imagine today.

Wheatland, Virginia, 1846

Wheatland is a tiny crossroads in Loudoun County near the northeastern tip of Virginia. About thirty-five miles northwest of Washington, D.C., even today it is fertile agricultural country, with large farms specializing in wheat, corn, and livestock. The low, rolling hills and expansive green fields give it a peaceful serenity. George Washington Johnson was most probably born in or near Wheatland in October 1846. Neither the place nor the exact date of birth may ever be known with certainty. According to one later report, he may have been born in Fluvanna County, eighty miles to the south, and brought as an infant to Wheatland, where he grew up. There was no birth certificate, as the birth of a poor black baby was not considered worth recording in these days. It is likely that Johnson himself did not know his exact birthdate.[7]

He was later said to have been born a slave, and that was probably true, although there is some contradictory evidence.[8] His father, Samuel, was a youth who worked as a laborer for white farmers in the area. In 1850 Samuel Johnson was working on the farm of one James Niscan (or Nixon) in Wheatland. But if Samuel was at that time a slave, he was soon freed. An old county court ledger entitled "Record of Free Negroes" indicates that in April 1853 a slave owner by the name of Thomas I. Marlow set free one Samuel Benjamin Johnson. "Said man may be said to be black, has a large black mole on the right cheek, has a large protruding scar on the right side of his neck and a similar one near the left ear. Aged about 20 years, 5 feet 8 inches high."[9] This is in all likelihood George's father.

Based on census entries Samuel would have been about fifteen when Johnson was born. His mother was even younger, a mere girl of twelve or thirteen at the time of the birth. Her name is variously shown as Druanna, or the even more melodious "Ann Pretty," which was probably her slave name.[10] Little more than this can be reconstructed about George Johnson's parents. They were two illiterate teenagers and were never spoken of in his later years. There was no legal marriage among slaves at the time, and the circumstances under which George was conceived can only be imagined.

Baby George, however, had a pleasant, happy temperament. Almost immediately he made an unusual friendship that would last more than half a century. Shortly after he was born he was placed as the companion of the young son of a prosperous white farmer, George L. Moore, whose farm was adjacent to that of James Niscan (Moore may have owned Johnson's father at the time). Moore's son, named Samuel, had been born in December 1845 and was therefore less than a year older than George. The white farmer's son and the black slave boy grew up together. Legally George was considered Samuel's "bodyservant," but among children the relationship was more likely that of playmate and best friend.

George L. Moore was a prosperous farmer who had married into another well-off family, the Russells, in 1834. His 250-acre farm, "Glenmore," was assembled by his father-in-law, who sold it to his son-in-law in 1851 for $14,000—a very substantial sum in those days.[11] While it was not what we would consider today an estate or plantation, it was a sizable property and the Moores were certainly upper middle class.

Moore and his wife, Ann, had ten children between 1835 and 1855, with young Master Samuel coming in the middle. Glenmore was no doubt a bustling place in the 1850s.[12] As Samuel's "bodyservant"/companion, George Johnson would have shared a great deal of the life of this hardworking, upwardly mobile white family. A local historian remarked to me, "I have a feeling that [slaves] were more servants than slaves in that area of small owners, they were more nearly members of the family, as suggested in the case of Sam Moore and George Johnson."[13] All of the Moore children helped out on the farm at one time or another, and the family was active in Loudoun County farming and church affairs. Several of the children would later become businesspeople and one of them, Jonathan, a doctor.

Perhaps because of his large family, George Moore had only a few permanent laborers living on his farm. The 1850 census listed only one (a white man) and the 1860 tally a free black, two adult slaves, and seven slave children (aged two to twelve), as well as twelve horses and mules.[14]

George Johnson gained more than a long-lasting friendship from this early entree into the white world. Master Samuel was given instruction on the flute at an early age. As Samuel developed into "an expert flute player," it was later reported, "the slave learned to imitate the notes. Johnson could soon whistle any tune that he had ever heard."[15] The seeds of Johnson's later musical career were planted. He gained something even more important from the Moores, as well. Although Johnson's parents were both illiterate, we know from census records that by the time he was in his early twenties he was literate.[16] It is likely that the Moore family taught Johnson to read and write, even though it was illegal in prewar Virginia to teach slaves those essential skills.

Perhaps equally important, young George, with his obvious intelligence and easygoing nature, learned how to get along in the white world. Although a servant, and very dark-skinned, he accepted his station with apparent good humor and in return was treated with kindness and genuine affection by the decent, religious family that had raised him. In later years the unfairness of black subservience would begin to eat at him, and he would become wily under a veneer of affability. But in antebellum Virginia of the 1850s the social order seemed graven in stone, unchangeable, and he accepted it without question. He was fortunate to be living with a white family who treated him so well. He was envied and no doubt taunted by the field hands whose lives were so much rougher.

The region had been settled in the 1700s by Quakers, who were both pacifist and antislavery, and their influence was strong, especially in the northern portion of the county around Wheatland. Slaves in the area seem to have been fairly well treated by the local farmers, sometimes taught to read and write (despite the statutes), and not infrequently given, or allowed to earn, their freedom. This was not the Deep South of "King Cotton" and ruthless overseers. Free blacks were more common in this area than in the South at large. In the 1850s one-third of Loudoun's population of 22,000 was black, about the same proportion as in the entire South; but of those 20 percent were free, compared to only 6 percent in the South as a whole.[17]

Nevertheless the "Peculiar Institution" was a fact of life, one that demeaned and sometimes brutalized its victims. The scars on George's father may bear mute testimony to this. A slave might sell for $1,000 to $1,500 during this period. There were occasional reports of slaves attacking their white masters, and at least some overseers were armed. "Problem cases" were sold to the Deep South, and families—perhaps including George Johnson's—were often broken up.

Public opinion on slavery was sharply divided in the area. The Quakers, led by the resolute Samuel Janney, denounced the human traffic and took action, secretly operating a station in the Underground Railroad at nearby Goose Creek to smuggle slaves out of the South. But they were outnumbered by farmers like the Moores who were determined that the economic order not be disrupted. Just how far the establishment would go to suppress the mere discussion of this sensitive issue became clear in a celebrated local trial that took place during Johnson's boyhood.[18]

In September 1849, a Southern Baptist minister named William A. Smith delivered a long, intemperate address at the county courthouse in Leesburg denouncing the Declaration of Independence and endorsing the view that slavery was "right in itself, and sanctioned by the Bible." Many in the audience applauded, and no opposing view was heard. This greatly distressed Janney, who proceeded to publish two rebuttals in the Leesburg *Washingtonian* (a third was withheld because of threats against the author). Shortly thereafter a county grand jury attempted to indict Janney on the grounds that his article "was calculated to incite persons of color to make insurrection or rebellion." The charge was dropped on a technicality, but those in power were determined to "get" the troublemaker and he was indicted again in November. Most of the justices who would hear the case were slaveholders.

After a series of delays, a "show trial" took place amid considerable publicity during the summer of 1850. Janney, a well-educated and respected man, pleaded his own case, arguing both legal technicalities and the broader issue of free speech. In the process he cleverly appealed to native pride. "Can it be possible," he thundered, "that freedom of speech and of the press are so completely prostrated in Virginia that a native citizen of the county may not be permitted to answer an address thus publicly delivered, in which were maintained doctrines at variance with the sentiments of Washington, Jefferson, Madison, Patrick Henry, and all the great statesmen of Virginia?"

The justices, fearful that Janney would become a martyr, reluctantly stopped the trial—but not before giving the Quaker a stern lecture on "the necessity of great care and caution in meddling with the delicate question of slavery." Publicly Janney ignored the lecture, but the trial may have had its intended effect. He was much less active as a crusader against slavery in the following years, shifting his attention instead to writing religious histories of the Quaker movement. No other Loudoun resident of similar stature took up the cause.

George Johnson certainly heard about this famous rebuke to the antislavery Quakers. He was also doubtless aware of the headline-making trial of a local man named Daniel Dangerfield, which took place in 1859, when Johnson was twelve. Dangerfield was a Loudoun-area slave who had escaped to Pennsylvania in 1853. Six years later he was tracked down by an acquaintance of his former owner and arrested by a U.S. marshal in Harrisburg, Pennsylvania, where he was quietly working as a fencemaker and raising a family. Dangerfield was transported to Philadelphia where the U.S. Commissioner would determine whether under the terms of the Fugitive Slave Act he must be forcibly returned to slavery in Loudoun County.

The hearing attracted a great deal of attention and much sympathy for the black man, as he had so obviously become a model citizen. In addition he had already suffered great tragedy in his life. Both of his young children had died, the most recent only a week before his arrest. Abolitionists seized upon the case and turned out in force to support him; hundreds of blacks gathered around the courthouse, and 400 policemen were dispatched to maintain order. The citizens of Pennsylvania (a free state) were clearly on his side. The hearing was turbulent, with arguments and counterarguments over legal technicalities, principally how long Dangerfield had been in Pennsylvania. Although the case against the defendant seemed strong, the commissioner was apparently cowed by the outburst of public support and set him free anyway. Dangerfield was driven through the streets of Philadelphia where he was cheered by a crowd of one thousand people. The verdict was denounced by some Loudoun newspapers and applauded by others.

Most Loudoun citizens supported slavery. A revealing item in a local paper some years earlier warned white citizens against teaching slaves to read, observing that under the law doing so could earn the perpetrator "three dollars for every offense" or "twenty lashes on his bare back, well laid on." The item concluded, "Negroes, teachers and justices look to it: the order of society must prevail over the notions of individuals."[19]

In 1853 George Johnson had gained, through his father's freedom, his own. Now as he approached adolescence he realized that he must begin to fend for himself. The Moores were kind, and Master Sam his closest friend, but Glenmore had more than enough help. By 1860, when Johnson was thirteen, he was working as a houseservant on a smaller farm owned by George W. Dorrell in Broad Run, about fifteen miles from Glenmore.[20] It is likely that Johnson moved around the county during his teens, working for various white employers.

He also spent time in Waterford, a village with a population of 300–400 which served the farmers in the Wheatland area. Samuel and Druanna, George's mother and father, were living there in 1860. By that time Samuel was working for another white man, Isaac Pearson. Druanna is found only in the census of 1860, living with Samuel and three minor children who were probably George's younger brothers and sisters—Mary, age nine, Annie, age eight, and a little boy named Goodloe, age two. After this point we lose track of them completely. They seemed to have little to do with eldest son George. In Johnson's later life his mother, father, and siblings were never mentioned.

George also knew the streets of Leesburg (pop. 1,600), the somewhat larger county seat a few miles south of Waterford. Leesburg boasted shops and mills, and even an "Opera House" that featured local entertainment and traveling performers. We can only guess whether black teenager George Johnson had his first glimpse of show business peeking through the windows of the whites-only Opera House, or perhaps watching performers on the streets of Leesburg.

One might expect that 150 years later these communities would be completely changed, overrun by modern shopping malls and condominiums. That is not the case. When I visited the area in 1989, I felt that I had entered a time warp. The region is steeped in history, and both Leesburg and Waterford have been immaculately preserved, much as they were in the mid-nineteenth century when George Johnson and the Moores walked their dusty streets. The entire village of Waterford has been declared a National Historic Landmark and is the site of a three-day historic festival each October. It is an area well worth visiting.

Unfortunately, the quiet, bucolic world in which George W. Johnson grew up was about to come to a violent end.

Johnson's World Disintegrates

The trouble began about ten miles north of Glenmore, at the convergence of the Shenandoah and Potomac Rivers. That was the location of Harpers Ferry, a bustling trading town that was also the site of a federal arsenal. On the night of October 16, 1859, without warning, the arsenal was attacked and seized by a band of sixteen whites and five blacks, led by the notorious white abolitionist John Brown. A violent man, Brown had been involved three years earlier in the slaughter of proslavery settlers in Kansas known as the "Pottawatomie Massacre." In 1858, at a remarkable convention of blacks and whites held in Canada, he had announced that he intended to establish in the mountains of Maryland and Virginia a free state to which black slaves might escape and where they could defend themselves. Apparently no one knew that he was lurking in the Harpers Ferry area, however, and the sudden attack—which threatened to instigate a slave uprising throughout the South— struck terror in the hearts of the white establishment.

George W. Johnson: The Early Years

Brown took some sixty local citizens hostage and held out for a day and a half before being overcome by a hastily dispatched detachment of Marines commanded by Col. Robert E. Lee. The fighting was fierce, with fifteen killed and Brown himself seriously wounded. As neither blacks nor whites in the area had any forewarning of the attack, there was no uprising to support him. Brown was quickly tried and on December 2 he was hanged, becoming one of the great martyrs of American history.

The white farmers and landowners of Loudoun County, just across the river from Harpers Ferry, reacted with what can only be described as panic. Rumors spread like wildfire of five hundred men in revolt a few miles to the north, a militia was quickly raised to "guard" the county's borders, and local newspapers railed against "the insane and atrocious attempt of the Abolitionists to excite a servile insurrection in Virginia and the South." The governor was petitioned to send arms, and travelers and transient peddlers were stopped for fear their real purpose might be to spread rebellion. Were more John Browns coming? As one historian put it, "the hysteria of Loudouners remained at a fever pitch into 1860."[21] Tension and suspicion between blacks and their masters in Loudoun County must have been considerable. Race was the one subject Johnson and his teenage white friend, Sam Moore, could not easily discuss.

The turmoil and fear of the winter of 1859–60 was only a prelude to the firestorm that would engulf George Johnson's world during the next five years. His own Loudoun County was about to become one of the major battlegrounds of the Civil War.

The Civil War

Tensions between North and South mounted steadily throughout the summer of 1860, as the presidential election approached. Loudouners were badly split, opposed to secession but unwilling to repudiate the old order. Abraham Lincoln, the Northern Republican strongly associated with abolitionism, had little local support in the four-way presidential race, but neither did either of the Democratic candidates, the South's fire-breathing John C. Breckenridge or the North's Stephen A. Douglas. Instead, Loudouners voted for John Bell of the Constitutional Union Party, who evaded the slavery issue and instead stressed preservation of the Union. Abraham Lincoln received only eleven out of the three thousand votes cast in the county.[22]

Even after Lincoln's election in November, and the secession of several Southern states, Loudoun's leaders struggled to find ways to keep Virginia in the Union. But events outraced them. A month after Lincoln was inaugurated on March 4, 1861, South Carolina fired on the federal garrison at Fort Sumter. Five days after that a special state convention in Richmond recommended that Virginia join the Confederacy (Loudoun's two representatives voted against secession). Public opinion turned swiftly as the North prepared for war, and secession was approved in a May 23 referendum (George Moore and his eldest son, Henry, voted "for").[23] The western portion of the state, a nonslave area, immediately took steps to separate and in 1863 West Virginia became a separate, Union, state.

George Johnson, now a teenager, appears to have remained in the area throughout the war, but it must have been a fearful time. The fury of the Civil War broke directly over his head. Confederate and Union armies alternately swept across the county, the former attempting to encircle Washington or seize Harpers Ferry and the latter attempting to beat them back. The Moore family sided with the Confederacy, and at least two of its sons, Henry and Samuel, joined the Confederate Army. Henry was killed in battle in 1864 in the Wilderness Campaign near Fredericksburg. His body was laid to rest in a small cemetery near Glenmore. Samuel, George Johnson's white friend, was only fifteen when hostilities broke out and did not join the Confederate Army until late in the war. He returned unscathed.

Forty-six battles and skirmishes took place in Loudoun County between 1861 and 1865, some just miles from Glenmore.[24] The fiercest battles occurred early in the war. These included, in 1861, the bloody battles of Manassas–Bull Run (twenty-five miles to the south) and of Ball's Bluff, and in 1862, Sharpsburg-Antietam (twenty miles north) and the capture of Harpers Ferry by the Confederates, the latter involving the largest Union surrender of the war, more than 12,500 men. There were constant troop movements through Loudoun, as Union armies chased the Confederates south following the battles of Gettysburg (1863) and Monocacy River (1864). At times, as after Antietam, the area around Wheatland and Waterford was filled with field hospitals full of wounded and dying soldiers from the nearby battlefields.

During 1863–65 Loudoun County became the principal operating territory for Confederate Colonel John S. Mosby, the "Gray Ghost," whose hit-and-run guerrilla tactics against Union forces became legendary. Vexed by the elusive Mosby, General Ulysses S. Grant in November 1864 finally sent in a Union division to destroy the entire agricultural capability of Loudoun, burning barns and crops and driving off livestock. Local farmers, including the Moores, were devastated.

Blacks did not take part in the battles but both slaves and free blacks were conscripted as laborers by both sides. Early in the war the Confederates used such conscripts to build fortifications around Leesburg.[25] Since George Johnson was in the area throughout the hostilities it is most likely that he took part in the "white man's war" at the end of a shovel. We get a glimpse of the world he was living in through the vivid memoirs of a Union soldier whose regiment marched through Leesburg in December 1862.

> By eight in the morning had fallen in and were ready to move. Soon we were off in an easterly direction. The road was dry and hard and smooth so we marched briskly. That afternoon we passed through Leesburg, a large old-fashioned town with many fine residences. The people were very "secesh" and did not seem to enjoy our coming. We gave them all the music we had; the fifes and drums, and sang "John Brown's Body" as well as we knew how. Only a few colored people showed themselves in the streets and the houses were fast closed. We camped that night beyond the town, footsore and lame.[26]

By the time the Confederacy crumbled in 1865, Loudoun's economy was in ruins. Many of its sons had been killed, and its crops and buildings had been burned. However, agricultural country can regenerate itself. George Moore and other landowners set to work rebuilding their lives and by 1870 Glenmore was valued at even more than it had been before the war—although the Moore family's personal wealth had suffered. Census records show that from 1860 to 1870 the value of the Moore property increased from $15,500 to $20,500; the family's personal estate, however, declined from $8,800 to $2,200.

George Johnson, now in his early twenties, remained in the area but he found paying work hard to come by and conditions oppressive. Most newly freed blacks became laborers or tenant farmers. While they were not subjected to the outrageous mistreatment common in other parts of the South (there was no Ku Klux Klan in Loudoun), they were still second-class citizens, frequently harassed and subject to stiff sentences for infractions of the law.

By 1870 George Johnson was employed as a laborer, living with Matthew and Ann Lee of Arcola, a few miles south of Leesburg (just outside the boundaries of present-day Dulles Airport). As this is his first census listing as an adult, we gain one more piece of firm information about him—he is able to read and write. According to one later report, he may have even taught school for a while.[27]

Moving North

For George Johnson, as for a great many other blacks in the rural, postwar South, the lure of the North was irresistible. Here was a chance to begin a new life, free from the oppression of an old order that, seemingly, would never change. Unfortunately we have only fleeting glimpses of him during the next twenty years. One article reported that he "came North" in 1873; his death certificate states that he had been a resident of New York City since 1876.[28]

Whenever it was that Johnson moved north—we shall assume it was in the mid-1870s, when he was in his late twenties—once there he eked out a marginal existence as a street musician. As a newspaper article later put it, "after slavery days he became a traveling musician and drifted to New York."[29] A 1900 Edison publicity piece painted an even more colorful picture of these years, saying "He was born a slave 'way back in '46 and has had a checkered career. He came North in 1873, and first attracted public notice as a whistler on excursion boats and on the ferries. Those were days when the signs 'Playing of Musical Instruments Positively Forbidden' were not in existence, and many a rich harvest he reaped by his novel entertainments. He made records for the Phonograph in 1877 when it was in the tin foil stage of existence, and they were wonderful records too, as the method of recording by indentations seemed to adapt itself wonderfully to whistling."[30]

A few comments are in order regarding the reference to tinfoil recordings. This must have occurred in 1878 or 1879, if it happened at all. Thomas Edison built the first working phonograph in December 1877 and introduced it to the public at large during the spring of the following year. It was demonstrated for President Rutherford B. Hayes at the White House in April 1878. From mid-1878 into 1879 it was exhibited widely by traveling showmen, who would charge a few cents to show a crowd the "miracle" of a machine that could talk, and record a few of the onlookers' voices.[31]

Recordings were made by wrapping a sheet of tinfoil around a grooved drum, then rotating the drum while speaking (or shouting) into a horn that created indentations in the soft foil. There were no "permanent" recordings, since after a few playbacks the soft indentations were worn flat, and the recording destroyed. Also, removing the tin foil from the drum immediately destroyed the recording. If George W. Johnson did make tinfoil recordings in the late 1870s it was probably as a street whistler employed by one of the itinerant showmen to demonstrate how wonderfully his piercing whistle could be reproduced.

There is conflicting evidence as to whether Johnson had any sort of larger show-business career during the 1870s and 1880s. No reference to him has been found in any contemporary theatrical source, and later accounts suggest that if he had any experience on the stage, it must have been minor. One later article did suggest that around 1872 he traveled to Europe with the famous Georgia Minstrels, married a white woman he met in Vienna, and fathered a daughter after they returned to the U.S. The story is puzzling, as all census reports list him as single, and there is no hint elsewhere that he ever had a child. He also does not seem to have had any permanent abode. The 1880 census showed him living in the household of a black laundress named Martha Erbey at 321 West 42nd Street, New York. According to New York City directories in 1884 he was living at 456 Ninth Avenue, in 1885 at 481 Seventh Avenue, and from 1888 to 1890 at 225 West 27th Street. These were all tenements in the Tenderloin or "Hell's Kitchen" section of the city. His occupation, interestingly, was given as "musician."[32]

Though Johnson's income was marginal, his friendly, engaging personality and ability to put white people at ease was evident from the beginning. He was able, it seems, to make friends in social classes far above his own. A fascinating item in 1899 reported that Johnson "got his start as a entertainer through a subscription of $100 raised by former Governor Levi P. Morton, on an occasion when Mr. Morton heard Johnson sing and whistle coon songs at a friend's house."[33]

Morton was an extremely influential New York businessman and politician. He served as a U.S. congressman from 1879 from 1881 and minister to France from 1881 to 1885, was elected vice-president of the United States under Benjamin Harrison (1889–93) and then governor of New York (1895–97). Briefly a candidate for president in 1896, he later became a wealthy banker. For such an important man to have "sponsored" this black street musician's early career suggests that Johnson was well-liked indeed.

Numerous references in later years indicate that Johnson was essentially a street entertainer, beloved in the slums on the west side of Manhattan. According to one, "Johnson, who is well known about the Tenderloin . . . was a slave in the South. He makes a living by whistling in the streets. His notes are as perfect, it is said, as those of a flute."[34] Another noted that "When not regularly employed, Johnson makes a living by whistling in the streets. His notes are as perfect as those of a flute."[35]

Up to 1890, at the age of forty-four, George W. Johnson had lived an interesting but not exceptional life. Then something happened that would put him in the history books.

2 Talking Machines!

After the exhibition of his first crude tinfoil apparatus in 1878–79, Thomas Edison virtually abandoned the phonograph to work on the electric light. He did not return to work on it until 1886, when the expiration of his major commitments to the electric light, and the hot breath of competition from other inventors working on sound recording, brought him back into the fray. By 1888 Edison had produced an "improved" phonograph, this one capable of producing permanent recordings on wax cylinders.

Eventually a sales organization called the North American Phonograph Company secured the rights to both Edison's new phonograph and a competing machine invented by Chichester Bell and Charles Sumner Tainter and began marketing them. The company divided the country into exclusive territories, each with its own local distributor owned by local interests. Since early attempts to market the phonograph as a business dictating machine foundered, several of these local companies turned to producing musical cylinders to be played on "coin-in-slot" machines that they set up in public places. By 1891 more than 1,250 such machines were in operation throughout the United States.[1]

Problems, of course, persisted. The recording equipment was crude and the sound faint. Patrons had to listen through rubber ear tubes. Stringed instruments such as pianos and violins, ensembles, and women singers did not record very well at all. Better results were obtained from brass instruments, flutes, and whistlers. Here was an opportunity for George W. Johnson's particular talent.

Enter Victor H. Emerson, a twenty-four-year-old telegraph operator and part-time employee of the struggling New Jersey Phonograph Company. Fascinated with the potential of this wondrous new talking machine, he enthusiastically pitched the idea of making musical recordings to the owners of the company. They initially resisted but, with their business on the brink of collapse, finally agreed. Emerson quickly set about finding some "talent." He later described what happened that summer day in 1890. "I set up ten recording machines and one day heard on the street a 'mud gutter band' of four pieces playing 'Boulanger's Patrol.' The leader said that they wouldn't work cheap—no use asking him. We finally closed the bargain at $3.50 for all of the four men for the afternoon. We made 500 records and sold them for two dollars each."[2]

Emerson needed more musicians, preferably cheap and loud. What about that middle-aged black man with the melodious whistle and hearty laugh he'd seen performing for coins at the Hudson River ferryboat terminal? Johnson listened to the proposition of the neatly dressed young man and said, "Why, sure . . . how much did you say you would pay?" "Twenty cents a song," said Emerson, "and you can work all afternoon." "Well, suh, just show me where you want me to go," said Johnson, throwing in one of his hearty laughs for free. Emerson had his second recording artist.

It was a surprisingly long trip, but Johnson did not complain. A ferry ride across the Hudson River, then a long trolley ride to Newark. Emerson led him to a small storefront at 758 Broad Street marked "New Jersey Phonograph Company." The front office was modest, striving to look like the home of a prosperous new business but not quite convincing. In the cluttered back room was the "recording laboratory"—a row of half a dozen battery-powered cylinder phonographs, about the size of small sewing machines, lined up in a shallow semicircle. Their straight black horns all faced the point where Johnson was to stand, like the rifles of a firing squad ready to exact a terrible price if he did not do as he was told.

These big, battery-driven phonographs did not look like the tinfoil machine that Johnson remembered from a dozen years earlier. That was a small, delicate-looking device that you cranked by hand as you bent over the revolving drum and bellowed into the small mouthpiece. Groups of them never ganged up on you. But Emerson assured him that these new machines worked more or less the same way. "Sing loudly and clearly," he said, "and *don't* make any mistakes. If you do we have to stop, shave down all the cylinders, and start all over again." Johnson himself had to announce each selection at the start, giving the title followed by his name. After all, the people hearing these disembodied songs on a machine in some distant place, at some future time, would not be able to see him.

What would he sing? Johnson knew all the popular street songs of the day, "Down Went McGinty," "Little Annie Rooney," "Listen to the Mocking Bird" (a favorite of whistlers). He could even whistle the new "Washington Post March" recently introduced by Sousa's U.S. Marine Band. But Emerson was more interested in a "coon song" novelty in which the black man made fun of himself. It is unlikely that Johnson enjoyed singing this insulting song, written a few years earlier by the

The earliest known picture of George W. Johnson, c. 1892, when he was in his mid-forties. This cut appeared in several catalogs. (*Phonogram,* Dec. 1892)

white vaudevillian Sam Devere and featured in touring minstrel shows, but it always brought a shower of nickels from the white folks. They seemed to find the sight of a portly, cheerful black man singing about his own fat lips and "cranium like a big baboon" uproariously funny. When you were hungry and needed money to eat, you sang whatever they wanted you to.

Emerson seemed like a nice enough young man, but like all the others was oblivious to what this might mean to a black man. Johnson didn't let on that it meant a thing to him. He simply positioned himself in front of the horns, while Emerson simultaneously started the six machines. As instructed, he announced as clearly as possible, "'The Whistling Coon,' as rendered by George W. Johnson." Then, as a bored-looking man at the beat-up piano began to play a tinkly accompaniment, he launched into his jaunty street song.

The Whistling Coon

Oh, I've seen in my time some very funny folks,
But the funniest of all I know,
Is a colored individual as sure as you're alive,
He's black as any black crow . . .
You may talk until you're tired, but you'll never get a word
From this very funny queer old coon . . .
He's a knock-kneed, double-jointed, hunky-plunky moke
But he's happy when he whistles this tune . . .
(Whistles refrain)

He's got a pair of lips, like a pound of liver split,
And a nose like an injun rubber shoe,
He's a limpy, happy, chuckle headed huckleberry nig,
And he whistles like a happy killy loo . . .
He's an independent, free and easy, fat and greasy ham,
With a cranium like a big baboon . . .
Say! I never heard him talk to anybody in my life,
But he's happy when he whistles this tune . . .
(Whistles refrain)

He'd whistle in the morning, thro' the day and thro' the night,
And he'd whistle like the devil going to bed . . .
Why, he'd whistle like a locomotive engine in his sleep,
And he whistled when his wife was dead . . .
One day a fellow hit him with a brick upon the mouth,
And his jaw swelled up like a balloon . . .
Now he goes along shaking like a monkey in a fit,
And this is how he whistles that tune . . .
(Whistles unsteadily)[3]

For his big ending, Johnson then whistled his way out with a bit of "Way Down upon the Swanee River" from Stephen Foster's "Old Folks at Home," an old favorite written nearly thirty years earlier. The comic third verse (shaky whistling after he's "hit upon the mouth"), followed by this unexpected bit of Southern pathos always wowed the crowd.

A traveling phonograph exhibitor in the early 1890s. Note the eartubes through which patrons listened to the glass-enclosed cylinder phonograph. Johnson's laughing and whistling songs were favorites with such exhibitors. (Library of Congress)

There were more verses to "The Whistling Coon," but this was all that would fit in the two- to three-minute recording time of the little brown wax cylinders. Emerson nodded, reset the machines, and slid on new blanks. Recordings could only be made one at a time—there was no way to duplicate them—and in order to build up enough stock to sell Johnson would have to keep singing and whistling this tune all afternoon. At twenty cents a "round," that was all right with him. He had strong lungs and had had plenty of practice. By the end of the afternoon he would be $4.00 or $5.00 richer. That was a week's work for a lot of people.

Emerson had reason to be pleased, too. He'd paid Johnson an average of five or six cents for each saleable cylinder (twenty cents for three or four at a time, more or less) and sold them to exhibitors for $1.00 to $1.50 each. Even taking into account overhead and the cost of the wax blank, there was money to be made.[4] Even greater profits awaited once the New Jersey company was able to install more of its own musical coin-slot machines in public places that fall. A single popular cylinder might bring in $20.00, $30.00, or even $50.00 in nickels before it wore out.[5]

At the same time he was making recordings for Emerson, Johnson was also selling his talents to another phonograph company. The New York Phonograph Company, located on Fifth Avenue in Manhattan, expanded its recording program during the spring of 1890 and upon hearing Johnson's sidewalk entertainment also wanted some cylinders. It is quite possible that Johnson recorded for New York first, since surviving ledgers for the company indicate that it was selling Johnson's cylinders as early as May 1890. At that time the company (through its affiliate the Metropolitan Phonograph Company) obtained its musical cylinders from an independent recording engineer named Charles Marshall, whom it paid and who in turn recorded and paid the artists. So Johnson may have originally been recruited by Marshall.

New York had Johnson's "Whistling Coon" and "Laughing Song" both in stock as of June 1890, and it began paying him directly for its own recording sessions beginning in late July. The first payment is dated July 22, followed by thirteen more sessions in 1890 alone. The ledgers indicate that Johnson was paid an average of $4.00 for each session, totaling $55.00 for the last six months of 1890—a healthy supplement indeed for a street musician used to living on perhaps a couple dollars a week.[6]

No files survive for the New Jersey company and no published catalogs earlier than late 1891. However, we have the rather specific reminiscence of Victor Emerson, in mid-1907, that Johnson was the second artist he recruited for them, seventeen years earlier. That would also backdate to mid-1890, when New Jersey was just getting into the coin-in-slot business. Johnson was definitely recording for both companies by the end of the year. Theoretically, since he lived in New York that company could have claimed him as its exclusive artist, but it apparently did not object to the New Jersey cylinders.[7]

Since Johnson began recording in early 1890 he was not, as Emerson later claimed, "the first man who made commercial records for the public," although he was clearly one of the first. The Edison laboratory had begun recording musical "phonograms" for the benefit of its local agents in late 1888, and the Columbia Phonograph Company of Washington, the New York Phonograph Company of New York State, and its affiliate the Metropolitan Phonograph Company of New York City all initiated their recording programs in 1889, at least on a small scale. Other local companies may also have begun recording in 1889. By early 1890 both the North American Phonograph Company and Columbia were publishing catalogs of their musical cylinders.[8]

In January 1891 the first industry trade paper, the *Phonogram,* was launched. It mentioned few recording artists in that first issue, but an interesting item in a chatter column remarked, "One of the hardest instruments that we have tried to [record] is the organ, and the easiest is the English concertina. Negroes take better than white singers, because their voices have a certain sharpness or harshness about them that a white man's has not. A barking dog, squalling cat, neighing horse, and, in fact, almost any beast's or bird's voice is excellent for the good repetition on the phonograph."[9]

Since no other black person is known to have recorded this early, and Johnson quickly became very well known, this January 1891 reference is almost certainly to him. In March a recording of "The Whistling Coon" (presumably Johnson's) was mentioned as requiring an encore at a phonograph exhibition given at New York's Standard Theatre, and in May Johnson's name appeared in print for the first time in connection with recording. A report of a "phonograph concert" held in Pittsburgh on May 14, 1891, listed nine titles as having been played for the assembled audience of two hundred, among them "The Whistling Coon" and "The Laughing Song" by George W. Johnson. These could have been either New Jersey or New York cylinders.[10]

"The Laughing Song" was Johnson's other big number, and it proved just as popular as "The Whistling Coon." It was evidently written by Johnson himself (at least, it was copyrighted by him, and no other composer was ever credited with it). Its clever, intricate lyrics, with phrases such as "a quiet bit of chaff" and "if he had not been a quince," suggest a talented, literate writer—or someone who had a lot of help. It was, however, the same "coon song" mockery of the black man.

The Laughing Song

As I was coming 'round the corner, I heard some people say,
Here comes the dandy darkey, here he comes this way . . .
His heel is like a snow plow, his mouth is like a trap,
And when he opens it gently you will see a fearful gap . . .
And then I laughed . . .
(Laughs heartily in time with the music)

They said his mother was a princess, his father was a prince,
And he'd been the apple of their eye if he had not been a quince . . .
But he'll be the king of Africa in the sweet bye and bye,
And when I heard them say it, why I'd laugh until I'd cry . . . And then I
    laughed . . .
(Laughs to the music)

So now kind friends just listen, to what I'm going to say,
I've tried my best to please you with my simple little lay . . .
Now whether you think it funny or a quiet bit of chaff,
Why all I'm going to do is just to end it with a laugh . . .
And then I laughed . . .
(Laughs to the music)[11]

What made this silly little song irresistible was its chorus, in which Johnson laughed in time with the music. It sounds nonsensical, and it was, but it never failed to draw grimaces, smirks, and guffaws from the most jaded listeners to the coin-slot machines. Who would not find amusement in the sound of uproarious laughter accompanied by a catchy melody?

Moreover Johnson's performance *sounded* authentic, just like the black panhandler on the street. This was far more unusual than it might seem, for in the early days of recording most artists sang in distinct, stilted, almost shouted tones, striving above all else to make the words very clear and understandable. When they imitated blacks, in sketches and song, they were so broad and mannered as to be almost cartoonish. But here was the real thing, a black street singer doing just what he did for nickels on the sidewalks of New York. More than in "The Whistling Coon" (a stage song), in "The Laughing Song" Johnson slurred phrases, used broad *as* and dropped his *gs* to great effect: "As I wuz comin' roun' the corner, I . . . heard some people saay / Here comes—a daandy daarkey, here 'e comes this waay . . ."

Later in the song, words like "gently" and "Africa" became "jintly" and "Afriker," and when he launched into his deep, full-throated laugh at the chorus he would interject, almost as if in a drunken slur, "I couldn'a help fr'm laffing, a-ha-ha-ha-ha-ha-ha!" Miraculously, he did it all in a way that was nevertheless quite intelligible, no mean feat on the primitive recordings of the day. No wonder these unique records fascinated the listening public.

Johnson's two songs, one showcasing his whistling and other his hearty laughter, quickly became the rage on coin machines around New York. So popular was "The Whistling Coon" that it was interpolated into the stage play *The Inspector*, performed by Johnson himself. The play, which opened in November 1890, was said to be a realistic depiction of New York City police work, and was set in part at the West 30th Street police station, in Johnson's real life neighborhood. Johnson also doubled as a "barker" in the play. The New York Sun commented, "George W. Johnson, the whistling Negro in the Battery scene of *The Inspector*, is a familiar figure on the North River ferryboats, where he whistles for pennies. . . . When dramatist [Will R.] Wilson approached Johnson on the subject of joining his company the whistler stuck out for a fair salary. He said that he could pick up over $15 on the boats, and get a regular salary from a phonograph company for whistling in their machines. Wilson had to pay him $25 a week. Since his engagement he has had an offer from Mrs. William K. Vanderbilt, who wishes him to whistle for her one night after the theater performance. Mrs. Vanderbilt will not go to a variety theatre, but she is anxious to see all the best performers."[12]

The following year brought proof that Johnson's surprise success with the two local phonograph companies was no fluke. Unlike the ephemeral popular songs of the day, his two specialties became instant standards, closely identified with the emerging entertainment phonograph. They never failed to entertain and their novelty never seemed to wear out; anyone operating a phonograph parlor or display *had* to have them. With such great demand—and no way to produce duplicates—the companies called Johnson back again and again to make more. According to its ledgers the New York company paid him for twenty-three sessions in 1891, and he probably did as many or more for Emerson in Newark. In addition, on June 1, 1891, Johnson spent two and a half hours at Edison's laboratory in West Orange, New Jersey, making cylinders for the parent North American Phonograph Company to distribute to companies around the country. Remarkably, log sheets for this session exist. No titles are shown, but they almost certainly included "The Whistling Coon" and "The Laughing Song." Johnson's specialty is given as "whistler and song" and he was accompanied on piano by Edward Issler, a well-known recording accompanist and bandleader of that day.[13] Additional sessions were held by North American in October 1891 and August 1892, and there may have been others.

The recording business was as intensively competitive at its birth as it is today, and Johnson's sudden success immediately attracted competing versions of "The Whistling Coon." This would be no free ride. The most serious threat was from the Columbia Phonograph Company of Washington, the most aggressive marketer of musical cylinders in the country. Columbia not only sold its products within its own territory but it was also accused of "poaching" on the other companies' exclusive territories by selling direct to their customers by mail. Almost as soon as Johnson's "Whistling Coon" began to catch on in New York, Columbia ordered copies from the New York company and then rushed out its own versions by its two most popular stars, the immensely popular U.S. Marine Band in November 1890 (instrumental), and "artistic whistler" John Y. AtLee in December (vocal and whistling). AtLee, a government clerk by day, was a diminutive white man with a large, drooping mustache and an exceptionally loud, piercing whistle. Columbia promoted him heavily, and his version of "The Whistling Coon" was featured in its catalog for the next four years. He added a version of "The Laughing Song" in 1892.

Other white artists copied Johnson's hits. Columbia had a second version of "The Whistling Coon," by A. C. Weaver, in its catalog in 1894.[14] However no other recorded versions came close to the success of Johnson's originals. This is truly remarkable considering Columbia's marketing might and the fact that *its* version was by a white man who, one might suppose, would be more acceptable to white patrons. In addition, songs were not generally associated with specific singers at this time; any company that could get its version to the customer first, and cheapest, would get the order. New Jersey fought back with a daring strategy for those race-conscious days. It not only publicized the fact that Johnson was black but even printed pictures revealing his very dark complexion. Johnson's obvious good nature (he was a "safe Negro"), and the comedy of a black man mocking his own race, won over listeners everywhere. The songs quickly became his alone. In his own quietly determined manner, he undoubtedly fought to keep it that way.

The song "The Whistling Coon" was quite popular at this time in live vaudeville performances, especially as sung and played by its composer, Sam Devere. Devere (1842–1907) was an old trouper and banjo virtuoso whose career stretched back to the 1860s. Evidence of the rough-and-tumble nature of touring shows is found in the story that Devere once killed a man with his banjo during a brawl in Texas.[15] He was still very popular in the 1890s, and "The Whistling Coon," published in 1878, was his biggest number. A January 1891 review of his troupe at Miner's Bowery Theatre in New York reported, "Sam Devere's company made its reappearance at this theatre Jan. 26, and packed the house at both performances. . . . The Bowery theatregoers are always with Sam Devere. The boys help him sing and whistle, and we think they would help him play his banjo if they could."[16] Devere never recorded.

Except for occasional Edison/North American sessions, Johnson seems to have recorded exclusively for the New Jersey and New York companies from 1890 until 1893. New York's ledgers show eight Johnson sessions in 1892 and two in the spring of 1893, after which the financially troubled company began to wind down its operations, eventually going bankrupt. Johnson continued as a best-seller for New

Jersey, however, and recorded exclusively for it from 1893 to 1895. Not content to let North American be its sales agent, the firm soon began shipping Johnson's cylinders throughout the United States. Many of the local companies developed exclusive "star" talent in a similar manner, distributing their cylinders both in their own territory and to other local companies for exhibition in other parts of the country. Few were as successful as New Jersey with its George W. Johnson records.

Johnson's cylinders found their way all over America. A traveling exhibitor in New England gave this report in the July 1892 *Phonogram.* It sheds light not only on Johnson's considerable popularity but also on how most Americans first heard the phonograph.

> I bought a treadle machine in Boston, and gave my first show at Haverhill the afternoon and evening of October 1, 1891. I took in nearly $18 that evening and have done as well many other evenings since. . . . I have taken about $75 in the past six days in Waterbury. . . . I came here a stranger, looked the ground over, secured a small open space on a good street, fixed a small platform and cotton canopy over all and opened up. Business has been good from the start, and I shall stay as long as it pays. I put up around my stand one or two nicely lettered signs, and the phonograph does the rest of the talking. I use no humbug or claptrap to secure attention.
>
> My patrons are of all classes—rich and poor, young and old, male and especially *female.* I go to schools, colleges, asylums, etc., etc., wherever I have paying inducements. I have lately had a call to go to a grove near this place for a Sunday exhibition, but I get about all the work I want during the six days, without [working] the seventh.
>
> I carry fifty selections and try to have them all good. . . . Johnson's "Whistling Coon" and laughing song are immensely popular, and I presume they will always be. There is more call for them than for any other selections. . . .
>
> My last customer after listening to ten selections remarked, as he laid down the ear tubes, "Well, that is d——d nice," and this is about what they all say.[17]

In July 1892 the New Jersey company, its business thriving, began regular advertising in the *Phonogram,* and Johnson's name was prominently displayed. In December he was featured in a pictorial gallery of fifteen "Famous Record-Makers." This line drawing is the first known picture of Johnson. He looks his age (about 45), is well dressed with a cravat, and appears older than most of the others, all of whom are white. The copy contains brief descriptions of the specialties of most of those pictured, ending with, "and last but not least, Mr. George W. Johnson, whose 'Whistling Coon' has been heard in all climes, even in the wilds of Africa. [It] must be heard in order to be appreciated."[18] This is the first, though not the last, reference to Johnson's cylinders being sold overseas.

In February 1893 a report on a phonograph concert in New England listed Johnson's "Laughing Song" as one of the cylinders played, in the all-important next-to-closing position, right after a quartet recording of "Dixie."[19] In March the New Jersey ad began referring to his titles as "always popular."[20] These were not mere passing novelties. They had obviously struck a chord; after two years, the public still couldn't get enough of them.

The March 1, 1894, catalog of "original records" issued by the New Jersey company, which was now called the United States Phonograph Company, revealed the first concrete information on Johnson's sales. Under his picture (the same one that appeared in the 1892 *Phonogram*), and just above the listing of "The Laughing Song" and "The Whistling Coon," appeared the words, "Up to date, over 25,000 records of these two songs have been made by this artist, and the orders for them seem to increase instead of diminish. Whole audiences are convulsed by simply hearing these songs reproduced. No exhibition box is complete without these two records."[21]

To appreciate what an incredible total this was for 1894, it is necessary to understand the limited scope of the industry in the early 1890s. There were very few phonographs in private homes, so nearly all of the 25,000 had to have been sold to exhibitors and coin-slot operators who played them over and over again for a fascinated, paying public. They must have worn out a lot of copies of these two songs. Second, techniques for duplicating cylinders were still primitive, and the New Jersey company promoted the fact that all of its products were "originals." Most of the 25,000 were apparently original recordings by Johnson.

With only three or four saleable recordings resulting from each "round," an afternoon's work might result in 60–100 saleable cylinders. Simple arithmetic tells us that to produce 25,000 cylinders for sale over a three-and-a-half-year period Johnson must have been a very busy man. Three hundred recording sessions, or about eighty per year, at $4 per session, would have netted him $320 per year. References in 1898–99 suggest that Johnson was then earning from $10 to $100 per week for his phonographic work.[22] This exceeded the income of the average white American worker at the time (about $500 per year), and it was of course on top of whatever Johnson was able to earn from his regular street singing and odd jobs, with which he had previously entirely supported himself.

These figures are, to be sure, entirely speculative. In a marathon recording session Johnson might turn out even more copies (and would be paid more). A 1906 article observed that "in the old days, it is said, he once sang the same song 56 times in one day, and his laugh had as much merriment in it at the conclusion as when he started."[23]

There is little evidence of Johnson's actual income, aside from periodic reports that he was doing quite well. The New York Phonograph Company ledgers indicate that he was paid approximately $40 to $80 per year for his work for that company, from 1890 to 1892, and his North American sessions netted $6 to $7 apiece.[24] His New Jersey income was no doubt higher. The 25,000 figure could be exaggerated, although the record industry was not as prone to "hype" in those days as it is now. Also, some of those 25,000 copies could have been—despite New Jersey's protestations—duplicates for which Johnson received no additional payment.[25] Johnson, like all artists at the time, was paid by the session. There were no royalties.

Whatever the exact figures, the obscure black street singer from Hell's Kitchen had become a well-known name across the United States, and even in foreign lands, thanks to this newfangled invention. Though he was by no means rich, his income had risen sharply. As he neared fifty, George W. Johnson must have felt he had whistled his way into the promised land. These were his salad days!

One of the most distinctive characteristics of Johnson's career—aside from the fact that he was the first black man to gain fame through recording—was his limited repertoire. His fame was based on just two numbers, "The Laughing Song" and "The Whistling Coon." Most successful artists of the day sang a wide variety of material, usually any song that was popular at the moment. None sold as many copies of a single title as did Johnson, however.

Despite the enormous popularity of his two hits, Johnson wanted to expand his recorded repertoire. Two additional titles by him, "The Laughing Darkey" and "Uncle Ned's Dream," appear in the October 1892 New Jersey catalog, but not thereafter.[26] No copies survive. A more significant expansion of his recording career began in 1894 thanks to an aggressive young hustler named Len Spencer.

Enter Len Spencer

Leonard Garfield Spencer was without doubt one of the most interesting characters in the early recording industry. Young, white, pushy, even a bit dangerous looking, he was undeniably talented and had made a name for himself in just a few short years. Len was the scion of a notable and progressive Washington, D.C., family. His grandfather had invented the Spencerian system of handwriting, a florid style that was taught to reluctant schoolchildren all over the country; the family had later founded the Spencerian Business College in Washington, which it still operated. Spencer's remarkable mother, Sara Andrews Spencer, was a political activist, suffragist, and a friend of Clara Barton. A domineering woman, and headmaster of the College, she was something most uncommon in the Victorian era—an advocate of women's rights.

The Spencers moved in rarefied social circles. The "Garfield" in Len's name was in honor of his godfather, President James A. Garfield, a family friend. Len, who was born in 1867, had taught at the College briefly in the late 1880s but became fascinated with the new phonograph (which was used at the school). He began recording for the local Columbia Phonograph Company almost as soon as it began operation in 1889, bringing to recording a distinctive baritone voice, a highly melodramatic style of delivery, and a talent for writing and organizing material.

He soon sold his talents to a higher bidder, the New Jersey Phonograph Company, for whom he began recording around 1890. His name quickly filled its catalog, alongside George Johnson's, doing an extraordinarily wide range of material. The 1892 New Jersey catalog included 140 selections by him, including sentimental songs ("You'll Miss Mother When She's Gone"), topical numbers ("It Used to Be Proper But It Don't Go Now"), and currently popular hits ("Ta-ra-ra Boom Der E"). So that he would not completely dominate the catalog, some of his cylinders were issued under the pseudonyms Garry Allen and Larry Leonard.

Around 1894 Spencer moved from Washington to New York to pursue his recording career and came up with a proposal for his employers. Minstrel shows were all the rage in the theater, and there had even been a few attempts to recreate miniature versions on cylinders.[27] Why not put out a whole series of such cylinders with a regular company of performers? These records would be based on the minstrel

Len Spencer, Johnson's friend and beneficiary, in the early 1890s. (Author's collection)

"first part," beginning with the traditional "Gentlemen, be seated!" followed by jokes, songs, and stories in which the cast interacted. (The minstrel second part, or "olio," consisted of stand-alone variety acts, while the finale was generally a walkaround or similar production by the entire cast.) Spencer put together an exceedingly slick package, complete with interlocutor, jokes by the endmen, and a featured number by a soloist (often himself), capped by a rousing chorus by the entire company. Only three minutes in length in order to fit the short playing time of a standard cylinder, these little productions were ingeniously paced to give the illusion of the variety and naturalness of an actual stage performance.

The first cylinders by the "Spencer, Williams and Quinn Minstrels" (later renamed the Imperial Minstrels) were announced in 1894. Len's little troupe included vaudevillian Billy Williams, tenor Dan W. Quinn, and George W. Johnson. It was described enthusiastically in the catalog:

These gentlemen have together produced a most decided novelty in their new minstrel records. Spencer and Quinn are well known to all users of the Phonograph, and comment on their work is unnecessary. They are ably assisted by Mr. Billy Williams, the aged-Negro delineator and comedian, as well as by George W. Johnson in his inimitable laughing specialty. Each record contains a complete minstrel first part, embracing overture with bones and tambourine accompaniment, several jokes and witty sayings, interspersed with laughter and applause by the audience, and finishing either with some comic Negro song or story by Spencer, or a pathetic song by Quinn or Williams. Wherever reproduced these records have made an instantaneous hit.[28]

Six records were initially announced, with the first described as follows. Note the prominent mention of Johnson.

No. I. "Be seated, gentlemen." Introductory Overture; the Black Serenaders, followed by applause; the Interlocutor ventures to ask Bones "How he finds things?" to which Bones replies, "Oh, I look for 'em." This strikes the audience as being a witty sally, and they applaud and laugh vociferously, Mr. Geo. W. Johnson's hearty laugh particularly being heard above the din and confusion. "How is business down at the tailor shop, Billy?" "Oh, sew-sew," which reply also invokes the risibilities of the audience. "How do you feel tonight, Dan?" "Kind of Chicago." "Why, how is that?" "Oh, fair." The Interlocutor then announces that Mr. Spencer will sing "A High Old Time," all joining heartily in the chorus, at the conclusion of which the audience show their approval by round after round of applause, laughter, whistling, etc., etc.[29]

The sixth cylinder in the original series featured Johnson's own "Laughing Song." The performance was raucous and fast-paced, with Spencer and Williams trading jokes in broad black dialect.

Announcer: The Imperial Minstrels, introducing their original minstrel first part. Be seated, gentlemen! (Music)
Announcer: Introductory overture (orchestra plays, followed by enthusiastic clapping and whistling.)
Len: Well, Billy . . .
Billy: What issit, Leonard?
Len: Thas'a, thas'a very ferocious necktie that yo' got on there.
Billy: Tha's one hand . . .
Len: I-I-I bet I know where you got it . . .
Billy: Come on, where, where?
Len: 'Round your neck! (great laughter)
Len: Hey, Billy . . .
Billy: What issit, Leonard?
Len: You'se very much intellectuality, can you tell me what it is that makes a coon dog spotted?
Billy: No, Leonard, I say, what is it that makes a coon dog spotted?
Len: Why, his spots! (great laughter)
Billy: Hey, Leonard . . .
Len: What is it Billy?
Billy: How long this intellectuality must go on . . . Did you ever notice down in a yard how the dog run around on the leash?
Len: Yeah.
Billy: Did you ever notice how fast he run when he go 'cross?
Len: I do, certainly.
Billy: What makes him do that?
Len: I don't know, Billy, what makes dem dere dogs go so fast?

Billy: Why he's just in a hurry to get to the other side! (laughter)
Announcer: Mr. George W. Johnson in his great "Laughing Song" . . .
(Johnson sings two verses and choruses)[30]

The minstrel records were an immediate hit, and Johnson became a regular member of Spencer's company. Frequent mention was made of his "hearty laughter" as an integral part of the show. But Johnson gained more than additional employment from his association with Len Spencer. Spencer, twenty-seven and wise to the ways of show business, seems to have "adopted" the cheerful, friendly, black man who was nearly twice his age, using him in various phonographic ventures and, as we shall see, caring for him in his declining years. They remained friends for the rest of Johnson's life.

As remarkable as the early 1890s had been for George Johnson, the second half of the decade was even more so. In 1894 the North American Phonograph Company and its network of exclusive local franchises collapsed in a storm of lawsuits and bankruptcies, and it was every man for himself in the newly competitive industry. Compounding the problems was a severe economic depression which lingered through 1893 and into 1894. Nevertheless, as soon as it was legally possible for it to operate nationally, the aggressive Columbia Phonograph Company, which had most heavily promoted musical cylinders, opened a studio in New York and began buying up competitors or driving them out of business.

One of its first victims was the New Jersey company. Chief recording engineer Victor Emerson was lured away in 1896, and best-selling artists followed. Len Spencer and his minstrels moved in June 1897 and began making even more elaborate productions for Columbia, still featuring George W. Johnson. The Columbia version of "The Laughing Song" minstrel routine was more mainstream than the comparable New Jersey cylinder, less raucous and definitely less "black." In it Len and his brother Henry Spencer (also a recording artist), speaking now in proper English, cracked a rather staid joke, Len did a little flag-waving, and then introduced his friend Johnson. The routine stayed in the Columbia catalog, in cylinder and disc versions, virtually unchanged for almost twenty years.

Announcer: The Imperial Minstrels, introducing their original minstrel first part, for the Columbia Phonograph Company of New York City. Gentlemen, be seated!
Len: I say, Mr. Henry, money is mighty cheap nowadays.
Henry: Money cheap, Leonard? Ha! I fail to get any of it.
Len: Why, you can get silver dollars for forty-five and fifty-five cents.
Henry: Why, that's absurd, nonsense.
Len: Everybody knows that forty-five cents and fifty-five cents makes a hundred cents, and you can get a dollar anywhere for that! (great laughter, whistles)
Len: Tell me, sir, why are the stars and stripes like the stars in the heavens?
Henry: Well, Leonard, why *are* the stars and stripes like the stars in the heavens?
Len (melodramatically): Because, sir, it's beyond the power of any nation on earth to ever pull them down. (cheers)
Len: George W. Johnson in his great "Laughing Song" . . .[31]

Johnson also recorded his "Laughing Song" and "Whistling Coon" specialties as solos for Columbia. Previously Columbia had promoted John Y. AtLee's versions, but as soon as it opened a New York studio in 1895 the label replaced them with Johnson's. The aging black man clearly had the patented versions of the songs, and with Len Spencer backing him he was determined to hold on to them.

A significant development in the fall of 1894 was the first wide sale of disc records by their inventor, Emile Berliner. Although discs did not offer the sound quality of the rapidly improving cylinders, they were louder, more durable, and could be produced in quantity. After a single recording session duplicates could be stamped out like pancakes, although at first this was limited to a few hundred copies. Johnson entered the Berliner studio in October 1895 to make his first discs, the ever-popular "Laughing Song" and "Whistling Coon." They sold so well that Berliner had him travel to Philadelphia to rerecord them in 1896, with additional sessions in 1897 and 1898. They also had him record a new title, "The Mocking Bird," but this does not appear to have sold very well.

Berliner's disc machines were small, cheap, and intended for home use. Edison and Columbia countered with low-priced, easy-to-use cylinder players in 1896, and the battle between cylinders and discs was on. Phonographs and records, including Johnson's, at last began to find their way into private homes in large quantities. Sales of Berliner's little seven-inch discs skyrocketed from about 25,000 during the first few months, to 100,000 in 1896, 250,000 in 1897, and over 700,000 in 1898.[32] Sales of cylinders, still the predominant medium, were probably three times this amount. The record industry was booming.

Since no one had an exclusive contract for his services, George Johnson also began appearing on other cylinder labels in the late 1890s—the Chicago Talking Machine Company in 1895, New York Cylinders (sold by Walcutt and Leeds) in 1896, Edison and Consolidated in 1897, Bettini in 1898, and probably others. Some of these, such as Chicago and Consolidated, may have been reselling another company's products under their own name, but the list illustrated the wide appeal of Johnson's titles. Columbia catalogs of 1895–97 said that the "Laughing Song" and "Whistling Coon" "have had a wider sale than any other specialties ever made. Johnson's laugh is simply irresistible." Walcutt and Leeds in 1896 called them "two great specialties that have been sold all over the world." Berliner in 1898 added, "Of all successful singers to the talking machine, no one has ever made two such popular records as his whistling solo and laughing song."

Sales figures were seldom published in the 1890s, but the success of Johnson's cylinders and discs was so great that several references to their actual sales do exist. In late 1895 the D. E. Boswell Company of Chicago, apparently reselling Johnson's New Jersey cylinders, reprinted the familiar 1892 picture and said, "Up to date we have made over 30,000 of his two songs. The demand is undiminished." Another unidentified catalog from the same period (probably from New Jersey itself) cited 38,000 made.[33] An even more aggressive claim was made on the cover of sheet music for the "Laughing Song," which was published in the late 1890s. It reads, "Over 50,000 records up to date for phonograph use all over the world."

This is a high but not impossible total. The new industry trade paper the *Phono-*

scope reported in 1896 that up to that time Len Spencer had made more than 62,000 records (that was, of course, the cumulative total sold of the estimated 600 titles he had recorded).[34] If we are to take the wording on the sheet music literally, however, the 50,000 figure refers just to "The Laughing Song" and just to cylinders, which were in those days identified as for use on the "phonograph" as opposed to the disc "gramophone." That would be incredible.

What is clear is that as of mid-decade, Johnson's two numbers remained the best-selling records in the country. The *Edison Phonographic News,* a publication of the Ohio Phonograph Company, commented on this directly in late 1894, saying, "'The Whistling Coon' sung by George W. Johnson . . . and (his) 'Laughing Song' are the most popular phonograph records ever taken, and seem always to be in demand." In answer to a reader's question about best-selling cylinders, it added, "We believe the 'Laughing Song' by Geo. W. Johnson has had the largest sale of any phonograph record made, and next 'The Whistling Coon' by the same individual—and a colored individual too. 'The Night Alarm,' by Holding's Band, no doubt comes next in order. Beyond this we can give no opinion on the respective sales of popular records. Just now 'Sweet Marie' seems to be ahead."[35]

Unable to steal these enormously popular titles, which had become so closely identified with Johnson, others imitated, translated, and even pirated them. In 1897 Reed and Dawson, a New York company, announced, "The New Laughing Song, or 'So Do I.' This is the only successful rival of Johnson's famous Laughing Song, and is regarded by many as far superior. The laughing is very natural and infectious, setting whole audiences in a roar."[36] Apparently "So Do I" sank without a trace. No copy has ever been found.

No more successful, but even more bizarre, were foreign-language versions of "The Whistling Coon." In late 1896 New Jersey announced a cylinder by Sr. Guiseppe Stoppa, an Italian tenor, singing the song in French. In May 1898 William Mattison attempted it in Swedish, calling it "Karl August," on Berliner disc no. 2981.[37]

The Berliner disc company was beset by pirates in the late 1890s who made counterfeit copies of its products with the manufacturer identification removed. There were no paper labels at this time; instead title, artist, and manufacturer were embossed in the center area of the disc. On the counterfeit copies, the embossed manufacturer information was removed by buffing. Not surprisingly, Johnson's best-selling titles have been found on these pirated discs. His cylinders were probably pirated as well, an even easier process achieved by simply dubbing from one cylinder player to another.

The publication of the sheet music for the "Laughing Song" must have been a particularly proud day in Johnson's life. On the cover was a new photograph of him, laughing heartily and identified as the "Whistling Coon and Laughing Darkey." The copyright date is given as 1894 (although he had recorded the song before that), and words and music were listed as by Johnson himself. The poor, black street musician was now a published composer. A clue as to who might have helped him with the complicated song may be found in the additional credit, "arranged by Frank Banta." Banta (1870–1903) was a young pianist who was extremely active during the

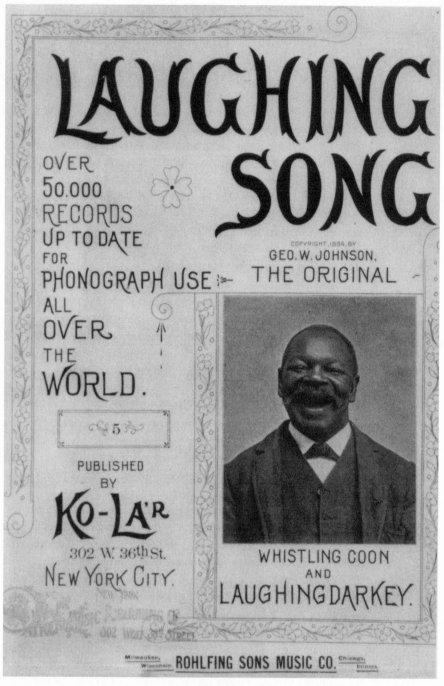

George W. Johnson's proudest moment? Cover to the sheet music for "The Laughing Song," published in 1894. (Author's collection)

phonograph's first decade, accompanying artists on Edison and other labels. The pianist accompanying Johnson on many of his early cylinders and discs may well be him.

Two New Songs

In 1897 Johnson was finally allowed to add two new songs to his permanent repertoire, recording "The Laughing Coon" and "The Whistling Girl" for Edison and Columbia. Although these new songs did not approach the enormous popularity of his first two specialties, they remained in print for many years. The author of neither is known. Perhaps it was Johnson himself, as both were uniquely tailored to reflect his image as "The Whistling Coon and Laughing Darkey." Both were jaunty numbers. "The Laughing Coon" was sung in "cut-four" rhythm, rather like "Little Brown Jug." Although sheet music has not been found, the lyrics are as follows, as closely as can be made out from the records.

> *The Laughing Coon*
>
> Away down south, where I was born,
> We used to hoe and weed that corn . . .
> Always low, walking slow, ha-ha-ha do you hear me now?
>
> *Chorus:*
> I'se gwine away to leave you, goodbye, goodbye,
> I'se gwine away to leave you, goodbye Liza Jane . . .
> I am the happy laughing coon, ha-ha-ha-ha-ha,
> I'm out in the valley and I look for the moon, ha-ha-ha-ha-ha,
> (laughs to music)
>
> The ducks play cards, the chickens drink wine,
> The monkeys doze on a large grapevine . . .
> Walk down low, always slow, ha-ha-ha do you hear me now?
> (repeat chorus)
>
> We went to walk, you and me,
> You got stung by a bumble bee . . .
> (unintelligible), sting me too, I'll not walk with you anymore . . .
> (repeat chorus)

The nonsense lyrics of "The Laughing Coon" have deep roots in folk music and minstrelsy. Essentially, the song seems to be a combination of preexisting songs and phrases, a common practice at the time. The first two verses and first two lines of the chorus are taken almost verbatim from "Good Bye, Liza Jane," as printed in *Delaney's Song Book* in 1896, the year before the Johnson recording. *Delaney* was widely distributed and may have been the source of Johnson's "inspiration." The song "Good Bye, Liza Jane" is much older than this, however, having been a favorite of minstrels since it was first published in 1871. The author is unknown; the original sheet music simply credited the arrangement to Eddie Fox.[38]

"The Whistling Girl" was a more traditional coon song, replete with stereotypes of high-dressing ladies, gambling ("4-11-44"), cakewalks, and razors. Though abhorrent today, such imagery was common and unquestioned in popular song at the turn of the century. At least it gave Johnson another opportunity to exhibit his whistling prowess.

The Whistling Girl

I know a little daisy, who lives in our street,
And when she hears the music, she cannot keep her feet . . .
I asked her if she'd marry me, she answered very soon,
I will marry you my dear, if you'll whistle me this tune . . .
(whistles chorus)

This gal of mine is dressy, and always looks so fine,
And soon we will be married, she has promised to be mine . . .
She's a reg'lar hot potater, a jolly, sporting coon,
And it's four-eleven-forty-four, and then whistles me this tune . . .
(whistles chorus)

The coons are getting jealous, you oughta heard 'em talk,
When the other night we took first prize down at the grand cake walk . . .
They all drew out their razors to carve the whistling coon,
Say don't you fear for I don't care, just whistle up this tune . . .
(whistles chorus)[39]

The cut-throat competition between phonograph companies in the late 1890s led to a surprising development in 1898, one that foreshadowed modern practices. Columbia announced that it had signed fifteen leading recording artists to make cylinders exclusively for its label during the coming year (although they could continue to make discs for Berliner).[40] An advertisement dated May 1, 1898, showed pictures and signatures of most of the artists, including George W. Johnson—as usual, the only black face in the crowd. The photo shows him smiling happily, while his signature looks rather stilted, as if he were a "lefty." In contrast, Len Spencer's ornate signature is a flowing work of art.

Johnson had been singing his original two songs for eight years, but their popularity showed no sign of waning. He was an established fixture in the burgeoning talking machine world. The July 1898 *Phonoscope* found a new term to describe him. "Geo. W. Johnson is *sui generis*. He sings 'coon' songs with a naturalness that is probably due to the fact that they were born in him. His specialties are laughing and whistling songs. He has a remarkable laugh which would make the fortune of any white minstrel performer who could successfully imitate it. Mr. Johnson has had considerable experience on the stage, where his peculiar ability has enabled him to make a decided hit. He is the only colored man who has achieved distinction in making records for talking machines and his fame is so well established that there will probably always be a demand for his coon songs."[41]

The reference to "considerable experience on the stage" is curious, as nothing has been found to corroborate this. Perhaps it is a polite way of referring to his "street theater"; or perhaps occasional engagements whistling and singing on stage. A newspaper in 1899 said that he was "known throughout the country as the 'Whis-

This blurry photograph may be the only shot of Johnson at work in the recording studio. It is much enlarged from a tiny, thumbnail illustration in the July 1898 *Phonoscope* accompanying an article on current record-makers, including Johnson. He was not specifically identified as the subject of the photo, but the physique and general appearance match his. (Library of Congress)

tling Coon' because of his appearance with theatrical companies," but this simply appears to be a garbled reference to his renown from the widespread coin-slot phonographs.[42]

As the 1890s came to a close America was in a very expansionist mood, and several of the phonograph companies were moving aggressively to establish overseas offices. Most of these foreign branches did their own local recording, but some U.S. best-sellers were exported, including George W. Johnson's two enormous hits. One wonders what proper Britons thought of his "Laughing Song" and "Whistling Coon," with their American racial stereotypes. Both were included in one of Berliner's first English catalogs, dated November 16, 1898.[43]

The French might be excused for being even more perplexed. The Bettini Company, which specialized in fine operatic recordings, included both titles (recorded in New York) in their French catalog of June 1901, along with a picture of Johnson. He looked distinctly out of place alongside the mustachioed operatic tenors and glamorous divas. His two "specialites Americaines" were presented to the French as "Le fou rire" and "La Chanson du sifflet," and priced at three francs each (about seventy-five cents).[44] They did not find many buyers on the Champs-Elysées.

Johnson's Personal Life in the 1890s

Although the widespread success of George W. Johnson's recordings in the 1890s substantially increased his income, it did not make him rich. As noted, performers were generally paid a flat fee for each session, royalties being unheard of. Those leather-lunged singers who landed the most recording sessions did the best, but no one became truly wealthy from recording, except perhaps the owners of the record companies.

Throughout the 1890s Johnson continued to live in cheap boardinghouses and tenements, mostly on the poor west side of Manhattan. From 1892 to 1895 he is found at 319 West 39th Street, in 1897 at 198 East Houston Street, and in 1899 at three addresses on West 41st Street. He does not seem to have ever been legally married or had any children, but he did have at least two "common law" wives, women with whom he lived for extended periods. The first relationship was described by police officer William Boyle during Johnson's legal problems in 1899: "He was living with a German woman in 1894–95, whom he quarreled with and beat frequently. This woman was found dead in bed in the fall of 1894 or spring of 1895. Johnson was arrested on suspicion of having caused her death, but the matter never got as far as the Police Court."[45]

In a separate statement Boyle said that he had known Johnson since 1893 and had also known the "German woman" (who was not named).[46] Because of the lack of a name, a precise date, or any charge being entered in the case, I have not been able to trace anything further about this woman. Also, we should not take too literally the statement about Johnson beating her, as it is both hearsay and at considerable variance with descriptions of him by his neighbors during the 1899 investigation.

Johnson's real problems began when he took up with a mulatto woman named Roskin Stuart in 1896. He was nearly 50, she was about 35. She was a real hell-raiser, and he, judging by later testimony, became almost a father figure to her. Their relationship was tumultuous.

Stuart was apparently a drifter. No one at Johnson's trial knew much about her background, and her death certificate gives no mother or father or place of birth (other than "U.S."). She seems to have lived in New York most of her life, and worked as a maid or housekeeper. According to later statements, she drank heavily. One of Johnson's neighbors, James Morton, contrasted her with Johnson, who he said had "a very good reputation." He added, "I have known Mr. Johnson for six or seven years and he always appeared to be a nice kind of a man, and I never knew him to have any trouble. Johnson never treated that woman bad. I have been around there, and Johnson never treated her bad and always treated as a father. I have seen him at the door of No. 236 telling her she ought not to bring [home] so much gin in her apron. She would cuss and say she bought it with her money and she would do as she chose, and Johnson laughed and came on the stoop with me."[47]

Another neighbor told the police, "I heard them quarreling many times. She usually started the quarrels, as a rule. She was full, and when she got any liquor in [her] she would start." A third added, "I have often told [Johnson] the woman was crazy. When she got gin in her she would yell and holler and whoop and abuse him."[48]

Stuart, it should be noted, gave at least one neighbor a different account of what was happening. Neighbor Lena Small reported that Stuart "quite often told me that Johnson used her badly. I saw her face black and blue. I didn't ask her who had been guilty of doing it, [and] she didn't tell me how it happened. She simply told me Johnson had been beating her, she told me that several times."[49] Interestingly Lena Small made no reference to Stuart's claims in later statements or on the witness stand. Perhaps because Stuart was known to hang out with a rough crowd, and no one believed that the friendly, easy-going Johnson would do such a thing, no one gave much credence to Stuart's complaints.

Johnson's domestic troubles soon escalated. At some time after the couple moved to 236 West 41st Street, Stuart fell or was pushed from the window of their second-floor apartment during a quarrel, into the yard on 40th Street. Some of the neighbors thought he had pushed her, and Johnson was arrested. However despite the fact that Stuart was in the hospital for twelve or fourteen days, "she refused to make any complaint, saying she would get 'hunk' with him when she got out." There were no witnesses, and the charges were dropped. A humorous item appeared in the February 1898 *Phonoscope* about an unnamed phonograph whistler "being arraigned for pushing a woman out of a second-story window recently"; this may refer to Johnson.[50]

By the summer of 1899 Johnson and Stuart were living at 234 West 41st, in the rear, and still quarreling. Then, apparently, she decided how to get "hunk." Herbert Small testified that one day, "She was drunk; I don't know whether he was drunk or not. I heard him say that she had his gun out of pawn. On this occasion Mrs. Johnson shot at Johnson with the pistol, and then he took the pistol from her and ran out on the street. . . . She was dispossessed out of No. 234 for disorderly conduct and general nuisance."[51]

Johnson, apparently struck in the ankle, was not seriously hurt. He moved to a basement apartment at 262 West 41st, where Stuart joined him a few weeks later. In the early morning of October 12, 1899, they had another of their loud arguments. Later that day Stuart was found beaten and unconscious in the apartment. She was taken to Bellevue Hospital where she died a few hours later. Johnson was arrested for murder.

Word traveled fast around the Tenderloin. The next day several New York papers carried stories about the incident, with the following headlines:

Woman's Mysterious Death—*New York Journal*

Woman Dead, Husband Held—*New York Herald*

Whistler Charged with Woman's Death . . . Found Insensible After Quarrel—*New York Evening Telegram*

A Negro Whistler Held on Suspicion of Killing His Common Law Wife—*New York Tribune*

George W. Johnson, the "Whistling Coon," In Trouble—*New York Times*

Most of the stories garbled the details, misspelling Stuart's name and giving various causes of death including poisoning and strangulation. There were apparently no witnesses. However, the reason Johnson was arrested was clear. Neighbors said they had heard him threaten to kill her during the heat of their late-night argument, and as Victor Emerson recalled years later, "two wives prior to this last one had met with violent deaths, and in New York when the third wife meets with a violent death the police sometimes become suspicious and so the poor man was arrested."[52] (Emerson was incorrect in referring to two previous wives; there was one, the "German woman.") The irony of the line in one of his great hits—"and he whistled when his wife was dead"—must not have been lost on Johnson or on those around him.

Johnson was arraigned in West Side Court, where he pleaded not guilty. He was held pending a coroner's inquest into the cause of Stuart's death. The inquest was held five days later, on October 17, by Coroner Jacob E. Bausch in the Criminal Court Building. Johnson, who was represented by an attorney named Edmund B. Brown, again pleaded not guilty. Statements were taken from five black neighbors and two white police officers—Herbert and Lena Small, John and Hattie Thomas, James Morton, and officers Michael McManus and William Boyle. The ten-person coroner's jury concluded that death was due to "cerebral hemorrhage, caused . . . at 262 West 41st St. by bodily violence at the hands of George W. Johnson." Johnson was remanded to New York's Tombs prison to await action by a Grand Jury.

Several other statements of interest are contained in the inquest file. Johnson stated he was 53, born in Virginia, and by profession a musician. An attending physician's statement from Bellevue Hospital stated that Stuart was admitted unconscious, suffering from "pulmonary ordinaria" with "contusions of face, neck and both arms and left shoulder." Her age was given as thirty-eight.

On November 13, 1899, a grand jury handed down an indictment of Johnson for murder in the first degree. The indictment painted a scenario in which Johnson "did then and there willfully, feloniously and of his malice aforethought strike, beat and kick with the hands and feet . . . upon the head, breast, belly, sides and other parts of the body of the said Roskin Stuart, and did . . . cast and throw the said Roskin Stuart down unto and upon the ground with great force and violence there, giving unto the said Roskin Stuart with the said beating, striking and kicking of her . . . divers mortal wounds . . . of which [she] did then and there die." Two days later new statements were taken from the seven persons who had testified at the coroner's inquest.

By the time of the indictment, something remarkable had begun to happen. Numerous people, black and white, had begun to rally to Johnson's side. According to a report in the *New York Sun,* "Victor H. Emerson, superintendent of records of the Columbia Phonograph Company, collected about $1,000 from men all over the country who knew and liked Johnson. This fund was used to hire counsel and make any fight on appeal that might be necessary. Rollin C. Wooster, one of the company's attorneys, gave his personal attention to the preparation of the case. . . . Lawyer Wooster said that probably twenty-one men of standing in this city, or who had come here for the trial, were ready to testify to Johnson's unfailing good nature."[53]

Emerson himself later recalled that "Johnson was always sober, industrious and gentlemanly, and nobody believed that Johnson would do it on account of the risk involved. Some of the talent held a meeting to provide ways and means to help him and after the object of the meeting was stated one of them said, 'Well boys, we ought to all chip in because there is no telling when some of us might be in the same fix.' The subscription after that speech was $2,100 on paper and we afterwards borrowed $100 real money (to hire counsel)."[54]

With the backing of Columbia, and a substantial defense fund, Johnson was assured of a strong defense team. Columbia's Wooster worked behind the scenes to help prepare the case. Representing Johnson before the grand jury and later at the trial was Emanuel M. Friend, described by the *New York Times* as "one of the best known criminal lawyers in the city." Friend, forty-six, had been practicing for twenty years and had won numerous highly publicized criminal cases. He also served as counsel for many theatrical companies and agencies; one of his most famous cases was representing boxers James J. Jeffries and Tom Sharkey against a showman who had exhibited motion pictures of their 1899 heavyweight championship fight without their permission. His victory established an important legal precedent.[55]

Johnson was much encouraged by the support he received while awaiting trial. The *New York Times* reported, perhaps with some exaggeration, that the "'Whistling Coon' seems to have suffered little from confinement and suspense. He spends much of his time in jail whistling for his own and other prisoners' diversion. He manages to keep from bursting into music in the courtroom by keeping his mouth firmly closed."[56]

Finally, the day of the trial arrived.

3   The Trial of George W. Johnson

In December 1899 New York City's many newspapers were filled with screaming headlines about the Insurrection in the Philippines, as well as lurid coverage of several murders and trials, most of them involving the rich and famous. The trial of the Tenderloin's "Whistling Coon" was not front-page news. It did, however, rate coverage in a number of major papers, including the *Times, Evening Telegram, Herald, World,* and *Sun.* (In addition, the *Journal* and *Tribune* had previously carried stories about his arrest.) Many of these stories included tidbits about Johnson's background. In fact, had it not been for this trial and the resulting coverage, we would know very little about George W. Johnson's life.

The trial opened on December 20 with a hundred spectators in attendance. Presiding was Judge Joseph E. Newburger, forty-six, who was in the early part of a long and distinguished career that would eventually take him to the New York Supreme Court.[1] Representing Johnson were not one but two white defense attorneys, Emanuel Friend and Edward Hymes. Hymes, twenty-eight, the junior member of the team, had been practicing for half a dozen years and, though not as eminent as Friend, he was certainly first-rate counsel, as well as an international chess champion. Hymes would go on to a long and successful career in New York law.[2] The prosecutor was Assistant District Attorney John F. Cowan. Judging by the trial transcript, he was thoroughly outclassed by the high-powered defense team.

The first day of the trial was occupied with jury selection. Eleven jurors were chosen, with the twelfth seated the next morning. The *New York Times* noted that one of the jurors, Martin Dodson, a real estate dealer, was "colored."

Cowan opened with a short summary of the state's case.[3] The prosecution would produce witnesses, he said, who had heard Johnson and Stuart arguing loudly around two o'clock on the morning of October 12; Stuart had accused Johnson of killing his first wife, and Johnson had replied that if Stuart once again called him "a certain scurrilous name," he would kill her. Later that day Johnson approached a police officer and told him that his wife needed medical help. She was removed to a hospital where she died that afternoon of injuries caused by violence.

No sooner had Cowan finished his opening remarks than Hymes moved for an immediate dismissal. Pointing out that the state's case was entirely circumstantial—no witnesses, no proof of violence by Johnson upon Stuart, not even clear evidence of what caused her death—he insisted, "If the Court please, the opening, as laid out by Mr. Cowan, points at evidence which, even if substantiated, would constitute no crime."

The motion was denied. Friend then asked that material witnesses be excluded from the courtroom until called to testify, and this was granted. He also indicated that all of the defense witnesses, except for a physician, would be character witnesses.

The first prosecution witness was Lena Small, one of Johnson's upstairs neighbors, who testified that Johnson had been living in the basement apartment at no. 262 for two or three months. The Stuart woman, she said, was known by both that name and as "Mrs. Johnson" ("she was living with him, and we generally called her that"). Prosecutor Cowan then asked Mrs. Small about the morning of October 12.

> Cowan: Where were you about half past two in the morning?
> Lena Small: My husband and I were just coming in about twenty minutes past two . . .
> Cowan: Was your attention attracted by anything?
> Lena Small: Just by one word, that is all . . .
> Cowan: Did you recognize the voices that you heard?
> Lena Small: Yes sir, I did.
> Cowan: Whose voices were they?
> Lena Small: It was Mrs. Stuart's voice.
> Cowan: Coming from what direction?
> Lena Small: Coming from the basement.
> Cowan: Can you tell whether or not it was coming from the apartment of the defendant, this man [indicating Johnson] and the woman?
> Lena Small: Yes, sir. I saw the shadow on the window. The curtain was raised, and there was a bright light in there . . . there was no fighting, or nothing like that—only words, that is all.
> Cowan: Now tell us just what words you heard, and who uttered them?
> Lena Small: I heard her making the remark, "You killed your first wife, but you will never kill me." Then he said, "If you call me," mentioning a certain name, "I will kill you."
> Cowan: What was the name?
> Lena Small: A black son of a bitch.

Cowan: He said, "If you call me a black son of a bitch, I will kill you"?
Lena Small: Yes, sir.

Mrs. Small then described how later that day she saw Stuart taken away by an ambulance. Here and throughout the trial the defense entered frequent objections when a witness appeared to be making assumptions. How could she be sure it was Stuart's voice? How did she know it was Stuart being taken away, since she didn't see the victim's face? Small stuck to her story, but in cross-examination the seeds of doubt were planted that this witness, at least, was making certain assumptions that went beyond what she had actually seen and heard.

The second prosecution witness was Mrs. Small's husband, Herbert, a Health Department worker. He repeated his wife's description of the overheard argument and the epithet Stuart used on Johnson ("Well, that remark was nothing unfamiliar with me. I have heard it so often that I didn't pay no attention to it"). He also made it clear that the Johnsons fought constantly, and this night seemed no different. In an earlier statement he said that his wife had remarked, "Come along up, they are having that same old row, as usual."[4] Small seemed much more cautious in his testimony than his wife had been, however. The voices he heard were *probably* those of Johnson and Stuart; the time *may* have been around 2:20 A.M.

On cross-examination, Herbert Small revealed some interesting information about Stuart's drinking habits, and, somewhat reluctantly, about his own involvement with her.

Hymes: You had known Mrs. Stuart for some years?
Small: Yes, sir.
Hymes: What was her habit as to drink?
Cowan: I object.
Judge: I will allow that.
Small: Mrs. Stuart, to my knowledge, was a habitual drunkard or fiend.
Cowan: A fiend?
Small: Yes, a fiend for gin.
Cowan: Did you ever see her drink gin?
Small: Yes, sir.
Cowan: Where did you see her drink gin?
Small: In 234 West 34th Street.
Cowan: Were you in her rooms upon those occasions?
Small: No, sir, but I have seen her send out after it and drink it.
Cowan: Where did she drink it, in her rooms?
Small: Yes, sir.
Cowan: Did you see her drink it?
Small: Yes, sir, I have seen her drink it.
Cowan: Were you in her rooms?
Small: Was I in her rooms?
Cowan: Yes?
Small: I have been in the rooms.
Cowan: Were you in her rooms on the occasions when you saw her drink gin?
Small: Yes, sir, many times, I have seen her drink gin in her rooms . . . possibly ten or twelve times.
Cowan: Were you familiar with her?

Small: No, sir, I never have been familiar with her any more than to speak to her.

Cowan: How did you come to go into her rooms; were they social visits?

Small: No, sir, not that. There was nothing concerned between her and me. She simply lived [downstairs].

Cowan: Tell us how you came to go into the rooms.

Small: I went in socially because she invited me . . .

Hymes: I object to that. It is an effort to impeach his own witness.

Judge: I will allow it. . . .

Small: I went in simply because I wanted to see her. It was a liberty that she permitted, and it was something that I felt I wanted to accept. . . .

Juror: To your knowledge, was Mrs. Stuart in the habit of having company at night at any and all hours . . . other than her husband?

Small: Only people that wanted to drink gin. Anybody was acceptable, if they had some gin with them. . . . Anybody, gentleman or lady—if they had the price of ten cents worth of gin, they were acceptable.

Small was then closely questioned about Stuart's drinking habits, but he stuck to his story, insisting "she was inclined to go with anybody who was inclined to give her the price of gin."

Next on the stand for the prosecution was Officer Michael J. McManus of the 20th Precinct. He said that the defendant, George W. Johnson, had approached him on 41st Street at 1:30 on the afternoon of October 12.

McManus: He came up and said, "Officer, I want you to go down to the house. There is a woman lying down there, and I don't know what is the matter with her . . ." I went to the house with him. I asked him who the woman was, and he told me that she was a woman that he was living with . . .

Cowan: What part of the house did you go to?

McManus: The basement . . . 262 West 41st Street.

Cowan: What did you find when you got there?

McManus: I found a woman lying on the sofa.

Cowan: Describe the condition of the woman as you found her.

Defense then objected that the witness was being asked to give expert medical testimony, but was overruled. Officer McManus continued that Stuart was lying on the sofa, unconscious.

McManus: I noticed that there was blood oozing from her mouth, and there was blood on her apron, and she was black in under here [indicating vicinity of right jaw], a dark black, and one of her eyes was discolored.

Cowan: Did you examine the wound on the lip?

McManus: Yes. There was a little kind of wound, like a hat pin was stuck in there [indicating a point under the right nostril].

Cowan: Did you notice the condition of the room?

McManus: Yes, sir . . . [there was] a sofa and a table, and a couple of chairs . . . I should say two or three at the most.

Cowan: Did you say anything to the defendant at that time? . . .

McManus: I asked him, when I saw the woman laying there, how she became that way. He said she came home about half past two in the morning, full of nigger gin, and when he got up at six o'clock in the morning he found her laying on the floor. He said that he picked her up and laid her on the sofa. I asked him did he have a private physician for her; he said "no." I asked him why he didn't notify somebody before the time he did me, and he said he saw her that way so often that he didn't think there was anything wrong with her. . . . I asked him about the marks on her and [the] blood, and he said he supposed she had been out with some of her companions, and that they had stabbed her with a hat pin.

Cowan: What did you do next?

McManus: I went out and rang up for an ambulance.

Officer McManus then arrested Johnson on suspicion and took him to the station house. No statements were taken at that time. When Stuart died later in the day, the charge was changed to murder.

Cross-examination added some detail about Johnson's living quarters. McManus reported that in addition to the spartan room that he had described, there was a bed in another room. The apartment was tidy, and there was a cuspidor in front of the sofa—with blood in it.

Next Hattie Thomas, another neighbor, was called as a prosecution witness. Johnson had approached her first, asking her to come look at Stuart. In an earlier statement Thomas related their conversation. "I said, 'What is the matter, drunk as usual?' He said, 'Yes, but she's breathing rather hard, come down and take a look at her.' I says, 'I will.' So I went down and she was lying on the lounge. I says 'That woman is dying!' He says, 'Do you think so?' I said, 'Yes . . . you had better call a doctor.'"[5] Mrs. Thomas described the bruises and the same wound on the lip, "that looked as if it had been done with a hat pin." She said Johnson had told her he found Stuart like that at eight o'clock that morning. She saw Stuart taken away in the ambulance but didn't know where she was buried, except that it was by the city.

Defense Attorney Hymes's cross-examination brought out the odd fact that Thomas had heard the deceased singing around 6:30 A.M. on the morning she died. A juror's question revealed that Stuart was a mulatto woman, "very light and fair." Another exchange with a juror brought out, inadvertently, more about Stuart's unsavory reputation.

Juror: What do you know as to the character of Mrs. Stuart?

Hattie Thomas: I know she was not a very nice woman.

Cowan: I move to strike that out.

Judge: Yes, strike that out. [To the juror:] You must not ask that question.

Defense attorney Friend then began to ask Mrs. Thomas about Stuart's drinking habits, whereupon Cowan again objected. This time the objection was sustained, the judge saying that he had erred in allowing such testimony earlier. Holding both sides to very strict standards, Judge Newburger then admonished the defense for even conceding that the body removed from the building was that of Stuart ("Let the prosecution prove it—Section 181"). This trial was to be conducted with scrupulous fairness.

Next on the stand was George Weissner, a morgue attendant at Bellevue Hospital. Stuart had been removed in a Roosevelt Hospital ambulance, but evidently because she was unable to pay the private hospital's fees, was detoured to the city-run Bellevue. In one of the trial's unintentionally amusing episodes, it transpired that the prosecution had called the wrong man; he was not the attendant on duty when Stuart's body came in.

> Cowan: Will you go back and tell them to send down the right man?
> Weissner: Yes, sir.
> Judge [curtly, to Cowan]: Telephone up there yourself.

Noting that the admitting doctor had not yet arrived, Cowan then requested a recess until the afternoon, which was granted. When court reconvened, Dr. William W. Beveridge of Bellevue Hospital took the stand. He had admitted Roskin Stuart.

> Cowan: Will you state to the jury what her condition was when you examined her?
> Dr. Beveridge: The patient, when she was admitted to the ward, was unconscious. She had some marks on her face and on her arms, both. There was a very large black and blue spot—a bruise it should be called, I presume—on the right arm, and also a cut on the lip, and she was unconscious, and had a condition of pulmonary edema. That frequently occurs before death. Her pulse at that time was fair; that is, strong and full . . .
> Cowan: The condition that this woman was in at the time that you saw her—was that serious or not?
> Dr. Beveridge: Very serious . . .
> Cowan: Could you say what cause produced her death?
> Dr. Beveridge: Well, it would be impossible to say the exact cause producing her death.

There followed a lengthy and inconclusive discussion of just what did cause Roskin Stuart's death. Dr. Beveridge repeatedly refused to identify any certain cause. Pulmonary edema, he explained, was normally a terminal symptom that could have been caused by either injury or disease. Cowan pressed him to state that it *could* have been caused by a violent blow, and Dr. Beveridge readily agreed, though he wouldn't identify exactly what kind.

On cross-examination the defense pressed equally hard to establish that the edema could have resulted from inflammation of the heart, or kidney disease (nephritis), and that the latter was often induced by excessive alcoholism. Dr. Beveridge agreed with this too, though he couldn't attest that this *was* the cause in Stuart's case. A urine test for cirrhosis of the liver had revealed nothing. However, it appears that the tests were not very comprehensive. Basically, the doctor said, her lungs failed and she died.

The testimony of coroner Philip F. O'Hanlon was then read. O'Hanlon had performed the autopsy and certified the cause of death as cerebral hemorrhage—again a terminal symptom, not the ultimate cause.

At this point, Defense Attorney Hymes moved for acquittal. The prosecution, he said, had utterly failed to demonstrate that Johnson had inflicted any violence upon Stuart. Yes, they had quarreled in the early morning hours, but Stuart was heard singing at 6:30 A.M.; Johnson's and Stuart's whereabouts between that time and the time he put her on the sofa at about 8 A.M. were not known; the cause of death had not been established; and the manner in which Johnson himself had called for help suggested his innocence.

Judge Newburger seemed rather dismayed by all this, asking if the fact that the defendant had been heard quarreling with the deceased was not enough to at least require him to give his side of the story. But Hymes pressed his argument. The prosecution had not made a case. It was not even known whether the observed injuries were received before or after the argument. "Myriads of things might have happened," he insisted. Finally, the judge turned to the prosecution.

Judge: Does the District Attorney desire to be heard?
Cowan: I will say very frankly, your Honor, that a conviction cannot be sustained in this case, and I think the [defense] Counsel has substantially stated the grounds in his application.
Judge: What does the District Attorney desire to do?
Cowan: I ask that the Court recommend an acquittal.
Judge: In other words, I understand that the District Attorney abandons the case?
Cowan: Yes, sir.
Judge: If that is so, that disposes of your motion [to acquit], Mr. Hymes.
Hymes: I would have wished to have heard a judicial disposition of it.
Judge: The District Attorney having abandoned the case, I do not think there is anything left for the Court to do but to direct an acquittal. Without passing on the merits of the case, or passing upon the manner in which it has been handled, I simply say to you, gentlemen of the jury, you are directed to acquit.

The jury thereupon rendered a verdict of not guilty.

Several things are evident from the transcript of George W. Johnson's trial. The defense was well prepared and very, very good. Objections were constantly being entered, whenever the prosecution seemed to be entering the realm of assumption. The judge, too, was determined that only observed facts were to be heard in this capital case—no hearsay. Even the admitting doctor got into trouble for reporting the results of a blood test that he had not personally conducted.

The prosecution, by contrast, was a shambles. Its own witnesses painted a dark picture of Stuart, leaving ample grounds to believe that her death was the result of her own carousing. No one had a bad word to say about Johnson. The wrong morgue attendant was subpoenaed, and neither the doctor nor the coroner could testify as to the actual cause of death. The only physical evidence—which was not introduced—was the clothing Johnson had been wearing when arrested, which bore some blood stains (he had picked up the woman), and a small pocket knife the police had taken from him.[6]

One wonders why the district attorney brought such a weak case to trial in the first place. There could be many reasons. Perhaps it was simply the blind wheels of the system turning without anyone noticing what was happening. Perhaps it was racism. Officer McManus gave a straightforward account of the events he saw that day, but earlier statements by Officer Boyle (who was not called to testify) suggest a certain dislike of this "uppity Negro." There was well-documented hatred of blacks in the New York City police force at this time, which would erupt in dreadful violence the very next year.

In any event, the defense team did its job well, seeing to it that neither Johnson nor any of his character witnesses even had to take the stand. We could have learned a great deal about Johnson if he and his friends had testified. However justice was certainly done.

According to news reports, the reading of the verdict set off an uproar in the packed courtroom, which was sternly suppressed by Judge Newburger. The scene outside the courtroom, as Johnson and his friends emerged, was pandemonium. A long and fascinating story in the *New York Sun* described the scene.

WHISTLING COON IS FREE
ACQUITTED OF MURDERING HIS COMMON-LAW WIFE

Women, Both White and Black, Rush Forward to Kiss Him—Big Demonstration in the Court House—Prosecution Abandons the Case for Lack of Evidence.

George Washington Johnson, known as the "Whistling Coon," was acquitted yesterday of the charge of murdering his common-law wife, Roskin Stuart, and went whistling out the Criminal Court Building a free man. A hundred persons had gone to court to watch his trial. Some were white and some were black. Nearly all came from the vicinity of Hell's Kitchen, where Johnson feels at home. . . . Johnson's friends crowded around him, the men shaking his hands and the women kissing him. An ovation of this kind was attempted in Judge Newburger's court room but was sternly suppressed. In the outer lobby the enthusiasm was unsuppressed. Besides the few white women who kissed him, white men, who had employed Johnson, and the son of the man who owned his father and himself as slaves before the war were there to congratulate him. As the Whistling Coon went down the Centre Street steps of the Court House he whistled shrilly, "I Don't Care If I Never Come Back."

The prosecution of Johnson was abandoned for lack of evidence. His defense, however, had been thoroughly prepared. Victor E. Emerson, superintendent of records of the Columbia Phonograph Company, had collected about $1,000 from men all over the country who knew and liked Johnson. This fund was used to hire counsel and make any fight on appeal that might be necessary. Rollin C. Wooster, one of the company's attorneys, gave his personal attention to the preparation of the case, although he did not represent the accused in court. A Mr. Moore, son of the man who owned Johnson's father, came on from Harper's Ferry to help in the fight. Mr. Moore and Johnson were born about the same year, and the colored boy started in life as the white boy's servant. Mr. Moore, who still resides on a plantation near Harper's Ferry, gave up his business for a week to come on here to help his old-time servant. Lawyer Wooster said that probably twenty-one men of standing in this city, or who had come here for the trial, were ready to testify to Johnson's unfailing good nature.

There followed a slightly garbled description of the facts of the case, and highlights of the testimony, including a description of Stuart as a "bad character." The article ended by recounting Johnson's side of the story, and a most interesting interview with Wooster on the courthouse steps.

Johnson's story to the police was that the Stuart woman had been beaten and jabbed with a hat pin before she got back to their rooms. The reference to [Stuart's claim about] his first wife was explained by a story that Johnson was usually so patient that the woman thought to make him angry by reference to the gossip about the German woman's taking-off. Judge Newburger directed a verdict of acquittal after Assistant District Attorney Cowan had declared that the prosecution must abandon the case.

"Johnson is what you would call a good coon," said Lawyer Wooster. "He is too good natured to ever have killed that woman. We're going to take him to a hotel tonight or to Mr. Emerson's home and give him a good dinner, sitting right down at the same table with him. I am glad that I was the first to shake hands with him after he was discharged. He can earn $35 to $100 a week singing and whistling."[7]

Johnson may have been beloved, but Wooster's approving reference to him as a "good coon"—someone you could even sit down and eat dinner with—speaks volumes about his true place in society. The song Johnson whistled on the courthouse steps, incidentally, was evidently a parody on the recent hit, "I Don't Care If You Never Come Back." Johnson certainly had a sense of humor.

Other papers carried shorter but equally enthusiastic stories about Johnson's acquittal. "Whistled Out to Freedom" said the New York World, referring to his song on the courthouse steps. "Clear of Murder, Negro Sang" proclaimed the New York Times. "At the announcement of the verdict there was a demonstration of joy in the court, which was suppressed with difficulty. Several persons ran up to Johnson and grasped him by the hand, and he was taken away singing and whistling by a party of friends to dinner at a hotel. . . . The courtroom was crowded by friends of the 'Whistling Coon.' The expenses of his defense were paid by a subscription started by Victor Emerson of a phonograph company, by which Johnson had been employed."[8]

Notice was taken of Johnson's trial outside of New York as well. The long New York Sun story was reprinted in its entirety by the Cleveland Gazette, a black newspaper, a week later.[9] There were probably stories in other black newspapers, too, though none have been located. Unfortunately, few black newspapers from this period survive.

The trial provides eloquent testimony to the esteem in which George W. Johnson was held by his many white and black friends, as well as to his marginal lifestyle at this time. There was self-interest at play, of course. As the New York Herald dryly observed, "Manufacturers of slot machines, so greatly had they become interested in Johnson's abilities, raised a fund to be used in his defense."[10] However, no recording artist was indispensable in these days, and Johnson, though valued, could certainly have been replaced. It is inconceivable that white businessmen would have come to his aid so fully had there been any belief that he was in fact guilty of murder.

Which raises one last question. Did Johnson kill Stuart? Or, for that matter, did he ever abuse either her or the "German woman"? The jury never ruled. I have been told that the reason this particular trial transcript was preserved, when most others from the period were destroyed, was that the authorities may have felt the case might someday be reopened. But it wasn't. Given the testimony and the affection so many people obviously felt for Johnson, I don't believe he would have done violence to anyone. We will never know for sure.

Johnson's Post-Trial Career

Following his exoneration Johnson resumed his recording career without difficulty. He was still under exclusive contract to Columbia, but when the label ended that practice in 1900 he and other artists once again began recording for anyone who would pay. One newspaper remarked that his "accomplishments are being whistled and sung by slot machines from one end of the country to the other."[11]

The major labels were experimenting at this time with oversized wax cylinders that were played on specially designed machines, and during 1899–1900 Johnson recorded his famous specialties in this format for Columbia, Edison, and Bettini. These "Grand" or "Concert" cylinders were a huge five inches in diameter and much louder than the regular size, but they were also very fragile. Few survive in playable condition today.

Johnson still chafed at the limits of his repertoire, but there seemed to be little he could do about it. "The Laughing Song" and "The Whistling Coon" kept right on selling. An amusing item in the May 1900 *Phonoscope* commented on this dilemma, which many artists shared.

> It seems very strange how some of the phonograph vocalists permit their ambitions to soar. George Johnson thinks that it is an imposition that they won't permit him to sing "The Blue and the Gray." Gaskin can't understand why four pages of the catalog are not filled with comic songs under his name. Dan Quinn thinks that he could sing almost anything in the catalog except "The Bedouin Love Song," and J. W. Myers fails to see why [George P.] Watson should do yodle songs while he is in the business. The only good things that Len Spencer ever put in the [catalog] were coon songs and readings from the Bible, and yet he aspires to ballads. The *Phonoscope* is wondering what the rest of the bunch "think" they can do. All of the above-mentioned artists are good in their respective lines, but the record buying public is wondering and hoping that they will follow the old adage, and "stick to what you can do the best."[12]

The thought of ex-slave George W. Johnson rendering the then-popular tearjerker about the Civil War is bizarre indeed.

Another concern was potential competition. George W. Johnson had been for ten years and still was the only well-known black man making records, but others were bound to emerge. There had already been a few. Louis "Bebe" Vasnier, a New Orleans "Creole of color," had made talking records and banjo solos for the Louisiana Phonograph Company in the early 1890s. Achieving somewhat wider circulation were the cylinders made by two black stage quartets, the Unique Quartette (first recorded in late 1890) and the Standard Quartette (1891). The Kentucky Jubilee Singers, a group that had toured for years, recorded in 1894, and in 1902 the Dinwiddie Quartet of Virginia made a series of discs for Victor. Very few of these recordings survive today, but those by the Standard, Unique, and Dinwiddie quartets are extremely interesting titles, mostly gospel-style "negro songs" rather than the demeaning comic "coon songs" of George Johnson.

Johnson's fame in the recording industry was apparent not only from his own records, but also by references to him by others. In October 1900 the Haydn Quartette, a popular white group, made the first recording of a sketch that would remain a popular seller for many years. The author is unknown, but may have been humorist Cal Stewart. "Negro Wedding in Southern Georgia" (sometimes more offensively called "Coon Wedding in Southern Georgia") was a recreation of a rural wedding, full of black stereotypes and dialect. In the midst of the proceedings the groom arrives and is announced as none other than "George Washington Johnson"! Johnson himself did not take part in any of the many recordings of this sketch, but the reference could only be to him. The text, as transcribed from period recordings, is as follows.

NEGRO WEDDING IN SOUTHERN GEORGIA

Parson: Brothers and sisters, I want to request the unfo'tunate parties who are about to participate in his hea'h catastrophe to stand up befo' me. [Bells ring; quartet sings "Hear Dem Bells"]

Parson: George Washington Johnson, does you promise to cherish and feed this lovely female through life, to the best of your abilousness?

Groom: Deed I do!

Parson: Lucinda Marguerita Jackson, am you willing to run the awful risk of takin' this hea'r black man, for better or for worser?

Bride [in screechy voice]: I'm gwinta if I can, parson! [giggles]

Groom: Look-a hea'r woman, stop that snivelin'.

Parson: Now you po' miserable sinners, by the law convested in me by the state of Georgia and the M.E. Church house, I denounces you tied hand and foot, and what the law has joined asunder, let no man separate together. [Loud cheers]

Deacon: The parson will now connubiate his august privilege of kissing the bride. [Loud smooching sounds]

Bystander: Look-a hea'h, parson, you ain't kissin' no cow! [Laughter]

Parson: The congregation will please come to order. While the parson am collectin' fo' dollars and two bits, the choir will render out, "Hail, Jerusalem, Hail." [Choir sings enthusiastically, interjecting shouts][13]

To heighten the humor, some versions used variations on Johnson's name, such as "George Washington Abraham Jackson" or "George Augustus Washington Chesterfield Johnson." Performers known to have recorded the routine include the Haydn, American, Columbia, Invincible, and Peerless quartets, and the Ramblers, on labels including Victor, Columbia, Edison, Zonophone, American, Busy Bee, Silver Star, Clico, D&R, and Indestructible. There was even a very short version on the small-sized fifteen-cent Little Wonder label in 1916. The sketch remained available, in one form or another, as late as 1926. As for Johnson's "Laughing Song," it was such a standard that it was incorporated into various medleys, including "The Laughing Medley," recorded by quartets on Edison and Zonophone in 1903.

The first few years of the new century brought a spurt of recording activity for Johnson. Improvements in recording technology, and the founding of new disc labels, meant work for him. "The Laughing Song" and "The Whistling Coon" seemed to have unending popularity, and every company wanted them on its list. In December 1900 he recorded all four of his tunes for the new "Improved" disc label, successor to Berliner (the sound was indeed improved over the noisy Berliners). The label name was soon changed to Victor, and in 1902 Johnson returned to the company's studio to sing them again, this time for issue in both seven-inch and ten-inch versions. The longer playing time of the ten-inch discs allowed him to slip in extra verses on those versions, and often the pianist had time for a raggy little coda as well.

Columbia was also going into the disc business, and it had Johnson record "The Laughing Song" and "The Whistling Coon" for its Climax disc label in late 1901 (the label name was changed to Columbia in 1902). Johnson returned to make ten-inch versions for them as well, which were issued on both Columbia and a number of allied labels including Harvard, Peerless, Oxford, Silvertone and Marconi. Len Spencer was also asked to remake his Imperial Minstrel routines for Columbia discs, and Johnson participated in those as well. Slightly later Johnson sang his songs for some smaller disc labels including Zonophone (1902), American (1904), and Imperial (1905). Zonophone even had Johnson record a new number, "Carving the Duck." Although this mysterious title remained in the catalog for several years it must have been a very small seller. No copy has ever been found, and it is not even certain whether it was a song or a sketch.[14]

Despite the temporary increase in work, the ability of the record companies to produce large quantities of discs from single master recordings through improved production methods was beginning to have a significant negative impact on artists' incomes. Fewer sessions were required to maintain the companies' stocks. Some rerecording was still done to take advantage of improved recording techniques and replace worn-out masters, but artists felt the effects of technological unemployment. Johnson, with his limited repertoire, was particularly hard-hit. For example his first Victor session took place in December 1900. He returned to the Victor studios in September 1902 and May 1903, but never again. Even though his recordings remained in the Victor catalog until 1910, his services were no longer needed. The same thing happened at Columbia.

The situation was the same for cylinders, now that mass molding had been introduced. Once he made "permanent" cylinder masters for Edison and Columbia between 1900 and 1905, he was no longer needed for that purpose either.

Johnson also lost work to white artists who finally succeeded in taking over some of his trademark songs. This was especially true of the whistling numbers. Perhaps Johnson was felt to be losing his "pucker," or perhaps recording executives felt that though he might be authentic, he was simply not as good as the professional whistlers who did most of the recorded work in that genre. Johnson had been one of an honored group of forty-two Edison artists photographed on the lawn of Thomas Edison's estate in New Jersey in 1900 (again, the only black). However when the inventor's company began making "permanent" masters in 1901 it employed white artists to record all of Johnson's songs. Cal Stewart took "The Laughing Song" and "Laughing Coon," while S. H. Dudley did the "Whistling Coon" and later "The

Whistling Girl." Eventually Edison had Johnson record new versions of his laughing songs, replacing those by Stewart, but Dudley retained the two whistling songs. Likewise Columbia had Billy Murray remake Johnson's "Whistling Coon" around 1902 or 1903, leaving Johnson with only his "Laughing Song" in the Columbia catalog. Murray completely changed the whistling song. His carefully enunciated, singsong delivery, combined with Joe Belmont's ornate, florid whistling stripped it of its "street" roughness and turned it into something resembling a children's novelty.

The situation was not much better on Berliner and its successors, Improved and Victor. In 1898 Johnson's old nemesis, John Y. AtLee, had reclaimed both "The Laughing Song" and "The Whistling Coon" on Berliner, and in 1900 he recorded "The Laughing Song" for Improved as well. However, this version was not released. While Victor recorded Johnson's versions of all four of his signature songs and kept them in its catalog until 1909–10, it also introduced a bland competing version of

Edison recording artists gathered on the lawn at Llewellyn Park, Thomas Edison's New Jersey estate, in 1900. Johnson is seated at the far right (no. 32). Others are: 1) Joe Belmont; 2) Nick Scholl; 3) A. Zimmerman; 4) L. W. Lipp; 5) Byron G. Harlan; 6) Fred Hager; 7) Arthur Collins; 8) S. H. Dudley; 9) W. C. Deusing; 10) W. Guarini; 11) William Tuson; 12) Will N. Steele; 13) Jim White; 14) Walter H. Miller (recording manager); 15) George Broderick; 16) Frank Kennedy; 17) A. L. Sweet; 18) B. Russell Throckmorton; 19) Harvey N. Emmons; 20) Ruby Brooks; 21) Samuel Siegel; 22) Albert Benzler; 23) Señorita Maria Godoy; 24) Joe Natus; 25) William F. Hooley; 26) May Kelso; 27) J. J. Fisher; 28) Will F. Denny; 29) John Bieling; 30) Marguerite Newton; 31) Fred Bachman; 32) George W. Johnson; 33) A. D. Madiera; 34) Frank Mazziotta; 35) Frank P. Banta, Sr.; 36) Charles D'Almaine; 37) George P. Watson; 38) Dan W. Quinn; 39) Harry Macdonough; 40) Edward M. Favor; 41) Albert Campbell; 42) Jere Mahoney. (Edison National Historic Site, West Orange, N.J.)

"The Whistling Coon" by S. H. Dudley (as "Frank Kernell") in 1903, which undoubt-edly cut into his sales. Victor sales were greater than those of any other disc label, and its Johnson titles are more frequently found today than those of any company except perhaps Edison. Later pressings on Victor are particularly valuable since manufacturing technology had improved immensely in a few short years, yielding much clearer reproduction than on the earlier cylinders and discs. Unfortunately Victor cut out all of its Johnson recordings by 1910. After that the only version of a Johnson song in its catalog was "The Whistling Coon" by Murray with Dudley do-ing the whistling. This remained available until 1927.

Cal Stewart, best known for his monologue character Uncle Josh, recorded a song called "And Then I Laughed," which seems to be a direct steal from Johnson's "Laughing Song." The tune is similar, and the title closely parallels a recurring line in Johnson's song. Some buyers probably bought the Stewart record thinking they were getting the original.

In 1898 Berliner had exported copies of Johnson's "Laughing Song" and "Whis-tling Coon" to be sold by its British affiliate. By 1900, however, successor label Gramophone had white artist Burt Shepard record both songs. "The Laughing Song" was so identified with Johnson that early versions were announced as "Johnson's Laughing Song," but nevertheless it was Shepard, not Johnson, who became identified with the song throughout most of the world outside the United States. Recording impresario Fred Gaisberg recalled in his 1942 memoirs the impact of Shepard's versions.

> Fat, jolly Bert [sic] Shepard, with his powerful tenor voice and clear diction, gave us our most successful results. . . . His repertoire comprised Negro airs, Irish and English ballads, comic and patter songs, parodies and yodels. The spontaneous and boisterous laugh he could conjure up was most infectious and was heard by thou-sands through his records. Bert Shepard's "Whistling Coon" and "The Laughing Song" were world-famous. In India alone over half a million records of the latter were sold. In the bazaars of India I have seen dozens of natives seated on their haunches round a gramophone, rocking with laughter, whilst playing Shepard's laughing record; in fact, this is the only time I have ever seen Indians laugh heart-ily. The record is still available there and I believe that to this day it sells in China, Africa and Japan as well.
>
> These songs I brought over from America, having transcribed them and taught them to Bert. I had acquired them from George W. Johnson, the tragic Negro men-tioned earlier.[15]

Shepard himself referred to the phenomenal popularity of these numbers in a 1907 interview in the English trade paper the *Talking Machine News*. "Mr. Shepard is confident he has made more records for the gramophone than any other artist, and all 'big sellers.' Take that laughing song of his, for instance. He has repeated his visits to their laboratory over and over again to make fresh masters of this popular record. 'More than one dealer has told me that it sells like wildfire. The natives of various parts of India especially would seem to like it very well. Friends write and tell me that all a native wants out there is a loin-cloth, a machine and my laughing record,' said Mr. Shepard."[16]

Shepard changed some lyrics to suit English sensibilities, for example, substituting "King of laughter" for "King of Africa" and "goon" for "coon." "The Laughing Song" was also recorded by English artist Wilson Hallett, and "The Whistling Coon" by Hallett, Mays and Hunter (banjo and ocarina), Burt Earl, and Albert Whelan, all between 1898 and 1906. In Sweden "The Whistling Coon" was recorded by Jens Larsen. Interestingly, European artists seemed to prefer the minor-key melody to "The Whistling Coon," rather than the major-key version utilized by Johnson. The minor-key melody, though interesting, was rarely heard in the United States.

None of this new international popularity of his songs benefited Johnson. Adding insult to injury, in 1907 Victor issued in the United States an unusual sketch called "Laughs You Have Met," containing the voices of five internationally known comics. Recorded in England, the disc ended with Burt Shepard doing a rousing excerpt from "The Laughing Song."[17]

George Johnson's income must have fallen dramatically. Although his sessions were now being used to record permanent masters, which produced no further income for him, he was paid little more than before for the time he spent in the studio. Edison cash payment books indicate that for a session on December 16, 1904, Johnson received $15; for another on February 6, 1905, to rerecord two of his numbers with orchestra, he was paid $30. For what must have been a very long session on February 23, 1906, taking part in six Edison minstrel records, Johnson received $20. Johnson was not being discriminated against. These were the standard rates for all noncelebrity talent at the time. The orchestra in his 1905 session divided up only $27.34.[18]

By 1905 George W. Johnson was fifty-nine years old, with little income and, in all likelihood, no savings. It must have been difficult for the aging black man to continue whistling for small change on the streets of Manhattan. The city directory shows him living at 177 East 102nd Street in Harlem in 1905 and 1906, no longer in the Tenderloin. Rent was no doubt cheaper there.

At this point one of Johnson's oldest friends in the recording business came to his aid. Len Spencer's career was flourishing. He was still popular as a solo artist. His rustic "Arkansas Traveler" routine was a steady best-seller on several labels, as were his melodramatic recitations of famous speeches ("Lincoln's Speech at Gettysburg," "Ingersoll at the Tomb of Napoleon"). In 1905 he had teamed with thirty-one-year-old Ada Jones, a buxom, foghorn-voiced singer with an exceptionally cheery style. Their Jones and Spencer sketches became extremely popular. Among the titles were "Pals," "Peaches and Cream," "Hans and Gretchen," "Chimmie and Maggie," "Becky and Izzy (A Musical Courtship)," "Si and Sis, the Musical Spoons," and "Louis and Lena at Luna Park." My own favorites are their mock-dramatic skits with Spencer as the pompous tragedian and Jones the willowy damsel, e.g., "The Hand of Fate" and "The Crushed Tragedian."

Len also operated a booking agency, which grew so rapidly that he opened a palatial new office—or "Lyceum"—on West 28th Street in 1906. An associate named Fred Rabenstein later recalled that "when Len opened his Lyceum he had a doorman in full regalia—he was none other than George W. Johnson, who made the old laughing song records. George was something to behold in his full dress admiral (or was it general?) uniform."[19]

Len also got Johnson some recording work. In early 1906 he used his friend on his sketch, "The Merry Mail Man," on Columbia. "This jocular record depicts the postman (Len Spencer) delivering letters and jests," said Columbia. "Passing from door to door he finally encounters George W. Johnson (the laughing coon), whose merry laugh concludes the record."[20]

"The Merry Mail Man" is particularly interesting as it gives us a chance to hear Johnson speaking, and in a comedy sketch at that. After funny encounters with a doctor, an Irishman, and a Jew, mailman Len reaches Johnson's door.

Len: Hello, here's a registered letter for George W. Johnson. I wonder if he's in?
[Dramatically:] I'll knock. [Knocks]

[They sing:]
Johnson: Stop that knocking . . .
Len: Here's the mail.
Johnson: Stop that knocking . . .
Len: Here's a letter.
Johnson: Oh, you'd better stop that knocking at my door . . .
Len: Let me in . . .
Johnson: Stop that knocking . . .
Len: Money for ya . . .
Johnson: Stop that knocking . . .
Len: All right.
Johnson: Oh, you'd better stop that knocking at my door!

[Speaking:]
Len: Better come down, this letter's pretty heavy. Had some money left ya?
Johnson: Yes, it left me long ago and I've been short ever since.
Len: Ah ha, but this is a money order.
Johnson: I didn't order any money, but if it's for Johnson give it to me.

Johnson then finishes the record doing his trademark laugh to the rollicking chorus of the old Christy Minstrels tune "Stop That Knocking at the Door."

In February 1906 Johnson took part in the aforementioned Edison Minstrels records, which also included Len Spencer. However, he was not a featured performer in any of the six resulting cylinders. One of Johnson's last recording sessions for a major label appears to have been in mid-1907, when he remade his venerable "Laughing Song" (now called "Negro Laughing Song") for Columbia's latest innovation, six-inch-long cylinders. These "LP" cylinders played for three minutes instead of two and were supposed to revolutionize the business, but they were so fragile that they soon disappeared from the market. Few survive today. Johnson's listing was accompanied by a new picture of him, probably the last ever taken, in which he looks distinctly old and tired. The copy was upbeat: "Actually the first ever recorded as well as the best of the laughing songs. Truly a most infectiously cheerful lyric, with the quaintest conceivable words and melody, sung by their genuine African originator, whose rhythmic merriment—as perpetuated by the Graphophone—will long continue to delight Columbia audiences the same as during the past twenty years or more; this is indeed a perennially popular selection. 'Laugh and the world laughs with you!' Listen to this record and you'll 'die laughing!'"[21]

Johnson's glory days were clearly past as he stood guard at Len Spencer's door, but he was certainly not forgotten. In late 1906 the New York musical journal *Music Trades Review* published the following rather exaggerated article about him, which was reprinted in England's *Talking Machine News.*

One of the most unique characters in the talking machine world is George Johnson, who is now working for all the companies, doing "laughing songs." Johnson is said to be the most infectious laugher in the country. He is described by the talking machine men as the original "haw-haw" man, and practically every laughing song heard on the phonograph is sung by him. He even figures in some songs which have only a few bars of laughing chorus or a laughing line. Johnson is a Negro who has been making a living by his exuberance for years. In the old days, it is said, he once sang the same song 56 times in one day, and his laugh had as much merriment in it at the conclusion as when he started.

A talking machine man tells of Johnson that he was in a Western city one day in a gallery at the theatre. A black comedian came out and did a laughing song. Johnson snorted after the first chorus. He moved about restlessly and at the end of the second verse shouted a protest. "You ain't singing dat song right!" he cried. "What's the reason I ain't?" declared the singer from the stage angrily. "P'raps you can sing it better!" "I sure can," declared Johnson. Johnson left the gallery, slipped into the stage entrance and took up the dare. He scored his usual success.[22]

It is obvious that by 1906 Johnson was not enjoying the success suggested in this article, although his records remained in print. The incident in the theatre in a "Western city" is a mystery, as Johnson does not seem to have traveled much; the "darky" dialect ("You ain't singing dat song right!") appears to be pure writer's fiction.

It is possible that Johnson had some minor stage exposure late in his career, perhaps through the auspices of Len Spencer's booking agency. An actor named George Johnson had a minor role as a "coal heaver" in the hit musical *The Time, the Place, and the Girl* as it toured the country during 1907. The musical, with a score by famed composer Joe Howard, debuted in Chicago in 1906 and made its way from the Midwest to New England and finally to New York where it opened in August 1907. From early 1907 through the New York run this "George Johnson" was in the supporting cast playing a role which, judging from the storyline, was probably black. No picture nor biography of the actor survives, however, so we cannot be certain that it is our George W. Johnson.

Another late Johnson recording session took place in 1909 or 1910 in a New York studio where masters were being stockpiled for a new cylinder company located in Cleveland. The U.S. Phonograph Company was formed by some former Edison executives and artists to market unbreakable cylinders under the "U.S. Everlasting" label. Edison's wax cylinders, by contrast, were *very* breakable. The inventor did not bring out an unbreakable cylinder, the celluloid Blue Amberol, until 1912. Johnson's two titles for U.S. Everlasting were, predictably, "The Laughing Song" and "The Whistling Coon." These were released in 1910 or 1911 and were available for only about two years. They are very rare today.

Johnson's last session seems to have been for Columbia, a label that had included him in its catalog since his glory days of the mid-1890s. By 1910 a great deal had changed. Cylinders were on the way out, discs had standardized at the large ten-inch (three-minute) size, and were now double-faced. Recording techniques had improved as well. Nearly all vocals were now recorded with orchestra accompaniment, but the single Johnson title still in the catalog ("The Laughing Song") was an old master with only a thin, tinkly piano accompaniment. Perhaps at Len Spencer's urging, Columbia brought the old man back into the studio one last time to rerecord his classic with full orchestra. It was used to replace an earlier master on one side of Columbia A297, a double-faced disc; on the other side was another old-timer of the 1890s, George J. Gaskin.

With the new technology Johnson only had to sing the song once or twice in order for the technicians to obtain a take suitable for issue. That was fortunate, as he was now sixty-three years old and very tired. The old laugh still came, but he probably could not have made it through one of the marathon recording sessions of his early days if he had wanted to.

Len Spencer's theatrical booking agency was bustling, with sidelines in colored song slides and musical coaching. A branch office was opened in Scranton, Pennsylvania. In 1910 the New York office moved to a huge loft over the opulent Crystal Theatre on Union Square and 14th Street. But all was not well with George Johnson. According to Fred Rabenstein, "It was all right for a while—George had a room at the Lyceum, but after they moved [to] 14th Street [from] 28th Street things caught up with George. He used to run errands and always being a little short of cash he used to borrow money from the clients. He never paid back and after a while he was afraid to go to some of the places. George could only do the 'Laughing Song' and therefore it was hard for him to pick up extra money. Then he liked to drink."

Reluctantly, Len had to let Johnson go.[23] Rabenstein continued, "Len did not get another doorman, but had an office boy. We understood that Len treated George all right, but was afraid to let him have much money because the 'doorman' would be indisposed for several days afterward."[24] No trace has been found of Johnson in the 1910 census. He was presumably still living in Len Spencer's offices at this time, and office buildings were skipped by the census-takers. Perhaps they did not realize that an elderly black man was living out his last years in a back room.

Newer black entertainers were finally coming into the recording limelight. Bert Williams had become a major star, and his Columbia records, including his comic lament "Nobody," were best-sellers. More African Americans began making records during 1908 and 1909, including baritone Carroll Clark, stage comedian Charley Case, the famous Fisk University Jubilee Quartette, and Polk Miller and his Old South Quartette. Most of them emphasized "respectable" black music, as opposed to the coon songs Johnson had been obliged to sing. Some blacks complained about Johnson's songs. In 1905 influential critic Sylvester Russell wrote in the *Freeman,* "Men who write words for songs can no longer write such mean rot as the words of 'Whistling Coon' and expect respectable publishers to accept it no matter how good the music may be. Composers should not set music to a set of words that are a direct insult or indirect insinuation to the colored race. This style of literature is no longer appreciated."[25]

The last known picture of Johnson, about sixty years of age but looking much older. (*Columbia Record,* Aug. 1907)

George Johnson's last days were bleak indeed. His income had long since dwindled to almost nothing, and gradually his name was fading from sight. His last Columbia cylinder had been deleted in 1908. Victor dropped the last of his records from its catalog in 1910, and Edison did the same in 1912. By 1913 only a single disc of his "Negro Laughing Song" was still available, made by Columbia years before, and his name was not even listed on the label. Instead of an artist credit, the label contained the simple words "an old standard." Len Spencer's minstrel routine featuring "The Laughing Song" was still in the catalog, but also without Johnson's name shown.

Johnson moved back to Harlem. On January 19, 1914, he was removed from his small tenement room at 44 West 137th Street to Central and Neurological Hospital, suffering from broncho-pneumonia and chronic myocarditis. He died four days later, on January 23, at 7:30 P.M. He was sixty-seven. His body was removed by the city and buried about a week later in Maple Grove Cemetery in Queens. He was laid to rest in a common, unmarked grave, along with twenty other destitute persons.

The world scarcely noticed Johnson's passing. Only a single obituary has been found, a small item buried in the pages of the *New York Age,* the city's leading black newspaper. "George Johnson Dead," it read, but the text suggested a certain embarrassment about the old Negro from another era who had gained fame catering to whites as "The Whistling Coon." It was now 1914, the NAACP had recently been founded, and the *Age* was at the forefront of the movement to promote a better self-image for blacks. The paper could not bring itself to print his odious nickname in its pages, substituting the previously unheard-of name "Laughing and Whistling Johnson."

George W. Johnson, better known as "Laughing and Whistling Johnson," whose songs are recorded through the phonographs manufactured by the Edison, Victor and Columbia companies, died in the City Home Hospital, New York, January 23.

His remains were buried by the various phonograph concerns, which were represented by the Rev. J. Henry Taylor, president of the Betterment League. The deceased was born a slave in Havana County, Va., 71 years ago, was educated in Lynn, Mass. He taught school in the South for a while.[26]

Many of the factual statements in this obituary are suspect. Johnson's death certificate gives the hospital as "Central and Neurological"; burial records indicate interment by the city, not by his former employers; there is no "Havana County, Va." (perhaps a corruption of Fluvanna?); and many sources establish that he was sixty-seven, not seventy-one. The allusions to his education in the North and his teaching school are a mystery.

Len Spencer found out about Johnson's death, probably after the fact, and looked after his effects. According to Rabenstein, "after George died Len started to clean out the room and in a closet they found remains of many lunches (bread, bottles, ham, etc.), including roaches and other livestock."

A Warm Summer's Day

On a warm summer's day in 1989 I visited George W. Johnson's grave. With no headstone, the spot could be located only by reference to old cemetery ledgers and maps. But somehow the site was appropriate. It was a small, grassy plot in the old section of the cemetery, nestled beneath a towering oak tree. A city street, lined with apartment buildings, lay only a short distance away, but it seemed much further. Here it was quiet and peaceful, a simple unmarked plot of land. One felt almost anonymous—like Johnson himself. Who *was* he? He had traveled a long journey from slavery, to the streets of Hell's Kitchen, to the recording studios that would preserve his voice and laughter for all time. Then he had slipped out of the world as he had entered it, quietly and virtually unnoticed.

Epilogue

On December 15, 1914, less than a year after his friend George Johnson had passed away, Len Spencer dropped dead at his desk in his bustling office. He was forty-seven. Ever the showman, Spencer had arranged for a specially made cylinder of himself reciting the Lord's Prayer and the Twenty-third Psalm to be played at his own funeral.

Victor Emerson, the man most responsible for Johnson's early career, went on to an illustrious and highly successful career in the recording industry. After twenty years with Columbia he left to found his own Emerson label in 1916, which lasted until the late 1920s. Although he lost control of the company in 1922, it later became an important manufacturer of radio and television sets, and his name survives in its trademark to this day. Emerson died in 1926, at the age of sixty.[27]

Samuel Moore, Johnson's white boyhood friend, died on September 27, 1927, in Waterford, Virginia, at the age of eighty. He was the last surviving of George and Anna Moore's ten children. He was a deacon in the Waterford Baptist Church and remained active in church affairs until the end of his life. In 1905 Samuel cofounded

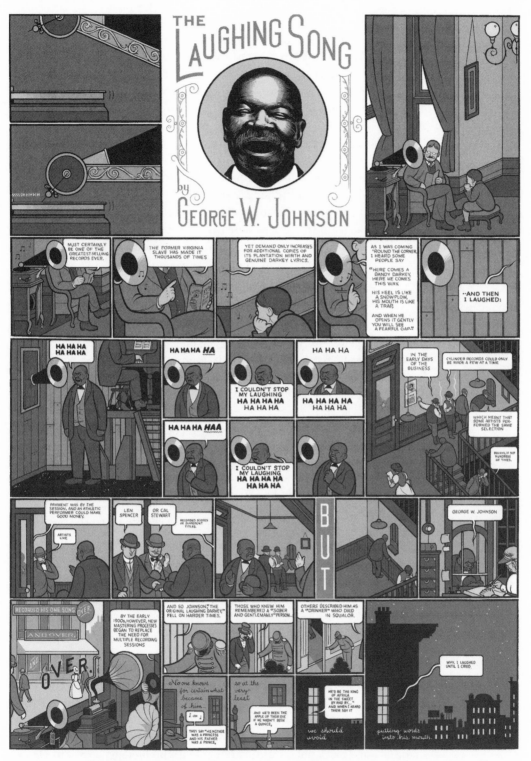

George W. Johnson's career remembered by cartoonist Chris Ware, nearly a century later. (Courtesy of Chris Ware)

the Moore-Clemens Insurance Company in Leesburg, which is still in existence. Glenmore, the family farm, was sold in 1900. It is still a working farm today.

Samuel was remembered by area residents as a busy, upright businessman who was "quick to see needs, eager to do at once what needed to be done, generous with his time and means, ready to speak for his Lord in private and public."[28] In light of this reputation, the fact that he rushed to his former slave's aid in 1899 is not surprising.

George Johnson's recordings quickly passed from the scene. His last listed disc was deleted from the Columbia catalog in 1915. His songs lasted only a little longer. In 1918 Edison issued two elaborately produced sketches built around "The Whistling Coon" and "The Laughing Song," performed by white artists Edward Meeker and the Empire Vaudeville Company on Blue Amberol cylinders. In the first of these, a group of World War I soldiers, passing the time singing old-time songs, recruit black soldier "Whistlin' Pete" (Meeker) to do the jauntiest tune of all. He obliges, ending in a "Whistling Coon" sing-along (whistle-along?).

The second sketch is a good-natured and very funny recreation of an amateur minstrel show. In it, the producer (Steve Porter) has a disappointment for his little cast (Billy Murray, John Young, and Donald Chalmers).[29]

> Porter: Say fellows, I've got a disappointment for you.
> Boys: You have? What do you mean? What is it?
> Porter: Why, I can't find anybody to sing Johnson's Laughing Song.
> Young: Oh Steve, you don't mean it . . .
> Murray: We've got to have it. Why it won't be a regular minstrel show without that song!
> Porter: Well I'm just as disappointed as you are. I've asked everybody I know.
> Murray: Have you asked Meeker?
> Porter: Why no, does he know it?
> Murray: Sure he does. I've heard him sing it.
> Chalmers: And he's up in the billiard room now.
> Porter: Fine! Give me the telephone and I'll see if he can come down right now. . . . Hello, hello? Is that you, Meek? Say Meek, listen. Can you sing Johnson's Laughing Song?
> Boys: What'd he say?
> Porter: You can! Well come right down. We're having a rehearsal. . . .
> Meeker [seconds later]: Thanks fellows. I accept the nomination!
> [Cheer]
> Porter: Now, Meek, for the Laughing Song.
> Meeker: Does the orchestra know it?
> Orchestra [shouts in unison]: DO—WE—KNOW—IT!!!

Meeker then launched into an enthusiastic version of the old song, accompanied by the orchestra and banjo virtuoso Vess L. Ossman. At the end, the entire cast joined in. It was an affectionate tribute. The two sketches were later issued on Edison Diamond Discs and remained available on cylinder and disc until 1929 when Edison quit the record business. Though entertaining, neither was a large seller.[30]

In the Jazz Age, black singers and instrumentalists proliferated on record. George W. Johnson, "The Whistling Coon" of the 1890s, was ancient history, remembered by only a few old-timers, and then, witness Gaisberg, not necessary too accurately.

His songs passed into folklore. In 1928 the Short Brothers, a country duo, recorded a ragged but fast-paced version of "The Whistling Coon" without author attribution (Okeh 45206). At the same time folklorists were already "collecting" the song from schoolchildren in the South and speculating as to its origins. One ethnomusicologist told readers that the song was "obtained by Julian P. Boyd in 1927 from Jeannette Tingle, one of his pupils in the school at Alliance, Pamlico county [North Carolina]," and that it might be "a product of the later minstrels (ca. 1900–1910)."[31]

The British comedian Charlie Penrose used the melody to "The Laughing Song" for his routine called "The Laughing Policeman," which he recorded several times in the 1920s and 1930s, but few of his listeners probably knew where the tune came from.

Johnson's records have essentially been out of print since 1915. In 1961 a rather noisy copy of his 1905 Edison cylinder of "The Laughing Song" was reissued on the Folkways LP *Phono-Cylinders,* volume 2; and in 1984 cylinders of "The Laughing Song" (with Spencer's minstrels) and "The Whistling Coon" appeared on the Mark 56 LP *The World's First Entertainment Recordings.* In 1989 an even noisier copy of a "The Laughing Song" Berliner showed up on the English CD *Emile Berliner's Gramophone.*[32] There have also been a few limited-distribution reissues by collectors.

George W. Johnson was, for most of his life, a happy, easygoing man with a ready laugh who wanted nothing more than to get by in a hostile world. He made many friends and brought pleasure to millions more. He probably never thought of himself as a pioneer, but as the first black recording artist he made history. Perhaps today, so long after his death in obscurity, his achievements will at last be remembered.

PART TWO

Black Recording Artists, 1890–99

4 The Unique Quartette

The Unique Quartette was the first black quartet to record commercially. Their story, as well as their sound, was almost lost in the mists of history. With public archives and present-day record companies virtually ignoring this earliest era of recording, it is nothing short of a miracle that a handful of the fragile wax cylinders made by the group in the early and mid-1890s have survived, in private hands. More may yet be found. They are fascinating sound documents, living examples of black stage quartet performance style more than a century ago.

After considerable research I have only a sketchy outline of the quartet's history, but it is enough to establish that this was no group of obscure singers brought together for the purpose of recording, as was often the case with early white quartets. Rather, it was a professional quartet with extensive stage experience and an interesting and distinctive repertoire. The quartet appears to have been founded by Joseph M. Moore in the mid-1880s, and performed primarily in the greater New York City area. It was not related to the Unique Trio, an earlier group that made appearances in New York singing "glees and plantation melodies" during 1883–84.[1]

The first known reference to the Unique Quartette appears in the November 27, 1886, issue of the *New York Clipper,* a white theatrical paper, which listed them on the bill at the National Theatre in the Bowery. The reviewer, who was not always complimentary to struggling performers, commented tersely but positively that "the Unique Quartette's vocalisms found much favor." Further listings in the *Clipper* show that the quartet was performing at Doris's Harlem Museum and Huber's Palace Museum in October and December 1890.[2] Such "museums" were well-known venues for middle- and lower-class entertainment in the city, combining stage shows with freak-show exhibits in different parts of the premises.

The quartet's first recordings were made during its Huber's engagement in December 1890. We will probably never know whether they sought out recording, or if the small recording company on Fifth Avenue found them. It wouldn't have been difficult for them to find each other. All a hard-pressed recording manager had to do was drop in on one of the many vaudeville shows then playing in the city, take a few notes about which musical acts might serve his purposes, and make them an offer. Most would gladly spend an afternoon at the "recording laboratory" turning out wax cylinders to pick up a few dollars.

The New York Phonograph Company was one of the more active local companies making musical records. Originally chartered to cover New York state excluding New York City, it absorbed the city's Metropolitan Phonograph Company in mid-1890.[3] Thereafter, from its headquarters at 257 Fifth Avenue, it continued Metropolitan's active program of recording to supply the many coin-slot cylinder phonographs located around the city. This was the same company that recorded George W. Johnson, the first successful black artist. For most of 1889 and 1890 a man named Charles Marshall served as the company's chief recording technician, and it may have been Marshall who recruited the Unique Quartette. If any of these primeval cylinders is ever found it should be readily identifiable, as Marshall is said to have announced each one, "record taken by Charles Marshall, New York City."[4]

The ledgers of the New York Phonograph Company indicate that the Unique Quartette, managed by "J. Moore," was first paid for making musical cylinders on December 19, 1890, with further payments on December 22, 24, and 29. The titles recorded are not indicated, but the group was paid $8 for the first session, and $10 for each session thereafter.[5] This was not an insignificant amount for the period, and seems to have been typical of the fees paid to artists, which ranged from $4 or $5 for a solo artist to $20 or more for a band. The amount may well have been determined by the number of usable cylinders produced. Moore's quartet was certainly not discriminated against financially.

The cylinders must have been heavily played on the coin-slot machines, as the quartet was called back repeatedly during 1891 to make additional copies. Thirteen different session payments are noted during that year, eleven between January and August, and two more in the fall. The fee for each session was $10.

Meanwhile the quartet's theatrical career was thriving. In the spring of 1891 they joined the cast of *O'Dowd's Neighbors,* a new musical play. Rehearsals began on March 2, and a few days later the *Clipper* reported that "as the time draws near for the opening of *O'Dowd's Neighbors,* the management almost daily announce some new advertising novelty, the latest being the engagement of the Unique Quartet—four dark skinned importations from the South—who will distribute on the streets a handsome illustrated bazaar of especial interest to the ladies."[6] The reference to the South suggests that the quartet might have been from outside New York, but the phrase probably represents editorial license. At least one of the members was later said to be a lifelong resident of the city.

O'Dowd's Neighbors opened on April 20, 1891, at the Windsor Theater. According to the *Clipper,* it was a farce-comedy by Con T. Murphy, and included many variety acts, among them "two Irish comedians, a German comedian, a female impersonator, some capital singers, a number of clever dancers, a negro quartet, a donkey and a puppy." Included in the cast were J. M. Moore, W. H. Tucker, J. E. Carson, and S. G. Baker—presumably, the "negro quartet."[7] The play went on to a long and successful run, touring during the 1892–93 season and finally closing in Kansas City in October 1893. It was revived several times between 1894 and 1896, and also produced a spinoff, *O'Dowd's Tribulations,* which opened in 1894.[8] The Unique Quartette did not stay with the show for its entire run, however, and by the fall of 1893 the Empire Quartette was being featured.

The Uniques continued to record for the New York Phonograph Company in 1892, albeit less frequently, with two sessions in April and one in June. The last session payment was on March 14, 1893, by which time mounting financial problems had caused the struggling company to begin winding down its business. The popular quartet then moved to the North American Phonograph Company, which was producing cylinders under the Edison name, recording at least twenty titles during the fall of 1893. There may well have been more, as many Edison release numbers from this period are untraced.

The titles of the Edison cylinders reveal the quartet's repertoire to consist primarily of black-themed material, especially songs that lent themselves to strong harmonizing. Many were novelty songs, and several were apparently specialties of the group, judging by their multiple later recordings of them. Among these specialties were "Mamma's Black Baby Boy," the quartet standard "I'se Gwine Back to Dixie," "Hot Corn Medley," and "Dancing on the Old Barn Floor," the latter with rooster sounds and duck calls. Other titles included the biblically themed "Who Built the Ark?," "Hand Down That Robe," and "Peter, Go Ring Dem Bells," and a "negro shout" called "Camp-Ground Jubilee." Most of the material seems to have avoided the harsher black stereotypes so prevalent in popular songs of the day, although there are a couple of straightforward "coon songs" ("The Colored Band," "Parthenia Took a Fancy to a Coon"). A few selections, surprisingly, were standard white parlor songs, including "The Last Farewell" and "Maid of the Mill" ("Golden years ago, in a mill beside the sea . . .").

At least one of these 1893 Edison cylinders has survived, in remarkably good condition. "Mamma's Black Baby Boy" is a fascinating example of black quartet singing in the 1890s. The cylinder is announced by a deep, rolling voice with a southern accent, possibly one of the quartet members, as follows: "Edison record six-ninety-four, Mamma's Black Baby Boy, as sung by the celebrated Unique Quartette." (This was a period when Edison announcements included the record number.) The song, sung a capella, is a gentle novelty about all the little problems a young black boy causes his mama, spilling things and running about. The second verse takes an unexpected and humorous turn.

> I stoled all the 'lasses from off of de shelf,
> I'm my mamma's black baby boy.
> I spilled all the sweetness all over myself,
> I'm my mamma's black baby boy.
> She would send me to school most every day,
> I'd pick up my books, and I'd run away,
> And when I'd come home my mamma she would say . . . (what would she say,
>   honey?)
> I'm her little black baby boy.
>
> I'm my mamma's baby boy, I'm my mamma's baby boy,
> Oh, dey [laugh at me and holler?], I'm my mamma's baby boy.
>
> She'd give me ten cents to buy me some gum,
> I'm my mamma's black baby boy.
> I slipped in a saloon, and I bought me some rum
> I'm my mamma's black baby boy.
> I staggered and stumbled all over this place,
> And the mud it did splatter all into my face,
> And the people all say, I was a disgrace,
> I'm my mamma's black baby boy.[9]

The lilting melody is sung by the lead tenor, who is joined in the chorus ("I'm my mamma's baby boy . . .") by the rest of the quartet, in strong, multipart harmony.

It is sung in call-and-response pattern, with impeccable timing. The entire performance is extremely professional, by obviously well-practiced performers. One modern reviewer has commented on its "gentle harmony and rolling melodicism."[10] The cylinder has been reissued on several modern CDs.

The song "Mamma's Black Baby Boy" was published in 1886.[11] Interestingly, the second verse was originally about the child going to a store and buying some gum, but the quartet changed this to "I slipped in a saloon, and I bought me some rum," probably to get a bigger laugh.

The quartet continued to be active in the New York area during 1893–94. In December 1893 Joe Moore was performing with Haxpie's Colored Georgia Minstrels in Paterson, New Jersey, presumably with his quartet. Also in the company were Billy Carson (possibly the quartet's "J. E. Carson" of 1891) and Jim Settlers (probably J. E. Settles, who is known to have been with the quartet in later years). In January 1894 the quartet was one of the members of the Colored Professional Club of New York who attended a reception for the touring *South Before the War* company.[12]

In the early fall of 1894 the Georgia Minstrels, including the Unique Quartette, began a long run at Worth's Museum at 30th Street and 6th Avenue. It was a fairly prominent troupe, judging by the presence of two major stars of the black stage, Bob Cole and Gussie L. Davis. During early 1895, while the quartet was still at Worth's, it recorded new cylinders for the New Jersey Phonograph Company of Newark.[13] By April, Haxpie's Colored Georgia Minstrels had morphed into C. V. Moore's Colored Minstrels and were in their fortieth week at Worth's. In the cast were Bob Cole, the Unique Quartette, and Ben Hunn, who would later sing with the quartet. Gussie L. Davis was the stage manager. In May C. V. Moore left Worth's to form a new touring minstrel troupe. A June news item listed the quartet among many black entertainers attending the New York Colored Theatrical Club summer outing, and during the fall they appeared as a solo act at Huber's Eighth Avenue museum.[14] There are scattered listings of a new "Unique Trio" playing eastern and midwestern theaters between 1895 and 1897, but this group was presumably not connected with Moore's quartet.

In late 1895 the quartet again recorded for a small Chicago company, D. E. Boswell. This was followed in mid-1896 by cylinders for Walcutt and Leeds (marketed as "New York Cylinders") and for the Phonograph Record and Supply Company of New York. A mid-1896 Walcutt and Leeds catalog described the group simply as a "colored quartette," while the Phonograph Record and Supply Company August–September listing commented, "this quartet is composed of the best negro talent obtainable and their records are loud and distinct. To those who are fond of negro melodies, we can commend these productions of the genuine article."

The titles recorded in 1895–96 largely duplicated those on the 1893 Edison list, including three more versions of "Mamma's Black Baby Boy" and three of "Dancing on the Old Barn Floor." It is possible, in fact, that some of these were the same recordings being sold by different companies. The only new titles were "Sunshine Will Come Again," the old standard "The Old Oaken Bucket," and the Williams and Walker comic song "Dora Dean," about a stylish black vaudeville entertainer.

Two additional surviving Unique Quartette cylinders are apparently from this period, although they are not listed in any known catalogs.[15] The first is announced,

"Who Broke the Lock, by the celebrated Unique Quartette," with no company mentioned. The smaller recording firms frequently did not mention their names in the announcements, since they often sold their products to other dealers who represented them as their own. The repetition of the phrase "celebrated Unique Quartette" indicates that the group was still trading on its stage reputation.

The song is a variation on the 1893 tune "Who Picked the Lock (on the Henhouse Door)" by Monroe and Mack.[16] The announcer on this cylinder is not the same as on the 1893 Edison, and the lead tenor also sounds different. The performance of the upbeat number, however, is just as professional as on the slower "Mamma's Black Baby Boy." Like the earlier number, it is sung a capella in a call-and-response arrangement with the tenor singing a rhythmic verse about the "coons" having a party and the rest of the quartet coming in on the chorus. A resonant bass dominates the ensemble sound.

The other cylinder is announced "Jubilee shout, The Old Camp Ground, sung by the famous Unique Quartette." The song, also known as "Down on the Old Camp Ground," had evidently been in the quartet's repertoire for a number of years, also appearing on Edison in 1893. Like the other Unique cylinders, it is sung a capella, in call-and-response pattern. The performance seems rather uninspired, as if made at the end of a long session. To be fair, however, the surviving copy is extremely noisy, making close analysis difficult. The song was later recorded by the Dinwiddie Colored Quartet in a rousing version on Victor in 1902.

Although the quartet's last known recordings were made in 1896, it continued as a successful stage act for several more years. In the fall of 1896 they appeared with the Primrose and West Minstrels, one of the major mixed-race touring companies ("40 whites and 30 blacks"). The members were now identified as Joseph Moore, Walter Dixon, William Tucker, and Ben Hunn. By 1898 they were an independent act playing Proctor's Pleasure Palace in New York with Miss Leola Mitchell. A March 1898 item called them "leading society and club entertainers of Greater New York." During the 1898–99 season the quartet toured with Al Reeves's Big Black and White Company.[17]

The lineup during 1898–99 was Moore, J. E. Settles, and Samuel Baker, but with a constantly changing bass—first Burt Lozier, then J. Carson ("Cayson"), (Thomas?) Craig, and finally (Frank?) DeLyons.[18] Table 1 gives an approximate reconstruction

Table 1. Unique Quartette Membership

Dec. 1890*	Moore, ——, ——, ——
Apr. 1891*	Moore, Tucker, Baker, Carson
Dec. 1893*	Moore, Settles, ——, Carson
Oct. 1896*	Moore, Tucker, Dixon, Hunn
Mar. 19, 1898	Moore, Settles, Baker, Lozier
Mar. 26, 1898	Moore, Settles, Baker, Carson
Aug. 1898	Moore, Settles, Baker, Craig
Oct. 1898	Moore, Settles, Baker, DeLyons
Feb. 1899	Moore, Settles, ——, ——

Note: An asterisk indicates that the group was recording at about this time.

of the quartet's membership, based on mentions in theatrical journals. Some of these attributions are by no means certain, as names were often misspelled or abbreviated in press reports.

The last known mention of the quartet was in February 1899 while they were touring with the Al Reeves show in Buffalo.[19] The quartet may have disbanded around this time, as it receives no further mention and most of its members are later reported in other roles.

It may seem strange that the Unique Quartette did not record for the nationally distributed record labels operating in the Northeast in the late 1890s, Columbia, Edison, and Berliner. It was well known, its cylinders seem to have sold well (judging by the many remakes), and it had a distinctive repertoire. It may be that a busy performing schedule prevented them from being available for the many sessions necessary to turn out the large number of copies needed by the larger labels. Also, as a popular stage act, they may have been too expensive for the record companies to employ regularly. Columbia already had one well-known black quartet (the Standard Quartette) and may not have needed another. The Unique Quartette's failure to record for more widely distributed labels, or for the more durable discs, may be our loss, but it is perfectly logical.

There seems to have been continuing demand for the Unique's repertoire after it ceased recording, as Edison had a white group, the Edison Male Quartette, record six of the Unique's songs in late 1897 or early 1898. The six titles were numbered consecutively (from 2210 to 2215), indicating that they were made as a group. They were "Mamma's Black Baby Boy," "Who Broke the Lock?," "Dancing on the Old Barn Floor," "Hambone Medley," "Hot Corn Medley," and "Tapioca."

It is instructive to compare the Unique's 1893 performance of "Mamma's Black Baby Boy" with the version by the white Edison quartet. The former has a certain infectious lyricism, with momentary pauses and bursts of enthusiasm, similar to those of the child who is the subject of the song. The Edison quartet, on the other hand, sings the song very deliberately, with attention to each note and syllable, but not much to its emotional underpinnings. At times its performance borders on a black parody, as in the following exchange between the tenor and bass:

Tenor: And when I'd come home, my mamma she would say . . .
Bass: What would she say, honey?
Tenor: I'm her little black baby boy.

As sung by the Uniques, the bass's line is a brief and spontaneous interjection, unexpected and therefore humorous. As rendered by the white quartet, however, it is a long and drawn-out declamation, with heavily exaggerated voice inflection, as if intended to mock black speech patterns. At several points the white quartet also replaces "mamma" with "mammy." This is only one small example of the different ways in which white and black singers of the period treated black repertoire, a subject that deserves further study.

Most of the singers who passed through the Unique Quartette over the years had independent stage careers, and their paths often crossed. Samuel G. Baker (c. 1865–1914) and William H. Tucker both left the quartet for a period around 1894 to tour with the Primrose and West Minstrels. By 1900 Baker had become a member of the Clover Leaf Quartette, which toured with the *On the Suwanee River* company for several years. When he died in 1914 at age forty-nine, his obituary said that he had been "well known in theatricals for 30 years." His death certificate reveals that he had been a lifelong resident of New York City, and he may well have been with Moore's quartet from its inception in the 1880s.[20]

Tucker went on to become a member of the Imperial Quartette, one of the featured acts with a white show called *A Female Drummer* (1899), starring female impersonator Johnstone Bennett. After the show closed the quartet was reconstituted as "The Drummer Quartet," which toured at least until 1904, at which time the lineup was Tucker, manager Phil Portlock, N. B. Collins, and former Unique Quartette basso J. Frank DeLyons. In 1909 Tucker was one of the charter members of the Colored Vaudeville Benevolent Association in New York, but nothing is known of him after that.[21] Baker and Tucker lived at various addresses in New York in the mid- and late 1890s, according to city directories.

Little is known of James Settles. In 1903 he toured the Northeast with one of Sam Cousins's Colored Comedy troupes, and he was later seen in *The Smart Set* and in his own summer show (1905).[22]

The two best-known (at the time) members of Moore's quartet appear to have sung with him briefly around the time of the 1896 recordings. Tenor Walter A. Dixon toured nationally with McCabe and Young's Minstrels (1890, 1891) and McCabe's Mastodon Minstrels (1894) in the early 1890s. In 1897 he starred in the original cast of Cole and Johnson's groundbreaking black musical, *A Trip to Coontown,* in the comedy role of Captain Fleetfoot. After two years with that show he spent the ensuing decade with a variety of big-name minstrel companies and shows, including Billy Kersands's Minstrels, Rusco and Holland's Big Minstrel Festival, Will Marion Cook's *The Southerners* and the European road company of Williams and Walker's *In Dahomey,* which starred Avery and Hart. He often played comic female characters, including the role of Aunt Matilda in *The Southerners.* While with Kersands in 1906 he was described by a reviewer as "a tenor singer with a slurring accent on his dissyllables, [who] sang 'Sweet Adeline' a trifle swift but sweetly and was well received." He is mentioned in 1907 singing with former Standard Quartette member Jube Johnson in the Excelsior Quartette, and he may also be the lyric tenor "W. A. Dixon" who toured the South with A. G. Allen's Troubadours in 1910.[23]

Even better known was Ben Hunn, who began his career in the early 1880s with a variety of minstrel troupes, including Sam T. Jack's Creoles, Billy Kersands's Genuine Colored Minstrels and Hicks and Sawyer's Colored Minstrels. He sometimes appeared with his brother Charles Hunn (c. 1850–97). Music publisher Edward Marks, in his autobiography *They All Sang,* referred to Charlie and Ben as "two Zulu giants who appeared in the Gus Hill colored shows." By 1895 Ben was in the stock company of Worth's Theatre in New York, said to be the first black-run theater in the city. In 1896 he was with the Primrose and West Minstrels, and in 1898 a reviewer called him a "cyclone of laughter" with Al Reeves's show. Another review, while he was with the Pat Chappelle Rabbit Foot Company in the summer of 1900, dubbed him "the greatest darky of them all." In 1901 he founded a vaudeville booking agency in Boston with Harry Eaton and fielded his own summer shows that toured New England fairs for several years. (This was evidently not bad work; one of his ads for talent read, "Wanted: 15 females, must be good looking.") During the winters he either toured on his own or joined such companies as Ernest Hogan and Billy McClain's *Smart Set* (1902–3). In May 1902 he married Lethia Liverpool, and they performed together as The Hunns during 1903–4.

By the early 1900s Hunn was considered an old-timer in the business, and some reviews suggested that he relied on rather dated material, interrupting the show for energetic renditions of ancient numbers such as "Turkey in the Straw." His big number in *The Smart Set* was a more recent song called "Gabie." Whatever his material, audiences seemed to love his energy and enthusiasm. Referred to as a "pioneer minstrel man," he wrote a long and interesting letter to the Indianapolis *Freeman* in 1902 describing the sad state of the black theater at that time, how black performers were being taken advantage of by white managers, and how blacks nevertheless seemed to do little to support "their own."[24]

Of the members who passed through the quartet briefly in 1898 (but did not record), mention should be made of bass singer "Craig," who may well be the basso Thomas Craig who made solo recordings for Berliner in that year. J. Frank DeLyons, originally a jubilee basso, had toured with tenor (and later critic) Sylvester Russell in the early 1890s. He stayed with Joseph Moore for a time in the early 1900s, but by 1904 had joined ex-quartet member William H. Tucker in the Drummer Quartette. He was still active in New York vaudeville in 1910, by then teamed with J. W. Jeffries.

After the Unique Quartette disbanded around 1899, its founder and guiding spirit, Joseph M. Moore, organized a small troupe called the New Orleans Minstrels, whose quartet initially included himself, Unique basso J. Frank DeLyons, James Robinson, and Charles Williams. He operated this group for at least ten years, appearing mostly in New York City, although it occasionally traveled in the Northeast. (It is not to be confused with another "New Orleans Minstrels," operated by A. G. Allen, which toured the Southern states.) Apparently his career as a manager served him well. An item in 1910 observed that "Joe Moore (of no more minstrel fame) . . . has money to burn," and that he had presented several gifts to the Colored Vaudeville Benevolent Association.[25] Nothing is known of him after that.

The Unique Quartette passed from the scene around 1899, after a career lasting nearly fifteen years, and most of its members seem to have left show business by 1910. The once-popular quartet was soon forgotten and virtually no references to it are found in later years. Even its repertoire, much of which consisted of relatively gentle, humorous, black-themed songs, seemed to pass out of favor in the early 1900s, an era that favored harsher, stereotypical "coon songs." Were it not for the few, fragile brown wax cylinders that have survived from the early and mid-1890s, we would know little of a style of black quartet singing that was polished, engaging, and highly popular in its day.

5 Louis "Bebe" Vasnier: Recording in Nineteenth-Century New Orleans

The Louisiana Phonograph Company has always held a special fascination for researchers due to the musical fertility of the Crescent City. What treasures *might* have been recorded by an enterprising firm that was active in New Orleans, the "cradle of jazz," in the 1890s, just at the time first glimmerings of "America's native music" were being heard in its streets?

Not much, it turns out. Although it was one of the earliest local phonograph agencies to record, this white-run enterprise stuck to fairly traditional repertoire for its mostly white, middle class clientele. The horn of the legendary Buddy Bolden may have been heard on the streets, but he was apparently not invited into the primitive recording studio, at least not to record commercially.[1]

The company did, however, record and promote another black artist. Louis Vasnier was a local performer and, unlike the nationally known musicians based in the Northeast, he has received little attention from modern researchers. The only substantive information about him located by this writer was in a short article in the *Jazz Archivist* (1989), published at Tulane University.[2] Yet Vasnier was apparently the third African American act to record commercially, preceded only by George W. Johnson and the Standard Quartette, both of whom began in 1890.

But before he could be heard, the phonograph itself had to make its way to New Orleans.

The Louisiana Phonograph Company

There had been demonstrations of Edison's original tinfoil phonograph in New Orleans in the early 1880s. However the inventor's improved machine arrived rather late, in 1891, more than two years after it was introduced in the north. Marketing of the Edison Phonograph was controlled by a national syndicate called the North American Phonograph Company, and the local sales franchise for Louisiana had been bought by two sets of brothers, H. Lee and Robert H. Sellers, and Hugh R. and Thomas Conyngton.

The four men had previously established the Texas Phonograph Company of Galveston. Founded in mid-1889, it had been one of the least successful of the thirty-odd local phonograph franchises. Several reasons were given for this, including its distance from New York (where the sometimes temperamental machines had to be sent for repairs), the lack of a large commercial center to support the company, and the sparse and scattered population throughout the rest of its territory. In addition, marketing emphasis had been upon the business uses of the phonograph, which proved to be a limited market. It was also suggested that Thomas

Conyngton, the general manager, had been unable to give the enterprise his full attention, being often absent.[3]

The Sellers and Conyngton brothers were nevertheless convinced of the possibilities of the phonograph and determined to try again. By late 1890 most of the desirable franchises had been sold, but nearby New Orleans remained unclaimed. It was a relatively large commercial center and had a vibrant musical and entertainment life. The Sellerses and Conyngtons applied for the Louisiana franchise, specifying that H. Lee Sellers would be president, Hugh Conyngton secretary/treasurer (the same position he had held in Texas), and Thomas Conyngton and Robert Sellers directors.

The brothers took a number of steps to avoid their previous mistakes, establishing their own repair facility and bringing in an experienced full-time general manager, Frank E. Clarkson, to run the business. Clarkson had begun his career in the infant telephone industry. In late 1888 and early 1889 he had assisted with the financial organization of the Metropolitan (New York City) and Minnesota Phonograph Companies. From March 1889 until late 1890 he had been general manager of the Georgia Phonograph Company. Unfortunately no sooner had Clarkson arrived in New Orleans than he died suddenly, at the age of thirty-two.[4] His responsibilities were assumed by Hugh Conyngton.

Perhaps the most important decision made by the brothers was to break with tradition and emphasize the entertainment uses of the phonograph from the start. Edison and the founders of the North American Phonograph Company felt that to push this aspect would "belittle" the invention as a toy and make it difficult to gain acceptance in the more lucrative business world. They railed against using the phonograph primarily for entertainment, even as the local companies were foundering trying to break into the office market. In desperation, several companies had taken the plunge into entertainment. They began to prosper as a result. The founders of the Louisiana Phonograph Company made no secret of their intentions.

> From its position as the last company organized, the Louisiana Company has been enabled to profit from the experience of the older companies and to avoid the errors and misfortunes inevitable to the development of an entirely new business. . . . The attention of the company was first turned to the social and exhibition uses of the machine, and as the first step in this direction the automatic [i.e., coin-slot] phonograph was introduced to the New Orleans public.
>   The company began its operations with the conviction that the phonograph was a legitimate and attractive source of amusement, and one that properly maintained need not lose its hold on public favor.[5]

The improved phonograph was introduced to New Orleans with a splash by H. Lee Sellers. On January 24, 1891, he held a demonstration for the press and on January 26 a lecture and demonstration at Tulane University for an invited audience of 200 community leaders. Both events were amply covered in the city's two leading newspapers, the *Daily States* and the *Times Picayune.* Possibly Sellers hoped to be in the field before Mardi Gras in February, which was then as now the city's biggest entertainment festival. He said the company would be chartered within "a few days," although in fact it took two months.

The audience listened politely to Sellers's predictions about how the phonograph would revolutionize American business, but it really came to life when the little machine began to sing. The *Daily States* reported on the press briefing as follows.

> The interview was enlivened by pleasing tests of the phonograph. Adapting to the machine at one end a rubber tube branching out into two parts at the other extremity, fitting upon each of those points with a piece of vulcanized rubber round in shape, and slipping a wax cylinder upon the mandrell, Mr. Sellers said to the *States* reporter, "Now, rest these rubber lobes gently into the orifices of your ears and listen." He then turned on the electric current and with a gentle whirr the cylinder began to revolve.
>
> Clear and distinct a voice was heard, announcing with that peculiar emphasis and tone that one hears so frequently from the stage, "Ladies and gentlemen, you will now hear a selection by the United States Marine Band of Washington, D.C., played for the North American Phonograph Company." And then—the band played. It played most delightfully. Every instrument was plainly heard. Beautiful concerted music it was, too. The tone, the timbre, the inflections, the rise and fall of the musical waves, the fleeting intervals between the bars; everything was as clear and distinct as could be desired. Mr. Sellers took out that cylinder and put on another, which gave out an amusing song, in the "plantation negro" dialect, with piano accompaniment.
>
> Next a dictated business letter was heard, every word from "my dear sir" to "yours truly, John Blank," being distinctly audible.[6]

The same paper found the Tulane audience just as enchanted with the machine's musical possibilities. After reciting Mr. Edison's obligatory ten uses of the phonograph (business dictation, talking books for the blind, the teaching of elocution, talking clocks, and so on—"reproduction of music" being strictly incidental), Sellers then set the phonograph to "speak for itself": "After treating the astonished and delighted audience to concerted music, chimes of bells of St. Andrews Church, New York; negro dialect songs; violin, violincello and flute selections; Mr. Sellers invited anyone in the audience to whistle or sing into the instrument. Prof. Brown Ayers volunteered and whistled 'Listen to the Mocking Bird' with variations. This was minutely reproduced by the phonograph, to the intense delight of the audience."[7]

The *Jazz Archivist* article speculated that Louis Vasnier's cylinders were played at this first demonstration, but it seems more likely that the "negro dialect songs" referred to were obtained from one of the northern companies, which were turning them out in quantity at this time.[8] The U.S. Marine Band and St. Andrews Church cylinders were definitely imported. It is possible that New York and New Jersey cylinders by black artist George W. Johnson, which were already very popular, may have been played.

After a frustrating delay, the company was finally incorporated on March 7, 1891, and on the same day placed its first coin-slot cylinder jukebox in Eugene May's fashionable Palace Drug Store at the corner of Canal and Chartres Streets. It was fabulously successful, taking in $1,430.80 in nickels in its first three months. This was reported to be the most profitable single location in the entire country.[9]

A limited number of additional coin-slot phonographs were placed throughout the city, and a twelve-machine arcade was established at West End, the city's popular summer resort by the shores of Lake Ponchartrain. The large, handsome, glass-enclosed phonographs, powered by large storage batteries and internally lit by electric lights, attracted patrons throughout the hot summer months. A considerable quantity and variety of musical cylinders were required to feed these machines. The company made clear on several occasions that it was buying prerecorded cylinders from most of the northern companies, and it may have even had recordings made for it by those companies. One collector has reported a cylinder by New York tenor J. W. Myers announced as a product of the Louisiana Phonograph Company. This might well have been made for Louisiana by one of the northern companies.[10]

The company recorded local talent as well, probably beginning in early or mid-1891. The identities of most of these artists are lost, as none of the company's catalogs or ledgers have ever been found (some cylinders may have been made solely for use on the company's own coin-slot machines, and therefore not listed in catalogs). How the company selected the two local artists it would promote nationally is not known. It was probably a combination of their salability and their willingness to work inexpensively for long hours in front of the recording horn, performing the same songs over and over to stockpile copies for sale.

The company's featured band was led by George Paoletti. His Paoletti's Southern Band was a popular local attraction for nearly thirty years, from the 1890s to the end of World War I. One of the band's more intriguing titles was "Dixie, as Rendered in the South." The chief vocal attraction was part-time minstrel Louis "Bebe" Vasnier, who had worked up a novelty he called his "Brudder Rasmus" sermons.

Louis Vasnier

Vasnier was born in May 1858 in Louisiana.[11] His father, Louis Sr. (1820–91), and mother, Louise (1826–92), were "Creoles of color" descended from French-speaking Creoles who were free before the Civil War. During the 1880s the middle-class Vasnier family lived at a variety of addresses in a racially mixed area east of downtown New Orleans.[12] Louis Sr. was a carpenter who, according the census, employed ten or more men. Louis Jr., or "Bebe," worked by day as a house painter and also employed several men.

Bebe had a sideline which he pursued in his spare time. An accomplished banjo player, he formed a semiprofessional minstrel company with a man named Johnson which appeared in local halls in the 1880s as Johnson and Vasnier's Colored Minstrels. One such appearance was advertised in the *Weekly Pelican,* a New Orleans newspaper, in 1887, as follows: "Johnson and Vasnier's colored minstrel company will give a performance Monday evening, February 14, at Friends of Hope Hall on Treme Street. Admission 25 cts. Performance commences at 8 o'clock." Subsequently the same newspaper noted that "they gave a credible performance."[13]

By the beginning of the 1890s Vasnier had established himself as a semiprofessional local musician. He was known only in the New Orleans area, and he could hardly have been called prominent even there, but this probably meant that the new phonograph enterprise could engage him at a reasonable rate. A January 1892 story on the new phonograph company referred to him as follows.

> In keeping up the standard and variety of its music, the Louisiana Phonograph Company has obtained records from almost every part of the country, and has in addition taken a very large amount of local music. New Orleans is perhaps the most generally musical city of our country and its musicians are very fine. In addition to all kinds of instrumental and vocal music, the company has gotten out a line of negro specialties of great popularity, consisting of old plantation songs, darkey melodies, etc. Probably the most successful specialty is the work of "Brudder Rasmus," whose sermons such as "Charity ob de Heart," "Adam and Eve and de Winter Apple," "Sinners, Chicken Stealers, etc." and "De Lottrey," with the characteristic participation of his congregation, are wonderfully realistic and attractive.[14]

Having had success within its own territory, by late 1891 the Louisiana company began to distribute its recordings nationally. In September it took out its first small advertisement in the *Phonogram,* the national trade paper of the phonograph industry, offering "finest musical records." No titles or artists were specified. A copy of its "catalogue list of musical records manufactured by the Louisiana Phonograph Co." was forwarded to the same paper, which commented in January 1892, "[The] price list includes a large variety of marches, schottisches, polkas, waltzes and a miscellaneous collection of arrangements from the best operatic musical authors. Paoletti's band, price $1.25 each. There are vocal selections: Vasnier, banjo quartettes, $1.25 each; Brady speeches, $1.25 each; artistic whistler, $1.25 each; United States Marine Band, $1.50 each; parlor orchestra, $1.25 each; vocal selections, $1.00 each. MUSIC LOUD AND CLEAR."[15] Some of these selections were obviously obtained from other companies (Brady monologues from the Ohio Phonograph Company, the artistic whistler—probably John Y. AtLee—from Columbia, the U.S. Marine Band from Columbia). Vasnier and Paoletti, however, were the company's own.

In the April–May 1892 issue of the *Phonogram,* Louisiana began advertising its artists by name in a full-page ad, listing forty-three titles by Paoletti, five "negro sermons" by Brudder Rasmus (now only $1.00 each), and eight songs with banjo accompaniment by Vasnier. Of the sermons it was said, "All of these are very popular, and good for the blues. Try them!" The titles given were said to be only a partial list, with a full catalog available on application (unfortunately, no copies seem to have survived). It was also made clear that these were first-grade cylinders, that is, directly recorded by the artists, which was important to exhibitors who needed the clearest, loudest copies possible. Second-grade duplicates, which were "nearly as good," were available at reduced prices.[16]

During the summer Louisiana sent samples of the Brudder Rasmus cylinders to the editor of the *Phonogram,* who commented, "they are original, quaint and interesting, and have to be heard to be appreciated."[17] Apparently copies were sent to Thomas A. Edison as well. The following letter to the inventor, dated August 4, 1892, has been found in the files at the Edison National Historic Site.

Thos. A. Edison, Esq.
Orange, N.J.
Dear Sir,

Some time ago the North American Phonograph Company ordered from us some sample records of our Negro Dialect series. They informed us that they wished them for you. Our company at once sent on some of our Negro Sermons which we consider the best we have in this line, and as they were for you sent them with the compliments of the La. Phono. Co., hoping that you would receive them and be afforded some amusement by their exceedingly good and realistic effects.

Hoping that you have received them in good shape, we remain,

Yours very truly,
La. Phono. Co., L't'd,
(signed) H. Lee Sellers, V.P.

The files indicate that Edison responded on August 24, but the answer has been lost. The pride that the Louisiana company had in these productions is evident, however.

What did Vasnier sound like? Only one example of this pioneering black artist has been found. It is a fragile wax cylinder of "Adam and Eve and de Winter Apple." This one copy passed through the hands of a series of private collectors over the years and as recently as the early 1980s was said to be relatively clear and understandable. No one, apparently, bothered to make a taped copy at the time. Unfortunately by the time it reached this writer in 1993 (and was immediately taped), it had deteriorated badly.[18]

A collector who heard the cylinder in the 1980s recalled the opening announcement as something like "Louis Vasnier will now tell the story of 'Adam and Eve and de Winter Apple.'" No company name was given, and the artist's name was pronounced *Vas*-nier. It consisted of talking only, with no musical accompaniment.[19] Listening today through the now extremely heavy surface noise, one can make out the deep-voiced Brudder Rasmus (Vasnier) delivering a mock "sermon" in broad dialect to his enthusiastic congregation, which responds with periodic exclamations and shouts of "uh huh!" A woman's voice (or imitation of same) seems to be part of the throng. Toward the end the Brudder breaks out in song, a sort of chant, and the congregation joins in. The rendition is not nearly as mannered as most white caricatures of black preaching at the time and seems to be an genuine attempt to capture the flavor of a real down-South church service.[20] Perhaps some future technology will allow us to recover more fully the text of this unique document.

An interesting item appeared in the *Phonogram* at about this time which reflected the difficulty the Louisiana company must have had in reaching beyond the white market. An Iowa reader inquiring about business opportunities received the following advice from the editor.

Q: Can you inform me if the South is a good territory?
A: The South is a good territory if properly worked.
Q: Will the whites and negroes patronize the same machines?
A: Don't think they will.[21]

Segregation was rigidly enforced at this time, and it is likely that Vasnier's cylinders had to be made available on separate coin-slot phonographs for white and black patrons at the resorts surrounding New Orleans.

Vasnier's other cylinders reflect the standard minstrel repertoire of the day. Songs like "Black Pickaninny" and "Coon with a Razor" were typical of the demeaning stereotypes that were deeply embedded in popular culture. Blacks and white alike sang them, and hardly anybody objected. "Turkey in de Straw" and "Old Gray Mule" (a takeoff on "Old Gray Mare"?) are from the folk tradition. The lyrics of some of Vasnier's selections have been located, and they suggest that he specialized in raucous comic songs. "Rock dat Ship" sounds like a spiritual but is probably "Rock dat Ship in de Morning," a lively minstrel tune written and sung by William J. Scanlan, in which Gabriel exhorts,

> Children, rock dat ship in the morning,
> And rock dat ship at night,
> Rock dat ship de whole day long,
> Be sure you rock it right![22]

"Good Bye, Susan Jane" is a comic song about a fickle sweetheart who leaves her beau for Rufus Andrew Jackson Payne. Instead of pining, the jilted boyfriend says, "I looked her in the face and said, Good bye Susan Jane!" Then he begins to mock her.

> Her mouth was like a cellar,
> Her foot was like a ham,
> Her eyes were like an owl's at night,
> Her voice was never calm.
> Her hair was long and curly,
> She looked just like a crane,
> I've bid farewell to all my love,
> Good Bye, Susan Jane.[23]

In August the Louisiana company changed its advertisement in the *Phonogram* to feature Vasnier exclusively, adding two new sermons, "Job" and the interestingly titled "Why You Are Black." It added, "These sermons, while very humorous, are characteristic Negro delineations and are faithful reproductions of a dusky style of pulpit oratory that is rapidly passing away. The sermons are very popular amongst both whites and blacks and have proved to be among the most profitable of exhibition records. All records are clear and distinct."[24]

The *Phonogram,* delighted to have the advertising, remarked in November, "We commend to our readers the laughable negro melodies, which are characteristic delineations of the colored preacher, as made by the Louisiana Phonograph Co. in their amusing series of 'Vasnier Records.' They will drive away the blues."[25] An item in January 1893 stated that "the proprietor of a popular [New York] uptown resort tells us he gathers more nickels from the 'Brudder Rasmus' sermons than any records they have. They are made by the Louisiana Phonograph Co., New Orleans."[26]

The Louisiana company continued its advertising featuring Vasnier's Brudder Rasmus cylinders right up until the last issue of the failing *Phonogram,* which was dated March–April 1893 (but probably published some months later). The publication reciprocated with kind words in its editorial columns. In the February issue the editor wrote, "The Louisiana Phonograph Co. gave some pleasant entertainments during Mardi Gras, at their phonographic parlor. The celebrated 'Vasnier Records' made a hit." The following issue was even more glowing.

> We received from a gentleman who was visiting New Orleans during the Mardi Gras festivities an account of the status of the Louisiana Phonograph Co., and learn that it was never more prosperous or more buoyant than now. The sales of machines are increasing, the people take an interest in the enterprise, and the entertainment afforded by the musical phonograph is greatly enjoyed.
> The musical records made by this company are of the finest. Wherever the French take up their abode one finds a grace, a perfection of detail and finish applied to the arts not met with elsewhere; and in New Orleans both the musical selections and the rendering of them is exceptionally good. Mr. Louis Vasnier's characteristic delineations of negro dialect continue very popular.[27]

Despite the upbeat reports, the United States was sliding into the worst economic depression of the decade, and the phonograph industry—a mere amusement business now—was sliding along with it. Most of the local phonograph companies were scaling down operations or going out of business entirely. Only the hardiest would weather the storm.

The fourth annual national convention of the local companies was held in Chicago in September 1893. The Louisiana company was represented by Hugh Conyngton and R. H. Sellers, but no mention was made of their Texas company. Most of the program was filled with educational sessions, and there no frank vetting of the industry's problems as had occurred during the previous three annual conventions, at least in the general sessions (transcripts of the executive sessions were not published).[28] It would be the last such convention for many years. The North American Phonograph Company itself went bankrupt in 1894.

The Louisiana Phonograph Company apparently wound down its activities during 1893–94. Nothing further is heard of it in scattered mentions of industry affairs during 1894–95, or in the *Phonoscope,* the new industry trade paper that debuted in late 1896. City directories indicate that the company moved out of its pricey Equitable Building offices in 1894 to Hugh Conyngton's residence at 130 Canal Street. In 1895 it was listed at 722 Canal Street where the partners ran a real estate and securities exchange firm. In 1896 the company was taken over by one T. Mauro, possibly a relation of American Graphophone Company lawyer Philip Mauro, and renamed the Louisiana Phonograph and Kinetoscope Agency. One suspects that by this time Edison's new motion-picture machine, the kinetoscope, was a more popular novelty than the phonograph. The company's last listing in the city directory was in 1897.

As for Louis Vasnier, he too disappeared from the city listings at about this time. His departure may have been connected with the deadly yellow fever epidemic that struck New Orleans in 1897. By 1898 he had relocated to St. Louis. An item in the July 23, 1898, Indianapolis *Freeman,* a national black newspaper, revealed that "Louie Vassinier [*sic*] of St. Louis, who, owing to illness last season was forced to resign the road, has improved wonderfully, not only in health, but new ideas as well, and will place some of them the coming season in many of the up-to-date vaudeville houses."[29]

Vasnier was still not pursuing a show business career full-time. During all of his years in New Orleans, and in St. Louis as well, he was always listed in the city directories as a house painter.[30] About a year after he arrived in St. Louis Vasnier was married (c. 1899) to a Mississippi woman named Lizzie, who was nine years his junior. Vasnier and his wife are listed in the 1900 U.S. Census as renting an apartment in a small home on South 14th Street in a racially mixed neighborhood. They had no children, and the census also reveals that both Louis and Lizzie could read and write. His occupation was given as "sign painter."

The last professional reference to Louis Vasnier that has been located is a small advertisement in the July 14, 1900, *Freeman.* Now in his early forties, he was still performing and looking for bookings for his distinctive act, which was vividly described.

LOUIS VASNIER
SINGING AND DIALECT COMEDIAN SKETCH AND SONG WRITER

In an original monologue turn, away from everybody else. (No elbow or chin holding). Natural facial expressions, in five different dialects, no make up—Negro, Dutch, Dago, Irish and French. I sing in all. The only colored comedian who can do it. "De proof of de eating vas in de puddings." "Sure it's the like of me dat can do it." "I tella fo you no lie." "Je ne mant pas." Address: LOUIS VASNIER, 110 S. 14th St., St. Louis, Mo.

Nothing further is known of Vasnier. His last listing in the St. Louis City Directory was in 1901. It is possible that he continued to perform in small-time vaudeville, although no reference to him has been found in the show business newspapers of the day. It is almost certain that he never again recorded. Despite the Louisiana company's attempts to promote his early 1890s recordings on a national level, there is no evidence that they ever achieved the popularity of the cylinders made by George W. Johnson, Len Spencer, the U.S. Marine Band, or other widely cited "stars." No copies beyond the one mentioned are known to exist today. No picture of Louis Vasnier has been located.

In fact, most of the fragile brown wax cylinders made by Vasnier during the early 1890s probably did not survive for more than a few years. Between the heavy wear of coin-slot phonographs and the heat and humidity of New Orleans, they were no doubt a dim memory by 1900—recalled only in memories of hot summer nights in the brightly lit amusement arcades of Lake Ponchartrain. For us Vasnier's music and humor is just barely audible beneath the surface noise of that one, deteriorating cylinder. The destruction of this important piece of black history at the hands of private collectors should serve as a wake-up call to historians. Hopefully, with further research and better preservation of what remains of our recorded legacy of the 1890s, we will one day discover more about this fascinating artist and his recordings.

Postscript

In 1994 I sent a tape of the Vasnier cylinder to Johnny Parth, proprietor of Document Records (an Austrian reissue label), as an example of something in such poor condition as to be beyond salvation even by his technology. Without warning, and to my amazement, Parth included the tape on a CD of rare early black recordings issued the following year, titled *Too Late Too Late*, vol. 4, *More Newly Discovered Titles and Alternate Takes, 1892–1937* (Document DOCD-5321). The writer of the liner notes scarcely knew what to make of the track ("a noise like the roaring of the sea . . . hardly anything can be understood of the story Vasnier tells"). However through the magic of digital technology it is now available for anyone who wants to try to make it out.

6 The Standard Quartette
and *South before the War*

The story of the Standard Quartette is closely intertwined with that of *South before the War*, a highly successful theatrical spectacle that toured the United States for most of the 1890s. The quartet was a featured act during at least three seasons of the long-running show, and the cylinders they made while with the show may well represent the only surviving "original cast recordings" from that production. They also represent valuable documentation of black quartet stage performance style in the 1890s.

The quartet seems to have been organized around 1890. Based in Chicago, it spent most of its history touring throughout the United States and there was a good deal of turnover in its membership over the years. The first press notices did not name the members, but slightly later reports (1893–95) listed four singers from the Midwest—Ed DeMoss, H. C. Williams, and Rufus L. Scott from Indianapolis, and William Cottrell from Toledo.[1] DeMoss was a tenor and Scott the bass. Nothing further is known about the backgrounds of these singers.

The earliest published reference to the quartet that has been located was in August 1891, while they were appearing at Huber and Gerhardt's Casino in Brooklyn, New York.[2] This coincides almost exactly with the date of their first recordings, which were made in the same month for the New York Phonograph Company, the firm that had previously recorded black artists George W. Johnson and the Unique Quartette. The Standard Quartette made two groups of cylinders for the company, on August 5 and 19, 1891, and was paid $10 for each session. This was a respectable amount of money for the period and was the same amount as the Unique Quartette was paid. Titles were not indicated.[3] Unlike the Unique Quartette, the Standards did not become regular artists for the company, probably because of their heavy touring schedule. The handful of cylinders they made were placed on coin-operated phonographs around the city while the quartet was appearing in New York. None are known to survive.

The quartet's activities for the next two seasons are untraced. In July 1893 they were back in New York, making one more batch of cylinders for the New York Phonograph Company while appearing at local theaters. Their major breakthrough would come that fall, when they joined the cast of the enormously popular touring show, *South before the War.*

South before the War had originated in Louisville, Kentucky, in 1892. According to one account, the idea for the show was conceived by black actor and musician Billy McClain, who pitched it to white theater owners John Whallen and Harry Martell. Sixty actors, singers, and dancers staged an energetic recreation of happy days in the Old South, through comedy, songs, and sketches. Spectacular panoramas were revealed as the curtains parted, including a plantation scene with black field hands singing spirituals in the midst of a real cottonfield, a levee scene on the old Mississippi, and a mammoth cakewalk. As one reviewer would later observe, with just a hint of sarcasm, *South before the War* offered "scenes in the sunny south in antebellum days, when the life of the colored folk had its bright moments, although they were slaves."[4]

The idea of "happy slave days" may seem grotesque today. However, the 1890s was an era when blacks were increasingly demanding an equal place in society. Many whites responded by romanticizing the Old South as a time when the "colored folk knew their place" and allegedly liked it. That attitude, and the show itself, were vividly described in the flowery prose of the following press release, believed to have been written by Harry Martell himself. Note the dismissive reference to "the Harriet Beecher Stowe class of literature" (i.e., *Uncle Tom's Cabin*) and similar tales of "whipping overseers" and "tyrannical masters." This was an Old South of "happy days and pleasant nights."

"THE SOUTH BEFORE THE WAR"

A generation has passed since the good old Antebellum days were with us, and with the decades now buried forever in the dim past, has disappeared forever the old-time plantation darkey, at least that interesting ebony individual has gone from actual life and lives now only in his counterfeit presentment upon the ever productive stage.

Those of use who knew the "Souf befo' the Wah," as the children of Ham put it, and who know what plantation life really was [like] before our great internecine struggle, and such of us as have not had our opinions colored by the Harriet Beecher Stowe class of literature, but can recall the happy days and pleasant nights spent by the darkies in the cotton fields and cane brakes, will have an opportunity of seeing and living over again those happy times at —— theatre by witnessing the inimitable performance given by Whallen and Martell's big *South before the War* company.

Sixty genuine southern darkies in genuine southern fun making. Sixty soulful singers and "rale divilish" dancers, buckers, wingers, jig reel and clog dancers. Soloists, duettists, trios, quartettes—a veritable quartette of quartettes, composed of two male and two female quartettes. Camp meeting shouters and shooters, acrobatic Salvationists, glee singers, jubilee singers, cotton picking, shindy kicking crap-shooting "coons."

No burnt-cork and velvet-breeched, inconsistent Ethiopian imitators, but calico-clad gunny-sacked, fun-loving, music-making, Momus-like "mokes" to whom terpsichorean tripping and sweet singing are necessary parts of their joyful existence.

The bill is a varied one, in which the three score participants have every opportunity of showing their versatility, from the loose-jointed and limber-limbed acrobat in "Silence and Fun" to the vociferous and leather lunged exhorter at "Camp Meeting" and the dandified darkey in the excruciatingly funny cakewalk. The scenery is simply excellent, the cotton field is true to nature, actual cotton plants "jes from de Souf" being plentifully placed upon the stage. The steamboat landing and steamboat [is] a piece of perfect realism seldom equaled in scenic effect. The costumes are particularly noticeable for lack of fashionable beauty, but irresistibly appealing because of the picturesqueness of their very paucity and vari-colored incongruity.

The music, when modern, is certainly brand new and matchlessly mellifluous, and where it is not modern consists of the "old but ever new" always pleasing airs. "My Old Kentucky Home," "The Poor Old Slave," "Carry Me Back," "The Suwanee River," and a score more of those soul inspiring ditties to which time but adds beauty and feeling, heartfelt songs whose plaudits come in tears.

There is an inexplicable charm about the performances, where in its higher flights it delights the audience with its truthful portrayal of nature, showing with photographic exactness its people as they were in fact, as well as by the noticeable absence of the whipping overseer and the tyrannical rather than the paternal master.

In a word, from the rising to the falling of the curtain one is transported through the pleasant media of song, dance, music and merriment in an inimitable manner back to the good old days of the past and "The South before the War."[5]

The spectacle toured the eastern United States and quickly became a major hit with theater-goers. Its arrival in most towns was treated not as a show but as an event. Among the high points were the comedy skits featuring Uncle Eph and Aunt Dinah, a rotund mammy usually played by a well-padded male; the much-imitated buck-and-wing dancing; and the big cakewalk competition. McClain later claimed that the show was a principal factor in popularizing that high-stepping dance across the country.[6] During the early seasons the cast included the Eclipse, Southern, Twilight and Buckingham Quartettes (the "quartet of quartets"), Billy McClain (who also served as stage manager), his wife Cordelia, comedian Billy Williams, and Ferry the Frog Man. The Standard Quartette joined in the fall of 1893.

The lineup at this time was DeMoss, Williams, Scott, and Cottrell. There is some evidence of turnover during the preceding year as basso Scott had appeared in (and provided music for) a show called *King Kalico*—described by one critic as a "dull absurdity"—during the summer of 1892.[7] H. C. Williams may be the Henry Williams who sang with the Southern Quartette in *South before the War* in early 1893.[8]

The Standard Quartette soon became an integral part of *SBW*'s large and varied cast, singing black-themed songs, both comic and religious. During a January 1894 New York City engagement a reviewer noted that "the olio consists of Katie Carter, a clever dialect; the Beantown Comedy Quartet in 'Washday on the Levee'; a prize

South before the War, a major touring show of the 1890s, featured the Standard Quartette and other black acts. (American Musical Theatre Collection, Yale University Music Library)

buck and wing dancing contest; Lo La Lanchmere, an importation from Hawaii; Ferry, the frog man, in a good act; Billy Williams, comedian; and the Buckingham, Twilight and Standard Quartettes. The performance concludes with a cake walk."[9]

The large show was constantly on the move throughout the Northeast and Midwest. For the 1893–94 season it opened in Lowell, Massachusetts, on October 18, 1893, then proceeded to Pittsburgh, Indianapolis, Cincinnati, Columbus, Baltimore, Washington, D.C., Cleveland, Buffalo, Meadville, Pa., New Castle, Pa., Girard, Pa., Dunkirk, N.Y., Buffalo, Rochester, New York City, New Haven, Worcester, Mass., Montreal, Boston, Providence, Philadelphia, Baltimore, Washington, D.C., Pittsburgh, Cleveland, Cincinnati, Louisville, Chicago, Pittsburgh, Baltimore, Wilmington, Del., Reading, Pa., New York City, and Brooklyn, closing in Hoboken on May 12, 1894. Most of these were full-week engagements, with some cities visited twice.

Both the Standard Quartette and fellow cast member Jessie Oliver (a white soprano) recorded while on the road with *South before the War,* producing what amounts to "original cast recordings." Amazingly, on some of these they appeared together, making them apparently the first interracial recordings ever marketed. On March 3, 1894, the Columbia Phonograph Company of Washington, D.C., an-

South before the War cast posing in front of its special railroad car. Could the Standard Quartette be in this picture? (American Musical Theatre Collection, Yale University Music Library)

nounced that it had "at last succeeded in obtaining first class records of the female voice. Miss Jessie Oliver is the first songstress whose work is both musically and phonographically satisfactory. Many others have tried but none have been sufficiently successful to continue. Miss Oliver gives a clear, loud record, without sacrificing any of the purity of the music or destroying the quality of the voice. The selections are the melodies which never grow old and are always in demand. The Standard Quartette have assisted in the chorus of some of the old-fashioned melodies, making a novelty which charms all hearers. The supply is limited." The titles were certainly standard fare: "Old Folks at Home," "My Old Kentucky Home," "Home, Sweet Home," "Annie Laurie," and "Love's Old Sweet Song."

The quartet also recorded on its own. Columbia announced on April 11, 1894, that "during a recent visit of this famous quartette to Washington, we obtained their services. They make a specialty of old-fashioned melodies and jubilee songs and have no equals in that line. They are all 'gentlemen of color' and sing their distinctive songs with harmony and sweetness." The nine titles listed were a mix of traditional Southern songs ("My Old Kentucky Home"), spirituals ("Swing Low, Sweet Chariot," "Steal Away to Jesus") and comic numbers ("Poor Mourner," "Who Broke the Lock on the Henhouse Door?" "Say Bo, Give Me Them Two Bits"). None were current popular songs, reinforcing the notion that the Standard Quartette—like the Unique Quartette—built their act around identifiably "black" material, serious and comic.

The dates of the recording sessions can be inferred from *SBW*'s itinerary. The show played Kernan's Lyceum in Washington, D.C., from November 17 to December 2, 1893, and again from February 19 to 24, 1894, and was extremely well received during both runs. A review after the first visit reported that the audience's "enthusiasm was unbounded"; another, following the second, noted that during a generally slow week in Washington *South before the War* had filled the house.[10] The cylinders announced in March and April were presumably made during the February engagement and placed on coin-slot machines around the city to capitalize on the show's success.

Miraculously, one of the cylinders made during the 1894 Washington engagement has survived, albeit in somewhat battered condition. It is "Keep Movin'," a serio-comic song with religious references. The faint announcement at the beginning of the cylinder seems to be "Keep Movin', as sung by the famous Standard Quartette, record taken by the Columbia Phonograph Company, Washington, D.C." The text, as reconstructed by several experts, is as follows.

> Tenor: Well, down in the hen house on my knees,
> I thought I heard a chicken sneeze.
> She sneezed so loud with the whooping cough,
> Sneezed her head and tail right off.
> Chorus
> Tenor: Now can't you hear the bells a-ringing?
> Quartet: Oh, I'll meet you,
> Tenor: Now don't you hear the darkies singing?
> Quartet: I'll meet you bye and bye.
> Tenor: Oooohh . . . good Lord.
>
> Quartet: Keep a-movin', movin', closer than Heaven.
> Movin', movin', it's a reg'lar old [word unintelligible] time. (repeat)
> Verse
> Tenor: As I was a-walkin' a-down the lane,
> I met old Satan on my way (spoken: Yes, you did)
> Says I, "Old Satan, How do you do?"
> He said, "I'm well, son, how are you?"
> (repeat chorus)
> Verse
> Tenor: And mind now you sisters how you step on the cross,
> Your foot might slip and your soul be lost.
> Some come a-crippled and a-some come lame,
> Some come a-harpin' on the Holy Name.
> (Chorus × 2)[11]

The a capella performance is infused with jubilee fervor. The chorus is call-and-response, with the tenor ("Now can't you hear the bells a-ringing?") alternating with the rest of the quartet ("Oh, I'll meet you . . ."), and then bursting into the soulful wail "Oooohh . . . good Lord!" This is followed by the ensemble chant, "Keep a-movin', movin' . . ." Despite the comic couplets, the entire performance has the air of a revival meeting. Nothing like this was heard in recordings by white quartets of the 1890s, most of which employed the carefully modulated, deliberate style familiar today in barbershop quartet singing.

South before the War ended a very successful season in May 1894, and the quartet was free to fill its own engagements during the summer. An item in September stated that they were starting the fall season with a new show, *The Old South,* which opened in Philadelphia on September 4.[12] However, *South before the War* opened in Louisville on October 8, and the quartet soon rejoined that show. During 1894–95 *SBW* toured Illinois, Ohio, New Jersey, New York, Ontario, Maryland, Pennsylvania, Massachusetts, Connecticut, Washington, D.C., Indiana, Kentucky, Tennessee, and Missouri, ending in New Orleans on April 27. Big crowds were reported at many stops, including the Bijou Theatre in New York, the Academy of Music in Chicago, and the St. Charles Theatre in New Orleans.

Although there were engagements in both Washington and New York, the quartet did not record in either of those cities. Instead they made a new group of cylinders for the Ohio Phonograph Company while appearing in that state. The Ohio company had an active recording program and operated a number of its own "phonograph arcades." It also published a promotional magazine, the *Edison Phonographic News,* which in January 1895 reported that "our Standard Quartettes have been called for so frequently that our supply became entirely exhausted. By the time this magazine reaches our readers, however, we shall have stocked up again, we believe, as the quartette has been engaged to sing for us again at a very early date."

An item in the March issue indicated how expert the quartet had become in dealing with the recording horn. "The reason it is so difficult to obtain good quartette records is because of the rapidity of the vibrations upon the diaphragm when a high note is held by four strong voices which must also be near enough to record on the lower notes, and to articulate distinctly. Our Standard Quartettes seem to have overcome these difficulties as far as it is possible to do so, and they are very loud, horn records also."[13]

The reference to "horn records" meant that in addition to being suitable for hearing through eartubes, the most common means of listening to cylinders at the time, they were also loud enough to be played through a open horn.

These cylinders were presumably made while *South before the War* was appearing in cities where the Ohio Phonograph Company had offices, namely Cleveland (November 5–10) and Cincinnati (February 17–23). The repertoire was similar to that recorded for Columbia during the previous season, including "Keep (a) Movin'" and "Who Broke the Lock." In addition to black comic and spiritual material, they also essayed "O Promise Me" and "My Old Kentucky Home."

Following the Cincinnati engagement the show moved on to Indianapolis, and that city's black newspaper, the *Freeman,* listed the quartet's members as Williams, DeMoss, Scott, and Cottrell, commenting that they were "making quite a reputation for themselves. . . . Their singing is one of the features of the show."[14]

After *South before the War* ended its season in April the quartet returned to the upper Midwest. In May it filled an engagement in Cincinnati and then took part in a "singing contest" with the Clay Gist Star Quartette at the 21st Baptist Church in Indianapolis. In June it was one of many black theatrical acts that turned out for the Colored Theatrical Club outing in New York. The quartet members were again listed and were the same as in February.[15]

For the next three seasons the quartet toured independently, filling engagements in the East and Midwest. No longer tied to the rigid touring schedule of *South before the War,* it did considerable recording, producing at least eleven new titles for Columbia, which were first listed in the company's late 1895–early 1896 catalog. The repertoire consisted mostly of standard titles (appropriate considering the group's name) familiar to black and white quartets, including "Annie Laurie," "The Old Oaken Bucket," "Rocked in the Cradle of the Deep," and "When the Mists Have Rolled Away." A couple sound like comic numbers ("Old Aunt Jemima," "Widdy Wink") and a couple were religious ("Almost Persuaded," "You May Talk about Jerusalem Morning").

Columbia frequently noted that it stocked additional titles not listed in its catalog, and this appears to have been the case with the Standard Quartette. A surviving cylinder from this period is announced, "Every Day Will Be Sunday Bye and Bye, sung by the Standard Quartette for the Columbia Phonograph Company of Washington, D.C." This is not listed in the catalog, but the physical appearance and style of announcement date it as c. 1894–95 (Columbia substituted the phrase "of New York City" in its announcements after it established offices there in late 1895).

The song is sung a capella, at a rather deliberate tempo, with the now familiar call-and-response pattern. Adapted from a spiritual about a hereafter of endless Sundays, it has the lead singing semi-religious (sometimes comic) couplets. After each line, the rest of the quartet harmonizes, "Ev'ry Day'll Be Sunday Bye and Bye . . ." For example,

> Tenor: As I went down in the valley to sin . . .
> Quartet: Ev'ry day'll be Sunday bye and bye.
> Ten: I met old Satan on my way . . .
> Quartet: Ev'ry day'll be Sunday bye and bye
> Tenor: Said I, "Old Satan, how do you do?"
> Quartet: Ev'ry day'll be Sunday bye and bye
> Tenor: He said, "I'm well son, how are you?"
> Quartet: Ev'ry day'll be Sunday bye and bye.

The fact that this verse is almost identical to one used in "Keep Movin'" is not unusual. Many couplets conveying religious or other imagery turn up repeatedly in spirituals and comic songs of the period. In these days before plagiarism lawsuits and battles over "intellectual property," songwriters felt free to copy, adapt, and build on the work of others. Other versions of the song contain entirely different verses, retaining only the repeated refrain, "Every day'll be Sunday bye and bye." For example a version recorded by a white quartet on Zonophone in 1906 was done as an unabashed "coon song."[16]

Another surviving Columbia cylinder is "Poor Mourner," a black quartet standby rendered in fine jubilee style, complete with a semi-spoken section. The song was originally recorded in Washington and listed in 1894, but the surviving copy is announced "New York" and therefore must be a remake from late 1895 or 1896.

During 1896–97 the quartet recorded for the U.S. Phonograph Company of Newark, New Jersey. Some selections duplicated those made earlier for Columbia ("The Old Oaken Bucket," "Way Down Yonder in the Cornfield," "Every Day'll Be Sunday Bye and Bye"), while others were familiar standards widely sung by white quartets ("Massa's in the Cold, Cold Ground," "High Old Time"). One, surprisingly, was a currently popular sentimental song quite unlike the rest of the group's specialized repertoire—"Just Tell Them That You Saw Me."

Meanwhile older cylinders by the quartet continued to be listed by Columbia. Apparently they were good sellers, as stocks were quickly depleted. Eleven titles were available in 1895, but only two remained in the August 1896 catalog and one in the November 1896 issue. By 1897 all were gone. Columbia then had the Manhasset Quartette (white) remake a number of the Standard Quartette titles, testimony to their continuing popularity. The last Standard Quartette cylinders to be sold were those made by the New Jersey company, which stopped selling cylinders about 1898.

South before the War continued playing to SRO business during 1895–98. The troupe now traveled in its own custom Pullman car, "The Hattie." Business was so good that at one point manager George Chennell remarked that he was going to open a hat store with all the hats he had won from Harry Martell, betting about business at the next stop.[17] During 1896–97 two companies operated simultaneously in the East and Midwest. In 1897–98 the company toured the West Coast for the first time, playing California, Oregon, Washington, and British Columbia. Numerous vocal groups rotated through the show's ranks, including the Diamond, Euclid, Alhambra and Eureka Quartettes, and the Virginia Trio. Competing shows sprang up, including *Black America, Darkest America,* and *Slavery Days.*

In the fall of 1898 the Standard Quartette returned to *South before the War* for one final season. The show toured the West that year, passing through Michigan, Minnesota, Manitoba, North Dakota, Montana, Idaho, Washington, British Columbia, Oregon, and California, then swung back through New Mexico, Nevada, Utah, Colorado, and Chicago, where the production was said to delight audiences with its "negro melodies and plantation atmosphere."[18] A major change had taken place in the quartet's lineup, which was now Cottrell, Jube Johnson, J. W. "West" Jenkins, and John Hill.

Two of the new members were well-known names in black theatrical circles. Tenor Julius "Jube" Johnson got his start as a soloist with Hicks and Sawyer's Minstrels (formed in 1886), and by early 1893 was in *South before the War* as a member of the Southern Quartette, with H. C. Williams. He appeared with the Virginia Students (aka the Imperial Quartet) in 1894, and with Sam T. Jack's Creoles in 1895. In 1896 he was in the original cast of John W. Isham's spectacle *Oriental America,* a melange of minstrel, popular, and classical music that has been called one of the productions that began the transition from minstrel show to modern musical and the first all-black musical to open on Broadway.[19] *Oriental America* toured the United States during 1896–97, then toured England and Scotland in 1897, although it is not known how long Johnson stayed with the show before joining the Standard Quartette.

John Wesley "West" Jenkins was born in Winchester, Virginia, in 1859. A talented singer as a youth, he organized his first quartet at age twelve. Three years later it toured with a production of *Uncle Tom's Cabin.* He later appeared with the New Orleans Jubilee Singers and formed the Oriole Quartet with basso John Hill. During his time with *South before the War* in the late 1890s he gave dramatic recitations ("The Johnstown Flood") and served as musical director of the company, as well as singing with the Standard Quartette. He was also a fine comic actor, and his depiction of the well-padded "Aunt Dinah" in *South before the War* was so memorable it earned him the sobriquet "the mammy of them all."[20]

William Cottrell (also spelled Cottrill) was the one holdover from the quartet's early days. He may have been related to Pauline Cottrell, a featured soloist with *SBW* during 1898–99, whose repertoire consisted of soprano showpieces such as "Russian Love Song." Little is known of John L. Hill, other than that he was from Memphis, Tennessee, and was with West Jenkins in the Oriole Quartette prior to their stint with the Standard Quartette. Apparently Hill's solos of basso specialties such as "A Hundred Fathoms Deep" were well received. A review of *South before the War* in February 1899 noted that Hill "responds to the encore which comes like a hurricane and takes it good naturedly and with a broad smile."[21]

After touring with *SBW* in 1898–99 the quartet returned to the vaudeville circuit, with appearances over the next several years in Chicago, San Francisco, and other major cities. There were further changes in the lineup. In 1902 it was reported to be Ed DeMoss, George Day, W. H. Culp, and J. R. Glover. In 1903 the quartet was reorganized again, becoming Ed DeMoss, Charles H. Morris, James Douglas, and Edward Hood.[22] The quartet's home base was still Chicago, and the *Freeman*'s Chicago correspondent remarked after the 1903 changes that "we hope the boys will continue to meet with success and hold up the barrier the Standard has made."

It is difficult to determine exactly how long the quartet continued to function because of the changing membership and the fact that other groups also used the name "Standard Quartette." One such group active in the early 1900s was sometimes called Miller's Standard Quartet; it toured with the shows *The Coontown 400* and *The White Slave* (1902). Its members were Harry Miller (tenor), James Chatman, Clarence Smith, and J. W. Jones. Still another Standard Quartette was reported in 1909, although it probably bore little resemblance to the group that recorded in the 1890s.

Although reports listing the members of the original Standard Quartette are scattered and fragmentary, two basic recording lineups emerge, both including William Cottrell. The lineup in the early 1890s appears to have been Cottrell, DeMoss, Williams, and Scott. The latter three left at some point after the summer of 1895, and the new lineup became Cottrell, Johnson, Jenkins, and Hill. It is almost certainly the Cottrell-DeMoss-Williams-Scott lineup that is heard on the 1894 cylinder "Keep Movin'." Although aural comparisons are difficult, "Every Day'll Be Sunday" is probably the later lineup; among other things, the bass sounds different. The leadership also apparently changed. Johnson was identified as the leader at the time of his departure in the middle of the 1898–99 season. No doubt there were others with the quartet for varying periods of time.

Several members went on to further success in the theater. Of the early members, tenor Ed DeMoss left to work as a solo act and is almost certainly the same "DeMoss" who made duet recordings with Sam Cousins for Berliner in 1898, as Cousins and DeMoss. He rejoined the Standard Quartette in 1902 and 1903, but nothing is known of him after that. Even less is known of the later career of H. C. Williams, who may be the Harry Williams who sang with the Plunger Quartette in 1898.[23] Basso Rufus Scott died in Indianapolis in April 1897, after an illness of several months. He was said to be one of the city's most prominent musical figures.[24]

Of the later members, John Hill had a minor role in Williams and Walker's *Abyssinia* (1905–6) and toured with Mahara's Minstrels (1906). Jube Johnson joined the Ponce de Leon Comedy Four with Mahara's Mammoth Minstrels in 1899, after his stint with the Standard Quartette. After that he toured with Tom Brown's Troubadours (1902–3) and S. H. Dudley's *Smart Set* (1905–7), and was still actively performing at the time of his death in Tewksbury, Massachusetts, on September 16, 1907.[25]

Probably the most successful of all quartet members was West Jenkins. Jenkins met his future wife, Mattie, while touring with *South before the War;* they were married on March 17, 1898. As of 1900 the couple was living in Chicago, according to U.S. Census records. Well-known in theatrical circles, they operated a boardinghouse for black actors, first in Chicago and later in Pittsburgh, during the early 1900s. Later they helped create the well-known "Bode of Education" sketch for Cole and Johnson's musical *The Shoo-Fly Regiment* (1905–7), in which they starred. Still later Jenkins was seen in the Black Patti Troubadours' *A Trip to Africa* (1908) and in Cole and Johnson's *The Red Moon* (1908–9), which played on Broadway. He then began acting in motion pictures, playing character parts in numerous films made by Vitagraph, Famous Players, Lasky, Selznick, Metro, Fox, Biograph, Universal, Goldwyn, and others from 1911 to 1930. One of these roles was in the Bert Williams comedy short *A Natural Born Gambler* (1916), in which Jenkins was Williams's principal support as "Brother Gardner." West Jenkins died in Brooklyn, New York, in 1930 at the age of seventy-one.[26]

South before the War continued its extraordinary run after the quartet's departure, although by the end of the 1890s its magic was finally beginning to fade. During 1899–1900 it toured the Midwest and South, while the 1900–1901 season seems to have consisted primarily of one-night stands in the Northeast. The last traced engagement was in Hoboken in February 1901. Harry Martell, who had taken over sole ownership in the mid-1890s, was with the production until the end. By the early 1900s the show's spectacular success was part of show business lore. Uncle Eph and Aunt Dinah routines continued to be performed in vaudeville; reviews of buck-and-wing dancers mentioned their indebtedness to the show; and one report of a packed house invoked the phrase, "not since the palmy days of *South before the War* . . .".[27]

As the new century dawned, however, the era of minstrel shows and "Old South" spectacles was coming to a close. Both *South before the War* and the Standard Quartette gradually faded from memory. The quartet's familiar repertoire did live on, but since it was not uniquely identified with them it did not serve to keep their name alive. The few cylinder recordings of this pioneering black quartet that survive are a fascinating glimpse into a performance style, and a major theatrical production, that has passed into history.

7 The Kentucky Jubilee Singers

This black chorus was formed in the mid-1870s, a period when scores of jubilee troupes were criss-crossing the country exploiting the vogue for spirituals ignited by the sudden and phenomenal success of the Fisk University Jubilee Singers. George C. D. Odell, a leading chronicler of the New York stage, reported that by 1875–76 "there was no end to jubilee singers," and of the 1876–77 season he said, "jubilee singing was by then an epidemic."[1] In the New York area alone he documented performances by the Hampton Colored Students, the Wilmington Jubilee Singers, the Virginia Jubilee Singers, the Juvenile Jubilee Singers, the Carolina Jubilee Singers, the Slave Troupe of Jubilee Singers from Virginia, Tinkler's Jubilee Singers, Slavin's Georgia Jubilee Singers, the Sheppard Colored Jubilee Singers, and numerous others.

The precise origins of the Kentucky Jubilee Singers are obscure. Odell first noted a New York area appearance by them on April 9, 1877, when "the old Kentucky Jubilee Singers were again to exalt the 'spiritual'—this time at the 4th Street M.P. Church" (a church in the Williamsburg section of Brooklyn). Later the same month they appeared at the Noble Street Baptist Church in the Greenpoint section of the city. The fact that they were referred to as "old" and singing "again" suggests that they may have been in existence for a number of years—although not *too* many, since jubilee groups did not begin to spring up until after the initial Fisk tour of 1871–72.

They were clearly a touring group and Odell only reports their appearances in the New York area. They must have been fairly well known because in 1879 they were immortalized by a popular instrumental number called "The Kentucky Jubilee Singers Schottische," by San Francisco composer Fred G. Carnes. Carnes was previously known for "Selika" (1877), written for African American concert soprano Marie Selika, who had made her debut in San Francisco in 1876. In 1883 he published a collection called *Songs of the Kentucky Jubilee Singers,* containing his arrangements of "Oh, Peter, Go Ring Dem Bells," "Swing Low, Sweet Chariot," "Darkies on the Levee," and "We'll Cross de Ribber ob Jordan." All of these songs and collections were published in San Francisco.

Unlike some of their fly-by-night competitors, the Kentucky Singers endured. In May 1885 they were appearing at Harry Hill's theater on Long Island, a venue which was said to feature jubilee singers every Sunday.[2] The identities of individual members of the troupe have not been located, although in 1891 the *Freeman* contained a short item seeking information about Miss Minnie Maurice, who was reported to have "traveled several years ago with the Kentucky Jubilee Singers."[3]

The Singers were still performing in the 1890s. In 1894 an entry appeared in the catalog of the U.S. Phonograph Company of New Jersey, a leading maker of cylinder records, stating "Kentucky Jubilee Singers—These records are novelties, but we do not recommend them for horn reproduction. They are made for slot and tube service. Sung by the colored Jubilee Singers, whose concerts are so popular. The company was complete, including the female voices. Price, $1.25 each." Four titles were then listed, "Roll, Jordan, Roll," "Adam and Eve," "Blow, Gabriel, Blow," and "On the Bank by the River's Side."

There are several interesting aspects of this announcement. The reference to the company being "complete" suggests that an entire chorus was recorded. That was highly unusual for the time, since the primitive recording technology of 1894 could not capture ensemble voices very well. The presence of female voices is also significant. Most recording at this time was by men, due to their stronger voices. This may document the first time black females were recorded.

The references to "horn reproduction" and "slot and tube service" indicate that the cylinders were fairly faint, perhaps because of their ensemble nature. Only the loudest cylinders of this era could be played through a open horn; other, fainter cylinders were intended to be heard through acoustic tubing attached to earphones. As for the repertoire, "Roll, Jordan, Roll" and "Blow, Gabriel" are familiar spirituals, and the other two titles were probably in the same vein.

These brown wax cylinders were most likely recorded at U.S. Phonograph's headquarters in Newark, New Jersey, while the Singers were appearing in the area. Since it was difficult to duplicate cylinders (at least cylinders as faint as these), they must have been individually recorded by the troupe, an arduous process that probably resulted in only a small quantity being made. The U.S. Phonograph Company catalog for the following year (1895) reported that all of them were out of stock. No further recordings by the Singers are known.

Despite the comment about the Singers' concerts being "so popular," no reference to them playing at a major venue has been found in this period, and they may have disbanded not long after the cylinders were made. Their name lived on, however, via Carnes's "Kentucky Jubilee Singers Schottische," a pleasant little tune that remained popular with dancers well into the twentieth century. It was one of the earliest dance numbers recorded by Edison for commercial sale in 1889, by Duffy and Imgrund's 5th Regiment Band and in violin and piano and clarinet and piano duets, and it was later featured on a Columbia cylinder (1897) and disc (c. 1902) by the Columbia Orchestra. The Columbia versions sold so well that the label had studio band leader Charles A. Prince rerecord the title in 1913 (with an orchestra) and in 1915 (with a band) in order to take advantage of improved recording technology. The latter version remained in the catalog until 1919. The song was recorded on other labels as well.[4]

The Kentucky Jubilee Singers name was revived in 1928 by an entrepreneur named Forbes Randolph, who organized an eight-man chorus by that name to serve as the centerpiece of a stage production about life in the South.[5] Dressed in overalls and bandannas, the troupe reenacted life in the cottonfields while singing spirituals and other songs. This incarnation of the Kentucky Jubilee Singers—which had nothing to do with the nineteenth-century group—made film shorts, recorded for Brunswick (as Forbes Randolph's Kentucky Jubilee Choir), and toured Australia and Europe until 1930, when Randolph abruptly deserted his singers and ran off with the payroll. The singers picked a new leader and continued touring, mostly in Europe, until the beginning of World War II. They then broke up, although a trio from the chorus continued performing until the 1950s under the name Day, Dawn, and Dusk.

No copies of the faint cylinders from 1894 are known to survive, and the chance that any will be found is remote, given the small quantities that were made. If one should turn up, however, it would represent a fascinating link with the very beginnings of spiritual singing by a group that traced its history back to the 1870s.

8 Bert Williams and George Walker

Bert Williams is often referred to as the first black "superstar" of the twentieth century. He achieved enormous success in vaudeville and on the Broadway stage, and was popular with black and white audiences alike. But we need not remember him only by old photographs and the memories of those who saw him. Often overlooked is the fact that in addition to being a top-rank actor and comedian, he was also an extremely popular recording artist and the best-selling black artist of the pre-1920 period by far. His recordings managed to convey his unique stage persona in a manner that appealed to both black and white record buyers. They serve as the soundtrack of his fabulous career.

He was born Egbert Austin Williams in Nassau, the Bahamas, on November 12, 1874.[1] A proud man, he was in later life quite secretive about his family. No picture of them is known to exist, and it is not even certain whether he had any brothers or sisters. His grandfather was a successful businessman, possibly in the citrus industry, and his father, Frederick, held a variety of jobs in that field. The family moved permanently to the United States when Bert was about ten, settling in California.

In 1893, while still in his teens, the light-skinned Bert briefly appeared with a West Coast traveling minstrel show run by Lew Johnson, where he impersonated a Hawaiian. Later in the year he joined Martin and Selig's Mastodon Minstrels. It was while in San Francisco with the latter troupe that he met his future partner, George Walker. Walker (born c. 1873 in Lawrence, Kansas) had just arrived in town from the Midwest with a traveling medicine show, and Williams got him a job as an endman with the Martin and Selig show. The two quickly became fast friends and began to talk about working together.

During the next three years Williams and Walker appeared in a variety of traveling shows and in solo appearances, gradually honing their act. At first Williams played the slick operator and Walker the "dumb coon," but they soon discovered that the comedy worked best when they switched roles. Over time Walker, lithe and sharp-featured, became the grinning, strutting dandy, while Williams played the slow moving, dimwitted oaf. Although he was a big man, Williams was extremely agile and would never fail to convulse audiences with his body language and unexpected bits of physical "business."

He was also a talented musician. By 1895 he had begun writing songs, some in collaboration with Walker, and several were published to modest success by Howley,

A young Williams and
Walker, the toast of New
York, at the start of their
career in 1897. (*Leslie's
Illustrated Weekly,* July 22,
1897; courtesy of David
Jasen)

Havel, and Company and Witmark Brothers in New York. Perhaps the first song to
become identified with the team was Williams's "Dora Dean," about the sharp-
dressing female half of the Johnson and Dean black vaudeville duo. It set the pattern for the clever, contemporary, sometimes slangy tone of their early material,
which spoke to a hip, young, urban audience.

Williams and Walker were still small-time, however, and they had their setbacks.
They joined John W. Isham's *The Octoroons* in Chicago during the winter of 1895–
96, but flopped and were dropped from the show. Finally, in September 1896, they
made it to New York, where their act was interpolated into a faltering musical written by Victor Herbert called *The Gold Bug.* They were rushed into the show on its
second night, but the orchestra had a hard time adjusting to their raggy material,
including their new comic song, "Oh, I Don't Know, You're Not So Warm." They
nevertheless made a favorable impression with their clever, energetic comedy.

Critics were not so kind to the rest of the show, and *The Gold Bug* quickly closed,
but Williams and Walker were able to parlay their good reviews into a booking at
Koster and Bial's, one of the city's premiere vaudeville houses, beginning on November 15. "You're Not So Warm" began to catch on, and a high-strutting cakewalk
finale, added in January, was a sensation. Soon they were packing the house, and
their run was continually extended, eventually totaling thirty-six weeks. Billing
themselves as "Two Real Coons" (to differentiate themselves from the many white
minstrels then performing in blackface), they were the surprise hit of New York's
1896–97 season.

It was during this breakthrough season that Bert Williams apparently made his first recording. One of the songs that Williams and Walker had written together, and were presumably using at Koster and Bial's, was a rather ordinary southern lullaby called "Mammy's Pickaninny Boy." Whether the team meant it as a parody, or simply counterpoint to their more raucous numbers, is not certain. It pictured an "old black mammy" down on the plantation, gently rocking her sleeping child and crooning,

> Mammy surely lobes her pickaninny,
> He am her only pride and joy,
> She am gwine to buy a great big stick of candy,
> And give it to her pickaninny boy.[2]

A cylinder record of the title is listed as a new release in the phonograph trade paper the *Phonoscope* for January–February 1897, followed by the name "Bert Williams."[3] The label was not specified but several other titles on the list appear to have been products of the short-lived Universal Phonograph Company run by the Joseph W. Stern publishing house. Stern had published several Williams and Walker songs (although not this one, which was published by Witmark) and frequently recruited visiting performers to make cylinders for it as well. In his memoirs Edward Marks recalled that Stern's recording studio was in a loft at 21 East Twentieth Street, a couple of doors west of the publishing office. "Any performer who came into our publishing house for professional copies was dragged down to the laboratory for a phonograph test. Lottie Gilson, Annie Hart and Meyer Cohen made records. The women's voices never sounded right, but their names looked good in the catalogue. . . . Our wide acquaintance with performers and our sense of popular taste gave us a jump over the Edison people."[4]

No doubt a cylinder by Bert Williams, then a brand-new sensation in vaudeville, would have been a coup for Stern. Relatively few copies could have been made, however, as the means for duplicating cylinders were limited at this time and Williams would not have had time to spend long hours in the studio stockpiling copies. No copies of this cylinder are known to survive.

Williams and Walker were mainly interested in expanding their stage career, of course. In the spring of 1897 they played other theaters with an act called "The Tobasco Senegambians," and in May they sailed to England to introduce their act at London's Empire Hall. They were not particularly successful and quickly returned to the United States to play vaudeville houses throughout the summer, including a return engagement at Koster and Bial's. During the 1897–98 season they toured the eastern half of the country with Hyde's Comedians (white), billed as "The Kings of Colored Comedians." Their new song, "I Don't Like No Cheap Man (Dat Spends His Money on de 'stallment Plan)," was a hit in early 1898. They also showed a knack for publicity by publicly challenging playboy socialite William K. Vanderbilt to a cakewalk contest. Vanderbilt did not respond.

In late 1897 they were approached by young composer Will Marion Cook, who pitched them with the idea for a full-scale musical comedy, cast entirely with blacks, to be called *Clorindy; or, The Origin of the Cakewalk*.[5] It would be a natural for them.

The high-stepping cakewalk was the rage of the moment, and Williams and Walker were among its chief practitioners. The idea of an all-black musical on a major New York stage was revolutionary; it simply had never been done. Unfortunately, Williams and Walker's prior commitments prevented them from accepting, and the show was ultimately staged—after much travail—in July starring leading black comedian Ernest Hogan. Although produced off-Broadway, it is today considered the first black musical and a landmark in the history of the American theater.

Undaunted, Cook and librettist/poet Paul Laurence Dunbar came up with another vehicle for Williams and Walker, *A Senegambian Carnival,* which premiered in Boston on August 29, 1898. Williams played a newly rich prospector named Dollar Bill, and Walker played Silver King, a confidence man out to fleece him. The supporting cast marked the beginning of the repertory company which was to remain with Williams and Walker through their great shows of the early 1900s. In the company were actress Lottie Thompson and dancer Aida Overton, the stars' future wives. The hit of the show was Williams's rendition of "Who Dat Say Chicken in Dis Crowd?" a song recycled from *Clorindy*.

The further exploits of Dollar Bill and Silver King were portrayed in Cook and Dunbar's *A Lucky Coon,* which succeeded *A Senegambian Carnival* in late 1898. In it Walker introduced "The Hottest Coon in Dixie." This was followed in October 1899 by *The Policy Players,* written by Williams and Walker themselves, with assistance from Jesse Shipp. In this one Dusty Cheapman (Williams) wins some money gambling and longs to use it to get into high society. Happy Hotstuff (Walker) obliges him, leading to a hilarious scene at the mansion of the Astrobilt family on the Hudson (no doubt a parody of the Astors and Vanderbilts, the latter having ignored the actors only a couple of years earlier). Williams and Walker sang "Kings of the Policy Shop," "The Medicine Man," and "The Ghost of a Coon," while Walker did "Broadway Coon," among others.

In 1899 George Walker married young star dancer Aida (born Ada) Overton, and the following year Williams married Lottie Thompson, also from the cast. Together, the foursome would be at the center of all future Williams and Walker shows.

Williams and Walker rose to stardom playing to mostly white audiences, but they faced continual reminders of the limits placed on them by that same white society. One particularly frightening incident almost cost them their lives. On an August night in 1900 a rumor began to race through the streets of Manhattan that a white detective had been shot by a black man. Seeking revenge, mobs of whites began roaming midtown attacking blacks wherever they could find them. As the crowds grew larger, Irish street cops, themselves resentful of the "uppity" blacks, did nothing or actively egged them on. Some blacks were pulled from streetcars and beaten while police stood by, others were chased down streets.

Unaware of the mounting violence outside, George Walker and Ernest Hogan left their respective theaters at the end of their shows and ran straight into the mob. According to one newspaper account, Walker caught the mob's full fury.

> Walker, of the famous team Williams and Walker, was nearly killed by an angry crowd at Thirty-fifth Street and Broadway. Walker was going uptown on a Sixth

Avenue [trolley] car. At Thirty-Fourth Street [he] was spied by the bloodthirsty crowd and before Walker knew what the trouble was, a dozen men had jumped on the car and dragged him off. He realized that his life was in danger and as soon as he landed in a heap upon the street, he jumped to his feet and sprinted up Broadway. More than 300 yelling men followed at his heels and caught him a block away.

He was knocked almost senseless by a blow from the foremost man of the pursuing crowds and was soon being trampled under the heels of the mob. He would have been killed had it not been for the timely appearance of a squad of police, who charged the crowd with their clubs and fought their way to Walker's side. The police almost carried him into the Marlborough Hotel, where kind hands dressed his wounds.[6]

The immaculately dressed Ernest Hogan was similarly set upon outside his theater by a mob screaming, "Get the nigger!" He barely escaped with his life through the back entrance of a building as a police detective held the mob at bay with a drawn revolver. Bert Williams, who happened to leave his theater in another direction, was apparently not hurt.

The white establishment did not condone such violence by the lower classes, but although there was much hand-wringing it did little in the aftermath to punish those responsible. It must have been with mixed emotions that the black stars laughed, sang, and danced for their white audiences during the nights that followed.

In September 1900 Williams and Walker staged their greatest hit to date, *Sons of Ham,* by the top-notch team of Jesse Shipp, book, Will Marion Cook, music, and Alex Rogers, lyrics. In addition to the stars and their wives, the cast included Hattie McIntosh, Jesse Shipp, Abbie Mitchell, and vaudeville acrobats the Reese Brothers. The plot concerned the attempts of Tobias Wormwood (Williams) and Harty Lafter (Walker) to masquerade as the sons of an old man named Ham, in order to inherit his fortune. They soon discovered that the real sons were away studying to be acrobats and were about to return. A great deal of physical comedy ensued before the impostors were finally forced to flee. The plot was hardly sophisticated, but most "musical comedies" at this time were really extended variety shows, held together by a thin story line and containing interpolated acts of all kinds. While plenty of its elements would be considered offensive today, it was relatively free of the extreme stereotypes found in other "black" shows then running. Williams and Walker had already begun to focus on human, rather than racial, comedy. Commented one black reviewer, "chicken stealing gags and crap game songs are conspicuous by their absence, which is delightfully refreshing."[7]

In October 1901, during the second season of *Sons of Ham,* Williams and Walker were lured into the Philadelphia studios of the Victor Talking Machine Company to make their first disc records. This was quite a coup for the young Victor company in heavy competition with the entrenched cylinder interests, and Victor paid handsomely for the privilege. The three sessions have long been considered historic due to the fact that they produced original cast recordings from one of the first black musicals. Some writers have even gone so far as to call Williams and Walker "the earliest documented black recording artists," though they obviously were not.[8] Victor was extremely proud of the results, announcing in its February 1902 catalog "The

most popular songs of the day are the 'Ragtime' or 'Coon Songs.' The greatest rec-
ommendation a song of this kind can have is that it is sung by Williams and Walker, the 'Two Real Coons.' Their selections are always from the brightest and best
songs with the most catchy and pleasing melodies. Although Williams and Walker
have been engaged to make records exclusively for us at the highest price ever paid
in the history of the talking machine business, and although their records are the
finest thing ever produced, being absolutely the real thing, we add them to our regular record list with no advance in price."[9]

Due to the limited technology in 1901 only about 500 to 1,000 copies could be
pressed of each recording. This was more than the limited number of duplicates that
could be made from a cylinder, but it ensured that few copies would survive today.
The situation would change within the next year as improved duplication techniques were developed for both cylinders and discs. Unfortunately, Williams and
Walker made their Victor recordings just before these advances were introduced.[10]
Consequently, the 1901 discs are extremely rare and are rabidly sought-after by
today's antiquarian collectors.

Enough of them do survive to give us a picture of what the famous duo sounded
like early in their career. I have been able to locate ten of the thirteen released titles,
in either seven-inch or ten-inch versions.[11] Most consist of specialty material from
Williams and Walker's stage act or shows, done in an uninhibited style that presumably mirrors their performance on stage. Both men had good recording voices, and
Williams's spare, ragtime piano accompaniment adds to the intimate "stage" feeling. All are introduced by a stiffly formal Victor studio announcer, probably Calvin
Child, which further heightens the comic effect when the loose and limber comedians begin to sing.

Although "I Don't Like That Face You Wear," by Ernest Hogan, is listed in the
Victor catalog as a duet, the disc heard is actually a solo by Walker. Williams may
make a few noises in the background. It is a typical (for the period) sarcastic "coon
song" sung fairly straight by Walker, who imitates a woman's voice part way
through. "In My Castle on the River Nile" and "The Phrenologist Coon," on the
other hand, are jaunty tunes sung with delicious irony by Williams. Both were featured in *Sons of Ham* and contain many of the offensive stereotypes of the genre ("If
his head looks like a razor, you can bet that coon will cut"), although the humor is
drawn more from generally relatable themes than from mockery of the black man.
"Castle" is about a black man who thinks he can rise in the social scheme because
he has traced his ancestry to royalty, while "Phrenologist Coon" is really about char-
latan doctors ("Just by feelin' in your pocket / I can tell what's in your head"). This
song was supposedly inspired by Williams's real-life interest in phrenology.

"Where Was Moses When the Light Went Out?" was a variation on an old riddle
(Q: "Where was Moses when the light went out?" A: "In the dark!"), originally published as a song in 1878. In this updated version, Deacon Moses Johnson raids a gambling den looking to extort cash, only to have the lights go out at the critical moment. When they come back on, the cash is gone and the gamblers cry out the title
line. But to the deacon's dismay, someone *else* made off with the cash.[12] Williams
acts out the scene effectively, with a partly spoken portion at the end. One can only

imagine the gestures and facial expressions that must have accompanied the performance on stage.

"(When It's) All Going Out and Nothing Coming In," from *Sons of Ham,* although done in dialect, is less a coon song than a funny and relatable lament about the problems when you have money, and the problems when you don't. It became one of Williams's best-known songs.

> But, oh, when your money is a-runnin' low,
> Times look bad, things look mighty blue,
> You look for help and find that all of your friends,
> Is paddlin' their own canoe.[13]

Williams delivers the song in his trademark deliberate style to a ragtime accompaniment with frills on the piano. There are no references to race, and it is easy to see how white audiences could identify with the singer's humorous problems. It is a precursor of Williams's most famous number, "Nobody," and in fact of his whole hard-luck persona of future years.

"Junie" is so trite ("Junie . . . spooney . . . like to be your coon-y") that one wonders if it was a parody. Perhaps not, as songs like this really were popular at the turn of the century. "Good Morning, Carrie," on the other hand, is a nicely constructed tune with an extremely catchy refrain. It exudes good cheer ("Good morning, Carrie, how ya do this morning?"), ending with the happy beau's proposal to his pretty maid. Although done in dialect, there are few stereotypes and the catchy tune must have sent audiences whistling from the theater. It is one of the few titles recorded in these sessions that was recorded by other artists as well, becoming a major hit. One analysis of popular songs of the period indicates that it was the most popular song in America during the fall of 1901.[14]

"Her Name's Miss Dinah Fair," by Williams's wife Lottie, is a straightforward coon song about a popular, sharp-dressing girl ("And when she goes out honey, goodness how she spends the money"). According to the announcement, Walker is "accompanied by Mr. Bert Williams," and Williams does not sing, establishing conclusively that on this disc, at least, it is Williams's own ragtime piano we are hearing. "She's Getting More Like the White Folks Every Day" is a clever little parody in which Williams's girlfriend is mistaken for a maid at a fancy hotel and promptly begins to ape the white ladies' pretentious customs ("Once she was stuck on calico patterns/Now all she want is silks and satins"). Williams sings the raggy melody with enthusiasm, curiously changing the published words in a couple of places to "she's gettin' more like the bucka-man every day," and then, as if he knows listeners will need an explanation, interjects at the end, "bucka-man means white folk!" Part of the team's appeal seemed to be this kind of use of black catchphrases and slang.[15]

No doubt the most unusual and fascinating of the extant recordings is "My Little Zulu Babe," from *Sons of Ham.* Ostensibly a love song set in Africa, it opens with a piano figure that sounds like a cat about to pounce, followed by jungle-like whinnies by Williams. Walker then takes the verse, as Williams howls and whoops in the background. The vocal interpolations resemble yodels or wails. Compared to the strait-laced tenors and quartets who filled the rest of the Victor catalog, such exuberance on disc was virtually unheard of in 1901. At the end the two harmonize. No one who hears this record fails to be taken aback by it. To have such vivid evidence of the energy, enthusiasm, and cleverness that made Williams and Walker stars preserved on disc is a treasure indeed (and a clear argument for the preservation of aural as well as visual materials as historical documents). Williams first recorded the number solo, on November 8, but it is the duet recorded two days later that best exemplifies the team's charisma.

None of the recordings made at these sessions remained in the Victor catalog for more than three years. Pressing information is available for only about half of them and is fragmentary at that, but it appears that fewer than 1000 copies were pressed of each title. "All Going Out and Nothing Coming In" apparently had the largest total, at 761 copies.[16] While these are valuable documents historically, it is unlikely that many people heard them at the time.

After a healthy two-year run Williams and Walker closed *Sons of Ham* and began work on their next vehicle, *In Dahomey,* with book by Shipp, music by Cook, and lyrics by Dunbar and Rogers. Opening in Boston on September 22, 1902, it became their most successful show of all. In February 1903 it moved to New York where it opened on Broadway—the first black musical ever to do so, a landmark event in the history of the American theater. This did not mean that everyone was equally welcome to the best seats in the house. Despite pressure to admit blacks, who lion-

Williams and Walker, starring in *In Dahomey,* c. 1903. (Courtesy of David Jasen)

ized Williams and Walker, the manager of the theater stoutly maintained, "we'll stand the lawsuits, if there are any . . . but the orchestra and boxes of this theatre are for our white patrons and no others."[17] It was claimed that the stars did not object as long as blacks were provided for in the galleries.

The action-packed plot of *In Dahomey* revolved around the exploits of Shylock Homestead (Williams) and Rareback Pinkerton (Walker) as they searched for treasure. One step ahead of the law, they eventually escaped to Africa, where, in the words of one song, "Every Dahkey Is a King." Songs included Cook's famous "Swing Along" sung by a chorus, "I May Be Crazy But I Ain't No Fool," "All Going Out and Nothing Coming In" (reprised from *Sons of Ham*), "I Wants to Be an Actor Lady" (sung by Aida Overton Walker), and Williams's famous "I'm a Jonah Man." More than any song to date "Jonah Man" defined Williams's emerging hard-luck persona, with hilarious tales of woe that cleverly spoke to the black condition without actually being *about* it. It was quite popular, and it is a shame that he never recorded it.

Following a very successful run during 1902–3 the entire company sailed for London on April 28, 1903, where they opened at the prestigious Shaftesbury Theatre. *In Dahomey* was a smashing success there as well, erasing memories of Williams and Walker's failure in the music halls six years earlier. The show received a boost in June when the company was asked to give a command performance for Edward VII at Buckingham Palace on the occasion of his grandson David's birthday (David later became Edward VIII, before abdicating in 1936). A newspaper report reflected the curiosity element that the show held for privileged Britons, remarking that "the juvenile members of the Royal Family came out from the Palace a little before four o'clock, their curiosity being thoroughly aroused at the prospect of seeing real niggers on the stage."[18]

Williams had a sudden case of stage fright before going on to sing "Every Dahkey Is a King," but the performance went without a hitch. Edward was extremely gracious. "The kindest, most courteous, most democratic man I ever met was the King of England, the late Edward VII," Williams later recalled. "I found the easiest, most responsive, most appreciative audience any [performer] could wish."[19] His Highness later invited Williams back to the palace to teach him the cakewalk and the card game of craps.

On June 5, 1903, shortly before the royal performance, Williams was induced by the Gramophone and Typewriter Company, Victor's affiliate in England, to record a song called "The Cake Walk." The dance was one of the high points of *In Dahomey*, but this vocal version went unissued.

At this point, Williams's recording history becomes very murky indeed. It has long been reported in various discographies that while in England he recorded numerous laughing and whistling songs. However, the repertoire bears no resemblance to anything Williams is known to have sung elsewhere, consisting of English music-hall novelties such as "He'd a Funny Little Way with Him (Laughing Song)" and "The Whistling Polka." Instead, these records appear to be by an English performer named Bert Williams who was recording at about the same time. The one example I have heard is definitely not by the American star. Although these records were listed in several English catalogs of 1903–5, they are excruciatingly rare, and noth-

Bert Williams

Exclusive Columbia Artist

Makes you chuckle with every word and laugh at every line when he sings:

| My Last Dollar
I'm Gonna Quit Saturday | A3356
10-inch
$1.00 |

Buy the records listed below and start your grafonola with a smile.

A-3305 10-inch $1.00	I Want to Know Where Tosti Went When He Said Good-bye Get Up	A-1504 10-inch $1.00	You Can't Get Away From It The Darktown Poker Club
A-2941 10-inch $1.00	Ten Little Bottles Unlucky Blues	A-2710 10-inch $1.00	Oh! Lawdy (Something's Done Got Be- tween Ebecaneezer and Me) Bring Back Those Wonderful Days
A-2849 10-inch $1.00	The Moon Shines on the Moonshine Somebody	A-6141 12-inch $1.25	Elder Eatmore's Sermon On Generosity Elder Eatmore's Sermon On Throwing Stones
A-1853 10-inch $1.00	Never Mo' Purpostus		
A-2750 10-inch $1.00	It's Nobody's Business But My Own Everybody Wants a Key to My Cellar	A-2877 10-inch $1.00	I'm Sorry I Ain't Got It You Could Have It If I Had It Blues Checkers (It's Your Move Now)
A-2979 10-inch $1.00	Save a Little Dram for Me Lonesome Alimony Blues	A-915 10-inch $1.00	Constantly I'll Lend You Anything

Bert Williams, the blackface "Jonah Man," with a group of his Columbia discs. (Columbia supplement, April 1921)

ing is known about the career of the "other" Bert Williams except that he was apparently a small-time Cockney music-hall comedian. He recorded for Columbia, Edison, Rex, and Lambert cylinders, and Odeon and Zonophone discs. Until evidence surfaces to the contrary, all of these records will be assumed to be by the English, not the American, Bert Williams.

After nearly a year and a half in England *In Dahomey* returned to the United States in August 1904. Much of the music was changed, new cast members were added, and the show had an additional profitable tour in 1904–5. At the end of the season the stars began working on their next vehicle. There were many delays, however, and to fill time they appeared as headliners in leading vaudeville houses.

An incident in December 1905 demonstrated that despite their fame, and their willingness to live within the "rules" of the day, they still encountered prejudice. Walter C. Kelly, a monologuist who was booked to appear with them at Hammerstein's Victoria Theatre in New York, refused to go on, saying he would not appear on the same stage with blacks. Kelly, a Southerner, was particularly irked that these men were occupying the star dressing room. In a widely quoted comment, "George Walker laughed when he was told of the incident. 'The man is foolish,' he said after a moment's thought. 'The day is past for that sort of thing. Both white men and black men have a right to earn a living in whatever manner they find most convenient, providing they injure no one else. . . . I do not think I will be thought conceited if I point to the fact that Williams and Walker are pretty well established, while Mr. Kelly's fame is still somewhat in retirement, as it were. Of course, if he is looking for a little advertisement, he will probably get it at our expense, but it is pretty small work at best.'"[20]

Kelly's fame may not have equaled that of Williams and Walker, but he was popular, and would remain so for many years. Beginning in 1920 Victor issued several of his "Virginian Judge" routines. They contained some of the most blatantly racist material ever issued on the Victor label—and they were best-sellers. In 1935 he made a film of the routine. Kelly was the uncle of the 1950s film star Grace Kelly.

In this case the show went on without a hitch, minus Kelly. But unfortunately the day was not past for "that sort of thing." Williams and Walker would encounter similar incidents—and Kelly himself—again.

By February 1906 the new show was finally ready. *Abyssinia,* with book and lyrics by Shipp and Rogers, and music by Will Marion Cook and Bert Williams, premiered at Broadway's Majestic Theatre to rave reviews. This time Jasmine Jenkins (Williams) and Rastus Johnson (Walker) were visiting Abyssinia (Ethiopia), where they of course got into trouble. It was an elaborate production with live camels. In contrast to previous shows, this time the Africans were sympathetic characters and the Americans were targets of humor. Songs included "Pretty Desdemone," "Here It Comes Again," and "Let It Alone."

In about April 1906 Williams and Walker returned to the studio to make their first American recordings since 1901. These would not be for Victor, but for that company's great rival, Columbia. The April session yielded a single title, a duet of "Pretty Desdemone," from the current hit *Abyssinia.* It was as loose and limber as the 1901 recordings, with laughter and chattering over the opening strains of the orchestra. Walker then took the lead, while Williams did the equivalent of vocal "mugging" in the background, sometimes harmonizing, sometimes interjecting various sounds. The total effect was very much like a stage performance, although the rather staid Columbia studio orchestra detracted somewhat.

"Pretty Desdemone" was Walker's last recording. Although his voice recorded well, his style on record was a bit stiff and essentially indistinguishable from that of numerous white baritones. Williams's vocal style, on the other hand, was unique, and he would return to the recording studio many times in years to come.

Two additional songs from *Abyssinia* were recorded in May and June, as solos by Bert Williams. One of them would become his most famous hit ever and his signature piece. "Nobody," with music by Williams and lyrics by Alex Rogers, had been introduced by Williams in vaudeville in 1905. It was first recorded in May 1905 by white "coon" singer Arthur Collins, who made versions for all three major labels, Victor, Columbia, and Edison.[21] By the time it was interpolated into *Abyssinia* in early 1906, it had become a major hit, inducing Columbia to obtain a recording by the originator.

The strength of the song was its brilliant marriage of ironic words, doleful but perfectly complementary music, and Williams's unique half-sung, half-spoken delivery. He began slowly, in his deepest voice, almost speaking:

> When life seems full of clouds and rain,
> And I am full of nothin' and pain,
> Who soothes my thumpin', bumpin' brain?
> [pause] Nobody.
>
> When Winter comes with snow and sleet,
> And me with hunger and cold feet,
> Who says "Here's twenty-five cents, go ahead and get something to eat"?
> [pause] Nobody!

Then he broke into his lamenting refrain.

> I ain't never done nothin' to nobody.
> I ain't never got nothin' from nobody, no time.
> Oh, until I get somethin' from somebody, some time,
> I'll never do nothin' for nobody, no time.
>
> When I was in that railroad wreck,
> And thought I'd cashed in my last check,
> Who took the engine off my neck?
> [Pause] Nobody!
>
> One time when things was lookin' bright,
> I started to whittle on a stick one night,
> Who cried out, just now, "That's dynamite"?
> [Pause] Not a soul.[22]

Williams's delivery was as much monologue as song, with exaggerated vocal interjections that must have matched the mugging he was famous for on stage. "Engine" became "en-giiine," and the conclusion of a verse might be accompanied by sounds of pondering followed by surprise when he realized the answer was, once again, "Nobody!" In his 1901 recordings, such as "All Going Out and Nothing Coming In," he was essentially singing. Here he was acting. It was a very unusual performance style for the time. Meanwhile the usually unimaginative Columbia studio orchestra outdid itself, providing a nice, subdued accompaniment that matched his drawling delivery, interrupted by trombone swoops and other effects when he broke into the chorus.

"Nobody" became so identified with Bert Williams that he was forced to sing it in almost every appearance he made. Williams himself made light of this, remarking in later years, "Before I got through with 'Nobody,' I could have wished that both the author of the words and the assembler of the tune had been strangled or drowned or talked to death. For seven whole years, I had to sing it. Month after month I tried to drop it and sing something new, but I could get nothing to replace it, and the audiences seemed to want nothing else. Every comedian at some point in his life learns to curse the particular stunt of his that was most popular. 'Nobody' was a particularly hard song to replace."[23] According to biographer Ann Charters, Williams eventually built an entire skit around the song, pretending he couldn't remember the words and hesitantly half-singing, half-talking as he searched for the words in a little notebook.

Williams and Walker's first two recordings for Columbia were released in July 1906. While Columbia was as pleased to have the stars as Victor had been, it clearly saw them as "coon" singers, the very characterization that they were trying to move away from. Perhaps Columbia felt that consumers would only buy that which was familiar, even if the message of the songs was subtly changed. The announcement read,

> [Vary] your program with the ebony emperors Williams and Walker, whose typi-cal coon harmony in their duet, "Pretty Desdemone"—10 in. disc No. 3410—with orchestra accompaniment, is truly delectable. The Ethiopian baritone Bert Williams sings his big hit, "Nobody"—10 in. disc No. 3423—in an extremely funny way, the haunting melody being supported by the trombone and orchestra. Both are selec-tions from Williams and Walker's recent musical production *Abyssinia,* which had a six weeks' run at the Majestic Theatre in New York. These negro artists sing ex-clusively for the Columbia Phonograph company.[24]

"Nobody" was released on a Columbia cylinder in October with the words, "The July record . . . 'Nobody' by Bert Williams created such a sensation that this merry monarch has sung it also on cylinder No. 33011, with orchestra accompaniment. Here is negro character by the funniest negro artist on earth, genuine colored phi-losophy by an African logician, whose records are made exclusively for the Colum-bia Phonograph Company."[25]

Columbia claimed that both disc and cylinder versions were among their best-sellers at the time of release.[26] Although promotional claims are always suspect, it is significant that this was the only one of Williams's 1906 titles for which this claim was made. "Nobody" remained in the Columbia catalog until the 1930s, and it has been frequently reissued since then. Part of its longevity must trace to that fact that it is not really a "coon song," but a human lament that almost anybody could iden-tify with. Bert Williams no longer needed to be one of the "Two Real Coons" or a high strutting cakewalker. Those were fads of the day. He had found a persona that transcended time and race.

"Here It Comes Again," from *Abyssinia,* recorded about a month later, was a simi-lar tale of woe by Rogers and Williams, but without the magic of "Nobody." The tune was rather ordinary, and although Williams gave it a similar performance it was sung more than acted. Issued on both cylinder and disc, it remained in the catalog for only a couple of years.

Williams returned to the Columbia studios at least five times during the fall of 1906, recording one more song from *Abyssinia* and six other tunes. They were writ-ten by a variety of songwriters (three by Williams himself), but nearly all reflected Williams's homey observations on life. None were really "coon songs"—although

Bert Williams and George Walker

virtually any song about blacks was called that in 1906. The genre was still extremely popular (one of the hits of the season was "If the Man in the Moon Were a Coon"), but Williams was now avoiding it.

"All In, Out and Down" was in the hard-luck mold of "Jonah Man" and "Nobody." It was recorded about three months after the release of Williams's "Nobody" and may have been an early attempt to cash in on the great popularity of his trademark song. Williams gave it the same deliberate, semi-talking performance, with ironic chuckles and asides, but although it remained in the catalog for many years it never achieved the enormous popularity of the earlier song. It is most notable for being Williams's first twelve-inch record, allowing him nearly four minutes to develop the song.

Two of the new numbers recorded in 1906 were "advice" songs. "Fare Thee! On My Way! Just Gone!" suggested what to do when trouble loomed, while "Let It Alone" from *Abyssinia* counseled the listener to stay out of other people's business. Columbia announced the release of "Let It Alone" in three different formats, a ten-inch disc, a standard four-inch cylinder that ran for two minutes, and one of the new six-inch "BC" cylinders that ran for three minutes. This simultaneous multiformat release suggests that Columbia did indeed think it could capitalize on the initial strong sales of the "Nobody" artist. The listing said, "A tremendously popular coon song hit in Williams and Walker's latest version of their *Abyssinia,* is written by the creators of 'Nobody' and recorded exclusively for the Columbia Phonograph Company, by the cleverest and most popular of real colored comedians, Bert A. Williams of Williams and Walker, the song being entitled 'Let It Alone'—10 in. disc No. 3504, BC cylinder No. 85086, cylinder No. 33025."

> Don't go 'round fo' flushin' an' puttin' on airs,
> An' dippin' yo' face in other people's affairs,
> But ef yuh doan' know, why jes' say so,
> An' go on 'bout yo' bizness an' Let it Alone![27]

The six-inch-cylinder format was marketed only by Columbia, from 1905 to 1909. Its expense and fragility doomed it to failure. Ten-inch discs played for about the same three minutes, so there was little reason for consumers to buy the special phonograph necessary to accommodate the long, clumsy cylinders. In all, three titles by Bert Williams were issued in this format, and all are extremely rare today.

Three of the titles recorded by Williams in the fall of 1906 were novelties, of the type being sung by many singers of the day. "He's a Cousin of Mine" and "The Mississippi Stoker" were written for white "coon shouter" and major star May Irwin and featured in her comedy *Mrs. Wilson-Andrews,* which opened on Broadway in November 1906.[28] "He's a Cousin of Mine" was a substantial hit, being a favorite of such white singers as Clarice Vance and Marie Cahill and was recorded by Victor, Columbia, and Edison. A catchy melody, with words to match, it remained in print for many years. Columbia commented, "Bert Williams, the genuine negro comedy king, records with orchestra accompaniment May Irwin's big hit in her new musical comedy success *Mrs. Wilson-Andrews,* the song being entitled 'He's a Cousin of

Mine' . . . wherein a very devoted darkey detects his fickle fiancee in the midst of a violent love-making with a perfect stranger who, however, she adroitly explains, is merely her dear long lost cousin. Subsequent indications cast considerable doubt upon their pretended relationship, the second verse furnishing an inexpressibly funny denouement. Truly the acme of Bert Williams' hits."[29]

"The Mississippi Stoker" was a rickety-tick, minstrel-type song about a black stoker "on the muddy Mississip'." Unusual for Williams, it contained mild ethnic references such as "my old mammy." It was not much of a hit. Columbia remarked that Williams had recorded it for them "because he likes the song."[30] The final number Williams recorded for Columbia in 1906 was also somewhat out of character and not very successful. "I've Such a Funny Feeling When I Look at You" was the closest thing he did to a love song, though delivered to an upbeat tempo.

Williams did not return to the recording studio for another three and a half years, but of the ten titles he made in 1906 six were sufficiently popular to remain in the catalog for extended periods. "Nobody," "Let It Alone," "I'm Tired of Eating in the Restaurants," "He's a Cousin of Mine," "The Mississippi Stoker," and "All In, Out and Down" were issued on double-faced discs when Columbia converted to that format in late 1908. "Nobody" (later rerecorded) remained in print until the 1930s, while the others were deleted between 1913 and 1919—by which time many new Williams recordings were available.

African Americans were justifiably proud of the achievements of Williams and Walker, the most popular actors of their race in American history. (The fact that Williams was of West Indian parentage was generally ignored; in everyone's view, he was black.) Coverage of their activities was extensive, especially in the black press, and so were the demands for them to positively represent "the race." They were cognizant of their role. In December 1907 the theatrical paper *Variety* published a most revealing letter from a black college professor in Kansas, addressed to the team.

> Gentlemen:
> I am one of the many cranks who persist in telling you how to run your business. However I have watched closely and studiously the effect, and after results, which your show leaves upon our people. You have a wonderful opportunity in this country. Your name is magic to our people, the characters you bring out in your plays, the vim and dash of Negro young manhood and womanhood have the effect of ideals which almost every Negro boy and girl, however far distant in the backwoods, seems to pounce upon, imitate, emulate and follow as the standard. . . .
> May I ask this question? Is it not possible that while at the same time you hold the old plantation Negro and the ludicrous darky and the scheming "grafter" up to entertain people, that you could likewise have a prominent character representative of Locke, the Negro student at Oxford, England . . . such as Pickens, who won the prize at Yale; Roscoe Conkling Bruce, who led the oratorical contest at Harvard; or the great colored football or baseball stars at Harvard, and make such characters heroes? Such would tend to lift the young Negro mind up to imitate and emulate these heroes . . .
> Making money is not the greatest thing in life. Bettering mankind, uplifting your fellow men, bring a far greater joy and personal contentment of the

mind and life spent in this world. You have the opportunity; can't you turn your tremendous influence more and more as you grow older and wiser along these lines?

In their reply Williams and Walker were neither condescending nor dismissive, but actually quite sympathetic to the professor's plea. They readily admitted that the progress of blacks in show business was still "in its infancy," but pointed out that important gains had been made in the past few years. For one thing, they were proud of the fact that their own shows were written, staged, and produced by blacks, "which required some thought and very careful deliberation before attempting to present them to the public." However, they said, most black theater-goers wanted to see characters who reminded them of respectable "white folks," while white patrons only wanted to see the antebellum darkey. So, they "averaged," concentrating on humorous character types rather than race per se.[31]

Leading black newspapers such as the *New York Age* and the Indianapolis *Freeman* mounted extended campaigns against demeaning titles of black shows and particularly the word "coon." In a 1909 editorial the *Freeman* maintained that,

> Williams & Walker are a great deal to blame for being the originators and establishing the name "coon" upon our race. They met a white man in San Francisco by the name of McConnell, who put them on the [vaudeville] circuit. In order to achieve success and to attract the attention of the public they branded themselves as "the two real coons." Their names, accompanied with "coon" songs, were soon heralded North, East, South and West. . . . Williams & Walker and Ernest Hogan were not old enough then to know the harm they had brought on the whole race. They needed the money, what little they received, and the white people needed the laugh [and made the money]. Colored men in general took no offense at the proceedings and laughed as heartily on hearing a "coon" song as the whites. But where the rub came is when the colored was called a "coon" outside of the [theater].[32]

No doubt such criticism stung, as Williams and Walker were deliberately trying to move away from the most offensive stereotypes while not alienating the white audiences who were the foundation of their success. They were walking a tightrope. George Walker, who was more outspoken on such issues than Williams, reflected in 1906 that the black man's progress would more likely come from within himself and his own heritage than from trying to become "white." "Talk to me about the infusion of white blood for the betterment of the Negro race. I do not believe in it. I tell you the black man's future lies in the development of his faculties—physical and mental— as a Negro. I think the white race has not realized the latent possibilities in us."[33]

Such considerations may have weighed on Williams and Walker's minds, but they did not change their successful formula as they developed their next show. *Bandanna Land,* with book and lyrics by Shipp and Rogers, and music by Cook, Rogers, and others, premiered in January 1908 and moved to Broadway on February 3. Besides the stars and their wives, the cast included Jesse Shipp, Alex Rogers, J. Leubrie Hill, Henry Troy, Abbie Mitchell, James Lightfoot, Sterling Rex, Ada Rex, and James M. Thomas. (Several of these cast members made recordings prior to 1920, and are covered elsewhere in this book.) Set in the south, the plot had Bud Jenkins (Walker) trying to relieve Skunkton Bowser (Williams) of his inheritance and swindle the railroad with the money; but in the end Bowser realized the con man's intentions, and got all the benefits himself. Included in the score were Will Marion Cook's famous choral number "Rain Song" ("'Tain't Gwine to Be No Rain Today") and "Exhortation." "I'm Tired of Eating in the Restaurants," previously performed and recorded by Williams, was an interpolation. The hit of the show was George Walker's lively "Bon Bon Buddy, the chocolate drop, dat's me," with which he closed the second act. Unfortunately he never recorded the song.

Bandanna Land also marked the debut of one of Bert Williams's most famous sketches, his pantomime poker game. In it the wide-eyed comedian would go through all the motions of winning, losing, suspecting, and slinking away when his luck ran out. It was perfectly suited for a physical comedian such as Williams, who could play out virtually every emotion on his rubber face. He performed it many times in vaudeville in years to come and even made a film of it in 1916.

In March 1908, during the run of *Bandanna Land,* Williams and Walker were asked by George M. Cohan to appear at a charity benefit at New York's Academy of Music. No sooner had they consented than Walter C. Kelly, the monologuist who had boycotted them once before, held a meeting and tried to influence the other performers not to appear on stage with the black comedians. Two acts did withdraw, but the show went on as scheduled and was a smashing success. It was also during 1908 that leading black entertainers, denied admission to white theatrical clubs such as the Lambs and the Players, founded their own club called the Frogs. George Walker was the first president, and Bert Williams later held the office.

Bandanna Land played successfully for more than a year, but by late 1908 the long-running Williams and Walker stock company had begun to disintegrate. Within less than a year the glory days of the great Williams and Walker musicals—and of black theater on Broadway—would be just a memory. First to leave was Williams's wife, Lottie, who, ill and tired, retired from the stage in December 1908. A more devastating blow was the physical deterioration of George Walker, who was in many ways the soul, and certainly the energy, of the Williams and Walker team. Suffering from paresis, apparently caused by syphilis, he began to slur his lines and struggle through performances. He carried on for as long as he humanly could, but by February 1909 he was forced to leave the show. His part was taken over by his wife, Aida Overton Walker, but she too left at the end of the season to pursue a promising solo career in vaudeville as a dancer.

Bert Williams, loyal to a fault, would not even suggest that he and Walker were breaking up. In May 1909, he told reporters that "when my old pal is alright . . . we will be back together again."[34] But it was not to be. With the Walkers gone, and his wife retired from the stage, Bert faced a crossroads in 1909. He had been with Walker for sixteen years, and no one—most of all Bert himself—knew whether he could carry an act alone. Many doubted it. George Walker had not only been the energetic counterpoint to Bert's slow-moving "darkey" on stage, he also was the business brains and spokesman for the pair. Some suggested that Williams should team with Aida Overton Walker to form a second "Williams and Walker." But Mrs. Walker had other plans, and there is no evidence they ever discussed it.

Williams's first, tentative foray as a single was in high-class vaudeville in the spring of 1909. He met with reassuring success. *Variety* described his act.

Three new songs and "Nobody," with a bit of talk worked in between the tunes, make up Williams' single specialty. Both songs and talk were highly amusing. Williams was never funnier. "That's a-Plenty" made a capital opening song. There followed a few minutes of talk adapted from his part of Skunkton in *Bandanna Land.* Even without a foil in his partner George Walker, Williams' stupid darkey was a scream. His second song failed to keep up the fast pace, but he picked up speed with a couple of stories and finished strong with a song about a dispute as to the naming of a baby, Williams' suggestion being something like George Washington, Abraham Lincoln, Booker T., and a lot more, until it was learned that the baby was a girl. The discussion ends when the mother announces Carrie Jones as the name. "Nobody" served admirably as an encore, and Williams had to repeat his inimitable "loose dance" several times before they would let him go.[35]

During the summer of 1909 Williams and his manager, F. Ray Comstock, put together a new show with many of the old supporting cast but starring Bert Williams alone. The book and lyrics of *Mr. Lode of Koal* were by Shipp and Rogers, with music by Williams and the brilliant composer J. Rosamond Johnson, formerly of Cole and Johnson. The story had King Big Smoke of the Isle of Koal (Williams) being kidnapped, whereupon Chester A. Lode (also played by Williams) impersonated him. After a good deal of comic business around the palace, the king was released and Lode forced to become a royal servant. Continuing the star's move away from stereotyped material, the setting was mythical rather than "black." *Mr. Lode of Koal* was a critical success but unfortunately a box-office failure, in part due to poor bookings that had it playing mostly second-class houses (Walker had always fought for first-class bookings). After limping along for a season, it closed abruptly in March 1910.

Williams talked bravely of "next season," but it would be difficult to mount another first-class show after the disappointing performance of *Mr. Lode of Koal.* He toyed with the idea of going into serious drama, a long-held dream; the famous producer David Belasco was interested in helping him to that end. But it was a most unlikely offer from an all-white musical revue that snared him. Producer Florenz Ziegfeld had founded his annual *Follies* only three years earlier, and he had an eye for first-rate talent that would catch the attention of both audiences and the press. The combination of the *Follies* and the comic genius Bert Williams seems natural in retrospect, but at the time it was unprecedented. There was some resentment at the prospect of America's most famous black entertainer appearing in a previously all-white show, especially one featuring platoons of beautiful white women. As a precaution, Williams's initial contract specified that the show would not tour in the south and "that at no time would he be on stage with any of the female members of the company."[36]

Nevertheless when Williams showed up for rehearsals there was a cast revolt. Some cast members reportedly told Ziegfeld, "either he goes or we go." But Ziegfeld would have none of it, replying, "Go if you want to. I can replace every one of you, except the man you want me to fire."[37] Still, Williams was given a cold shoulder and the writers didn't even have any material for him to perform until shortly before the opening. There was speculation that he would not be in the *Follies* at all.

But when the *Follies of 1910* opened on June 20, 1910, there he was, the star of the show. Among his sketches was a burlesque on the arty French play *Chantecler,* with the big comedian dressed as a rooster. Williams provoked gales of laughter making "an awkward entrance out of a large papier-mache egg."[38] One of the riskier sketches, added shortly after the premiere, was "A Scene in Reno," his takeoff on the hugely publicized Jack Johnson–Jim Jeffries heavyweight championship fight that took place in Reno on July 4, 1910. Johnson, a high-living black man who had done everything but spit in white America's face, had secured his championship against the "great white hope" Jeffries. His knockout victory had sparked race riots in cities across the United States, in which several people were killed. Motion pictures of the fight were widely banned for fear of stirring further racial strife. Emotions ran high for many weeks afterwards. Comedy was perhaps the best way to defuse the situation.

Many considered the debut of young comedienne Fanny Brice to be the hit of the 1910 *Follies,* but reviews of Williams's solo act were also glowing. Ashton Stevens of the Chicago *Examiner* called him "the Mark Twain of his color";[39] the *New York Herald* called Williams "the real star of the evening."[40] But the most appreciated tribute came from none other than Booker T. Washington, perhaps the most famous black leader in America. Washington wrote in a 1910 magazine:

> Vaudeville performances, as a rule, strike me as tiresome . . . but Bert Williams' humor strikes me as the real thing. I suppose the best reason I can give for liking his quaint songs and humorous sayings is that he puts into this form some of the quality and philosophy of the Negro race. . . .
>
> Bert Williams is a tremendous asset to the Negro race. He is an asset because he has succeeded in actually doing something, and because he has succeeded, the fact of his success helps the Negro many times more than he could help the Negro by merely contenting himself to whine and complain about racial difficulties and racial discriminations.[41]

What was the "specialty" that so impressed theater-goers and critics in the *Follies* and elsewhere? Unique in the noisy world of 1910s vaudeville, it was quiet, underplayed, and visually hilarious. The mere sight of the lanky, bedraggled, sad-faced black man in an ill-fitting formal suit, hesitantly shuffling onto the stage, would provoke gales of laughter. Langston Hughes described his entrance. "A spotlight would make a great white circle against the black velvet curtain at the left of the stage, the orchestra would strike a few chords. Then out of the wings would protrude a lone hand in a white glove, then another white-gloved hand with slowly moving fingers. And just the droll motion of those two hands, before Bert Williams himself came into view, would make an audience shake with laughter. Then Williams would emerge, sing a little and talk a little, and disappear."[42]

Williams, who was naturally light-skinned, used blackface makeup that exaggerated his eyes and mouth and gave him a downcast look. Those who cannot understand the appeal of his slow, thoughtful songs should imagine the visual presentation Williams gave them.

Williams made a second major decision during the summer of 1910, resuming his recording career in earnest. During June or July, just as he joined the *Follies,* he recorded four numbers from the show for Columbia. The label was delighted to have him back and responded with a full page of flowery compliments and paeans to his greatness in its November 1910 supplement. There was no more talk of "ebony emperors" or "coon harmony." Williams had become a star who transcended race, to the extent that was possible in 1910. Henceforth Williams's recordings would not be coupled with those of any other artist, and they would not be leased to other labels (as were those of Columbia's other singers). He would be accorded star treatment.

Under the headline "Bert Williams—The World-Famous Comedian Now Makes Records Exclusively for the Columbia," the label proudly announced:

> Through an arrangement recently concluded we have acquired the sole right to record and reproduce the absolutely unique and inimitable art of Bert Williams, one of the greatest comedians the stage has ever known, and the highest priced artist in vaudeville in America at this writing. . . .
>
> As senior member of the comedy team of Williams and Walker, Williams kept the theater-going public of America amused and in good humor for over twelve years, earning in that time a reputation for individual cleverness and skill in comedy work such as no amount of money could buy. We need only hark back to the days when we laughed at his drolleries in "Bandanna Land," "Arabia" [*sic*] and the many other productions in which this team starred to realize how significant and important a factor he has been in the amusement field. After the enforced dissolution of the Williams & Walker partnership through the illness of Mr. Walker, Williams accepted one of the many offers awaiting him to enter vaudeville, and has since been a headliner whenever booked. . . . In *The Follies of 1910,* Ziegfeld's latest production at the Jarden de Paris, playing all this summer, Williams has made one of the biggest hits of his career.
>
> Bert Williams' humor is of that genuine sort that relies on no clap-trap, horse-play or stage-setting for its effect. It goes straight to the mark by a direct appeal to the intelligence through the sense of humor and perception of the grotesque and the ridiculous. The Columbia Records of Bert Williams' work are masterpieces. They reproduce with the last degree of faithfulness every trick of expression and vocal inflection that goes to form the sum total of the comedian's entertaining strength.[43]

The new recordings, his first in more than three years, are aural evidence of how much he had refined his style. Bert realized that he was not a singer, but a storyteller, and the performances reflect that. They are essentially monologues with orchestra accompaniment, interspersed with asides and vocal effects. Only at the chorus does he generally break into song.

The least imaginative of the four is "Constantly," an obvious knockoff of "Nobody." The speaker relates a litany of bad-luck stories, ending every one by saying how this happens to him, ". . . constantly!" Whereas "Nobody" sounded genuinely fresh in 1906, by this time Williams had turned his *de rigueur* hard-luck songs into an act that was more about him singing a predictable song than about the song itself. His performance is "over the top," as is that of the orchestra, complete with the trademark trombone swoops lifted from "Nobody."

"I'll Lend You Anything I've Got Except My Wife" is one of the making-fun-of-the-little-woman songs so popular at the turn of the century (Irving Berlin's "My Wife's Gone to the Country, Hurrah!" had been a hit the year before). The punch line was "and I'll make you a present of her." "Something You Don't Expect" related the tale of Madame Lee, a fortuneteller whose philandering husband made the mistake of giving Madame's jewelry to his young lady friend. When the young woman came in to have her fortune read, both she and the husband got "something you don't expect."

The most famous of the four songs was "Play That Barbershop Chord," which is still heard occasionally today. It was introduced by Williams during his vaudeville run at Hammerstein's Victoria Theatre, earlier in the year, then incorporated into the *Follies* when he joined that show. According to musicologist Lynn Abbott it was "the first popular song *about* barbershop harmony, and it has been credited as a major factor in ameliorating the term and disseminating it into the American mainstream."[44] It is about a black piano player in a rathskeller named Jefferson Lord who caught the eye of "a kinky haired lady they called Chocolate Sadie," when he played the magic minor-key notes:

> She cried, "Mr. Jefferson Lord,
> Oh play that barbershop chord,
> It's got that soothing harmony,
> It makes an awful, awful, awful hit with me!"

The song was a substantial hit and was the only one of the four songs to be widely recorded by other artists. However, all four titles sold well for Bert Williams. "I'll Lend You Anything" and "Constantly" were issued in November, while "Something That You Don't Expect" and "Play That Barbershop Chord" were coupled the following month. The two discs remained in the catalog until 1930 and 1928, respectively.

Bert Williams's embrace of recording as an integral part of his career was unusual. Few stage stars at this time did so. He had a special talent for it, however, adapting well to the peculiar requirements of acoustic recording. In theaters, which had no amplification, clarity and strong voice projection were required simply to be heard in the back rows. Often singers used broad gestures to aid in the communication process, illustrating what they were singing about, and of course there was plenty of time to "put a song over." In the recording studio, on the other hand, gestures were pointless and movement was discouraged, lest the singer move out of range of the narrowly focused recording horn, or, worse yet, bump into it. Voice projection had to be toned down considerably or "blasting" would result. Simultaneously a singer had to remember to enunciate very carefully, adhere to strict timing, so as not to run over the maximum three minutes that would fit on a single disc, and make no mistakes (no editing was possible)—all of this while sounding natural and not rushed.

It was no wonder that the record companies generally used professional studio musicians specially trained in handling all of these strange mechanical requirements. Celebrities often did not (or could not) record well. Bert Williams was an exception. Most of his songs were recorded in just one or two takes, and they sounded as natural as if he was standing in the room.

The 1910 *Follies* was a smashing success, putting to rest any questions about whether Bert Williams's career could survive the loss of his beloved partner, George Walker. Walker's worsening condition was a constant emotional drain on Williams. Little could be done for him; the present-day treatment for syphilis, penicillin, had not yet been developed. After a lingering illness Walker died on January 6, 1911. Williams heard the news as he was about to go on stage in New York, and it is said that he broke down and cried like a baby. Only four people attended the private funeral, Bert and Lottie Williams, Walker's mother, and his widow, Aida. The floral pieces were numerous, including one from Bert with a simple card reading, "My Dear Old Pal."

To the world at large Walker's death was anticlimactic, receiving relatively little press coverage. Williams and Walker were almost forgotten. They had been totally eclipsed by the new media star, Bert Williams.

There was no question that Bert would appear again in the next year's edition of the *Follies,* now called the *Ziegfeld Follies* in honor of its creator. The big show opened on June 26, 1911. Among the sketches were a parody of the allegorical play *Everywoman,* called "Everywife" (the *Follies* liked to mock the "higher" arts). The characters had names like Everyhusband, Happiness, Rhyme, Drink, and Gamble. Williams appeared as a one-man Greek chorus called—what else—"Nobody." He intoned, "What is the plot of the Follies? Nobody knows. What is the moral pointed out by the Follies? Don't ask me—Nobody knows."[45]

The big comedian also essayed physical comedy with rubber-legged white comedian Leon Errol on girders high above the stage, in a sketch about the building of Grand Central Terminal, then under construction. Williams and the Aussie Errol worked well together, ad-libbing, improvising, and often stealing the show. The *New York World* said they "brought down the house"; the *New York Post* called the scene "excruciatingly funny."[46] Williams also did his famous poker sketch and sang a song called "Woodman, Woodman, Spare That Tree."

Apparently Columbia's 1910 contract with Williams was short-term, for he did no more recording in 1911 or 1912. Instead, he played with the *Follies* through the 1911–12 season, then went into the 1912 edition, which opened late on October 21, 1912. Some of the old fears had been put to rest, and he now appeared on stage with the beautiful women of the cast and with the other principals. One of the highlights of the 1912 edition reunited him with Leon Errol in a sketch about a black cabman helping a drunken bon vivant (Errol) find his way home. Williams and Errol worked up the sketch themselves, and the critics loved it.

Columbia finally signed the star to a new contract and got him back into its New York studios in January 1913. He recorded eight titles, four of them from the *Follies.* The *Follies* numbers were Irving Berlin's "Woodman, Woodman, Spare That Tree" from the 1911 edition, and "My Landlady," "Borrow from Me," and "You're on the Right Road (But You're Going the Wrong Way)" from 1912. The last three all had music by Williams himself. All were novelty songs, but none was particularly outstanding, and none enjoyed any substantial popularity beyond the show. "Woodman" was about a henpecked husband who sought refuge in a favorite elm tree whenever his wife went on the warpath and had to persuade a woodman not to chop it down. "It's the only tree my wife can't climb," he lamented.[47] The three songs from the 1912 *Follies* were all about various character types: the snooping busybody ("My Landlady"), the person who's always asking for something ("Borrow from Me"), and an amorous widow who drives off her intended beau by constantly chattering to him about how much everything cost ("You're on the Right Road"). The man appreciated the meal she prepared for him but said as he got up to leave, "I ain't gonna marry no price list."

"I Certainly Was Going Some" was a novelty with a rickety-tick sound, about a black man who always runs at the first sign of trouble (similar to "Fare Thee! On My Way! Jes' Gone"). All of these were delivered in Williams's now-trademark half-spoken, half-sung style, as if he was acting them out on stage.

In some ways the most interesting titles recorded in the 1913 sessions were the two unaccompanied monologues, which serve as invaluable evidence of his storytelling style. Recorded on twelve-inch discs, they allowed Williams a full four minutes to develop the stories. "You Can't Do Nothin' Till Martin Gets Here" is a particularly funny tale about a black preacher who takes refuge in a haunted house during a storm. The fearless preacher lights a roaring fire in the fireplace and settles down with the Good Book. A kitten comes down the stairs, jumps into the fire, washes its face in the hot ashes, then curls up next to him. He is unfazed. A few minutes later a larger cat, the size of a bulldog, bounds down the stairs, plunges into the fire, washes itself in the hot ashes, and jumps up beside the preacher; it asks the kitten what they should do next. "Do nothin' till Martin gets here" answers the kitten. The preacher is still unmoved. Then down the stairs ("ka-blook, ka-blook, ka-blook") comes an even bigger cat, this one the size of a Newfoundland dog. It washes itself with some burning coals (the ashes aren't hot enough), joins the other two, and asks the same question. The kitten looks at him and replies, "We can't do nothin' till Martin gets here." Whereupon the preacher calmly stands up and says, "Well, when Martin gets here, you all just tell him I been here, but I'm *gone!*"

Williams delivered the yarn in wonderfully understated style, doling out one surprise after another, until the climax was reached. The other monologue, "How? Fried!," was about how an old black man's incredible memory kept him from becoming the property of the devil. Although Williams was renowned for his storytelling ability, neither of these recorded examples was released at the time. Columbia apparently preferred to market only his familiar character songs. In fact, no purely spoken monologues by Bert Williams were released until 1920, when the runaway success of the "Elder Eatmore" stories led Columbia to exhume these two 1913 examples from its vault.

The other two titles recorded in 1913 provide evidence that Williams was not an improviser who constantly changed his delivery, but rather an actor who stuck (or, at least, could stick) pretty closely to the script. The first was a rerecording of his great hit "Nobody." It is this 1913 version, issued on Columbia A1289, that is most commonly found today on old 78s and is most often reissued. It is instructive to compare it with the 1906 original. The rerecording seems to have been made to take advantage of improved recording technology, which had advanced substantially in the intervening seven years. Although A1289 is still an acoustic recording, the orchestra sounds much richer and fuller than in the pinched, tinny 1906 version.

Williams's 1913 performance is quite close to that of 1906, right down to the asides and inflections. It is almost as if he listened to the earlier recording before making this one and intentionally tried to duplicate it, disregarding the embellishments he had been making in live performances over the years. There are some subtle differences, however. The opening verses in the 1906 original are masterfully underplayed, delivered in a sort of sorrowful drone that heightens the humor when the inevitable punch line arrives ("Nobody!"). The 1913 version is closer to being sung and is generally a more stylized "performance." The orchestra also intrudes more, with loud trombone bleats, which the singer answers. Despite the improved sound, it is not quite as interesting a rendition in my view.

The one major difference in the text is the substitution of a new verse for the one about whittling on a stick of dynamite:

When summer comes all cool and clear,
And friends they see me drawing near,
Who says "Come in and have a beer?"
[pause] Nobody.

"Woodman, Woodman, Spare That Tree" is revealing because different takes were issued on different pressings, allowing further analysis of the consistency of Williams's performance style. Take five, recorded in 1913, has a fairly straightforward, unembellished accompaniment. Take eight, recorded in 1920, features a much livelier orchestra, with trumpet flourishes and little musical jokes, some of which Williams answers. Just before the vocal begins there is a trumpet run and a trombone swoop. However, Williams performs the song almost identically in both cases, once again suggesting that he "stuck to the script" even in takes made years apart.[48]

Columbia welcomed back its star with open arms, treating him with the respect deserved by a major celebrity. The announcement included a handsome photo of him in street clothes, without the blackface makeup he still wore on stage. However, it persisted in called his songs "coon songs," a generic term for almost any song about a black individual. Williams never used such derogatory terms in his songs anymore. "Again the 'one and only' Bert Williams, the greatest comedian of his kind the American stage has ever known, has made a number of records for the Columbia under a new exclusive contract—and such records of coon songs as were never before heard or issued. Of course the excellence of the new record of 'Nobody' goes without saying. 'Nobody' without Bert Williams to sing it would be 'Hamlet with Hamlet left out.' This is the most artistically executed coon song ever issued to the public and one of the most inexhaustible mirth producers that has ever been heard."[49]

Six recordings from the 1913 sessions were coupled on three two-sided discs and issued between May and September of that year. They appear to have been good sellers, all remaining in the catalog for a dozen years or more. The cumulative list of Williams's recordings in Columbia's annual general catalog was becoming longer. It was now accompanied by a photo and a paragraph of flowery praise, including the inaccurate statement that "throughout his stage career the Columbia has had the sole right to record and reproduce the unique and inimitable art of Bert Williams."[50]

Williams took a year off from the *Follies* in 1913–14. He certainly didn't need the work, as he was in enormous demand for vaudeville and other appearances. This was also a time of other changes in his life. His father, Frederick, had died in 1912. In 1913 his sister-in-law passed away, and Bert and Lottie adopted her three girls. In August 1913 he appeared in the Frogs' annual Summer Frolic at Manhattan Casino with Aida Overton Walker, his erstwhile partner, then went into high-class vaudeville doing "Nobody," his famous pantomime poker game, and a new song he had cowritten called "The Darktown Poker Club." In it one Bill Jackson joined the local poker club; "his money seemed like it had wings" until he caught on to the many tricks the players were using, resulting in a humorous confrontation.

In February 1914 Williams recorded this number and a topical song called "You Can't Get Away from It." The latter was a clever but typical Tin Pan Alley creation about the ragtime craze ("Syncopation rules this nation, you can't get away from it . . .") and was not very well suited to the comedian's unique conversational style. It was an unusual performance for him, being sung the whole way through, without his usual asides or half-spoken interludes. His rough-hewn baritone was certainly distinctive, but he would do few straight songs in the future.

When Williams returned to the *Follies* in June 1914 the year-old "Darktown Poker Club" was interpolated and was one of his featured numbers, but no new song hits emerged from this edition. The rave reviews for Williams instead focused on his physical comedy, particularly when he was reunited with the limber Australian Leon Errol. Williams had four spots in the show, including one in which he played a caddy to Errol's amateur golfer on the Mexican border (then a war zone), and another in which the two were workmen on the 1,313th floor of a skyscraper under construction. As they teetered on the girders Errol tried to persuade him that they were as safe as if they were in bed at home. Williams retorted, "I may be dark, but I ain't no crow."[51] Also in this edition were dancer Ann Pennington and comedian Ed Wynn.

While Williams was appearing in the *Follies* that fall, news came that another integral part of his earlier career was gone. After leaving the last Williams and Walker show, *Bandanna Land,* in 1909, Aida Overton Walker had launched a successful act as an artistic dancer in vaudeville. Though not a star of Williams's magnitude, she had attracted excellent notices and seemed set for a long and prosperous career. She performed through the summer of 1914, then in late September suddenly became ill. Less than six weeks later, on October 11, she died. She was only thirty-four. The cause of death is not certain, with some reports citing a nervous breakdown and others, kidney disease. Relations between her and Williams were evidently strained, and newspaper articles did not mention whether he attended her funeral.[52]

As for the "new" Bert Williams, he seemed to be going from triumph to triumph. When the 1915 edition of the *Ziegfeld Follies* opened on June 21 of that year, he was in several sketches, including a lampoon of the George Bernard Shaw play *Androcles and the Lion* (as the playwright, "O. Shaw"). There was more comedy with Leon Errol and new cast member W. C. Fields, and of course new songs. One of these was a topical song about the war that had recently broken out in Europe, called "I'm Neutral."

On August 2, a few weeks after the show had opened, Williams returned to Columbia's New York studio to record "I'm Neutral" and several other numbers. During the next month and a half he recorded a total of eight titles, at least four of which he wrote or cowrote. Several had a topical flavor, something that Williams was beginning to turn to with increasing frequency (as in "You Can't Get Away from It"); four contained references to the European conflict. In "I'm Neutral" he went downtown to look at the bulletins from the front and found himself in the middle of a scrap.

> Somebody hopped the Kaiser, and I don't know the reason why,
> A Frenchman took a swing at me and dug a trench right 'neath my eye,
> A Russian saw my color, and he hollered "Kill the Turk!"
> Then the Allies all got my range and started in to work,
> But I'm neutral!
> I am, and is, and shall remain . . .

Although "I'm Neutral" is the only title from these sessions known to have been in the *Follies of 1915*, "Samuel" bears a close resemblance to one of Williams's featured sketches in that show. In the sketch he played a West Indian hotel clerk dealing with the self-absorbed tenants. In "Samuel," "Big Sam Thompson" is a hotel attendant similarly at everyone's beck and call. "Where's that flim-flam, ram-tam, Sam-u-el?" they cry. He resolves to tell them all to go to Europe!

"Purpostus" ("preposterous") was Williams's chuckling reflections on the absurdities of modern life, including newfangled child-rearing methods and war fever. The label read "song monolog," accurately describing his unique half-spoken style. In "Everybody" he joins the militia, but everybody gets out of fighting except him. "Never Mo'" is an odd, slow, moody song about Edgar Allen Poe's raven and its famous utterance ("Quoth the raven, nevermore"). In Williams's version, the raven "used to sit above the do' / Of Mr. Po' / And keep on quotin', 'never mo',' 'never mo'.'"

Six of the titles recorded were released between November 1915 and March 1916 on three double-sided discs, accompanied by flowery but uninformative prose from Columbia. Perhaps accurately, the company's promotional writers remarked that "we could never say anything half as funny about Bert Williams's last records as the records themselves." They added proudly that his records were "full of the cleanest and most enjoyable humor imaginable."[53]

Four of the titles released from the 1915 sessions were written or cowritten by Williams, as was much of his material up to this time. It is notable that after this date, however, he virtually stopped writing his own songs. He never again recorded a new song of his own.

Two titles, "Hard Times" and "Eph Calls Up the Boss," were never released, a rare occurrence for Williams. Virtually all of his prior recordings had been released in some form. The Columbia files give no clue why these weren't; the file card for "Hard Times" clearly indicates one take as being approved for issue, while the notations for "Eph" are less clear. Perhaps Columbia simply felt that four Bert Williams discs at once would be a glut on the market. The masters are no longer in Columbia's vaults and are presumed lost.

Another important part of Williams's legacy that is now mostly lost is his work on film. He had begun making silent movies around 1910. The first is believed to have been an all-black movie called *The Pullman Porter* by pioneer black film pro-

ducer William Foster, and costarring Lottie Grady from the cast of *Mr. Lode of Koal.*
Williams may also have been in Foster's *The Railroad Porter* (1912).[54] He made at least
two more films for Biograph in 1914, *Darktown Jubilee* and *The Indian.* All of these
are now lost.

Williams made two films in 1916, both silent two-reelers. *Fish* was described as
featuring him "as a country boy who, among other things, fishes and hawks his
catch to white folks."[55] A brief scene survives. The other was *A Natural Born Gambler,* which committed to film his most famous routine, the pantomime poker game.
It is the most frequently seen film of the comedian in modern retrospectives and
may be the only full motion picture of his work to survive. It takes place in an all-
black clubhouse, where Williams has gone to make a killing. However, the place is
raided and he winds up dealing out imaginary hands behind the bars of a jail cell.
His slow, deliberate gestures and facial expressions at each unfortunate turn of fate
give us a glimpse of the magic of his stage performance style. He appears in exaggerated blackface and tattered dress clothes, as he did on stage. The film lasts about
fourteen minutes.

Despite his stage and recording fame, Bert Williams had little success in films.
His friend and lawyer Henry Herzbrun attributed this to racism, saying, "There is
no market. All of the representatives of the releasing concerns were approached and
they were unanimous in their decision that the Southern territory [of the United
States] would resent and would not exhibit the pictures of a Negro star; they were
also unanimous in regretting that this was so."[56]

This has been a popular explanation with modern writers as well. According to
film historian David Ragan, 1914's "*Darktown Jubilee* [was] historically of note because it was the first attempt to star a black in a movie. At its opening, white audiences—accustomed only to seeing a black in a tom role and rejecting this star—
jeered the film off the screen, precipitating a race riot."[57]

This explanation is a bit glib, however. Audiences certainly did not jeer Williams
himself off the stage, either in New York or on tour, and they bought his records in
huge quantities. Even assuming that the southern territory was lost (the *Follies*
didn't tour there either), with his talent for mime, he should have been as successful in movies as in other media. It may be that he simply wasn't presented well in
early silent comedies.

The *Ziegfeld Follies of 1916,* which opened in June, produced no new Bert Williams song hits, but it did feature him in several well-received sketches. In a travesty
of *Othello* he choked his Desdemona until he was tired, then beat her with a sledge-
hammer, but it only irritated her. In "Recruiting on Broadway" he was compelled
to enlist as a soldier, although he preferred running to fighting. Elsewhere in the
show he burlesqued ballet star Nijinsky (in a skit with Fanny Brice), Mexican revolutionary Pancho Villa, and a Hawaiian hula dancer.

Shortly after this edition of the *Follies* opened, Williams returned to the nearby
Columbia studios in July to cut two new songs. "The Lee Family" was about a hick
who changes his family members' names to those of products he sees on city signs;
"I'm Gone Before I Go" is an uptempo buck-and-wing song, unusual for Williams,
in which he hears of the war in Mexico and promptly enlists. But when he finds out

that soldiers can actually get killed, he quickly changes his tune ("I 'spect I'm gone before I go!"). The song includes several other topical references, including one to black heavyweight champion Jack Johnson and even an unusual (for Williams), sidelong reference to lynching. Although it was not one of his larger sellers, the title, "I'm gone before I go," became one of his comic catchphrases. Neither of these songs is known to have been used in the *Follies*, although the latter sounds suspiciously like the "Recruiting on Broadway" sketch.

During 1917 trade papers made passing reference to the effect that Williams would be appearing in a new series of one-reel comedies for independent filmmaker William Selig.[58] It is not certain whether these were ever made.

The *Ziegfeld Follies of 1917*, which opened in June of that year, featured an incredible array of talent, including W. C. Fields, Ann Pennington, Will Rogers, Fanny Brice, and Eddie Cantor, as well as long-time star Bert Williams. Williams appeared in one sketch as an illiterate railroad-station porter who could barely put up with the affectations of his college-educated son, played by Cantor (who was then working in blackface). Cantor later related in his autobiography, *As I Remember Them,* that he expected Williams to be resentful of a hyperkinetic young white actor playing opposite him in blackface, but the opposite was true. Williams was open and helpful to younger members of the profession, if they were willing to accept him, and he became something of a mentor to young Cantor. It was the beginning of a sincere friendship between the two.

Williams recorded two new titles for Columbia in September 1917. "The headliner of *Ziegfeld Follies 1917* is just as much funnier as he is days older since his last Columbia record," enthused the catalog.[59] "No Place Like Home" was from the show and was a typical Williams monologue with music; it compared the strife between various members of his household with the war in Europe. "Europe never was so slaughterous as right at my home," he intoned. The composer of this bit of topical pap was none other than humorist Ring Lardner. "Twenty Years" was the tale of old Judge Grimes who doled out stern punishment for the most ridiculous infractions.

By 1918 America was at war, with massive exhibitions of patriotism ranging from bond drives to Irving Berlin's soldier spectacle *Yip Yip Yaphank*. Bert Williams, who was born in the Bahamas, a British colony, took the opportunity to finally become a naturalized citizen. He did not return to the *Ziegfeld Follies* when the 1918 edition opened in June. After years of appearances, sometimes with rather thin material, he apparently felt that the writers had simply not been able to come up with adequate sketches for him.

Ziegfeld and Williams both denied that there had been a split. That was probably true since Williams appeared instead in the *Ziegfeld Midnight Frolic,* a variety show that was staged in the New Amsterdam Theatre's roof garden after the main show ended downstairs. According to the reviews, the arrival of the beloved star in this more intimate setting was greeted with a "storm of applause" that lasted almost five minutes.[60]

During Williams's hiatus from the *Follies* he increased his recording activity, a change in priorities that would continue for the rest of his career. During August and September 1918 he waxed three new titles for Columbia. "O Death Where Is Thy

Sting?" was about black preacher Parson Brown whose fiery sermon portrayed Hell as full of "vampire women, whiskey, gin and dice"; on hearing this, Mose Jackson jumped up from his pew and declared that he wanted to go! Williams could not entirely escape such throwbacks to the "coon song" tradition, mocking his race.

"When I Return," by black composer Will Vodery, was a topical song about the fad for "transmigration," the belief that a person will come back in another form after death and thus live "a thousand lives." Williams sang that he wanted to come back as an insect tormenting the judge who sent him to jail or as a pampered pet Pekingese.

Beginning in December and extending through the spring of 1919, Williams periodically left the *Midnight Frolic* to fill engagements in high-class vaudeville. He was warmly greeted at every appearance, and he tried out numerous new songs, no doubt including some of those he recorded during several visits to the Columbia studios between February and June 1919.

The repertoire Williams chose for these early 1919 sessions is interesting, as it represents the two main themes of his recorded music toward the end of his career. On the one hand he continued to look for topical subjects that would freshen his act. Prohibition was in the news and was the theme of many Tin Pan Alley songs (the Eighteenth Amendment had passed in January 1919, and Prohibition was to take effect on "July thirst"). Williams first mentioned it in "Bring Back Those Wonderful Days," which lamented many of the changes taking place in modern America, among them inflation, the income tax, installment buying, and even "red flag [Communist] agitators." The reference to inflation was ironic as the very Columbia record on which the song was issued bore a sticker raising its price from 85 cents to $1.00! As for Prohibition, Williams related in his folksy monotone, "Drinking ginger ale / Makes me weak and pale."

Even more explicitly based on Prohibition was "Everybody Wants a Key to My Cellar," which explained that "even folks who never ever gave me a tumble" wanted to get to his stash of now-forbidden liquor. Prohibition and "drunk" songs such as these were among Bert Williams's all-time best-sellers, and they became mainstays of his repertoire during the following years.

The other main theme in Williams's late recorded repertoire was an unfortunate return to "coon songs" mocking blacks. He had never been able to abandon the genre entirely and in the period immediately after World War I, a time when racial strife was resurgent in America, this type of material had renewed popularity. One of the beneficiaries was Williams and Walker's old nemesis, Walter C. Kelly, whose racist "Virginian Judge" routines on Victor were enormous sellers during the early 1920s.

We can only speculate why Williams consented to record such material. Of course it was not considered offensive by most people, merely "character humor" about a colorful minority. Virtually all minorities were the butt of humor at the time, with popular songs mocking Italians, Poles, Chinese, Irish, Jews, and even people with disabilities ("You Tell Her, I Stutter"). Some of these songs were actually rather appreciative of their subjects. Nora Bayes had a best-seller intriguingly titled, "The Argentines, the Portuguese, and the Greeks," in which she recounted how those immigrants had taken over everything, but ended with,

They don't know the language, they don't know the law,
But they vote in the country of the free,
And the funny thing, when you start to sing, "My Country 'Tis of Thee,"
None of us know the words, [except] the Argentines,
and the Portuguese,
and the Greeks![61]

Many of Williams's "black" songs were written by African Americans, including Henry Creamer, Turner Layton, and Alex Rogers. And of course, unlike white
performers such as Kelly, Williams never used pejorative terms such as "nigger" or
"coon" in his songs. His entire career suggests that while he softened stereotypes
when he could, and used character rather than racial humor, he never wanted to
be a crusader. He avoided confrontation wherever possible, hoping that the example
he set, the dignity he projected in his private life, and the entree he helped obtain
for others of his race were more important than taking a rigid, and probably hopeless, stand.

The Elder Eatmore sermons were the first straight monologues by Williams to
be released (though not, as we have seen, the first to be recorded). Evidently uncertain of Williams's appeal as a monologuist, Columbia withheld them for nearly a
year before finally releasing them in the spring of 1920. Both routines were written
by Williams's close friend and colleague Alex Rogers and recorded on twelve-inch
discs, which allowed four minutes of playing time. In "Elder Eatmore's Sermon on
Generosity" the good parson exhorts his fractious congregation to bring him a little
more food and sustenance. "I need everything, from my hat down, and from my
overcoat in," he complains. "If somethin' ain't done, your shepherd is gawn!" The
choir begins to sing, led by a strong female voice and accompanied by an organ,
while coins clatter into the collection plate. As the record ends the parson declares,
"Now I'm gonna count it." Assisting Williams were Alex Rogers, Bob Slater, and
Mary Straine. The additional voices make this a much fuller and more varied performance than is usual on Williams's records (since the days of Williams and Walker, he had never appeared on record with anyone else).

In "Elder Eatmore's Sermon on Throwing Stones" the parson is in a foul mood
because the congregation has been whispering that he stole a turkey. Throw stones
at me, he roars, and I'll throw 'em right back at you. He then calls on the chief ru-
mor-monger to lead the congregation in prayer, whereupon the man begins singing reverently about how the elder is crazy, that he was so full of apple jack one night
that he had to carry him home, that he stole the lodge's money, that . . . Before he
can get any further the elder quickly calls for the Doxology and shoos everybody
out. The assisting male voice on this side is unidentified but may be Rogers or Slater.

In addition to these two sides, Williams recorded two black-themed songs in
early 1919. In "Oh Lawdy (Something's Done Got Between Ebecaneezer and Me)" a
black groom is killed in a razor fight on his way to his wedding, whereupon his
would-be bride "loudly sang the blues" about her lost insurance money and chance
to beat him up herself. "It's Nobody's Business but My Own" tells the story of Parson Brown, who, when confronted by a delegation of deacons inquiring about his
scandalous behavior, tells them to get lost. The chorus of Williams's most famous

song "Nobody" is played by the orchestra in a couple of spots, perhaps to bolster the weak material. The Columbia supplement called this song "number six of the famous 'Deacon' series," but what the other five were is unknown.

Columbia also had Williams rerecord one of his earlier numbers, "Indoor Sports," around this time, presumably to replace the 1915 master. Since 1910 none of Bert Williams's recordings had gone out of print, and the list in the annual catalog was becoming quite long, occupying nearly a full page. It was uncommon for Columbia to keep all of a performer's recordings in print this way and is evidence of how well Williams's records continued to sell.

The strain of being away from the *Follies* and on his own for the first time in years took its toll. In May 1919, exhausted, Williams retreated to an Indiana sanatorium for a week's recuperation. The stay must have given him time to think about his career. It had been years since the great Williams and Walker shows of 1900–1908 and since his debut in the all-white *Ziegfeld Follies* had garnered so much attention in 1910. He was famous and beloved, but many new stars had arisen to steal the spotlight (none of them, interestingly, were black). At forty-four, Bert Williams was in danger of becoming an "old favorite," Broadway's "token Negro," whose great successes were mostly in the past.

His first reaction was to return to the scene of his greatest solo triumphs. Perhaps the *Follies,* which constantly renewed itself, could do the same for him. The 1919 edition was indeed spectacular, and arguably the greatest *Follies* edition of all, with a cast that included Eddie Cantor, Marilyn Miller, John Steel, and Van and Schenck, in addition to Williams. It opened on June 16 amid turmoil on Broadway, as the Actor's Equity union prepared to strike over long-standing pay and working-condition abuses by producers. The strike began in early August and closed down nearly every show on Broadway, including the *Follies*. It ended after five weeks when the producers finally capitulated.[62] Bert Williams, anxious as ever to avoid confrontation, sidestepped taking sides by being away from the theater when the *Follies* walkout took place.

After this rocky start the 1919 *Follies* went on to a smashing success. Williams was featured in a number of sketches. In one he played a janitor in a resort full of comedians, and in another he was the unwilling "William Tell" for a cowboy marksman. In the opulent minstrel show that closed act 1 he was Mr. Bones to Eddie Cantor's Tambo, and sang "I Want to See a Minstrel Show" as a duet with George Lemaire.

The real star of the *Follies of 1919,* however, was the hit-laden score by Irving Berlin. Several of the stars had best-selling records of their featured numbers; these included young heartthrob John Steel ("A Pretty Girl Is Like a Melody"), the animated Eddie Cantor ("You'd Be Surprised"), and comedians Van and Schenck ("Mandy"). Bert Williams's big production number was another prohibition song, "You Cannot Make Your Shimmy Shake on Tea," which he did not record. However Williams also had a solo spot in act 2, in front of the curtain (while the next sketch was being set up behind), in which he used a wide variety of songs and stories during the run of the show. These were not listed in the program so we cannot know for sure what he sang on most nights, but it is likely that he incorporated all of his recently recorded titles at one time or another, giving a significant boost to their sales. One song he is known to have used was "It's Nobody's Business but My Own." Columbia was able to rush this into stores just after the *Follies* opened, and it became one of his biggest sellers ever.

Approximate production figures are available for some of Bert Williams's late releases. "O Death Where Is Thy Sting" backed with "When I Return" shipped more than 100,000 copies. "Bring Back" / "Oh Lawdy" shipped about 75,000, while "Everybody Wants a Key" / "It's Nobody's Business" shipped nearly 200,000. At a time when few major-label releases sold more than 100,000 copies, these were certainly good sales. It should be noted that these figures represent "copies shipped," not necessarily sold. Since Columbia continued to issue new titles by Williams and ship additional copies of old ones, however, it seems likely that the earlier stock was in fact being sold by dealers. The huge numbers found in collections today confirm this. The record business at this time was not geared to guaranteed returns and "dumping" of unsold stock as it is today; rather, records were produced as dealer orders came in.

A pleased Columbia had its star back in the studio three times during November and December 1919 to record four more titles. All four were reminiscent of his previous work in one way or another. The most popular was "The Moon Shines on the Moonshine," a prohibition song he sang in the *Follies,* in which he lamented in his usual, lugubrious tones the closing of "the old distillery."

> But in the mountaintops,
> Far from the eyes of cops,
> Oh how the moon shines, on the moonshine, so merrily,
> Oh, oh.[63]

A nice, subdued orchestra provided humorous counterpoint, including bits of "How Dry I Am" at appropriate moments.

"I'm Sorry I Ain't Got It, You Could Have It if I Had It Blues" was Williams's first use of the term "blues" in a title, although the song hardly qualifies in the usual sense. "Blues," like the term "jazz," was being slapped on almost everything at the time. The rest of the clever title is lifted from Williams's 1906 song "All In, Out and Down," and the text is heavily reminiscent of the "hard luck" songs he relied on so heavily in his earlier years ("If money grew on chestnut trees / I'd starve to death, hangin' around for a breeze").[64]

"Somebody," like the 1915 tune "Everybody," was evidently meant to sound like a sequel to the famous "Nobody." In this one Williams is presented with some dubious wonderful opportunities that await "somebody," but concludes each time that they're for "somebody else, not me!" "Checkers" was a topical song about the current rage for the board game, in which Sam Johnson gets into trouble with his wife because he plays the game day and night. She gets a judge to rule that he must pay her support, then tells him "it's your move now."

"I'm Sorry I Ain't Got It" / "Checkers" was one of Williams's poorest sellers of the period, shipping only about 32,000 copies. "The Moon Shines on the Moonshine," backed with "Somebody," was possibly his best seller ever, logging nearly 250,000 copies. It remained in the Columbia catalog longer than any other, until the mid-

1930s. Although "The Moon Shines" is hardly the best representation of Williams's work, it has been frequently reissued over the years, perhaps because a nice clean master recording exists at Columbia. It is currently available on several CDs.

Bert Williams's other runaway best-seller in early 1920 was a twelve-inch disc containing the two "Elder Eatmore" monologues. Released in April, this eventually shipped 185,000 copies, an astounding total for a premium-priced twelve-inch recording.

Basking in the glow of these strong sales, Columbia brought the cooperative Williams back for at least seven additional sessions during the first half of 1920. Recording was clearly occupying a larger portion of his time than ever before. In several of these sessions he rerecorded some of his earlier titles that Columbia wished to retain in the catalog. Presumably either the earlier masters had worn out, or freshened accompaniment was desired. The rerecorded titles were "Woodman, Woodman, Spare That Tree" (originally recorded in 1913), "Everybody" (1915), "Never Mo'" (1915), and "I'm Neutral" (1915).

Williams also recorded five new titles in early 1920, two of them additions to his growing list of drinking songs. "Ten Little Bottles" was a variation on the old tune "Ninety-nine bottles of beer on the wall," except that here all sorts of odd happenings successively reduced the stock by one bottle after another. When only one is left, he takes a swig and utters a satisfied "ahhhh!" "Save a Little Dram for Me" concerns Parson Johnson, who sniffs some gin in the congregation during the service and declares, "Brethren if you want mo' preachin', save a little dram for me." "Get Up" is a typical Williams "trouble" song, delivered in his trademark style. He wants to sleep all day but his wife and mother-in-law keep telling him to "get up and find yourself some work"; he then enters a prize fight "with a dark-skinned brother" only to get knocked out and have the bystanders shout at him to "get up, get up." In Williams's world there was no rest for the weary.

Perhaps the most interesting of the early 1920 recordings are the two "blues" titles. Here for the first time Williams actually tried singing in a bluesy style, not unlike that being used so successfully by both black and white "blues shouters" in vaudeville at the time. The result is a sort of resonant growl, a little like that for which Louis Armstrong later became famous. Williams's performance is not at all inappropriate to the material. Unfortunately, the songs were ersatz "blues," ground out by white Tin Pan Alley songwriters and filled with every imaginable blues cliché: the mailman brings nothing but bad news, gals turn him down, the landlord's after him, and he tries to jump into the river and drown (all that in "Unlucky Blues")! The situation isn't helped by the stiff Columbia studio orchestra, which tries but fails utterly to swing. Who knows what Williams might have been able to accomplish with better material and a genuine jazz band?

The *Ziegfeld Follies of 1919* would be Bert Williams's last. The reasons for his leaving are not clear, but it may have been that he simply wanted to try something new. Certainly Broadway in 1920 was a much different place than it had been when he began, and that meant new opportunities. He decided to appear in a new revue being staged by some breakaway Ziegfeld stars including George Lemaire and Eddie Cantor. Ziegfeld's giant shows were so sprawling, and so dependent on spectacle, that it was hard to get the writers to focus on a single performer's special needs. Perhaps in a more manageable setting he could stand out more.

The new show was called *Broadway Brevities of 1920,* in anticipation of hoped-for annual editions, and it opened on September 29, 1920, at the Winter Garden. Bert Williams appeared in sketches with Lemaire, as a prison inmate ("Ninety Days from Broadway") and a shoe-store customer, as well as composing the music for a burlesque ballet called "The Kiss." Among his songs were two that he previously had recorded, "The Moon Shines on the Moonshine" (from the *Follies*) and "Save a Little Dram for Me." Critics were unkind to *Broadway Brevities,* which never did see another season. Nevertheless, as historian Gerald Bordman put it, "Cantor and Williams helped keep the revue alive [for] thirteen weeks."[65]

Columbia had Williams back in the studio during the fall to record six more titles, including three from *Brevities.* The standout was black songwriter Chris Smith's clever parody on the overexposed art song, "Good-Bye (Addio)," by Italian composer F. Paolo Tosti. Originally published in 1861, the florid melody was enjoying a resurgence in popularity and had been recorded by everyone from Enrico Caruso to Mrs. A. Stewart Holt. There were seven versions in the Victor catalog alone. In Smith's song the singer, who says he "ain't got no education," proceeds to recite a long list of random facts he has memorized, but then ruefully admits,

> I can solve most any mystery,
> But there's one thing that's been puzzling me,
> I want to know . . .
> Where Tosti went,
> When he said . . . "Good-bye!"[66]

The punch line is delivered in a soulful wail that was a hilarious takeoff on second-rate art singers and incidentally an example of what a good voice Bert Williams really had when he wanted to use it.

The rest of the repertoire followed a familiar pattern: three "black" songs, one hard-luck number, and one novelty, delivered in Williams's conversational style. "You'll Never Need a Doctor No More," from the *Brevities,* was about Dr. Bones and Deacon Jones, old enemies who meet when the deacon becomes ill. Bones tries to finish off the deacon and other patients he doesn't like by stuffing them full of food. "You Can't Trust Nobody" tried to capitalize on the blues craze by describing a dark-brown lady who sang a "wicked blues." "I'm Gonna Quit Saturday" was about a lazy southern black who recoils when a northern foreman actually expects him to work. Asked to unload a circus train, he responds with a rare, direct reference to his color—"I know that lions love dark meat, so I'm gonna quit Saturday!"

No list of new Bert Williams records would be complete without a "Nobody"-style hard-luck song, and this had one called "My Last Dollar," which he said was your only true friend when you're down and out. The title was delivered in a sort of a wail. "Eve Cost Adam Just One Bone," from the *Brevities,* was a collection of Garden of Eden jokes.

The material may have been mostly unexceptional, but as the Columbia supplement observed, "There are few artists so capable of putting over their individual

Bert Williams in the recording studio, c. 1920. (Author's collection)

personality through records as the famous 'Bert.' 'Bert' can put enough fun into ten inches of recorded humor to last an evening."[67] "I Want To Know Where Tosti Went" / "Get Up" shipped more than 120,000 copies, a very strong total considering that overall record sales were declining sharply due to the worsening economic situation in the United States. "Eve Cost Adam" / "You'll Never Need a Doctor" and "My Last Dollar" / "I'm Gonna Quit Saturday" shipped about 80,000–90,000 each.

Although it limped along for thirteen weeks, *Brevities* was the least successful show in which Bert Williams had appeared for many years. Finding himself at liberty when it closed in mid-season, he looked about for an opportunity to do something totally new. He was impressed, and even envious, of the acclaim being re-

Bert Williams and George Walker

ceived by a black actor named Charles Gilpin in the title role of Eugene O'Neill's drama *The Emperor Jones.* He too had long yearned to try serious drama, but would his loving public accept him in such a role?

He obtained a somber script based on a voodoo theme, possibly *Taboo* by Mary Hoyt Wiborg.[68] But when the play eventually opened, it was with Paul Robeson in the leading role. Bert Williams filled most of 1921 with vaudeville appearances and more recording sessions. During July and October he rerecorded another of his old songs ("My Landlady") and four new numbers.

Of the four new songs, two were never released. "'Tain't No Disgrace to Run When You're Skeered" was a 1903 coon song by Ernest Hogan and Chris Smith about a black man who thinks he's the "bravest coon" in a southern town until he runs into a ghost.[69] The other unissued side, "I Ain't Afraid of Nothin' Dat's Alive," was a recently published number by white vaudevillian Al Bernard (known for his "black" material), and presumably had a similar theme. It is surprising that in 1921 Bert Williams would consent to record such stereotypical material, and tempting to suppose that his better judgment prevailed before it could be issued. The Columbia files simply say that the recordings were unacceptable to the label's music committee, which approved all issues. This usually indicated technical problems, although we cannot be sure what the reason was in this case.

"Brother Low Down" was another number by Bernard, about an itinerant preacher "down in New Orleans" who tries to clean the place up. Set to a ragtime rhythm typical of Bernard's songs, it is sung in a "blues shouter" style by Williams, who was evidently trying to capitalize on the current blues craze. "Unexpectedly" was more in line with Williams's typical "Nobody" type of song, a half-spoken litany of the unfortunate things that happen to him so "unexpectedly." The latter two songs were released as a mid-month special in January 1922 with the following comments:

> If your grouch be as deep as the sea or as wide as the universe; if you have a case of the blues of a shade so dark it is almost black; if you're feeling at all out of sorts, there is always one remedy—a record-full of Bert Williams taken now and then on your phonograph.
>
> "Unexpectedly" was written specially for Bert. It graphically pictures the things that are apt to creep up behind a fellow and catch him unawares when he has something special to do.
>
> "Brother Low Down" was a colored preacher down in New Orleans. He was anxious to save souls—for a money consideration. His text was, "If you want to keep from sin, drop your little nickels in and help poor Brother Low Down." Bert's two latest are guaranteed to make you shake well while taking.[70]

The disc shipped just under 60,000 copies, a respectable total considering that overall record sales were declining rapidly at the time. Recording remained an important part of Williams's income, as evidenced by figures in a 1922 article. He was reported to be one of the most highly paid popular recording artists in America, in the same league as Al Jolson and Nora Bayes, having received approximately $16,000 in royalties in just two months in 1921.[71]

By the time "Unexpectedly" / "Brother Low Down" came out, Bert Williams was already immersed in his next project. Once again he had decided to forgo his "serious" aspirations and return to a familiar format. An all-black musical called *Shuffle Along,* starring Sissle and Blake and Miller and Lyles, had opened in May and become a surprise smash hit during the summer. After more than ten years, black musical theatre was suddenly back on Broadway in a big way. Perhaps in reaction, Williams decided to launch a book musical of his own, his first since *Mr. Lode of Koal.* Called *Under the Bamboo Tree,* it was in the style of the great Williams and Walker shows of the early 1900s, with numerous songs and energetic dance routines tied together with a comic storyline. This time, however, Williams headed an all-white cast. The plot had hotel porter Anania Washington (Williams) trying to locate a buried treasure by finding the pieces of a secret map, at the same time the hotel guests (and various others) were trying to do the same thing. His big number was a song called "Puppy Dog," in which he commiserated with a real dog. He never recorded it, however.

Under the Bamboo Tree opened in Cincinnati on December 4, 1921, and almost immediately ran into trouble. Although critics raved about Bert Williams's comic genius, and crowds still turned out to see him, little else was memorable about the show. It moved to Chicago for an extended run on December 11 but lost money during half of its first twelve weeks.[72] Determined that this would not be another *Mr. Lode of Koal,* Williams redoubled his efforts, in a desperate attempt to save the show. His health was beginning to break under the strain. A stubborn cold threatened to turn into pneumonia, but he refused to let up. Without him, he knew, the show would fold.

Meanwhile, Columbia Records was becoming desperate for new Williams material during his extended time away from New York. Record sales were plummeting in a worsening recession, and the overextended label was in deep financial trouble. Bert Williams was one of its few artists who could be counted on to score respectable sales with each new release. To accommodate its star, Columbia arranged for an unusual Chicago recording session on February 14. Only one title was recorded, "Not Lately," a typical character song with topical references to prohibition. Delivered in Williams's conversation style, with chuckles, it contained the ironic line, "Things don't seem to be coming my way—not lately."

Columbia no doubt intended further sessions with Williams soon after this to stockpile additional releasable material, but they would never have the chance. Less than two weeks after the Chicago session, on February 27, Williams collapsed during a performance in Detroit. Suffering from neuritis and lumbar pneumonia, he had insisted upon going on, but lasted only ten minutes. Cast members John Dancy and Sammy White helped him to his dressing room. "When [we] laid him out on a couch in his dressing room, I whispered to him, 'Bert, the audience laughed because they didn't know you were sick.' He looked up at me and said, 'Mistuh White, that's a nice way to die—they was laughing when I made my last exit.'"[73]

The following day he was carried to a train, which took him back to New York. There his condition rapidly worsened, aggravated by a long-standing heart condition. He received a transfusion from his young friend and protege Will Vodery and briefly rallied, but on the evening of March 4, 1922, he died. He was forty-seven years old.

Until the final week few people even knew that Bert Williams was sick, and his death sent shock waves across the country. He was beloved, one of the icons of American popular culture. According to the *New York Times* more than five thousand people filed past his casket, and thousands more were unable to get into the church. Tributes flowed in from Florenz Ziegfeld, Eddie Cantor, and other colleagues; honorary pallbearers at his funeral included Leon Errol, Harry T. Burleigh, Noble Sissle, Chris Smith, and others who worked with and admired him, both black and white. Much was written about his massive contributions to the musical theater and how much the new generation of black performers owed to his pioneering efforts.

There was a predictable surge in sales of his recordings immediately after his death. In June Columbia posthumously released his last recording, "Not Lately," coupled with a previously unreleased title from 1920, "It's Getting so You Can't Trust Nobody." The announcement was respectful, but not sorrowful. "Bert Williams' Columbia records are more than 'moanful' songs of humor, they are perfect character studies of this greatest of comedians himself, that will live as long as people laugh. Listening to 'You Can't Trust Nobody,' you can just picture him standing before you, feet turned out, shoulders hunched forlornly, hands gesturing with his own indescribable 'flop'; while he lugubriously sings this song about a pathetic lady who was deceived in love."[74]

The disc shipped a respectable 41,000 copies. Three months later, in September, Columbia released one last Bert Williams disc, a twelve-inch coupling of the long-withheld 1913 monologues "You Can't Do Nothin' Till Martin Gets Here" and "How? Fried." It sold poorly.

Sales of Bert Williams's Recordings

Williams's earliest records were available only briefly. The 1897 Universal cylinder, if it existed at all, must have been on sale only locally in New York and only for a few months. The 1901 Victor recordings were also produced in limited quantities and had all been deleted by 1904 (Victor must have wished it could produce more of them when Williams became a solo superstar in the 1910s). Whatever records Williams may have made in England in 1903–4 also seem to have had very little circulation.

Bert Williams's first big sellers were the discs and cylinders he made for Columbia in 1906, especially his original recording of "Nobody." The cylinders were deleted in 1908, but six of the ten single-sided discs recorded in 1906 were transferred to the new double-sided format in 1908 and retained until the teens. Most were also leased out to minor labels, as was Columbia's custom at the time. Interestingly, one of the four titles dropped in 1908 was "Pretty Desdemone," the last Williams and Walker duet.

Everything Williams recorded for Columbia from 1910 on stayed in the catalog at least until the changeover to electrical recording in 1925. Nearly all of his Columbia recordings were of specialty material, written for or by him; he rarely recorded current popular songs of the day. As a result his records were not dependent on the transitory popularity of current hits. They were "Bert Williams songs," and few of them were recorded by anybody else.

Williams's list in the annual Columbia catalog became quite long, eventually occupying more than a full page, accompanied by his picture. While sales figures are not available until the late 1910s, Bert Williams was undoubtedly one of Columbia's best-selling artists from the day he set foot in their studios. Most of his double-faced discs (issued after 1908) are fairly frequently found today. Most common are his Columbias from the late teens and early 1920s, and their large sales are born out by surviving documentation. Table 2 is a ranking of releases for which totals are known.

The figures represent total shipments from release to deletion, generally eight to ten years. Bert Williams records were certainly long-term sellers, but the bulk of shipments (usually 90 percent or more) were within the first year of issue, suggesting that most of these were best-sellers when they came out, rather than merely accumulating their totals gradually over a long span of time.

It will be noted that some of Bert Williams's most famous songs, including "Nobody," are not on the list. This does not indicate lack of sales, but rather lack of information. We can make some estimates. Total industry sales were much smaller prior to World War I than afterwards, averaging 25 to 30 million units per year during the early 1910s versus more than 100 million per year from 1919 to 1921.[75] Despite the wishful thinking of some current writers, it is unlikely that individual discs or cylinders were "million-sellers" during this period.

Partial data are available for "Nobody" (A1289), and it shows nearly 50,000 copies being shipped to dealers from 1915 until deletion in the 1930s. Most copies found today are this issue (not the 1906 recording), with a label style indicating a mid- or

Table 2. Shipments of Selected Columbia Records by Bert Williams

	Released	Copies Shipped
"The Moon Shines on the Moonshine" / "Somebody" (A2849)	1920	246,000
"Everybody Wants a Key to My Cellar" / "It's Nobody's Business But My Own" (A2750)	1919	188,200
"Elder Eatmore's Sermon on Generosity" / ". . . On Throwing Stones" (A6141)	1920	185,200
"Ten Little Bottles" / "Unlucky Blues" (A2941)	1920	183,800
"Save a Little Dram for Me" / "Lonesome Alimony Blues" (A2979)	1920	129,700
"I Want to Know Where Tosti Went" / "Get Up" (A3305)	1920	121,900
"Eve Cost Adam Just One Bone" / "You'll Never Need a Doctor No More" (A3339)	1921	89,000
"My Last Dollar" / "I'm Gonna Quit Saturday" (A3356)	1921	84,300
"Oh Lawdy" / "Bring Back Those Wonderful Days" (A2710)	1919	76,600
"Unexpectedly" / "Brother Low Down" (A3508)	1922	58,900
"You Can't Trust Nobody" / "Not Lately" (A3589)	1922	41,000
"I'm Sorry I Ain't Got It" / "Checkers" (A2877)	1920	31,700
"You Can't Do Nothin' Till Martin Gets Here" / "How? Fried!" (A6216)	1922	16,200

late 1910s pressing. So even taking all versions together (1906 disc and cylinder, 1913 remake), I would estimate that Columbia sold between 100,000 and 150,000 copies of "Nobody." It was certainly no million-seller and would probably rank after several of the titles on the foregoing list.

None of Williams's other pre-1919 recordings is likely to have exceeded the top-ranked totals shown previously either. Partial data is available for "All In, Out and Down" (A5031), indicating only 11,000 copies shipped after 1915. Some of the others may have done better, but it is unlikely that any exceeded 150,000 copies in total sales. That, of course, would have been a very high total for the period.

We can also estimate Bert Williams's total record sales by year from 1918 on (see table 3). Figures are available for his new issues and "Nobody," and a margin is added for continuing sales of other older releases to arrive at an estimated total.

It is apparent that Williams enjoyed an enormous surge in sales on the heels of his final season in the *Follies,* 1919–20. The fact that the record business in general was booming, particularly for major labels such as Columbia, didn't hurt. The sharp fall-off in 1921 could be in part due to the decline in the business generally and the sudden upsurge in competition from small, low-priced labels then flooding the market. Most of the decline, though, is undoubtedly due to Williams himself. He produced no new hits like "Moon Shines on the Moonshine" and "Elder Eatmore." In fact, due to Williams's unavailability few new sides were recorded in that year.

With the star's death in March 1922, sales fell off drastically. Nevertheless, Columbia retained all of its existing listings in its catalog until 1925 and about half of them for several years after that (despite the fact that most other acoustic recordings had been deleted). The company could not be choosy; it was in great financial difficulty during the mid-1920s and in fact went into receivership in 1923. It continued to operate under court supervision but needed every seventy-five-cent sale it could get from backlist titles like those of Bert Williams.

Table 3. Bert Williams: Estimated Total Shipments

	Number of Discs in Catalog	Shipments
1918	12	200,000
1919	14	300,000
1920	14	1,000,000
1921	18	175,000
1922	22	120,000
1923	25	30,000
1924	25	18,000
1925	25	10,000
1926	20	8,000
1927	15	3,100
1928	15	1,300
1929	12	600
1930	7	200
1931	4	100
		1,866,300

By the early 1930s only four of Williams's records were left in the catalog, "Nobody," "Everybody Wants a Key to My Cellar," "The Moon Shines on the Moonshine," and "Elder Eatmore." Acoustically recorded up to twenty years earlier, they must have sounded very dated, and all were gone by the middle of the decade. After nearly thirty years of continuous availability, Bert Williams's records were no longer on sale.

Epilogue

Bert Williams was fondly remembered in the years following his death. A few months after he died his famous poker routine was recreated in a short-lived show called *Keep It Up* (1922). In 1924 a much more successful show, Lew Leslie's *Dixie to Broadway,* included tributes to both George Walker and Bert Williams. The first (and for many years, only) book-length biography of Williams, by Mabel Rowland, was published in 1923. It was titled *Bert Williams, Son of Laughter.* The black community especially missed him. There was even a tribute record (rare for the period) on the black-owned Black Swan label, called "So Long Bert."[76]

Williams was recalled in books and articles about great black Americans, and many contemporary entertainers acknowledged his pioneering efforts. Others tried to exploit his fame (or continue his legacy, depending on how you look at it). During 1925–26 a vaudeville entertainer named Ham Tree Harrington, billed as "the Pint-Sized Bert Williams," made a series of records for Brunswick and Vocalion that are very much in the Williams style; in fact, some of his songs were virtual clones of Williams's tunes (e.g., "Nobody Never Let Me in on Nothin'," a close copy of "Nobody"). Singer/songwriters Shelton Brooks and Eddie Hunter also recorded in the Williams style, as did various others.[77]

In 1925 Robbins-Engel published a collection of ten of his songs, entitled *Bert Williams: Folio of Ne'er-to-be Forgotten Songs.* New recordings of Williams's songs were made periodically, but their success had been so dependent on his unique delivery that the new versions did not sell well. As early as 1922, the year of his death, Edison issued "Save a Little Dram for Me" by a Williams soundalike named Duke Rogers.[78] Three years later the same label issued two more of the great comedian's specialty numbers, "O Death Where Is Thy Sting" and "You're Going to Get Something You Don't Expect" by another Williams imitator, Guy Hunter. In 1928 George Moran and Charles Mack, a blackface comedy duo who were extremely popular on record with an Amos 'n' Andy–type routine, recorded "Elder Eatmore's Sermon on Throwing Stones." None of these sold very well.

Williams continued to be remembered in the 1930s and his songs occasionally performed. An ASCAP log shows several hundred plays of "Nobody" on radio in 1937, and the great Louis Armstrong recorded the two Elder Eatmore sermons in 1938.[79] The next great burst of interest came in 1940, when Duke Ellington recorded his own composition, "A Portrait of Bert Williams," on Victor. The renewed interest that this generated led Columbia to undertake a unusual reissue of Williams's recordings (reissues of such old recordings being quite uncommon at the time). Eight titles recorded between 1918 and 1921 were remastered, renumbered, and issued as a four-disc 78-rpm album set called *Famous Songs of Bert Williams*. Oddly, "Nobody" was not included. Issued in October 1940, the set remained in print until the late 1940s. They were probably the only acoustic popular records in the Columbia catalog at that late date.

A major promoter of Williams's work was white bandleader-comedian Phil Harris, a radio star who specialized in novelty songs about the south. Harris had been using Williams material for many years, recording "Constantly" as early as 1931 for Victor. In 1937 he recorded three Williams titles for Vocalion ("Nobody," "Woodman, Woodman, Spare That Tree," and "Constantly"); "Nobody" and "Woodman" were reissued on Okeh in 1941 to take advantage of that period of interest in Bert Williams.[80]

In 1945 Harris recorded "The Darktown Poker Club" for the small ARA label of Los Angeles, rerecording it for Victor when he joined that label in 1946. Both versions were substantial sellers, placing on the *Billboard* charts in 1946 and 1947. In early 1948 Victor issued a 78-rpm album set by Harris, including both "Darktown" and a new version of "Woodman," which remained on sale until the early 1950s.[81] When Harris's version of "The Darktown Poker Club" was reviewed in *Variety* the reviewer called it "disgusting" and said that he was embarrassed at having played the disc for his black maid.[82] Apparently the reviewer knew nothing of Bert Williams or the context in which the song was performed. Harris continued to use Williams material for years and as late as 1972 included three Williams titles on an LP for the small Mega label of Nashville.

Surprisingly, Williams's songs also endured in the country music field. Red Foley recorded "Nobody" as early as 1941; later country artists to record it included Riley Shepard, J. E. Mainer, and Merle Travis. The 1940s also saw a Liberty Ship built with Harlem war-bond subscriptions named the *Bert Williams*.[83]

The 1950s were a period of eclipse, during which Williams was remembered mostly by academicians. Probably the first serious study of his recordings was Jim Walsh's multipart series in *Hobbies* magazine in 1950. His great song "Nobody" was incorporated into the 1955 Paramount film *The Seven Little Foys,* sung by Bob Hope portraying vaudevillian Eddie Foy. Recorded versions of the song were issued in that year by Perry Como and Bing Crosby, but neither attracted much attention. Como's smooth version was delivered in his trademark crooning style, about as far from the song's "tale of woe" beginnings as one could imagine.

The civil rights era of the 1960s, with its renewed interest in black history, brought new attention to one of the race's great pioneers. Ann Charter's *Nobody: The Story of Bert Williams* (1970) was the first full-length biography of Williams since 1923. "Nobody" was sung by Avon Long in the hit Broadway musical *Bubbling Brown Sugar* in 1976, and Ben Vereen impersonated Williams at Ronald Reagan's inaugural gala in 1981. The latter was intended as a tribute to a great black performer but caused some consternation when Vereen's introduction setting the scene was deleted, leaving the assembled dignitaries watching a unexplained "shuffling darkey" act that many did not understand.

Various small theatrical revues based on Bert Williams (and on Williams and Walker) were staged in the 1970s and 1980s. Probably the longest running was

Vincent D. Smith's *Williams and Walker,* a collection of original songs and sketches by the pair augmented by some modern sermonizing about the injustices they suffered. Premiering in 1979 at the University of Maryland, it was staged off-Broadway in 1986 at New York's American Place Theater, starring Ben Harney and Vondie Curtis-Hall, and in other small theaters into the 1990s.[84] Some of Bert Williams's records once again became available via specialized LP reissues. A few are now available on CD, including, for the first time, a number of the long-unavailable and historically important 1901 Victors. A new biography, *Bert Williams: A Biography of the Pioneer Black Comedian,* by Eric Ledell Smith, was published in 1992.

Williams has certainly been remembered, though more for his contributions as a black man than for his talents as an entertainer. Had he been white, his career would have been long forgotten. Appreciation of his accomplishments has been tempered somewhat by modern discomfort with the mere acknowledgment of the racial climate in which he lived. Any mention of coon songs, blackface humor, and his "shuffling darkey" persona still makes some people uncomfortable. (According to several sources, a planned scholarly reissue of the 1901 Victor recordings by the Smithsonian Institution in the 1970s was suppressed due to complaints by a black staff member.) To ignore these realities is to ignore the very forces against which he had to struggle, and thus to misunderstand profoundly the contributions he made.

Jim Walsh called his 1950 article "Bert Williams, a Thwarted Genius." Perhaps. Williams was acutely aware of the limitations placed on him by white audiences, which he accepted with a certain stoicism. Clearly, in his *Follies* days, he missed the all-black environment in which he had worked during the earlier part of his career. In the white world he was an outsider. In one of the most famous quotes about him, his friend W. C. Fields later said, "Bert Williams was the funniest man I ever saw and the saddest man I ever knew." "I often wonder whether other people sensed what I did in him—that deep undercurrent of pathos. . . . With all his philosophy, and he had a well grounded philosophy, he would occasionally say, 'Well, there is no way for me to know this or that thing, which you say is going on—I'm just relegated—I don't belong.' It was not said in a bitter tone, but it did sound sadly hopeless."[85]

Williams clearly chose his own path. When he had the opportunity to pursue "higher" art, with the Belasco offer in 1910 and with the dramatic play *Taboo* in 1921, he opted instead for the safe and profitable course of least resistance: blackface comedy. One wonders if his choice might have been different had the far more aggressive George Walker still been at his side.

> People sometimes ask me if I would not give anything to be white, I answer, in the words of the song, most emphatically, "No." How do I know what I might be if I were a white man? I might be a sand-hog, burrowing away and losing my health for $8 a day. I might be a street-car conductor at $12 or $15 a week. There is many a white man less fortunate and less well equipped than I am. In fact, I have never been able to discover that there was anything disgraceful in being a colored man. But I have often found it inconvenient—in America.[86]

Bert Williams would have wanted to be remembered not with a tear but with a chuckle. Despite the prejudice he endured as a black man, and the fact that audiences never let him break completely free of black stereotypes, he bore no anger. "I have no grievance whatsoever against the world or the people in it," he once said. "I'm having a grand time."[87]

A thwarted genius? Williams himself never expressed it that way. He was not a firebrand, but a quiet, persistent man who worked within the system. He was grateful for what he had been able to achieve against towering odds, and for the doors he had been able to open for so many who followed him. Most blacks and unbiased whites of the day apparently felt the same way. Perhaps we should as well.

9 Cousins and DeMoss

The recordings by Cousins and DeMoss represent a bit of a mystery. They appear to give us a glimpse inside the world of black vaudeville in the late 1890s, but we must say "appear to" because the identities of the two artists have not been conclusively proven. There are no first names on the label, and no catalog listing or advertising has been found. However, it is almost certain that these were Sam Cousins and Ed DeMoss, two experienced if somewhat minor black entertainers who were active on the vaudeville and minstrel stage at the turn of the century.

Sam Cousins and Ed DeMoss both performed frequently in the New York area, although they did not normally appear as a duet. Cousins, the better known of the two, was a comedian and monologuist with a long list of credits. During the 1898–99 season he was with producer John W. Isham's popular touring show *The Octoroons,* in one- and two-act comedy sketches including "Darktown Aristocracy" and "A Tenderloin Coon." Audiences loved his songs and topical humor. Following a November appearance one reviewer commented that "Sam Cossins [*sic*] keeps them roaring with his monologue, and some parodies he has written on late popular hits." Another, following an engagement in Canada in February, remarked that "Mr. Sam Cousins, monologue artist and comedian, never fails to please the audience with his funny sayings and parodies which are up to date."[1]

Life on the road was grueling, but also brought good times and camaraderie. A February column in the *Freeman* reported that Cousins and other members of the *Octoroons* cast had attended a reception in London, Ontario, where they smoked expensive cigars and posed for a "flash light picture." In March Cousins took out an advertisement in the *Freeman,* in which he listed his specialties and current engagement and noted that he was currently singing Cole and Johnson's "I Wonder What Is That Coon's Game?" The ad included a photograph of Cousins, who appeared to be in his twenties.[2]

Tenor Ed DeMoss was best known for his years with the Standard Quartette (q.v.), of *South before the War* fame, in the early 1890s. He was familiar with recording from his experiences with that group, which had made numerous cylinders for the New York and Ohio Phonograph companies, and for Columbia. After leaving the quartet around 1895 he became a solo performer, based in New York. A Decem-

A WARM MEMBER

SAM COUSIN,

MONOLOGUIST AND COMEDIAN

And doing what? Why closing the olio with Jno. W. Isham's Octoroons.

A grainy photo of Sam Cousin(s), of Cousins and DeMoss—the only one known—from the *Freeman,* March 11, 1899.

ber 1898 item referred to him as a "popular vocalist" who had just returned from a four-week engagement outside New York.[3]

The two known recordings by Cousins and DeMoss were made for Berliner in New York, most likely during the summer of 1898.[4] That the duo recorded at all seems to have been an accident of time and place. Both were frequently in the city, and they may have even performed together occasionally. The Berliner Gramophone Company, struggling to establish disc records in an industry heavily dominated by cylinders, was busy in the late 1890s trying to build up its catalog. Many varied artists were invited into its recording laboratories in New York and Washington, and the company seems to have been open to experimentation in order to add some distinctiveness to its listings. It recorded choruses, Broadway actresses, famous orators, and an operatic tenor, as well as the usual run of studio regulars familiar to cylinder buyers—mostly obscure baritones and tenors and brass bands. It was also open to black artists, recording George W. Johnson and black basso Thomas Craig.

Two titles have been documented by Cousins and DeMoss, both numbered in Berliner's 3000 series, which was reserved for "duets." Both are fascinating recordings of old folk/gospel tunes. "Poor Mourner" begins with an opening announcement by one of the artists, "Poor Mourner, as sung by Cousins and DeMoss," followed by an enthusiastic rendition of the song sometimes known as "Mourner, You Shall Be Free."[5] The two singers alternate verses while one or both provide energetic banjo accompaniment. The performance is remarkably loose and fervent for the period and very much in the black gospel tradition, with the singers overlapping and interjecting exclamations ("Ohhh!" "Hallelujah!") as counterpoint to the main melody line. The tempo varies, gradually accelerating throughout the record.

The text is barely decipherable, but seems to contain the usual collection of comic and semireligious couplets favored in black-themed songs of the period. For example it includes the following lines, also heard in the Standard Quartette's 1894 cylinder "Keep Movin'": "Now mind now sister how you step on the cross / Your foot might slip and your soul be lost."

The song "Poor Mourner" turns up on many other recordings, including a version made by the Standard Quartette in 1894 when DeMoss was a member. It was revived in later years as well, most notably in a slick 1930s dance band version by Ted Weems, called "Oh, Mo'nah!"

The second title by the duo was "Who Broke the Lock," another black-themed number that had previously been recorded by both the Unique and Standard Quartettes. It is sung with equal enthusiasm and abandon. Ed DeMoss had performed both of these songs with the Standard Quartette, and it is likely that Sam Cousins used them in his act as well. There are numerical gaps before, between, and after these two discs (numbered 3010 and 3012), suggesting that Cousins and DeMoss recorded other titles that are as yet untraced.

Following this brief encounter with disc recording, both artists resumed their stage careers, their paths often crossing those of other early black recording artists. After spending the 1898–99 season with *The Octoroons,* Cousins joined Cole and Johnson's landmark musical *A Trip to Coontown,* which was then in its third season (1899–1900). This show is often cited as the first true black musical comedy. Also in the cast was a Myrtle Cousins, Thomas Craig (who had also been in *The Octoroons*), and former Unique Quartette member Walter Dixon. In later years Cousins alternated between starring in his own small troupes and appearing in larger shows. In 1901–2 he toured the Northeast with his own *Coontown Golf Club,* then in 1902 joined Jolly John Larkins's *A Trip to the Jungles* (1902), whose cast also included one Bertha Cousins, doubling as actor and stage manager. This was followed in 1902–3 by a stint with the touring company of Williams and Walker's *Sons of Ham,* starring Avery and Hart. Cousins took over the role of Old Ham (originated by Jesse Shipp), doddering father of the two stars, and also had a routine in which he imitated Booker T. Washington as a drunk. By 1903 Cousins was once again fronting his own summer troupe, "Sam Cousins' Colored Comedy," which played towns in the Northeast with a cast including James Settles (formerly of the Unique Quartette), Rosa Ball, Josephine Norris, Mattie Brown, Ella Stevens, and "Buddie Gilmare" (possibly Buddy Gilmore, later the drummer with Jim Europe's pioneering proto-jazz orchestra). In 1905 he partnered with banjoist Will Humphreys, and the two performed as a duo on the East Coast.[6] After that he dropped from sight.

DeMoss eventually returned to the Standard Quartette, performing with them in 1902–3, and possibly later. Details of his later life are also unknown.

Cousins and DeMoss may have been "accidental" recording artists, whose few discs were made because they happened to be performing down the street when the record company needed some exotic material. However accidental, their recordings are an irreplaceable snapshot of black vaudeville in the 1890s.

10 Thomas Craig

Berliner disc catalogs from 1898 and 1899 list two selections by an obscure artist named Thomas Craig, intriguingly billed as "the colored basso." No information was provided about him, but like nearly all black artists who recorded during the phonograph's first decade, he in fact had an active stage career around the turn of the century.

Craig was based in New York and appeared primarily in the Northeast. The first season for which he has been traced is 1896–97, when he toured with the Primrose and West Minstrels. After spending the summer of 1897 in New York, he traveled to Boston in August to join Harkins and Barbour's production of *Uncle Tom's Cabin*, appearing "with his quartet."[1] (Stagings of the 1852 Harriet Beecher Stowe novel were so numerous in the 1890s that theatrical papers referred to them by the initials "U.T.C. companies.") The play evidently had a short run.

Craig appears to have recorded for Berliner in New York during the summer of 1898, judging by known recording dates for surrounding issues.[2] This was about the same time that Cousins and DeMoss recorded for the company. The first of his two titles was Stephen Foster's "Old Black Joe," an appropriate choice for a basso but hardly distinctive as it was featured by multitudes of artists, black and white. Accompanied by piano, Craig sang in a straightforward style, with no particular mannerisms or even much emotion. Nor was his voice particularly resonant. It is a pedestrian performance, although it may be unfair to judge the artist by this single, rather poorly recorded example.

The second title, listed in the catalog as "Good Ole Georgie," is probably "Good Old Georgia," a song featured in minstrel shows of the period. No copy has been found. Both discs first appeared in the October 1898 catalog under the heading "Old Plantation Songs." Craig may have recorded other titles for the label, as nearby catalog numbers are untraced.

After depositing his rather thin bass voice on disc for posterity (and for a few dollars), Craig resumed his stage career. During the 1898–99 season he was in the cast of John W. Isham's *The Octoroons*, along with comedian Sam Cousins and black singers Belle Davis and Madah Hyers. The *Octoroons* troupe featured comedy sketches and musical performances, and Craig's solo numbers were well received. A report of a performance in Canada in February 1899 began, "Mr. Thomas Craig, New York's favorite basso, is certainly a wonder," then quoted the *Montreal Canada News* as saying, "Craig is the possessor of a deep and resonant voice which was heard to good advantage in such selections as 'Old Black Joe' and 'Rocked in the Cradle of the Deep.'" Another item, from March 1899, reported that Craig was receiving applause nightly singing with *The Octoroons* in upstate New York.[3]

During the following two seasons Craig traveled with Cole and Johnson's landmark musical *A Trip to Coontown*, which was still drawing good audiences in its third and fourth seasons on the road. With him in 1899–1900 were Sam and Myrtle Cousins, and former Unique Quartette member Walter Dixon. It is obvious that in the small world of black minstrelsy and vaudeville, many of the artists who recorded knew each other. Craig was frequently praised during his two years with the show—perhaps with some exaggeration—as the "renowned basso" and as having "the greatest voice of its kind extant." His specialty was said to be old plantation songs.[4]

The basso spent 1901–2 with the touring company of Williams and Walker's *Sons of Ham,* starring Avery and Hart. Also in the cast was Sam Cousins. After that, Craig disappeared from sight.

Thomas Craig was a journeyman black vaudeville performer whose single surviving recording is rather undistinguished. Perhaps additional recordings, if they could be located, would shed further light on the little-known voice that drew such good reviews.

PART THREE

Black Recording Artists, 1900–1909

11 The Dinwiddie Quartet

Dinwiddie County is a poor, rural county in the southeast corner of Virginia, near the North Carolina border. Named for Robert Dinwiddie, lieutenant governor of Virginia in 1752 (when it was formed), it was the site of some notable military actions during the Civil War. By 1900 its population was about 15,000, mostly farmers and sharecroppers. More than 60 percent of its citizens were black, and living standards were low.[1]

In 1898 a group of white philanthropists founded the Dinwiddie Normal and Industrial School (also known as the John A. Dix Industrial School) about fifteen miles south of Petersburg, Virginia, to help ameliorate the poor conditions under which blacks in the area lived. Like most such schools, it was continually in need of funds to sustain its mission, and like others it quickly formed a "jubilee quartet" to go on tour and raise money. Under the leadership of Charles B. Cheshire, the original Dinwiddie Quartet spent the next two years singing in YMCAs, churches, and similar venues, raising thousands of dollars for the school.[2] The members of the quartet at this time are unknown, and it is not known whether they were students or professionals.

Upon Cheshire's death about 1900, the quartet went into vaudeville. A newspaper item in May 1901 indicates that the manager at that time was J. A. Porter, and that the quartet was still touring the country on the school's behalf.[3] In the fall of 1902, now under the management of a young Philadelphian named Sterling Rex, the quartet joined a new touring show called *The Smart Set,* starring vaudeville headliners Ernest Hogan and Billy McClain. By this time the quartet seems to have been operating independently of the Dinwiddie School. No mention is made of fundraising or a school connection. The membership was Sterling Rex, first tenor and leader, J. Clarence Meredith, second tenor, Harry B. Cruder, first bass, and J. Mantell Thomas, second bass.

The Smart Set was an immediate hit. Sylvester Russell, the notoriously hard-to-please critic of the Indianapolis *Freeman,* called it "the smartest colored comedy ever produced in America," and the public embraced it as well.[4] *The Smart Set* would go on to become one of the longest running shows in the history of black theater, playing until 1923. The role of the Dinwiddie Quartet was to provide musical interludes in the playlets that comprised most of the show, as described in the following review of an October 18, 1902, performance at the Empire Theatre in Newark, New Jersey. The plot was set in Honolulu. The character played by Ernest Hogan was getting initiated into a lodge, where he and his wife sang "Tell Me, Dusky Maiden." Then, "The scene changes. The Dinwiddie Quartet comes in on its way to the Rooster's lodge and sings 'The Palms' in a manner unsurpassed. S. C. Rex, the leader, has a light baritone voice of much sympathy and sweetness and J. M. Thomas, the basso, is very fine; together with J. C. Meredith and H. B. Coyer [sic], they make the most harmony and display the best artistic methods of any colored quartette now before the public."[5]

On Monday, October 27 *The Smart Set* opened at the National Theatre in Philadelphia, again impressing the critics. *"Smart Set* captivates Philadelphia," wrote one, adding "the Dinwiddie Quartet, a feature of the show, sustained their well-earned reputation by delightfully rendering 'The Palms' and 'Come Out Dinah on the Green.'"[6]

Just two days later, Rex and his quartet traveled the short distance to the studios of the Victor Talking Machine Company at Tenth and Lombard Streets in Philadelphia to record three selections on seven- and ten-inch discs. On October 31 they returned to make three more. These were not the popular selections cited in reviews of the show, but rather characteristically "black" material that Victor evidently felt would add novelty to its catalog. To make sure customers would understand exactly what they were getting, Victor called the group "The Dinwiddie Colored Quartet" on its labels.

These six historic a capella sides were the first jubilee recordings ever made by Victor. The first title recorded on the first day, "Down on the Old Camp Ground," would become a particular favorite, remaining in the Victor catalog for eight years and being reissued in recent times on LP and CD. Labeled a "coon shout," it is a lively, rhythmic performance of a favorite black folk tune of the period, which had been recorded earlier on cylinder by the Unique Quartette. The Dinwiddies sing it quite fast, in the familiar call-and-response, or "floating verse," jubilee style. An energetic tenor (probably Rex) sings the lead, alternating with the rest of the quartet in a performance so contemporary sounding that one modern writer has called it, "the first rhythm and blues vocal group record."[7]

The record begins with the announcement, "'Down on the Old Camp Ground,' coon shout, by the Dinwiddie Colored Quartet." The four verses contain a mix of religious references and comic stanzas, including the familiar "down in the barnyard on my knees . . .," which is also heard on other black-themed songs of the period, including the Standard Quartette's "Keep Movin'."

Chorus

Quartet: There's a jubilee,
      There's a jubilee,
      There's a jubilee,
      Way down on the old camp ground.
      (repeat)

Tenor: The little white cart came a-rollin' down,
Quartet: Way down on the old camp ground,
Tenor: And it rolled like thunder to the ground,
Quartet: Way down on the old camp ground,
Tenor: You say you're aiming for the sky,
Quartet: Way down on the old camp ground,
Tenor: Why don't you stop your tellin' lies?
Quartet: Way down on the old camp ground.

Chorus

Tenor: You say your Jesus set you free,
Quartet: Way down on the old camp ground,
Tenor: Why don't you let your neighbors be?
Quartet: Way down on the old camp ground,
Tenor: Some go to church for to sing and shout,
Quartet: Way down on the old camp ground,
Tenor: And before six months they done turned out.
Quartet: Way down on the old camp ground.

Chorus

Tenor: You come to my house for to drink-a my tea,
Quartet: Way down on the old camp ground,
Tenor: Then you run around town and you talk about me.
Quartet: Way down on the old camp ground,
Tenor: Some go to church for to show their clothes,
Quartet: Way down on the old camp ground,
Tenor: And always jumpin' up a-runnin' outdoors.
Quartet: Way down on the old camp ground.

Chorus

Tenor: Down in the barnyard on my knees,
Quartet: Way down on the old camp ground,
Tenor: I thought I heard that chicken sneeze.
Quartet: Way down on the old camp ground,
Tenor: He sneezed so hard with the whoopin' cough,
Quartet: Way down on the old camp ground,
Tenor: That he sneezed his head and tail right off.
Quartet: Way down on the old camp ground.

Chorus[8]

Five of the six songs recorded in the two sessions were in fast or medium tempo, suggesting that upbeat numbers were a specialty of the group. Many phrases are shared with other songs, as was customary in the folk repertoire. In fact, "Poor Mourner," with its refrain, "you shall be free . . .," opens with the same verse ("down in the barnyard on my knees . . .") heard at the end of "Down on the Old Camp Ground"—the previous selection recorded at the same session. "Gabriel's Trumpet" quotes two familiar phrases. The quartet's recurring response to the tenor is "Glory hallelujah to the lamb!" while the chorus is "In the morning, / In the morning by the bright light, / When Gabriel blows his trumpet in the morning."

The performances are tight and well practiced, and the arrangements varied, with different members featured on different recordings. Even one of the basses gets a solo line on "My Way Is Cloudy." Other titles were "We'll Anchor Bye-and-Bye" and "Steal Away." The only slow-tempo number recorded was "Steal Away," in which one of the tenors takes a dramatic solo ("My lord he calls me, he calls me by the thunder!"). It is, nevertheless, less effective than the Dinwiddies' rhythm numbers.

The six titles were released as a group in December 1902, a little more than a month after they were recorded, in both seven- and ten-inch versions. "These are genuine Jubilee and camp meeting shouts," boasted the catalog, "sung as only negroes can sing them." Although they stayed in the catalog as long as eight years (the last, "Down on the Old Camp Ground," was deleted in 1910), they appear to have been modest sellers. Fragmentary data in the Victor files suggest that fewer than a thousand copies were pressed of "Poor Mourner," "Steal Away," and "My Way Is Cloudy." Pressing figures are missing for the others. "Down on the Old Camp Ground" probably sold best, being found somewhat more frequently than the others, but all are rare today.

The Dinwiddie Quartet toured with *The Smart Set* for the 1902–3 season. In January the show played to a standing-room crowd in Hamilton, Ontario, where a review noted the vocal contributions of the quartet and a chorus of thirty people. By March the show reached New York City.[9] The quartet then left *The Smart Set* and went into the three-a-day vaudeville circuit for the 1903–4 season. One report referred to them as "the Dinwiddie Quartet of Philadelphia," suggesting that city was their home base. Items as late as June 1904 show them still on tour and scoring notable success. Nevertheless there are no further reports of them after 1904, and according to a later reminiscence they disbanded in that year.[10]

Two quartet members, both in their twenties at the time, went on to fairly notable careers. Tenor and leader Sterling C. Rex (born c. 1879–80, in Pennsylvania) and bass James Mantell Thomas (born c. 1875) joined the Williams and Walker theatrical company shortly after the dissolution of the Dinwiddie Quartet. In August of 1905 both were in the sixteen-member Williams and Walker Glee Club, organized by George Walker to provide the young men of the company with summer employment. In the same year Rex married Ada Guigesse, an actress in the troupe.[11]

Rex subsequently played supporting roles in Williams and Walker's hit shows *Abyssinia* (1906) and *Bandanna Land* (1908) and Williams's solo show *Mr. Lode of Koal* (1909). It is not known whether Thomas was in *Abyssinia,* but he did appear in the latter two shows. In *Mr. Lode of Koal* Rex, Thomas, James Lightfoot, and Charles Redd (or Reed) appeared as a quartet of singing lieutenants who harmonized with their captain, costar Henry Troy, in the well-received number "Happy Days in Dixie."[12] So popular was this number, in fact, that after *Mr. Lode of Koal* closed in March 1910 Henry Troy and the singing lieutenants (Rex, Thomas, Lightfoot, Redd) played in vaudeville together for several weeks.

Rex then formed an act with his wife, Ada, who had also appeared in *Abyssinia, Bandanna Land* and *Mr. Lode of Koal.* They were known as Guy and Rex. One review noted that Rex had one of the funniest scenes in *Bandanna Land* and was using the same makeup (and act?) in vaudeville.[13]

Rex continued to appear in vaudeville, both with his wife and as a solo act, for the next several years. An August 1914 item announced that they were joining that season's edition of *The Smart Set.* Both made occasional concert appearances in the Philadelphia area, for example, Sterling with the Philadelphia Concert Orchestra (1912) and Ada with tenor Roland Hayes (1916).[14] Their home base was Philadelphia, and censuses and city directories after 1910 show them living there at various addresses, finally settling at 1826 Fitzwater. Around 1920 Sterling entered medical school and in 1921 began a second career as a chiropodist. By now one of the pillars of Philadelphia's black cultural scene, he continued to give classical and charity concerts in the area, as a "singing doctor." In 1933 he toured for a time with a production of *Green Pastures* as a vocalist. The last directory listing for him that has been located is in 1938, when he would have been about fifty-nine. Although no obituary has been found, it is presumed that he died around this time.[15]

James Mantell Thomas settled in New York City and also seems to have had a minor vaudeville career in the early 1910s.[16] In 1912 he joined James Lightfoot and three others in forming the Right Quintette, a lively cabaret act that appeared in the New York area for at least the next six years and recorded for Columbia in 1915. Thomas sang bass and played the banjo.

Following the dissolution of the Right Quintette around 1918 Thomas continued to work as a musician in the New York City area (at least he is listed thus in the city directories). The 1925 city census shows him living in a tenement on West 136th Street with his wife, Daisy, and older brother John, also a musician. Thomas died of heart disease on July 3, 1925, at the age of fifty-one.

No information has been found on the other two members of the Dinwiddie Quartet, J. Clarence Meredith and Harry B. Cruder. Moreover, no photograph of the quartet has been located.

The Dinwiddie Normal and Industrial School was incorporated into the public school system in 1936, becoming the county's only black high school. It is still in existence today.

The Dinwiddie Quartet was in existence for a relatively short period of time, but its 1902 Victor recordings are landmarks in the history of recorded jubilees and spirituals. "Down on the Old Camp Ground," in particular, has captured the imagination of modern writers with its lively harmonies, presaging more modern musical styles.

12 Carroll Clark

Carroll Clark was one of the most prolific black recording artists of the early 1900s. Between 1908 and 1924 at least forty sides by him were released on five principal labels, with reissues on many other labels. His specialties were plantation and dialect songs about the Old South, which he rendered with uncommon sensitivity. He also recorded art songs and spirituals. Some of his records—particularly those made for Columbia between 1908 and 1910—were substantial sellers, judging by the frequency with which they are found today.

Yet, ironically, Clark was one of the least-known black recording artists of the period, and practically nothing has been written about him in recent times. Whereas the Fisk Jubilee Singers and Bert Williams were record "stars," Clark was just a name on a label. One reason for this anonymity was the fact that his principal label, Columbia, never published any information about him, never included his picture in any of its literature, and in fact never even indicated that he was black. Nor did his reper-

Carroll Clark at the time of his first
recordings in 1908. (*New York Age,* Oct.
29, 1908)

toire, mostly genteel Southern songs by white songwriters such as Stephen Foster,
suggest his race, something Clark was to become rather bitter about in later years.

Because of the dearth of information published about him, tracing Clark's life has
been a challenge. From U.S. Census entries we know that he was born Clarence
Carroll Clark in October 1885 in Indiana. His mother, Evaline A. Clark, was a native
of Indiana, having been born there in February 1849, but based on later statements
that he was "at least three generations removed from slavery," it appears that she was
a free black.[1] His father's name is uncertain (see below), but we do know that he had
twin older brothers, Raymond A. and Roy Clark, born in Indiana in April 1883.

In 1890 Evaline and her three young sons moved to Denver, taking up residence
in a single-family house at 1856 California Street. With them at this address during
most of the 1890s were two adult males, William J. Clark and Charles H. Clark, who
may have been related. One of them might have been Clarence's father. According
to city directories William and Charles held various jobs, including coachman, butler, and porter. Evaline could read and write and evidently wanted her sons to have
an education, as all three of them were still in school in 1900. Raymond also worked
at Hyman's Cigar and Importing Company as a porter, and by 1902, when he was
sixteen, Clarence was working there as well. Around 1899 the Clarks moved to 1928
California Street, and in 1904 to 335 Adams, where they remained until the end of
the decade. By the early 1900s William and Charles are found at other addresses in
Denver, so apparently the Clark family had begun to break up by that time.[2]

Around 1905 young Clarence began studying voice under Mme. Amelie Hild at
her studio at 48 Barth Street (later in the 401 Charles Building), while continuing

to work as a porter at Hyman's. In 1908 he was offered a major opportunity, the chance to make his East Coast debut at a concert being organized by the famous artist, educator, and philanthropist Mme. E. Azalia Hackley.

Hackley (1867–1922) was a Detroit teacher who in 1894 had married lawyer and journalist Edwin Hackley and moved to Denver. Interested in music since childhood, and possessed of a beautiful high soprano voice, she decided to pursue a professional career and in 1900 or 1901 was the first African American to graduate from the University of Denver School of Music, where she was awarded a bachelor of music degree with honors. In 1901 she separated from her husband and began a long series of concert tours, eventually settling in Philadelphia. Hackley was also a social activist and a strong promoter of black talent, and in time decided to devote her life to the training and advancement of others.[3] It was no doubt through her continuing close ties to Denver that she became aware of the young baritone who was studying at Mme. Hild's studio, and offered to add him to the program of the "new artists" concert she was organizing.

The concert, which took place on October 22, 1908, at the Philadelphia Academy of Music, featured eight young artists from various parts of the country—soprano Marie E. Burton, contralto Lulu Vere Childers, baritone Clark, violinist Virginia Moore, cornetist John W. Johnston, pianists R. Nathaniel Dett and Nellie Moore, and dramatic reader Richard B. Harrison, plus a chorus of 250 trained voices under the direction of W. H. Wright. Opening the program was pianist Dett (1882–1943), who would later become a noted composer and director of music at Hampton Institute.

Of Clarence Carroll Clark, who turned twenty-three in the month the concert was held, the *New York Age* said, "By the stage presence of Mr. Clarence C. Clark, baritone, of Denver, Colorado, one would quickly judge that he had not appeared in public to any extent. But with the sweet, sympathetic voice he possesses he should some day, after hard study, rank as one of the leading baritones of the race."[4] Clark's picture was published, along with those of three of the other artists. Shorter reviews of the concert in the *Philadelphia Inquirer* and the *Philadelphia Public Ledger* did not mention him.[5]

It was presumably during this trip to the East Coast that Clark made contact with the Columbia Phonograph Company in New York. Why Columbia wanted a young black artist to sing standard southern selections for them is uncertain, when they had numerous white vocalists on call. They must have liked his sweet, trained baritone, his ability to sensitively communicate sentimental songs and lullabies in dialect, and his ability to project for the recording horn. They would use him almost exclusively for sentimental material, mostly plantation songs portraying life in the Old South in a positive, nostalgic light.

At least three selections were recorded during November and December 1908. (Additional sides may have been made but not issued; we cannot be certain as Columbia files are missing for this period.) The first, an 1899 lullaby by Albert Noll called "Doan Ye Cry, Ma Honey," was in some ways one of Clark's best performances. It was a simple song about a black man reminiscing about the days when his mother would cradle him in her arms.

Doan ye cry, ma honey,
Doan ye weep no mo',
Mammy's gwine to hold her baby.
All the udder black trash sleepin' on de flo',
Mammy only lubs her boy.

In the second verse the man gets "emancipation," goes north and marries, and his wife sings the same lullaby to his own child.[6] Clark delivered the song with careful enunciation but naturally and with great sensitivity, occasionally humming as would the mother herself. The use of dialect was natural and not at all overdone, and a studio orchestra provided suitably restrained accompaniment. For the type of material, it was an admirable performance.

"Sweet Miss Mary" (1906) and "Some Day Melinda" (1908) were love songs, recently published but also meant to evoke gentle images of the Old South. The former was contained in a collection called *Southern Dialect Songs.* While all of these songs were presumably about blacks, there was not a hint of mockery or reference to anything but heartfelt sentiment.

"Doan Ye Cry, Ma Honey" and "Some Day Melinda" were released in February and April 1909. In each case the Clark recording was coupled with a song by a different artist, as was customary for the period. For some reason Columbia called its new artist "Carroll Clark," using his middle name rather than his first. He would be known as Carroll Clark, or by variations on that name ("Carroll C. Clark," "C. Carroll Clark"), for the remainder of his career. Columbia told its patrons little about him. His first release, "Doan Ye Cry, Ma Honey," was described in the February 1909 supplement as follows: "A soft Southern lullaby of most unusual beauty, beyond question destined to be as universal a favorite as the famous 'Sleep, Kentucky Babe,' with which it may be classified as a companion piece. In this record Mr. Clark makes his bow to Columbia users, and we predict for him instant popularity. His voice is rich, tuneful and expressive, of true baritone quality and admirably controlled."

The reasons for Columbia's reticence to say much about its new artist are unknown but would continue throughout his association with the company. It cannot be attributed simply to corporate racism. Columbia had pictured and promoted George W. Johnson ("The Whistling Coon") in its catalogs in the 1890s and certainly made no effort to downplay the race of Broadway star Bert Williams. Perhaps these sentimental songs about the Old South, with their rosy picture of slavery days, were intended to appeal primarily to conservative, older customers in rural areas and the south, who might be offended by the thought of buying records by a black man. There was presumed to be no market among blacks themselves, and Clark's trained baritone did not suggest his race, so Columbia simply avoided the issue by not characterizing him at all. In a world where blacks were expected to specialize in either coon songs or spirituals, he was simply a talented singer of another genre.

Clark's first records must have been successful since in April 1909 he returned to Columbia's New York studios and during the next four months made five more issued sides. First was "Hush a Bye, O Baby," called a "Georgia Lullaby" upon its original publication in 1899. Rendered in a minor key, it ended with a nod to the most famous of all such Negro lullabies, the huge 1896 hit "Kentucky Babe" ("Hush-a-bye . . . and sleep . . ."). The orchestra accompaniment was stately.

For his next recording Columbia replaced the orchestra with a simple but highly effective banjo accompaniment. "De Little Old Log Cabin in de Lane" (1871), by prolific composer Will S. Hayes, was a favorite of minstrel troupes and male quartets, and probably the most famous song Clark had so far been assigned to record. As the banjoist (probably Vess L. Ossman) strummed along, Clark tenderly recounted the story of the elderly black man sitting in his decaying cabin recalling happy days of long ago and waiting for the angels to take him away.

> I'm a-getting old and feeble now,
> I cannot work no more,
> I've laid de rusty blade and hoe to rest,
> Ole massa and ole missus am dead, sleeping side by side,
> Deir spirits now are roaming with the blest.
>
> De scene am changed about de place,
> De darkies am all gone,
> I'll nebber hear dem singing in de cane.
> And I'se de only one dat's left with dis old dog of mine,
> In de little old log cabin in de lane.

Three more titles were recorded in the early summer of 1909, all with orchestra accompaniment. The lullaby "Sleep Time, Mah Honey" and "Daddy's Piccaninny Boy," both in dialect, were coupled on two sides of a single record. The third song was B. R. Hanby's famous "Darling Nelly Gray" (1856), a real "weeper" sung with great feeling by Clark. Interestingly the song was originally written as an antislavery piece, the reminiscence of an escaped slave in the North. After recalling happy years with his love Nelly Gray, the narrator tells how one night "the white man bound her with his chains" and took her to Georgia "for to wear her life away" in the cottonfields.

> Oh my poor Nelly Gray, they have taken you away,
> And I'll never see my darling any more.
> I'm sitting by the river and I'm weeping all the day,
> For you've gone from the old Kentucky shore.

Much like *Uncle Tom's Cabin,* the pathetic song is said to have been an important factor in arousing Northern sympathy for the slaves in the years prior to the Civil War. Clark's version omits the verse about the white men seizing Nelly Gray, but the meaning of the story, and its reflection on the cruelty of slavery, must have been clear to most listeners. Not in dialect, it was perhaps the most overtly political song—certainly the most sympathetic to the black experience—that Clark had been allowed to sing up to this time.

The titles recorded during the spring and summer of 1909 were released beginning in July of that year. "De Little Old Cabin in de Lane" benefited from being coupled with the enormously popular standard "Dixie," as rendered by Byron G.

Harlan and Frank C. Stanley. It was subsequently released on at least ten different labels and remained in the Columbia catalog until 1925. It is the Carroll Clark record most frequently found today, and was probably his all-time bestseller.

Once again Columbia said little of substance about these records when releasing them, and less about the artist, preferring to rhapsodize in general terms about his performances. Of "De Little Old Log Cabin": "Mr. Clark is so well known to our patrons as a supreme artist in the singing of this class of songs that little more need be said." Of "Sweet Miss Mary": "Mr. Clark displays in this his usual finished vocalism, with just enough dialect to give the right touch of piquancy and naturalness to his rendition." Of "Darling Nelly Gray": "If you have never heard 'My Darling Nellie [sic] Gray' sung the way it ought to be sung—with sympathy, intelligence of diction and tonal purity—there is a treat waiting for you in this record."

Although Columbia did not acknowledge Clark's race, the black press took some pride in the fact that "one of its own" was recording. An item in the December 30, 1909, New York Age noted, "Clarence Carroll Clark, baritone, claims the distinction of being the only Negro in America who is actively engaged in singing for records for the Columbia Phonograph Company. Among his recent numbers are 'Sleep Time, Mah Honey' and 'Daddy's Piccaninny Boy.'"

In early 1910 Clark was invited back to the Columbia studios to record another long series of sentimental songs. The label's regard for him must have grown, as he was given even better material to record, including three Stephen Foster songs. In all, ten issued sides were cut between January and May 1910.

"Little Black Lamb," a 1907 song by white composer Theodore Morse, was even more explicitly sympathetic to the black experience than "Darling Nelly Gray,"and a good deal more contemporary. It was one of a class of song popular at the time that reflected on the cruelty and unfairness of racial prejudice extending even to innocent children. In the song, a little black child attempts to join some white children at play, only to be rejected because of his color.

A little piccaninny saw, while romping 'round one day,
Some happy white folk's children, and he joined them in their play.
Said one of them in anger, "You're unwelcome don't you see,
So go away you black boy, for you cannot play with me!"

As tearfully he pleaded, "Chillun' won't you let me stay?"
They called him little kinky head and ordered him away.
With heavy heart he toddled home, his shiny eyes grown dim,
And daddy took him in his arms and softly said to him . . .

The boy's father then comforted him, assuring him that "down in yo' heart you'se as white as they." Clark's recording omitted the even more pathetic second verse, in which the boy dies and goes to a place where "dey'll not call him kinky head and taunt him 'cause he's black." The omission of this rather clichéd ending, if anything, adds dignity and relevance to Clark's quietly expressive performance.

Two other songs recorded in early 1910 also dealt with children. They were "Two Dirty Little Hands" by Cobb and Edwards, a contemporary number about a mischievous child; and "Baby's Lullaby" by Chapman, a typical black lullaby ("Little eyes am tired...").

The other seven songs recorded in this group were all much older, dating from 1852 to 1874. Three were Stephen Foster songs, all sung with banjo accompaniment. "Old Dog Tray" (1853) is a sweet ballad about an old man and his faithful canine companion ("He's gentle he is kind / I'll never, never find / a better friend than old dog Tray"). "Gentle Annie" (1856), one of Foster's lesser-known songs, is a weepy lament to a love who has passed away. The famous "Massa's in the Cold, Cold Ground" (1852), on the other hand, is written in dialect and conveys a delicious irony about slaves' feelings toward a departed master. Although it is written in the sad, mournful style of Foster's other laments, and conveys the appropriate "happy darky" sentiments, the very fact that Massa is six feet under and his slaves are not is a reminder that the powerful, too, will one day meet their maker.

> Down in de cornfield,
> Heah dat mournful sound:
> All de darkeys am a-weeping,
> Massa's in de cold, cold ground.

Clark sang these pretty melodies in his usual, sensitive style. The banjo accompaniment (all probably by banjo virtuoso Vess L. Ossman) is restrained, with a faster break between verses. It gives the performances an appropriate "Old South" feeling.

Two additional titles also done with banjo accompaniment were "I Want to See the Old Home" (1873) by Frank Dumont and James K. Stewart, and "Carry Me Back to Tennessee" (1865) by Septimus Winner. Both are about newly freed slaves longing for the happy days on the old plantation. The latter was also known as "Ellie Rhee." Although it is about a love who had been left behind, it was performed in a more sprightly tempo, which allowed time for two verses. Like the chorus of "I Want to See the Old Home" ("I want to see the cotton fields / and the dear old home again"), the words must have seemed ironic to Clark.

> Oh why did I from day to day,
> Keep wishing to be free,
> And from my massa run away,
> And leave my Ellie Rhee.

> They said that I would soon be free,
> And happy all de day,
> But if dey take me back again,
> I'll never run away.

Also recorded in early 1910, this time with orchestra accompaniment, were "Lilly Dale" (1852), whose plot can be described simply as "girl dies, boy pines," and "Trabbling Back to Georgia" (1874), another pining-for-home song.

Comparison of these recordings with the corresponding sheet music reveals that Clark seldom strayed from the published text, rendering even the sometimes awkward dialect (written by whites) exactly as it appeared on the page. Never, however, did he exaggerate for effect or offer the slightest suggestion of mockery. The quiet naturalness of his phrasing was a large part of the appeal of these recordings. Another indication of his professionalism is that different takes of the same recording are virtually identical performances.

Most of Clark's early 1910 recordings were released between April 1910 and February 1911, with several remaining in the catalog until the end of the decade, and one ("Massa's in the Cold, Cold Ground") until the end of the acoustic era in 1925. The release announcements still said nothing of substance about the artist. Two titles, "Baby's Lullaby" and "Gentle Annie," were held back and released in March 1912, nearly two years after they were recorded. The catalog editors, though a bit flowery and long-winded, did seem glad to have him back. "The reappearance of Carroll Clark in our list with two solos of the type of which he is so pre-eminently a master and with which his name has been so often associated in our catalogue in the past will be the cause of much felicitation on the part of many of our patrons who have enjoyed the melodious voice of this artists and his unique interpretation of the old plantation songs of the South."

Most of Clark's 1908–10 Columbia recordings were also leased to other labels, including those sold nationwide by Sears, Roebuck (Oxford, Silvertone) and a consortium of Chicago mail-order dealers (Harmony, Standard, United, Aretino). Although his name might or might not appear on these reissues, they gave the recordings even greater distribution, particularly in the south and midwest. Some of his sides were even issued by Columbia's English affiliate, where in at least one instance he was called "Billy Newsome."

For a short time after he began recording in late 1908 Clark continued to maintain his residence in Denver. His last listing in the Denver City Directory was in mid-1909, when he and his brother Raymond are shown at 335 Adams Street (his mother was now at another address). By 1910, however, Clark had apparently moved east. There are periodic notices of recitals featuring him at New York area churches beginning in 1910 and continuing into the 1920s. His regular occupation and place of residence are untraced, although a 1914 recital notice referred to him as a resident of Pittsburgh.[7] Clark was apparently attempting to cultivate a career in serious music. His formal music training was stressed. The notice for a recital sponsored by the Literary League of Greater New York in 1911 referred to him as "C. Carroll Clark" and noted that he was "a student of the Hilde Musical Studio, Denver, Colorado."[8] One writer states that he worked for a while at New York's Music School Settlement for Colored People, which was in operation from 1911 to 1919.[9]

Perhaps as a reflection of his new, serious direction, Clark made no more recordings of plantation melodies for Columbia for many years. A single session in December 1910 resulted in a duet recording with New York concert artist Daisy Tapley of the stately hymn "I Surrender All." (Tapley, an interesting figure whose biography is given in chapter 17, was one of the first black women to make a commercial recording.) The recording is a slow, solemn performance accompanied by an organ, with the two singers singing in harmony throughout. It was apparently a poor seller and is seldom found today.

While Clark stopped recording for Columbia, he did make at least one cylinder record for the U.S. Everlasting label in 1910 or 1911. The song, a dialect number called "Rockin' in de Win'" (1904), was subtitled a "raccoon lullaby" and was about a real raccoon "in de tree a-swingin'" and the efforts of its "mammy" to protect it from hunters. It was released in July 1911, but no copy has been located.[10]

Despite his absence from the studio, Clark's earlier records continued to sell well. Up to seventeen of his titles were listed under a special heading in the Columbia catalog, although as usual the label said little about him ("probably the best singer of old plantation melodies anywhere to be found, a favorite with all Columbia users").[11]

After an absence of six years Clark returned to Columbia's New York studios in December 1917 to record two additional titles by Stephen Foster, "Nellie Was a Lady" (1849) and the immortal "The Old Folks at Home" (1851), which Columbia called by its colloquial title, "Swanee River." Accompaniment was with banjo, this time played by Fred Van Eps, who had replaced the older Vess L. Ossman as the premiere studio banjoist of the period. Detailed recording files exist from this period, and they show how laborious the acoustic recording process could be. Three sessions and eight takes over a period of two months were required to obtain a suitable recording of "Swanee River." The following problems were noted in the files, most of them not due to Clark.

> Take 1: "break in voice near finish"
> Take 2: "poor tone"
> Take 3: "poor banjo at start"
> Take 4: "poor banjo at start"
> Take 5: "banjo thin tone"
> Take 6: "bad appearance" (a problem with the master record?)
> Take 7: "OK"
> Take 8: "break in banjo"

Finally, take seven was authorized for issue. "Nellie Was a Lady" caused even more problems, with nine takes required, most of which were rejected due to problems with the banjo. The performances were slow, with great feeling. (The difficulty of playing the banjo at such a slow tempo may have caused some of the problems.) Clark's voice seems to have deepened over time, and he sounds here almost like a basso.

The choice of repertoire suggests the high regard Columbia had for Clark's treatment of this class of song. There were already two versions of "Nellie Was a Lady" and four of "Swanee River" in the catalog. Columbia must have felt that Clark's distinctive delivery, and the popularity of his earlier recordings of similar material, warranted still another version of each.

The songs, on two sides of a single disc, were released in August 1917. By this time Columbia was routinely featuring pictures of its artists in its supplements, but all readers got with the announcement of the Clark recording was a picture of the river. It read, "'All the world am sad and dreary'—in 'Swanee River' Foster has given his deepest reading of negro nature. Carroll Clark has found the true beauty in Foster's music. Only such a singer can really sing Foster's melodies. Not everyone knows there is a real 'Swanee River': there is and our photograph was taken on the bank of the Southern river itself."

The *Crisis,* journal of the NAACP, proudly noted that "Mr. C. C. Clark, a colored baritone, sings for the Columbia Graphophone Co., and has his photograph in their new catalog."[12] However, as noted, no photo of Clark has been found in any Columbia literature.

"Nellie Was a Lady" / "Swanee River" remained in the catalog for only two years. Nevertheless the label wanted more by Clark, and between 1917 and 1920 it booked sessions for rerecordings of "De Little Old Log Cabin in De Lane," "Old Dog Tray," and "Doan Ye Cry, Ma Honey" and new recordings of "Ma Curly Headed Baby," "Dah's Gwinter Be Er Landslide," and "Don't You Mind It, Honey." None of these sides were issued. The files indicate a number of problems, including poor banjo tone, problems with the master record, and sometimes problems with Clark's performance (one session is noted "voice hoarse"). "Dah's Gwinter Be Er Landslide," a performance piece in the style of a "Negro sermon," was noted as "unsuitable to artist." Different banjoists were used on several of these unissued recordings, old-timer Vess L. Ossman (in one of his last recordings), and minstrel man Harry C. Browne. It is unfortunate that the masters have not survived.

By 1921 Carroll Clark was in his mid-thirties and frustrated. His concert career was limited to small venues and relative obscurity. He had been recording for thirteen years but had been restricted by Columbia to "plantation songs," received little personal promotion, and been given no opportunity to tackle the more serious repertoire he favored. Meanwhile, the revived Fisk Jubilee Singers were renowned in the field of spirituals, and Roland Hayes was building a career as the premiere black concert singer.

In early 1921 Clark was approached by Harry H. Pace, a black publisher who admired his work, and who was planning to start the first major record label to be run by, and exclusively feature, blacks. It would be called Black Swan, named after Elizabeth Taylor Greenfield, the great black diva of the nineteenth century. Unlike earlier black-run mail-order labels, Pace's label would be sold in stores, ensuring wider distribution. He also wanted to feature a wide range of music, including jazz, blues, spirituals, art songs, and concert selections. He enlisted young pianist Fletcher Henderson as his musical director and composer/arranger William Grant Still as his staff arranger.

According to publicity put out by Pace, Black Swan caused a stir in the industry. "When the announcement was made that a company had been formed to manufacture phonograph records of selections by our [black] artists a great uproar was caused among white phonograph record companies who resented the idea of having a Race company enter what they felt was an exclusive field." Pace would later claim that the white companies had tried to prevent him from lining up pressing facilities, even going so far as to buy a failing pressing plant he was using in order to shut him out. He later bought the plant himself.[13]

Carroll Clark's initial recordings for Pace were made in early 1921. A fascinating article in the June 4, 1921, issue of the *Chicago Defender* describes a reporter's visit to the Black Swan studios while Clark was recording. As one of the few contemporary accounts of Clark at work, it is worth quoting at length.

Listening critically to the record [he had just made] stood the singer, Carroll Clark; the musical director of the corporation, F. H. Henderson; and the arranger, W. G. Still. The singer, the darkest of the three, was probably the oldest, although it did not mean that he was more than thirty. Medium sized, of athletic build, his dark, alert countenance pictured all the shades of expression of the artist who gives critical attention to his own production. His voice, a rich baritone, reproduced well as phonograph renditions go, but of the three listeners he evidenced the least satisfaction with the record, a fact which was laughingly noted by the others.

Mr. Clark came here from Denver, Colo., where he studied singing for several years. A balladist who can stand comparison with McCormack, a white phonograph corporation employed him, and after permitting him to sing "The Suwanee River" and such songs, insisted that if they granted his request to have his picture published it must not be identified with the finer ballads, but with the type of song which has come to be associated in the popular mind with the smart, sophisticated "coon" who furnishes us with ragtime and jazz.

Mr. Clark, a cultured Negro with a fine and well trained voice, justly rebelled against the imposition of this demand that he cheapen his art and belittle his race and left the employ of the white concern. He sings now in one of the highest class restaurants in the theater district, but the songs with which he favors his hearers are such as do justice to his talent and credit to his race.[14]

After discussing other artists recording for Black Swan and the importance of black spirituals, the writer returned to Clark and the spiritual he had just recorded.

At my request Mr. Clark sang for me "Swing Low, Sweet Chariot," with its quietly exultant "Comin' for to carry me home!," and although he too is three generations removed from slavery, there crept into his voice more than a hint of the longing for escape from suffering which must have inspired the original to a poignant degree.

Prosperous, cultured, well-groomed and alert, the peculiar musical sensibility and emotional force of his race found sympathetic expression in this old slave song of his forefathers. I listened, and wondered at the crass stupidity of the white folk who had wanted to keep him down to "coon shouting."

Clark recorded six titles for Black Swan between February and May 1921. The first two were the well-known art songs "For All Eternity" by Mascheroni and "Dear Little Boy of Mine" by Ernest R. Ball, the type of material favored by some of the leading white concert singers of the day. Accompanied by J. Cordie Williams on violin and Fletcher Henderson on piano, Clark delivered each in stately fashion, in a deep, strong voice reminiscent of a thousand competent white concert baritones. At one point, he even rolled his *r*s. He sang deeper and much more forcefully than on his Columbias, abandoning the restrained style that had made his early records so successful. While he had brought a special sensitivity to the sweetly nostalgic plantation melodies he sang for Columbia, here he was good but practically indistinguishable from numerous other booming baritones, either in delivery or choice of material. Caruso and Stracciari did this type of song better.

Much the same could be said of two other art songs Clark recorded, both of which had been recorded by many prominent white singers. "By the Waters of

Carroll Clark in 1921.
(*Crisis*, July 1921)

C. CARROLL CLARK
Premier Baritone Soloist of the race

Minnetonka" was done in medium tempo with accompaniment by piano, violin, and a barely heard saxophone. Though it was certainly a competent performance of an interesting piece, the song challenges an artist's upper registers, an area in which Clark was not at his best (particularly the rather weak ending on a high note). "One Sweetly Solemn Thought" was a religious song done in a slow, formal style with piano, violin, and cello.

The final two sides were spirituals, a type of music that had lately come into considerable prominence thanks to the work of the Fisk Jubilee Singers, Harry T. Burleigh, and Roland Hayes among others. Many white singers were now featuring spirituals in their concerts, and numerous recordings were available on the major labels. Black Swan needed some in its catalog, and who better to tackle them than Carroll Clark?

As with the art songs, "Nobody Knows de Trouble I've Seen" was done rather forcefully, quite competently, but without the subtlety of the recorded performances by Roland Hayes and (later) Paul Robeson. "Swing Low, Sweet Chariot" was perhaps more successful. Here Clark varied the tempo, communicating nicely the song's alternation between hope and melancholy. A violin obbligato, presumably by Cordie Williams, provided counterpoint.

The Clark recordings were announced in a series of advertisements in the *Chicago Defender, Crisis,* and other black publications beginning in May 1921. Some ads included his photo (at last!), with the modest caption, "premiere baritone soloist of the race."[15] A September 1921 ad made an even bolder claim.

COMPARE THEM

For the sake of comparison play on your machine Caruso's Victor record number 8333 of "For All Eternity." Then with the same kind of needle and at the same speed play Carroll Clark's Black Swan Record, No. 2002, of the same song.

We leave the verdict to you. Try it. There is a delightful surprise awaiting YOU.[16]

To confer further dignity, after his first release Clark was billed by Black Swan as "C. Carroll Clark."

Some writers have claimed that Clark's Black Swan records sold poorly.[17] They may not have achieved the circulation of the label's later blues recordings by Ethel Waters, Alberta Hunter, and others, but they are not uncommon today. In addition, they were later reissued on a number of allied labels, an indicator of continuing popularity. The success of his Black Swan recordings led to sessions with other labels in 1923 and 1924. By this time Clark appears to have moved permanently to New York City, making him available for more frequent recording work. He is first found in a city directory in 1922, living at 118 West 137th Street in Harlem, with his occupation given as "musician."

In November 1922 Clark recorded two spirituals for Okeh, "Ain't That Good News?" and "Were You There?" both rather bland performances. At about the same time he began recording hymns and spirituals for Paramount, a Wisconsin-based label with studios in New York, which included good deal of race material in its catalog. Based on the examples heard, these were done in the same deep-voiced, forceful style employed on his Black Swans. Titles included "Dear Lord, Remember Me," "Jesus Is Coming Soon," "I'm Glad Trouble Don't Last Alway," "The Home Beyond," and the Burleigh arrangements of "By an' By," "Oh! Didn't It Rain," "Swing Low, Sweet Chariot," and "I Stood on de Ribber ob Jordan." In addition, in the following year Paramount began leasing the Black Swan catalog and reissued on its own label all six of Clark's 1921 sides.

In October 1923 Clark recorded two spirituals for Pathé ("Oh Didn't It Rain!" and "O Lord What a Morning"), accompanied by Fletcher Henderson on piano, but these were not released. All of this recording activity in a concentrated period suggests that Clark was shopping his talents around, hoping to land a steady engagement with one of the many record labels headquartered in the New York area.

Finally in December 1923 he returned to the Columbia studios for the first time in more than four years to record for his original label a number of the now-popular spirituals. His piano accompanist was Fletcher Henderson, now freelancing since the recent demise of Black Swan. After a second session in February 1924 to obtain additional takes, two titles were released in August 1924. The Burleigh arrangement of "Deep River" was sung in a deep, reverent style, so low he was almost singing as a basso. R. Nathaniel Dett's "I'm So Glad Trouble Don't Last Alway" displayed the same deep bass, although sung in a slightly higher register. Both sides featured the careful phrasing, intonation, and emotional intensity characteristic of Clark's performances over the years. They reveal that although he had changed his repertoire and style of delivery somewhat over the years, Carroll Clark was at the peak of his vocal power.

The two sides were released on a single disc in August 1924, joining in the catalog two Columbia discs made long ago ("De Little Old Log Cabin in de Lane" and "Carry Me Back to Tennessee" / "Massa's in the Cold, Cold Ground"). All were deleted in the mass changeover to electrical recordings in 1925–26.

The February 1924 session, in fact, was to be Clark's last. He never recorded electrically, which is our loss as well as his. Aside from an obscure later reissue on Paramount, his recordings were all out of print by the late 1920s. It is believed that he continued to appear at restaurants, churches, and clubs in the New York area for a number of years. His last listing in the city directory is in 1924, at the West 137th Street Harlem address; however, the phone book lists a "Clarence Clark" (the same?) nearby at 300 East 126th until 1928. One writer states that he "sang in high class restaurants and at concerts and in churches until at least 1929; occasionally at the Lafayette Theater, New York (1925), and with the Happy Rhone or Allie Ross Orchestras."[18]

After that, and while still in his forties, Carroll Clark simply disappeared. What became of him is one of the mysteries of this field. One modern writer speculated that he might have been killed in a traffic accident in 1933, but that turned out to be a different Carroll Clark.[19] In fact there are numerous Carroll Clarks, C. Carroll Clarks, Clarence C. Clarks, and so on, in various directories of the period, any of whom might be him.[20]

Whatever his fate, the baritone Carroll Clark left us with a legacy of fine recordings of both popular and art music dating back to the early days of the industry. His training and good taste was in evidence whenever he sang, and his contributions should be recognized in any history of African Americans and early recording.

13 Charley Case: Passing for White?

Charley Case has one of the more fascinating stories among early recording artists. A popular monologuist whose droll, low-key style and offbeat observations about human nature are reminiscent of Bert Williams, Will Rogers, and in more recent times Bill Cosby, Case had a very successful career in vaudeville. He toured the major white circuits for more than twenty-five years and recorded for America's biggest record label. However, the circumstances of his death—by self-inflicted gunshot wound—are shrouded in mystery. Was it an accident or suicide brought on by the pressures on a man of mixed race who spent his life "passing for white"?

Modern references to Case uniformly assume that he was black, or of mixed race, as did many of his contemporaries. Others at this time assumed he was white. New research only deepens the mystery of his true racial identity. We will probably never know for sure. Whatever Case's ethnicity, his story is a fascinating tale of the phenomenon of "passing for white," and the reasons for it, and is well worth considering here for that reason alone.

The following incorporates new research into Case's story and may bring this amiable man of mystery into a little clearer focus. The main thing we know about Charley Case is that his stories were not racial but about basic human nature, and they remain funny and relatable today.

Charles M. Case was born in Lockport, in upstate New York, on August 27, 1858, to Moses and Catherine (Kate) Martin Case. Moses (1825–85) was born in Indiana and Kate (1840–c. 1888) in Ireland; although both were listed in census reports as "Caucasian," one later account said that Kate was an albino.[1] Moses had lived in Erie County, New York, for most of his life, and many other Cases lived nearby. He was apparently quite a character and was involved in small-time show business in some way. A 1862 newspaper item reported that he put on a show in LeRoy, New York, "which was largely attended by the elite of the village." In the 1866 Lockport City Directory he is listed as a musician. The Cases seem to have been reasonably well off. According to the 1875 state census they owned their frame house and had a net worth of $2,000.

If the Cases had a mixed-race background, they hid it well. Nothing in the official records suggests that they were anything other than a typical, white, small-town family. Young Charley attended Lockport's Union School, which was for white kids (a separate school was maintained across town for blacks). His first goal after graduation was to become a lawyer, and in 1880 he was admitted to the New York State bar and opened an office on Main Street. He soon discovered, as he put it, that he was destined to become a "$5 lawyer." He later told the story of his first client, a man who had been accused of stealing a cow. He figured the man was guilty and so instructed him to act crazy in his cell, so that he could plead insanity. The man gave a good performance but made the mistake of boasting about it to a cellmate. The judge found out, so Case had to quickly come up with another explanation. He told the court that his client had been walking along the road and had seen a piece of rope. He picked it up, thinking it might come in handy, and threw it over his shoulder. When he reached home he found, to his amazement, that attached to the other end of the rope was a cow. While the story was a masterpiece, the defendant was found guilty and sent to jail.

Years later Case used this story in his monologue, and reporters were naturally skeptical as to whether it had really happened. To prove his point to a San Francisco newspaperman, Case wired the Lockport police chief, who promptly wired back confirming the story and giving details of the suspect's incarceration.[2]

Counselor Case had few clients and spent much of his time in his office idly playing the banjo. By 1882 he had opened a saloon and, when that failed, a combination ice cream parlor and confectionery store, which stayed in the family for many years. In October 1883 he started a second line of work, opening a "Detective

Agency" in the Hodge Opera House, the city's largest vaudeville theater. His principal clients appeared to be local store owners, who employed him to check the locks on their stores each night and protect their premises.

On March 12, 1883, Case married Charlotte Bush (b. 1861), the daughter of prominent local citizen Capt. W. W. Bush, a Civil War veteran who had raised the first regiment of volunteers from Niagara County. Within the space of a few years the couple had five children, only two of whom survived to adulthood—an unfortunately common occurrence in those days. The two, both sons, were Charley Jr. (b. 1886) and William (b. 1888). Their father, incidentally, preferred the spelling "Charley" for his first name, although numerous later reports used "Charlie."

Though he was listed in city directories from 1883 to 1887 as a "detective," Case was bored and wanted to try something else. He later claimed that, among other things, he tried peddling patent medicine—for one day. Soon he was bitten by the show business bug. "I had a little store in Lockport and I had never been beyond the township line save to go up to Buffalo. Fellows would drop into my place and casually talk of things I knew nothing about. They would take it for granted I had traveled and would ask me if I had seen such and such a thing in New York or Boston or Chicago. It made me anxious to see a little of the world."[3]

He may have been inspired by a young man about his age who had lived in Lockport around the time Case was growing up, and who had already gone on to become a globetrotting actor—Chauncey Olcott (1857–1932). Quiet and unassuming, Case was a natural storyteller, a talent that he thought might help him on the stage. However, he had a wife and two small children to support, so he had to figure out how to make some money.

> I thought at first that since I could not sing or juggle, that the thing to do was to copy someone who had been successful. I had seen Lew Dockstader, and I began practicing his mannerisms before the mirror at home, working with my cuffs, etc. But pretty soon George Wilson came along and I decided I could do him better than I could Dockstader, so I began practicing him. After Wilson I tried George Thatcher, and then it occurred to me that, after all, I was simply trying to do imitations and stuff that gave me no personality, and I made up my mind to be as unlike anybody else as I possibly could, and ended up by doing nothing but standing still and fumbling with a string . . .
>
> At first I thought of using political jokes, but then I thought they might hurt people sometimes, so I selected Father as the butt of all my puns. In confining things to my own family in this way, I couldn't see how anybody could take offense at what I said.[4]

Case's choice of his family for his material was safe in other ways as well. His parents had divorced in the late 1870s, and Moses Case had died in 1885. Kate is believed to have passed away in the late 1880s. One can only guess how many of Charley's colorful stories about his n'er-do-well "father" were based on his own small-time showman dad. Case appears to have had no siblings, so stories about "Brother Hank" and "Sister Mary" were products of his fertile imagination.

In late 1887 or early 1888 Case put together a minstrel show with local talent to benefit an actor who had fallen sick in Lockport. "It wasn't charity at all with me," he later said. "I just wanted a chance to appear in a show." When this went well he took a little troupe of his friends on the road as the Big Four Minstrels, and they got as far as Michigan before their manager absconded with their earnings. Undeterred, he then joined the Ward and West Minstrels, performing as an endman and doing a monologue in the olio. According to an item in the *Lockport Daily Journal,* he was with Ward and West by March 1888.[5] The following season he lined up some bookings in the East, making his "real" debut at Harry Williams's Academy of Music in Pittsburgh.[6] He soon discovered that his quiet, rather sophisticated material went over better with urban audiences than with the "rubes."

Still, it was a long journey to fame. By the early 1890s Case began to attract some attention in national theatrical journals. In 1891 he joined the newly formed Fields and Hanson's Drawing Cards, which played Tony Pastor's Music Hall in New York among other major venues.[7] He remained with Fields and Hanson for at least three years, moving in 1895 to Gus Hill's New York Stars. He then toured as a solo act, working in blackface. One review referred to him as a "burnt cork entertainer."[8]

Over the next dozen years Case carefully honed his routine. He would amble on to the stage, seemingly absentmindedly, wearing exaggerated blackface makeup (common for the period). Standing stock still in the center of the stage he would begin his stories, almost as a chat with the audience, while fiddling with his trademark piece of string. There was no "darkey" dialect or outlandish gestures, just an easy, conversational tone. Most of the stories were about his mother, brother, sister, or, most of all, his good-for-nothing father, who seemed to be a bottomless pit of ineptness, malapropisms, and misplaced intentions. The stories were full of subtle puns, unexpected turns of phrase, and irony, which could slip by an audience used to broad comedy. Here are a few short examples.

> Father was always a great drinker, but he always knew when to quit. He never drank more than he could stand. Whenever he saw he couldn't stand anymore, he'd stop a while. Then when he could stand again, he'd take another drink.

> Mother is the family historian. History's her specialty all right. She knew all about our town before it was founded. And you bet she knows the family tree of everybody in that town, in all its branches. Little incidents in their lives, you know—the number of times they've been arrested, for instance. Pop only stuck her once on history, and even then he felt so sheepish he wouldn't look at anybody for weeks. Of course, he could only see a little out of one eye, but nevertheless . . .

> Nobody was ever sent away hungry from my mother's house kitchen. They would go to the kitchen door, take one look, and go away of their own accord.[9]

Audiences sometimes took a while to warm up to Case, not realizing at first what he was up to. "Case is different from the general monologuists," remarked *Variety* in one review. "He has a peculiar droll delivery, growing funnier as he proceeds. The impression of one man in the second row sums up. When Mr. Case first came on he remarked to his companion, 'punk'; in about a minute he changed this to 'not bad'; and a little later it was 'good'; then 'immense.' At the finish this man was laughing his head off. The monologuist takes his family for the sole subject. It isn't what he says of them, it is what he doesn't say but infers."[10]

Then there was the string. Case was always fiddling with that little piece of string, winding it around his fingers, then unwinding it, as he talked. It was such a trademark he became known as "The Man Who Talks with a String." He told several reporters the story of how it had come about.

It began in this way. When I first went into the business I used to wear a pair of black gloves and during my talk carelessly toyed with one of them, picking at the fingers. In the course of time, naturally, a hole appeared in one of the fingers, and as I continued to work with it it grew and, instead of getting a new glove, when it became too dilapidated to wear any longer, I took it off and blackened my hand, carrying the glove, at which I still continued to pick.

Now in a few months this glove had become little more than a rag, and after a while all that was left of it was a string, and this too in time wore out. But . . . I noticed that the audiences were commenting on this peculiarity, so when the last thread of the glove had disappeared I got a string in its place. I also learned that I had become so accustomed to it that I couldn't get along without it, and now I might almost as well be without my hands.

But stringing, that is, joking aside, that's the true story of my string. However I have had worse experiences than forgetting my string. Yes, I have delivered my monologue in Canada. Imagine telling fifteen minutes of what you think is humor and never getting a laugh. I tell you, being a joker is no joke sometimes.[11]

Another routine developed by Case in later years involved singing/reciting mock 1890s-style moralistic ballads. Even when they were new these pathetic ballads drew snickers from more sophisticated listeners, and mocking by entertainers like Case helped end their vogue. Musicologist Dr. Sigmund Spaeth, in fact, later gave Case considerable credit for the death of the genre, by making "an uproarious joke of all the platitudes of sentimentality that Americans of the past century had taken so seriously."[12] For example, there was the tale of a young girl who had gone to New York to seek her lost lover, Jack. The last verse revealed what befell her on a street car, ending with a hilarious twist.

Then up spoke the conductor, and said,
"I'll never doubt you more!"
And he tore off his false whiskers and it was Jack!
Just then she received a telegram,
That her father's knee was better,
And her aunt had died and left her $58,000.

Two of Case's most popular parodies were "A Warning to Girls" and "A Warning to Boys." In the former, he sang:

Homeward to her mother a working girl did come,
Weary with her honest toil and lighted up with rum,
Supper was not ready, she aimed the brutal blow,
When the bright baby stopped her, saying, "Sister, don't do so!"

Don't swat dear mother, girls,
Just 'cause she's old,
Don't mop her face with the floor!
Think how her love is a treasure of gold,
Don't shove her head through the door.
Don't put the rocking chair next to her eye,
Don't bounce the lamp off her bean,
Angels are watching you up in the sky,
Don't swat your mother—it's mean![13]

In "A Warning to Boys" a decent young man leaves the country for the city and falls in with a group of bounders who get him to drink his first glass of beer.

When he saw what he had done,
He dashed the liquor to the floor
And staggered through the door with delirium tremens.
While in the grip of liquor
He met a Salvation Army lassie,
And cruelly broke her tambourine!
All she said was "Heaven bless you!"
And placed a mark upon his brow,
With a kick that she had learned,
Before she was saved.
So kind friends, take my advice,
And shun the fatal curse of drink,
And don't go around breaking people's tambourines.

Critics loved Case's subtle, intelligent humor and the totally unexpected twists in his stories. Amy Leslie, the highly regarded critic for the *Chicago News,* gave him a rare rave review in 1903, which was widely reprinted ("He is one of the greatest entertainers in vaudeville [with] a pack of new and solemn stories, irresistible and original").[14] Another remarked, "Now if all vaudeville was as good as Case what a delight we would have."[15]

Personally, Charley Case was a quiet, introspective man. One writer described him as "different from the average vaudeville performer. He is of a quiet and retiring disposition when off the stage, and to see him on the street or at his hotel one would never take him for a comedian who makes thousands of people laugh each season. He never 'talks shop,' never even refers to his professional work unless asked."[16] Nor did he mix much with his performing colleagues. By the early 1900s he had adopted a number of hobbies to keep him occupied while on the road. One was collecting fine pipes; another was studying the heavens with a telescope he carried with him. After a show, instead of heading for the nearest saloon with the other performers, he made his way to the roof of the building and spent hours observing the stars. He also assembled a library of books on the subject.[17]

Case toured only during the winter months, returning to Lockport each summer to be with his family. His unwillingness to alter this schedule was legendary and gave rise to a much-told story about him. He was in Lockport one summer, enjoying the company of old friends at the local tavern, when a telegram arrived. It was from Mike Shea, manager of the Court Street Theater in nearby Buffalo, and it was urgent. A key performer had fallen ill; could Case please come and take his place for the remaining three days of the week, for $300? Case smiled, showed the telegram to his companions, then scribbled his laconic reply on the back. "Can't come, am painting the barn." Shea was said to have displayed the response prominently on his office wall for many years. "Can't come, am painting the barn" was pure Charley Case.

Case's summers in Lockport were not just for relaxation. The family store was still in business, operated by his wife (who was sometimes listed in directories as a "confectioner"). In 1902 Charley announced that he would build a road on his extensive property and begin constructing houses. The project was delayed by illness, but by 1905 the street, called Case Court, was in place, and three homes had been built and occupied. In 1903 Case arranged for the *Lockport Journal* to publish a 131-page paperback book of his monologues called *Charley Case's Father*. At least five thousand copies were printed.[18]

Case's isolation on the road may have been in part due to his quiet nature and in part due to rumors of a mixed racial background. When and how those stories originated is not known. No one wrote about it while he was alive (the press was very polite about personal matters in those days), but when he died it became clear that his racial identity had been the subject of much speculation within the business. Some believed that he was at least part black, others did not. Judging by known photographs of him he did not have any facial features that might denote an African heritage, nor did he act or speak in a way that would identify him with the race. On stage, blackface makeup was a wonderful mask; it was widely used by both black and white performers and revealed nothing of the person underneath. It was generally used to mock blacks, but in Case's act it merely served to heighten the irony as he delivered what was essentially a "white" act in blackface.

The rumors about his race must have reached him and bothered a person as sensitive as Case, even if it was not spoken about publicly. If he was, in fact, "passing for white," he was indulging in a well-accepted practice of the time. Even some individuals who were known to be black were allowed to live a "white" lifestyle (at least in the north), if their skin was light enough. But of course they knew, and at least some others knew, that they were not really Caucasian.

Whether it was because of these concerns, the wear of many years on the road, or frustration at being at age forty-nine still a second-tier performer (he rarely headlined), Case left the business in late 1907. The reason given was illness; stories circulated that his physician had urged on him "some new occupation in which the nervous strain would not be so severe as that imposed by work on the stage."[19] He may have suffered a nervous breakdown. It was said that he would devote his energies to managing his real estate in Lockport.

The retirement was brief. By the fall of 1908 Case was once again on stage. Welcomed back as an "old favorite," he saw his career reach new heights during the next few years. Though still not generally a headliner, review after review remarked on how he could brighten a multiact bill, outshine bigger acts that came before or af-

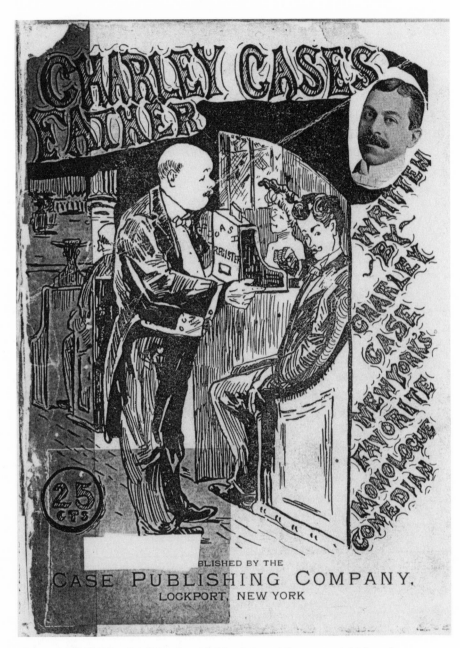

The cover of Charley Case's book, with his picture at the upper right (1904).

ter him, and leave listeners howling at his understated humor. One article claimed that he had become one of the highest-priced single acts in vaudeville.[20]

A review in 1909 caught the offbeat flavor of his act at this time.

It's all about a little girl in a red merino dress, and the song, sailing along in monotonous fashion, excites the laughing interest of every person in the audience.

And then it stops, right there in the middle. You never know any more about that little girl or the dress or the thousand dollars. Instead Charlie Case goes on to tell you all about his family, his sister, his mother, and particularly his father. He just delights in telling stories about his father and you just can't stop laughing from the moment he begins until he closes with a few stories about himself. Charlie is an original and Keith audiences this week are enjoying him to the limit.

Charlie prefers the blackface. He stands in one place on the stage throughout his act. Once in a while he moves his hands but never his feet. He meanders on from story to story, each one funnier than its predecessor and you are really wishing he would stop long enough for you to get your breath. But he keeps right on.

What becomes of the little girl of seven years of whom never a breath of scandal has been heard? No one knows except Charlie, and he won't give away the secret. He tells yarns about that father of his, his love for whiskey and his singing ability and finally swings around to stories about himself. You sit there bent over in your seat, laughing, laughing, laughing every minute that he's on stage. Charlie certainly knows how to bring the laughs.[21]

On the heels of this revival of his career Charley Case either approached, or was approached by, the Victor Talking Machine Company about recording some of his routines. The record labels of the day occasionally offered celebrity monologues, but usually only those of major stars (e.g., Nat M. Wills, Digby Bell) or those with famous set-pieces (DeWolf Hopper's "Casey at the Bat," Joseph Jefferson's "Rip Van Winkle"). It is testimony to Case's celebrity in 1909 that Victor was interested in having him represented in its catalog by some routines of his choosing.

A session was scheduled for Thursday, March 18, 1909, and three of Case's routines were selected. All of them—or variations—had appeared in his 1903 book, so Case was apparently working from an established body of material. Two takes were made of each, as was customary, but in each instance the first take was approved for issue. Case was practiced and at ease in front of the recording horn. His voice was a trifle nasal, which was fine for recording, and his delivery was natural, if a bit hurried. His deadpan description of events contrasted nicely with the ironic words. On these records he sounds as if he is patiently explaining something, without a clue as to the absurdity of it all.

One routine was about Case's favorite topic, dear old Dad. It was called "Father as a Scientist," although in typical Case fashion the title had practically nothing to do with the story that unfolded. It was reminiscent of his "lawyer" story.

Now you know, my father was an educated man. He was a kind of a scientist, a professor, a man who was always trying to make some new discovery. Why, if Father was going along the street and saw anything on the sidewalk he'd stoop down and pick it up to examine it—tobacco or anything. You know, and he was one of these men. . . . I remember one morning he and I were coming home from downtown about three o'clock and we cut through the next-door neighbor's yard. Well, while we were going through this neighbor's yard Father saw something on the ground and out of curiosity he stooped down and picked it up to examine it.

Well, when we got it over to our house where the light was we discovered that it was an armful of wood. Well, the man who lived there had been missing wood for quite a while, and he was watching the woodpile. So when he came out and saw

Father with this wood he thought of course that Father intended to steal it. Why, nothing of the kind! Why, the idea of my father stealing a man's wood when we had a cellar half full of wood just like it!

So the first thing this fellow did was begin to fight with my father, and I remember the first thing he did was to strike a blow at him, but Father is an experienced boxer, you know, and he happened to get his eye on this blow just in time. But of course by the time he got his eye off again, why, the eye was closed.

Well, I noticed that Father had succeeded pretty soon in getting the thumb hold on this other fellow. You know, the thumb hold, that's the hold where you stick your thumb in the other fellow's mouth and holler. Well, Father got it on him all right and hollered and everything, but the other fellow wouldn't let go. And that made Father mad and he called this fellow everything he could think of, but the fellow stood there actually afraid to open his mouth. Well, Father is one of these experienced boxers, you know, like Fitzsimmons, and he was watching all the time for an opening, and he happened to see an opening—in the fence—and he went for it. But the other fellow headed him off and hit him right in the mouth. But that

CHARLEY CASE'S FATHER.

Charley's reprobate father, as imagined by an illustrator. (From *Charley Case's Father,* 1904, author's collection)

Father could get along with anybody.

blow didn't amount to anything, that didn't do any damage at all, because those four teeth had been troubling Father for quite a while anyhow.

Well, I remember they wrestled around on the ground there, sometimes my father being under and sometimes the other fellow would be on top. And that's the way it would go. Well, of course, you know when the neighbors heard about my father fighting they were all surprised because they knew he had such a lovable disposition. You know you couldn't make him mad. I never saw him really angry but once and that was the day that Barnum's circus was in town. I remember one of the girls in the ladies' dressing room stuck her finger through a little hole in the tent and it happened to hit my father in the eye![22]

It is easy to see why not everybody "got" Charley Case's humor. It is humor built on mental images, with the reverent words about Father only gradually revealing that the old man is really an incompetent crook. Listeners had to pay attention or they could easily miss the absurdity of the "thumb hold," the mysterious object that turns out to be an armful of wood, or "sometimes my father was under and sometimes the other fellow was on top."

Also recorded that day was "How Mother Made the Soup," a story that Case had been using on stage for many years. This one was a little more obvious.

You know my sister Mary, amongst the young folks I s'pose she was one of the most popular girls in town. I'll tell you how popular she was. You know, we used to go to parties and we used to play games there. And one of the games we'd play, the way we'd play it, we'd blindfold one of the girls. Then she'd go around among the boys, and put her hands on one of them and if she guessed who he was, he'd either have to kiss her or else give her a dollar. Why, sometimes Mary'd come away from there with $35 or $40.

Now Mother was one of these women—you know, everybody liked her because she had everything so neat and clean around the house, why you could actually eat right off the floor. In fact, we used to do it. And, you know, Mother was one of these women—I remember she was all the time getting recipes out of the newspaper, how to cook things. I remember one time Mother found a recipe in the newspaper directing how to make farmer's soup, and Mother went at this soup and it took her about half a day to make it. And when she had it made she put it on the table and I didn't like the smell of it, so I didn't eat any of it, but Hank, my brother, ate some of his and it made him sick!

Well, Father thought it couldn't be very good, from the way Hank acted, but he made up his mind that he'd try it and get it over with as soon as he could. So he closed his eyes and drank a big bowl full of it, and he fell over on the floor in a fit. And I said to Hank, I said, "Hank, run for the doctor quick!" and Hank started off on a run and after he had gone I took Mother into the other room and I said, "Mother, I guess you've poisoned them!" And she said, "No, I haven't." She said, "That soup, I made it just according to the directions in the newspaper." And I looked in the paper and I says "I can't find where it says "soup." And mother says, "Well, what's the matter with you, are you blind? There it is right in front of your face and eyes, 'S-O-A-P,' soup!" And I told her, "Why, Mother, that spells soap. You've filled Father and Hank full of soft soap!"

Well, you know Hank ran all the way to the doctor and by the time he got there, from running and one thing and another, why the poor fellow was so full of suds he couldn't speak, and the doctor threw him down and put a muzzle on him—thought he had hydrophobia.

Well, while I was talking to Mother, every once in a while I could hear the baby in the other room. She'd begin to laugh and clap her hands, and I went in there to see what was making the baby laugh, and Father lay there on the floor, on his back, coughing. And every time he coughed he'd blow a soap bubble![23]

"How Mother Made the Soup" was certainly one of Case's more easily understood routines, less sly and more slapstick than "Father as a Scientist." Audiences must have roared at the description of Mother mistaking "soap" for "soup," and Father on his back blowing bubbles while the baby laughed and clapped.

Case also made fun of himself, mocking his own reputation as a beloved "old-timer." The last of the three routines recorded in 1909 used this theme and is called "Experiences in the Show Business." It contains fascinating references to show-business practices and people, including F. F. Proctor, one of the top vaudeville impresarios of the day.

I'm glad you like my singing. You know, I sang that song once in California and it made an awful hit. In San Francisco the people liked my singing so well they didn't want me to come away from there at all. One of the newspapers there—one of the leading newspapers in San Francisco!—came out and stated they wished I could stay there forever. I have the note, it's right here in my pocket. I can show you. There it is. It says, "Charley Case closed his engagement at the Orpheum Theatre last night and leaves California tomorrow morning for the East. We would like to have him stay forever."

Now you know I sang this song the other morning for Mr. Proctor at a trial performance, and he thought it was all right. In fact, he told me he was very much pleased with it. And while I was singing the song, as bad luck would have it, one of the stage hands went to throw a brick out of the window and it accidentally hit me on top of the head. You know, it was all I could do to finish the song, but still, if I do say myself, I never sang it better in all my life. As I say, Mr. Proctor said he was very much pleased with it, and I said to 'im, I said, "Now, if you're very much pleased I wish you would put that in writing and then I can publish it in the paper, and it can help me get some work." And he said he would. And I told him, I said, "You might mention in the letter that I was injured at the time and singing under difficulties and that'll make the letter all the stronger." And he said, "Why, certainly." And he wrote me a beautiful letter. I have it right here. I'll read it to you. It says, "This is to certify that Charley Case sang for me this morning at a trial performance. While he was singing his ballad somebody dropped a brick on his head and nearly killed him. I was very much pleased."

Now you might have read about my singing in some of the newspapers. Still, I don't think you'd know it was me because at that time I was traveling under my right name. You know, Charley Case—that's only a stage name. My right name is Cass, John Cass. I took the name Case, because it sounded like it. And I liked the name John Cass, and I probably would have kept it, only I noticed sometimes some of the people who'd come out of the theater and they'd be speaking about my act, instead of calling me *John* Cass, they'd call me Jack.

Now down in my town—down in Lockport, New York where I was born, why, they all knew my right name down there. You know, speaking about being born in Lockport, there were quite a few cities claimed me. You know how it is. When a person goes in show business and he's anyway successful then every city wants to claim he was born there. Now there are Buffalo and Rochester, two rival towns down our way that are all the time making fun of one another and each claims to have the better city. You know, they've been arguing over my birthplace for over five years. The Buffalo people claim I was born in Rochester and the Rochester people claim I was born in Buffalo.[24]

The way Case spun out the gag about his real name being John Cass was typical. It was up to the listener to make the connection: what audiences were calling him was "Jack Cass," or in other words, "jackass!" While this kind of subtle wordplay endeared him to sophisticated audiences, it must have gone over the heads of many. One c. 1909 review from Spokane, Washington, remarked that during his act at the Orpheum Theatre, "his exposition . . . that his real name was Cass and that he had to change it because people persisted in calling him Jack instead of John found ready response . . . but the tardiness with which one matinee patron 'caught on' came near to stopping the act."[25]

Contemporary audiences were not the only ones fooled by Case's deadpan sincerity. Historian Jim Walsh, writing about the comedian in 1979, believed the foregoing story and stated unequivocally that Charley's real name was John Cass.[26] "Jack Cass" is most likely a reference to Dr. John Cass, a real physician who lived in Lockport while Charley was growing up. Perhaps the kids in Lockport originated the gag, and Case later decided to use it in his act.

The first of the Victor records to be released was "How Mother Made the Soup," on a single-faced disc in June 1909. The announcement implied that he was already well known to Victor customers. "Every frequenter of vaudeville knows Charley Case; and many a man has gone to the theater feeling blue and despondent, but was obliged to laugh when Charley began to talk about that poor old imaginary (we hope) father of his. Here is a record of one of Case's best stories; and if any buyer of this record fails to smile by the time the father-baby-soap-bubble incident is reached, he should see a doctor at once."

The record sold well. It was reissued on a double-faced disc in 1910, coupled with a comic selection by Golden and Hughes, and remained in the catalog until 1926. It then appeared in a special 1927 catalog of "Victor Records of Historical and Personal Interest," which listed older acoustic records that were still available by special order.[27] It is the Case record most frequently found today.

"Father as a Scientist" was released a month later, in July 1909, coupled with a novelty routine by Harlan and Stanley. The supplement said little about this record ("Charley Case tells another of his scandalous stories about father"), but it remained available for more than ten years.

The listing for the final recording, "Experiences in the Show Business," is in some ways the most interesting because it is accompanied by one of the few known photographs of Case. He appears without his stage makeup, looking like a mild-mannered, middle-aged businessman with a high collar and a thick mustache. The routine was coupled with a comic song by Billy Murray. The supplement said, "Charley takes us into his confidence here and gives away all the secrets of the 'show business.' He has nothing to say about 'father,' however—doubtless intending to give the old gentleman a much-needed rest."

"Show Business" was the least successful disc of the three and was deleted in 1915. Nevertheless the three Victor releases, taken together, appear to have enhanced Case's fame even further. One interviewer, on meeting him, wrote, "I had often seen his name in big type in various papers, and had often heard his peculiar and amusing line of talk in talking machines, but this was the first glimpse I had ever had of the famous comedian."[28]

Around this time Case experimented with dropping blackface and performing "straight," but he soon went back to his familiar persona.[29] A 1914 article explained why.

> While black-face comedians are passing one by one—the last two to dispense with the darkey make-up being Eddie Leonard and Jack Wilson—Charlie Case declares he will continue to cling to the burnt cork and piece of string that helped make him famous.
>
> "Yet the black-face makeup has many drawbacks," he admits. "In the first place it is a terrible ordeal to 'black up' twice a day. It is costly too. The burnt cork is no small item of expense, the cleansing necessities are costly and the cleaning-up process is terrible on the nervous system and on the skin on the face and hands. Those who have deserted black-face did so by accident. I know Mr. Leonard's trunks arrived late one Monday afternoon, he went on without blacking up and the novelty of it was appealing, so he kept it up. As for myself, though, I shall stick to this line of work, for I wouldn't feel at home on the stage in any other makeup."[30]

Numerous clippings from the early 1910s attest to Case's continued popularity on the vaudeville circuit. Most of these articles were in the general (white) press, which assumed he was a white man. Reporters liked him because he was articulate and would almost always share with them a funny story to enliven their column. He seemed to have no problem seeing his best material in print, which contributes to his legacy, if not his exclusivity at the time.

He continued to tour widely, not headlining but always a popular performer on the bill. Although this kept him away from his family and a well-earned retirement (he was now in his fifties), he did not complain, at least in public. In December 1909 he remarked, "Speaking of New York and audiences, I played twenty-five weeks around here last season, and I never was better contented with my lot. As for the audiences, well, they pick up a point here quicker than in other places I go. I mean by that chiefly the little hidden points that are half under cover. Sometimes I am surprised, though, at the way they fail to take up the simplest ones."[31]

In 1910 he spent the spring in Chicago, then traveled to London. Promoters had long been after him to perform in Europe, but he had always declined. When asked why he did not accept these flattering offers, his reply was that he might get seasick on the way over, and when urged to accept, he added that he probably would go later "when the bridge was built." It was his way of getting out of doing something that he didn't want to do.[32]

Once he made the trip, he was sorry he had. British music-hall audiences didn't understand him at all. In an interview Case recounted in hilarious fashion how he had sung in London his "Warning to Boys," ending with the Salvation Army lassie planting a swift kick on the forehead of the errant drunk, and how they had taken the story entirely seriously. He produced a sober review that said, "It would be interesting to hear a discussion . . . by the clergy, as to whether a religion which is rather more emotional than dogmatic is sufficient to prevent its believers from relapsing, as in this instance, to primitive habits and customs."

"I am trying to forget," said Charles yesterday with tears in his voice. "They liked me in London, but they said it was because I appealed to the nobler nature; that I was so serious and uplifting that I raised the audiences above the silly commonplaces that so many music hall performers delighted in."

The saddened Mr. Case does not use any of the jokes and gibes that were wont to set his hearers in a roar. "I used 'em in London," said Mr. Case. "I will never use them again. I sold them to a publisher on the Strand and he is bringing them out this fall in a book called *Golden Gems for Every Day; or, Struggling Toward the Nobler Life*."[33]

The English, it is said, did not understand Case's humor. (Unidentified newspaper, 1910)

The interview concluded, "There are tear stains on the English newspaper clippings. The tears fell from the eyes of Mr. C. Case."

A series of reviews from 1912 show Case performing in Cleveland, St. Louis, and Duluth, where one of his fellow performers hid his string!

> Just a moment or two before the time came for his act, he looked for the string and it was gone. A frantic search began, but the string could not be found. He appealed to the property man, but the property man was out of string, probably for the first time in his life. The orchestra was playing the introductory bars for his appearance, and repeated them. Mr. Case was frantic. Finally he drew a knife from his pocket and slashed a strip from the lining of his coat. Twirling this about his fingers he made his appearance, but the grinning performers noticed it was several minutes before the cold perspiration disappeared from his forehead.[34]

Appearances in 1913 included Baltimore and Toledo, where he was referred to as an "old school black-face comedian" and an "old-time monologuist." The next year brought "a tour of the suburbs," including Rhode Island, Pittsburgh, Ohio, Chicago, St. Louis, Denver, and Los Angeles. In the latter city Case showed a reporter a stack of "complimentary" clippings, all of which seemed to imply he should go somewhere else! He delighted in making fun of himself.

> I hardly know how to proceed with my act before you—you seem to be such a Missourified kind of an audience. Sometimes I just sing a song, walk off, and let the audience call me back. And sometimes they fool me.
> The manager of this theater is a very good friend of mine. He never kids people, but he's genuinely complimentary. I met him in San Francisco Monday morning before I came down here, and he asked me if I was going to sing. I told him yes, I had a brand new song with just one word in it. He said he was glad of that. Wasn't that lovely of him?[35]

Clippings from 1915 and 1916 suggest that Case was by then touring mostly in the East, and that his career was past its peak. He was now fifty-eight, still living in hotels, still separated from family, still a second-tier performer. In 1916 he hit a dry spell, not performing for many months. During the fall he roomed for several weeks at the Palace Hotel on West 45th Street in New York, waiting for his next bookings to come through. At length an arrangement was in sight for him to appear in Erie, Pennsylvania, and a money order was supposed to be on the way.

Then, during the early morning hours of Monday, November 27, 1916, Charley Case died suddenly under what can only be described as bizarre circumstances. Reports of the incident appeared in at least two city newspapers, as well as in the theatrical paper *Variety*. The following account is believed to be from the *New York Telegraph*.

> Albert Cutler, another actor and a close friend of Case's, returned to his room at the hotel at an early [morning] hour. Noticing a light shining through the transom of Case's apartment, Cutler knocked on the door and was admitted. After a short talk the pair made a breakfast engagement together, as Case was scheduled to leave for

Erie, Pa., to fill a theatrical engagement there. Cutler had scarcely closed the door after him, however, when he heard the report of a revolver shot.

Rushing back into the room, he found Case lying across his bed with the revolver clutched in one hand. "Pardon me," the dying man muttered, as his friend came up to the bedside.

A physician was summoned at once, but Case died before his arrival. The vaude-villian leaves a wife and two children. His home is at 613 Breckinridge Street, Buffalo, where the funeral services will probably be held tomorrow morning.[36]

Compounding the tragedy, when a friend sent a wire to Case's wife in Buffalo, notifying her of what had happened, she dropped dead at the news. "'She was killed by the shock at the news of her husband's sudden death,' said the doctor who examined her."[37]

The *New York American* gave a more pathetic account of the events, suggesting that Case was waiting for funds to allow him to visit "his little family" in Buffalo, and that the couple's "two children were now alone in the world." *Variety,* however, said that "he was reputed to be quite wealthy, owning considerable property in Lockport," and that his two sons were grown.[38] A photograph of Case's Buffalo home, taken many years later, shows a rather substantial residence.[39] *Variety* also gave a slightly different account of Case's death, saying that Cutler had invited Case to his room for a bottle of beer, and that Case had agreed, but when Cutler returned to tell Case the beer was ready he heard the fatal shot.

All three accounts called the shooting accidental, saying that Case had been cleaning his automatic revolver when he shot himself in the heart. Case's death certificate, interestingly, gives the cause of death as "bullet wound of abdomen." If true, this might support the theory that the death was accidental, although it also raises the question of why a wound in such a place would have killed him so quickly. According to *Variety,* "When Sam Salvain, proprietor of the hotel, reached the room a few minutes after the shot, there was a bottle of oil on the floor and a cleaning cloth in the dead man's hand." Since no one else was in the room when the shot was fired, we cannot know for sure exactly what happened.

It should be noted that press reports in this era were sometimes less than candid when it came to reporting unsavory events, especially those concerning respected citizens. For better or worse, America had not yet entered the "tell all" era. It is significant that neither of the mainstream newspapers that reported Case's death mentioned that he may have been mixed race. But others did so. According to Jim Walsh, who interviewed people who had known Case, "After his death some of Case's associates inclined to the belief that his shooting was intentional, and was caused by long brooding over his mixed racial heritage."[40] Lending strong credence to this theory, a remarkable article appeared a few days later in New York's leading black newspaper, the *New York Age,* written by its theater critic, Lester A. Walton. While repeating the story that the death was accidental, Walton used it as a springboard for a discussion of the curious custom of "passing for white." The article was unusual for the *Age,* a respected paper not known for scandal-mongering, and is significant for its reflections on the shadowy practice.

CHARLIE CASE
BY LESTER A. WALTON

Colored members of the theatrical profession, who behind closed doors have been wont to class Charlie Case, the well known black-face comedian, as "a colored man passing for white," were shocked to learn of his tragic death Monday when he accidentally killed himself while cleaning a revolver in his room in the Palace Hotel on Forty-fifth street. The comedian had been booked to fill a vaudeville engagement in Erie, Pa., this week.

Dispatches from Buffalo, where Case resided with his family, tell the sad news that after receiving word of her husband's death Mrs. Case became unconscious and never recovered. Her physician said the shock killed her. . . .

The position occupied by Case was most unusual in that hundreds of white people harbored the impression that he was a colored man. A number of years ago Case and a big colored musical act divided headline honors at Hammerstein's Victoria Theatre. In discussing the merits of Case as a comedian an attache of the theatre confidentially remarked to a member of the colored act, "Charlie Case is a colored man!" The performer showed mock surprise, for he had been discussing the comedian's racial identity only a few minutes before with some of his colored actor friends.

The inconsistent attitude of the white man on the color question was never more glaring than in the case of the deceased comedian. Many believed him to be colored, yet they always [treated] him as a white man and did not despise him because he married a white woman. Some believed the rumor that he was other than white untrue, others did not hesitate to express opinions in the affirmative; and yet no attempt was ever made to draw the color line.

Along Broadway one may find a number of stars and near stars who started life as colored men and women, but who today are known as white, except to certain Negroes and a few white people. As in many other avenues of endeavor, there are on the stage those who not only play make believe on but also off. Coming to New York and finding the numerous handicaps which the ambitious must face, and soon learning that the path trod by the colored performer is far more rocky than that of the white performer, many have buried their true racial identity and secured work as Caucasians. In the field of drama, in musical comedy and in vaudeville, the colored American of light complexion may be found "passing for white." As a rule they do not forget their intimate colored acquaintances of former years, and are never happier than when with them for a few hours, which are taken up in talking of years gone by and the success achieved on the stage by the one-time Negro. The colored American is often accused of talking too much, but there is not a case on record where the identity of these successful actors has been disclosed by a former colored associate. Colored people are usually glad to see one of their race "getting by," and among one another they point with pride to a Negro who has been able to perform such a feat.

On the day Charlie Case met his death I was strolling down Broadway and chanced to pass two members of the race who have found it profitable to pose as white people in the theatrical world. I regarded this as a strange coincidence. Standing in front of one of the larger hotels frequented by theatrical folk was one who has made an enviable reputation in vaudeville, and his demeanor plainly showed that long ago he had put aside the race problem and left it for the Booker T. Washingtons to solve. Further down the street I came across a comely miss who is regarded as one of the best chorus girls on Broadway. But with her she has found it hard to get far away from the race and is often seen with colored female friends in Harlem.

"Passing for white" is a game played by hundreds of colored Americans today, not as a diversion but as a necessity. No one can blame these people for lessening the obstacles confronting them in this great struggle for existence. Negroes have a feeling of aversion for but one class of colored Americans who "pass for white": those who want to be white and don't know you today, but who want to be colored and enjoy your society tomorrow.[41]

Case's true racial heritage remains a mystery. I have found nothing published during his lifetime that suggests that he was anything other than white, though that would not be unusual for those polite times. Not until his death did the rumors that he was part black begin to surface in print. In addition to the *New York Age* article, Broadway historian Joe Laurie Jr. insisted that it was true. Laurie (1892–1954), a vaudeville performer, radio personality, and longtime *Variety* columnist, knew Case personally. In his book *Vaudeville* (1953) he devotes nearly a page to the comedian, saying, "Case was partly colored," and later adding, "I believe that Charlie Case and Bert Williams were two of the greatest artists the Negroes gave to vaudeville." Laurie made similar statements to Jim Walsh. That Laurie did not always get his details right is evident in the fact that he claimed Case's wife was "a very black woman," and that "his mother was a Negro and his father of Irish stock."[42] Case's mother was from Ireland, his father from Indiana. Nevertheless both Walton and Laurie knew Case personally and were well connected in the theatrical world. Their first-hand accounts must be given credence.

Over time the legend grew. In 1931 the famous columnist Franklin P. Adams ("F.P.A."), writing in the *New York Tribune,* said, "he was a Negro; despite his high merit as an original comedian he never got the big salaries that were current. About a dozen years ago he killed himself; or so-called civilization murdered him. . . . Debts and taxes! What the world needs is a moratorium on the cruelty of prejudice."[43] Walsh in his seminal 1979 article stated as fact that Case was part black, as have virtually all modern references that I have seen.[44]

But was he? Official records such as the U.S. Census and his death certificate might seem to be conclusive, but anyone who has done genealogical work knows that official records can be wrong. Census entries reflect either what the subject reports or what the census-taker observes ("looks white, lives in a white neighborhood, must be white"). There is no investigation. If there had, in fact, been miscegenation in Moses's or Kate's background, it would hardly have been in their interests—or Charley's—to admit it. (Quite the opposite, in fact, in those segregated times.) One clue may lie in the *Variety* obituary, which stated that Kate was an albino. Lack of normal skin coloration is not necessarily the result of mixed race breeding, but it can be.

When all is said and done, it probably doesn't matter. The rumor that Charley Case was "passing for white" is clearly not a modern invention but was widespread while he was alive. Knowledgeable sources such as the *New York Age* and *Variety* would not have published such speculation unless they thought it might be true, but they didn't know for sure, and neither can we.

There was apparently some consideration given to allowing Case's eldest son, Charley Jr., to enter show business like his father and grandfather. At the age of seventeen he appeared with his dad at a local appearance, playing a violin solo. In the same year (1903) he was reported to be running the family business, Case's Country Store, on Main Street in Lockport, where he also opened a small restaurant called Case's Country Kitchen. Laudatory items in the local paper emphasized that "a strong point with Mr. Case [Jr.] is his coffee, not the kind of coffee that is usually served in restaurants, but *real* coffee."[45] Despite the fine coffee the restaurant closed in June 1904. Shortly thereafter Charley Jr. moved to the New York City area, accepting an "important clerkship" in a Wall Street broker's office.[46] He enlisted in the Army during World War I and is believed to have been killed during the war. The other son, William B. Case, remained in the Lockport area, eventually becoming manager of the Crescent Distributing Company. He died around 1938 or 1939. William and his wife, Florence (a one-time city clerk), had one son, William M. Case, who is also now deceased.

After his death Charley Case's name quickly faded from memory. He is seldom mentioned in general histories of early twentieth-century show business, which generally dwell on a few famous headliners. His influence may have been greater than this lack of attention suggests, however. One wonders whether storytellers such as Bert Williams and Will Rogers were influenced by his low-key, humanistic style. They certainly must have been aware of him, as each got his start while Case was still active. Two of Case's parodies outlived him. "A Warning to Girls" and "A Warning to Boys" were both recorded by Vernon Dalhart in 1928, and "A Warning to Boys" turned up in the 1933 W. C. Fields film short *A Fatal Glass of Beer*.[47] In the 1950s it was being used by comedian George Gobel on his television show, and as late as 1963 the Weavers performed it at their famous Carnegie Hall concert, later released on LP. Mention of Case by Joe Laurie Jr. in his 1953 book, a lengthy article on the comedian by Jim Walsh in 1979, and entries for him in such modern references as *The Complete Entertainment Discography* (1989) and *The Encyclopedia of Popular American Recording Pioneers* (1999) have kept Case's name alive among collectors and specialists.

Charley Case's 1909 Victor recordings serve as a tribute to a humorist who brought an unusual brand of subtle, intelligent humor to a broad audience. The 1927 Victor catalog, the last one to list Case's recordings, could have been referring to him when it said, in its introduction, "Some [of these records] are the work of artists now dead; and these, of course, will remain unique. Others embody music which may not again be recorded. As with old books, their interest will not diminish but grow with time."

14 The Fisk Jubilee Singers and the Popularization of Negro Spirituals

The saga of the Fisk University Jubilee Singers is one of the most remarkable chapters in the annals of African American music. This unassuming chorus from a small southern college was the first performing group to bring black music suitable for the concert stage to an American public that had previously seen the race mostly though the prism of minstrel stereotypes. The few black concert performers who preceded them, such as Elizabeth Taylor Greenfield (known as the Black Swan), who was active in the 1850s and 1860s, had emphasized standard white repertoire. The great and lasting contribution of the Fisks was the introduction of the spiritual to America's musical literature.

The impact this music would have cannot be overstated. In the oft-quoted words of the eminent Bohemian composer Antonin Dvořák, "These beautiful and varied themes are the product of the soil. They are American. They are the folksongs of America, and your composers must turn to them. In the Negro melodies of America I discover all that is needed for a great and noble school of music."[1]

Although there are few modern books about the Fisk Jubilee Singers, their early years are summarized in most histories of black culture.[2] Less well known is the story of the Fisks' later career, their recordings, and the pivotal role those recordings played in bringing black concert music to mainstream America. To my knowledge there has been no serious discussion of these recordings, which are—or should be—essential source materials for scholars studying either the Fisks or more generally the spread of black music in twentieth-century America. It is my contention that it was through these widely distributed records—marketed with a mix of respect and condescension—that middle-class whites in the early twentieth century became familiar with this important aspect of African American culture.

The best-known African American recording artists prior to the Fisks, such as George W. Johnson and Bert Williams, had specialized in vaudeville fare, much of it mocking their own race. The Fisk Jubilee Quartet reminded America that there was another side to black culture.

Origins of the Fisk Jubilee Singers

Fisk University, located in Nashville, Tennessee, was founded in 1865 by the American Missionary Association (which had ties to the Congregational Church) to provide badly needed education for newly freed slaves. From the day it opened its doors on January 9, 1866, the school attracted an abundance of students but suffered from a severe shortage of funds. Housed in flimsy, abandoned Union Army barracks, Fisk's all-white faculty worked for minimal pay and with barely adequate supplies. The new "Fisk School" was on the verge of financial—and physical—collapse.

In April 1867 Fisk treasurer and part-time music instructor George L. White conceived the idea of presenting some of the more musical students in concert in Nashville and surrounding areas. The repertoire was the standard white "art" repertoire of the day, designed to show how much these former slaves had benefited from higher education. Their reception was unexceptional. White persevered, however, and over the next three years both he and his charges gained confidence and polish. With financial pressures mounting, in 1871 White proposed sending the student chorus on a fundraising tour to the East, where the liberal white establishment would surely come to the aid of a struggling black college. His ambitious goal was to raise $20,000 for the university. Many of his colleagues viewed this as impractical and foolhardy, but White prevailed and on October 6, 1871, White, a ladies' chaperone, and nine students (five women and four men) embarked on their daring journey. It was daring because at the time the American public viewed black entertainers almost exclusively as minstrels and comedians. Never had a serious attempt been made to present an ensemble in a "high-class" setting.

At first White's detractors appeared to be right. Audiences in Cincinnati and other midwestern cities were lukewarm to the mélange of operatic arias, temperance songs, and parlor songs such as "The Old Folks at Home" and "Home, Sweet Home." But White noticed that the occasional authentic black spiritual on the program drew a strong response. The students had sung these semireligious "sorrow songs," most with biblical themes, in chapel at Fisk. In singing the songs, drawn in part from their own backgrounds, the singers conveyed an emotional intensity unmatched in their other repertoire.

Some writers suggest that spirituals were previously known only in the cottonfields of the South. This is a bit of an exaggeration, as a number of these songs were already in print. "Go Down Moses" was first published in 1861 and "Roll, Jordan, Roll" in 1862. A group of white Northerners had published the landmark collection *Slave Songs of the United States* in 1867.[3] Another Northerner, Thomas Higginson, wrote an influential article about the music for *Atlantic Monthly* in mid-1867.[4] As Epstein notes, these early efforts had fairly limited circulation, and the music was initially regarded by many as "shrieking, screaming [or] mere noise."[5] Still, the groundwork had been laid, and the curiosity of northern liberals piqued just as the Fisk Singers came on the scene. Their timing was impeccable.

Soon spirituals were featured regularly in the Fisk Singers' concerts. In October 1871, while in Columbus, Ohio, White made the inspired decision to change the name of the group to "The Jubilee Singers"—after the blacks' long awaited "year of jubilee," or emancipation. The catchy name immediately attracted attention. As the tour progressed, engagements were more and more warmly received, as well as financially successful. A highlight was an appearance at Henry Ward Beecher's Plymouth Congregational Church in Brooklyn, New York, where the Singers attracted national attention and generous donations. In all, they remained in the New York area for six weeks. By the time the troupe returned to Nashville in the spring they had raised the full $20,000 White had promised. But this proved to be just the beginning. Almost immediately White was invited to bring his Singers to a gigantic music festival being planned in Boston by noted bandmaster Patrick S. Gilmore.

With its orchestra of two thousand pieces and chorus of twenty thousand voices Gilmore's World Peace Jubilee was in danger of collapsing under its own weight. But in the midst of a July 1872 ensemble performance the Fisk Jubilee Singers broke though, electrifying the arena with their fervent performance of "The Battle Hymn of the Republic." In the words of one observer, "The great audience was carried away with a whirlwind of delight. The men threw their hats in the air and the Coliseum rang with cheers and shouts of 'The Jubilees! The Jubilees forever!'"[6] Their reputation soared.

Embraced by the liberal Northeast, and viewed with warm curiosity by much of the rest of the country (excluding the Deep South), the Jubilee Singers set out on a fabulously successful season of touring in 1872–73. Articles and books were published about them, including the best-selling *The Jubilee Singers and Their Campaign for Twenty Thousand Dollars* by Gustavus D. Pike (1873), which included both their story and sixty-one spirituals and which had far wider circulation than *Slave Songs*.[7] Their "sorrow songs," like "Roll, Jordan, Roll" and "Swing Low, Sweet Chariot" began to enter the public consciousness. Many in the press didn't know what to make of this new, serious music, insisting that it must be some new type of minstrel show.

In April 1873 White took his troupe to England, where they performed "Steal Away to Jesus" and "Go Down, Moses" for Queen Victoria. They were a sensation in that country as well. The Singers returned to the United States in May 1874, but another long tour of Europe followed from May 1875 to July 1878. By the time they returned, they had raised an estimated $150,000 for the university, which was used to buy new land and erect its first major structure, appropriately named Jubilee Hall.

Spirituals in the Late Nineteenth Century

The "official" Fisk Jubilee Singers then disbanded, although Fisk did allow White and a former Singers member named Frederick J. Loudin to field private groups under the Fisk name. Their success had brought many imitators into the field, some with similarly noble purposes (e.g., the Hampton Institute Singers, who raised money for that black institution), but also many charlatans out to make a buck by implying that they were somehow connected with the now-famous Fisk. Many unsanctioned "jubilee singers" toured widely during the 1880s and 1890s, carrying African American music and, by association, the name of Fisk throughout the world. Unfortunately, the musical standards of some of these hastily contrived (often white-controlled) commercial groups were low. They were in it for the money, and there definitely was money to be made. One newspaper sarcastically observed in 1900 that "the moment a company of jubilee singers arrives in town the cash registers even take on an unusually bright, glistening appearance."[8]

By the turn of the century spiritual singing had fallen into some disrepute because of its exploitation by second-rate groups. The music itself needed rescuing. In 1903 W. E. B. Du Bois spoke of the Fisks and their legacy in his classic book *The Souls of Black Folk,* as follows: "Since their day they have been imitated—sometimes well, by the singers of Hampton and Atlanta, sometimes ill, by straggling quartettes.

Caricature has sought again to spoil the quaint beauty of the music, and has filled the air with many debased melodies which vulgar ears scarce know from the real."[9]

The *Freeman,* a black newspaper, described the state of affairs in even more vivid terms in 1901. The occasion was the debut of the Tennessee Jubilee Singers, a group evidently dedicated to raising standards in the field.

> It is the ambition of the company to rescue jubilee singing from the mire of mediocrity, and place it on the high plane left vacant by the Donavin and the original Fisk companies. The rule in the organization of jubilee companies has been about two real singers with six or seven very, very rotten ones. Good people, owing to the cheap salaries of these "punk babies," have been forced to seek more profitable lines. The Tennesseans will set the pace in the hope there will be other companies of its kind to follow. The more good companies there are the better it is for all parties concerned. The rotten singers, along with the "whiskey heads," must be put on the incline plane of popular disapproval and sent down to oblivion.[10]

Spirituals were mocked in vaudeville and on early records. One example is a popular routine called "A Characteristic Negro Medley," first recorded by white quartets on Edison and Columbia in 1902 and filled with stereotypes of gambling, fighting with razors, and chicken-stealing. In the middle of the record the quartet breaks into the spiritual "Keep a-Hammering on My Soul," complete with verses about gambling, bedbugs, and fleas.[11] In the even more popular "A Coon Wedding in Southern Georgia," white singers imitated a "jubilee quartet" singing "Hail Jerusalem" and "Hallelujah to the Lamb." "Coon Wedding" was first recorded in 1900 and appeared on numerous labels, including Victor, Columbia, Edison, Zonophone, American, Busy Bee, and Indestructible.[12] Spirituals were in danger of being marginalized.

Such was the sorry state of affairs when, around 1898, a twenty-five-year-old black faculty member named John Wesley Work II (1872–1925) organized a new "official" Fisk Jubilee Singers, which embarked on several fundraising tours. Work not only led the group but served as first tenor and, with his brother Frederick J. Work, was a pioneering black folklorist. John and Frederick Work published a number of landmark collections, including *New Jubilee Songs as Sung by the Fisk Jubilee Singers* and *Folk Songs of the American Negro,* enriching the troupe's repertoire even further.[13]

First Recordings

In 1909, as he was about to embark on a new tour, John Work reached an exclusive agreement with the Victor Talking Machine Company which would bring the Singers' music to both a contemporary audience far larger than those in the previous forty-odd years and to us as well. This was a bold move on the company's part, and quite a departure from the repertoire then on record. Victor catalogs of this period were redolent of white, middle-class America, with pictures of male singers stiffly posed in suits and ties and ladies in formal dress, often with large hats. All were

The Fisk Quartet that recorded for Victor in 1909. *Left to right:* King, Myers, Ryder, Work. (Courtesy of Doug Seroff)

white. There was not a black or Asian face to be seen in the Victor General catalog, and little to suggest any sort of music outside of the European tradition. The Fisks would be the first respectable blacks in the neighborhood.

During December 1909 a quartet from the larger Fisk chorus visited the Victor studios in Camden, New Jersey, four times, recording twelve titles, ten of which would eventually be issued. Most of these were completed in one or two takes, testimony to the practiced professionalism of the quartet, which at this time consisted of Work, second tenor James A. Myers, first bass Alfred King, and bass/baritone Noah Ryder. It was the first time the music of the Fisks had ever been committed to record.

Technical limitations no doubt dictated that only a male quartet from the Fisk Jubilee Singers would record. Fortunately, the four chosen recorded quite well (not all voices did). Moreover, it appears that the singers were given considerable artistic freedom by Victor. The repertoire was that featured in their concerts and the performance style was the same as that employed on numerous future recordings on different labels—suggesting that it was *their* style, not Victor's. These recordings may not reflect the way African American fieldhands had sung these songs before the Civil War, but they do appear to be a good representation of the way they were presented in concert by the Fisks.[14]

The repertoire initially recorded was varied, no doubt reflecting the strongest titles then in the Fisks' program. Upbeat numbers such as "Little David" and "Golden Slippers" (which is not the James A. Bland minstrel song) had an energetic, clean sound, with tenors Work or Myers taking the lead and the others answering in a classic call-and-response arrangement. (I believe Work is the lead on the former, Myers on the latter.) "Swing Low, Sweet Chariot" and "I Couldn't Hear Nobody

Pray" were slower, with the four voices interweaving, but quite distinct. "Roll, Jordan, Roll," which is sometimes performed in an almost dirge-like manner, is notable here for its oddly shifting harmonies. These are unique and practiced performances by an obviously well-rehearsed group. As on all Fisk recordings, the group sang unaccompanied.

Perhaps the least successful number, interestingly, is Stephen Foster's "Old Black Joe," which had been widely recorded by white basses and baritones. The Fisk bass is not particularly resonant and the arrangement undistinguished. At heart, "Old Black Joe" is a white man's "Southern song." It is perhaps for similar reasons that Victor chose not to issue the one other Foster song recorded, "My Old Kentucky Home," which would have been even more familiar to record buyers from multitudinous earlier versions. Victor alone had seven versions of the song in its 1910 catalog.[15]

Two of the ten titles recorded were recitations by Reverend Myers of poems by the famous black poet Paul Laurence Dunbar (1872–1906). These are extraordinary sound documents, a rare example of serious spoken-word recordings in this era, and apparently the first time Dunbar's poetry had been recorded. (He was also a lyricist.) Moreover, they are presented as performed in concert by the leading black vocal ensemble of the day.

Dunbar was highly regarded by the black establishment for his sensitive depiction of life in a simpler, pre–Civil War era, although his work has not been kindly received by many modern critics. For one thing his most famous work is in dialect, which fairly or unfairly is considered bad form today. These are simple scenes from the dusty roads of the Old South, rarely mentioning the horrible injustices suffered by black people at the hands of white society.[16] Reverend Myers reads both of these examples forcefully and with obvious feeling, without excessive exaggeration. "Banjo Song" is about the joy brought to an old man by that instrument ("music from that banjo sets my cabin all a-ring"), while "When Malindy Sings" humorously extols the virtues of the best church singer in town. Supposedly about Dunbar's mother, it was perhaps his most famous single poem.

> Easy 'nough fu' folks to hollah,
> Lookin' at de lines an' dots,
> When dey ain't no once kin sence it,
> An' de chune comes in, in spots . . .
>
> Y'ought to hyeah dat gal a-wa'blin',
> Robins, la'ks, an' all dem things,
> Heish dey moufs an' hides dey faces,
> When Malindy sings.[17]

The manner in which these recordings were presented to the public suggests that they were considered quite different from what had appeared on record before. For one thing, Victor treated the music with some respect, describing it as "folk" music, a term rarely seen in record catalogs up to this time. Virtually all recordings of black-related material prior to this date had been lumped into the general category of "coon songs." No one was likely to call the Fisk repertoire that.

Victor was clearly proud to have signed such a prestigious group. In announcing the first four titles in February 1910 it said, "The Jubilee Songs collected and introduced to the world by Fisk University, and which might be called Negro Folk Songs, are without parallel among musical productions. They touch the heart with their pathos; and although intensely religious, they sometimes excite to laughter by their quaint conceptions of religious ideas or Biblical facts. Kept fresh and living by contact with the people, and sung by trained vocalists who are thoroughly in sympathy with the emotional nature of their originators, they have a unique and powerful appeal to all classes."[18]

The label also went to great lengths to assure its customers that these singers were the real thing, the world-famous Fisk Jubilee Singers. The introductory copy traced the history of the Jubilee Singers since 1871, extolled Fisk University as housing "practically the only musical conservatory for Negroes in the world," and described the voices on the record as the "genuine Fisk Quartet," not to be confused with the many imitators still active. To emphasize the latter point, pictures of Work, Myers, King, and Ryder were printed, and their names shown on the label of the initial twelve-inch disc. Later, when the somewhat cluttered Victor label was simplified by the removal of several lines of patent information (the 1914 "bat-wing label"), their names were included on the ten-inch discs as well. It was very unusual for a record label in this era to contain a personnel listing.

As the first "serious" African American recordings to be widely distributed, the Fisk recordings would become quite influential. Still, they were seen basically as novelties for Victor's overwhelmingly white clientele. The religious references were presented as "quaint" and perhaps even humorous.

Additional titles were announced in the March, April, and June 1910 Victor supplements. The March release was accompanied by a picture of Jubilee Hall on the Fisk campus ("erected by efforts of the original company of Fisk Jubilee Singers"), and the boast, "The records of the Fisk singers have attracted wide notice, and the announcement that the Victor had secured their exclusive services was looked upon as another evidence of the enterprise of the Company. . . . This month two famous old Jubilee songs are presented, and the correct and authentic renditions given by the Quartet are most interesting, in view of the indifferent way these numbers have been sometimes done in the past."[19]

The success of the 1909 recordings naturally led to a demand for more, and in February 1911 the quartet returned to the Victor studios for three more sessions. The membership was the same except that King had been replaced by baritone Leon P. O'Hara. This time the quartet stuck to the repertoire they knew best, and all ten sides recorded were issued. This second batch was dominated by somewhat less well-known songs, however, and sales do not seem to have been quite as large as for the first group. Two of the five releases were dropped from the catalog within four years, although the others remained available until 1926.

Most of the 1911 titles were upbeat numbers, dominated by the strong tenor voice of John W. Work. The other members generally harmonized, or sometimes hummed in the background as in "My Soul Is a Witness." On "Band of Gideon" the two tenors harmonized. Even more than in the 1909 recordings, these seemed to be a showcase for the first tenor. Once again Reverend Myers offered recitations of two Dunbar poems, "In the Morning" and "I Like to Hear the Old Tunes . . . in the Old Fashioned Way."

Victor welcomed the quartet back to its catalog with long write-ups and pictures of Myers and Jubilee Hall. Evidently Victor felt these recordings had a nostalgia value. As one announcement noted, "everybody who is more than forty years old, and many who are less, will remember the Fisk Jubilee Singers who traveled through the country from 1871 to 1878, singing the old plantation songs of the South with a sweetness and fervor that was never surpassed."[20]

The members of the quartet were again named in the supplement and, for a time at least, on the record labels as well. The supplement text was at first largely repeated from previously used copy, but in June 1911 Victor added some new information.

> Many of the songs which have been harmonized by the Fisk Singers were brought to the University by students who learned them from their mothers; or at the "big meetings" (camp meetings) and the "basket meetings"—gatherings of negroes who brought food enough to last them through an all-day service of song and prayer. Students are also sent out among the plantations to collect these almost forgotten songs. One young negro was out six weeks during the past summer and brought back more than seventy songs. Not all of these, of course, could be used, but some of the finest songs now in the repertoire of the quartet were taken from this collection.[21]

And in July 1911:

> An interesting feature of one of the Fisk Quartet's recent tours was the concert given at the Henry Street Settlement in New York, when the Quartet sang many of their songs for the people of the neighborhood. Never, perhaps, in the history of settlement work have representatives of so many different races been brought together. The singers, sons of slaves and freedmen, gave the folk-songs of their own race, which differed so widely in character from those of the various peoples in the audience, composed mainly of immigrants—Russians, Polish Jews, Italians, etc. The concert was a great success in every way, the audience evincing the liveliest interest in every number given.[22]

It is fortunate that the Fisk Singers signed with Victor, the world's largest record company, which ensured not only high technical quality but also wide distribution (although not, apparently, outside the United States).[23] Spirituals were already known, of course, through songbooks, sheet music, and the Fisks' own live performances, but they had infrequently been available on record. A search of the catalogs of the Big Three record companies of the day—Victor, Columbia, and Edison—for the years just prior to 1910 reveals no versions of spirituals such as "Little David" or "Swing Low." The Standard Quartette in the mid-1890s and the Dinwiddie Colored Quartet in 1902 had recorded some such material, but their records had limited distribution and were long out of print. A great many Americans, black and white, were no doubt introduced to black concert-hall music by these historic recordings.

The appearance of the high-quality Fisk recordings had no noticeable effect on the vast market for coarser black fare. In fact, on the page opposite the announcement of the first Fisk release, Victor advertised "Down Where the Big Bananas Grow" by white comedians Collins and Harlan as "another of those real darky shouts by the ever welcome 'Kings of Comedy.'" Nor did all blacks necessarily appreciate spirituals, which some considered reminders of slave days. In December 1909 black students at Howard University protested when they were asked to sing such songs.[24]

The Singers accepted an engagement with Edison while in the New York area in December 1911. Either the exclusive Victor contract expired during 1911, or it covered only lateral disc recording, as opposed to Edison's vertically cut cylinders.

Only two members remained from the quartet that had recorded for Victor. J. W. Work was first tenor and leader. The new second tenor was twenty-four-year-old Roland W. Hayes, a strong-willed but very talented singer who had left Fisk University the previous year after a dispute with a faculty member. Hayes was now studying voice in Boston and hoped to establish himself as a concert tenor—no mean ambition for a black man in 1911. Despite many obstacles, he would eventually succeed beyond anyone's wildest dreams and become an important recording artist in his own right. It is a testament to Work's artistic taste and open-mindedness that he was willing to offer Hayes a position after the young man's problems at Fisk. Completing the lineup were Leon P. O'Hara, now listed as a bass, and Charles Wesley, both graduates of Fisk then studying at Yale University. Both were said to have had "several years experience with the Jubilee Quartet."[25]

Nine selections were recorded during the last week of December, seven of them duplicating material previously released on Victor. New were "Crossing the Bar" and the infectious "All Over This World."

Weepin' and-a moanin' will soon be over with,
Soon be over with, soon be over with,
Weepin' and a-moanin' will soon be over with,
All over this world . . .

Thanks to the detailed records kept by the Edison company we know that on December 27 the quartet was paid $1,500 for its work, a very substantial sum, and that in addition to nine four-minute cylinders they recorded two experimental, vertically cut discs. The discs were never released (Edison did not enter the disc business until 1913).

Despite the longer playing time of the Edison Amberol cylinders (up to four minutes versus three for the ten-inch Victors), the quartet used identical arrangements and tempos as on the earlier recordings. And although two of the four members had changed, the sound is quite similar to the Victors due to the dominance of Work's lead tenor, which was alternately soaring ("Little David") and fervent ("Great Camp Meeting"). In fact on most Fisk recordings of this period the remainder of the quartet served primarily as background for Work, richly textured but without other standout individual voices. Even the strong tenor of Roland Hayes, who would become the most famous singer to come out of the Fisk chorus, is not distinctly audible, at least on the examples I have heard.[26]

Unfortunately, the technical quality of these cylinders is inferior to that of the Victor discs. Edison introduced the four-minute wax Amberol cylinder in 1908 to combat the rising popularity of Victor and Columbia discs (which ran for three or four minutes, depending on size, compared to the two-minute length of Edison's earlier cylinders). The Amberol's fine grooves were prone to breakdown, and the examples I have heard are much less clear than contemporary Victor discs or than Edison's own celluloid cylinders, which were introduced the following year.

All nine cylinders were released as a group in May 1912, accompanied by a special four-page flyer picturing the quartet and describing its members, Fisk University, and the repertoire. Although Edison, too, was proud to have signed the famous quartet, its descriptions of "Negro Songs" were clearly written with curious white patrons in mind. The copywriter takes an "us versus them" point of view, depicting the music as quaint and even peculiar.

> Many of us have never attended a negro camp-meeting, but it is a matter of common knowledge that the negro is highly imaginative and deeply religious, being particularly susceptible of religious exhortations at the hands of professional revivalists. When the negro "gets religion" his feelings are generally best expressed by songs, usually a fanciful adaptation of the scenes and deeds recorded in Scripture.
>
> The Fisk University Jubilee Quartet has sung for the Edison some of the very best and most typical of these campmeeting songs, expressing in the negro's own inimitable way his Biblical ideas, his picture of Heaven and his dread of certain sins. "Roll, Jordan, Roll" and "The Great Campmeeting" are excellent examples of the racial peculiarity of negro music—the flat seventh in place of the usual natural in the scale.[27]

Another Edison publication took an even more condescending tone, saying, "It is through [the Fisks'] untiring efforts that we have our present-day knowledge of the old-time darkey's religious passion. Being superstitious and of a highly imaginative turn of mind, he took a great many religious fables and allegories too literally, as many of the old songs show."[28]

These cylinders may have been intended primarily for whites, but they were sold throughout the country. Edison's dealer newsletter, the *Edison Phonograph Monthly,* stated that "freight shipment of these records was begun about February 26, starting with the Southern territories and working North and West as rapidly as possible. These records may be placed on sale as soon as they are received."[29]

Despite the introductory publicity, the Edison cylinders were on sale for only five months. When the company abruptly replaced wax cylinders with sturdier Blue Amberol celluloid cylinders in October 1912, the Fisk recordings were not reissued in the new format. For the next eight years all of them were out of print. In 1920 the lively "All Over This World" was reissued as a Blue Amberol, and during 1926–27 seven more of the 1911 recordings were released in that format. However by this time cylinder sales were practically nonexistent, and Edison was obviously combing his vault for material to reissue. Nevertheless, the virtually unbreakable celluloid cylinders are found at least as often as the fragile wax versions of 1912.

Under Work's direction the Fisks continued to tour during the early 1910s, although membership was constantly changing (Roland Hayes remained with the group only a short time). The Victor records sold in steadily increasing quantities, further spreading their fame.

The influence of the early Fisk recordings was quickly felt within the recording industry. In mid-1910 Columbia released the first recordings by Kitty Cheatham (1864–1945), a white performer and diseuse, who featured respectful renditions of Negro folk music in her concerts. Some very interesting and rarely recorded material appears on these records, including "Scandalize My Name" and "When Malindy Sings." Cheatham later recorded titles including "Swing Low, Sweet Chariot" and "Walk in Jerusalem Just Like John" for Victor in 1916.[30]

Jealous that Victor had snared the prestigious Fisks, Columbia also attempted to cash in on the demand for spirituals in 1912 by bringing out a disc by an unknown but apparently black quartet called the Apollo Jubilee Quartette. In 1914 Columbia issued two Will Marion Cook songs by Cook's own Afro-American Folk Song Singers, a black chorus. Neither of these discs sold well. In early 1915 Victor upped the ante by releasing the first discs by another famous black aggregation, the Tuskegee Institute Singers (a double male quartet).

In the fall of 1915 Columbia scored a coup by luring the Fisk Quartet away from Victor and signing them to its own exclusive contract. It had evidently been trying to secure their services for three years. Columbia was a major label with a large roster of famous talent, but the arrival of the Fisks at its New York City studios was something of an event, as described in the following newspaper account: "The Singers . . . sang one song. J. C. Jell, manager of the recording department, then called all of the employees of the company together, telling them that they were to hear something extraordinary. When asked by the Singers for an endorsement, he said, 'Write any endorsement you please and sign it with my name. You can't be too extravagant in your expression. I never heard anything equal to this.'"[31]

Unlike Victor and Edison, Columbia did not identify the individual members, but the quartet now consisted of lead tenor John Work, second tenor and reader James A. Myers, baritone J. Everett Harris, and bass Lemuel L. Foster. The quartet immediately set about recording its most popular Victor titles for Columbia in a series of six sessions held in New York in October 1915 and February 1916. Their "Swing Low," "Shout All Over God's Heaven," and "Couldn't Hear Nobody Pray" would now be found on Columbia as well as Victor. In addition there was new material, including "Oh Mary, Don't You Weep, Don't You Mourn," "Steal Away to Jesus," and "In That Great Gettin' Up Mawnin'" (which is in slow tempo and is not the modern upbeat number). Twelve titles were released, seven of which had previously been available on Victor. Three titles went unissued, "Old Black Joe" and two recitations by Reverend Myers of Paul Laurence Dunbar poems.

The Fisks continued to use their familiar arrangements on these new recordings, combining the strong tenor lead of John W. Work with the closely woven background harmonies of the other three members. For example, "There Is a Light Shining for Me" and "Oh Mary, Don't You Weep" have Work deftly interweaving with the quartet, leading to a rhythmic refrain. Only "Swing Low" sounds different from previous performances. It is a rather doleful rendition with an unusual falsetto lead.

Columbia announced the first of its Fisk recordings with obvious pride in its January 1916 supplement. Columbia, like Victor, considered them to be novelties. The term "spiritual" was printed in quotes.

The old negro "spirituals" can quite logically be called American folk songs. Naturally, every American will want some native folk songs in his musical collection. With this idea in mind, the Columbia has made an exclusive contract with the Fisk University Jubilee Singers to sing a collection of their most famous numbers.

The humor, simplicity, pathos and imagination of the whole negro race is sung into the rhythmical mono-melodies of "Swing Low Sweet Chariot" and "Shout All Over God's Heaven," two "spirituals" typical of all that makes negro music so intense and soulful. The recordings are flawless—you can hear the negro voices with all the sweetness and pathos so connected with this character of singing.[32]

This announcement was accompanied by a small line drawing of the quartet, standing together informally, but no identification of the individual members.

Later issues were also treated as folksong novelties for the white trade. Of "There Is a Light Shining for Me," Columbia observed: "It is almost a mystery how words, in themselves almost ludicrous, can be sung with such inborn religious spirit that they seem serious and solemn. 'There Is a Light Shining for Me' is such a negro 'spiritual.' 'O Mary, Don't You Weep,' however, is certainly one of the strangest songs of sympathy one could imagine, but to those who understand the true negro character, thoroughly typical."[33] Of "Couldn't Hear Nobody Pray," "one of the famous 'rocking' songs. When sung at the spiritual meetings the men, women and children rock and sway to the music, beating their arms and crooning accompaniments to the wail of the tenor and the reiterated complaint of the bass as the words go on and on, 'I Couldn't Hear Nobody Pray . . .'"[34] Of "Good News, the Chariot's Coming," "it almost seems as if the gift of singing has been given the colored race to compensate for the 'slings and arrows of outrageous fortune.' Surely no other race could sing such a hopesong as 'Good News' with such a mixture of joy and pathos."[35] In fact, all of the early Columbia titles were identified on the labels as "folk songs." In most cases no authors or arrangers were given, although some Columbia issues of "Little David" specified "arrangement of Fisk University Singers."

Although "Little David" was one of the Fisks' most popular numbers, which they recorded for virtually every label they were associated with over the years, Columbia did not immediately release the version it recorded in 1915. It finally saw the light of day in 1920, backed with "Steal Away to Jesus," a title long featured in the Fisks' concerts but not previously recorded by them. The Columbia recordings also appeared on other labels. Unlike its rivals, Columbia routinely leased its masters to smaller labels, and Fisk recordings from 1915 and 1916 can be found on Standard, Consolidated, Silvertone, and probably others not yet identified. At least two titles, "Shout All Over God's Heaven" and "Good News," were released on Columbia's affiliated label in England.

Columbia now claimed the Fisks as exclusive artists, but this apparently covered only lateral-cut discs. In July 1916 the quartet made three more vertical-cut tests for Edison on disc. Thomas A. Edison himself evaluated these tests. Cantankerous as ever, the tone-deaf inventor scribbled in his notebook, "might take one disc of this trash as a novelty."[36] Nothing by the Fisks was issued on Edison discs.

The much-in-demand Fisk Quartet was more favorably received by another, smaller label specializing in vertical-cut discs. The Starr label was the initial imprint of the Starr Piano Company of Richmond, Indiana, which would later gain fame for its jazz-oriented Gennett label in the 1920s. Starr had very limited distribution, but the Fisks appear to have recorded at least four titles for the company in its New York studios. The thick, fine-grooved discs were rather crudely recorded and while an example in my collection undeniably features Fisk arrangements of two of their trademark songs, it cannot be certain whether the quartet members are the same as on the Columbia discs. It is likely that they are. American-made Starr recordings (not to be confused with the Canadian Starr label of a few years later) are quite rare today.

A picture of the Fisk University Singers in the June 1, 1916, *New York Age* showed a sextet: Work, Myers, Harris, Foster, Mrs. John W. Work, and Miss Johnella Frazer. This is the group that was appearing in concerts at the time, although only the four men recorded. At the end of 1916 John W. Work was fired as leader of the university-sponsored Singers. His promotion of spirituals had long been vehemently opposed by music department chairman Jennie Robinson (who also ousted Roland Hayes from Fisk). Fayette McKenzie, who assumed the presidency of the university in 1915, sided with her and dismissed Work from most of his positions the following year.[37] Despite Work's enormous contributions to the university, and to the cause of black concert music in America, he was defeated in his lifetime by the intense intramural politics of Fisk.

The Singers then became a professional group led by James A. Myers (c. 1877–1928). According to researcher Doug Seroff, Myers was never on the faculty.[38] However, from the early 1900s to the 1940s, he and his wife, separately or together, were continually associated with the Singers.

By late 1919 Columbia was ready for more recordings by the group. Sessions were held in December of that year, yielding both remakes of earlier titles and new songs, but only two of the many recordings made were issued: "Most Done Traveling" and "Oh! Reign Massa Jesus Reign." The Columbia files say only that the rejected sides were "unacceptable to [music] committee."

Sales and Influence of the Early Fisk Recordings

The Fisk Singers recorded for the two largest labels in the United States, which provided distribution and marketing in every corner of the country. Columbia claimed 17,000 dealers throughout the United States,[39] while Victor was even more omnipresent. An artist I once interviewed, who had recorded for Victor during the acoustic era, put it this way: "The Victor company, the big Victor company, was like the United States postage stamp in many ways . . . long before you were born. Every place you went there was a Victor store . . . every inky dinky town, not only in the biggest cities."[40]

Both the Victor and Columbia recordings sold steadily during the late 1910s. Although we do not have sales figures for Victor, fairly complete production data does exist for Columbia. It shows the Fisks to have enjoyed steady sales from their initial release on that label in 1916 until the mid-1920s, with a surge in sales during and immediately after World War I. Sales during this period were much smaller than in our day, and the totals are impressive for their time (see table 4). The boom in

Table 4. The Fisk Jubilee Singers: Estimated Total
Columbia Shipments

	Number of Discs in Catalog	Shipments
1916	4	25,000
1917	5	25,000
1918	5	80,000
1919	6	200,000
1920	7	170,000
1921	8	50,000
1922	11	60,000
1923	14	90,000
1924	15	50,000
1925	15	30,000
1926	17	50,000
1927	16	10,000
1928	13	3,500
1929	13	2,000
1930	7	300
		845,800

Note: Copies shipped and copies sold are not necessarily the same,
of course, but given the ongoing shipments of catalog titles such as
these, the figures are undoubtedly close.

1919–20 was aided by a huge surge in record sales overall, coupled with a limited
supply of new releases, and the 1921 decline was caused by an economic recession
that devastated the entertainment industry in that year.

Although individual Fisk records may not have been major "hits," some accu-
mulated substantial sales over time. A best-selling record on Columbia prior to
World War I might ship 20,000 copies during its catalog life; during the 1919–20
boom years this rose to perhaps 50,000 or more (see table 5).

Figures are not available for Victor, but it is apparent from the long catalog life
of the 1909 and 1911 recordings and the frequency with which they are found today that they were also bestsellers, probably bigger than the Columbias. Most remained available until the end of the acoustic era, and the last of them ("Swing
Low") was not deleted until 1928. Copies found today generally bear labels that date
from the mid-1910s to the early 1920s, and it was probably during that period that

Table 5. Shipments of Selected Columbia Records by the Fisk Singers, 1916–21

	Released	Copies Shipped
"Swing Low" / "Shout All Over" (A1883)	Jan. 1916	108,100
"Couldn't Hear Nobody" / "River of Jordan" (A1932)	June 1916	103,300
"Steal Away" / "Little David" (A2803)	Jan. 1920	103,100
"Oh! Reign" / "Most Done" (A2901)	June 1920	83,600
"Ezekiel" / "You're Going to Reap" (A3370)	May 1921	60,800

Note: Figures are missing for several well-known numbers from 1916–17, specifically "Oh Mary, Don't You
Weep" (A1895), "Great Camp Meeting" (A2072), and "Great Gettin' Up Mawnin'" (A2342). These were also
probably in the 80,000–100,000 range.

Victor sales were also at their height. In terms of overall record production Victor was considerably larger than Columbia. Based on the Columbia production figures shown earlier, I would estimate total Fisk sales on Victor plus Columbia to be well in excess of two million copies. The Fisks were already famous when they began recording in 1909, and for many years they had no real competition in the field of recorded spirituals. They were probably the second best-selling African American vocal artists of the pre-1920 period, after Broadway star Bert Williams.

Who bought and played these millions of records? We cannot learn the answer from contemporary press coverage or reviews. The record industry received very little attention in the general press at the time, and until the 1920s recordings were rarely reviewed or even commented on outside of the promotional literature produced by the record companies themselves. While reviews appeared as early as 1906 in Germany, the first independent consumer periodicals devoted to recordings were the *Gramophone* in England (1923) and the *Phonograph Monthly Review* in the United States (1926).[41]

The phonograph had spread deep into American middle- and lower-middle-class homes long before this. The 1910s were boom years for phonograph sales, driven by heavy marketing and extraordinarily wide dealer networks controlled until late in the decade by three companies: Victor, Columbia, and Edison. Between 1910 and 1920 approximately 10 million phonographs were manufactured in the United States, including 2.2 million during 1919 alone.[42] There were 24 million households in the United States in 1920,[43] so penetration by then had presumably reached 40 percent to 50 percent of all homes (some phonographs made prior to 1910 were no doubt still in use).

The mantra of the phonograph industry in the 1910s was "a phonograph in every home," and Thomas A. Edison even went so far as to declare, "There is no family in America so poor that it can not buy a talking machine, provided that there is any fund at all available for amusement."[44] Literature from both companies and articles in trade papers make it clear that the primary sales target was middle-class, white consumers. Dealer-oriented publications, such as the *Voice of the Victor* and the *Columbia Record,* and the leading trade paper, *Talking Machine World,* regularly ran articles giving sales tips and exhorting the sales force. The subject of black consumers was rarely if ever mentioned. This is not surprising. Phonographs and records were relatively expensive (records typically cost seventy-five cents to a dollar each), which ruled out most of the poor as customers. Few recordings were made specifically for the black market until the surprise success of minor-label blues records in the early 1920s.

Promotional copy for the Fisk recordings at the time of their release, previously cited, reinforces the notion that they were intended for the white trade, as does the fact that they were always released in the general numerical series rather than in a specialty "ethnic" series. This ensured the widest possible distribution to dealers. Every new release received featured treatment in the monthly catalog supplement that was the primary means of advertising new records at this time. The annual or semiannual general catalogs published by Victor and Columbia also did not just list the Fisk recordings but gave them special headings and descriptions. The Columbia catalog even included a photograph of the quartet, something usually reserved for featured artists. The records themselves, particularly the Victors and the early Columbias, are today found frequently in collections of 78s from this period, intermixed with popular tunes and novelties of the day.

One might think the Fisk records would have been a source of pride among blacks. No doubt they were for some, but throughout the 1910s there is little mention of the Fisks, and virtually no notice of their recordings, in the pages of such black publications as the *Freeman,* the *New York Age,* and the *Crisis* (the official publication of the NAACP). All of these made a point of celebrating black accomplishments in the arts. Instead we find occasional laments about the lack of serious black artists on record, a theme that continued when the first black-owned record labels were founded around 1918–21 to advance that cause.[45] Even blacks seemed to believe that the Fisks were performing primarily for whites.

Live appearances by the Fisk Jubilee Singers were generally staged in churches and concert halls, and thus accessible primarily to the subset of the population that frequented such venues. Sheet music and songbooks of their repertoire were available, although it is questionable how often middle-class whites sang "Swing Low, Sweet Chariot" at their parlor pianos.

The phonograph record, on the other hand, reached almost every stratum of white society, directly or indirectly, and required no personal involvement with the music. It is probably not an exaggeration to say that the Fisks' widely distributed Victor and Columbia records introduced their music into middle-class homes across America. Indeed, these records may have helped spark the early twentieth-century interest in spirituals, which by the late 1910s had entered the performing mainstream. According to Harry T. Burleigh biographer Anne Key Simpson, Burleigh's 1917 arrangement of "Deep River" was performed in concert by John McCormack, Evan Williams, Oscar Seagle, Marcella Sembrich, Mary Jordan (to whom it was dedicated), and "nearly every other concert artist in subsequent years."[46] During World War I the *Musical Courier* published a listing of "Songs the Soldiers Like" which placed "Negro spirituals" in first position.[47]

Standards such as "Swing Low, Sweet Chariot" were recorded by such prestigious artists as Mabel Garrison and Dame Nellie Melba on the Victor Red Seal (classical) label.[48] The music was also adopted by the pop mainstream. Bandleader Vincent Lopez released a medley of spirituals in fox-trot tempo,[49] and the Burleigh arrangement of "Deep River" became so well known that songwriters Henry Creamer and Turner Layton adapted it into a popular song called "Dear Old Southland" (1921), which was widely recorded. This renaissance of interest in spirituals in the early 1900s, and the effect it had on the spread of other forms of African American culture, deserves to be more thoroughly studied by scholars.

The Fisk Jubilee Singers in the 1920s and Beyond

Beginning with the 1919 sessions Columbia stopped calling the group the Fisk University Male Quartet and began billing it as the Fisk University Jubilee Singers. Some researchers believe this means that the recording group became a mixed quintet at this time, with Mrs. Myers taking part.[50] Indeed, from 1923 to 1925 the catalog carried a large picture of the "Fisk University Jubilee Singers" showing five members, including Mrs. Myers (dressed rather severely in short hair, a dark suit, and a tie).

While it is obviously not known who sang on the unissued sides, all but one of the discs released from the 1919–24 sessions are explicitly identified as by a "male quartet" on the label, in the Columbia supplement, and/or in the company files.[51] In addition, all of them *sound* like a male quartet, with no female voice in evidence. It is my belief that the recordings are as labeled, by a quartet consisting of the four men, without Mrs. Myers's vocal participation. The recordings made in 1919 are presumably by the quartet that was performing at the time: J. A. Myers, tenor R. W. Houston, baritone Alfred T. Clark, and bass Theodore H. Moore. "Most Done Traveling" and "Oh! Reign Massa Jesus" are both moderate tempo numbers and not as distinctive harmonically as many of the sides by Work's quartet.

Columbia said little of substance about these and most later Fisk issues, preferring to rhapsodize about the exotic nature of spirituals in general. A Eurocentric attitude was certainly in evidence as the supplement spoke of "their music" and "us": "Where for ages the Congo has cut its golden thread through the dark green of the African jungles negro music was born. Through all the vicissitudes of the negro race their music still brings to us echoes of distant barbaric melody. In the singing of the Fisk University Jubilee Singers there is a rhythm as of vanished beating feet and the monotony of the simple three chord harmony of primitive music. The singing of this negro quartette is very appealing."[52]

The Fisks returned to the Columbia studios exactly one year later for eight additional sessions. The December 1920 sessions were more productive than those in 1919, producing twelve new titles for issue, as well as remakes of earlier selections. The quartet members were the same as in 1919, except that Carl Barbour had replaced R. W. Houston as second tenor.

The new selections included two that are now standards of the spiritual repertoire ("Ezekiel Saw de Wheel" and "I Ain't Goin' to Study War No More") and several others that showed promise. Unfortunately, Myers's arrangements were much blander than those of his predecessor. No longer did the lead tenor soar or the quartet evoke rich harmonic textures. Reverend Myers was reported to be a charismatic performer in person, but on most of these recordings there was a sort of mellow crooning, while a tenor or baritone took an occasional, uninspired lead. "Were You There (When They Crucified My Lord)," which could be electrifying when performed by Roland Hayes, for example, here sounds drained of emotion. "Roll, Jordan, Roll" sounds like a dirge. The Fisks had become perhaps too dignified.

A few items stand out. "You May Carry Me, You May Bury Me" has some interesting four-part harmony in the refrain; "I Done Done What You Told Me to Do" is a rhythm number; and "I Ain't Goin' to Study War No More" served as the basis of the modern pop song, "Down by the Riverside." Four sides from the 1920 sessions went unreleased, including "Po Mourner's Got a Home at Last" and Reverend Myers's two Dunbar recitations, "When Malindy Sings" and "In the Morning." The rest were issued over the next three years to steadily decreasing sales.

It took a series of recordings by a young black bass singer to spark a new wave of interest in recorded spirituals. Victor first recorded twenty-seven-year-old Paul Robeson in 1925, and over the next two years his fervent renditions of traditional spirituals—including duets with his accompanist Lawrence Brown—were bestsellers. Robeson showed that songs like "Swing Low," "Ezekiel," and "Bye and Bye" could be infused with real energy and emotion, and suddenly the refined, stately versions by the Fisks seemed a little old-fashioned by comparison.

Quite a few other spiritual singing groups appeared on record during the 1920s; it almost seemed that every label now wanted to have a few of these records in its catalog. Some examples were the Norfolk Jubilee Quartet and the Elkins-Payne Jubilee Quartet on Paramount, the Pace Jubilee Singers and the Utica Institute Jubilee Singers on Victor, the Birmingham Jubilee Singers on Columbia, the Dixie Jubilee Singers on Brunswick, the Biddle University Quintet on Pathé, Bryant's Jubilee Quartet on Gennett, the Commonwealth Quartet on Banner, and the Cotton Belt Quartet on Vocalion. None of these approached the fame of the Fisks, but they meant that the Fisk Singers no longer had the field to themselves.

It was once believed that the Fisks recorded for Edison in 1921 under the pseudonym "The Southern 4."[53] The repertoire is that of the Fisks ("Couldn't Hear Nobody Pray," "Swing Low," and so on). However, the Edison announcement of the group in May 1922 stated that they were all believed to be graduates of Hampton Institute.[54] This appears to be an example of the Edison practice of "cloning" celebrity artists it could not get with imitators who sang the same material in the same style. For example, someone named Glen Ellison did Harry Lauder songs for Edison, while Guy Hunter imitated Bert Williams. Some sources have also confused the Bethel Jubilee Quartet with the Fisks, since two of the latter's 1909 Victor sides were remade by this group in 1924 and even released with the same catalog number.[55]

The Fisk Jubilee Singers continued to make appearances and in 1924 announced their first European tour since 1878. Shortly before their departure they visited the Columbia studios for another series of recordings, in April and May 1924. The lineup was now Myers, Barbour, Horatio O'Bannon, baritone, and Ludie David Collins, bass. Although seven titles were recorded on four different dates, with as many as six takes per title, only two were issued. "Hope I'll Join the Band" was perhaps the more interesting of the two, with nicely developed counterpoint between the lead and the rest of the quartet. However, better efforts were to come.

The 1924 European tour was successful and was followed by another in 1925. In January 1926 the Fisks returned to Columbia's New York studio to record ten selections using the new electrical recording process. Six of these had previously been released in acoustic versions, while others had been attempted acoustically but not released. A total of seven titles were issued, including a mix of old material ("Little David") and new ("Keep a'Inchin' Along").

Electrical recording, with its much wider frequency range, offered better reproduction of group harmonics, which was exactly what the Fisks needed. The 1926 recordings are a considerable advance musically over Myers's earlier efforts for Columbia. On a slow number like "Steal Away to Jesus" the delicate textures are vivid and dramatic; on an upbeat selection such as "Shout All Over God's Heaven" one can hear the group "answering" the tenor in multipart harmony, rather than the ensemble sound of the earlier versions. Although the Singers still lacked a tenor as strong as John W. Work, the voices were now distinct and engaging. This is perhaps nowhere as evident as on "Ezekiel," especially the ending chords. Overall, these new recordings must have been a revelation for those who had heard the Fisk Jubilee Singers only on acoustic records.

One of the few consumer reviews located for a Fisk recording of this period, in the *Phonograph Monthly Review,* evaluated "Keep a'Inchin' Along" and "Shout All Over God's Heaven." It gave a brief, and ultimately positive, critique: "I liked this record much better on second hearing than at first. It is almost perfect singing of negro spirituals, and almost perfect recording in the second number. The first one is marred just a bit by one or two shrill spots. Yet this is one of the few records not to be missed."[56] There are several possible reasons for the improved performances. The group may have adapted its arrangements to take advantage of the new technology, which now allowed them to sing less loudly and with more subtlety; the group may have simply improved over time; or someone other than Reverend Myers may have been directing.

The last explanation is given credence by Mrs. Myers's increased involvement in recording. For the first time Columbia did in fact record the Fisk Jubilee Singers as a quintet. The recording files indicate "5 voices" for the January 20 session, and although they do not give names it is presumably the 1924 lineup plus Mrs. Myers. Close listening to the released discs does not reveal a woman's voice being featured on any of them; she can possibly be heard in the ensemble on "Keep a'Inchin' Along." Mrs. Myers's contribution was evidently subtle. A review published in the French journal *La Musique* during the 1925 tour stated, "The woman's voice merges itself with the male voices so discreetly and with such amazing subtlety and delicacy that it is impossible for the most sensitive ear to detach it from the other voices in the ensemble." In a later interview she referred to her vocal contribution as "intoning." "I just take my voice and weave their voices together. I interlace them, going from one part to another as they need it."[57] The Fisk sound continued to be male-dominated, although with these recordings it began to evolve toward a fuller, more choral sound.

It is noteworthy that the files indicate that the same recording engineer, a Mr. Freiberg, was responsible for the 1924 (acoustic) and 1926 (electric) sessions. Perhaps by 1926 he had found a way to resolve the problems that had caused so many takes from the earlier sessions to be rejected.

As late as 1925 the Columbia catalog had fifteen Fisk discs and Victor had eight. Label styles on surviving copies suggest that both the Victors and the Columbias continued to sell well until the end of the acoustic era (1925).

Although the 1926 electrical recordings were superior in many ways to those that had gone before, they were much less successful commercially, remaining in the catalog for only a few years. By 1931 all but one ("Steal Away to Jesus") had been deleted. As noted in table 4 above, sales of Fisk recordings were fairly steady in the early 1920s, but at lower levels than during the boom years of 1919–20. In the late 1920s they declined dramatically. Sales of individual titles mirrored this trend (see table 6).

Table 6. Shipments of Selected Columbia Records by the Fisk Singers (1920s)

	Released	Copies Shipped
"Roll Jordan" / "Lord Laid His Hand" (A3657)	Oct. 1922	25,600
"Soul is Witness" / "Give Way" (A3819)	May 1923	23,700
"Another Building" / "Want to Be Ready" (A3726)	Jan. 1923	23,000
"Ain't Goin' to Study" / "Hear the Lambs" (A3596)	July 1922	17,700
"I Done Done" / "Were You There?" (A3919)	Sept. 1923	15,400
"Steal Away" / "Every Time" (562D)	Apr. 1926	13,600
"Hope I'll Join" / "Get Somebody" (163D)	Sept. 1924	12,300

In comparison, the runaway bestseller on Columbia in 1927 was a comedy monologue called "The Two Black Crows," in which white comedians Moran and Mack imitated two lazy black men. It sold over 1.3 *million* copies.

The Edison cylinders were a minor factor in disseminating the music of the Fisks. They were available only briefly in 1912, then again in the 1920s when the company reissued most of them on celluloid Blue Amberol cylinders. Why Edison did not keep these recordings available on cylinder or disc during the 1910s, when Victor and Columbia were selling large quantities of Fisk records, is a mystery. However, Edison was noted for its somewhat irrational marketing practices.

"All Over This World," which was released on Edison Blue Amberol 4045 in 1920, may have had a decent sale, as cylinder sales were still reasonably healthy in the early 1920s. By 1927, when the other seven were released, the market for cylinder records had collapsed and sales were pitifully small (see table 7).[58]

The Fisks' style of singing was passing out of vogue on record. The group remained popular in personal appearances, however. The Fisk name was by now legendary and closely associated with the way educated whites thought the old spirituals should be sung. Blacks were divided on the matter. An older generation may have appreciated the dignity their style brought to the black heritage, but a younger generation looked on it as something of a throwback. The hard-driving jazz and blues of the 1920s was closer to their language.

Fisk University itself went through a period of upheaval in the mid-1920s over similar issues. In early 1925 black students and alumni went on strike to protest the administration of President Fayette Avery McKenzie. McKenzie, a white man, had done much during the previous ten years to expand the curriculum, raise faculty sala-

Table 7. Production Totals for Edison Cylinders

	Released	Copies Manufactured
5216 "Swing Low"	Oct. 1926	1,280
5273 "Roll Jordan Roll"	Jan. 1927	985
5302 "Shout All Over God's"	Mar. 1927	995
5328 "Great Camp Meeting"	May 1927	990
5379 "Crossing the Bar"	Aug. 1927	510
5397 "Peter on the Sea"	Oct. 1927	530
5442 "Band of Gideon"	Dec. 1927	350

Note: Production figures from the Edison files. No complete figures exist for 4045.

ries, and improve facilities. He was especially effective as a fund raiser among wealthy white patrons. Although he was credited with launching a new era at the struggling university, many students and alumni resented his retention of Jim Crow practices and his perceived closeness to the white establishment. Racial pride was becoming equally important with the university's physical well-being. After a period of turmoil, which was supported by black leaders including W. E. B. Du Bois, McKenzie was forced out and replaced by Thomas Elsa Jones, who redressed grievances and during the next twenty years led Fisk through a period of unprecedented growth.[59]

During a third European tour in 1926–27 Reverend Myers suffered a heart attack that forced him to retire from singing. He died on February 16, 1928, at the age of fifty, while the Singers were on a fourth European tour. His widow, Henrietta Myers, who had been singing with the group, then became director. She led the group for the next nineteen years, always billed as Mrs. James A. Myers.

By 1935 the Singers were appearing on a transcribed radio program called *Magnolia Blossoms*. The transcriptions, some of which have survived, were made at sta-

The Fisk Jubilee Singers in the 1930s. *Left to right, top:* Billy Holland, Edward Mitchell, Arthur Bostic. *Seated:* Luther King, William Coller, Mrs. Myers, Cecil Reeves, Oswald Lampkins. (Courtesy of Doug Seroff)

tion WSM in Nashville. Another group of transcriptions for *Magnolia Blossoms* was made at WSM in 1940. The Singers' theme song on the show was "Swing Low, Sweet Chariot."[60] Also in 1935 the Singers are believed to have recorded at least eight sides at the Studebaker Theater in Chicago. The date is inferred by Seroff from information he received in an interview with member William Collier in 1983 and cannot be independently confirmed. The recordings were not released until a decade later, on Rainbow, a tiny gospel label headquartered in Winona Lake, Indiana. They must have had minuscule distribution, as neither the recordings nor the record company itself is known to most experts. Rainbow was apparently an offshoot of the 1920s gospel label of the same name, which had been founded by evangelical singer Homer Rodeheaver. Rodeheaver claimed to have a factory in Winona Lake, and the later label may have been operated from that location by his daughter.[61]

The Rainbow recordings, which were very well made, reveal the Singers now to be recording primarily as a choral group. There appear to be eight voices—a double quartet—led by Mrs. Myers, but with no other holdovers from the 1920s quartet. All except Mrs. Myers were men, and the sound is that of a male chorus as she is not individually audible. The performances are mostly straightforward, with feeling but without the multipart harmonies heard on earlier Fisk recordings. In fact, on a number such as "Dry Bones," one could be listening to Fred Waring's Pennsylvanians, a popular white chorus that also made a specialty of that song. "Ev'ry Time I Feel the Spirit" is an upbeat number featuring an engaging lead tenor, sung in a tight, rhythmic style that would be popularized in the late 1930s by the Golden Gate Quartet and other jazz-oriented groups.

The repertoire, interestingly, was not primarily old Fisk standards such as "Shout All Over God's Heaven" or "Little David," but rather spirituals that had come into vogue more recently (e.g., "Dry Bones"). All of these are "old" songs, of course, but even old songs go into and out of vogue. Six of the ten titles released on Rainbow had not previously been available by the Fisks.

Interest in traditional spiritual singing declined noticeably during the 1930s and 1940s, and many schools discontinued their singing troupes. Fisk itself decided to disband the Jubilee Singers in 1932, but Mrs. Myers—a very determined woman—refused to go along. Against the express wishes of the school administration she organized a male octet made up of the best student voices and fielded a new touring group; eventually, the university relented. Through her hard work, the Fisk Jubilee Singers remained intact and active for the next fifteen years. Finally jealousies in the music department reached such a level that in 1947 she was dismissed, and the Singers were converted back to a student chorus led by the chairman of the music department, John Wesley Work III (sweet revenge for his father's sacking more than thirty years before). The indomitable Mrs. Myers then organized her own "Famous Jubilee Singers" in order to continue her life's work of spreading the gospel of spiritual singing. After some difficult years this group toured Europe, South America, and Asia in the 1950s and recorded for the Pathé, Bullet, and Kapp labels. Belatedly honored by the university in the 1960s, Mrs. Myers died in 1968 at the age of eighty-nine.[62]

The Rainbow discs were the last known Fisk Jubilee Singers recordings issued during the 78-rpm era. Many years would elapse before the Fisk name again appeared on record, this time on three LPs issued during the mid- and late 1950s. The first was on Folkways, a specialty label devoted to preserving American folk culture of all types. Released in 1955 it presented a large mixed chorus directed by John W. Work III and prominently featuring a number of female soloists. The program included early standards ("Couldn't Hear Nobody Pray," "Were You There") along with newer material. Next came a 1957 LP on Word, a gospel label, also directed by Work. Finally in mid-1958 Harmony released a live recording of the Fisk Jubilee Singers made at a 1956 concert in Paris. Again, a large chorus dominated by female voices presented a program of Fisk standards and newer songs. Throughout the early 1900s—even under Mrs. Myers—the Singers had a very male-dominated sound, but their recordings in the LP era emphasized female voices.

The "official" Fisk Jubilee Singers toured the United States and Europe during the 1950s. John Work III retired in 1957 and was succeeded by his one-time student and later Fisk professor Matthew W. Kennedy, who led the Singers (with some gaps) until 1986.[63] The Fisk Singers, as a chorus, continue to perform to this day.

Epilogue

Since the late 1920s, releases by the Fisks have been restricted to small specialty labels with sales to match. For years their only available recording was the Folkways LP, which in later years was sold on cassette by special order. Scholarly acknowledgment of the importance of their early recordings was slow in coming, even from discographers. *Blues and Gospel Records,* the standard discographical reference in the field, deliberately omitted the Singers in its first three editions, stating that they sang principally for white audiences and had "little authentic gospel quality."[64] This

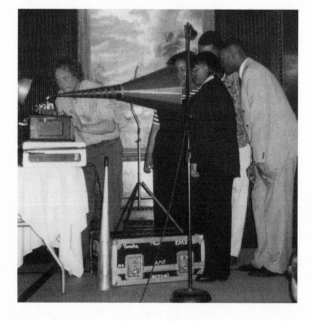

Four members of the modern Fisk Jubilee Singers record a cylinder in 1997; recording expert Peter Dilg is at the left. (Courtesy of Steven Ramm)

outrageous statement was finally removed in the fourth edition (1997), and a discography added. Also in 1997 their early twentieth-century recordings were finally reissued, by Europe's Document label.

On a spring day in 1997 in Nashville, a select audience witnessed an unusual recreation of the scene when the Fisk Jubilee Singers had made recording history. The occasion was a session at the annual conference of the Association for Recorded Sound Collections. Following my talk on the history of the Singers, a quartet from the current student chorus stepped onto the stage, positioned themselves in front of an antique recording horn, and proceeded to make a new cylinder record, on original equipment. The faint sounds that poured forth when the small wax cylinder was played back were a fitting tribute to their predecessors, the pioneers who had first embraced recording almost a century earlier.

The original Fisk University Jubilee Singers were pioneers in introducing black music into the American concert hall in the late nineteenth century, and their early and frequent use of recording in the early 1900s helped to spread that music to every corner of the country. It is unfortunate that their recorded legacy is so little recognized today.

15 Polk Miller and His Old South Quartette

Why, you might ask, would a wealthy, white, southern businessman, former Confederate soldier, and apologist for slavery be the subject of a chapter in this book? Polk Miller was a remarkable man. He organized, toured with, and recorded with a black quartet. Those recordings, made in 1909 and very nearly not released, provide perhaps the most direct aural link we have with the music of black America in antebellum times.

To appreciate Miller's contribution, it is necessary to separate his music from the social beliefs he espoused. A successful businessman who entered show business late in life, he was one of a wave of turn-of-the-century entertainers who catered to white nostalgia for the pre–Civil War South. A Confederate Army veteran and confirmed "son of the Old South," he used songs and stories to paint a rosy picture of "happy darkies" and banjos ringing 'round the old cabin door, as if slavery had been some beneficent, paternalistic system that even the slaves enjoyed. This version of history may seem repugnant today, but it was a major theme of American popular culture at the time. It was reflected in books and articles, minstrelsy, immensely popular traveling shows (e.g., *South before the War*), and songs ("Little Old Log Cabin in De Lane," "Carry Me Back to Old Virginny," "I Want to See the Old Home").

Many blacks found employment singing these songs and appearing in these traveling shows. Miller's presentation included a quartet of "genuine Negro singers," and his recordings with his group—from a rare early integrated recording session—represent a glimpse into a curious branch of American entertainment. Miller's career is particularly well documented, in part due to scrapbooks that he kept

New Edison Record Talent

POLK MILLER

POLK MILLER'S "OLD SOUTH QUARTETTE"

Polk Miller and His Old South Quartette. (*Edison Phonograph Monthly,* Jan. 1910)

in the 1890s which are now preserved in public archives.[1] Much of the following information about Miller's stage career is drawn from the clippings in these scrapbooks, augmented by new genealogical research into his background.

Miller was, as his daughter later put it, "quite a character."[2] His real name was James A. Miller, and he was born on August 2, 1844, in Grape Lawn, Virginia, a tiny hamlet in Prince Edward County, near Burkeville. He was the fifth child of Giles A. Miller, a wealthy tobacco farmer, and his wife, Jane Webster Miller. Later publicity stressed that Polk was raised on a large plantation, and public records bear this out. Giles Miller owned extensive property stretching over several counties southwest of Richmond. According to the 1860 census, his Prince Edward County holdings consisted of nearly thirteen hundred acres, with a net value of more than $35,000. He owned dozens of slaves who worked his farms. He was a prominent local citizen and a member of the state legislature.

Polk grew up surrounded by blacks in a setting of unquestioned white supremacy. An athletic youngster, he also had an ear for music and a curiosity about the songs he heard in the fields and around the slave cabins. He later reminisced, "I was raised on a plantation where niggers were thicker than hops, and it was there that I learned to 'pick upon de ole banjo.'"[3] His interest in black music (or "nigger music," as he called it) was unusual for a white boy in the South at this time. Most whites considered blacks little more than animal chattel and disparaged, or ignored completely, evidences of their culture. On some plantations music-making was forbidden. Because ruling whites tended to ignore evidences of black culture, there is little written record of music among blacks in the antebellum South.[4]

In February 1860, at the age of fifteen, Polk moved to Richmond, about fifty miles away, and took a job in the Meade and Baker store alongside his older brother, Giles Jr. (b. 1840). He later said that "when my father sent me here he told his friends, in my presence, that he wanted to get the country green off me."[5] It was a smart move. Meade and Baker was frequented by many of the important men of the city, who gathered there to discuss the issues of the day. Miller, though a country youth, learned to be comfortable around them and was welcomed into their discussions. A hard-working, intelligent youth, he attracted attention.

It was a tumultuous, exciting time for a young man who believed in preserving the Southern way of life. Just as Miller arrived in Richmond events were rapidly unfolding that would plunge American into a civil war. After years of tension and inflammatory rhetoric, the November 1860 election of Northern Republican Abraham Lincoln as president led to the secession of eleven states from the Union, followed by the formation of the Confederate States of America in early 1861. In April Southern soldiers fired on federal troops at Fort Sumter, South Carolina. Jefferson Davis was named president of the Confederacy, and after a short time Richmond became its capital. By 1862, with the war raging, Polk Miller reached eighteen and was eager to enlist in the Confederate Army. His son Withers later wrote that, "on one occasion, when waiting on Mrs. Jefferson Davis, who was a patron at the store, he remarked to her that probably that would be the last time he would have the pleasure of serving her, as he had arranged to enlist for the war. She expressed her regrets and left the store, but in a few days an order was issued by President Davis that he should be detailed to retain his position with Meade & Baker. But it did not take long before [Miller's] patriotism overcame the force of the detail and he joined the Second Company of Howitzers."[6]

Miller served with the unit in its Valley campaign and also as a hospital steward. His brother Giles served as a musician in the army band, indicating that there was more than one musically inclined sibling in the large Miller clan. Less than three years later, in April 1865, Polk was at Appomattox Court House, not far from the plantation where he had grown up, witnessing the surrender of the "Lost Cause."

The end of the war left the local economy in ruins. His father lost his slaves, his Prince Edward County plantation, and much—though not all—of his fortune. Records from 1870 show Giles Sr. in adjacent Amelia County, his estate worth a still substantial $11,000. Young Polk worked for a time on a farm outside Richmond, then took a position with the Richmond drug firm of Powhatan Dupuy. Soon he was ready to strike out on his own, and in 1871 he opened his own small drugstore at 500 East Marshall Street.[7] On November 29, 1871, he married Maude Lee Withers, the daughter of a local physician. It was at about this time that he adopted the name "Polk" Miller. He may have had his name legally changed; he used no other for the rest of his life, even on official documents. Miller and his wife would eventually have three children, Withers (b. 1873), Maude (b. 1875), and Virginia (b. 1892).

The next twenty years were spent building up his drug business, which proved to be quite successful. He bought a second store at Ninth and Main, and, combining his love for animals with his fascination with the field of "chemistry," he formulated and sold medications for hunting dogs, among other things. Soon "Polk

Miller" animal medications were being widely distributed. An avid sportsman and hunter, he also became president of the Virginia Field Sport Association.

Miller downplayed his interest in music during this period. As he later put it,

> I was soon so mixed up in "physics" that I didn't have time to keep up with my music. Indeed, I wouldn't tell anybody that I even "knowed how" to play the banjo, because it was looked upon as a "nigger insterment" and beneath the notice of the cultivated. For years I longed for the time when it would come in fashion, and I could play on my favorite musical instrument without disgracing myself in the eyes of my city friends. . . .
>
> I do play the "nigger banjer," and now and then as I pass along the road. . . . I delight in getting behind a Negro cabin and singing a plantation melody "jes" to see 'em come a-crallin' out to see who is dat out dar a-playin' on dat banjer.[8]

By the time he was in his late forties Miller was evidently rich enough to do what he wished and not worry about what his "city friends" might think. His son Withers had earned a degree in pharmacy from a local college and entered the family business in 1890. He was now ready to assume its management. Polk decided to work up an act about his beloved "Old South," and in 1892 he began appearing at benefits in the Richmond area. These were so well received that the following year he turned his business over to his son and began accepting professional engagements. His big breakthrough came in February 1894. Following a successful appearance at the University Club in New York City, Miller was called from the audience at Madison Square Garden to join Mark Twain on stage during one of the celebrated author's highly publicized public appearances. Twain introduced him by saying, "Mr. Miller is thoroughly competent to entertain you with his sketches of the old-time Negro, and I not only commend him to your intelligent notice but personally endorse him. The stories I have heard him tell are the best I have ever heard."[9]

Armed with the endorsement of one of the most famous authors and lecturers in America, Miller began touring extensively. His was not a vaudeville act—in fact, he hated comparison with the blackface vaudevillians and minstrels then burlesquing blacks. "The word 'show' as some people call my entertainments, was always nauseating to me," he later told a reporter. "I hated the name, for if it were merely that and nothing more, no one would have ever seen me on the platform."[10] Instead he presented himself as a lecturer, storyteller, and dialectician, from whom younger listeners could learn as well as be entertained. His stories and solo songs (he did not yet have a quartet with him) were meant to recreate, authentically, life on plantations in the antebellum South—at least his version of it. He also had a message to communicate. He later said that "it has been my aim to vindicate the slave holding class against the charge of cruelty and inhumanity to the Negro of the old time."[11]

Appearances were advertised with phrases like "Lecture and Ball—Old Times in the South," "Dialect Recital and Character Sketches," and "An Evening of Story and Song." At the same time, Miller did not want audiences to think his presentation was overly dry and formal. One flyer explained, "This entertainment is in no sense a lecture, but is an evening of story and song on 'Old Times Down South.'" Added another, "dialect stories, songs and recitations follow each other in quick succession, making an entertainment of about two hours' duration. There are no disagreeable waits for the shifting of scenery and no letting down of curtains during the performance."[12]

Repertoire consisted of both religious and comic songs, most of them uptempo and spirited. Among the religiously themed numbers were "Jordan Is a Hard Road to Travel," "Rise and Shine," and "Keep in De Middle ob De Road"; among the secular, "Arkansas Traveler," "Run, Nigger, Run," "Little Log Cabin in de Lane," "Gwine Back to Dixie," "Old Folks at Home," and "Go Tell All the Coons I'm Gone." There would sometimes be a ballad, such as "Carry Me Back to Old Virginny." Some songs were composed by Miller himself, such as "The Huckleberry Picnic" and "Going Back to Ole Virginny." A highlight would be a rousing rendition of the famous Confederate battle song "The Bonnie Blue Flag."

Despite the blatantly racist overtones, Miller presented his material with respect, as a recreation of earlier times. He never used blackface, and most of the songs dated from the period before or shortly after the Civil War. Currently popular "coon songs" mocking blacks were not a principal part of his repertoire. He also gave the songs some context; he would not just sing "The Arkansas Traveler," for example, but would talk a bit about its origins. Most important, he did have a claim to authenticity. He *had* grown up on a plantation and, unlike most whites, *had* listened to the music being played and sung by the slaves at the time. (He did bend this rule on occasion; it is doubtful that fieldhands of the 1850s were singing Stephen Foster's "Old Folks at Home.")

As for Miller's banjo playing, according to reports as well as the evidence of the recordings, it was both expert and enthusiastic. Was it authentic? One historian has observed that it represented "a compelling study of a direct transmission of black folk banjo style, from plantation slave banjo players to Polk Miller." The eminent writer Joel Chandler Harris (Uncle Remus) put it a little more crudely: "There is a live 'nigger' hidden somewhere in Polk Miller's banjo, and you look for him to jump out and go to dancing when Miller strikes a string."[13]

Appropriate to his type of presentation, Miller appeared mostly at social clubs, lecture halls, business conventions, benefits, and chautauqua gatherings rather than in vaudeville theaters. An 1898 item in the *New York Dramatic Mirror* shows him at the National Rifles Armory, in Washington, D.C.[14] For obvious reasons, he was a favorite performer at reunions of Confederate soldiers.

Sometime between 1899 and 1903 Miller took the rather daring step of adding a black quartet to his presentation. The leader was said to be Anderson Eppes, one of his old family servants who, like Miller, had "chased de possum and de coon."[15] Mixed-race entertainment in a serious setting was practically unheard of at the time. Miller took pains to emphasize that the purpose of the quartet was to "illustrate my work," demonstrating how the old songs were sung. He called the group his "Old South Quartette." The name was not unique. An "Old South Quartette" had toured with a show called *The Old South* during the 1894–95 season, but it was presumably unrelated to Miller's group.[16] Miller said that he had assembled his quartet from men in "various places of work . . . who had been singing on the street corners and in the barrooms of this city [Richmond] at night to motley crowds of hoodlums and barroom loafers and handing around the hat. . . . I could get a dozen quartettes from the good singing material among the Negroes in the tobacco factories here."[17] Given Miller's excellent musicianship, it is likely that he auditioned numerous candidates before arriving at a quartet that met his requirements. It is also likely that he drilled them extensively in the style of singing he wanted.

Like the rest of his presentation, that style was meant to recreate as closely as possible Miller's vision of the music of plantation days. One of his program brochures from 1910 pictured the quartet in the middle of a performance, standing side by side informally, smiling and snapping their fingers. One is strumming on a guitar. The brochure made it very clear what Miller was after. Note the swipe at dandified "colored university" singers (e.g., the Fisk Jubilee Singers) and the professed authenticity of Miller's version.

GENUINE NEGROES
THEY LOOK, ACT AND SING LIKE THE "OLD TIMES"

With a view to giving the general public a true and faithful reproduction of Plantation Life and Scenes before the War, Mr. Polk Miller of Virginia, who is recognized as the very best delineator of Southern life and character in his Negro sketches, has organized and drilled for the purpose a quartette of the best Negro singers ever heard on the platform. They are taken from the tobacco factories of Richmond, Virginia, and, as types of his subject, could not be improved on. Their singing is not of the kind that has been heard by the students from *"Colored Universities,"* who dress in pigeon-tailed coats, patent leather shoes, white shirt fronts, and who are advertised to sing *Plantation Melodies* but do not. They do not try to let you see how nearly a Negro can act *the White Man* while parading in a dark skin, but they dress, act and sing like the real *Southern Darkey* in his "workin'" clothes. As to their voices, they are the *sweet,* though uncultivated, result of nature, producing a *harmony* unequaled by the professionals, and because it is natural, goes straight to the hearts of the people. To the old Southerner it will be *"Sounds from the Old Home of Long Ago."* To others who know of Southern Plantation Life from much reading, it will be a pleasant and *Educational Pastime.*[18]

Another brochure contrasted the quartet with Williams and Walker–style "stage Negroes": "These men do not imitate white folks in their style of singing, nor do they give the Vaudeville Dude Negro's way of acting, which is so disgusting to people who know the *real* thing. They dress plainly, in their everyday working clothes, and do not assume the airs of the CAKE WALKIN' dude who thinks that to please, he must play the part of a MONKEY. They are natural, and in every way try to please as Negroes, without being ashamed of the fact."[19]

Despite the remark about "workin' clothes," the quartet pictured is dressed neatly in suits. Other photographs of the quartet also show them in suits, looking not unlike the "colored university" singers mocked in the first passage. Miller also dressed formally. His was a respectable, "educational" presentation, even if the songs were lively hoedowns, and the message was that slavery had been right, and black Americans should be respected—as long as they stayed "in their place." One wonders if Miller shared any audience at all with the enlightened Northerners who supported rule-challenging groups such as the Fisk Jubilee Singers.

Some of Miller's fans lauded his presentation without necessarily agreeing with his endorsement of the old order. One pastor wrote in 1894, "The Negro is undergoing a wonderful transformation, and the *old type* which Mr. Miller describes is rapidly disappearing. Hence it is important to hear one who knew and loved and thoroughly understood the Negro of the antebellum days."[20]

Mark Twain remained a devoted fan, and he particularly liked the new quartet. He provided the following quote about one of their performances; "Prince Henry" is a reference to a Prussian nobleman who was visiting America at the time. "I think that Prince Henry in being out West, and not hearing Polk Miller and his *wonderful four* in Carnegie Hall last night, has missed about the *only thing* the country can furnish that is originally and utterly American. Possibly it can furnish something that is more enjoyable, but I must doubt it until I forget that pair of *Musical Earthquakes,* 'The Watermelon Song' and 'Old Dan Tucker.'"[21]

Judging by the venues he played, the company he kept (such as Mark Twain, Joel Chandler Harris, and novelist Thomas Nelson Page), and the semiformal style of presentation, it is clear that Miller was playing not to the rabble but to middle and upper classes. Although the majority of his appearances seem to have been in the south, he was also well received in the north, with positive reviews from Philadelphia, New York, and Boston. A quote from the *Brooklyn (N.Y.) Life* remarked that "Mr. Miller appeared on Thursday evening at the Hamilton Club, under the auspices of the Art and Literature Committee, and the members were charmed both by his personality and wit."[22]

The Art and Literature Committee! It is a fascinating reflection on the racial cross-currents of the times that an educated white middle class could support both culturally "liberated" blacks such as the Fisks and the racial regression of Polk Miller and His Old South Quartette.

By 1909 Miller was sufficiently famous to attract the attention of the Edison company, which had a large southern and rural clientele. Possibly at the urging of C. B. Haynes, the Edison distributor in Richmond and a friend of Edison's, a recording team was sent to the city in early November to record Miller and his quartette. This was a most unusual arrangement; recordings were rarely made on location at this time, artists normally being required to travel to record company studios in New York and environs. Nor did the major labels generally make records of purely regional interest.

The trip resulted in seven master cylinders being taken, four of the new four-minute ("Amberol") length and three of the older two-minute duration. These recordings were extraordinary on many levels. Polk Miller was sixty-five years old at the time and one of the few Civil War veterans ever to record commercially. He was probably the only person from the Civil War era who had first-hand knowledge of black music of that era and committed it to record. He sang with a black quartet at a time when integrated sessions were highly unusual. And, of course, these were "creator" recordings from a prominent stage act.

The repertoire was a mix of religious and secular songs, and the performances were loose and lively. The evident enthusiasm on many of these records was reminiscent of a revival meeting, or perhaps a raucous get-together of old-timers. Yet the level of musicianship was high. The performances were quite unlike what was usually heard on record at the time.

Miller himself sang lead on three of the recordings; one is known to feature Randall Graves, the first tenor of the quartet. The leads on the other three are uncertain, but they sound like at least two other voices. It appears that Miller was giving nearly every member of his quartet a chance to be featured. Despite the publicity about Miller's banjo playing, only one of the cylinders ("Bonnie Blue Flag") has banjo accompaniment. Four are accompanied by guitar, and two are unaccompanied.

Miller takes the lead on "Rise and Shine," a typical, lively revival song propelled by a fast, strumming guitar. Miller had a strong and slightly nasal voice quality, sounding not unlike "old-timey" country musicians of a later era such as Uncle Dave Macon. In fact, if it were not for the acoustic audio many of these records could easily be mistaken for traditional country recordings of the 1930s. Miller periodically interjected a trademark upward inflection of his voice, a sort of whoop that gave the lyrics a real punch. The quartet then came strongly in on the chorus ("I'm gwine home to glory, glory!"), with the powerful bass of James L. Stamper prominently heard.

Miller delivers the famous hymn "The Old Time Religion" ("is good enough for me") in a similar vein, making even greater use of his "whoop!" to end each line. It sounds almost like a chant, made more effective by being rendered a capella, with the quartet again coming in on the choruses. The identity of the lead vocalist on "What a Time" is uncertain. This is a very fast-paced revival number, full of religious imagery ("Jesus, Jesus stand by me / And keep the devil away from me!") and thigh-slapping rhythm. There is call-and-response between the lead and the rest of the quartet, which sometimes breaks into multipart harmony. It is easy to see how Miller could bring down the house in live performance with fast, tightly arranged numbers like this.

The variety of performances on these cylinders is nowhere more evident than on "Jerusalem Mornin'" (which Edison misspelled "Jerusalem Mournin'"). The song is actually "I'll Be Ready When de Great Day Comes" by James S. Putnam, published in 1882. Edison publicity called it "probably the catchiest of the seven numbers," and in some ways it is.[23] Sung a capella, it sounds like a preacher with his congregation, starting slowly and then suddenly breaking into a fast tempo at the chorus.

> Tenor: Are you talkin' about Jerusalem mornin'?
> Quartet: Yaass, good lord . . .
> Tenor: Are you talkin' about Jerusalem mornin'?
> Quartet: Yaass, good lord . . .
> Tenor: For Daniel in the lion's den!
> Quartet: Yes, brother!
> Tenor: He said unto some colored men!
> Quartet: What'd he say?
> Tenor: Put on your long white robe and your starry crown too,
> Tenor [much faster]: So get ready when the great day comes.
> Chorus [fast tempo]
> Ensemble: Yes I be ready, I be ready, yeah!
> Good Lord I'll be ready when the great day comes!
> [Repeat]

It is an expert, well-honed performance, with the bass adding rhythmic vocal counterpoint in the chorus ("bom-bom-bom-bom") to accentuate the tempo.

Among the secular numbers, "Laughing Song" is a generic name for a type of song in which singers laugh in time with the music. It is unrelated to the "Negro Laughing Song" made famous by George W. Johnson. This one is done in waltz tempo, with strummed guitar accompaniment. The refrain is "oysters and wine at two A.M.," and it was later recorded under that title. After the cylinder was issued an Edison customer wrote to the company to say, "Will you kindly publish . . . the words of Polk Miller's 'Laughing Song,' Amberol record no. 390? The record is melodious and entertaining, but I am unable to reconcile some of the words and sentences. They seem to be without much sense or connection." The editor replied, "It is not at all surprising that you should have difficulty making sense out of certain parts of the song. . . . This song, written by genuine Southern plantation darkeys with little or no education, contains phrases and expressions which are coined and introduced haphazard. . . . The fact that the words and phrases are meaningless and loosely strung together does not detract from the attractiveness of the song . . . the melody and harmony are there and the fact that the words are truly characteristic of the darkey as *he is* rather enhances the attractiveness of the record."

The words are as follows, with the lead apparently sung by the unidentified second tenor.

A journey to Long Branch is pleasant,
And always delightful to me,
While strolling the beach at moonlight,
While the wild waves are rolling the sea.

Then give me a lady for waltzing,
Such pleasures to me they are grand,
And quickly passed by it is finished,
We have oysters and wine at two.

Chorus: Oysters and wine at two A.M., two A.M., two A.M.,
    We have oysters and wine at two A.M.,
    We have oysters and wine at two.

We fought while the stars were shining,
We fought for the friends that are true,
And quickly passed by it is finished,
We'll have oysters and wine at two.[24]

During the choruses the lead laughs in tempo behind the quartet, giving the song a jovial air. This hardly sounds like a song written by "genuine Southern plantation darkeys with little or no education," however. It is in the style of the waltz songs, some romantic, some with nonsense lyrics, that were highly popular in the first decade of the century.

"The Watermelon Party" is another upbeat comic number, sung with prominent guitar accompaniment. This is one of the numbers Mark Twain called "a musical earthquake." The lead is possibly tenor Randall Graves. The song was described in the Edison release announcement as "an original 'makeup' by James L. Stamper, the basso of the quartette, and for which no music has ever been written." This probably comes closest of any of the numbers recorded to "coon song"–style imagery, as a supposed love for watermelon filled many contemporary songs mocking blacks. It is notable, however, given Miller's racist message, how restrained most of his material was in terms of overtly burlesquing blacks.

The final number recorded was no doubt the *pièce de résistance* at Polk Miller recitals. It was the stirring Confederate battle song, "The Bonnie Blue Flag," sung with enthusiasm by Miller, accompanied by his own loudly strummed banjo. The quartet chimed in on the chorus ("Hurrah! Hurrah!").

> We are a band of brothers,
> Native of the soil,
> Fighting for the property,
> We gained by honest toil,
> When first our rights were threaten'd,
> And a cry rose near and far,
> We raised on high the Bonnie Blue Flag, that bears a single star!

> Chorus: Hurrah! Hurrah! For Southern rights Hurrah!
>   Hurrah! for the Bonnie Blue Flag that bears a single star!
>   Hurrah! Hurrah! For Southern rights Hurrah!
>   We'll rally around the Bonnie Blue Flag that bears a single star!

Miller goes on to sing five full verses in the nearly four-minute record, making it probably the most complete version of the Southern anthem recorded up to this time. The later verses outline how, one by one, additional states joined South Carolina in the rebellion, until at last "the single star of the Bonnie Blue Flag has grown to be eleven." It is interesting to note what Miller altered or omitted, as compared with original sheet music published during the Civil War.[25] Some versions of the original had the rebels "fighting for our liberty / with treasure, blood and toil." Here they are fighting for their *property,* a characterization that must have been particularly significant for Miller, whose father lost his slave holdings and much of his fortune in the war. Even more significant, the second verse of the original set the stage for the Southern states to secede:

> As long as the Union was faithful to her trust,
> Like friends and like brothers kind were we and just,
> But now when Northern treachery attempts our rights to mar,
> We hoist on high the Bonnie Blue Flag that bears a single star.

The attack on Northern "treachery" must have been a little too direct for Miller's audiences in the early 1900s—or at least, for the Edison company—and this verse was omitted. One wonders if Miller sang it at Confederate Army reunions?

According to cash books at the Edison National Historic Site, Polk Miller was paid $175 on November 13, 1909, a Saturday. Another entry on the same day, presumably referring to transportation for the engineers, says "Werner (to Richmond)—$73.80."

The recording trip to Richmond in early November 1909 was just the beginning of a behind-the-scenes drama within the Edison company. Judging by correspondence surviving in the Edison files, these historic recordings came close to not being released at all. On November 15 C. B. Haynes wrote to the Edison home office.

Nov. 15th, 1909
Gentlemen:
Men from your Recording Department were here last week, and made some records from the Polk Miller organization which is very prominent throughout the South. We would like to have you strain a point and get these records out with an extra slip [i.e., brochure] so we can revive some holiday business with them. We understood they made four (4) Four-Minute and three (3) Two-Minute Records. You can enter our order for two hundred (200) each providing you will make special effort and put them out right away. Give them their respective numbers so they will appear in the regular catalogue, but give us the printed matter and the slips for same as we want to feature them. We would like to hear from you whether you will be able to do this or not. If you cannot get them out until after the holidays cancel this order and we will make up another.

Awaiting your reply, we are yours very truly
C. B. Haynes & Co.

The letter was received the following day (the mail was fast in 1909!). F. K. Dolbeer, manager of sales, responded in the negative.

Nov. 16th, 1909
Gentlemen:
We have at hand your communication of November 15th, and upon taking this matter up with our Recording Department, we find that they did have some records made by the Polk Miller Co., but at the present time we will consider listing them only in the regular way, and then only one at a time. . . .

Yours very truly,
F. K. Dolbeer, Manager of Sales

But Haynes was persistent, responding to Dolbeer as follows:

Nov. 17th, 1909
Dear Sir:
Your favor of the 16th relative to Polk Miller Records received in which you say you will only list one at a time, by this it will be six months before we get them all. This is very disappointing to us. Under the circumstances we thought you might make a special list of these records. You have no idea of the amount of business we could create with them, people are coming in and writing in about them every day. The newspapers were full of the account. Thought perhaps you would overstep yourself a little in this case. We want something to revive business, we can tell you honestly we have never experienced such dull business. This part of the country has never recovered from the [financial] panic [of 1907–8] yet, and collections are simply terrible. Thought this would revive them, records by talent they all know. Will not please have your folks reconsider this and change your decision in this matter. If we can get them all at once we can make a hit with them. We want to put

them out while the iron is hot and derive some benefit from them. Please let us hear from you again on this subject.

Yours very truly,
C. B. Haynes & Co.

The reference to newspaper articles is particularly interesting, but a search of Richmond newspapers of this period has failed to locate them. Discussions and memos followed within the Edison organization. When an answer went out to Mr. Haynes it was even more firmly in the negative.

Nov. 20, 1909
Gentlemen:
   Replying to your favor of November 17th in which you again take up the question of the Polk Miller records, you state that while it may be true that you are in a position to sell a quantity of these records, the Polk Miller organization is not well known throughout the United States, and we have always avoided making special records for any one section of the country, for the reason that the other Jobbers [distributors] would have a perfect right to object, and we do not feel inclined at this time to list seven of these records, where at best there can only be a limited sale for them, if they were placed upon a special list.
   We propose giving this matter further consideration, and the samples will probably be placed before the [Sales] Committee for its consideration on the 23rd, at which time action will be taken as to how these are to be listed.

Yours very truly,
F. K. Dolbeer, Manager of Sales

Haynes then wrote to Frank Dyer, president of the Edison company.

Nov. 22nd, 1909
Dear Sir:
   Your Recording Department had some men down here taking some records of the celebrated Polk Miller organization, known all over the South and a great many places in the North. They sing old time songs in strictly negor [sic] dialect. We have had thousands of calls [for] them. Had a little notice in the newspapers here and ever since then we have inquiries from all over the South.
   We have taken this up with Mr. Dolbeer and he has given us no satisfaction in the matter more than to take them up in the regular way. That would make it more than six (6) months before we could get all the records here. Isn't there some way you can make a special list of these six or seven records, put them out on a special list, give them their regular numbers so they will appear in the regular catalogue later on? We are willing to buy two hundred (200) each of them on our first order. We do not know today of any six or seven records in your catalogue we would order two hundred (200) of. That is just the condition of things down here. Good times have not come to us yet. Business is very quiet, and we want something to stir them up before the holidays.
   Trust you will give this your serious consideration at your meeting on the 23rd, when your Committee meets to hear these records.

Yours very truly,
C. B. Haynes & Co.

More internal correspondence ensued within Edison. After the sales committee met on November 23, one of the participants noted, "only one record was submitted last night, and the consensus of opinion of the Committee is that it is not suitable for our regular list. If the remainder are as poor, I question whether it would be advisable to place them upon the market, either in the regular list or as a special." Dyer responded to Haynes, with an even firmer "no."

Nov. 26, 1909
Gentlemen:
I have only heard one of the Polk Miller records, but from this as a sample I would have no hesitation in saying that we would make a great mistake to put them all out at one time. We contemplate putting out the first of these records in March, and then if the sales warrant it we might consider putting out all the others in a single list; but candidly I do not expect this record will have even an averagely good sale. Of course you understand that these Polk Miller records are not records of special new popular music which may have only a very limited life and the records of which should be put on the market quickly. I have no doubt that the records will be just as interesting in six months time as at present.
Regretting that I cannot see a way towards helping you out in this matter, believe me,

Yours very truly,
Frank L. Dyer, President

Like a dog with a bone, Haynes would not let go, and he immediately responded to Dyer.

Nov. 27th, 1909
Dear Sir:
Your favor of the 26th received and fully noted. If you do think these records will only be sold by us principally [why have you] gone to the expense of making the masters? Will you consider our order for three hundred (300) each of them, every one you make? Send a list to every jobber you have in the South and you will be surprised at the orders you will receive for them. If you do not think they are going to sell, what quantity do you want us to order to give us the control of them? We think this quartette is more popular than you have any idea, because the songs they sing have made appeal to the whole country south of Mason and Dixon's line. We are willing to take hold of them and handle them [ourselves] if we can get them within any reasonable time.
Please let us hear from you again on this subject.

Yours very truly,
C. B. Haynes & Co.

One more letter followed from Dyer to Haynes, in which the Edison president adamantly refused to reconsider, saying that one record would be put out in March, and that the company "might" put out the rest after that, but only if sales warranted (which he obviously didn't think they would). He maintained that an order for three hundred would not pay for the cost of making the molds (for mass production), and he turned Haynes down cold on the latter's offer to assume all the risk, saying, "we could not consider any proposition to let you have the control of them even if we felt that by doing so we would receive a greater return than by putting them out [ourselves]." The door seemed to be firmly slammed shut.

However, the matter obviously did not end there. Although the paper trail in the Edison files ends, the company almost immediately did a complete about-face. In all likelihood, Haynes went directly to Thomas Edison himself. The mercurial inventor, who had a legendary distrust of his executives and a willingness to overrule them, may have ordered Dyer to put the records out. By this time it was physically impossible to get them out for the Christmas trade, but a special list of all seven was rushed out on January 3, 1910, along with a set of "special Masonic records," perhaps to deflect criticism that the company was catering to a single jobber's desires. It was too late to get them into the regular monthly brochure that dealers gave to customers.

The catalog writers put the best possible face on things. "The Bonnie Blue Flag" was called "one of the most popular war songs of the South, surpassing in popularity even the world-famous 'Dixie' in the days from '61 to '65. It was sung by Polk Miller around army campfires and he sings it now at reunions of Confederate veterans." Of "Laughing Song," "it takes a genuine Southern negro to sing this song, which is typical of the happy darkey nature. The laughter of the quartette is natural and contagious." Of "Rise and Shine," "Polk Miller, whose imitations of the darkey character are as inimitable as enjoyable, sings the selection just as the old darkies used to sing it on his father's plantation before the war. The harmonization of the quartette's voices is sweet and appealing." And of "Jerusalem Mornin'," "A favorite camp-meeting song, whose fame is by no means confined to the South." Separate pictures of Polk Miller and of his quartet were published (they were never pictured together), but little was said about them.

In an outcome that must have pleased Haynes, Messrs. Dolbeer, Dyer, and the rest of the "suits" at company headquarters were proven totally wrong about the appeal of the Polk Miller cylinders. Eating a large helping of crow, the company published the following announcement in the March 1910 dealer newsletter.

POLK MILLER RECORDS A SURPRISE

The seven records made by Polk Miller and his "Old South Quartette," which went on sale January 3rd, have proven a tremendous surprise. We expected that the demand for these records would be confined almost exclusively to the South, as the request that they be catalogued emanated from that section. In this we were mistaken, for while naturally the demand was greatest in the South, still the North took them very kindly and some sections of the West simply cannot get enough of them. One enthusiastic Kansas dealer wrote in to the factory suggesting that we make one thousand records of the same order. The popularity of the records proves that the real "darkey" plantation melody still has a firm grip upon the affections of the American public, irrespective of locality. Dealers will do very well to advertise and push these records in every way. Polk Miller and his "Old South Quartette" are conceded to be the best delineators of the Southern plantation darkey before the public, and the selections are the very best numbers in their repertory.[26]

This was apparently not just hype. The original Polk Miller wax cylinders are found with reasonable frequency, even though they were available for only a couple of years, until celluloid Blue Amberol cylinders were introduced in 1912. In 1914 the four four-minute selections were reissued in the celluloid format, and they remained in the catalog until the end of cylinder production in 1929. Two of them appeared in a special "Golden Treasury" catalog in 1927. Sales figures for individual cylinders do not exist prior to the very last days of cylinder production, in 1928–29, when demand for this recording format was virtually nil. Even then, however, copies of the four Polk Miller cylinders were occasionally being ordered by Edison customers.

Apparently Haynes, a loyal Edison man, bore no grudges. He was a member of the distributors' committee that organized an opulent testimonial dinner for F. K. Dolbeer on the latter's retirement from the Edison company in 1914.[27]

Despite this success Polk Miller made no more recordings for Edison, or for any other company. Chances are, as a wealthy man, now in his late sixties, he didn't need the work. He continued to appear in concert however, including joint appearances with Colonel Tom Booker as "Two Old Confederates, in Old Times Down South." He apparently allowed his Old South Quartette to make solo appearances as well. A March 1910 article mentions an engagement by "Polk Miller's Original Quartette" at a black Baptist church in Richmond.[28]

Polk Miller's long run with his quartet came to an abrupt and somewhat surprising end in 1911. The very racial inequality that he tried to excuse made it impossible for him to continue touring with black musicians. He explained the situation to a reporter for the *Richmond Journal* in January 1912 in an article titled, "Abandons Show Biz: Polk Miller's Famous Negro Quartette Is No More." His reflections on contemporary attitudes, and his continuing feelings of paternalism for "his boys"—just like an old-time slaveholder—make fascinating reading.

> There is a deep-seated, cruel and foolish prejudice in the North . . . against the Negro as a race of people. Some of the Northern towns which wanted me would write, "We are exceedingly anxious to have you, but our people don't want the quartette, as our people do not like the Negro." There is a certain class of whites in the South, whose ancestors never owned Negroes . . . this class of people made it very uncomfortable for my Negroes. My solicitude for the comfort of my men, and many times for the safety of them in going from the halls to their quarters worried me very much, and unfitted me for my work. This fact, with the inborn dislike of the Negro on the part of the hoodlum element, intensified my troubles when on the road and in some places I had to call on the police force to guard my men. . . . The better class of white people knew that I used these Negroes for a purpose—to illustrate my work . . . but the commoner classes could not understand why Polk Miller, who posed as a gentleman, could bring a lot of "niggers" there to entertain white people.[29]

The reporter then asked Miller if he had had the same men in his quartet from the beginning. "By no means, I made frequent changes during the time. I never discharged one of them for a fault, but they had to give up for other reasons. One of my best men was paralyzed four years ago and he is my porter in the drug store now. . . . Others had throat troubles and had to give up. . . . I have had about twenty men in all, I reckon, since I first began using a Negro quartette. . . . For local purposes (entertaining here at home) I will perhaps organize a good one, but shall never again take a Negro quartette on the road with me."

The reporter asked, "Didn't your men become very stuck up?" Miller replied, "Well, it was natural that after my men had shaken hands with men like Grover Cleveland, Mark Hanna, Bishop Potter and other 'big bugs,' they should have felt that they were 'some pumpkins,' but they were always respectful and considerate in their demeanor towards me."

On the following day the newspaper editorialized, "Mr. Miller, always the personification of amiability . . . touches the subject so politely that the casual reader would hardly grasp in full the fact that he has been compelled to give up his Negro quartette because of the rank prejudice against the Negro. . . . He is deeply grieved over the necessity of givin' up his quartette, and a cherished purpose, which, because of prejudice against the Negro race, has defeated its own ends."[30]

Miller's attitude toward African Americans was clearly more complex than it might appear on the surface. On the one hand, his message was to explain and defend the "old order"—that is, slavery—which in effect meant white supremacy. However, unlike many racists, he seemed to have a great respect for blacks as people. One columnist contrasted him with a race-baiting speaker named Senator Tillman, saying Miller "tried to tell of the good points in the character of the Negro, rather than the bad ones."[31] Said another, "he never failed bitterly to condemn the injustice to the Negro himself of an act which set free millions of people hitherto entirely dependent on their masters, without at the same time providing in any way for their maintenance or support."[32] He was perfectly willing to perform in public with blacks and denounced the "cruel and foolish prejudice" that drove his quartet off the stage. Yet his embrace of a system that considered human beings chattel—even if he did grow up in it—can hardly be called enlightened.

This was not the end of the Old South Quartette. Miller told the *Journal* reporter, "I farmed them out to a New York man for five weeks. He was so much taken with them that he has taken them for good and all, for which I am profoundly grateful." The quartet did continue to appear, at least in 1912. An item in the April 1, 1912, *New York Age* notes an appearance by the "Polk Miller Quartette" at Daly's Theater in Baltimore.

After more than three thousand performances Polk Miller retired from the stage, although he continued to be active in his business. He died suddenly of an apparent heart attack on October 20, 1913, in Richmond, and was buried in that city's Hollywood Cemetery. He was sixty-nine. A detail of Confederate veterans, in uniform, assembled in his honor. His epitaph read, "Honest Citizen, Faithful Friend, Confederate Patriot, Christian Gentleman, Virginia's Son, Loving and Beloved. Peace to His Ashes."[33]

No mention of the Old South Quartette has been found for the next fifteen years, either in black newspapers or in the general press. Perhaps some obscure listing is yet to be uncovered, but if they continued to perform, they did so quietly. Then in 1928, as if through some incredible time warp, a group calling itself "The Old South

Quartette" suddenly reappeared and made seven sides for the small QRS label in Long Island City, New York. Not only was the name the same, but two of the selections were among those recorded in 1909, done in a style closely modeled on that of Miller's original quartet. No literature from the company is known to survive to explain who this "new" Old South Quartette was, but a connection with the long-dead Polk Miller (some of whose cylinders were still being sold by the Edison company) was clearly intended. A photograph in a rare QRS flyer pictures four black men in tuxedos, one holding a banjo and another, a guitar.[34] Although identification is difficult from the fuzzy photograph, two appear to be younger and two older, perhaps veterans of an earlier incarnation of the Polk Miller group.

The two songs repeated from the 1909 session were "The Watermelon Party" and "Laughing Song" (retitled "Oysters and Wine at 2 A.M."). The performances are less polished than those of Miller's original quartet, almost as if the quartet was a group of out-of-practice old-timers—which perhaps they were. The arrangements were identical. "Oysters and Wine" sounds particularly dated, as waltz songs had long been out of vogue by this time, but the looseness, enthusiasm, and old-timey atmosphere that was Polk Miller's musical trademark was still in evidence.

As in 1909 different members of the quartet take the lead vocal on different sides. All are accompanied by a strumming guitar except for the jubilee song, "Oh What He's Done for Me," which features a rather tame banjo. "No Hiding Place Down Here" is a sort of rhythmic chant, done in call-and-response. Perhaps most unusual is "Bohunkus and Josephus." The only known copy is a mislabeled alternate label issue, and so the correct title is uncertain. According to researcher Doug Seroff the song is similar to "Bohunkus and Josephus," recorded by the Birmingham Jubilee Singers on Columbia in 1927.[35] It is a mock religious service, with the "preacher" leading his "congregation" in a nonsense song about two brothers, here called Tobias and Keechungus. Sample lyric:

Now these two boys, they had a cow
and that old cow was blind
She had a pair of legs in front
And another pair behind.

The lyrics are sung to the tune of "Auld Lang Syne" ("Sing it, chillun!").

A number that Polk Miller probably *wouldn't* have performed was "Pussy Cat Rag," a vaguely scatological novelty song from the mid-1910s about an old maid and her cats. Filled with meows, barks, and choruses of "kit-kit-kitty," it is part of long tradition of quartet novelty songs about cats and other animals. It was first recorded in 1914 as a kind of childish novelty, with the best-known version being by Ada Jones and the Peerless Quartet on Victor and Columbia. The performance here seems to be more like the sexually frank blues songs popular in the 1920s.

The final number recorded is a musical adaptation of black poet Paul Laurence Dunbar's famous dialect poem, "When de Corn Pone's Hot." Set to a catchy, rhythmic melody, it describes a domestic scene of happiness around the kitchen table when the food and Mammy's love were plentiful.

Why, de 'lectric light o' heaven,
Seems to settle on de spot,
When yo' mammy ses de blessin'
An' de co'n pone is hot.

The quartet sings it with a buoyancy and cheerfulness that fit the scene perfectly, and a very natural use of dialect with no hint of exaggeration. It is altogether a very appealing marriage of words and music, and one wonders why it is not better known. This seems to be the only recording ever made of the song.

Several master numbers are untraced within the numerical range used for the seven issued QRS recordings, indicating that other recordings may have been made. The QRS releases apparently had very limited distribution, as they are extremely rare today. The Old South Quartette was never heard from again.

Besides his remarkable recordings, Polk Miller left another legacy. He did not sever his connection with the field of animal medicine when he entered show business in the 1890s, as evidenced by the publication of his book, *Dogs: Their Ailments and How to Treat Them,* in 1903.[36] The Polk Miller Drug Company continued to prosper after his death, issuing several guidebooks during the 1920s and later, includ-

Polk Miller and his dog, Sergeant. (*Polk Miller's Dog Book,* 10th ed., © 1925)

ing *Save the Dog* and *Polk Miller's Dog Book.* The latter apparently achieved wide circulation, judging by the number of copies found today. As late as the 1960s canine
medicines were being marketed under the Polk Miller name. In 1901 the company
adopted the trade name "Sergeant's" (the name of Miller's favorite hunting dog) for
remedies it sold through other outlets. By 1926 Sergeant's products were available
throughout the United States, and in 1965 the company introduced its best-known
product, a flea and tick collar. Today Sergeant's Pet Products—named after Polk
Miller's dog—is a division of the giant ConAgra food conglomerate.[37]

As one obituary put it, "Polk Miller was a perfect walking encyclopedia in matters pertaining to the old regime in the South, and, being a sort of connecting link
which binds the old to the new South, there was very little about either in which
he was not well informed. He had twenty-one years of what is known as plantation
life in Virginia before the war closed, and passed through the period of hard times
and reconstruction and the various panics, which were enough to crush the spirit
of one who had been raised in affluence."[38] He had a message for later generations
about that bygone time, which he didn't want them to forget. He was, as his daughter commented, "quite a character," and he preserved for posterity perhaps the most
authentic aural link to the antebellum South that we are likely to find.

PART FOUR

Black Recording Artists, 1910–15

16 Jack Johnson

It may seem a bit odd to find a profile of the first black heavyweight boxing champion in these pages. Jack Johnson was one of the most inflammatory black men in America in the early 1900s, lionized by most blacks and despised by many whites. It is not generally known—and biographies omit to mention—that he visited the recording studios several times during his heyday, recording descriptions of his fights (including the famous "Great White Hope" fight in 1910), talking about his exploits outside the ring, and giving advice on health and fitness. Not only do we have silent films of this extraordinary athlete and lightning rod for racial tensions, we have his own voice describing his life and philosophy.

Prizefighters in the early 1900s frequently exploited their fame by going into vaudeville. A glib, loquacious man and a major celebrity, Johnson spent many years on stage, both during and after his reign as heavyweight champ, giving exhibition bouts and spinning stories about the sports world. His recordings were a natural, if unusual, extension of this aspect of his career.

John Arthur Johnson was born in Galveston, Texas, on March 31, 1878, the son of a caretaker and part-time preacher, and was said to be of pure African Coromante stock. An adventurous youth, he later claimed to have run away from home around 1890 with the intention of hoboing his way to New York City.[1] His goal was to meet Steve Brodie, the man alleged to have jumped off the Brooklyn Bridge. It is not known whether Johnson actually did meet Brodie; he spent the next several years bumming around the country, picking up odd jobs as a dishwasher or stable cleaner and trying to avoid the white thugs who frequented the railyards looking for black hobos to brutalize (a favorite tactic being to throw a victim under the rolling wheels of a train). Johnson also spent a good deal of time in libraries, museums, and art galleries, in part to educate himself, in part to keep warm.[2]

One journey took Johnson to the Northeast as a stowaway on a freighter, where a brutal white cook discovered him and beat him severely. According to his friend and biographer Robert deCoy, "Jack admitted that his humiliation and suffering aboard ship was the thing that had changed him from a happy-go-lucky, adventuresome boy into a hardened man, knowing his first hatred, preferring to die rather than be subjected to such cruelty at the hands of any white man again."[3] He also learned that not all whites were cruel. The passengers, learning of his mistreatment, took up a collection to pay his expenses for the remainder of the trip to Boston.

From time to time Johnson made his way back to Galveston, but he had grown too large and strong to receive much discipline from his worried parents. They could do little more than look on as their strapping son supported himself though a series of odd jobs, including stable boy and bakery apprentice (he loved and became quite good at cooking).

Johnson's first amateur boxing matches are said to have occurred around 1893–94. A job as sparring partner for black welterweight boxer Joe Walcott, "The Barba-

Jack Johnson at the Edison Bell Studios, England; possibly a mock-up picture. (*Sound Wave,* Aug. 1914; courtesy of British Library)

dos Demon" (not to be confused with "Jersey Joe" Walcott of the mid-twentieth century), introduced him to the world of big-time professional boxing. Boxing was one of the few arenas in which blacks were allowed to compete directly with whites, violently at that, and it offered the proud, strong young teenager (now six feet tall and 150 pounds) an opportunity to vent his rage in an acceptable forum. In Galveston he worked at a gym and fought many "pick-up" fights on the streets and docks of the city, slowly learning what would become his trade. By most accounts his first major bouts were in 1899, by which time the lanky fighter was known around town as "Li'l Arthur."

Around 1898 Johnson made a brief stab at settling down, moving in with a light-skinned black woman named Mary Austin (wife number 1).[4] Cultured and refined, she disapproved of his fighting and eventually deserted him. He hit the road once again, to the West Coast and then Chicago, fighting small-time bouts and working as a sparring partner. He seldom lost a bout, and his reputation gradually grew. Johnson was less lucky with women, however. He took up with another black woman, Clara "Sadie" Kerr (wife number 2), who conspired with her lover, Johnson's friend Willie Bryant, and Jack's then-manager Frank Cordella to pick him clean and drug him before a big fight in March 1902. She and Willie then ran off with Johnson's possessions.

By 1904 Johnson was well enough known to open a café and bar in Chicago with black vaudevillian S. H. Dudley.[5] He also began to attract what today would be called "groupies," young women (both black and white) entranced with the virile young fighter and determined to get their chance in bed with him—a favor that he not infrequently bestowed. He began living with a white prostitute named Belle Schreiber but declined to marry her. Instead, he later claimed to have married another white woman, Hattie McLay (wife number 3), who had continual battles with jealous girlfriend Belle. The tabloid press had a field day with stories about the rising, womanizing young fighter, picturing him as deflowering every innocent white virgin in sight. Pornographic comic books appeared with titles like *Jack Johnson and His Girls* and *Black Ape Splitting the White Princess*. It was about this time that one of the more famous stories about Johnson apparently originated. As ever more colorful tales circulated about his sexual prowess, Jack decided to satisfy (or mock?) his detractors by showing up for sparring sessions with gauze stuffed in his trunks, then strut around the ring, arms raised, displaying what seemed to be outsized genitals.

How did a black man in 1905 get away with this kind of baiting of the white population? For one thing many considered boxing a somewhat seedy branch of show business. Prizefights were banned outright in many cities, and the whole "sport" was considered beneath contempt by upward aspiring whites and blacks (Booker T. Washington denounced Johnson). But it had its fans as well, and a great deal of money could be made from title fights, especially those attracting the kind of notoriety that had begun to follow Jack Johnson. Savvy white managers caught on quickly to the profit-making potential of a talented, in-your-face young black man like Johnson, and they protected him from serious interference by the authorities. Money trumps race. Johnson was party to this devil's bargain, of course. A canny showman as well as a showoff, he seemed to know how far he could go, how outrageous he could get, and when, at the last minute, to pull back—or appear humble—in front of "the Man."

Another aspect of Jack Johnson that attracted attention was his love of automobiles, especially big, flashy, fast ones. As soon as speeding tickets were invented he started to get them, always paying cheerfully for the thrill of "racing" down the bumpy roads of the time. He challenged the leading race-car driver of the time, Barney Oldfield, to a race on Long Island, which Oldfield won when Johnson's big 690 Thompson developed motor trouble.

Johnson and his white manager, Sam Fitzpatrick, spent much of 1908 chasing heavyweight champion Tommy Burns around Europe, trying to corner him into a title fight. Even King Edward IV of England called Burns "a Yankee bluffer" seeking to dodge the ambitious up-and-comer. Burns finally assented, and the match was held at Rushcutter's Bay on the outskirts of Sydney, Australia, on December 26, 1908. Taunting the arrogant Burns from the moment he stepped into the ring, Johnson completely dominated the fight, reducing his opponent to a bloody pulp. In the fourteenth round the police stepped into the ring and stopped the fight, and Jack Johnson was named the new heavyweight champion.

White sportswriters, led by racist journalist/author Jack London, were apoplectic and immediately began a campaign to negate Johnson's victory. They claimed that since longtime champ Jim Jeffries had retired undefeated in 1905, Johnson could not really be crowned champion until he defeated *him*. Wrote London, "Jim Jeffries must now emerge from his alfalfa farm and remove the golden smile from

Jack Johnson's face. JEFF, IT'S UP TO YOU! The White Man must be rescued."[6] Thus began the eighteen-month campaign to find "The Great White Hope" who would put this infuriating black man in his place.

Johnson dumped his manager and Hattie McLay (he said the two had been having an affair) and began a new phase of his career, alternating between highly promoted nontitle fights and well-paid exhibition appearances in vaudeville. A review in *Variety* of a 1909 appearance at Hammerstein's Victoria Theatre in New York gave the flavor of his nine-minute "act."

> There were no preliminaries about the act. . . . An announcer proclaimed Johnson the undefeated champion of the world. The hisses which greeted this speech drowned the applause. The gallery held many colored people. Johnson stepped on the stage, disregarding the disturbance, and went at the bag. On the third punch it flew in the balcony. The stage hands removed the apparatus without further ado, and Johnson proceeded to box his sparring partner, Kid Cutler, a white man, three one-minute rounds. The white man, handicapped by height and reach, could not touch Johnson, who toyed with him. The audience offered much advice. At the conclusion of the bout . . . [Johnson,] stepping forward, made the following speech, which turned the tide in his favor, winning him some genuine applause to close with: "Ladies and *gentlemen,* kindly give me three minutes of your valuable time. Today I have deposited with the *New York American* $5,000 as a deposit on a side bet for $10,000 to fight any man in the world. If there is a fight, I hope the best man will win."
>
> Johnson is a drawing card and seems to attract even those hostile to him [because of] his color. His bearing while making the speech and the language proved the black champion is no novice on the stage.[7]

Jack Johnson was now a major celebrity, whether or not his championship was contested, and his racing, womanizing, ostentatious displays of wealth, and disparagement of his opponents provided continuous copy for tabloid writers. Among his nicknames were "The Big Smoak" and "The Big Black Fire." There were parodies galore. In Bert Williams's 1909 musical *Mr. Lode of Koal,* the ruler of the mythical island of Koal is called "Big Smoke," leading a reviewer in the Indianapolis *Freeman* to dub Williams "the Big Smoak of colored and white artists, [as] Jack Johnson is the Big Smoak of all prizefighters." Williams also referred to Johnson in one of his songs, "My Ole Man." In early 1910 a minstrel troupe toured with a sketch called "Jack Johnson's Return," in which a couple of dumb hobos posed as the prizefighter and his trainer. In the final scene the victorious boxer knocked out his opponent, and everyone else within reach, until he finally became disgusted and knocked himself out.[8]

Meanwhile the real Jack Johnson resumed his relationship with the prostitute Belle Schreiber, then moved in with another white woman, Etta Duryea. When former wife Hattie McLay committed suicide, he used films of her funeral in his vaudeville act. Between November 1909 and February 1910 Johnson toured the European music halls, doing the cakewalk, with Etta as part of the cast. He continued to fight a succession of white challengers, including an up-and-comer named Victor McLaglen, who would later become a movie actor. During a match with Stanley Ketchel in October 1909 someone spiked Johnson's water. He defeated

Ketchel anyway, knocking out his teeth. Johnson then hired an "official taster," who was poisoned while pretasting Johnson's drink a few months later.

By the end of 1909 serious negotiations for a championship bout between revered ex-champ James J. Jeffries and Jack Johnson were underway. This would decide once and for all whether, for the first time in history, a black man could call himself the uncontested world heavyweight champion. The publicity buildup during early 1910 was considerable, and the press coverage of the negotiations, the insults flying back and forth between Johnson and Jeffries, and the riotous behavior at the training camps (especially Johnson's, where "Li'l Arthur" was now attended by a bevy of white female hangers-on) made for colorful copy. July 4 was chosen as the date, and San Francisco as the location, with the backing of the governor and mayor. The promoter, Tex Rickard, would serve as referee (supposedly English writers H. G. Wells and Sir Arthur Conan Doyle were offered the honor but declined). In the middle of June Governor James N. Gillett, under intense political pressure, abruptly banned the fight. After some fast negotiations the site was moved to Reno, Nevada, where Governor Denver S. Dickerson was eager to have his small state host such a major event.

The nascent film industry was also anxious to cash in, with films from Johnson's training camp being advertised in early June.[9] Rights to film the big fight were sold to Essanay, Selig, and Vitagraph. Working together, cameramen from the three companies set up nine cameras on raised platforms around the outdoor ring so that every moment of the action would be captured. The estimated cost of staging the fight was $125,000, the estimated gate $360,000, and the total amount of bets placed on the fight in the United States alone more than $3 million. The winner stood to make approximately $135,000, and the loser about $100,000.[10] On the day of the fight more than eighteen thousand spectators were on hand, including approximately six hundred reporters. Guns, knives, and other weapons were confiscated at the door, and a special train was said to be standing by, ready to whisk Johnson away if serious trouble erupted. Thousands more listened for the results in theaters and other public places across the country. A throng estimated at thirty thousand—virtually all white—gathered in New York's Times Square to watch fight bulletins posted on the large, revolving blackboards on the Times Building. This would be one of the biggest media events of the new century.

The fight began at 2:30 in the afternoon on a hot Monday. By all accounts the agile Johnson demolished the lumbering white champ, while tossing taunts and making wisecracks to the screaming ringside partisans. Battered and bruised, Jeffries gamely took the beating until Johnson was finally declared the winner in the fifteenth round.

The aftermath was explosive. There were reports of race riots around the country as incensed whites vented their fury on hapless blacks, especially those who had the temerity to brag about their hero's victory (a black man in New Orleans was reportedly shot for walking into a restaurant and saying, "gimme eggs, beat and scrambled, like Jim Jeffries"). In some cases blacks attacked whites. The true extent of the violence was the subject of debate even at the time. While the tabloid press screamed of mass rioting, other newspapers (such as the *New York Age*) said that many of these reports were exaggerated. There clearly was violence, and racial tensions were high. On the morning of July 5 the *New York Times* reported that eight people had been killed in fight-related incidents the previous night, and many others injured. The *Times* led with four pages of detailed reports, including twin page-one headlines: "Johnson Wins in 15 Rounds" on the right, and "Eight Killed in Fight Riots" on the left. It also reported that the huge Times Square crowd had been overwhelmingly pro-Jeffries but had dispersed silently after the final bulletin was displayed ("Not a cheer for Johnson, but everybody was sorry for Jeffries"). The few blacks at the fringes of the crowd wisely scattered.[11]

Fearing the incitement of further violence, officials in many cities banned the showing of the fight films that had been rushed east immediately after the bout. Movie industry trade papers railed against this abrogation of filmmakers' constitutional rights, arguing that suppressing the films would simply make them "forbidden fruit."[12] Clearly racism was at play, although writers at the time tended to tiptoe around this aspect of the issue. Many fight films had been exhibited in the past without incident, although of course this bout was different. Rising to the challenge, the film companies quickly produced recreations of the fight, sequences of still pictures, and even parodies (e.g., two cats fighting) for exhibition where the real fight films could not be shown.

Perhaps the most unusual attempt to get around the film bans, and the one that led to Jack Johnson's first recordings, was made by the American Cinephone Company of New York City. This small firm specialized in a primitive type of sound film, which operated by running a silent film and simultaneously playing a specially recorded disc record containing appropriate sounds (not necessarily in sync with the film). Johnson was filmed in street clothes, calmly describing the fight, blow by blow. A series of discs, made at the studios of the Columbia Phonograph Company, reproduced his voice. According to the following advertisement by American Cinephone, "these pictures can be shown anywhere."

JACK JOHNSON'S OWN STORY OF THE BIG FIGHT

Jack Johnson has spoken into the phonograph his own story, by rounds, of the big fight at Reno, Nevada, and has posed in street attire for moving pictures to accompany his monologue. These pictures can be shown anywhere. Wherever the fight pictures are barred for any reason, the value and drawing power of the Jack Johnson pictures are enhanced beyond measurement.

Jack Johnson received $10,000 for making these exclusive pictures and records containing the only authentic and authorized version of the big fight. . . . In these talking and moving pictures he gives a complete description of the fight, very much more comprehensive than in his "turn" in the regular vaudeville theaters. . . . One reel, two twelve-inch records. Absolute perfection secured.[13]

The advertisement was signed by Milton W. Blumenberg of the American Cinephone Company, and the pictures were said to be on exhibition at the company's offices at 125 East 25th Street, New York City.

Apparently Johnson's talk was recorded in three parts, parts one and three on two sides of one twelve-inch disc, and part two on one side of another (so that they could be changed smoothly while the film ran). Only the disc containing the first and third parts has been located, but it reveals a Jack Johnson who is in stark contrast with the braggart and inflamer of white hatred often portrayed in print. He is calm and well spoken, delivering his scripted talk in forceful, measured phrases, like a somewhat stiff public speaker. One listener compared his delivery to that of a ring announcer. His English is impeccable—there is no use of slang—with only an occasional hint of an accent (he says "woid" instead of "word"). There is also no hint of braggadocio; in fact, he goes out of his way to compliment his vanquished rival. The polite, educated-sounding voice is so different from what we have been led to expect by sensationalizing latter-day biographers (including deCoy) that one expert told me it could not really be Johnson but must be a white elocutionist imitating him. "A black man wouldn't sound like that." This is the height of racial stereotyping. It is indeed Johnson, proven by comparison with his later recordings as well as a sound film he made in the 1920s.

Johnson's polite, conciliatory speech (similar to the one he used in his vaudeville act) offers a clue as to how he managed to win over fair-minded whites. He won his title fairly, was courteous to all, and did not brag excessively about his victory. References to fairness ("may the best man win") were a recurring theme in his public statements. This was a basic American value on which sportsmen prided themselves, and Johnson cleverly turned it to his advantage. Even former champ John L. Sullivan, while acknowledging "my well-known antipathy to his race," conceded that Johnson was "one of the craftiest, cunningest boxers that ever stepped into the ring . . . the best man won, and I was one of the first to congratulate him."[14] Johnson, who allowed Sullivan free access to his training camp, referred to the white man cordially as "Cap'n John."[15]

Johnson began his recorded description of the fight as follows.

> Ladies and gentlemen, with your kind indulgence I will endeavor to say a few words in regards of the great heavyweight battle which took place Fourth of July of this year between myself and one of the gamest, and greatest, heavyweights that ever laced on a boxing glove. And the name, Mr. James J. Jeffries. Allow me to state that on the fourth day of July Mr. Jeffries entered into the ring with a world of confidence. I did likewise. And the fight was strictly on its merits. Mr. Jeffries fought with the very best of his ability and self-knowledge.
>
> During the second round Mr. Jeffries [seized] a left hand uppercut to the eye, which closed the eye entirely. Paralyzed both sides of his face. [He] fought a great uphill battle, something an ordinary man could not withstood [sic]. I have fought over a hundred and seventy odd battles, and during that time I have met America's greatest and also the greatest that Europe can find, and Australia. But, the whole of my career, I have never seen or heard of a man that could undergo the punishment that Mr. James J. Jeffries had gone through on that day. The fight was a fight that one who has seen it can never forget. For the public at large wanted it and they got it. There was folks from all parts of the world, and at the end of the battle they were well satisfied, and they say it was the greatest that was ever.[16]

He then described each round, passing quickly over those in which there was little action. Finally he reached the climactic fifteenth round.

Round fifteen was the round that Jeffries met his Waterloo. And a great round it was. I fought with all the courage, all the science, and gameness combined that I had in me. And then a left to the jaw that staggered Jeffries, and a right hand uppercut which knocked him down. And then he was assisted to his feet by a few of his seconds, [James J.] Corbett and [Sam] Berger and some unknown newspaperman. He rises, only to be put down again with a left hook to the jaw. This time Berger jumped into the ring and shoved me back. [Referee] Rickard, during the excitement, waved me to my corner. But I did not go, and we mix again, and Jeffries went down, and I was declared the winner. And the sports at the ringside considered me one of the greatest of the modern times. And they all wished me well, and the battle was fought strictly on the level, and the best man won.

Johnson recorded at least two versions of his commentary. On the double-faced disc quoted he describes round two in part one, and rounds five through fifteen in part three. There is also an original master recording in the Columbia Records vault, labeled "Part III, Second Set," on which Johnson describes rounds *seven* through fifteen and uses different wording. This master begins with a throat being cleared and an unidentified voice saying, "ready." The Columbia file card for this master contains a cryptic date of "July 24, 1910," which could be the recording date. Johnson ends this alternate version a little differently: "I sent a telegram home to my mother telling her that I've brought the bacon home and wished her good luck and told her that I would leave on the first train for Chicago. And I am champion now and I will try and retain that position and to defend it against all comers. It makes no difference whom I may meet, let us all wish, and hope, may the best man win."

The advertisement for the Cinephone film and records appeared in *Moving Picture World* on August 13, 1910. Two weeks later the following ad appeared in the *New York Age,* proving that the records were also sold separately.

HEAR JACK JOHNSON'S VOICE
HIS OWN STORY OF HIS GREAT VICTORY

The heavyweight champion of the world, the unconquerable Jack Johnson, has told into the phonograph his own story of his contest with Jeffries at Reno, July 4. The story occupies both sides of a twelve-inch phonograph record. It can be reproduced on any talking machine using disk records. A letter from Johnson, in facsimile, certifying to the authenticity of the record and commending it to his friends, goes with each record. You hear Jack Johnson's own voice telling how he won the big fight. Price $2.50 Delivered.

A few minor discrepancies should be noted. This ad cites one disc, whereas the Cinephone ad mentioned two. The address given (124 East 25th Street) was across the street from the Cinephone office. It seems likely that these were the same records, however. Since not much happened in rounds three and four, perhaps buyers simply got the coupling of parts one and three, as transcribed above.

Moving Picture World reviewed Johnson's talking film in its August 20 issue. Although it was not particularly impressed with either Johnson or the film, its speculation on the future of "topical talking pictures" was prescient.

Mr. J. A. Johnson, a colored pugilist, who recently "defeated" Mr. James J. Jeffries, is a loquacious man. His loquacity is golden in that as a result of his victory he has been paid very large sums of money to talk on the vaudeville stage. More recently he has been induced to talk for the purpose of making phonographic records, which are heard in connection with the picture. In other words, Mr. Johnson has been converted into talking pictures through the agency of the American Cinephone Company.

As our readers well know, we are no particular admirers of these pugilists; but the other evening we sat and listened to Mr. Johnson talking in the production room of the American Cinephone Company. Orally, Mr. Johnson was a success; photographically and histrionically, Mr. Johnson was not a success. He just stood there on the screen, unaccompanied by the fistic gestures we naturally look for, and quietly described his fight with Mr. Jeffries. As we have said, he did not suit the action to the word, and the result was some disappointment. Probably there were difficulties in the way of securing the best kind of photographic and acting results. We will make allowances, while congratulating the American Cinephone Company on its enterprise.

As we sat and watched the picture and heard the phonograph we seemed to perceive possibilities in the way of topical talking pictures. Already we have the singing and talking picture in dramatic form, but so far the purely topical picture has not often been attempted or presented. But of course expedition will have to be used in these matters. It is now six weeks since the fight took place. Interest in it has not disappeared, it is true, but then the exhibition was of somewhat exceptional interest. Maybe in future times when a Mr. Roosevelt returns from abroad we shall be witnessing talking pictures of him that same night. Or, again, when any great public event takes place it will be phonographed and photographed and presented to the public within a few hours. This is some of the possibilities that lie before the talking picture.[17]

Despite the allusion to "singing and talking pictures," sound films were rare at this time. It would be more than a dozen years and the debut of *The Jazz Singer* (1927) before "talkies" became the norm.

Neither the Johnson film nor the records seem to have achieved much notice. The records are extremely rare, and it is not known whether any prints of the film still exist. Jack Johnson's first foray into the recording studio produced a fascinating historical artifact, but little else.

The next five years were tumultuous, to say the least, as Johnson exploited his championship while being pursued by vindictive whites determined to bring him down. At first, in the afterglow of the Big Fight, everyone wanted to see him. He returned to the East by special train immediately after the fight, stopping in Chicago to see his mother, Tiny. He then began a three-week engagement at the Victoria Theatre in Manhattan, at $2,500 per week, playing to packed houses. After punching the bag and giving a three-round exhibition match with Walter Monohan, the champ gave a short speech that was as gracious as the one he recorded.

I thank you from the bottom of my heart for this ovation. When I was in this city some time ago, before the match between Mr. Jeffries and myself was made, I said that Mr. Jeffries was one of the greatest fighters in the world. Since that time I have had a practical experience of Mr. Jeffries' worth, and I have had no occasion to change my opinion. You all know how the fight was prohibited in California and was transferred to Reno, where we fought it out. Mr. Jeffries is game to the core. He put up a game fight and took a terrible grueling without flinching. He fought a fine battle and did not attempt in any way to foul. He did all he could to win a fair battle, and took his defeat in a manly way. While I hold the position in the pugilistic world that I do, I will try to defend my title against all comers.[18]

The *New York Age* (a friendly paper, to be sure) reported "vociferous applause" at each appearance. On August 2 Johnson sailed for London to begin a thirty-week tour of the musical halls, for which he was said to be earning $3,000 per week.

The further violence that authorities feared did not materialize, in part, one imagines, because of the obvious fairness of Johnson's victory and the conciliatory tone he took in his public statements. The aftermath of the Big Fight lasted for many months. In the fall a song dedicated to him was being advertised, called "Mamma, I've Brought Home the Bacon." Bert Williams, the great Broadway star, appeared in his first *Ziegfeld Follies* portraying Johnson in a comedy sketch called "A Scene in Reno."[19]

Johnson returned to the United States in early 1911 and on January 18 married Etta Duryea (wife number 4), the white woman with whom he had been living. That fall he opened a sumptuous cabaret called Café de Champion at 42 West 31st Street in Chicago, with the golden champ's belt hanging above the bar. He lived upstairs with Etta in his "harem room."[20] He was constantly in the news. When the *Titanic* sank in April 1912, it was rumored that Johnson was supposed to have been aboard but had been denied passage. A series of matches with other "White Hopes" took place, but none gained the white-hot media attention of the Jeffries battle, and Johnson easily prevailed in all of them.

Living with the larger-than-life black legend took its toll on Etta Duryea, and there were rumors that she would divorce him. Instead, on September 11, 1912, she committed suicide by shooting herself in the head. Johnson was despondent, but a few months later he met another white woman, nineteen-year-old Lucille Cameron, who took over his business affairs. It was not clear whether he was living with her, but Lucille's mother, Mrs. Cameron-Falconet, was enraged anyway, hiring a lawyer and beginning her own campaign to bring down the black devil. In this she had considerable support from the authorities. Two years earlier U.S. Representative James R. Mann of Illinois had introduced into Congress a bill to make illegal the transportation of a woman across state lines for immoral purposes. It was widely interpreted at the time as aimed at Jack Johnson, but the authorities had never been able to make it stick because none of the women involved with Johnson would testify against him. Neither would Lucille, even though she was imprisoned without bail (as a "material witness") and heavily pressured to do so. The city shut down his cabaret by revoking its liquor license.

Finally the Chicago police tracked down Belle Schreiber, the discarded prostitute, who was still smarting from Johnson's unwillingness to marry her. After years of what she perceived as unrequited loyalty, and perhaps sensing her own chance at fame and fortune, she agreed to testify that Johnson had transported *her* across state lines for immoral purposes. Ignoring the fact that "immoral acts" were her line of work, the police immediately swooped in and arrested Johnson. Bail was initially set at an incredibly high $65,000, and the racist judge even refused to accept cash to cover it ("there is a human cry in this case that cannot be overlooked," he self-righteously declared).[21] Johnson's lawyers quickly prevailed over these shenanigans, and the champ was released. Lucille was released from prison and fled to Canada to escape her mother.

Lucille soon returned to Chicago and, two weeks after Johnson's release, married him (wife number 5). Mrs. Cameron-Falconet was beside herself. The trial of Jack Johnson began on May 13, 1913. His team of lawyers put up a convincing defense, pointing out, among other things, that the alleged acts had taken place *before* the Mann Act went into effect. But the jury wasn't listening and quickly convicted him, whereupon the judge sentenced him to a year in prison and a fine of one thousand dollars. Johnson was freed while his case was on appeal, but by now was convinced that the white-controlled system was going to get him one way or another. Deciding to flee the country, he escaped to Canada in early July, ostensibly to go on a "fishing trip," then proceeded to Paris, where he received a huge welcome. There were accusations that FBI agents had accepted a huge bribe to let him get away, but nothing was ever proven.

Once in France Johnson was safe; the Europeans had no interest in extraditing a black man convicted of such dubious charges. He played the Folies Bergère, and began touring with his show *Seconds Out*. The part in the show once played by Etta was now played by Lucille. By fall he was playing the musical halls in England, giving boxing demonstrations. After run-ins with members of the British aristocracy offended by his display of wealth, however, and a denunciation by Winston Churchill, he was expelled from that country. He then proceeded to Russia, where he hit it off famously with the "Mad Monk" Rasputin, the power behind the Russian throne.

Continuing to defend his title, he defeated Jim Johnson, a black man, in Paris in late 1913. Although he broke his arm (previously fractured in an auto accident) in this match, Jack Johnson participated in a wrestling match in Spain in early 1914 in order to raise funds. He won that by punching his opponent unconscious. In June he defeated Dr. Frank Moran in a title fight in Paris, but his winnings were impounded by the authorities because of claims that he tried to rig the fight. Short of funds, he accepted engagements wherever he could. Among them was an offer from Edison Bell Records in London to record two sides for them on the subject of "Physical Culture."

The manner in which these recordings came to be made was related in a story in the English trade paper, *Talking Machine News*.

> Jack Johnson, the heavyweight champion of the world, is a frequent visitor to the West End depot of the Edison Bell Co. in Cranbourn Street, and Mr. Willis, the manager thereof, tells me he is very much interested in the records, and will listen for a long while to the entertainment provided thereby, especially in march music. As a natural result it happens that the enterprising directorate in the recording part of the business thought it would be a good idea to get "Jack" to give a few views of his system of training on the record for the benefit of those who can never hope to attain any of the prominence that he has, but would like to have a few hints as to the manner in which he obtains [his] natural fitness. . . .

On Tuesday last, Jack Johnson, accompanied by his wife, motored over to Glengall Road, Peckham, to the works of J. H. Hough, Ltd., to fulfill an appointment to make a talking record to the effect as I have mentioned. And right here it may be mentioned that the celebrated pugilist is very far removed from the ordinary conception of a coloured fighting man. As a matter of fact, save for the few peculiarities in the matter of nasal twang and drawl inseparable to the negro race, he is a very fine specimen of what a man should be. His father, he told me, was a preacher at a chapel in the Western States, and as a youngster he received a good education.[22]

The session was also covered in another industry publication, the *Sound Wave*, in a long, rambling article that quoted E. T. Hough as saying that his dealings with Johnson were quite agreeable, and that the champ was "a black man, a pugilist and—a gentleman." It also mentioned that an interesting photograph was taken as Johnson was leaving the premises and about to enter his motor car. "He is depicted with his wife, a charming American lady, and Mr. E. T. Hough, and surrounded by the latter gentleman's employees. The 'black velvet face' among the other 'velvet faces' forms an attractive picture, quite a colour harmony, in fact."[23]

The Edison Bell recordings, made c. June 30, 1914, reveal a Jack Johnson who sounded calm and confident, despite his legal and financial troubles. His delivery was much like that of the 1910 recordings, slow, stentorian, and in measured phrases, like a ring announcer. His advice to his listeners was eminently sensible.

Ladies and gentlemen, first of all I want to thank each and every one for this grand occasion. I am here this afternoon to speak a few words on physical culture. Some

Jack Johnson recording at Edison Bell, apparently without a script! (*Talking Machine News*, July 1914; courtesy of British Library)

Jack Johnson and his wife, Lucille, surrounded by onlookers, outside the Edison Bell Studios. (*Sound Wave,* Aug. 1914; courtesy of British Library)

people seem to think that one that is fat, to get that fat off, that they will have to diet themselves. It is absolutely untrue. First you must take exercise—strut, and walk, and perhaps a little run. You can use dumbbells. You can use the medicine ball. You can also use what we term as a punching ball. That alone will take all of the excess flesh [?] off of anyone that will use it.

Some people seem to think if you drink water it will make you fat. Water is the most strengthening thing that we can possibly use. We can go two or three days without food, but we cannot go so long without water. Water, it makes the blood . . . rich, but also gives strength to the heart. And you will notice, one that drinks a lot of water, he, or maybe she, will never have any trouble with their kidneys. And they always have regular beats of the heart, and it also gives one a very enticed appetite. I myself, after a long, hard jog on the road, before breakfast, I will come in, and after I have my rubdown, I will partake perhaps a quart of water or a little more. Then I have gained some two or three pounds of strength. Not in weight, strength alone [that] will help one to overcome any pain.

Johnson went on to promote vigorous walking ("it makes one's heartbeat greater"), a medicine ball to strengthen the abdominal muscles, and dumbbells (not too heavy, though) for the arm muscles. Most of all, however, he advocated clean, clear water. "The first thing in the morning when he, or she, gets up, they should take one glass of water and then, about a hour from that, they should drink two. And that will wash the kidneys out and make the body healthy."

The 1914 "Physical Culture" records are in their own way as interesting as the 1910 description of the Jeffries fight. They confirm what was widely written, that Johnson approached his training seriously and with careful planning, using techniques that, by and large, are well accepted today.

By late 1914 Johnson was back in Russia, which was in political turmoil. Thugs tried to assassinate him, and his baggage was seized. There is some evidence that British authorities, impressed with his access to Rasputin and the tsar, recruited him to spy for them, suggesting that if he cooperated they would intervene with the American authorities to allow him to return to the United States without fear of imprisonment. Nevertheless he remained a highly controversial figure wherever he went, and he was attacked in London as well.

To retain his heavyweight title Johnson had to keep fighting challengers, and in early 1915 he agreed to fight Jess Willard in Mexico City. President Carranza, in the midst of a revolution, forbade the fight. Rebel leader Pancho Villa offered to host it, and there was some talk of staging it in El Paso, Texas (if it could be declared a "safe haven"), but Johnson's manager, Jack Curley, opted for Havana instead. The date was set for April 15, 1915. The fight, which lasted for a marathon twenty-six rounds, is controversial to this day. Johnson partisans claim he "took a fall," either tired from the years of exile or having been promised a pardon in the United States if he did so. The thirty-seven-year-old Johnson fought well, but Willard, younger, bigger, and stronger, outlasted him and Johnson finally went down for the count. There was no pardon forthcoming from America.

His manager tried to steal the fight films, but Johnson followed him to London, recovered them, and went on to alternate between stage appearances (with his show, *Seconds Out*) and nontitle fights, which he usually won. His chances of getting another title fight appeared to be slipping away, however. He settled in Spain for a period (helped by references from the admiring president of Cuba), where he acted in his first film, *False Nobility,* wrestled, and opened a boxing school. In a celebrated 1916 adventure he became a bullfighter, coached by famed bullfighters Belmonte and Joselito. He also, allegedly, engaged in some espionage for the United States, but still received no pardon. He was not even allowed to return for the funeral of his beloved mother, Tiny, who died in 1916.

In 1919 Johnson arrived in Mexico, the guest of the restored President Carranza. He had several close brushes with death, once when his boat was caught in a storm, and later when his train was ambushed by bandits in northern Mexico. When the bandits found out who was on the train, however, they lionized him ("You are a champion of the poor people. You have spoken out on our behalf") and invited him to join them at their camp. He politely declined, and the train was allowed to proceed unmolested. He then opened a gambling-cabaret in Tijuana with his two loyal companions, Lucille and his nephew, Gus Rhodes. He fought several more bouts, but Jess Willard, the white champ, refused to fight him.

Finally, on July 20, 1920, in a prearranged ceremony, with reporters crowding around, Jack Johnson stepped across the border and surrendered to U.S. authorities. He was whisked to Chicago for a rehearing, obviously hoping for clemency now that he was no longer champion and had voluntarily surrendered. But American was still a deeply racist country, and he still had a white wife. Judge George A. Carpenter thundered that "Johnson has behaved in a manner to indicate a complete disregard for the laws and institutions of this country," and remanded him to the federal penitentiary at Leavenworth, Kansas, to serve his full sentence. So-called white justice would be served.

In some ways, the resilient ex-champ had the last laugh. The prison superintendent turned out to be none other than Denver S. Dickerson, former governor of Nevada and Johnson's old friend. Dickerson made sure that Johnson's time at his facility was as painless as possible, even allowing exhibition bouts within the prison walls. He was released a year later, in July 1921.

Still a major celebrity, he then embarked on a vaudeville tour with a jazz band led by Fletcher Henderson.[24] During 1921 and 1922 he appeared in at least three films, *As the World Rolls On* (helping a young kid learn sports), *For His Mother's Sake,* and *Black Thunderbolt.*[25] He continued to fight, but Jack Dempsey, the new champ, refused to meet him. His vaudeville act took on a new, more entertaining tone. No longer was it enough to simply appear as "the champ" and give a conciliatory speech; audiences expected more. So Johnson began to tell humorous stories. A natural actor, he was good at it. In March 1924 the small Ajax record label of Chicago induced him to record several of these stories. Ajax was owned by the Compo Company of Montreal, Canada, where the sides were evidently recorded.

Johnson was accompanied on these sides by a group of admirers (presumably black), who provided encouragement and interjections. The first routine, "Runnin' Down the Title Holder," occupied two sides of a ten-inch record. Johnson opened with a hearty laugh.

> Johnson: Ha-ha-ha-ha, Ha-ha-ha-ha, Ha-ha-ha-haa-ha. Yessir, this is Lit'l Arthur Johnson, better known as Jack Johnson. Ha! Glad to be with you. [Crowd cheers.]
> Voice #1: Mr Johnson, tell us sumthin' about your prizefighting.
> JJ: As a prizefighter, I'm a runnin' fool. I started running after Tommy Burns, and run from one end of the world to the other. Oh, boy! I was runnin'. And before you could tell it, I had done run clean all over here.
> Crowd: Come on, Jack.
> JJ: When I entered the ring with Tommy, I looked over the big crowd [and] sittin' way back on the fence, behind everybody, I saw one, just one, colored man. Well sir, Burns made a swing at me. I ducked, but he swung so hard that it must have excited my colored brother, and he fell clean off the fence. He ain't got back on that fence yet! [Crowd laughter]

Johnson then launched into a long story about jogging outside his training camp in Australia and encountering a tribe of native wild men. After a certain amount of interplay with them ("I had done heard that them wild men was crazy about dark meat") he broke free and escaped. How? "It was one of them cases of, I'm runnin' . . . I broke all of those Australian traffic laws, and if I didn't break them, it was because they don't mind a man runnin' sixty miles an hour. . . . And you bet, when I got to the training party I found that I had lost 22 pounds, my socks, and still, both of my shoes was tied on just as tight as they could be. Friends, I was running!"

"Bull Fightin' in Spain" recounted Johnson's famous 1916 bullfighting exploits, in humorous fashion. In this version he says he thought he was signing a contract for a boxing match, but the opponent turned out to be a bull ("Great balls of fire!"). He told the promoter, "I can't fight no bull. I can throw the bull, but I ain't fightin' nobody's bull." But fight it he did, surviving by jumping on the bull's back. Johnson raucously sings a bit of "La Paloma" on this side, whereupon his unnamed sidekick interjects, "Mr. Jack, I don't mind hearin' ya talk, and laugh, but please suh, don't sing!"

"Up in Bear Mountain" was a yarn about Johnson encountering a grizzly bear one evening outside his camp while training for the Jeffries fight. "Well, it was getting dark. The bear was dark. I was dark. And it looked mighty dark for poor L'il Jack." As the bear drew closer and closer, Jack finally decided that there was nothing left to do but go in for the clinch. "The next morning, the game warden was out at our training quarters trying to find out who had done killed a bear out of hunting season." His sidekick was incredulous: "You killed a bear, huggin'?" "Yessuh, yessuh," shot back Johnson. "When they crowd me!"

Both of these latter sketches are credited to "Grainger," which may mean pianist Porter Grainger. It is unknown who assisted Johnson in the studio, although the piano briefly heard in "Bull Fightin'" could be Grainger. The records were advertised in *Phonograph and Talking Machine Weekly* as part of the Ajax race record series, under a picture captioned "Jack Johnson (himself)."[26] The ad boasted that "L'il Arthur's record is a sure fire hit wherever race records are sold," but copies of the two Ajax discs are quite rare today and they probably had limited circulation.

Nineteen twenty-four was another tumultuous year for Johnson professionally and matrimonially. He officially retired from the ring at the age of forty-six, after one last victory over a little-known young fighter named Homer Smith in Montreal. Although he was still in good fighting form, the days when he was considered a serious challenger for the championship were long past, a fact that must have been difficult for him to acknowledge. However, the humiliation suffered by former champs who had tried to make comebacks—including Jim Jeffries—must have been on his mind. Around the same time, Lucille Cameron filed for a divorce on grounds of adultery and infidelity, which Johnson did not contest. They had been married for nearly twelve years, his longest relationship yet. Eager newspaper reporters tried to get her to "dish the dirt" about the champ or write a tell-all book, but she refused, retiring quietly from the limelight. At least her mother, the angry Mrs. Cameron-Falconet (who was still alive) could now die in peace.

Only a few months passed before Johnson met and fell in love with yet another white woman, Irene Pineau, the estranged wife of an advertising executive. After she divorced her husband she married Johnson in August 1925 (wife number 6). Newspaper columnists once again went on the attack, outraged that the former champ had now married not one, but *four* white women, two of whom had committed suicide. Irene, a quiet, intelligent woman, wrote letters in his defense, including two celebrated letters to *Vanity Fair,* which had called Johnson "a subhuman black, with supernatural, hypnotic powers over white women." Irene responded, describing the day they were married.

What a wonderful day it was for both of us! How different is the real soul-stirring love from that which we often mistake for real love, but that which is no more than a passing infatuation. What great things are not possible, when one loves and is also loved, truly and deeply?

Since our marriage we have not changed one iota, except to have our love for each other grow stronger as time goes on. As a husband Mr. Johnson is everything he could possibly be, loving, considerate to the smallest details, generous to the nth degree, loyal and kind. To many people who might be a bit skeptical about marrying a man of a different race, let me say that there could not be a man from any race in the world more worthy of being loved and honored than is my husband.

It took him to show me what a real love and a happy home is, and in comparing mine with the lives of all my friends and acquaintances, I can say without fear of contradiction that none can boast of a more harmonious and happy home than we. A prejudiced writer once said of my husband "that Jack Johnson has a sinister influence over women, white women." And I answer, "if to be a man, in every sense of the word . . . and to treat a woman with utmost respect, kindness and loyalty is 'sinister,' then a lot of men would make this world a better place, to emulate my husband and become 'sinister' too."[27]

With his finances suffering Johnson found "celebrity" work wherever he could during the years that followed. In 1926 he was touring on the T.O.B.A. black vaudeville circuit. His autobiography, *Jack Johnson—in the Ring—and Out,* was published the following year. While containing some suspiciously "tall tales" from his youth, it was remarkably free from bitterness. In 1929 Johnson opened the Checkers Club in Harlem, with a black orchestra and floor show. While performing there he made a short sound film with his band, a hot jazz aggregation. Opening the festivities was big Jack in his tuxedo, grinning broadly and declaring, "Ladies and gentlemen, I have been requested by many to tell just how I knocked out so many of my opponents. As far as I'm concerned, that day has gone. And today, I have a new way of knocking them out, and I will show you!"[28]

The eleven-piece band then ripped into a wild version of "Tiger Rag," while Johnson waved a baton and did an energetic little dance that looked a lot like he was attacking a punching bag in a gym. Three takes of the film exist, with closeups of band members and Johnson, including his shuffling feet. It's a fascinating picture of Harlem jazz at the end of the Roaring Twenties. The film is dated December 21, 1929.

During the 1930s Johnson engaged in a variety of activities. He sold stocks, did celebrity endorsements, made nightclub appearances and worked as a movie extra. At one point he had a walk-on role in *Aida.* One writer observed, "He even brought excitement as a lecturer in a flea circus, and excelled as a traveling sideshow freak, placing his foot on a handkerchief in a circus ten boxing ring, taking on all comers, offering a cash prize to those who could hit him solidly enough to make him move." Joe Louis, the next black heavyweight champion, wanted nothing to do with him, saying, "We're still paying for him. When I was coming up back in 1934 and '35, they didn't forget about old Jack. I had to live like a saint to get a break."[29] Old hatreds die hard.

Jack Johnson lived to the ripe old age of sixty-eight, and died as he had lived, furiously and at high speed. He was killed in a automobile wreck on June 10, 1946, while speeding down a highway near Raleigh, North Carolina.

Postscript

The legend of Jack Johnson does not end there. As America emerged, slowly, from the darkness of institutionalized intolerance and racism, he began to be viewed more favorably as a pioneer in the long struggle for black equality. He was particularly appealing during the rebellious 1960s, and in 1967 a hit Broadway play was produced based on his famous 1910 fight with Jim Jeffries, called *The Great White Hope.* It won a Pulitzer Prize as well as Tony Awards for the both the play and its stars, James Earl Jones (whose character was called "Jack Jefferson") and Jane Alexander. In 1970 the play was made into a Twentieth-Century Fox feature film, also starring Jones and Alexander. Both this film and a documentary, *Jack Johnson: The Big Fights,* were nominated for Oscars that year. Several books about Johnson were issued, or reissued, most of them playing up the controversy and spirit of rebellion that had followed him throughout his life. Some were less about Johnson than they were vitriolic attacks on racism (the biography by his friend Robert deCoy, for example, uses the "n word" on practically every page).

Few writers seem to have known about his recordings or the voice that presented a somewhat different picture—an intelligent, thoughtful man who knew exactly what he was doing. Jack Johnson was a rule-breaker, but he led by his own example of excellence, not by being a firebrand. As Irene Pineau Johnson wrote to the editors of *Vanity Fair* in 1926, "You writers from whom words and stories flow so glibly, most of the time will not look beneath the surface to even see the facts in a case. . . . How many men would be willing to survive the uphill climb and struggle, enduring the bitterness and heartaches, as Jack Johnson has done, and who could still remain the steady, temperate man he is today? Very few! These virtues have not the earmarks of a 'levee Negro.' You are entirely mistaken in your impression of him. Signed / Mrs. Irene Johnson."

17 Daisy Tapley

The contralto Daisy Tapley may have been the first African American woman to record commercially in the United States.[1] We must say "may have been," because we cannot be sure who is on all the lost brown wax cylinders of the 1890s. The elusive Kentucky Jubilee Singers cylinders (1894), if they truly existed, may have contained female voices. Moreover, if Tapley *was* the first, it was on the basis of a single duet recording in which she did not take a solo line.

Tapley's impact on recorded history may have been slight, but her contribution to the world of black music was considerable, making her one record of special interest. She was born Daisy Robinson in Big Rapids, Michigan, c. 1882, the daughter of Harvey and Martha Robinson.[2] Shortly thereafter her family moved to Grand Rapids, and, in 1890, to Chicago. Daisy showed great musical promise and as a child studied with organist Clarence Eddy and pianist Emil Liebling, among others. At age twelve she became the organist at Quinn Chapel. At age seventeen she entered show business, joining the three Winslow sisters to form an act called "The Colored Nightingales," which played at the Alhambra Theatre in Chicago in 1899.[3] This was followed during 1900 and 1901 by various engagements in Chicago, with the Slayton Jubilee Singers, Prof. N. Clark Smith, and others.

Shortly thereafter she met a young actor named Green Henry Tapley, a member of the Williams and Walker theatrical troupe. They were married around 1903,[4] and Daisy joined the company, traveling with it to London where she met the great composer Samuel Coleridge-Taylor and others. Back in the United States she appeared with Williams and Walker in vaudeville in December 1905, at the same Alhambra Theatre where she had debuted as a teenager.

Green (who styled himself somewhat grandiosely as "G. Henri Tapley") had been with the great comedians since their first major show, appearing in supporting roles in *Sons of Ham* (1900) and *In Dahomey* (1903) as an actor and singer. He was a well-respected member of the troupe and was especially close to its "business brains," George W. Walker. He eventually became Walker's personal secretary, caring for the actor and acting as his spokesperson to the press during Walker's final illness. Also in the Williams and Walker troupe was a singer/actress named Minnie Brown, who became Daisy's closest friend and companion, remaining with her for the rest of her life. Daisy, Minnie, and Green Tapley all appear to have had small roles in Williams and Walker's *Abyssinia* (1906) and *Bandanna Land* (1908), as well as in Bert Williams's first solo effort after Walker's retirement, *Mr. Lode of Koal* (1909).[5]

Nineteen-ten was a turning point for Daisy Tapley. In that year the Williams and Walker company broke up, and she apparently separated from her husband (although she continued to carry his name). With her friend Minnie Brown she settled in New York City, where she became a teacher of piano, organ, and voice. Dedicating herself to the more refined types of music, and to the promotion of black artists, she quickly became friendly with many of the leading black concert musicians of the day. In the words of one obituary, she was soon "the center of a large musical circle."[6]

It was no doubt through this widening circle of friends that she came into contact with Carroll Clark, a young baritone who was attempting to build his own career as a concert singer. Clark had been recording since 1908, and in December 1910 he and Tapley were invited to the Columbia studios in New York to record the hymn "I Surrender All." The recording is a very sober, straightforward performance, with Tapley and Clark singing in unison throughout, neither taking any solo lines. Tapley's voice is strong and clear, although the whole performance is rather restrained. Accompaniment is by a thin-sounding reed organ, probably a small studio model.

This single duet by Tapley and Clark was released in March 1911, coupled with another sacred selection by Harrison and Anthony. Columbia intimated that cus-

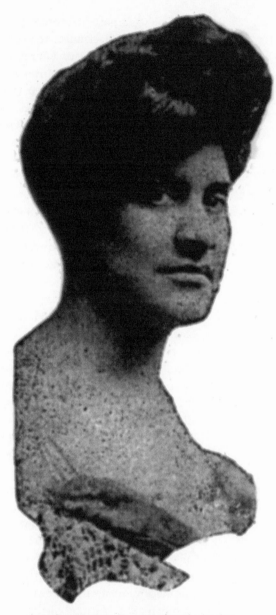

A determined Daisy
Tapley in 1912. (*Pittsburgh
Courier,* Oct. 18, 1912)

MRS. DAISY ROBINSON TAPLEY.

tomers might be hearing more from the new Tapley-Clark combination, but that
was not to be. Although the disc remained in the catalog until 1919 it was evidently
a poor seller. Few copies are found today, and the masters were not leased to other
labels. It would be Tapley's only recording.

Following this, Daisy Tapley returned to her work of teaching, performing, and
organizing recitals. Many notices are found in the black New York press about her
activities. To cite just a few, in 1912 she performed at a charity ball at the Manhat-

tan Casino; in 1913 she was in charge of vocal music at the big Emancipation pageant at the 12th Regiment Armory; in 1914 she trained an employees' chorus for the Lincoln Day celebration at Wanamaker's Department Store, appearing with them in concert (the first black woman to do so); in 1915 she appeared in recital in New York and Boston as part of a quartet including Roland Hayes, Harry T. Burleigh, and Minnie Brown, and sang contralto solos at the annual recital at the Martin-Smith Music School; in 1916 she appeared at a music festival at Hampton Institute in Virginia, and also at the Southwestern Negro Music Festival in Dallas; and in 1917 she accompanied Roland Hayes in concert at the Casino Theatre, New York. In early 1918 she sponsored the New York City debut of teenage soprano Florence Cole-Talbert, who would later become a notable figure in black concert music. Other activities during this period included directing the YWCA Glee Club of Brooklyn for twelve years and the choir of Concord Baptist Church for eight.

In some instances Tapley performed as a soloist, in others she was a choir director, in yet others a piano or organ accompanist. She seems to have been a very accomplished musician. Minnie Brown appeared with her at some of these concerts. There is never any mention of her husband, Green Tapley, who in the mid-1910s was living just a few blocks from her Harlem apartment and who still worked as a musician.[7] Census records in 1915 and 1920 show Daisy living with Minnie Brown, who was variously described as her sister or a lodger. They also reveal a certain amount of vanity on Tapley's part; in 1915 she reported her age as thirty-four, and in 1920 as thirty.[8]

In early 1918 an article in the *New York Age* reported that Tapley had angrily canceled a recital at the YMCA when she learned that the organization would not allow a mixed-race audience.[9] Instead, with Minnie Brown, she initiated her own series of "educational recitals"—approximately one a month during the winter—featuring the best black concert talent of the day. The series continued for the next three years, "at a financial loss because of her desire to increase the artistic appreciation of the colored race."[10] They featured such well known names as Florence Cole-Talbert, Roland Hayes, Clarence Cameron White, Harry T. Burleigh, and lecturer W. E. B. Du Bois.

A 1920 item noted that Tapley was then treasurer of the New York chapter of the National Association of Negro Musicians (Minnie Brown was vice-president). More projects followed in the early 1920s, including directing the chorus for productions at the 71st Regiment Armory and at Carnegie Hall (1921). The latter engagement led to her founding the Negro Singing Society of New York.

Daisy Tapley's busy life came to a sudden halt when she was stricken with ovarian cancer in mid-1924. Eight months later, on February 5, 1925, at age forty-two, she passed away at her apartment on West 136th Street. Minnie Brown was by her side. Her funeral drew a large crowd of musicians of both races. One newspaper reported that "the procession was a lengthy one, and the streets were choked for some time with cars containing actresses from the Broadway theater districts and colored artists from Harlem. Every dramatic and musical association in Harlem was represented both in person and [by] floral designs."[11] There were numerous tributes in the black press, one obituary noting that she was "one of the most prominent colored women in the country [with] a wide reputation as a contralto singer and pianist."[12] Interestingly, none of the obituaries mentioned her husband; condolences were received by her companion, Minnie Brown. Interment was at Tapley's summer home at Sag Harbor, Long Island, New York.

Had it not been for her single venture into the recording studio in 1910, Daisy Tapley's voice would have been stilled forever. As it is, we have that piece of audio to remind us of a woman who contributed much to the advancement of black concert music.

18 Apollo Jubilee Quartette

There is little we can do other than speculate about the identity of the mystery group called the Apollo Jubilee Quartette. Columbia released a single disc by the quartet, in August 1912, but said little about them. It is no mystery, though, why Columbia wanted some jubilee selections in its catalog. In February 1910 Victor had announced the first recordings of spirituals by the famed Fisk Jubilee Singers. These represented a major innovation for the record industry, presenting to the public a type of music not previously widely available on record. They were bestsellers. In May 1912 Edison got into the act, releasing several cylinders by the Fisks.

With spirituals by the Fisks on both Victor and Edison, Columbia felt it had to be represented in this field. No other organization of the Fisks' caliber was immediately available, so somehow Columbia came up with a previously unknown group called the Apollo Jubilee Quartette. They recorded four traditional spirituals in New York City on February 26 and 27, 1912. According to company files two titles ("Little David" and "Camp Meeting") were rejected by the music committee. The other two, "Swing Low, Sweet Chariot" and "Shout All Over God's Heaven," were released in August with little fanfare and a catalog description that spoke mostly of the music and said nothing about the singers. "A novelty that cannot fail to attract attention. The peculiar rhythms and harmonies of the genuine old time jubilee singing are unmistakable, defying imitation. Above all things this class of song stands alone as an expression of the Afro-American temperament, its curious vociferation and reiteration being practically unique with musical expression of this particular type. Of the abilities of the Apollo Quartette of jubilee singers our records leave no question."[1]

The disc remained in the Columbia catalog only until 1915, when Columbia secured the services of the real Fisk Jubilee Singers. The Fisks immediately recorded the same two titles as their first release for Columbia, and the Apollos disappeared, never to be heard from again.

Despite the short shrift they were given, based on their two issued sides the Apollo Quartette was a very competent group, giving creditable and practiced renditions of the two standards. Both were sung with feeling, in tight performances reminiscent of the Fisks. In fact the two issued titles use arrangements virtually identical to those of the Fisk Jubilee Quartet and are particularly close in sound to the Fisks' Edison cylinders. This was no doubt intentional.

Who were they? Apollo is, of course, the Greek god of music and poetry, and the name was used widely for musical clubs and performing ensembles across the country. In fact there was an Apollo (Male) Quartet on Victor at the time. However, its single selection, released in June 1911, was the old minstrel tune "When the Corn Is Waving, Annie Dear," making it unlikely that this was the same as the Columbia jubilee group.[2] The "Apollo" name was used on records for a number of other groups that were presumably or definitely white, including the Apollo Quartet (Berliner, 1898), the Apollo Quartet of Boston (Edison, 1916 on), the Apollo Trio (Columbia ethnic, 1923), and the Apollo Male Trio and Quartet (Perfect, 1920s).

Of course we cannot even be positive that Columbia's Apollo Jubilee Quartette was black. However, the repertoire, the performance style, and even the vague catalog copy strongly suggest that they are. They are a close, and no doubt intentional, copy of the Fisks. The most intriguing possibility is that they were in fact related to the Fisk Quartet, which was in New York recording at almost exactly the same time. The latter made their Edison cylinder recordings in December 1911 and were back in the New York area making addition disc tests for Edison in February 1912. A possible connection can be found in the background of two Fisk members, second tenor Roland Hayes and basso Leon P. O'Hara. Hayes and O'Hara had been singing together since their student days at Fisk University, and while at Fisk they had both been members of a student quartet formed by Hayes called, coincidentally, the Apollo Quartet.[3] Hayes was an ambitious young man who would soon leave the Fisk quartet to launch a solo career. It is possible that while in New York he put together a quartet for Columbia, perhaps using Fisk arrangements and personnel, and used the quartet name he had used at Fisk.

While the Apollo arrangements are virtually identical to those used by the Fisks on Edison, the Edison cylinders had not yet been released at the time of the Columbia sessions. Thus Columbia could not have simply copied them from the cylinders. This lends credence to the idea that Hayes brought them with him. On the other hand, they are fairly common arrangements and were no doubt used by the Fisks in concert.

I don't think that the Apollo Quartette was simply the Fisk Quartet in disguise. The Apollo's lead tenor does not sound like the tenor on Edison (John W. Work) or, for that matter, like Roland Hayes, by aural comparison with the latter's version of "Swing Low" recorded six years later. The Apollo tenor's voice is a little deeper. It is hard to be certain, given the sonic limitations of these early recordings. The evidence of an Apollo-Fisk connection is interesting but inconclusive.

Whoever the Apollo Jubilee Quartette was, they left us fine versions of two great spiritual standards. Perhaps the identities of those who created them will one day be discovered.

19 Edward Sterling Wright and the Poetry of Paul Laurence Dunbar

Public speaking was a respected and popular profession in the late nineteenth and early twentieth century, a time when bettering oneself through education was just beginning to become a widespread pursuit. Private lectures were patronized both by the snobbish elite who wanted to show off their education and by lower classes who wanted to get some. Celebrity was not essential for success as a speaker. Any good orator with a popular subject could fill a hall.

Most "platform speakers" were white, but African Americans understood better than most the value of education (which they had been long denied), and some of their own entered the field. One of these was New York's Edward Sterling Wright, who left us an unusual legacy in the form of readings of the poetry of the famous black poet Paul Laurence Dunbar, recorded on Edison cylinders in 1913. These are among the earliest spoken-word recordings dealing with serious literature. Wright's early life was summarized in Edison publicity.

> Edward Sterling Wright, the noted Negro reader and impersonator, was born in New York in 1876. He sold papers to help his mother along while attending school, and was inspired to strive to attain a higher sphere in life when he was refused employment in a factory on the ground of color. This refusal landed him in the Emerson College of Oratory, Boston. Dr. Charles Wesley Emerson became interested in his new pupil. He took Mr. Wright to live with him in his home at Millis, Mass., and at Rochester, Vt. This close association and personal influence exerted on the student by this most skillful master of elocution, together with his close application to the requirements of his profession, has made Mr. Wright one of the most versatile, artistic and thoroughly competent entertainers before the public.[1]

According to his death certificate, Wright was born in New York in 1878, and was a lifelong resident of the city. His parents were Henry and Sarah Jacobson Wright.[2] No student records have been located at Emerson College for Wright.[3] Even if he was not regularly enrolled, it is certainly plausible that he attended Emerson around the turn of the century and received personal instruction from its white founder. The college was opened by Dr. Emerson in 1880 with the goal of "qualifying students to become professors and teachers of elocution and oratory in the colleges and high schools of the land. . . . The college is also designed as a means of liberal culture; its aim is not merely to make readers, but thinkers as well."[4] Dr. Emerson was evidently liberal on matters of race. Booker T. Washington was invited to speak at the institution in 1900, and black students are known to have been in the student body at that time. Dr. Emerson remained actively involved in the affairs of the college until 1903.

By the 1910s Wright's profession was listed in the *New York City Directory* as "lecturer," and he evidently supplemented his income by acting in area productions.[5]

A 1911 item in the *New York Age* reported that "Earle Wright [*sic*], the well known dramatic reader and vocalist, has signed a contract to play in the spectacular production *Marching through Georgia* at the Hippodrome, New York, beginning March 6, for two months."[6] This is more than likely our subject.

Paul Laurence Dunbar

On the lecture platform Wright was known for his interpretations of the poetry of Paul Laurence Dunbar (1872–1906). Dunbar, who had died at a young age just a few years earlier, was a cultural hero to blacks and was popular among whites as well. The son of former slaves, he was born in Ohio and raised by his widowed mother, who told him stories of happier times "befo' de wah." Because she omitted the more brutal aspects of life under slavery, Dunbar developed a romanticized notion of the era which he incorporated into his early poems and stories. For this he has been much condemned by latter-day critics and historians, although it certainly was a popular notion at the time.

Dunbar was an excellent student and by 1889, two years before he graduated from high school, he had already published poems in the local newspaper. Lacking the funds for a college education he had to settle for menial jobs in Dayton, including work as an elevator operator. He continued to write, and his poetry attracted wealthy white sponsors who helped him self-publish his first book of verse, *Oak and Ivy,* in 1893, which he sold from his elevator post and after recitals. A highly favorable review by the eminent critic William Dean Howells in *Harper's Weekly* brought further attention. Eventually the young poet was invited to work on a number of projects, including collaboration with composer Will Marion Cook on the pioneering black musical *Clorindy; or, The Origin of the Cakewalk* (1898). He also traveled to England and collaborated with the famous black composer Samuel Coleridge-Taylor. Dunbar was, in fact, extremely versatile, writing short stories, novels, and poetry, as well as lyrics to popular songs. He wrote in both standard English and Negro dialect, but became known almost solely for the latter, a fact that disturbed him greatly.

Dunbar's dialect poetry portrays simple, happy times growing up, often with a humorous twist. While many authors were writing in this style at the time, Dunbar's work is considered especially realistic and sensitive. One modern analysis comments that "he portrayed these events with ironic tenderness that conveys the emotions and thoughts of his uneducated, inarticulate subjects. Even Dunbar's detractors admit that his dialect poetry vividly captures the folklife and beliefs of late nineteenth-century black Americans."[7]

Dunbar was wracked by illness in his last years and despondent that his more "serious" work had found so little acceptance. Although he began to confront racial injustice more directly in his later work, it was his earlier, humorous, dialect pieces that continued to find favor. Dunbar died of tuberculosis in 1906, believing his life had been "a national joke and a failure." In the decades since then reaction to his work has alternated between acceptance (the first great black poet) and rejection (a kind of Uncle Tom, sugarcoating a horrific era). A common view in today's academic community seems to be that he is worthy of study because he was black, an attitude he would have hated. Also, the use of dialect itself is today controversial, to say the least. Nevertheless, he has many admirers, and his work is available in print and on the Internet.

The Recordings

However history may have treated him, Dunbar's short, romantic life, combined with his work in a popular genre of poetry, made him a much-admired figure in the 1910s. It was probably due to his association with Dunbar's work that Edward Sterling Wright, a relatively minor name on the lecture circuit, was engaged to record several of Dunbar's poems for Edison in the fall of 1913. We don't know if Wright had known or heard Dunbar, but he certainly could have, as he was living in New York while Dunbar was active there. Wright was not the first person to record Dunbar's poetry. Reverend James A. Myers of the Fisk Jubilee Quartet had done so

Edward Sterling Wright at the time of his Edison recordings. (*Edison Phonograph Monthly*, Dec. 1913)

EDWARD S. WRIGHT
Impersonator

as early as 1909, on Victor. But Wright's readings are especially realistic, delivered by someone who was an actor as well as a reader. One can almost see him gesturing in front of the recording horn as he recreated the simple scenes that Dunbar had envisioned. His use of dialect is pronounced when it serves the scene, restrained otherwise. These are intelligent and sensitive readings, without a trace of mockery.

Three four-minute cylinders were released, containing full readings of six short poems. According to the Edison files, two other cylinders (titles not known) were recorded but not released. Of the three released, Edison 2153—"When de Co'n Pone's Hot" and "Possum"—seems to have had the widest sale.

"When de Co'n Pone's Hot" is a lyrical evocation of the scene in a kitchen when Mammy's cooking wiped away the cares of the day.

> When you sit down at de table,
> Kin' of weary lak and sad,
> An' you feel a little tired,
> An' purhaps a little mad;
> How yo' gloom tu'ns into gladness,
> How yo' joy drives out de doubt
> When that oven do' is opened,
> An' de smell comes po'in out;
> Why, de 'lectric light 'o Heaven
> Seems to settle on de spot,
> When yo' mammy ses de blessin'
> An' de co'n pones hot.

Comparison with the printed poem indicates that Wright did change a word here or there, but the reading is certainly true to Dunbar's intent. Parts of this poem were set to music and recorded, years later, in a rollicking version by the Old South Quartette.

"'Possum" celebrates a favorite dish and tells white folks they just don't know how to eat it since they take the skin off.

> Now, white folks t'ink dey knows 'bout cookin',
> An' I reckon dat dey do,
> Have a little idea,
> 'Bout a middlin' dish er two;
> But dey ain't a t'ing dey knows of
> Dat I reckon cain't be beat
> When you set down at de table
> To a unskun [unskinned] possum's meat!

Edison 2152 contained "Howdy, Honey, Howdy!" and "Little Christmas Basket." The former is a humorous story about a nervous beau trying to work up the courage to approach a girl, while the latter is a lecture on generosity that shows the poet's more serious side.

> What's de use a-tellin' chillun about a Santy an' a Nick,
> And the stories that a body all is tol',

When de hearth is gray with ashes and we haven't got a stick,
For to warm 'em when their little toes is cold?
What's de use of preachin' 'ligion to a man dat's starved to death,
An'a-tellin' him de Maaster will provide?
If you want to catch his feelin', save yo' sarmen and yo' breath,
And take a little Christmas basket by his side.

The final issued cylinder (2253) contained "Jes' Gib Him One ob Mine" and "In de Mornin'." The former is a humorous little story about a black urchin who finds a cigar butt and wants to light it, but doesn't have a match. So he buys a box of matches for a penny, then gives the box back to the storekeeper, saying if anyone else wants a light, "jes' gib him one ob mine!" "In de Mornin'" is a humorous tale about a mammy trying to rouse her lazy little Elias from bed in the morning, get him to wash, brush his teeth, and sit down at the table. It ends with her lecturing the rambunctious youngster, in a scene to which any parent could relate.

Fol' yo' hands an' bow yo' haid,
An' wait until de blessin's said;
"Lawd . . . have mussy on our souls . . ."
Don' you DARE to tech dem rolls!
"Bless de food we's 'bout to eat . . ."
You set STILL—I see yo' feet!
You jes' try dat trick again.
"Bring us peace an' joy . . . Amen!"

This last poem was also recorded by Reverend Myers on Victor. Both Myers and Wright "act out" the scene with suitable inflection and changes of tempo, but Wright seems to put a little more edge in his voice, as if his mammy really *is* mad at the recalcitrant youngster. One can tell that he is more of an actor than Myers.

The first two cylinders by Wright were released in February 1914, with the lecturer's picture prominently displayed in the *Edison Phonograph Monthly* (which called him, interestingly, an "impersonator").

Mr. Wright was the first artist to discover the entertaining feature, as well as the instructive qualities, of Paul Laurence Dunbar's poetic works. He is today under the management of the largest Lyceum Bureau in the country, and is accomplishing a most noteworthy work with remarkable success in a new and unique field, unfolding to the public in inimitable and charming dialect, the pathos, reverence, humor and drollery, which are the basis of all folklore stories of antebellum days. One of the most comprehensive things that has ever been said about Mr. Wright was a remark made by one of his auditors at a recital recently. "To hear him is to laugh with one eye and cry with t'other."[8]

The blurb added, insightfully, that "much has been written about Mr. Wright, and perhaps because of his race, his talent has earned him a greater fame than it otherwise would."

The final cylinder (2235) was released in April. The first two remained in the catalog until the end of cylinder production in 1929, although 2235 was deleted in

1918. None were issued on Diamond Discs. According to the Edison files Wright was paid $125 on October 17, 1913, for all five four-minute recordings. This seems to have been a normal rate for this kind of work.

During the following years Wright remained active as a lecturer and actor. His most notable stage exposure came in April 1916, when he starred in the title role in *Othello* at Harlem's Lafayette Theatre. Produced in celebration of the Shakespeare tercentenary, this was considered a fairly important production at the time. It was said to be the first time Shakespeare's tragic tale of love between the white Desdemona and the Moor, Othello, had been played by an all-black cast (which, of course, robbed it of at least one level of meaning). On April 3 Wright previewed a scene for the eminent English actor Sir Herbert Beerbohm Tree, who praised the proposed production.[9] The play opened on April 24, receiving mixed but generally positive reviews by the critics, who seemed mainly impressed by the fact that a troupe of semiprofessionals (most of the cast were not professional actors) could creditably perform such a difficult work with only two weeks' rehearsal.

Writing in the *New York Age,* theater critic Lucien H. White ventured that "the performance as a whole was meritorious." He reminded readers that blacks had not generally been trained in classical theater, making the achievement here all the more impressive. "There are shortcomings, but there is also a great amount of talent [in the production]." He was particularly impressed with Wright's performance. Although a small man, not of the commanding stature one might expect of the powerful Moorish soldier, Wright infused the role with an intelligent, almost intellectual air. "Othello offers a character easily overplayed. . . . It speaks volumes for Mr. Wright's ability that he was able to hold a curb on himself in the tempestuous passages, and it was this characteristic that enabled him to make a deep impression upon the audience."[10]

After a week (April 24–30) at the Lafayette, producer Rudolph Voelckel (former manager of the Black Patti Troubadours) took the troupe to Boston where they played for a week at the Grand Opera House. They then returned to New York for a professional matinee for white actors at the York Theater, which was well received, although the *New York Telegraph* felt obliged to take a few racist swipes ("And now Darktown is to take a whack at the Shakespeare Tercentenary thing . . . razors may be checked at the door").[11] A few days later the same paper published a lengthier review, saying, "the novelty of the enterprise is probably the chief reason for its success thus far, for there are many causes which must prevent it from being an artistic or enduring success."[12] The *Telegraph*'s main objection seemed to be that an all-black cast negated the black-white tension. Of Wright, it said,

> Edward Sterling Wright, whose ambition it is to become the recognized colored Othello of all time, seemed yesterday to be fully warranted in his aspirations. In one respect, at least, nature has favored him over any other actor who has yet essayed the role. . . . Mr. Wright's Othello is without doubt the blackest Othello in the history of the stage. He gives to his interpretation an earnest quality of dignity that would be heightened if he were to gesticulate less, for he is neither sufficiently familiar with his curved Moorish scimitar nor with his strange Venetian surround-

ings to brandish his keen-edged and uncomfortable weapon with the same gay and careless abandon that marks the way of a barber with his blade. In the midnight broil of drunken Cassio, Mr. Wright does things with his scimitar that would seem to imperil even more than the wigs and whiskers of Roderigo, Iago, Ledovico and other innocent bystanders.

The reviewer later added that "sincerity, dignity and admirable intentions mark the performance as one of which the colored race may well be proud."

The company then played for a week beginning May 22 at the Walnut Street Theatre in Philadelphia, to audiences composed about equally of blacks and whites. Once again white critics were intrigued. Wrote the *Philadelphia Public Ledger,* "they are a group of intelligent young men and women, some of whom have had wider experience in acting than others, but it was evident that all approached the work with sincerity and intense seriousness of purpose. They are deserving of praise for their courage in undertaking such a task at a time when some professional managers are just beginning to be persuaded that Shakespeare does not spell ruin." The *Philadelphia North American* called it a "creditable performance" and an "effective entertainment," while the *Philadelphia Telegraph* observed, after some sarcastic opening remarks, "in all seriousness, it is no slight thing for a company to give so adequate a performance as that staged last night under any circumstances."[13]

Wright was singled out for praise. The *Ledger* felt he "played the name role with requisite dignity, and his reading of the lines, although given at times to somewhat of the older method of exaggeration, was precise, entirely understandable and by no means devoid of poetic feeling. He denoted the gradual growth of jealousy with a deal of artistry, and his handling of the culmination of the tragedy was forceful without being ranting." The *Telegraph* opined that "Mr. Wright's conception of Othello seemed not to be the bluff, all conquering soldier turned into a raging beast by jealousy, but rather that of a man of the finest sensibilities roused to fury. In the third act with Iago his gradual development of the character was notably good, and in the final act he played with potency and power." The *Philadelphia Evening Bulletin* was reminded of the great nineteenth-century Negro tragedian Ira Aldridge, who had played Othello in England for many years.

There was talk of a western tour for the play, but despite the favorable reception in the East this apparently did not transpire. Wright may have restaged the play at the Lafayette Theatre in 1919, although this is not certain.[14] That he was dedicating himself to the cause of serious black theater is demonstrated by his involvement with *Goat Alley,* at New York's Bijou Theatre in June 1921. This rather heavy drama by white playwright Ernest Howard Culbertson was billed as a realistic but tragic portrait of life in the Washington, D.C., ghettos. A failure, it closed after five performances. Although not in the principal cast, Wright was apparently involved in some way.

Edward Sterling Wright's life was cut short when he was struck by an automobile on Queens Boulevard in Long Island City, New York, on December 8, 1921. He died at nearby St. John's Hospital on January 16, 1922, and was buried in Evergreen Cemetery. An obituary in the *Chicago Defender* described him as a dramatic lecturer in the schools of Boston and New York, and recalled his involvement with *Othello* and "the unfortunate *Goat Alley*." It said he left a wife, Bessie Wright, of 668 Third Avenue.[15] No children are mentioned, but an Edward S. Wright is listed at the same address in the 1924 New York city directory, and there are listings for an Edward Sterling Wright in Harlem phone books from the 1930s to the 1960s, so he may have had a son.

Although a little-known figure in black history, Edward Sterling Wright made important contributions both in popularizing the work of Paul Laurence Dunbar and in furthering the growth of black theater. His three Edison cylinders are his aural legacy.

20 James Reese Europe

One of the most influential and revered black musicians of the 1910s is, paradoxically, one of the less remembered today. Murdered at the age of thirty-nine, James Reese Europe was in the early stages of a brilliant and colorful career that might well have earned him a more prominent place in history books had he lived into the 1920s. As it is, we know him primarily from a handful of interesting and innovative recordings. He was the first black bandleader to record in the United States, and his records are fascinating precursors of big band jazz.

Jim Europe was born in Mobile, Alabama, on February 22, 1880, the fourth of five children of Henry and Lorraine Europe.[1] The Europes were a middle-class black family. Henry, who had been born a slave, was a civil servant who prospered under Republican patronage, as well as an active worker in church affairs, while Lorraine was the freeborn daughter of a prominent Mobile family. Music and study were encouraged, and two of Jim's siblings, John (1875–1932) and Mary (1885–1947), also became professional musicians.

In 1889 the family moved to Washington, D.C., where Henry accepted a position with the National Postal Service in the new Republican administration of Benjamin Harrison. Jim studied violin under Enrico Hurlei, the assistant director of the U.S. Marine Band, and began to make a name for himself in recitals and competitions. At age fourteen he won second prize in a citywide music composition contest; sister Mary placed first.

The sudden death of Henry Europe in 1899 left his family in a somewhat precarious position. The two eldest daughters lived in Alabama, and neither Jim nor his siblings John and Mary had established careers that would allow them to support the family. So John moved to New York City, where he found work as a piano player in clubs. He was followed during the winter of 1902–3 by Jim, who first sought employment at a violinist and, when that failed, as a mandolin and piano player. A gregarious sort, Jim hung out with other black musicians and actors at the famed Marshall Hotel on West 53rd Street.

The Marshall was a meeting place for New York's black creative community, and the friendships Jim made there led to several opportunities. He formed a string quartet that played for the Wanamakers, leading to a lasting relationship with that prominent New York family. In the fall of 1904 he was engaged as conductor for John Larkins's musical *A Trip to Africa,* which opened on October 17 at the Third Avenue Theatre. It was Europe's first big break, and almost his last. The opening was a disaster. The *Freeman,* which was normally friendly to any black production, called this one a sorry mess, reserving special criticism for the conductor ("the orchestra was vile, cues were not taken up fast enough by the director"). Europe complained that he had been engaged at the last minute, but the reporter for the *Freeman* obviously didn't believe him.[2]

Recovering from this debacle Europe began to write songs, some with Larkins, including instrumental numbers and marches. In early 1905 he became one of the original members of Ernest Hogan's successful Memphis Students company, playing ragtime and other syncopated music. When the Students left for England in the fall, led by composer Will Marion Cook, Europe remained behind and joined Cole and Johnson's new musical *The Shoo Fly Regiment* as conductor. One of his songs, "On the Gay Luneta," was included in the show. He remained with Cole and Johnson through a long road tour in 1906 and early 1907, leaving in March 1907 to begin work developing a musical for black comedian S. H. Dudley's Smart Set Company.

The Black Politician opened on September 14, 1907, with book by R. C. McPherson and music by Europe, and starring Dudley. This time the *Freeman* was cautiously complimentary. "James Reese Europe, whose reputation has not yet quite caught up with the length of his name, is accredited as composer of all the music. He is leader of the orchestra and a very good one. His music gives evidence that he possesses more ability as a composer then he has hitherto been given a chance to exhibit, and we will look forth encouragingly for what his demand may create in the future."[3]

Europe's career in New York theater continued to prosper as the decade came to a close. In April 1908 he left the Smart Set Company to begin work on a new Cole and Johnson project, *The Red Moon,* which opened October 24 in Chicago. The *Freeman* now enthused, "James Reese Europe, musical director and composer of some of the music of the show, handled the orchestra and the chorus in a masterly way. He worked every minute he was in the pit and between the acts. The show has 21 big numbers and every one takes two or more encores. The musical director in the big league has to work these days."[4]

During the summer of 1908 Europe was one of the original members of the Frogs Club, a black actor's society founded that year with George Walker (of Williams and Walker) as its first president. He toured with *The Red Moon* throughout 1909, leaving at the end of the year to join Bert Williams's *Mr. Lode of Koal* as musical director.

Many of Europe's contemporaries would have been, and were, content with a successful career composing and conducting for the musical theater. But Jim Europe had bigger goals. An ambitious man, and a natural leader, he could not help but notice how disorganized and exploited ordinary black musicians were in New York. The white musicians' union had little interest in them, and influential theatrical societies such as the Lambs and the White Rats were rigidly segregated. As a result, black musicians—when they worked at all—worked for minimum wages under the worst possible conditions.

There had been attempts to redress the situation, by organizations including the Frogs, the New Amsterdam Musical Association (founded in the early 1900s) and the Colored Vaudeville Benevolent Association (1909), but black musicians still had no central booking agency effectively promoting their interests. In the spring of 1910, shortly after the closing of *Mr. Lode of Koal,* Europe and some of his friends from the Marshall decided to launch a new organization, the Clef Club. Europe was elected its first president with cabaret pianist Dan Kildare as vice-president.

Europe plunged into this new project with his accustomed energy. A tall, imposing, yet outgoing man, he did not easily take "no" for an answer and usually got things done. Realizing that more than a fancy name and a letterhead would be necessary to change entrenched attitudes, he immediately set in motion an ambitious plan to draw attention to the club. The first order of business was to organize a Clef Club Symphony Orchestra and then make arrangements for its well-publicized debut. The gala benefit at Manhattan Casino on May 27 was a smashing success. Europe led a one-hundred-piece orchestra, assisted by Joe Jordan and Al Johns, playing both standard repertoire and syncopated music. The instrumentation was unique, consisting of ten pianos and dozens of mandolins, banjos, and related string instruments, This did not look or sound like the "normal" white orchestra and it attracted a good deal of attention.

Clef Club concerts thereafter became semiannual affairs, held each spring and fall. The musicians' enthusiasm was evident in ads appearing in the *New York Age* for the second concert. "Yea Bo!" exulted the headline, "The Clef Club of the City of New York Will Present the Clef Club Symphony Orchestra of 100 Musicians (Using 11 Pianos), Personally Conducted by James Reese Europe, in Their Second Grand Concert . . . 8:15 sharp, Dancing from 11 until dawn."[5] The club also set up a musician's hotline and began providing orchestras for clubs and private parties. By December it had moved to a two-floor clubhouse on West 53rd Street and published its first membership directory.

Although the Clef Club benefited black musicians throughout New York, it gave a special boost to the career of Jim Europe. A first-rate musician and showman, he drilled his musicians until they became a tight ensemble, one that could "swing" with the most syncopated, contemporary music of the day. Increasingly callers to the Club's booking line wanted Europe himself. He found himself organizing several orchestras, sometimes shuttling between them on a single night, leading each for a few minutes before handing the baton to an assistant conductor and moving on. Eubie Blake, who joined Europe a few years later, vividly described the scene.

> Europe was a big, tall man, very commanding. Stood up straight, like a West Point soldier. *He* knew his music—studied arranging and conducting at Columbia. We all called him Jim . . . very flexible. At home or in the White House, it was all the same to him. You couldn't *make* him mad. And he had a brain! My God, he could see around corners. He could always figure out what was going to happen and be prepared for it. He knew how to make a plan and stick to it.
>
> Play? Well, he used to *sit* at a piano and *hold* a violin. I was the assistant conductor, and Jim used to hand me the baton almost every number after he started it off, then he'd go mingle with the people.

Now the white bands all had their music stands, see, but the people wanted to believe that Negroes couldn't learn to read music but had a natural talent for it. So we never played with no music. Now this is the truth. Europe's orchestra was filled with readin' *sharks*. That cornet player, Russell Smith! If a fly landed on the music, he'd play it, see, like *that*. But we weren't supposed to read music. . . . All the high-tone, big-time folks would say, "Isn't it wonderful how these untrained, primitive musicians can pick up all the latest songs instantly without being able to read music?"[6]

Europe did not stint in his efforts to help other black musicians. Besides presiding over the thriving Clef Club, he helped David Mannes, son-in-law of eminent conductor Walter Damrosch, found the Music School Settlement for Colored People in Harlem in 1911 with the aid of white philanthropists. In May 1912 the Clef Club staged its most spectacular concert yet, at Carnegie Hall. A black orchestra performing popular music in that august temple of white culture was revolutionary and attracted some resistance, even within the black community. The eccentric "grand old man" of black music in New York, composer Will Marion Cook, opposed it, claiming Europe knew nothing of serious conducting, and that the project would "set the Negro race back fifty years." He refused to participate—until the last minute, when he quietly slipped into the orchestra with his violin and began to play under Europe's baton. The concert was a stunning success.[7]

In January 1913 Europe married Willie Angrom Starke (1877–1930), a widow "of some social standing within New York's black community."[8] However biographer Reid Badger notes that this was not Europe's only romantic involvement. Around 1908, during the run of *The Red Moon,* he had met Bessie Simms (1889–1931), an attractive young dancer with whom he had a long-term relationship. He continued to see her even after his marriage, and in 1917 she had a son, his only child. Presumably Willie, and Jim's strait-laced family, knew about this, but they said nothing, at least publicly.

During the remainder of the year Europe produced and/or conducted the Negro Players' production *The Old Man's Boy* in Philadelphia, the *Frog Frolics* (which toured in the summer), and several Clef Club concerts, including a tour of the East Coast. His own orchestras were extremely busy playing for white society in New York and Newport. At one of these engagements in the late summer Europe met superstar dancers Vernon and Irene Castle, who were so impressed with his musicianship and personality that they hired him as their personal conductor. Vernon was especially taken with the infectious dance rhythms played by Europe's orchestra. Castle began taking drum lessons from the band's star drummer, Buddy Gilmore, and developed into a more than competent drummer himself.

It is difficult to overstate how popular the Castles were at this time. Slender, athletic Vernon and winsome Irene were trendy, ultra-chic and very, very contemporary. They had burst on the scene in 1912 as exhibition dancers in the swankiest clubs in Paris and New York. Astutely managed by Elizabeth Marbury, a literary agent with close ties to high society, their youth and style captured the imagination of America. How appropriate that such an utterly modern act would use the best syncopated black orchestra in New York (the music hadn't evolved into jazz yet) for its accompaniment. White dancers appearing with a black orchestra would, of course, be an anathema in some parts of the country, but the Castles didn't appear in the South. They were stars of the urban, liberal Northeast, and Europe and his musicians were in any event perceived as their employees, not their equals.

Europe's association with the Castles catapulted him from a prominent position within the black musical world to some celebrity in the much larger world of white entertainment, a rarefied level attained by few blacks aside from the phenomenally popular Bert Williams. It undoubtedly led to the unprecedented offer from the Victor Talking Machine Company for him to record several dance selections for them, under the name Europe's Society Orchestra. This appears to be the first time a black orchestra was recorded by any major label for commercial release in the United States.[9]

On December 29, 1913, Europe assembled twelve of his best men at the Victor studios in New York in front of the big recording horn used for orchestras and choruses. According to the recording ledgers five banjo mandolins, three violins, one clarinet, one cornet, one trap drum, and one piano ("2 playing it") were used. The unusual instrumentation must have been a challenge for the Victor recording technicians; in these premicrophone days each player had to be placed at exactly the right distance from the large horn to achieve a proper sound balance. Victor's experts were among the best in the business, but they were used to the standard instrumentation of brass bands and string orchestras, which seldom featured mandolins or hard-to-record drums. Nevertheless the sound, while subject to the limitations of acoustic recording, was reasonably full and defined.

Four selections were recorded that day, and it is a testament to the proficiency of the musicians that in three out of four cases Victor's finicky experts approved the first take for issue. First was an English import called "Too Much Mustard" (or "Tres Moutarde"), a fast-paced one-step/Turkey Trot that was a favorite in the dance clubs. Europe had often played it for the Castles. The orchestra gave it an unbelievably rough and ready performance, with shouts from the bandmembers, cymbal crashes, and frantic drumming (complete with military drum rolls) by the energetic Buddy Gilmore. Edgar Campbell's clarinet took the lead, with Gilmore's drumming prominent behind him, a most unusual arrangement for the time. The high energy performance lasted nearly four minutes on a twelve-inch record and must have exhausted dancers who tried to keep up with it.

Comparison with other recorded versions reveals how different Europe's performance style was. The Columbia version of "Too Much Mustard" was by its studio orchestra, led by Charles A. Prince. It is taken at the same fast tempo but in strict military time, with cornet and trombone predominating and blocks for rhythm (the drums are not even audible). It is a stiff and mechanical performance compared to Europe's Victor. Most Victor dance records of the period were by the Victor Military Band, led by Walter B. Rogers, which had recorded the popular "Too Much Mustard" about a year earlier. Rogers's reading is not as stiff as Columbia's but still has traditional military band instrumentation, with brass taking the lead, and a tuba for rhythm (no drums audible). Certainly there were no exuberant shouts from the well-disciplined musicians of either band.

The second selection recorded was "Down Home Rag," by black composer and bandleader Wilbur Sweatman. It is also a one-step or Turkey Trot and is played even faster than "Too Much Mustard." Violins and drums predominate, egged on by encouraging shouts from the musicians. At times the drums fade out, leaving the fast-sawing violins to go solo, lending an even more varied sound; at the end the whole ensemble plays a fast "shave and a haircut, two bits" figure, as if to exclaim "that's all, folks!" It sounded like a party in progress. The Victor studios had seldom seen anything like this.

The final two titles demonstrated the orchestra's versatility. They were "Amapa," a Brazilian maxixe, and "El Irresistible," an Argentine tango, both taken at a moderate tempo, with mandolins, violins, and castanets predominating. The latter was given a rather dramatic reading with the stops and starts characteristic of the tango and a trombone evident at times. Europe's men produced a smooth, full-bodied sound, demonstrating how they were able to accompany the Castles quite expertly in any type of dance routine. There were no more shouts from the orchestra.

Six weeks later, on February 10, 1914, Europe returned to the Victor studios, this time accompanied by Vernon and Irene Castle who, for publicity purposes, had agreed to "supervise" the recordings. The instrumentation was somewhat different, omitting the five mandolins and adding a flute, 'cello, and baritone horn for a total of ten instruments. Once again the piano was played by two men, Leonard Smith and Ford Dabney.

Four titles were recorded, three of them written or cowritten by Europe especially for the Castles. The ledgers indicate changes being made on the spot, perhaps at the suggestion of Vernon and Irene. Annotations indicate that Europe's "The Castles in Europe" was retitled "Castle House Rag," while the title "Castle's Lame Duck" was crossed out and renamed "Congratulations Waltz."[10]

First to be recorded was a then-popular but now forgotten Broadway show tune called "You're Here and I'm Here" by Jerome Kern, which was being featured at the time in the musical *The Laughing Husband.* All the major record companies issued versions of the hit tune, vocal and/or instrumental, and Victor, needing an quick instrumental, assigned it to Europe—perhaps because he happened to be in the studio that day. It is the only example from these early sessions of the Europe orchestra playing a current pop tune, something they no doubt did frequently in appearances. A lively one-step, it is played with as much distinctiveness as the orchestra can manage, violins carrying the melody with prominent drumming (alternating with blocks) providing the rhythm. Buddy Gilmore's enthusiastic drumming is in fact the most distinctive feature of Europe's 1913–14 recordings, setting them apart from other dance records of the period, in which drums were seldom heard.

With "Castle House Rag" (aka "The Castles in Europe"), another one-step, the Europe orchestra was back in familiar territory. There were no shouts from the band members in this session, but otherwise the performance was similar to the frenetic "Too Much Mustard" and "Down Home Rag" from December, with fast sawing violins in the lead, backed by fancy drumming. The arrangement was more varied than that of "Down Home Rag," with bells and other instruments coming in and out. "Castle Walk," by Europe and Dabney, was billed as a "one-step or trot" (the Castles liked fast dances) but was a little more lyrical than some of the other numbers. Here the violins were accompanied by rim shots on the drums, which sounded like gun-shots punctuating the music.

The final number, "Congratulations," showed another side of the band's abilities, providing a stately waltz to be danced as a "hesitation or Boston." The longest of the early recordings at four minutes and fifteen seconds, its steady one-two-three rhythm makes it sound like a real dance instruction recording, quite competently played.

It should be noted that a white Castle House Orchestra, directed by Frank W. McKee, recorded maxixes, tangos, and waltzes for Victor at about this time. Vernon Castle also supervised these sessions, but Jim Europe, who was essentially the Castles' "hot" orchestra leader, does not appear to have been involved. McKee later made many recordings for Victor with his own string orchestra.[11]

The social dancing craze was at its peak during the winter of 1913–14, and dance records were selling like hotcakes. Victor and Columbia rushed to get on top of the trend, churning out dozens of new releases covering all of the new steps. Victor, as usual, was one step ahead of its rival Columbia (both outscored the laggardly Edison). Under the heading "dance records," the November 1914 Victor general catalog listed the following categories: Barn Dances, Boston, Cakewalks, Castle Polka, Castle Walk, Clog Dances, Fish Walk, Fox Trots, Gavotte, Grand Marches, Half and Half, Hesitation (or Boston), Jigs, Lu Lu Fado, Maxixe, One-Step, Pavlowa Gavotte, Quadrilles, Reels, Schottisches, Ta Tao, Tango/Maxixe, Three Steps, Trot, Two Steps, and Waltzes. A curious note added that an additional five records "were recorded when the One-Step and Trot were first introduced, and are rather slow for present use, but can be used for Barn Dance and Schottische." In all there were almost four hundred entries (with some duplication), the vast majority by military bands led by Walter B. Rogers or Arthur Pryor.

Europe's first two releases, the raucous "Too Much Mustard" / "Down Home Rag" and "Irresistible" / "Amapa," were announced in a special list rushed out in early February 1914. The other four titles were released in April.

The announcement of the signing of the Castles, together with a large picture of the pair, appeared in the April 1914 supplement, and special brochures were issued showing the couple demonstrating some of their steps. One of these reprinted a letter from Vernon, dated March 2, 1914, on Castle House stationery, stating that "Mrs. Castle and I, after a thorough trial of other sound reproducing instruments, have decided to use the Victor and Victor Records exclusively at Castle House. . . . I also take great pleasure in announcing that I have given to the Victor Company the exclusive services of the Castle House Orchestra for the making of dance records, and also that I will personally superintend the making of Victor Dance Records."[12] The labels of Europe's February recordings even bore the unusual statement, "Recorded under the personal supervision of Mr. and Mrs. Vernon Castle."

Columbia countered with a blaze of publicity, stating that it had engaged well-known dance instructor G. Hepburn Wilson, who operated several dancing schools in New York, to supervise *its* records. It also signed the Clef Club orchestra led by Europe associate Dan Kildare (q.v.), which played for Castle rival Joan Sawyer, and even claimed that Vernon Castle had also endorsed its records.[13] But the stiff Columbia renditions, mostly by Prince's Military Band, paled beside the Victor releases, especially those by Europe. The Victor April supplement enthused, "Many of these [records were] made with drums and other trap effects, which seem to be quite popular, as they not only accentuate the rhythm, but probably increase the high spirit of the dancers! The Europe Orchestra records have made a hit, and our customers will note with pleasure four more up-to-the-minute selections by this famous organization, made under the personal direction of Mr. Castle."[14]

Although no sales figures are available for Victor records of this period, the number of surviving copies suggests that Europe's releases sold quite well, especially the one-steps and rags. Two of them were also released in England. Some of Jim Europe's compositions for the Castles were recorded by others as well. "Castle Walk" and "Congratulations" appeared on Columbia (by Prince's Band), and the "Castle House Rag" on an Edison cylinder (by the National Promenade Band). Another popular Europe-Dabney number, "Castle's Half and Half," was released on Columbia and Edison.[15] According to Badger, Europe composed at least nine songs with "Castle" in the title, most during the spring of 1914.

Despite all this activity Europe did not receive much personal publicity from Victor. Perhaps because it was nervous about publicizing a black orchestra, perhaps because the emphasis was on the Castles, Victor said nothing about him in its catalogs and supplements and printed no picture of him after an introductory flyer for his first two discs (even though it customarily did so for its new artists).[16] The name on the label read simply "Europe's Society Orchestra," and many buyers outside the New York area must have been unaware that it was a black orchestra that was making these exciting sounds. Similarly, Columbia never gave any indication that Joan Sawyer's Persian Garden Orchestra was black.

Jim Europe made one more trip to the Victor studios, on October 1, 1914, but neither of the titles recorded at that session was released. That is a pity, because both were apparently songs composed by him, "Fiora Waltz" and "Fox Trot." It is uncertain what the proper title of the latter number is, but since Europe is supposed to have devised the fox trot—one of the most popular dances of the twentieth century—for the Castles, it would be interesting to hear a contemporary recording of it by him. Europe and Dabney also made piano rolls for the Welte-Mignon Company in Poughkeepsie, New York, during April 1914.[17]

As historic as Jim Europe's 1913–14 recordings appear today, they were not the most important event in his busy life at the time. More startling to his contemporaries was his abrupt and unexpected resignation from the Clef Club, which he had founded and labored so hard to build, in late December 1913. No one who was there has left us a clear account of exactly what happened, but the likely reason was infighting and jealousy within the ranks.

Europe's rapidly growing fame, as a result of his association with the Castles, must have raised the hackles of some of his colleagues. His was the name that appeared frequently in the black press, his was the orchestra that was called for constantly for the most prestigious venues, he was the man asked to lead the first recordings ever by an African American orchestra. The breaking point may have been a November 20 story in the *New York Age,* which described in glowing terms the latest Clef Club Concert at Manhattan Casino, gave extreme praise to its conductor, and rhapsodized that "Mr. Europe is so completely identified with the public appearance of the Clef Club that a concert without Europe would be similar to seeing Hamlet played with no Hamlet present."[18]

No amount of modesty and attentiveness to the needs of others could have overcome the jealousy of some of his colleagues in the face of such paeans. Europe disliked politics and infighting, so rather than force the issue, it appears he simply quit. Faced with the loss of their president and founder, club members met on December 30 (the day after some of them had participated in Europe's first recording session) and elected a successor, former vice-president Dan Kildare.[19] One wonders if the charming Kildare, a ladies' man with an aggressive streak (he later killed two women, and himself, in a murder-suicide), had something to do with the turmoil.

In any event no one seemed to bear any grudges, at least not in public, even when Europe founded a competing musicians' organization, the Tempo Club, in early January with the assistance of Ford Dabney and William Tyers.[20] Europe remained a "financial member" of the Clef Club, and members of both clubs performed together. So great was the demand for black musicians in New York that both organizations prospered during the following years, although the Clef Club (even under Dan Kildare's mismanagement) remained predominant.

Another historic event took place on January 12 when, as the *Age* reported, "For the first time in the history of New York, theatre-goers witnessed the unusual spectacle of a colored orchestra playing in the pit of a first class theatre for white artists. The scene was enacted at two houses in one afternoon—Hammerstein's Victoria Theatre and the Palace Theatre. Such an unusual condition was due to the insistence of Mr. and Mrs. Vernon Castle, known in the Four Hundred as society dancers, that James Reese Europe's Society Orchestra play their dance music."[21]

The white musicians who normally played in these theaters at first disdained the black band members, but when the latter received loud ovations and demands for encores the white musicians insisted the black men move on to the stage, where they could be considered "performers" rather than a pit orchestra. Europe complied.

The remainder of the year was filled with concerts and a twenty-eight-day tour with the Castles. Among the concerts were several by the National Negro Symphony Orchestra, which was an outgrowth of the Clef Club Symphony Orchestra and a pet project of Europe's. It appeared at a March 11 benefit at Carnegie Hall, accompanying such celebrities as Will Marion Cook, Abbie Mitchell, Harry T. Burleigh and Cook's Afro-American Folk Song Singers. Another performance took place on April 8 with Vernon and Irene Castle demonstrating dances for the black audience as a tribute to Europe and Dabney. The Castles also appeared at a Tempo Club show in October.

During 1914 Jim Europe gave two long and thoughtful newspaper interviews in which he articulated his thoughts about the future of Negro music. The first appeared in the *New York Post* in March.

> The reason that he had made a success of his musical enterprises, according to Mr. Europe, is that he has recognized the principle that the negro should stick to his own specialties and not try to imitate the white man's work. His attitude is that in

his own musical field the negro is safe from all competition, so why should he go to the useless task of attempting to interpret a music that is foreign to all the elements in his character?

"You see, we colored people have our own music that is part of us," he explained. "It's us; it's the product of our souls; it's been created by the sufferings and miseries of our race. Some of the old melodies we played Wednesday night were made up by slaves of the old days, and others were handed down from the days before we left Africa. Our symphony orchestra never tries to play white folks' music. We should be foolish to attempt such a thing. We are no more fitted for that than a white orchestra is fitted to play our music. . . .

"I know of no white man who has written negro music that rings true. Indeed, how could such a thing be possible? How could a white man feel in his heart the music that a black man feels? There is a great deal of alleged negro music by white composers, but it is not real. Even the negro ragtime music of white composers falls far short of the genuine dance compositions of negro musicians. . . . Music breathes the spirit of a race, and, strictly speaking, it is a part only of the race which creates it."

Nor, he added, was his orchestra organized along the lines of a white ensemble.

"For instance, although we have first violins, the place of the second violins with us is taken by mandolins and banjos. This gives that peculiar steady strumming accompaniment to our music which all people comment on, and which is something like that of the Russian Balalaika Orchestra, I believe. Then, for background, we employ ten pianos. That, in itself, is sufficient to amuse the average white musician who attends one of our concerts for the first time. The result, however, is a background of chords which are essentially typical of negro harmony . . . we have developed a kind of symphony music that, no matter what else you may think, is different and distinctive, and that lends itself to the playing of the peculiar compositions of our race."[22]

In a November interview with the *New York Tribune* Europe explained the realities of working in his world.

The Tempo Club contains about two hundred members, all musicians, and from this body I supply at present a majority of the orchestras which play in the various cafes of the city and also at the private dances. Our Negro musicians have nearly cleared the field of the so called gypsy orchestras. . . .

Yet we Negroes are under a great handicap. For "The Castle Lame Duck Waltz" I receive only one cent a copy [sheet music] royalty and the phonographic royalties in like proportion. A white man would receive from six to twelve times the royalty I receive, and compositions far less popular than mine, but written by white men, gain for their composers vastly greater rewards. I have done my best to put a stop to this discrimination, but I have found that it was no use. The music world is controlled by a trust, and the Negro must submit to its demands or fail to have his compositions produced. I am not bitter about it. It is, after all, but a slight proportion of the price my race must pay in its at times almost hopeless fight for a place in the sun. Someday it will be different and justice will prevail.

He also said of the music of black composers, "These songs are the only folk music America possesses, and folk music being the basis of so much that is most beautiful in the world, there is indeed hope for the art product of our race."[23]

It was also during 1914 that Europe and Vernon Castle worked out the music and steps to the fox trot, which would arguably become the Castles' most enduring legacy. Vernon credited Europe with the piece, but Europe modestly gave credit to W. C. Handy's recently published "Memphis Blues" as providing his inspiration.[24] The dance became so popular it was featured in the Castles' hit Broadway musical *Watch Your Step,* which opened in December (Europe was supposed to play for the Castles in this show but dropped out at the last minute for unknown reasons).

Europe continued to appear regularly with the Castles during the first half of 1915, until Vernon, a patriotic Englishman, left to join the Royal Air Corps as a combat pilot during the summer. Irene continued as a solo, but with less need for Europe's services. Vernon survived more than one hundred missions behind German lines, only to be killed during a training mission near Fort Worth, Texas, in early 1918.

His association with the Castles winding down, Europe turned his attention to collaborating with the cranky but talented composer Will Marion Cook on a new musical called *Darkydom.* It starred comedians Miller and Lyles in their first major show but had only a short run in New York and Washington during the fall. Cook and Europe alternated conducting the orchestra.

Two musicians who would be particularly important to Europe's later career and legacy joined the band in early 1916. They were Noble Sissle, a handsome young tenor, and his friend, pianist Eubie Blake. Both were composers and collaborated with Europe on new songs. Sissle, a natural leader, became Europe's right-hand man.

In May 1916 an intriguing story in the *New York Age* reported, "On Tuesday of this week James Reese Europe's Castles in the Air Band played for Holbrook Blinn, who is [appearing in] a picture which is being made at Fort Lee, N.J. Those who took part in the making of the film were William Tyers, conductor; Elias Bowman, bandolin; Sylvester Williams, saxophone; Clarence Jones, flute; Russell Smith, cornet; Frank Withers, trombone; Buddy Gilmore, drums; Nelson Kincaid, clarinet; Lawrence Costner, bass; Isadore Myers, piano; Joe Lynas, violin; Hall Johnson, violin."[25]

Blinn was a major silent-movie star who made eight dramatic features during 1916 and 1917; it is uncertain which one this was, or whether Europe's band was in the finished film. Even without Jim Europe himself present, it would be fascinating to see his band, including such recording notables as Buddy Gilmore and Russell Smith, in a motion picture. Unfortunately no copies of the film have been found.

Jim Europe's career took a new turn in mid-1916 when he was approached by Colonel William Hayward, commander of the 15th New York Infantry, to take over the regimental band. The 15th was an all-black National Guard regiment under white officers which, despite the national mood of preparedness, was finding enlistments slow. A first-rate band under a respected figure like Europe might help.

Europe was at first skeptical. He was patriotic, but his standards were high and he would have little money or equipment to work with. Hayward was persistent, and when he raised $10,000 from white philanthropist Daniel G. Reid to outfit the band, Europe finally agreed. He signed up in September, replacing bandleader E. E. Thompson, and within weeks had molded the regimental band into a first-class outfit. Appearances at recruiting drives followed, and enlistments boomed.

In December Europe was commissioned a lieutenant, one of the first black officers in the regiment. He continued to fine-tune the regimental band while simultaneously managing his civilian organizations. Noble Sissle also enlisted and became his drum major and star vocalist. Eugene Mikell, another close associate, was persuaded to join as assistant conductor. But lining up all the right men for the world-class military band he envisioned was not easy, and Europe was forced to make a quick trip to Puerto Rico in May 1917 to find reed players.

The United States declared war on Germany on April 6, 1917, and the first American forces landed in France in June. The 15th Regiment was called into active service on July 15 and began training at Camp Whitman, near Poughkeepsie, New York. In early October it was sent to Spartanburg, South Carolina, for further training, which proved to be a serious mistake as the southern town bitterly resented black soldiers in its midst. Lieutenant Europe, Sergeant Sissle, and other leaders did their best to avoid confrontations (basically, the black soldiers were told to take any abuse and not fight back), but after two weeks of increasingly serious incidents and a near riot the regiment was abruptly shipped back north. There it encountered further racism, including a shooting incident with Alabama troops at Camp Mills, Long Island.[26]

Finally, after several false starts, the 15th sailed for France in December, arriving on January 1, 1918. It was first assigned to support activities. By April it was renamed the 369th Infantry, attached to the 4th French Army, and assigned a frontline position in the Argonne Forest. Eager to see action, Europe got himself assigned to a machine-gun company and became the first black officer to lead troops in combat during the war.[27] Caught in a gas attack in June, he was taken to a hospital where he recuperated and returned to bandmaster duties in August. Meanwhile, the black soldiers of the 369th so distinguished themselves in battle they earned the unit the moniker "Hell Fighters," a name that was attached to Europe's band as well.

The Army recognized that Europe's real value was as a bandleader. His well-trained band gained fame both throughout the AEF and with the French for its ability to play peculiarly American black syncopated music (now being called "jas" or "jazz"). They toured recreation centers and hospitals throughout France, cheering the Americans and winning the hearts of the French with sounds they had never heard before—*le jazz hot*. Generals began to compete for their services, and the band was eventually posted to 1st Army Headquarters in Paris. Other black American army bands were also making names for themselves at this time, including those of Tim Brymn, E. E. Thompson, and Will Vodery, but Europe's 369th "Hell Fighters" were by acclamation the best. Stories about their triumphs began to appear in newspapers and magazines back home, and there were popular songs about black soldiers bringing ragtime and jazz to France ("When Alexander Takes His Ragtime Band to France," "When Uncle Joe Steps into France"). There was even a song dedicated to Lieutenant James Reese Europe, with the somewhat awkward title, "When the Good Lord Makes a Record of a Hero's Deed, He Draws No Color Line."[28]

When the war ended the 369th Regiment returned to a hero's welcome with a giant parade up New York City's Fifth Avenue on February 17, 1919. Jim Europe's 369th Infantry Regiment Band were the stars of the day, playing hotter and hotter as they marched toward Harlem. They were lionized.

Jim Europe and his sixty-piece military band on the cover of the sheet music for one of his biggest hits (1919).

It was some affectionate howdy; it was some day. . . . Never in the history of Father Knickerbocker has such a rousing royal welcome been given returning heroes from the field of battle; not for many a day is it likely that thousands of white and colored citizens will participate in such a tumultuous and enthusiastic demonstration. . . .

Fifth Avenue gave Col. Hayward's braves a noisy welcome, but in Harlem the greeting bordered on riot. Amid exciting scenes and the band playing "Here Comes My Daddy Now," the Hell Fighters marched between two howling walls of human-ity from 125th to 140th Street. Those unable to secure standing room on the side-walk [hung from windows and lampposts], while from the rooftops thousands stood and whooped things up.[29]

James Reese Europe, now an authentic war hero, was at the pinnacle of his ca-reer. As always, he was full of ambitious plans to advance black popular music in America. The Tempo Club, which had become dormant during the war, needed to be revived. The new "jazz" music, a sort of primitive, cacophonous wail, was sweep-ing the country played mostly by white groups such as the Original Dixieland Jazz Band, Earl Fuller's Band, the Louisiana Five, Frisco Jass Band, and Yerkes Jazarimba Orchestra. This was black music, *his* music, and he would take it to another level. There were songs to write, shows to produce (perhaps with his pals Sissle and Blake), and perhaps ultimately his dreamt-of goal of a permanent National Negro Sym-phony Orchestra.

Europe immediately set about arranging a triumphal national tour of his 369th Infantry "Hell Fighters" Band, to bring his veteran musicians to the American pub-lic. This would not be simply a series of concerts, but a full-fledged musical variety show, with vocalists, instrumentalists, quartets, and choruses, and music ranging from current popular hits to spirituals, snatches of the classics, novelty numbers, and, of course, his own brand of big band jazz.

Simultaneously he made plans to return to the recording studio for the first time in nearly five years. It is interesting to speculate why he wasn't signed by either Vic-tor or Columbia, the two giants of the industry. Perhaps they thought they had enough jazz bands already, perhaps his demands for artistic control were too great (the major labels were notorious for forcing artists to conform to their own tried and true approaches). In any event he signed with a relatively small but nationally dis-tributed New York label, Pathé, which had previously recorded at least three of his own bandmembers, Eubie Blake, Noble Sissle, and Opal Cooper. Perhaps they steered him toward the label. Another possible connection was a senior Pathé ex-ecutive named Barrett Andrews, who had recently joined the label after serving on General Pershing's staff in France, where he would undoubtedly have heard Europe's band first-hand.[30]

In a marathon series of sessions "Lieut. Jim Europe's 369th U.S. Infantry ('Hell Fighters') Band" would record an astounding variety of material, including jazz, popular, and serious music, presumably reflecting the full range of his upcoming concerts. Lucky for us.

The sessions began during the first week in March 1919 at the Pathé studios on 42nd Street. Probably ten to fifteen men were in the studio; the limited technology of the day could not capture the ninety or more who had marched down Fifth Avenue

Sensational, Money-Making Jazz Records

Lieutenant Jim

EUROPE'S

HELL FIGHTERS 369th U.S. Infantry **JAZZ BAND**

How Pathé saw its new recording star, Jim Europe. (*Talking Machine World,* May 15, 1919).

a few weeks before.[31] Recording for this small label must have been a somewhat different experience from the Victor sessions five years earlier. Victor was the giant of the industry, and its studios were run by expert musicians who tended to be involved in every aspect of an artist's performance. Pathé promised a somewhat looser atmosphere, one that may have allowed Europe's band to sound the way *he* wanted it to.[32]

No files survive for the Pathé label, so the exact recording dates are not known, but we can estimate them fairly closely from issued recordings. Twenty-two titles appear to have been recorded, fourteen between Monday, March 3 and Friday, March 7, and eight more, all vocal recordings, on Friday, March 14. Fully half were Tin Pan Alley pop tunes, but the rest were an interesting mixture of blues, rags, spirituals, and specialty numbers that accompanied production sequences in the concerts.

The band is shown to best advantage in the three "blues" and the two rags. While not quite as uninhibited as in the wild 1913 Victors (no shouts from the band-members), it is an extraordinarily loose aggregation, exuding enthusiasm and good cheer. There are jazzy riffs, buzz cornets, hot clarinets and even an occasional "shave-and-a-haircut" stinger. A number of small combos were beginning to loosen things up in the recording studio around this time, including the Original Dixieland Jazz Band on Victor and Wilbur Sweatman's Band on Columbia, but no one had made a big band swing like this. Certainly no military band had ever sounded like this on record.

The three blues were all by W. C. Handy. "St. Louis Blues" is replete with hot clarinets, "buzz" cornets, and blues effects. Instruments play off each other in a decidedly nonstandard show arrangement that may sound familiar today but must have been electrifying at the time. It is among the earliest recordings of the famous tune and possibly the first to give it an authentic jazz performance, at least in the United States.[33] "Hesitating Blues" is another good reading, dominated by trombones and other brass instruments until, toward the end, a hot clarinet, à la Wilbur Sweatman, starts peeling the wallpaper off the wall. The third Handy number, "The Memphis Blues," is given a similarly intense treatment dominated by cornets and trombones, with interjected flutes, clarinet squeals, and even a little military bugle flourish.

Musicologist Lawrence Gushee, in his perceptive notes to a 1977 reissue, marveled at the latitude Europe gave his musicians on this last number. "Behind this recording may be a written arrangement treated with considerable nonchalance. The playing is often quite free, with many short ad-libs by solo instruments in addition to the breaks at the end. The clarinets often disagree on pitch and attack . . . the brass sometimes play with great precision, other times not. This, together with surges of volume and a rather nervous pulse, makes an unusual effect, as of going in and out of focus."[34]

"That Moaning Trombone" is a trombone showpiece, a novelty rag with a fast, jazzy rhythm and trombone swoops against the background of a full military band. "Russian Rag," based on Rachmaninoff's Prelude in C Sharp Minor, is even more gimmicky, opening with a "Volga Boatman"–type minor key strain, and featuring buzz effects and trombone swoops. It ends with a triple "shave-and-a-haircut" figure, played by three different instruments.

Europe's stage show was not all hot blues and rags, however. One can almost see the scene change as the band went into a sentimental medley of old Southern airs called "Plantation Echoes." It opens with a fast little dance, followed by a lugubrious reading of "Massa's in de Cold, Cold Ground," a heartfelt vocal rendition of "The Old Folks at Home" by Noble Sissle, and finally a rousing finale of "Dixie." Jim Europe's all-black band playing "Dixie"! Now *that's* show business!

Hardly less surprising is "On Patrol in No Man's Land," a production number written by Sissle and Europe in France and delivered here with gusto by Sissle. Meant to recreate the sounds and excitement of the front for audiences back home, it is full of instruments imitating explosions, rat-tat-tat machine guns, wailing sirens, and whistling shells. Sissle sings, "Nerve gas, put on your mask!" followed by the shouts of a sergeant and troops cheering as the enemy is repelled.[35] Accompanied by a good light show, it must have been quite an entertainment.

Another complete change of pace is heard in four spirituals sung by Europe's male chorus, the Singing Serenaders. The exact composition of this group is not known and evidently changed from performance to performance. On the records it sounds like a quartet or quintet, although Badger calls it a sextet[36] and articles in the phonograph trade papers sometimes referred to it as a double quartet.[37] Badger identifies Messrs. Bumpford, Zabriske, Whitney, L. Gibbs, C. Smith, W. Viney, T. Lee, and Arthur Payne as possible members.

The most striking of the four is Alex Rogers and Will Marion Cook's dramatic "Exhortation (A Negro Sermon)." "Remember!" thundered bass/baritone Creighton Thompson,

If a brudder smotes de on de lef' cheek,
Turn roun' and han' him de odder!

Cause . . .
If you kaint 'turn good fu' evil . . .
What's de good o' bein' a brudder?[38]

A discreet piano accompaniment (perhaps by Europe himself) and backing vocal by the Serenaders served as accompaniment to what must have been Thompson's star turn during the concerts.

More familiar today is the traditional "Little David Play on Your Harp," sung a capella by tenor Noble Sissle and the chorus. Sissle sings the old song with real fervor, alternating with the Serenaders' rhythmic backing; the song ends with an enthusiastic "yeah!"

Also sung a capella were two others by the Serenaders. "Ev'rybody Dat Talks about Heaven Ain't Goin' There" is better known today as "Goin' to Shout All Over God's Heaven." Led by a baritone (apparently not Thompson), the group sings in the familiar call-and-response pattern. "Roll Jordan Roll" is a black "sorrow song," sung slowly and with conviction by the same baritone-led ensemble.

The remaining eleven titles were mostly ephemeral Tin Pan Alley pop tunes. Most sound very "white," even though a few of them were written by black composers including Sissle, Blake, and Europe himself. It is interesting to speculate why Europe, who a few years earlier had spoken so eloquently about the need for black musicians to reflect their own heritage, would himself begin mimicking white Tin Pan Alley's most crass conventions.

Probably the best of the lot was the rousing end-of-war hit, "How Ya Gonna Keep 'Em Down on the Farm (After They've Seen Paree)?" Many bands and vocalists recorded this smash hit, but none with such drive and enthusiasm as Europe's musicians—who had, after all, lived the song's lyrics. Cornets and trombones alternated with flutes in a fast, vaudeville-style opening, followed by a clever bridge and then a vocal chorus by Noble Sissle, who almost shouted the words in a style reminiscent of Eddie Cantor (who was featuring the song in vaudeville at the time). By the time Sissle was finishing the band was really cooking; barely able to be restrained, it came charging back in on top of the end of his vocal, never losing momentum as the song built to a exhilarating conclusion. One wonders if Europe simply signaled the band to "go for it" during the last thirty seconds or so. The finale is so striking that it was reissued by itself—just the finale—on one modern reissue.[39]

Another interesting performance is "Darktown Strutters' Ball," by black songwriter Shelton Brooks, which is given a novelty treatment complete with slide whistle, trombone swoops, and triple-tongued cornet. It is more vaudeville than jazz, but nevertheless a distinctive performance. In comparison, the "Broadway 'Hit' Medley" (including the monster hit "Smiles") sounds lifeless and pedestrian, seemingly read right off the sheet music. "Arabian Nights" was a minor-key "exotic" number along the lines of the currently popular "Hindustan," while "Indianola" was another minor-key instrumental novelty, laden with trombone swoops, tomtom effects, and a buzz cornet. "Arabian Nights" and "Indianola" were both coauthored by Pathé's musical director, Dominic Savino (using a pseudonym), which might have had something to do with their selection.[40] The monotonous hit "Ja-Da" is at least enlivened by a raggy clarinet solo toward the end.

The rest of the pop songs were vocal recordings on which the band merely provided subdued background accompaniment. One was by Creighton Thompson, whose resonant bass was sorely misused on the insouciant "Jazz Baby"—which he sings stiffly. Nor did Sissle do much better with "Mirandy (That Girl o' Mine)," a bit of fluff by Sissle, Blake, and Europe, which he tried to salvage with a bouncy, jittery performance. Sissle and Europe's "All of No Man's Land Is Ours" is similarly trite with its moon/June lyrics (about a soldier calling his honey as soon as he returns home), as is the team's "When the Bees Make Honey (Down in Sunny Alabam')" (heading for home, sweet home). Finally, the current jazz craze was described in the novelty song "Jazzola," sung by Sissle in his usual animated style ("Nobody knows its origination / It's just a dance full of syncopation").

Europe's busy musicians had little time to rest after all this recording activity. Just two days after the last session the band, eighty-five members strong, commenced its triumphal homecoming tour at the Manhattan Opera House, on March 16, 1919. Vocal soloist Noble Sissle, writing years later about the event, rhapsodized about the irony of Europe's black musicians filling this temple of classical music with the sounds of jazz. "Ere the last strains of the opening selection of Jim Europe's 369th Infantry Jazz Band had reverberated through the halls of the Manhattan Opera House, there burst forth a spontaneous applause from the jewel-bedecked patrons in the stage boxes to the last row of the gallery—the volume of which was conclusive of the merits of this original interpretation of what had been looked on by many as a desecration."[41]

Reported the *New York Sun,* "There was a flood of good music, a gorgeous racket of syncopation and jazzing, extraordinarily pleasing violin and cornet solos and many other features that bands seldom offer . . . echoes of camp meetings and of the traditional darkey life that seems almost of have disappeared." Classical adaptations such as the "Russian Rag," a Broadway medley, "Plantation Echoes" and Handy's "St. Louis Blues" (all just recorded) were included in the program; the *Sun* commented that Europe's organization was more than a band, "they are a complete circus." The highlight, and finale, was an "ear splitting crash of jazz music that caused the audience to explode [with] cheering and laughter."[42]

The band then began a ten-week tour of eighteen east and midwest cities, including Brooklyn, Boston, Springfield, Albany, Syracuse, Buffalo, Cleveland, Indianapolis, St. Louis, Terre Haute, Fort Wayne, Chicago, Pittsburgh, and Philadelphia. While in Chicago from April 27 to May 3, Europe auditioned new members for the troupe, hiring a black vaudeville quartet called the Four Harmony Kings, but rejecting a dance-band clarinetist named Sidney Bechet.[43]

While in the Midwest Europe received word that the Pathé company back in New York was rushing out the first releases from the band's March sessions and would mount a major advertising campaign on their behalf. According to an item in *Phonograph and Talking Machine Weekly,* the first five discs (ten sides) were released on April 20, barely six weeks after recording—a fast turnaround for this period.[44]

Although the issue numbers (between 22080 and 22085) correspond to regular re-leases that would come out in June or July, Pathé was rush-releasing current hits via special "popular supplements" at this time.[45] "Another Big Scoop for Pathe!" the *P&TMW* article began.

> Lt. Jim Europe, the "Jazz King," and his famous 369th "U.S. Infantry" Hell Fighters Band are now recording exclusively for Pathe records the music that put pep into our boys over there, who put pep into the war and settled it.
>
> This famous overseas band is now making a two-year [*sic*] triumphal tour of the country, from Maine to California, playing every matinee and evening to packed houses in every city. Everybody is wild about the lively jazzing and syncopated rhythm, played as only Jim Europe's band can play it. When you hear the wonder-ful music you can't sit still. Your head and shoulders have to sway. "It's Jaz as is!"
>
> Lt. Noble Sissle, the finest colored tenor in America, and Creighton Thompson, popular colored baritone, two of the band's favorite soloists, are singing the latest ballads and song hits; the Singing Serenaders and the Hell Fighters' Double Quar-tet harmonize real Southern jubilee songs.

Talking Machine World, under a picture of the Europe band marching down Fifth Avenue, wrote that "Jim Europe is today without doubt the leading exponent of jazz music," and Sissle "sings Southern songs the way they should be sung."[46] Another story reported, with perhaps a bit of exaggeration, how fast Pathé had rushed out the records. "The recording organization of the Pathe Freres Phonograph Co. points with pride to the remarkable record which it established in the production of the Pathe records made by Lieut. 'Jim' Europe's Jazz Band. . . . Within two weeks after Lieut. Europe's Jazz Band had visited the recording laboratories and made several records these records were ready for shipment to the dealers."[47]

A full-page ad appeared in the May trade papers, headlined "Sensational Money-Making Jazz Records" and illustrated with a "darkey" caricature of Europe's band in France. Less offensive was a two-page spread in June, offering dealers a Jim Europe poster and calling the records "best sellers of the year."[48]

It is interesting to note that both Pathé and the trade press emphasized the jazz content of Europe's work, not the pop tunes, specialty numbers, or spirituals. It is likely that they considered everything the band did to be "jazz"—the name was being applied to virtually everything that was the least bit syncopated at this time. The company clearly hoped to sell black music to a white audience, which was most unusual for the period, and to capitalize on the band's status as authentic war he-roes. One advertisement related the following story:

> One of the boys in our office went to war.
>
> On his return I asked him what American effort most impressed him and he an-swered JIM (Lieut.) EUROPE'S BAND.
>
> He said that the French and British bands would play and one would say to him-self, "what beautiful music!" But when Europe's band came along no one, whatever his race, could keep still. There was that pep, that something of life and animation that made everybody want to do something.[49]

The troupe returned east during the first week in May, with stops in Toledo and Pittsburgh.[50] After a Philadelphia concert on Wednesday, May 7, it planned to head for Boston for an encore performance, to be followed by a big, final concert in New York on May 12. While en route from Philadelphia to Boston (on May 7 or 8), the band stopped at the Pathé studios in New York for an additional recording session.

Once again Europe set an ambitious schedule for his musicians. Six sides were to be recorded in a single day, two of them with vocal choruses by Sissle. The band members may have not have had as much stamina as their leader; the long weeks of touring seem to have worn them down. Compared to the March sides, the band here sounds a little tired—the jazz improvisations are less frequent and less inspired, and the ensemble playing sounds not just loose, but at times ragged, at least to this listener. Nevertheless, loyal to their leader, the musicians did their best.

The four instrumentals were all interesting jazz or blues material. "The Dancing Deacon" was a syncopated dance number, dedicated to the current president of the Clef Club, Fred "Deacon" Johnson.[51] "That's Got 'Em" was a Wilbur Sweatman tune played in the cacophonous style of the Original Dixieland Jazz Band. Rather repetitive, it arguably sounded better in the Columbia recording by Sweatman's own small (six-man) combo. In the Sweatman recording individual instruments, even the piano, stood out; here we have a sort of 1919 version of Phil Spector's 1960s "wall of sound." It is instructive to compare the clarinet-led chorus on "How Ya Gonna Keep 'Em Down on the Farm," with its biting attack, with the dreadful muddle by the same instruments on "That's Got 'Em." Something that was there in March was gone in May.

Similar comments could be made about "Clarinet Marmalade," by Original Dixieland Jazz Band members Henry Ragas and Larry Shields. In Europe's version massed clarinets carry the melody, whereas the ODJB Victor recording is dominated by Shields's solo clarinet. The two versions make an interesting comparison in other ways as well. It is the ODJB's small unit arrangement that sounds familiar to us today; Dixieland music is now almost always played that way. Europe was moving toward a big band sound, but he had not quite developed the mix of tight ensemble playing and solo breaks that made the swing bands of the 1930s and 1940s so successful musically. Nevertheless he clearly was their precursor and leagues ahead of his 1919 contemporaries. (The muddy sound of the Pathés versus the clean, crisp Victors also doesn't help as we compare these early recordings.)

"Missouri Blues" is a bluesy adaptation of the much-recorded "Missouri Waltz," a huge hit in 1916–17.[52] The final two selections were vaudeville-style novelty songs with vocal choruses by Noble Sissle. Both had war-is-over themes appropriate to the Hell Fighters' show. In "Dixie Is Dixie Once More," a kind of vaudeville strut along the lines of "Are You from Dixie?" Sissle belts out the chorus:

> There'll be happy days in Dixie,
> Happy days and nights,
> All our boys are back once more,
> Celebrating 'cause they won the war. . . .

"My Choc'late Soldier Sammy Boy" is hardly less trite and even shamelessly steals a little from "Waiting for the Robert E. Lee." Sissle energetically sings,

See him marching along,
Hear him humming a song . . .
Come, come, come to your mammy,
My choc'late soldier Sammy boy!

"Sammy" was period slang for one of Uncle Sam's soldier boys.

In addition to the band recordings the newly hired Four Harmony Kings re-corded two sides under Europe's auspices, billed as "Lieut. Jim Europe's Four Har-mony Kings." Since the Kings were actually a preexisting, independent quartet that had appeared with Europe for only two weeks and their recordings were sung a capella, with no involvement by the band, their discs will be discussed in a separate chapter.

Europe proceeded directly from the recording session to Boston for the next-to-last appearance of the tour. Meanwhile, the New York papers were already going to press with ads promoting the May 12 grand finale in that city: "engagement extraor-dinary—climax of triumphant tour—last concert, at Manhattan Casino."[53] Creighton Thompson, the Four Harmony Kings, and "superstar Lieut. Noble Sissle" would all appear.

Characteristically, Europe was also busy planning summer appearances for those of his musicians who wanted to continue to work, then a worldwide concert tour for his band in the fall, including a triumphal return to France. Longer term, there was the resuscitation of his beloved National Negro Symphony Orchestra, and per-haps a Broadway show with bandmembers Noble Sissle and Eubie Blake. No one could have guessed how suddenly, and with what finality, all these plans would be destroyed in Boston.

Europe and his band arrived early on Friday, May 9 and immediately made preparations for a matinee and evening performance at drafty old Mechanics' Hall. It was cold and miserable, but there were bright spots. Al Jolson and several mem-bers of his musical, *Sinbad,* attended the afternoon show, and Gov. Calvin Coolidge extended an invitation for the band to play at a ceremony on the State House steps the next morning. Although Europe was fighting a bad cold that threatened to turn into pneumonia, he persevered and the matinee went without incident. As the evening show began he began to have trouble with diminutive drummer Herbert Wright, one of the "Percussion Twins," who had previously disrupted concerts with unpredictable fits of giggling and walking about the stage.

Wright was an orphan who had been informally "adopted" by the fatherly Eu-rope, and who had performed with the band for the past two years. He and Steven Wright (no kin) formed a novelty drumming act. Herbert was of limited intelligence, and his behavior had become increasingly erratic. During a short intermission Eu-rope called him into his dressing room to talk with him. Noble Sissle was also in the dressing room and later recalled the exact sequence of events.[54]

Before Europe could get very far with Wright, a distinguished visitor, concert tenor Roland Hayes (who lived in Boston), entered the room accompanied by three of the four Harmony Kings. Sissle quietly ushered Wright out of the room. Then, brooding about perceived injustices, Wright rushed back in and to the astonishment of those present, brandished a pocket knife and screamed, "I'll kill anybody that takes advantage of me! Jim Europe, I'll kill you!"

> Jim backed up between the table and the wall, and raised a chair in between himself and the menacing dwarf, as he stood there in his distorted position, crouching as a ferocious animal preparing to lunge upon its victim. Jim Europe, standing six feet tall with a large chair between him and his attacker, was apparently safe from harm.
>
> We all hollered, "Knock that knife out of his hand, Jim!" Jim grasped the chair in an attitude as though he was about to carry out our warning, when all of a sudden there came over him some thought, God knows what, that caused him to completely relax his whole body and set the chair down. [He] was about to mutter "Herbert, get out of here!" when to our amazement, before any of us could move from our track, like a panther Herbert Wright hurled himself over the chair. As he came through the air, Jim clasped his body and whirled it away from him, but as the demon had made up his mind to carry out his murderous attack with a back hand blow, he made a wild swing of the knife, brought it down in the direction of Jim Europe's face.
>
> [Wright] fell, scrambling in the chair, and before he could regain his feet, I had grasped him by the shoulder. Quite unconscious as the rest of us were that he had struck Jim Europe the blow, immediately after I touched him, and as soon as I had spoken to him he became as calm and quiet as a child.

At first none of those present realized that Wright had managed to stab Europe with a glancing blow to the neck. Even when the wound became apparent, it did not look life-threatening. Europe asked Sissle to take over and have assistant conductor Felix Weir complete the concert, while he left by a back door so as not to disturb the audience. He told Sissle,

> "Sissle, don't forget to have the band down before the State House at 9:00 in the morning. I am going to the hospital, and I will have my wound dressed and I will be at the Commons in the morning, in time to conduct the band. See that the rest of the program is gone through with. I leave everything for you to carry on."
>
> With that he was hastily carried from the room, the last time that I ever saw Lieutenant Europe, my best pal, in life.

A few hours later word came that Europe had taken a sudden turn for the worse. Sissle and others rushed to the hospital ready to give blood for a transfusion, but it was too late. Their leader, their hero, was dead.

Wright, who was confused and distraught, was immediately arrested and charged with murder. Although he was not found insane, doctors judged him to be "of such low type of mentality that there was a question as to his entire responsibility." He was ultimately sentenced to ten to fifteen years in Massachusetts State Penitentiary.[55]

Reaction to Europe's death was overwhelming. There was a huge turnout for his funeral in New York City on May 13, reportedly the first ever public funeral for an African American in the city's history.[56] Thousands filed past his casket at a funeral home on 131st Street. Among those paying their respects were Bert and Lottie Williams, John Wanamaker Jr., Colonel William Hayward, representatives of the French Army, and many others both black and white.[57] Among the floral tributes was one from Irene Castle. Deacon Johnson, president of Jim's beloved Clef Club, gave a eulogy. "Before Jim Europe came to New York, the colored man knew nothing but Negro dances and porter's work. All that has been changed. Jim Europe was the living open sesame to the colored porters of this city. He took them from their porter's places and raised them to positions of importance as real musicians. I think the suffering public ought to know that in Jim Europe the race has lost a leader, a benefactor, and a true friend."[58]

A quartet led by Creighton Thompson sang "Dear Old Pal of Mine," and Harry T. Burleigh ended the service by rendering "Now Take Thy Rest." Europe's body was transported to Washington, D.C., where he was laid to rest at Arlington National Military Cemetery.

Europe's death and funeral was widely reported in the mainstream press, including a front-page story in the *New York Times*. That august pinnacle of white American newspaperdom had never seen fit to report on Europe while he was alive; not until he died did he merit coverage in its pages.[59]

Without their creator and driving force, the future of the Hell Fighters Band and of Europe's other projects looked dim. There were attempts to carry on. Jim's brother, John Europe, briefly replaced him, but he was not the leader Jim had been and so the baton passed to close associate Lieutenant F. Eugene (Gene) Mikell. The Hell Fighters continued to make sporadic appearances for another year, finally disbanding in May 1920.[60] Eugene Mikell returned to teaching.

Europe's sudden death also caught Pathé by surprise. The May 15 *Talking Machine World* contained several mentions of his recently made recordings and a big Pathé ad promoting them, while on a back page appeared a short, hastily inserted obituary.[61] Following the five discs released in April came six more in May. Though no specific sales figures survive, sales appear to have been reasonably good at first. At least, copies of these now very desirable records do turn up in modern collections.

Sales dwindled rather rapidly in the months that followed for several reasons. Primary, of course, was Europe's death. While there may have been a brief spurt of interest following his demise, record sales seldom survived an artist for very long in those days. This was also true following the death of superstar Bert Williams a few years later. In addition, Pathé did not have the distribution or marketing muscle of the mighty Victor and Columbia oligopolies; its special "sapphire ball" groove cut meant that its discs could only be played on specially equipped machines, limiting their appeal to the average record buyer. The fact that the records were released in the spring, just before the summer sales doldrums, probably didn't help either. Significantly, Victor did not think there was sufficient interest to warrant the reissue of any of its Jim Europe sides from 1913 to 1914.

Four additional titles were released in August, and one last disc, "The Dancing Deacon–Fox Trot" / "Clarinet Marmalade–One Step," in October. Pathé remained upbeat, saying of the last-named disc, "Once more the leading 'jazz' exponents of the world add to the gaiety and joy of the dance by two characteristic contributions which must certainly rank among the very best of all the exciting novelties recorded by the irrepressible 'Hell Fighters.' Both the fox trot and the one-step present musical dishes highly spiced with joyous 'ginger' and toe-tickling 'pep.'"[62]

Did Europe record any unreleased titles during his long sessions for Pathé? In the absence of company ledgers we cannot be certain, but a July 1919 advertisement for the Pace and Handy Music Company (a black publishing firm co-owned by W. C. Handy) did claim that Europe had recorded the firm's "Mauvoleyne Waltz" by Frederick M. Bryan for Pathé.[63] Several matrix and issue numbers were skipped in and around the sequences assigned to Europe, which may indicate unissued or withdrawn recordings. Perry Bradford, composer of "Crazy Blues," claimed in his autobiography that "[Noble] Sissle told me that James Europe made a fine record of 'Crazy Blues' for Pathe with 22 men, and he sang the vocal." However this seems unlikely. "Crazy Blues" was not published until 1920 and the earliest recording otherwise known is Mamie Smith's version for Okeh in August 1920, followed by others during the winter of 1920–21, when the song became popular.[64]

Even if unissued takes were made it is highly unlikely that they still exist. Pathé recorded, uniquely, on large wax master cylinders that were then used to dub the recording on to various formats (e.g., wide groove, narrow groove) for issue. The U.S. Pathé label shut down in 1930 and none of its masters are known to survive.

Pathé did reissue a few of Europe's sides, including four instrumentals and all of the Singing Serenaders and Four Harmony Kings titles, on its lateral cut Pathé Actuelle and Perfect labels between 1921 and 1923. None of these sold particularly well, judging by their rarity today. Curiously, none of the Pathés appears to have been issued in France, where Jim Europe was presumably well remembered, even though that was the home of Pathé Freres.

Despite Jim Europe's major contributions to black advancement, and to the development and popularization of jazz, he is little remembered today outside of scholarly circles. His recordings are today considered "pre-jazz" or "transitional." Jazz bands flourished during the 1920s in smaller combinations, usually eight to twelve men (e.g., Duke Ellington, Fletcher Henderson, Coon-Sanders, the Virginians), sometimes fewer (Original Memphis Five). Only show bands such as that of Paul Whiteman were sometimes larger, and they played a refined, arranged style of syncopation that was hardly relevant to what was going on in Harlem. So, Europe's experimental "big band" sounded out of date almost immediately. The big swing bands that arose in the 1930s and 1940s used substantially different instrumentation and arrangements.

The Tempo Club folded after the war, although the Clef Club continued until the 1940s. Its functions were eventually taken over by a liberalized musician's union. Most of Europe's musicians dispersed to minor careers with jazz and dance bands of the 1920s and 1930s. Some, including Creighton Thompson, Opal Cooper, and Buddy Gilmore, spent many years performing overseas.[65] No doubt the most successful Europe alumni were Noble Sissle and Eubie Blake, who went on to coauthor the hit Broadway show *Shuffle Along* and make many recordings, individually and together. Blake, of course, became one of the more important popular composers of the twentieth century, living to the grand old age of one hundred.

Most of Europe's immediate family passed away in the 1920s and 1930s. His wife,

Willie, died in 1930, and his girlfriend, Bessie Simms, in 1931, unacknowledged by the family. The last surviving family member, sister Mary, died in 1947. Europe's son, Jim Europe Jr., was, sadly, rejected by the family (Lorraine, his strong-willed grandmother, literally slammed the door in his face when he attempted to make contact with the family after his mother's death).[66] "Little Jim" nevertheless went on to a responsible career, serving in World War II and later becoming a member of the New York City police and fire departments and a drug abuse counselor. He is believed to still be alive at this writing, living on Long Island.

Badger lists eighty-nine compositions by Europe, many in collaboration with such songwriters as Bob Cole, R. C. McPherson, Henry Creamer, and Sissle and Blake.[67] None have survived into the contemporary repertoire. His band recordings have been periodically reissued, with two lavishly produced CDs of the complete Pathé sessions being released simultaneously in 1996. Symptomatic of the uncertainty surrounding these recordings, the two CDs sound quite different because the producers made wildly different assumptions about the correct speed at which the original discs should be played! The six sides by the Singing Serenaders and the Four Harmony Kings were reissued on an Austrian CD in 1994, from originals owned by (and with notes by) this author.[68]

Jim Europe was lovingly remembered in a long chapter in *Reminiscing with Sissle and Blake,* an opulent and well-researched coffee-table book compiled by Robert Kimball and William Bolcom and published in 1973. Noble Sissle's first-hand reminiscence, "Memoirs of Lieutenant 'Jim' Europe," written in 1942, has never been published. A major event was the 1995 publication of the first book-length biography of Europe, the immaculately researched *A Life in Ragtime* by Professor Reid Badger. This book is essential reading for anyone interested in Europe's life.

In 1989 conductor Maurice Peress staged a recreation of Europe's historic 1912 Carnegie Hall Clef Club Concert at Carnegie Hall in New York. The original program was reproduced as closely as possible, complete with ten pianos and a large section of banjos and mandolins (harp-guitar and bandoris players were by this time hard to find). Baritone William Warfield, mezzo soprano Barbara Conrad, and eighty-eight-year-old conductor and actor Jester Hairston appeared, along with James Europe Jr. The evening was well reviewed, but primarily as a historical curiosity rather than as "living music."[69]

Perhaps Europe is best remembered in the words of two of his contemporaries and friends. From Eubie Blake: "People don't realize yet today what we lost when we lost Jim Europe. He was the savior of Negro musicians. He was in a class with Booker T. Washington and Martin Luther King. I met all three of them. Before Europe, Negro musicians were just like wandering minstrels. Play in a saloon and pass the hat and that's it. Before Jim, they weren't even supposed to be human beings. Jim Europe changed all that. He made a profession for us out of music. All of that we owe to Jim. If only people would realize it."[70]

W. C. Handy, who was then living in New York City, recalled feeling depressed and sleepless on the night Jim Europe was killed. Unaware of the events in Boston, he spent the night aimlessly riding the subways. When he emerged into the daylight the next morning he heard the 135th Street newsboys shouting, "Extra! Extra!

All about the Murder of Jim Europe!": "The man who had just come through the baptism of war's fire and steel without a mark had been stabbed by one of his own musicians during a band performance in Boston. No wonder I couldn't sleep. No wonder the rumble of the empty subway had been a ghostly sound without music. I felt that I could at last put my finger on the strange restlessness that had troubled me. . . . The sun was in the sky. The new day promised peace. But all suns had gone down for Jim Europe, and Harlem didn't seem the same."[71]

21 Will Marion Cook and the Afro-American Folk Song Singers

Will Marion Cook was one of the most respected black composers of the early 1900s. His career extended from the beginnings of the black musical theater at the turn of the century to the spread of jazz in the 1920s, and he was a key figure in both. His name is frequently cited in histories of black music in America. As with a number of icons of black musical history, though, it is not generally known that he recorded some of his own best-known works.

Will Marion Cook was born on January 27, 1869, in Washington, D.C., to Dr. John H. Cook, a law professor at Howard University.[1] Displaying musical talent as a child, he was sent to the Oberlin Conservatory of Music at age fifteen. He studied under the great German violinist Josef Joachim in Berlin from 1887 to 1889 and made his debut as a concert violinist in Washington, D.C., in December 1889. His reputation as a violinist grew rapidly during the early 1890s, and from 1894 to 1895 he studied with Antonín Dvořák at the National Conservatory of Music in New York. Cook's prickly nature was already beginning to evidence itself. A perfectionist, and somewhat rigid in his ideas, he squabbled with the great composer, who he thought favored young baritone Harry T. Burleigh over himself. Shortly thereafter Cook abruptly gave up his concert career when he found himself being referred to as "the greatest Negro violinist"—he wanted to be considered the greatest violinist, period.

In the late 1890s Cook concentrated on conducting and composing. He began to mix with the New York theatrical crowd, where he engaged in heated debates with another young composer, Bob Cole, over the direction black theater should take. Cole believed that blacks should strive for excellence by competing directly with whites, producing shows that would prove that blacks were the equal of whites in every aspect of stagecraft. Cook argued that "Negroes should eschew white patterns" and produce shows that reflected their own distinctive heritage. The two argued so violently that friends had to keep them apart.[2] Each went his own way, and separately they developed two shows that revolutionized the theater. Cole's show, *A Trip to Coontown,* was patterned after the mainstream theatrical hit of the early 1890s, *A Trip to Chinatown.* Opening off-Broadway on April 4, 1898, it became a substantial hit. Cook's show, *Clorindy; or, The Origin of the Cakewalk,* was really more of a musical sketch, written in collaboration with young poet/lyricist Paul Laurence Dunbar.

Will Marion Cook. (Author's collection)

It opened on July 5 on Broadway, or, to be precise, on the roof garden of the Casino Theatre, above Broadway, following the main presentation in the big theater below. It too became a success, producing such hit songs as "Who Dat Say Chicken in Dis Crowd?," "Hottest Coon in Dixie," and "Darktown Is Out Tonight." Together, these two 1898 shows are credited with giving birth to black musical comedy.

In 1899 Cook married Abbie Mitchell (1884–1960), a beautiful teenaged actress who had appeared in *Clorindy*. They had two children, Marion in 1900 and Will Mercer in 1903. After their divorce around 1906, they continued to appear together professionally.

On the heels of their initial success, Cook and Dunbar collaborated on additional productions, including *A Senegambian Carnival* (1898) and *A Lucky Coon* (1899), both starring rising young comedians Bert Williams and George Walker. During the following two years Cook was musical director for Williams and Walker's *Policy Players* company (1899), contributed to the white musical *The Casino Girl* (1900), and with Dunbar composed *Jes Lak White Folks* (1900) and the sketch *Uncle Eph's Christmas* (1900), for popular black vaudevillian Ernest Hogan. Cook was becoming closely associated with Williams and Walker, and in 1900 he provided the music for their first hit musical, *Sons of Ham*. A year or so later he began working with Dunbar on a follow-up, *In Dahomey*, but the Cook-Dunbar partnership was beginning to fray. The bombastic composer and the sensitive poet fought constantly. Finally Dunbar walked out. Mutual friend James Weldon Johnson tried to get him to return, but he said, "No, I won't do it. I just can't work with Cook, he irritates me beyond endurance."[3]

Though deprived of his favorite lyricist, Cook proved he could work with others, including Williams and Walker favorites Jesse Shipp and Alex Rogers. In fact, Cook became the virtual "house composer" for Williams and Walker, providing the music for their great hits *In Dahomey* (1902), *Abyssinia* (1906), and *Bandanna Land* (1908). He also found time for many other activities during this period, contributing music to the white show *The Southerners* (1904), musical revues at Chicago's black Pekin Theater, and the Memphis Students, a musical revue starring his wife and Ernest Hogan. He wrestled ownership of the latter show away from Hogan and took it to Europe in 1905, where it scored a substantial hit with its ragtime rhythms.

Cook was also closely associated with Gotham Music Company (later Gotham-Attucks), the first major black publisher, and in 1909 established the "Marion School of Vocal Music" on its premises with help from Harry T. Burleigh.

During the early 1900s Cook was a major figure in the black New York musical world, not only contributing to shows but mentoring younger musicians (when they could stand him). He clearly rubbed some people the wrong way. Sylvester Russell, the influential theater critic of the *New York Age,* accused him of blatant self-promotion, but Cook was undeniably talented and driven by a desire to advance the cause of black theater.[4] His interests veered increasingly toward choral music. Although he had begun his career composing "coon songs" like "Darktown Is Out Tonight" and "Who Dat Say Chicken in Dis Crowd?" (using the pen name "Will Marion," perhaps to distance himself from the material), he now began to focus on texts and settings more sensitive to, and evocative of, the black experience—just the sort of thing he used to argue with Bob Cole about. This produced some of his most lasting music, including "Swing Along," a lilting celebration of black pride sung by a chorus in *In Dahomey;* and "Rain Song" and "Exhortation," imaginative numbers drawn from African American folkways, and performed in *Bandanna Land.* The latter two songs both had lyrics by Alex Rogers. One writer later observed, "Much of Williams and Walker's success with *Bandanna Land* was attributed to Will Marion Cook's ensemble numbers, which tended to give the production a classical tone and helped significantly in making it a Broadway production."[5]

In the early 1910s, with black musical theater in decline, Cook contributed music to a succession of minor shows, including *In the Jungles* (1911), *The Traitors* (1912), *In Darkeydom* (1914), and *The Cannibal King* (1914). A highlight of this period was his reluctant participation in the historic Clef Club Concert at Carnegie Hall on May 2, 1912. Cook had initially vehemently opposed the concert, which was organized by Clef Club president James Reese Europe to bring black music to the greatest white temple of culture in America. The risk of failure, Cook argued, was too great. Europe prevailed, and at the last minute Cook showed up to participate as a violinist in the orchestra, asking not to be recognized, even though his works were being featured. However when the 125-piece Clef Club Orchestra and chorus performed "Swing Along," the reception was so enthusiastic—requiring three encores—that Cook was forced to take a bow. According to one eyewitness account, he was so overcome "he began to weep tears of joy and when he tried to speak he couldn't say a word. All he could do was just bow."[6]

Another project led to Cook's first and only recordings of two of his most famous songs. In the fall of 1913 Mrs. Harriet Gibbs Marshall, president of the Washington Conservatory of Music, sponsored the organization of a large mixed chorus called the Afro-American Folk Song Singers, directed by Cook. On November 21, 1913, the Singers presented a concert at Washington's Metropolitan A.M.E. Church, with Cook conducting and Abbie Mitchell among the soloists. The program was a mix of classical, art, and folk selections, including Mendelssohn's "Rondo Capriccioso," Coleridge-Taylor's "Spring Song," Marshall's "I Hear You Calling Me," and Shelly's "De Coppah Moon." Abbie Mitchell sang the spirituals "Steal Away" and "Nobody Knows." Cook compositions on the program included "Swing Along," "Rain Song," and "Exhortation," sung by the chorus.[7] The next traced appearance by the Singers was on February 28, 1914, at the Howard Theater in Washington, D.C., where Abbie Mitchell, Harry T. Burleigh, and Lottie Wallace were soloists, and James Reese Europe led the chorus in "Swing Along" and "Rain Song." Probably the highlight of the season, however, was an appearance at Carnegie Hall on March 11 at a concert sponsored by New York's Music School Settlement for Colored People. On the program were the school chorus, the Afro-American Folk Song Singers, Europe's Negro Symphony Orchestra and soloists Mitchell, Burleigh, and J. Rosamond Johnson. The following day, under the heading "Negroes Give a Concert," the *New York Times* reported as follows.

> It was an interesting concert, and one calculated to stimulate the musical imagination. Perhaps its most significant feature was a demonstration of what may be expected of Negro composers trained in the modern technique, as they are affected by their racial traits in music. The fact that the program consisted largely of plantation melodies and spirituals, which were in each case "harmonized," "arranged," or "developed," showed that these composers are beginning to form an art of their own on the basis of their folk material . . . the subject of Negro music is receiving a good deal of attention nowadays in various directions among people not of the race, for which reason the music presented last night was all the more interesting.[8]

Musical America, reflecting the classical music "establishment" of the period, was a little less charitable. While praising the concert as "more creditable" than Europe's two previous concerts at Carnegie Hall, and noting the positive audience response, it criticized the inclusion of popular black-oriented material, such as "Why Adam Sinned" and "Under the Bamboo Tree," and advised the Negro Symphony Orchestra that if it wanted to be taken seriously it should apply itself to some Haydn symphonies.[9]

The day after their successful Carnegie Hall appearance Cook marched his chorus over to the studios of the Columbia Phonograph Company to record, under his direction, two of the numbers they had been performing all season.[10] The Columbia files for this period are sketchy and do not reveal exactly who participated, but it was most likely a lineup similar to that which had been with him on tour. The closest surviving program with a detailed personnel listing is for the February 28 appearance in Washington, D.C., which lists six sopranos, five contraltos, five tenors, and seven basses. Piano accompaniment was by Mary L. Europe, Jim Europe's sister.

The first selection recorded, "Swing Along," is a remarkable song for its period, a lilting melody with lyrics encouraging black children to be proud of who they are. The sheet music states that it should be sung "brightly, joyously."

> Swing along, chillun, swing along de lane,
> Lif' yo' head and you' heels mighty high,
> Swing along chillun, 'tain't a-goin' to rain,
> Sun's as red as a rose in de sky.
> Come along Mandy, come along Sue,
> White folks watchin' and seein' what you do,
> White folks jealous when you'se walkin' two by two,
> So swing along, chillun', swing along!

Chorus:
> Well-a swing along, yes-a swing along,
> An' a lif'-a yo' heads up high,
> Wif pride an' gladness beaming from yo' eye!
> Well-a swing along, yes-a swing along,
> From a-early morn till night,
> Lif' yo' head an' yo' heels mighty high,
> An'a swing bof lef' an' right.

It seems unlikely all twenty-three members of the chorus listed in the February 28 program took part in the recording session. The limited technology of the day made it difficult to record more than four or five voices distinctly, and Columbia rarely issued records by larger groups. However this clearly is a sizable chorus, with at least a dozen voices standing out at various times. The sound is predictably muddy, which perhaps contributed to the record's short life in the catalog. The arrangement no doubt reflects how Cook performed the piece in concert. It lasts for a full three minutes and forty-five seconds, which is extraordinarily long for a ten-inch record; the grooves on the author's copy run practically into the label area. This must have been a challenging session for the Columbia engineers. One wonders why it wasn't issued on a twelve-inch disc.

The chorus opens with the verse at a sprightly trot, like kids skipping down a lane, followed by a more deliberate tempo for the initial chorus. They then repeat. Multipart harmony is prominently used, with the basses sometimes singing counterpoint to the rest of the chorus. The finale is an elaborate arrangement of variations on the main theme, building to a gradual and extended crescendo. One can imagine the engineers frantically signaling Cook to "wind up!" before the cutting needle ran clear off the ten-inch wax master, and the perfectionist Cook just as deliberately ignoring them as he strived to get exactly the effect he wanted. Despite the difficulties that must have attended this remarkable recording, only two takes were made, and take one was issued.

"The Rain Song" is a musical setting of a scene in which black folks are sitting around talking about all the signs of rain ("When de ducks quack loud . . . when de air it stan's stock still"). The sound is, if anything, even muddier than on "Swing Along," making it impossible to follow the lyrics without sheet music. Nevertheless the outlines of Cook's complex arrangement are clearly discernible, with various male vocalists taking solo lines, answering each other, and the ensemble voices dramatically swelling in the chorus ("Dar ain' gwine be no rain today"). The pianist (possibly Mary Europe?) provides a gently syncopated accompaniment. This one came in at just under three minutes.

It is not clear what expectations Columbia had for this unusual recording, but it was announced with some pride of purpose in the August 1914 supplement. There was no picture of Cook or the chorus, although he is specifically named as directing the session.

> A noteworthy and novel departure in recording is found in this double disc of genuine Afro-American folk music, sung authentically by the best trained chorus of

Negro singers to be found in the United States. The songs by Will Marion Cook have long come into their own as representing with incomparable fidelity the varying phases of the Negro character and temperament. They do this likewise in a manner that is musicianly and authoritative with an insight into the emotional nature of the real passion for melody that exists in the American Negro that has never been surpassed. The chorus, which has been heard in concert notably in New York City and Washington, has been trained by Mr. Cook and the records were made under his personal direction.

Noteworthy it may have been, but the muddy, indistinct recording apparently did not sell well and was pulled from the catalog after only a few months. It had been deleted by the time the April 1915 catalog was issued. It is seldom found today.

The Afro-American Folk Song Singers seemed to have performed on an occasional basis during the seasons that followed. Only occasional press mentions of them have been located, although a program exists for an April 4, 1919, concert at the Academy of Music in Philadelphia. They are referred to as "The Afro-American Folk Song Singers of Washington, D.C." and appeared with Cook, Burleigh, Carl Diton, and Nathaniel Dett. This concert emphasized spirituals and black songs (no Mendelssohn), with Cook's "Swing Along" and "Exhortation" and Burleigh's arrangements of spirituals prominently featured. Stanley Brooks, Louise Reynolds Robinson, and Richard Henri Nugent were listed as soloists. In July 1920 the Singers performed at the second annual convention of the National Association of Negro Musicians in New York.

During the late 1910s Cook's contributions to black shows declined (there weren't as many shows being staged) and he seems to have emphasized teaching, conducting, and speaking out on musical matters. In a September 1918 article in the *New York Age* he issued a ringing call to fellow black musicians "to bring [our] distinctive type of American music prominently before the public." In his view, "developed Negro music has just begun in America. The colored American is finding himself. He has thrown aside puerile imitations of the white man. He has learned that a thorough study of the masters gives knowledge of what is good and how to create. From the Russian he has learned to get his inspiration from within; that his inexhaustible wealth of folklore legends and songs furnish him with material for compositions that will establish a great school of music and enrich musical literature."[11]

Following his own advice, late that year he led the Clef Club Orchestra on a tour of the Northeast, spreading his gospel of "authentic" black music. Then, in January 1919, Cook embarked on perhaps the greatest adventure of his career, launching the New York Syncopated Orchestra, managed by George W. Lattimore. The big show included a thirty-five-piece orchestra, and fifteen quartets and soloists, including Florence Cole-Talbert. Advertising called it "by far the most meritorious effort put forth to place the musical art of the Negro—truly American, distinctive, characteristic, sublime—in the sphere in which it properly belongs."[12] After touring cities in the East and Midwest, it played for a week at the Nora Bayes Theatre on New York's 44th Street, "presenting an enjoyable entertainment of ragtime jazz, syncopation and song." "Not for years has a colored aggregation been housed in a Broadway Theater," enthused the *New York Age*.[13] But this was just the beginning.

In late May and early June, Cook and most of his company sailed to England to play what was to be a six-month engagement there. It turned into a three-year stay, as the orchestra (renamed the Southern Syncopated Orchestra) brought ragtime rhythms as well as Cook's beloved "characteristic Negro melodies" to adoring Europeans. Cook's "Swing Along" and "Exhortation" were a prominent part of the program. The orchestra scored a hit at London's Philharmonic Hall and played a command performance for King George V. Reviews contrasted the musical literacy and varied repertoire of the SSO with the wild music being played by another American group then creating a sensation in London, the Original Dixieland Jazz Band.

There was a certain amount of dissension within the group, and at one point two competing "Syncopated Orchestras" were touring England, one led by Cook and the other by Lattimore, with lawsuits flying between them. Turmoil and artistic achievement seem to have followed Cook throughout his life. By the end of 1920 he had returned to the United States, but the SSO continued to tour, in one form or another, until early 1922. After that several of its members opted to remain in Europe.

Back in America Cook spent the 1920s composing, conducting, and serving as a father figure to a new generation of black composers and musicians. A young Duke Ellington (born in 1899) was an eager disciple. Ellington, who called the older composer "Dad," wrote in his autobiography, "Several times after I had played some tune I had written but not really completed, I would say, 'Now Dad, what is the logical way to develop this theme? What direction should I take?' 'You know you should go to the conservatory,' he would answer, 'but since you won't, I'll tell you. First you find the logical way, and when you find it, avoid it, and let your inner self break through and guide you. Don't try to be anybody but yourself.'"[14]

Cook's glory days in the theater were long past, but he continued to contribute to productions such as *Just for Fun* (1923) and *Negro Nuances* (1924). The latter, starring Miller and Lyles and ex-wife Abbie Mitchell (with whom he evidently remained on good terms), was performed by a new Cook group called the Negro Folk Music and Drama Society and "traced the musical history of blacks starting in Africa, moving with the slave ships, the lamentations of pre–Civil War days to the Reconstruction Period as typified by the early minstrels of Jim Bland's day."[15]

He also continued to write songs, and in 1926 collaborated with a Trinidad-born former member of his orchestra named Donald Heywood on a song called "I'm Comin' Virginia." This led to Cook's involvement with another recording session, when in September 1926 he led a chorus backing Ethel Waters in her Columbia recording of the song. The record was billed as by "Ethel Waters and Her Singing Orchestra," and was mostly a solo vocal by her. Cook's chorus came in only briefly toward the end. Nevertheless anything Will Marion Cook was involved in invariably bore his stamp, so this can be considered a "creator" recording of the song.

In July 1927 "I'm Comin' Virginia" was interpolated into Waters's hit show *Africana,* which had a score by Heywood. There were a number of contemporary recordings of the song, including versions by Fletcher Henderson, Frankie Trumbauer, the Original Indiana Five, and the Singing Sophomores. Perhaps the best remembered version, and certainly the most often reissued, is the jazzy version by

Paul Whiteman and His Orchestra, with vocals by the Rhythm Boys, including a young Bing Crosby. The song went on to become a jazz standard and was especially popular during the swing era. There were versions over the next fifteen years by Bunny Berigan (1935), Maxine Sullivan (1937), Les Brown (1937), Fats Waller (1937), Teddy Wilson (1937), Benny Carter (1938), Will Bradley (1939), Woody Herman (1939), Artie Shaw (1939), Art Tatum (1939), Charlie Barnet (1941), Sidney Bechet (1941), and Stephane Grappelly (1942), among others. Benny Goodman featured it in his famous 1938 Carnegie Hall concert.

In 1929 Cook created an opera with his son, Mercer, called *St. Louis 'Ooman,* but this was not performed. Also in that year he wrote a show called *Swing Along* with Will Vodery, and was choral director for Vincent Youmans's Broadway show *Great Day*. The latter show was set in the Old South and introduced Youmans's classic hits "Without a Song" and "Great Day," sung by one of the leads backed by a chorus of plantation hands. Cook also continued to speak out on behalf of black music. In a 1926 letter published in the *New York Times,* he complained about white producer George White (of *George White's Scandals*) being given credit for creating the dances "The Charleston" and "The Black Bottom." After treating readers to a short history of black dance, he concluded, "Messrs. White et al are great men and great producers. Why, with their immense flocks of dramatic and musical sheep, should they wish to reach out and grab our little ewe lamb of originality?"[16]

Will Marion Cook died in New York City on July 19, 1944, at the age of seventy-five, having made immense contributions to the growth of indigenous black music in America. His few recordings are particularly valuable as "creator" recordings of some of his most famous songs.

22 Dan Kildare and Joan Sawyer's Persian Garden Orchestra

The name of pianist Dan Kildare is virtually unknown to most collectors of early jazz and black music, despite the fact that he was the second black bandleader to record for a major label in the United States (Jim Europe was the first, a few months earlier). A colleague of Europe's, and a central figure in New York's fabled Clef Club, Kildare skirted the margins of jazz and commercial dance music, and his recordings are a vivid reminder that not everything that came out of New York's burgeoning black music scene in the 1910s was nascent jazz. The African American influences in his music are striking. His obscurity today is largely due to the fact that he never recorded under his own full name. Who would expect to find a black Clef Club band playing waltzes under the name Joan Sawyer's Persian Garden Orchestra?

Nathaniel Augustus (Dan) Kildare was born in Kingston, Jamaica, on January 13, 1879. He later claimed that his birth occurred "during the temporary residence there of my parents," although he told officials in London that his father was Paymaster

The dashingly handsome
Dan Kildare. (1915 pass-
port photo)

of Constabulary in Kingston. His brother, George Walter Kildare, was born in Kingston on September 5, 1885. According to author Jeffrey Green, Dan was "from Jamaica, [but] later claimed American parentage."[1]

Whatever his origins, Kildare soon moved to the United States. Census documents indicate that he was resident in the United States by c. 1895, and in 1900 and
1901 he was musical conductor of J. W. Gorman's Alabama Troubadours, one of the
largest summer park shows then touring the East Coast. In his book *One Hundred
Years of the Negro in Show Business,* old showman Tom Fletcher recalled working with
him in that show during the summer of 1901. In addition to Fletcher and his partner, Al Bailey, the large cast included vaudeville headliner Sam Lucas, Madam Flowers ("The Bronze Melba"), and dancer Bill "Bojangles" Robinson. As orchestra leader,
twenty-two-year-old Dan was referred to as "Professor" Kildare.[2]

The next glimpse we have of Kildare is in 1909, when he is listed in *Trow's New
York City Directory* as living at 26 West 136th Street, a Harlem boardinghouse popu-
lated primarily by West Indians. He was by this time working as a cabaret musician.
A handsome, personable young man, he mixed well with other musicians—as well
as with the ladies—and displayed leadership abilities early on. One of his acquaintances was James Reese Europe, a twenty-eight-year-old composer and conductor
who had become a leading figure in the New York musical theater. The ambitious
Europe was laying plans for the first Negro booking agency, the Clef Club, which

was incorporated on April 11, 1910, with Europe as its first president and Dan Kildare as vice-president. In the next year's city directory Europe proudly listed his profession as "president," while Kildare listed his as "vice president."

Headquartered at a rented "clubhouse" on West 53rd Street near the theatrical district, the new organization served as both a one-stop booking agency and a social club for black musicians. In order to attract attention, Europe at once set about organizing the "Clefties'" debut concert. It took place on the evening of May 27 at the Manhattan Casino on 155th Street in Harlem and was a rousing success. Europe led a Clef Club Orchestra of one hundred musicians, including ten pianos—one of them no doubt played by Kildare. Kildare also appeared on the bill as a member of the Long Beach Quartette, together with Harvey White (with whom he would later record in England), Wesley Johnson and George Watters.[3] Many more Clef Club concerts would follow, including a landmark 1912 appearance at Carnegie Hall that many consider one of the turning points in modern American music.

During 1910–13 opportunities for musicians in New York were booming, fueled in part by the rapidly growing popularity of social dancing. It was an exciting time for black musicians. Dance clubs were opening all over the city, and the rich hired orchestras for private dance parties at their estates. Black orchestras were particularly "trendy" among the liberal elite. Jim Europe instilled the Club's members with both discipline and his own highly developed musicianship, resulting in plenty of work for all. The Clef Club was at the center of the activity.

Nevertheless there was trouble brewing. In mid-December 1913 Jim Europe abruptly resigned from the organization he had founded and a short time later launched a new one, the Tempo Club. The reasons for Europe's sudden departure have never been fully explained, but it appears that his growing personal popularity may have stirred jealousies within the ranks (see the chapter on Jim Europe for further details). On December 30 the Clef Club held a meeting to decide on Europe's successor. Dan Kildare was elected president, defeating William Humphreys. For the next year he presided over a still-thriving organization, which seems to have been in no way diminished by Europe's sudden departure. Kildare appears to have been a popular leader, less authoritarian than the stern, though undeniably talented, Europe. A 1915 photograph of Kildare shows a light-skinned, dapper young man with a confidant smile—looking younger, perhaps, than his 36 years.[4]

On February 15, 1914, shortly after Kildare took over, the Clefties held a beefsteak dinner, with entertainment, at Reisenweber's restaurant. A big picture on the front page of the *New York Age* shows perhaps sixty musicians, in suits and white bibs, obviously having a roaring good time.[5] A dozen notables spoke, including President Kildare. An even more pointed indication of the organization's continuing viability came in June with the fourth annual Clef Club Concert and Dancefest at the Manhattan Casino in Harlem. The Clef Club Symphony Orchestra was under the direction of Tim Brymn, and the assistant conductor and chorus master was the eminent composer/conductor Will Marion Cook. Among the members of the huge orchestra were forty-six mandolins and bandoris, eight violins, eleven banjos, twenty-seven harp guitars, one saxophone, one bass tuba, thirteen cellos, one tympani, five traps, two bass violins, and thirty pianists, the latter including Kildare, Clarence Williams,

William Tyers, and Jim Europe's brother, John Europe. Also on the bill were famed concert baritone Harry T. Burleigh, J. Rosamond Johnson, Abbie Mitchell, Bill "Bojangles" Robinson, and Tom Fletcher. "As a directing genius Mr. Kildare has won laurels for himself, and the success of the 1914 Clef Club affair is due largely to his efforts," enthused the *New York Age.* "Brymn, Kildare and [James C.] Hunt made up a team that achieved a success unsurpassed by any effort of the past." In a sidelong reference to the recent turmoil in the Club's leadership, the reviewer added, "Notwithstanding certain changes that have occurred during the past year, the most critical listener could find no fault with the musical achievement of the club."[6]

In October Kildare announced the second Clef Club tour of the East Coast.[7] Evidently not a shy man, he now listed himself in *Trow's Directory* as "President, Clef Club," and paid to have the entry printed in bold type.

Kildare's own career took a most unexpected turn during his term as Clef Club president, leading to his first recordings. Early in the year the Club was approached by a very determined white woman entrepreneur who wanted a black band—one every bit as good as the Castles'—to perform in her new dance club. With Jim Europe already spoken for, she settled for nothing less than a band led by the new president of the Club, Dan Kildare.

Joan Sawyer

Joan Sawyer was a remarkable woman. Because of her role in sponsoring early black musicians, and the paucity of information about her available today (what there is often being inaccurate), it seems worthwhile to outline her career here.[8] Her talent for publicity and legend-building during her years of fame were so great that it is a bit difficult to sort out the facts from the many rags-to-riches press accounts. She was born Bessie J. Morrison about 1880 in Cincinnati, Ohio (she later shaved ten years off her age), and raised in El Paso, Texas, by a family named the Waltons. Returning to Ohio as Bessie Walton, she attended school there until age fifteen. Then, with $150 given to her by an uncle, she left to find fame in show business.

Fame proved an elusive suitor. Sixteen years of struggle followed, during which she was married in Canada to one Alvah Sawyer, in 1902.[9] The marriage was short-lived, but she retained his name for the rest of her career. Her first break, if one can call it that, came in 1907, when she joined the replacement cast of a fairly successful play called *The Vanderbilt Cup* as a chorus girl. This was followed by minor parts in *The Hurdy Gurdy Girl* in late 1907, and in Raymond Hitchcock's *The Merry-Go-Round* in early 1908. She first hit the headlines in the fall of 1908, not for her acting, but for a $100,000 breach-of-promise suit against a young Boston playboy who, she claimed, had lived with her and promised to marry her.

Apparently the suit was none too successful (the playboy's lawyers acidly observed that she had failed to reveal she was already married), and more years of scuffling followed. Around 1911 Sawyer decided to try to capitalize on the emerging dance craze, and finally something clicked. "Discovered" (no doubt with a lot of pushing on her part) more or less simultaneously by Maurice Mouvet, one of the leading dancers of the day, and by literary lion and dance promoter Jeanette Gilder,

Among other things, Joan Sawyer (shown here dancing) claimed she invented the fox trot. (Columbia brochure, 1915)

Sawyer began to move up in the world of exhibition dancing in New York. In late 1913 Gilder wrangled an offer from theatrical mogul Lee Shubert for Sawyer to manage and headline a new dance club called the Persian Garden to be located in Shubert's Winter Garden Theater building.

The room opened in January 1914, opulently decorated and with "Joan Sawyer's Persian Garden" in lights above the door. Accompanied by a blaze of well orchestrated publicity, it was an instant hit with New York's smart set for afternoon teas and after-theater dancing. Joan greeted each patron and gave regular exhibitions of the latest dances with a variety of professional partners. She cleverly positioned herself as the elegant, high-class alternative to the athletic Castles. They featured such demanding dances as the Texas Tommy; she was the "Waltz Queen." Irene Castle bobbed her hair; Joan dressed in high fashion, but always conservatively. She was safe, yet oh-so-up-to-date, and like the Castles she had her own private Negro orchestra.

Dan Kildare at the Persian Garden

It is uncertain whether Dan Kildare and his seven-piece Clef Club orchestra were at the Persian Garden on opening night, but press clippings from February through October identify him as her sole bandleader. He also accompanied her in her vaudeville appearances, which continued concurrently with her club work. They spent at least two weeks at the Palace in February 1914; later venues included the Brooklyn Orpheum in April, Philadelphia's Lyric Theater and Boston's Shubert Theatre in May, and back at the Palace in June. *Variety*'s review of the June appearance observed that "Dan Kildare's Clef Club colored orchestra of eight pieces made the hit of the turn. . . . It has a drummer who doesn't go wild and a leader who can rag on the violin." This latter reference is a little puzzling, as Kildare usually played piano, not violin. It might perhaps explain another puzzle that we will encounter shortly.[10]

Sawyer was by all accounts an extraordinarily graceful dancer, and her exhibitions were often artistic, bordering on ballet. Kildare's orchestra played an important part in her act. A July 1914 review described a performance as follows: "Lightning flashes, the dusky orchestra drummer evokes the thunder of a summer shower, and the dancers come forward to do a little duet scarf dance. . . . After the Negro Clef Club orchestra has played a little dancing melody, Miss Sawyer, in picturesque Gypsy garb, and [her partner] Mr. Sloden return to do the polka tango." Another review, in May, complimented "Dan Kildare's Clef Club Orchestra of colored musicians, who furnished some of the few demonstrations seen here this season of the real charm of syncopation properly done." Still another remarked that "the orchestra is composed of colored musicians with a remarkable sense of time and harmony. Even the audience can't make its feet behave when that orchestra gets to work—and it's working all evening."[11]

The release of Jim Europe's Victor recordings in March and April 1914 ("recorded under the personal supervision of Mr. and Mrs. Vernon Castle") created a sensation, and Columbia was quick to respond. Who was the second most prominent dancer in New York, with her own orchestra? Joan Sawyer, of course. On May 5 and 6, 1914, six titles were recorded. Two of them, "The Joan Waltz" and "Bregeiro (Rio Brazilian Maxixe)," were chosen for issue and rushed into production, reaching stores in July and listed in the August supplement.

The Columbia files do not give session personnel, but notices in the trade journal *The Talking Machine World* were fairly explicit about who was in the studio. One story began, "Joan Sawyer with Columbia . . . well-known conductor of Persian Garden arranges to supervise the making of a special series of dance records for the Columbia Graphophone Company." Sawyer was then quoted as saying, "I have decided to have you make records for me of the dances I have been using in my own work and shall loan you for that purpose *my special dance orchestra from the Persian Garden, New York*" (italics added). An advertisement added that Sawyer had "her own Persian Garden Orchestra making Columbia dance records." Since Dan Kildare was her sole orchestra leader during this period, it was almost certainly him with her in the studio that day. This is corroborated by entries in the files of the English HMV label, which in 1915 noted that Kildare had previously recorded for Columbia in the United States.[12]

Nevertheless the twelve-inch record that was issued was credited to "Joan Sawyer's Persian Garden Orchestra," with no acknowledgment of Kildare. It also bore the legend "recorded under the personal supervision of Joan Sawyer." No doubt her name was thought more likely to sell records than his.

Kildare toured with Sawyer in vaudeville during the summer of 1914, until she was struck with appendicitis in mid-August. After a seven-week convalescence she reopened a renovated Persian Garden Room on October 5, with Kildare returning as her bandleader. Another Columbia session followed on about October 16, with no sides released.

Then, about late October, disaster struck. The New York musicians' union had long maintained a policy of excluding most blacks. Realizing that jobs at many of the new dance clubs were going to nonunion musicians as a result, the union suddenly did an about-face. It announced that blacks were now being accepted into its ranks and that henceforth all musicians working at the city's dance clubs must be union members. In other words, join immediately or lose your job.

Black musicians were deeply divided over what to do. They suspected that the white-run union simply wanted a piece of their earnings or wanted to force its way into the clubs so it could eventually replace them with white musicians. Editorialized the *New York Age,* "Already the white musicians of the union have stirred up a lot of strife by seeing to it that non-union colored men were replaced by colored musicians affiliated with the union at the Jardin de Danse on top of the New York Theatre" (the Jardin de Danse complex included Sawyer's Persian Garden Room). "Sixteen colored musicians are said to be working at the Jardin de Danse in the place of 23 colored musicians who were let out because they did not join the union." The *Age* also complained that the union was undercutting the value of black musicians by substituting its own easy admission test for the Clef Club's more stringent musical screening.[13]

The files of the union have long since disappeared, and it is not known whether Kildare and his men joined or were fired. Although Sawyer continued to receive a great deal of press, there is no mention of the identity of her bandleader between October 1914 and March 1915. A black orchestra led by William Blacklock, described as "direct from Joan Sawyer's Persian Gardens of New York," is mentioned in the *Age* in early December, but this is in connection with that band's extended tour of the south, without Sawyer.[14] Someone else must have been playing back in New York.

The turmoil makes it uncertain who led the orchestra at the final Joan Sawyer sessions for Columbia, which were held on November 30 and December 4, 1914. My guess is that it was still Kildare. Even if he had been ousted from the Persian Garden a few weeks earlier, which is not certain, Sawyer probably would have used the leader she had been working with for nearly a year rather than risk someone new for such an important assignment. Whoever was leading Sawyer's orchestra, it recorded seven more twelve-inch sides during the November–December sessions, of which two were released. At first these were planned to be "Valse Boston" and "Passing of Salome" on two sides of a disc, but this coupling was withdrawn at the last minute. Instead "Valse Boston" was coupled with a one-step called "When You're a Long, Long Way from Home," which was released in March 1915. Like the earlier release, the disc bore the legend "recorded under the personal supervision of Joan Sawyer." Miss Sawyer's autograph also appeared in the wax.

The two discs by "Joan Sawyer's Persian Garden Orchestra" are hardly jazz, but like the 1913–14 Jim Europe Victors they are fascinating examples of what black Clef Club orchestras sounded like at the time. There is a looseness and enthusiasm not heard from white studio groups like Prince's Band. "Bregeiro" is a maxixe, enthusiastically and rhythmically performed, with a mandolin (or bandolin) playing lead (mandolins and related instruments were favored in Clef Club concerts). The one-step "When You're a Long, Long Way from Home" is a little more subdued, although the drummer's riffs do sound influenced by the frantic Buddy Gilmore style heard on the Europe recordings.

Of the issued waltzes, "Joan Waltz-Hesitation" also has a mandolin lead, while the "Valse Boston," better known as "Drigo's Serenade," is a long, repetitive rendering of the famous waltz by a somewhat amateurish violinist, accompanied by a subdued orchestra. Remarkably, a pressing of the unissued "Passing of Salome" waltz has also surfaced. This is a sinuous, oriental-styled number, again with a violin lead, no doubt intended to accompany one of Miss Sawyer's artistic dances. It is technically fine, and the reason Columbia decided not to issue it must have been commercial rather than musical. Who is playing the violin on these numbers? Kildare was a pianist and Sawyer herself did not play an instrument. If the June 1914 *Variety* review quoted earlier is correct, it may be Kildare struggling along on an unfamiliar instrument. Perhaps not coincidentally, some of the "Dan and Harvey's Jazz Band" recordings made by Kildare and Harvey White several years later in England feature a similarly unsteady violinist.

Dan Kildare's term as Clef Club president ended in December 1914, and he was succeeded by Fred "Deacon" Johnson, who held the post for the next several years. Writers at the time complimented Kildare on his successful administration, but later references suggest that in fact he left the club in a shambles. A 1917 item in the *Age* noted that when Johnson took over things were in a bad way, with membership down and the treasury empty. A later article in the same publication described how Johnson "rescued" the Club and brought it back to health.[15]

While there is no direct evidence as to whether Kildare continued to lead Sawyer's orchestra after October 1914, news items do indicate that she continued to use a black band. In early March 1915 Sawyer headlined at B. F. Keith's in Philadelphia ("music of a semi-barbaric variety is provided by her own Persian Garden Orchestra from New York") and later the same month scored a big hit at Rochester's Temple Theatre, headlining over Eddie Cantor and Helen Trix, among others (her "colored orchestra contributes its full share to the presentation of a thoroughly delighting and never tiring performance").[16] The first mention of Kildare's replacement appears in the March 11, 1915, *New York Age,* which reported that "the Persian Garden Sextet Orchestra, comprising William Reilly, E. Weeks, V. Lowry, P. Jones, J. R. Burroughs and J. D. Barnes, members of the Clef Club, supported Miss Joan Sawyer at Keith's last week." Later items in March, June, and August 1915 identify her bandleader as mandolin player Seth Weeks (presumably the "E. Weeks" mentioned above).

Kildare had probably left Sawyer by early 1915, as an item in early February shows him playing Dover, New Jersey. (His brother, Walter Kildare, was simultaneously appearing in Brooklyn.) However, Dan's career was about to take a dramatic new turn. In March came the startling report that "A Clef Club Orchestra of seven men sail for Europe on or about March 18. Dan Kildare is the leader." Few black American bands had permanently moved to Europe before this, but many would follow in the years to come. Kildare led the way, and his great success encouraged others.[17]

A big Clef Club "mulliganfest" dinner was held for Kildare and his men on Sunday, March 21, at the clubhouse, and the following day Kildare applied for a passport, giving his address as 30 West 136th Street. According to the application he was five feet, six and three-quarter inches tall, light-skinned and with brown eyes. In his passport photo he is handsome and well dressed, looking every bit the leader. Traveling with him were band members Walter Kildare (age 29, cello), Seth Jones (27, banjo), Joseph Meyers (26, banjo), Louis Mitchell (29, drums and vocal), John Ricks (36, bass violin), and George Watters (38, banjo). On March 27 they sailed for England on the White Star Line's *Megantic.*[18] Dan Kildare could hardly have foreseen the combination of spectacular success and tragedy that awaited him during the next five years in London.

Kildare's party arrived in Liverpool on April 9 and proceeded to London, where they had a contract for a year's engagement at the elegant new Ciro's Restaurant. Ciro's had been launched in Monte Carlo with an American bar at the Galerie Charles III. Ciro later sold the business to a British syndicate, which expanded by opening several Ciro's in France, including one in Paris. The London Ciro's was the latest addition and was still under construction when Kildare arrived. Located on the site of the Westminster Public Baths on London's Orange Street, behind the National Gallery, it was decorated in Louis XVI style with a sliding roof and a dance floor on springs that could be tightened or loosened as needed. The premises also included a gallery and a grill room. It was operated basically as a private club for the upper crust, who were not about to let wartime stringencies get in the way of having a night on the town.

Construction was finished on April 17, 1915, and the club opened the following evening to a crowd of six hundred, including many celebrities of the London stage. Proceeds of opening night were donated to the *Daily Telegraph* Belgian fund. There was much coverage of the gala event, and several articles made note of the exotic black "ragtime" orchestra that had been imported from America to play for the dancers. The *Daily Telegraph* reported that "Mr. Dan Kildare's coloured orchestra from the Clef Club, New York, was in attendance, and the selections which it provided were greatly enjoyed." *Town Topics* said, "the Negro band made music which is rather remarkable in its way, for it consists of the newest ragtime and fox-trot melodies, with a Central African feeling for the tom tom and other instruments of percussion running through it all." A little later a less sympathetic reporter said the band consisted of "many indefatigable black men who bang drums and cymbals and even sound motor horns."[19]

Ciro's quickly became one of the trendiest night spots in London and had little trouble attracting patrons. As of March 7, 1915, 450 members were signed up, but by January 1916 the total had reached 2,207. It did not need to advertise, which makes tracing its activities from week to week a bit difficult. Its original hours were noon to five A.M., although closing was later cut back to between one and two A.M. One of the chief attractions was dancing to Kildare's orchestra. "Eve," the gossip columnist for the society magazine *Tatler,* confided in September 1916, "I don't know what one would do to keep one's spirits if it weren't for the theatres and restaurants, and the little dances, with Ciro's band to bang away till breakfast time. The coon music, by the way, isn't getting depressed at all—in fact it's madder than ever, I do b'lieve, if anything, and goes to one's feet so badly that—well, it's a good thing frocks are as flimsy as they're curtailed. Otherwise some of us might get hot."[20]

Kildare's band remained in residence at Ciro's for about two years, also playing outside engagements from time to time, mostly at society functions. Eve described one in 1915: "Down at Coombe Court, Lady Ripon's been having open-air concerts for her convalescing soldiers ever since the weather got good enough, and the other day she had Ciro's black ragtime band to play for them—she's a Ciro-ite herself, you know. The men simply loved it, of course; shrieked the ragtime choruses and reveled in the fearful din and encored everything, and altogether were a much more appreciative audience than the usual Ciro's ones, who are generally busy eating, of course."[21]

Other reported functions at which Kildare's band appeared included a 1915 party given by Mrs. Evelyn Walsh McLean for Americans in London, attended by the prince of Wales (Tallulah Bankhead and the Dolly Sisters entertained); and a 1916 benefit luncheon and garden party at Grosvenor House to aid the Three Arts Women's Employment Fund, graced by Queen Alexandra, the duke of Westminster, Lord Asquith, Winston Churchill, and various dukes and duchesses. Reporting on the latter, the *Times* described "in the various rooms . . . a variety entertainment with an all-star programme, [including] Ciro's nigger band."[22]

Early reports indicated that the transplanted musicians met with great success. Shortly after arriving in April 1915 Joe Meyers and his wife sent a card to Clef Club president Deacon Johnson back in New York saying that everything pointed to "a bright future of the Clefties on [this] side of the water." An article in the May 6, 1915, *New York Age* reported on the success of black entertainers in London, saying, "as a result of the European War colored entertainers are in great demand in the London theatres and cafes, and . . . before many months have passed, colored musicians and singers will be doing most of the cabaret work in London." Referring to Kildare at Ciro's and banjoist Gus Haston's Versatile Four at Murray's Club, it continued, "Kildare, until recently president of the Clef Club, assumed the onerous duties of amusing the fastidious and high-class patrons of Ciro's. He has seven men in his aggregation, which is known as Dan Kildare's Clef Club Orchestra. They are making a big hit, and as Murray's and Ciro's are generally regarded as the leading establishments of their kind, the opinion prevails that other well known cafes will soon adopt the policy of employing colored entertainers."[23]

The article pointed out that because of the war German musicians, who had previously been favored in London's night spots, were being replaced, offering major opportunities for Americans. It then issued a stern warning.

> This new state of affairs should make it possible for colored entertainers to ultimately corner the cabaret work in London, unless they make a mess of things, as is so often done. . . . With such alluring prospects in sight for colored entertainers abroad, we respectfully beg of those who go to England to use good judgment and to remember that while it is important that their work be of high order, it is equally important that their CONDUCT be above reproach. For no matter how highly their work is regarded, if they become obnoxious because of their CONDUCT, their stay abroad will be painfully short.
>
> It behooves every colored musician in England to be on his good behavior, for just as . . . the producers of *The Birth of a Nation* are seeking to create a false impression in this country regarding the Negro, so are agencies for America at work abroad doing their utmost to sow the seeds of race hatred. Let the colored Americans in London show their loyalty [to] their race by being gentlemen at all times and in all places. If they pursue this policy they will be rendering incalculable service to their people.

There was considerable turnover in personnel, making the exact lineup of the band at any point in time difficult to ascertain. Drummer Louis Mitchell left around July 1915 to tour the music halls with Joe Jordan and was apparently replaced by Hughes Pollard. George Watters was killed in an accidental shooting in September 1915.[24] Others leaving were Meyers, Ricks, and possibly Jones. Dan Kildare returned to the United States in April 1916 for a month's visit, bringing back new musicians (Ferdinand Allen, Vance Lowry, Sumner Edwards) to replace those who had left the band. Kildare's future partner, drummer Harvey White, arrived in England in mid-1916, although it is not known whether he joined the band at Ciro's at this time.

A New York City census taken in June 1915 indicates that Kildare may have had more to do in New York than simply round up new musicians. Entries for 78–81 West 141st Street in Harlem, an apartment house occupied mostly by white immigrants, show a husband and wife named Daniel and Ena Kildear, with the former listed as a thirty-five-year-old musician born in the British West Indies. They had a daughter named Francis, aged nine. That this is our Dan Kildare is proven by the fact that his will, made out in 1920, mentions a daughter named Carmin Francis, living with one Ena Kildare. Dan had left New York by this time the census was taken, but census-takers were instructed to list all persons whose "usual place of abode" was the premises, even if they were not in residence. It is the first indication that he was married.

Ena was twenty-seven years old at the time, and her entry indicates that she was born in the United States, although, like Dan, she was classified as an "alien." All three family members are listed as "white." This was not unusual in mixed-race situations where some inhabitants were light-skinned blacks (as was the case with Dan).

Dan Kildare and Joan Sawyer's Persian Garden Orchestra

Three years later, when Dan married again in England, he described himself as a "widower," but it seems more likely that he and Ena divorced, as he named her and his daughter in his will two years after that.

Shortly after Dan arrived in London he evidently approached the local recording companies. An entry dated July 1915 in the files of the Gramophone Company (HMV) noted that at that time, barely three months after arriving in England, Kildare's Ciro's Club Sextette was willing to record. Instead, in 1916 he accepted an offer from Columbia, the British branch of the company for which he had recorded in the United States. The company was evidently interested in capitalizing on the success of the band everyone was talking about at the trendy Ciro's night spot. For recording purposes, Columbia gave the group the ghastly name "Ciro's Club Coon Orchestra."

The first sessions were held in August 1916 and consisted of six currently popular U.S. show tunes, giving an indication of the high-class (and almost exclusively white) repertoire in which the group specialized. Three songs were from Jerome Kern's *Very Good, Eddie,* two from *Hip-Hip-Hooray,* and one was actor Raymond Hitchcock's specialty piece, "I Can Dance with Everybody but My Wife," from *Sybil,* shows that had not necessarily opened in London yet. Most standard discographies list the band at this time as consisting of Dan Kildare, piano and leader, Vance Lowry, banjo, Ferdinand Allen, banjoline, Walter Kildare, 'cello, Sumner Edwards, string bass, Hughes Pollard, drums, and Seth Jones, vocals, although Jones is most in question.[25] The sound was dominated by the banjos, making the group resemble a loud banjo orchestra with rhythm accompaniment. Dan's piano is virtually inaudible amid the racket. Most of the performances are very fast-paced, loose, and "live" sounding, and give the impression of a wild party going on—which was exactly the atmosphere at Ciro's, late into the night.

The vocals by Seth Jones (or whoever it is) are the icing on the cake. A deep, resonant bass/baritone who sounds like he ought to be singing "Asleep in the Deep" or "Nearer My God to Thee," he comes in periodically during the wild proceedings with short choruses in a style that is at once slightly dignified and slightly loose. The aural picture is two A.M. at Ciro's with a distinguished baritone, his tuxedo rumpled and his bowtie hanging loose, jumping in to join the fray as the banjos crank out one silly novelty after another.

Perhaps the best example is "On the Shore at Le-Lei-Wei," from *Very Good, Eddie,* also known as "On the Beach at Waikiki" (which is how Jones sings it). As the banjos plunk along furiously for nearly four minutes, Jones seems to hum along, coming in three times for short choruses in his booming baritone.

> Honika-u a wiki-wiki,
> On the beach at Waikiki,
> And she gave me language lessons,
> On the beach at Waikiki!

On "Some Sort of Somebody" (also from *Very Good, Eddie*) Jones is almost drowned out by the banjos. Banjoists Lowry and Allen get a real workout on these recordings, and they are very good. So is drummer Pollard, who at times uses blocks to accent the rhythm.

It could be called "A Night at Ciro's." These performances are hardly jazz, but they do owe a lot to New York's Clef Club sound, with its acres of mandolins and other stringed instruments, and reliance on a loose sort of playing that was in sharp contrast with the careful, note-by-note readings of most white orchestras at the time. It would be only a short step to the improvisation that marked the evolution of jazz in the twenties. Kildare's sound was not entirely new to record-buyers in 1916. A few months earlier, in February 1916, HMV had recorded a quartet of black American musicians called the Versatile Four in some raucous, ragtime-flavored numbers. Banjos were used on their recordings as well, though drums and vocals were more prominent.

However we view Kildare's recordings today, they were sold at the time as a souvenir of glamorous Ciro's for its elite patrons, and as a peek inside the place for those who could never dream of getting in. The first discs were released by Columbia in October 1916, with the following description in the industry trade paper *Sound Wave:* "An exclusive engagement of the popular orchestra of the most famous night club in the world—Ciro's—is announced on Columbia this month. . . . All the latest in music is played by the Club Orchestra and the atmosphere of the club is reflected in these first records—gaiety in excelsis."[26]

A photograph of the band appeared with the announcement, but it pictured the original band of 1915, some of whose members were certainly gone by this time. If nothing else, this suggests a perceived continuity in the Ciro's band, and the fact that the specific members were considered of little importance by the record company or presumably by the patrons. All African Americans looked alike to them. None of the bandmembers was named.

Although these records are fairly scarce today, they evidently showed enough promise to encourage Columbia to want more. About October 1916 another session took place, this time resulting in seven issued sides. Among them were more show tunes, including Harbach and Friml's "Something Seems Tingle-Ingleing" from *High Jinks,* and several currently popular novelties. Among the latter were "(They Made It Twice as Nice as Paradise, and) They Called It Dixieland," "Yaaka Hula Hickey Dula," "Hello, Hawaii, How Are You," and "Never Let Your Right Hand Know What Your Left Hand's Going to Do." The booming baritone vocalist is heard on most sides, fairly briefly. On "Yaaka Hula" he wordlessly vocalizes along, "La-la-la-la . . ." "My Mother's Rosary" is particularly amusing, a seemingly serious ballad done at an ironic fast tempo, with Jones apparently oblivious to the lyrics he's singing. Several of the sides have flashy, razzle-dazzle endings by the banjoists, and on "Never Let Your Right Hand Know" the drummer even appears to incorporate tom-toms.

The sound was so novel that even writers at the time had trouble—as we do today—sorting out exactly what instruments were being heard on these records. Wrote the *Sound Wave* in 1917, "We have found ourselves striving with more or less heroic resolve but with scant success to locate the tonal identity of the peculiar—very—though distinctly enticing quality of the instrument or instruments comprising this original orchestra. After much searching of heart, and so far as we can make out, it is a kind of blend of banjo and guitar, spiced with a flavouring of mandoline." *Talking Machine News* was more decisive, though not necessarily right, when it described "a combination of capital banjo players."[27] To the ears of my fellow researcher Howard Rye, "on many of the records, it sounds as though a conventional banjo is being used alongside an instrument hybrid between banjo and mandolin which is presumably a banjoline. Though three banjos or whatever were used at the club, there are only two on the records."[28]

Beginning at least as early as June 1916 Kildare's band entertained at private functions at the Grafton Galleries on Grafton Street in London following their sets at Ciro's. The Grafton parties went on long into the night, and there were complaints to police about the noise. An investigation resulted that sheds some light on the band's activities at the time. In November 1916 Inspector Lummus of the Metropolitan Police reported that on several dates in June and July music, dancing, and singing were heard coming from the Grafton Galleries between 12:30 and 4 A.M., and carriage drivers confirmed that they had brought revelers there from Ciro's after it closed. "Ragtime dances and loud singing by a nigger troupe could be heard in the neighboring street on these days," he wrote. "On three occasions I saw the band leave the Galleries between four and five A.M. and recognized it as the same band which I had seen leave Ciro's Club on other nights. One morning, the members of the band, who are very dark-skinned, were evidently under the influence of drink and were shouting loudly in Albemarle Street, but as I approached them they went quietly away."[29] Another citizen, complaining about the noise, testified that "Ciro's nigger band went to the Galleries almost nightly after Ciro's closed." Later a new club opened in the Old Bond Street Galleries and witnesses testified that Ciro's band had played there. Inspector Lummus reported "a rowdy noise of singing, music and dancing . . . commencing about 12:30 A.M. and continuing until 4 A.M."

Kildare and his musicians were no doubt making a good deal of money from their multiple engagements. However public resentment was beginning to build against these clubs as blatant examples of the upper classes continuing to live the "high life" even in wartime. Rumors were rampant that the crowd at Ciro's included aristocrats, diplomats, and even younger members of the British royal family. The official investigation began to center on whether Ciro's business was effectively being transferred after closing hours to the Grafton Galleries and later to the Old Bond Street Galleries for the purpose of evading regulations governing closing hours for establishments dispensing liquor.

Finally the authorities began to close in on Ciro's itself. Undercover investigators infiltrated the club in mid-October and "found about 250 persons in this room, a large number of whom were dancing to the music of a nigger band in the centre of same." A full-scale police raid took place on Sunday, October 22, 1916, at 11 P.M. Following the raid one police official reported that "between 60 and 70 ladies and gentlemen were dancing to ragtime music from a nigger band." Another stated that the music was "of a rather crude and riotous character . . . [meaning] that the music was rather rough, the musicians evidently struck the notes of their own accord . . . the music was not classical or such as one would expect to hear on a Sunday."

Club officials were summoned before Bow Street magistrates on November 9 to "show cause why the club should not be struck off the register on the grounds that it was not conducted in good faith; that it was habitually used for an unlawful purpose; that illegal sales of intoxicants had taken place; and the supply of intoxicants was not under the control of the members of the committee appointed by the members." Summonses were issued for selling liquor after 9:30 P.M. and for selling liquor without a license. The *Times* headlined "A Raid at Ciro's," much to the delight, no doubt, of those who wanted to put an end to all this hedonism. Columnist Eve spoke for the fun-loving customers, writing in the *Tatler,* "So after all, they're going to prosecute our last and only night club—hard luck, what? No one thought, you know, they'd have the nerve to, considering the very distinguished crowd they'd got there on the Sunday night they went and raided it; but, lor, you never know what'll happen these days, and positively no one's safe."[30]

The case went to trial on November 24 and dragged on into December. The Club put on a strong defense, citing among other things the obvious musical prejudices of the investigating officers. Defense counsel stated that £100 per week was being paid for the band's services, and that it was "the finest we could get." However, music was not the issue. The magistrate found against the Club, imposing substantial fines, striking the Club off the register, and ordering that no liquor be served on the premises for twelve months. The judgment was appealed, but the appeal was dropped on January 18, 1917.[31]

There was unfavorable comment during the trial that the names of famous and well-connected patrons of the Club were being withheld. Official documents related to the raid were sealed for an extraordinary seventy-five years, and when they were finally made public in the early 1990s they proved to contain no name of special distinction other than that of the Russian naval attaché. As Howard Rye notes, if the names of distinguished citizens (or of the band) were ever in the file they had been judiciously removed.

Despite the suspension of its liquor license Ciro's continued to operate for dining and dancing, and Kildare's musicians kept their jobs, while the authorities kept up the pressure to shut the Club down permanently. A police superintendent visited on December 22, 1916, and found that "the nigger band of six performers was playing, between fifty and sixty persons were in the restaurant including eight couples dancing." To placate the authorities the Club primly announced in January that "a special feature will be made of the Afternoon Teas, at which Ciro's Orchestra will perform, and Dancing will take place daily." The military had by this time decreed that officers in uniform could not dine but were permitted to dance. Said Eve in the *Tatler* in February, "there's always Ciro's as a place in which to get exercise on a dull Sunday afternoon."[32]

The controversy about the club continued. In Parliament on February 27, 1917, Labour M.P. James O'Grady stated that Ciro's intended to spend £3,000 to open a new cabaret. This opened on March 3, with Melville Gideon providing the music, but Dan Kildare advertised as the "Chef d'Orchestre" of Ciro's Club Orchestra. On March 3 Conservative M.P. Sir John Butcher referred to a function that had taken place at Ciro's as an "orgy." Other M.P.'s lodged complaints about the Club as well.[33]

The fatal blow fell on March 13, 1917, when Ciro's was placed off-limits for all troops and it was announced that the Club would be picketed beginning the following day. As Eve in the *Tatler* lamented, "Ciro's sans a single ossifer . . . you can't run a cabaret without men, can you? and after all there's a very small percentage left of civilians." She also referred to the "loss of that gorgeously—swung dancing floor, and wonderful nigger band," so it seems apparent that Kildare's band remained until the very end, which is believed to have come in early April. The premises were loaned for the duration of the war to the YMCA, whose patrons were promised "classical and light music of the best kind."[34]

Despite the closing of Ciro's and the loss of their lucrative engagement, the band did not immediately break up. Lowry, Allen, Walter Kildare, Edwards, and Jones—the entire band minus Dan Kildare and drummer Pollard—promptly embarked on a tour of the British music halls under the leadership of former drummer Louis Mitchell, billing themselves as the Seven Spades, "the Syncopated Band from Ciro's Supper Club, London." (The "seventh spade" was a "mad dancer" named F. Jones, possibly Seth Jones's wife.)[35] Their first traced engagement was on April 9. Mitchell had been playing the halls for some time, and was a highly efficient self-publicist. It appears that he wrested the band away from Dan Kildare, complete with Dan's brother.

Columbia still wanted the Ciro's band for recordings, and most experts believe that Dan led the band in the recording sessions held during March, June, and September 1917. Possibly he held the recording contract. Aurally it is the same Ciro's band that had recorded during 1916 with the sound dominated by ace banjoists Lowry and Allen.

The March 1917 session(s), held right about the time Ciro's was being censored and picketed, resulted in nine issued titles. Most of these are not quite as frantically fast-paced as the 1916 sides, but they capture the same loose, happy "party" atmosphere. Among them were top pop tunes of the day, including "Poor Butterfly," "Hello Frisco," "Oh! How She Could Yacki, Wicki, Wacki, Woo," and "Where Did Robinson Crusoe Go with Friday on Saturday Night?" (Al Jolson's big hit from *Robinson Crusoe, Jr.*). For the first time the band also tackled a couple of numbers by black composers, namely Shelton Brooks's "Walkin' the Dog" and Jim Europe's "Clef Club March." The latter was the first recording ever of that trademark number and shows that Kildare's men had not forgotten their roots as members of New York's fabled Clef Club.

Some of these sides contain truly extraordinary banjo picking. Note in particular the shifting tempos and rhythms of "Oh! How She Could Yacki . . ." and the bluesy accompaniment to "Walkin' the Dog." Once in a while extraneous sounds would be introduced, such as a slide whistle in "Where Did Robinson Crusoe Go." It is possibly Seth Jones who comes in periodically with his booming vocals, although another deep-voiced vocalist may be present on "Walkin' the Dog." This is believed to be Louis Mitchell.

The June session resulted in four more issued sides, consisting of more pop tunes ("What Do You Want to Make Those Eyes at Me For?") and novelties ("She'd a Hole in Her Stocking"). Jones and Mitchell are believed to have alternated vocals on these, although their voice quality is so close it's hard to tell. The fact that some of the vocals are rather faint, as if the vocalist was too far from the recording horn, doesn't help. The lead banjos (or banjo and banjoline) play some nice harmonies and counterpoint in "She'd a Hole."

Saving the best for last, in some ways, the Ciro's band in September 1917 recorded W. C. Handy's immortal "St. Louis Blues." It is given a suitably bluesy treatment, with the vocalist (probably Mitchell) interjecting whoops and vocal slides. It is one of the earliest vocal recordings of the song and an interesting performance. The other title made at this session, "Chinese Blues," is another good syncopated number, with the drummer accenting the beat with blocks. There is a long raggy section toward the end, with the vocalist coming in and out. Ending on a high note, Ciro's Club Coon Orchestra would be heard no more.

Dan Kildare's activities between April and November, aside from the recording sessions, are uncertain. It is even possible that he joined Mitchell's Seven Spades, although it seems unlikely that he would become a sideman in his own band. By November he had teamed with a New York friend, drummer/vocalist Harvey White, in a new act called Dan and Harvey's Jazz Band. Their first traced engagement was at London's Shoreditch Empire Theatre in November. A review commented, "Dan and Harvey, two coloured artistes in an act new to London, introducing singing, dancing, piano and trap drum, made an immediate hit. Dan is a pianist of more than the usual ability, who can play ragtime as skillfully as he can a good classical selection. Harvey has a good baritone voice, can dance in first-rate style, and manipulate the trap-drum without making too much noise. With just a little more briskness infused into the show, the boys should have a busy time in store, as far as dates were concerned. They were called before the tabs." Another review said their act consisted of "ragtime and other selections."[36]

Dan and Harvey continued to work together through 1918 and 1919. They were also active songwriters. During 1918 they placed their song "I Love Them All, Just a Little Bit" (music by Dan, words by Harvey) in the hit revue *Hullo, America,* which opened at the Palace Theatre on September 25, 1918. It was sung in the show by star Elsie Janis and Irene Magley. Kildare also co-composed a song called "The Jazz Band" with Elsie Janis for the same show, and a facsimile of Kildare's signature appeared on the published sheet music for both songs. A later report said, "his big income came from songs he had written for Elsie Janis, among others," but these are the only two published songs that have been traced.[37]

During the summers of 1918 and 1919 a band called "The Famous Coloured Orchestra (late of Ciro's)" was billed at the Karsino resort, located on an island in the River Thames outside London. No personnel were given, but it seems likely that Kildare was involved. Louis Mitchell's Seven Spades had gone to France in January 1918 but had split with Mitchell during an engagement in Paris in mid-1918, and thus might have been available to rejoin Dan during the summer. That, of course, is speculation.

Kildare still had connections in the recording industry, and in December 1918 he landed the first of two sessions with Columbia for his new Dan and Harvey combination. Six titles were recorded, again concentrating on white show tunes and popular hits of the day. Among them were "The Missouri Waltz," "If You Look in Her Eyes" (from *Going Up*), and "Allah's Holiday" (from *Katinka*). His own two numbers from *Hullo America* ("The Jazz Band" and "I Love Them All") were also committed to wax, but unfortunately not released.

Dan and Harvey's Jazz Band was a quartet consisting (presumably) of Dan on piano, Harvey on drums, and unknown musicians on violin and banjo. Musically, the results were much less satisfying than those of the old Ciro's band. Whereas the Ciro's band spotlighted banjos, on the Dan and Harvey sides the violinist dominated the sound, and he was noticeably unsteady, with a rather thin tone. He sounds like the amateurish violinist on Joan Sawyer's 1914 Columbia of "Valse Boston," though this may be merely a coincidence. The drummer (White) clatters along without much rhythm, sometimes using blocks or tom-toms ("Allah's Holiday"), while the piano and banjo contribute what they can. It is altogether rather "weak tea," as the British would say, and certainly has none of the energy and excitement of some of the Ciro's sides, sounding at times like an amateur combination at a failed audition.

Despite this musical mess, Columbia wanted more, and in late April 1919 Dan and Harvey's combo was back in the studio to record three more sides, the popular hits "Smiles," "Till the Clouds Roll By," and "Hindustan." On the first two Harvey White contributed competent vocal choruses in the deep baritone style of Seth Jones and Louis Mitchell. Unfortunately he was overwhelmed by that awful violinist and his squeaky strings. Kildare added a cute little piano coda at the end of some sides.

Seven of the nine songs recorded in the two sessions were released in mid-1919, in a joint release with some Columbia sides by the Original Dixieland Jazz Band. The contrast couldn't have been greater. The press-release writer did his best to put a positive spin on things, claiming, under the headline "Genuine Jazz on Columbia," that "those who desire to know the difference between 'jazzed' music and the ordinarily acceptable variety should hear 'The Missouri Waltz' or 'Smiles' played by an ordinary orchestra, and then 'jazzed' as Dan and Harvey's Jazz Band do it on Columbia." As jazz researcher Brian Rust later put it, "If that is a jazz band, I'm Ludwig van Beethoven."[38]

In late August 1919 newspaper items began to appear saying that the fabled Ciro's would reopen in October with a house band and dancing every evening after dinner. There was much anticipation, with the *Dancing Times* predicting "a special band with giant drum and several saxophones from America," and the *Sketch* saying "there is to be a real coon band." Eve of the *Tatler* enthused about "a surprise band to dance to—shouldn't wonder if it's an even bigger success than the old one."[39]

Kildare was not there on opening night—instead, a band called the White Lyers entertained. In January 1920 Kildare began a six-month engagement as leader of the new Ciro's jazz band, "presiding at the piano." The remainder of the personnel are unknown. It is quite possible that Harvey White may have been a member, but most of the rest of the old band—Lowry, Allen, Edwards, and Jones—were reported to be playing at Ciro's in Monte Carlo.[40]

On April 9, 1918, after about three years in London, thirty-nine-year-old Dan Kildare, describing himself as a widower, married Mary Rose Frances Fink, a twenty-nine-year-old English widow. He liked his new surroundings, and it looked as if he wanted to settle down. He was prosperous for a musician. His long stay at Ciro's (not to mention the many other engagements) had no doubt brought him a considerable income, and he was a successful songwriter as well. One later report claimed he could make over $200 a night playing the piano. His new bride had two small children, Charles and Doris, from her former marriage. She was also the owner of the Bell public house (bar) at 15 Little Titchfield Street in London, which she had inherited from her late husband. Kildare was at the time living at 1 Gower Street in London, where he had a studio for a time.[41]

We cannot know what caused Dan Kildare's personal life to begin its downward spiral. Seemingly he was quite successful. There are clues, perhaps, in his apparent mismanagement of the Clef Club, evident only after the fact, and his failure to be reelected for a second term. He apparently lied to his second wife, saying he was a widower. There was also the wildly uneven quality of his bands—when surrounded at Ciro's by first-rate musicians inherited from the Clef Club, it was superb; but when he went out on his own, with Harvey White, it was distinctly second-rate. He seems to have been a smooth talker and a ladies' man. Personality traits like that can come back to haunt one. It was reported at the time of his death that he was drinking heavily and using drugs.

His marriage, not surprisingly, was an unhappy one. Dan and Mary Rose separated after a short time, then reunited, then separated again. By 1920 there were incidents of violence and suggestions of infidelity. According to the *Times* there were frequent quarrels. "Kildare, it is said by neighbours, often assaulted her, and he did not appear to have kindly feelings toward his step-children." In January 1920 he was charged with an offense "in connection with one of his wife's barmaids" but was not convicted. He was said to have threatened his wife on several occasions and was at one time "in the hands of the police on a charge of wrecking his wife's home." In early June 1920 the police were called to intervene in a marital dispute, and he was charged with assaulting an officer. Mary Rose resumed using the name of her first husband and instituted divorce proceedings. Some thought he believed she was trying to get him deported, although it would have been legally impossible to deport someone born in Jamaica, a British territory.

Kildare's friends gave a somewhat different version. One later wrote, "he had come to England in 1915, married an English woman, and had opened a flourishing bar in London. He made piles of money and royally maintained his wife's family— wife, mother-in-law, sister-in-law, etc. . . . Married for two years, he and his wife did not understand one another." There were also intimations of racial tension between the two.[42]

Events came to a horrific climax on the night of June 21, 1920. According to the account in the *Times,* at about 6:10 P.M. "Kildare entered the bar of the public house, and inquired of [his wife's sister] Mrs. Ludlow where his wife was, as he wanted to speak with her. Mrs. Kildare then came into the kitchen, which is quite close to the bar, and it is said told her husband to speak to Mrs. Ludlow and not to her. She then went back into the kitchen, and Kildare followed her, although two barmaids, fearing there might be trouble, tried to prevent him. He got past them, however, and entered the room. Almost immediately afterwards the women in the bar were horrified to hear a revolver shot. The kitchen door had somehow become locked on the outside, and it is stated that in order to get back again into the bar Kildare blew off the lock with his revolver. He then attacked Mrs. Ludlow, and shot her dead."

He then shot Matilda Heiser, a nurse who was apparently employed as a maid at the Bell, and turned the gun on Kathleen M'Millan, a shorthand typist who was visiting with Lucy Ludlow. She testified at the inquest that "He seemed to frown and changed his mind and turned the thing round in his hand and put it right up against his left temple. There was a report and he fell." When police arrived they found Mary Rose dead in the kitchen (shot in the head), and her sister and Kildare dead in the bar. Heiser would survive. The verdict at the inquest was murder in the case of the two women, and suicide in the case of Kildare. The coroner ruled that Kildare was sane at the time of the crime and suggested that the laws on carrying firearms ought to be tightened.[43]

Needless to say, the sensational crime received wide coverage in the London press, with headlines such as "Shooting Affray in London" (the *Times*), "Triple Tragedy of Jealousy" (the *People*), "Fourfold Crime by Jazz Musician" (*Daily Express*), "Coloured Musician's Jealousy" (*Holborn Guardian*), and "Slaughter in a Public House" (*Daily Herald*). The general consensus was that jealousy was the motive, and there was surprisingly little allusion to the racial aspects of the case. One wonders if that would have been true if the crime had occurred in the racially tense United States. Kildare was referred to as a West Indian. According to Rye racial intolerance would grow rapidly in Britain in the years that followed.

After Kildare's death evidence surfaced that the murders may have been premeditated. Just two days before the shootings Dan had made out a new will, assigning his £10,000 life insurance policy to his daughter, Carmin Francis Kildare, who he indicated was living in Montreal, Canada, with his first wife, Ena. (The money may not have been paid, since he committed suicide.) The remainder of his estate was bequeathed to his brother, Walter, then living in Brussels, Belgium, a garage owner named Thomas Owen, and one Lydia Sharpe. Walter and Owen were appointed executors.[44]

Back in America Kildare's death received muted coverage, perhaps because he had been gone so long and was less well known there. Most reports were short, factual, and sometimes inaccurate. New York's leading black newspaper, the *New York Age,* ran a very short page-one report headlined "Dan Kildare Kills 3 and Commits Suicide," recalling that he was a one-time president of the Clef Club. There were short obituaries in *Variety* and *Billboard,* and probably elsewhere, but little discussion of the case.[45]

It is not known what became of Kildare's first wife, Ena, or daughter, Francis. His brother Walter, who left to join Louis Mitchell's band after Ciro's closed in 1917, recorded with Mitchell's Jazz Kings in Paris in 1922 and 1923 but is not heard from thereafter.

There is no telling what Dan Kildare might have accomplished had he lived. He was said to be a prolific songwriter, and the secretary at Ciro's described him as "exceptionally well educated . . . his soul seemed to be full of old melody." His original songs were said "to number many hundreds, but they were never published, because he forgot all about them a few hours after they were composed. Night after night, when he arrived to take charge of his jazz band, he would sit at the piano, compose a melody, decide it was good, and give his musicians their instructions: they would promptly swing into it and make it a hit. The next morning Kildare would not have the faintest idea of what his composition had been, and, although members of his band preserved a few, the wonderful melodies which came from his brain have not been recorded."[46] He was a pioneer black recording artist both in England and the United States. What we have left on record are mostly interpretations of white pop songs, albeit with a distinctively Afro-American flavor.

Postscript on Joan Sawyer

Dan Kildare's Clef Club orchestra played for Joan Sawyer during her moment of greatest triumph, from the opening of the Persian Garden in January 1914 through the fall of that year. Guided by her astute and well-connected manager, Jeanette Gilder, Sawyer garnered a tremendous amount of favorable press coverage in the popular newspapers (but not in the *New York Times,* which did *not* mention mere popular dancers) The world of dance clubs was highly competitive, and when the Persian Garden reopened for the fall in October 1914 it was upstaged by Maurice and Walton's even trendier club one floor down in the same building. The Persian Garden evidently closed the following year.

Joan Sawyer continued to draw rave reviews and big salaries for her appearances in vaudeville across the country during 1915 and 1916. She garnered much publicity during the summer of 1915 for a cross-country motor trip promoting women's suffrage (ironically, her manager Jeanette Gilder was a leading antisuffragist).[47] She continued to maintain her own orchestra but changed dancing partners with alarming frequency. The most famous, in retrospect at least, was "Signor Rudolfo," an obscure twenty-year-old Italian immigrant named Rodolfo Alfonzo Raffaele Pierre Philbert Gugliemi, who would later go to Hollywood and find international fame as Rudolph Valentino. Sawyer employed him as her partner for about six months in early 1916 and then dismissed him. That would prove to be a mistake.

Sawyer's success in vaudeville and personal appearances continued after Jeanette Gilder's death in January 1916. She even made a Fox feature film, *Love's Law,* in the fall of 1916. Then in December of that year she was named co-respondent in the divorce trial of two very wealthy socialites, Bianca de Saulles (a niece of the former president of Chile) and American playboy Jack de Saulles. Joan, said Bianca, had stolen Jack's affections. Sawyer's ex-partner, Signor Rudolfo, testified against her. (Never mind that other sources suggest that Bianca and Rudolfo were an item.) The divorce and its aftermath simmered on until August 1917, when Bianca, fearing she would lose custody of her only son to Jack, shot and killed her ex-husband in front of his father and sister at their Long Island estate. A sensational trial ensued, during which Joan Sawyer's name was dragged through the mud and her career effectively ended.

Little is known of Sawyer's life after this. She played a little while longer in vaudeville, to increasingly negative reviews. In March 1918 a trial recording was made at Columbia apparently under her auspices—but not by her (the file card gives the artist as "Miss Baker c/o Joan Sawyer"). By 1921 she had tangoed off the stage, never to be heard from again. I would like to believe that at Valentino's huge funeral in 1926, which jammed the streets of New York City and attracted enormous media attention, standing at the back of the crowds was a forgotten but proud woman dressed in black, who "used to be" Joan Sawyer. But that is merely speculation.

It is ironic that Joan Sawyer and scores of other highly successful exhibition dancers of the period are almost completely forgotten today. Only the Castles are remembered. Her promotion of black dance music, long before it became widely popular, should ensure her at least a footnote in musical history.

23 The Tuskegee Institute Singers

The historic 1909 Victor recordings by the Fisk University Jubilee Quartet were instrumental in bringing Negro spirituals to the twentieth-century American public. In their wake white artists began to include such music in their concerts, and recordings of black "concert" music slowly began to turn up in record company catalogs by artists both black (Will Marion Cook, the Apollo Jubilee Quartette) and white (Kitty Cheatham, Reed Miller). One of the most prestigious black groups to begin recording after the Fisks was the Tuskegee Institute Singers, the first to record choral versions of spirituals.

Their home base, Tuskegee Institute, was the product of a rather crass political deal, but one that would benefit black Americans for generations to come. In 1880 Lewis Adams, a black political leader in Macon County, Alabama, struck a deal with two white candidates to "deliver" the black vote if the two white men would sponsor legislation to build a school for blacks in the area. The two candidates were elected and, true to their word, pushed a measure through the Alabama legislature establishing the "Tuskegee State Normal School" for the training of black teachers. General Samuel Armstrong, principal of Virginia's successful Hampton Institute for Blacks, was asked to recommend a white teacher to take charge of the new school. Armstrong instead recommended one of his own black students, an exceptionally bright and driven young man named Booker T. Washington.

Washington (1856–1915) was born a slave on a small farm in Virginia. He never knew the identity of his father; his mother later married a slave named Washington Ferguson, and the youngster took his step-father's first name as his own surname. Following the Civil War the family moved to West Virginia, where young Booker worked in a coal mine and salt furnace, and then became a houseboy for the wife of the mine owner, who encouraged him to pursue his education. In 1872 he wrangled his way into Hampton Institute, graduating at the top of his class in 1875. Armstrong became his mentor. After a few years teaching, he was offered the job at Tuskegee, which would become the great work of his life.

It certainly was a challenge. When the school opened on July 4, 1881, twenty-five-year-old Washington was the only teacher. The state had provided just enough money for salaries, with nothing for land, buildings, or equipment. Washington borrowed money from Hampton Institute to buy an abandoned plantation outside Tuskegee and set up shop in a shanty building owned by a local church. If funding

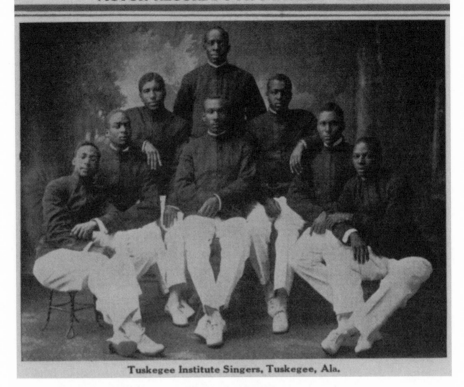

VICTOR RECORDS FOR JANUARY—1915

Tuskegee Institute Singers, Tuskegee, Ala.

The Tuskegee Institute Singers at the time of their first recordings. (Victor supplement, Jan. 1915)

was scarce, his goals were clear: to teach a generation of free blacks not theory or philosophy, but rather the practical skills they needed to make a living. This included farming, carpentry, brickmaking, shoemaking, printing, and cabinet-making. Their workshop was Tuskegee itself; they cleared land, laid foundations, made bricks, and erected the buildings the school needed for its own operation. They made its furniture, printed its literature, and raised its food. Tuskegee was truly a school built from the ground up by its own students.

Washington, a stern taskmaster, instilled in his students a strict work ethic and standards of personal behavior that would serve them well in the unfriendly world outside. He discouraged political activity or overt challenges to the southern social order, which endeared him to the local white power structure and brought funding to his school. His philosophy, espoused throughout his life, was that blacks should concentrate on achieving economic independence through self-help, hard work, and a practical education before demanding social equality. Once they had economic power, he believed, equality would follow. It was a philosophy that would come increasingly controversial in years to come, but one that the white establishment—and many blacks—embraced in those hard times. Washington spent many years on the lecture circuit and was extremely successful in extracting large contributions from white philanthropists such as Andrew Carnegie and John D. Rockefeller, who felt comfortable with his policies.

In 1895 Washington delivered a landmark address at the Atlanta Exposition promoting this vision, which elevated him to the role of acknowledged spokesman for American blacks and political heir to the revered, recently deceased Frederick Douglass (c. 1817–95). He was courted by presidents and captains of industry. President McKinley visited Tuskegee, and Washington dined at the White House with Theodore Roosevelt, much to the discomfiture of southern whites. His close ties with powerful white Americans brought funding to his beloved Tuskegee, which by the time of his death had a staff of nearly 200, a student population of 2,000, and an endowment of $2 million. Top-notch teachers were attracted to the school, notably the great agriculturist George Washington Carver (1864–1943), who was recruited by Washington in 1896 and whose research there helped revolutionize the agrarian economy of the south.

Tuskegee opened in 1881, after the initial heyday of the Fisk University Jubilee Singers in the 1870s, but Washington was keenly aware of the value of music in fundraising and in building bridges to white America. From the early years of the school he insisted on the singing of African American spirituals at the weekly chapel worship services, a tradition that continues to the present day. In 1884 he sent the school's first male quartet out on tour to raise money for Tuskegee and spread its name. Concurrently, in 1886, a school choir was organized.[1] In the years that followed male quartets and quintets traveled north on fundraising tours. Life on the road was not always easy for these groups. Around 1900 Isaac Fisher, who traveled with the Tuskegee Quartet, wrote to Dr. Washington that black minstrel entertainers were making their life difficult. "We are told to our faces often that though our quartet is one of the best that has been heard up here, they would like us better if we would 'play the Nigger'—their own words—more . . . every day we are made to understand that if there was less refinement about us and more fool, we would do better." He added that the "coon" acts made considerably more money than they did, as much as $40 a performance to the $12 or so they might raise. Nevertheless, he did not give in. "When I have about three persons ask for the [spirituals] and about four score ask that we dance and sing songs which tell of Negroes stealing chickens, I make no pretensions to try to please."[2]

Surprisingly, there is no detailed history of the Tuskegee musical groups or their personnel. We do know that Alvin J. Neely, later the school's registrar and dean of men, led the touring quartet (which was reorganized in 1909) in the 1910s and may have been its leader when it was approached by the Victor Talking Machine Company in 1914 to record.[3] Booker T. Washington himself was almost certainly aware of the arrangements, as he was involved in almost every aspect of Tuskegee's operations, and he was still active at this time (he died in November 1915).

Having scored major, and surprising, sales with its Fisk quartet recordings, Victor may have been looking to extend its coverage of the field with the Tuskegee chorus. The Fisks had evidently been in negotiation with Columbia for some time, and Victor may have known that it might lose that group (which had not recorded for it since 1911) to its rival. In any event, a double quartet of Tuskegee singers arrived at the Victor studios in Camden, New Jersey, on August 31, 1914, to record seven sides, four of which would ultimately be issued.[4] The marking "Edu." on the original recording sheets indicates that they were intended for the educational catalog.

All of the titles were traditional spirituals, similar to but generally not duplicating those previously recorded by the Fisk quartet (only one title, "Good News," was available on Victor by the Fisks). The sound was quite different, too. There was no single prominent lead voice on the early Tuskegee recordings, in contrast with the early Fisk Victors, which often served as a showcase for tenor John W. Work. The eight-member Tuskegee Singers emphasized close group harmony, often lingering on, almost caressing, particularly harmonious chords. Sometimes the baritones would drop out and the tenors would harmonize. When a single voice did take the lead, as in a call-and-response passage, it was usually brief. Although aural interpretation is difficult, three different voices appear to take solo passages on the four sides issued from the August 1914 session—a baritone and two tenors. On "Live a-Humble" a tenor takes a relatively long solo, while the rest of the chorus hums along behind him. On "Go Down Moses," a bass/baritone takes the few solo lines. Most of the selections were in moderate tempo, with only "Good News" done at a relatively fast clip. These were clearly intended to illustrate a style of choral singing not often heard on record in the 1910s.

Such harmony-reliant performances must have been hard to capture with the acoustic recording process. Three of the selections recorded in August were not deemed suitable for issue, and two ("Heaven Song" and "Steal Away") were attempted again at the next session, a year later. Those takes were not considered adequate either, and still another try had to be made in early 1916 before issued takes were achieved. Close listening is required to detect the careful harmonies being executed here. Unlike electrical recording (introduced in 1925), the acoustic "horn" method was not particularly sensitive to subtle vocal textures.

That may have been one reason why the Tuskegee recordings were less successful commercially than the those of the Fisks. Victor clearly considered them specialty items for the study of the music rather than popular releases. The first four Tuskegee sides were released on two ten-inch discs in January and February 1915 under the heading "Educational Records." The dignified announcement of "Good News" and "Live a-Humble," in the January supplement, was as follows. Note the reference to "weird harmonies" and the odd musical analysis.

> In our American Music Series we add this month two songs of the very old Negro spirituals. We take pleasure in presenting these by the Tuskegee Institute Singers— from the famous school of Dr. Booker T. Washington, Tuskegee, Ala.—who sing these inherited old "Spirituals" as did their grandfathers, in deep reverential spirit, with all the native, peculiar richness of tone-coloring and harmonies that make these songs of real use in an educational and historical sense.
>
> There are no more beautiful examples of genuine folk-songs anywhere in the world than those that have grown up in the peculiar conditions of the development of singing among our American Negroes. The roots of melody and rhythm and weird harmonies were brought, no doubt, from Africa, but the application to the

needs of expression in religious fervor, unity of effort in labor, in cotton field or levee, are wholly American.

Perhaps we shall one day know why the Negro is a natural harmonist, while all other primitive peoples were monodists. All early music of the Hebrews, Egyptians, Orientals, Greeks, Indians, etc. is always in one part, but set any three Colored people singing, at any time or place, and instantly you hear an accompanying part to the melody.[5]

The facing page in the supplement contained the announcement for "Five Shakespeare Songs," sung by Raymond Dixon, Reinald Werrenrath, and Harry Macdonough (Victor 17634 and 17662). Clearly the Tuskegee Singers were in a respectable neighborhood.

The following month saw the release of "Go Down Moses" and "I Want to Be Like Jesus," of which the supplement observed, "'Go Down Moses' is a very old song, much used in the cotton fields as a working song. Large numbers of pickers work together to its slow, swaying rhythm, and cheer themselves with singing in these weird harmonies. 'I Want to Be Like Jesus' is evidently of later development, but a gentleman who heard these singers sing it at a Chautauqua this summer said, 'I am not easily moved, but the tears ran down my face, stirred by the deep religious feeling they put into the song.'"[6]

None of the individual singers was named, although a large group picture was published with the announcements. The eight men are seated together, dressed neatly in matching dark jackets and white pants. Most appear to be relatively youthful, in their twenties or even late teens, and could easily have been students at Tuskegee. (The young man who is second from the right looks strikingly like a youthful Booker T. Washington, but this is obviously a coincidence.) Two somewhat more mature-looking men are at the center. As noted earlier, Tuskegee faculty member and tenor Alvin J. Neely may well have been the leader. Others believed to have been in the group at this time were tenors William J. Williams, Charles Edgar Clayton, and Leroy Brown, baritone William P. Smith, and basses Alfred Taylor and William Wiley.[7] *Blues and Gospel Records* speculates that the eighth member may have been William Levi Dawson (1899–1990), later a noted composer. However, he entered Tuskegee at the age of fourteen in 1914, and no one in the photograph looks quite that young. Dawson later became director of the Tuskegee Choir and chairman of the Music School. Other evidence suggests that he joined the Singers after these initial recordings.[8]

More than a year later, on September 20, 1915, the Singers returned to the Victor studios to cut ten sides, including two remakes of unissued songs from 1914. The session was not very productive, as only one of the ten was issued. "Roll Jordan Roll," one of the Fisks' signature numbers, was done in moderate tempo, again with much emphasis on the group (and tenors) harmonizing. Interestingly, "Go Down Moses" was remade at this time, even though the take from the 1914 session had already been issued.

The Singers returned one more time, on February 14, 1916, mostly to remake unsuccessful sides from the previous two sessions. This time things went better, and out of ten sides attempted, nine were issued. Once again the emphasis was on group harmony, especially on such key lines as "My lord he calls me, he calls my by the thunder!" (in "Steal Away") and "Sometimes I'm up, sometimes I'm down" (in "Nobody Knows"). The same, slightly thin tenor voice takes an occasional solo line on most of these sides. This is quite possibly Alvin Neely. On "I've Been Buked and I've Been Scorned" a different, deeper voiced tenor is heard. He is quite good and gets rather lengthy, featured treatment on this one number. Tempi were mostly moderate, although "Heaven Song" is upbeat and "I Want to Be Ready" has some interesting alternation between slow and fast tempi.

By this time the Singers were beginning to duplicate more of the Fisks' recorded repertoire. There were only so many well-known spirituals to go around. "Heaven Song" is actually "Shout All Over God's Heaven," and "I Want to Be Ready" was also known as "Walk in Jerusalem Just Like John." Inexplicably, "Go Down Moses" was recorded once again but was the one side not issued.

The numerous sides resulting from the 1915–16 sessions were released over the next two years. Booker T. Washington had passed away in late 1915, and announcements of the Tuskegee recordings made mention of him and his great work at the school. There was also analysis of the "weird" music itself, as in the following, which says much about the white writer's understanding (or misunderstanding) of the black experience. Blacks, he said, had "imperfect understanding" of religion, operated on "blind faith," and found solace in "vague aspirations" and "religious ecstasy." "Swing Low" was described on the record label as a "Primitive Negro Chant." Victor seemed to feel that it was doing everyone a great favor by preserving such "primitive" music. What would Booker T. Washington have thought of this analysis?

These old spirituals are the perfect and spontaneous expression of the Negro slaves of the Old South. They voice the black man's imperfect understanding of religious teaching and his blind faith in a future life. Words and melody seem to have been made for one another, so perfectly do they express the sorrow of racial bondage, relieved by vague aspirations and the joy of religious ecstasy. The weird natural harmony, the unusual slides in the tonal effects and the long-sustained notes are characteristic of this music. Another remarkable feature is the absence of triple rhythm, the even measure being due to the regular beating of the foot and swaying of the body which always accompany the singing of these camp-meeting songs. Most of the spirituals begin with the chorus or refrain, then a verse is introduced, which is followed by the refrain. In the new era of educational progress of the Negro in the South, the spirituals in their oldest and purest form are fast disappearing. Fortunately for future generations the Victor is preserving a number of these characteristic songs, given in their original form, unaccompanied, by the famous Tuskegee Institute Singers of Alabama.[9]

Tuskegee Institute continued to prosper after the death of its founder. Washington's successor, Robert Russa Morton, built upon the foundation Washington had laid, and in 1927 expanded the trade school into a full-scale, degree-granting college. Many of the faculty he recruited remained, including George Washington Carver, who stayed and worked at Tuskegee for the rest of his life.

In December 1926 and January 1927, after the advent of electrical recording, a quartet from the Tuskegee chorus made several more recordings for Victor. Thanks to the improved recording techniques, as well as the reduced size of the ensemble, these have a cleaner sound than the 1914–16 choral sides. The members of the quartet were Neely (leader and tenor), Brown (tenor) and Wiley (bass) from the original octet, plus Nathaniel McCray, baritone.

Even though a smaller group was recording, the emphasis was still on close harmony. Notes are held for extended periods to emphasize the vocal textures. Virtually everything is sung at moderate or slow tempo, although sometime this is varied for effect, as in "Good News" ("Dar's a starry crown in the heaven I know"). In several cases the two tenors harmonize high above the bass and baritone, for example, in "Live a-Humble," "I Want to Be Like Jesus," and "Steal Away." This vocal device could be used in place of a more traditional solo tenor. Where short solos were used on these recordings they all seem to have been by the same person, probably Neely.

This focus on carefully wrought harmonies did not preclude putting emotion into the music. In "Live a-Humble" and "I Want to Be Like Jesus" the tenors sing with some feeling. An interesting comparison can be made between two of the Tuskegee titles and the same two titles as recorded by the Fisk Singers (at this point a quintet) for Columbia in 1926. There is a clear difference between the two groups' versions. On "Steal Away" the Fisk version is quieter and even more intense than that of the Tuskegees; the Fisks seem to be paying more attention to the emotional message of the song than to careful harmonies, and the effect is eerily touching. On "Heaven Song" (aka "Shout All over God's Heaven") the Fisks are energetic, almost jubilant, while the Tuskegees are once again careful and deliberate, paying attention to every note. With their appropriately upbeat performance, the Fisks better communicate the offhand sarcasm of a line like "Everybody dat talk about heaven ain't goin' there!" As a study in harmonization the Tuskegee singers are unparalleled. To touch the heart, one might argue that the Fisks are superior.

The 1926–27 Tuskegee Victors were intended specifically for the educational market and were not listed in the monthly supplements promoting new popular releases. They were included in the annual general catalog, however (as well as in educational catalogs), and they remained in print until 1944. Thus recordings by Tuskegee groups were available on the Victor label continuously for nearly thirty years.

Music remained an important part of Tuskegee, with a music department being established by former student William L. Dawson in 1930. Instructors included such notables as Abbie Mitchell, Florence Cole-Talbert, and pianist Hazel Harrison.[10]

Singing groups from Tuskegee continued to tour, particularly after a new choir was organized by Dawson in 1931. Dawson would head the music program at Tuskegee for the next twenty-five years. In 1932 his choir leapt to national prominence when it was invited by Samuel "Roxy" Rothafel to sing at the opening of Radio City Music Hall in New York, on December 27, 1932. The 110-voice choir remained for a four-week engagement, after which it sang at the birthday party of President-elect Franklin D. Roosevelt in Hyde Park, New York, in concert at Carnegie Hall, and in a performance at the White House at the invitation of President Herbert Hoover. It was later heard on radio network broadcasts on NBC (1937–38), CBS (1945), and ABC (1946), as well as on local station WAPI in Birmingham, Alabama. In 1946 it was the first African American performing organization to appear at the previously segregated Constitution Hall in Washington. In the 1950s it appeared on such television shows as *The Kate Smith Show* (1952), *Ed Sullivan's Toast of the Town* (1952), *The Eddie Fisher Show* (1953, 1954), and *Arthur Godfrey and His Friends* (1954). Historian John Lovell reports that it was especially popular in the south and with predominantly white audiences.[11]

In 1933 new stained-glass windows were installed at the chapel at Tuskegee, commemorating the spirituals for which the school had become famous. Each panel reproduced the words of a famous spiritual, such as "Roll, Jordan, Roll" and "Shout All Over God's Heaven." Years later the panels were destroyed in a fire but were restored.

Dawson also gained individual recognition as a composer. His *Negro Folk Symphony,* composed in 1931, received its world premiere in November 1934 in a performance by the Philadelphia Symphony Orchestra conducted by Leopold Stokowski. He was also known for his arrangements of spirituals.[12]

The choir recorded at least one title for the U.S. Department of Agriculture in 1937 and reportedly some unreleased sides for the Cosmo Record Company in the 1940s. This label was headquartered in New York and was active from about 1945 to 1947. All four members of the 1926 quartet were still active at the college in the early 1940s. In 1955 the choir recorded an LP for the Westminster label, titled *The Tuskegee Institute Choir Sings Spirituals,* which remained in print for more than fifteen years. An original advertisement for the LP shows a large, mixed choir in robes, with Dawson standing in front.[13] Another album, *Tuskegee Institute Choir—Live,* was recorded in 1979. The choir has continued to perform to the present day, singing at the White House in 1997.

The original 1914–16 Victor recordings by the Tuskegee Institute Singers brought a new choral dimension to the recorded spiritual. They are a fitting legacy for a school with a long and proud history, and a more than a century of dedication to the advancement of African American music.

24 The Right Quintette

The recordings of the Right Quintette provide a rare glimpse into the thriving New York cabaret scene of the 1910s. This very successful act was fortunate enough to be able to record performances that seem to have mirrored their lively stage style.

The quintet was formed by veteran singer James Escort Lightfoot in 1912, during a period of general realignment of black talent from the musical theater to other forms of work. Black musicals such as those of Williams and Walker and Cole and Johnson were passing out of favor, and many experienced stage performers found it necessary to seek employment in revues and cabarets. Lightfoot's career in music extended back to the early 1890s. He was born in Hamilton, Ontario, probably in 1871 (different sources give different birthdates).[1] He must have retained a youthful appearance in early manhood, since around 1891 he joined the Canadian Jubilee Singers billed as "Jimmie Lightfoot, the boy basso." Even though he was presumably in his twenties, he retained that billing for several years.

New York's lively Right Quintette. (Columbia supplement, Aug. 1916)

Reviews in theatrical papers indicate that the Singers toured widely in the United States and Canada, and that Lightfoot was a featured act. An 1895 item said that he was "still surprising the people with his voice." Another, in 1897, said he had added new bass solos, and "his rendition of 'Rocked in the Cradle of the Deep' as arranged by himself is spoken of in the highest terms." Other songs in his repertoire included "The Armorer's Song" from *Robin Hood* and "True Til Death." During his later years with the troupe he doubled as its orchestra leader and played mandolin in a specialty act with soprano Mrs. A. A. Lightfoot, who may have been related. Another soprano with the troupe was Mrs. E. Lightfoot, so this may have been a family affair.[2]

In 1898 Lightfoot left the Canadian Jubilee Singers and joined the even more successful Black Patti Troubadours, still singing his bass specialties. An 1899 item reported, "James E. Lightfoot, who sang 'The Armorer's Song' last season, is singing 'The Gypsy Love Song' from *The Fortune Teller* and repeating his success. . . . The press speaks of him as an excellent baritone with a well trained sympathetic voice of good quality." Another item said that he assisted Mme. Sissieretta Jones, the star of the show, with this number.[3] After touring with Black Patti for about three seasons he was evidently much in demand and was able to spend the next three years doing short engagements with various major companies. During 1901–4 he toured with Rusco and Holland's Big Minstrel Festival as a "conversationalist and baritone," assisting stars S. H. Dudley and Billy Kersands, and staging a burlesque of the "Lucia Sextette"; appeared with Avery and Hart; and spent a few months with Richards and

Pringle's Georgia Minstrels singing the booming hit "In the Shade of the Palm." He wintered in Palm Beach, Florida, where he managed the Poinciana Hotel Quartet.

In mid-1904 Lightfoot entered a new phase of his career, switching from minstrelsy to the theater. He joined Bert Williams and George Walker, who had just returned from England, in a new production of their stage hit *In Dahomey*. Remaining with Williams and Walker for the next six years, he had speaking roles as well as singing in *Abyssinia* (1906), *Bandanna Land* (1908), and Williams's solo effort, *Mr. Lode of Koal* (1909). When the latter closed in the spring of 1910 he toured in vaudeville for a number of months backing Henry Troy as a member of the "Mr. Lode of Koal Quartette." He then joined S. H. Dudley's Smart Set company for the 1910–11 season, appearing in the production, *His Honor the Barber*.

Following another winter engagement in Palm Beach, he returned to New York City in the summer of 1912 with the idea of forming a cabaret act. It would feature current popular songs, as well as specialty material and a little comedy. He named it the Gardenia Quintette, no doubt inspired by the hotel he had worked for in Florida. The remainder of the quintet would be made up of other veterans of black music and minstrelsy, all of whom Lightfoot most likely knew from his years of touring.

Tenor Clarence Tisdale was born on September 17, 1878, in Louisville, Kentucky, and may have spent a brief time with Williams and Walker in the early 1900s.[4] Around 1902 he relocated to Australia, where he spent eight successful years touring Australia and New Zealand with McAdoo's Jubilee Singers and the Fisk Jubilee Singers. He received featured billing as "the Great American Tenor," and one review noted that "the charming singing of Mr. Clarence Tisdale is alone sufficient for the success of the delightful concerts given in the Town Hall by the Fisk Jubilee Singers. Last night Mr. Tisdale was in excellent voice, and a treble encore was the penalty of the popularity."[5] He later played Australian vaudeville in a singing and dancing act.

In 1910 Tisdale returned to the United States, settled in Chicago, and began playing vaudeville in the Midwest. He was a member of Chicago's Pekin Theater stock company during 1910 and 1911 before joining Lightfoot in New York in 1912.

Bass James Mantell Thomas (born c. 1875) recorded early in his career as a member of the Dinwiddie Quartet, later joining the Williams and Walker theatrical company and appearing in *Bandanna Land* and *Mr. Lode of Koal*. He sang with James Lightfoot in the "Mr. Lode of Koal Quartet" in the show and in vaudeville afterwards.

The youngest members of the quintet were tenor James W. Loguen (born c. 1886) and pianist Leon Adger (born c. 1883), both in their late twenties in 1912. Little is known about their earlier careers, although a notice has been found indicating that Adger had been a recital accompanist in the New York area.[6]

Lightfoot's quintet made its debut in 1912 as regulars at the famous Reisenweber's restaurant in Manhattan, augmented by occasional appearances elsewhere. A July 1912 advertisement for Young's Casino refers to them as "The Incomparable Reisenweber Gardenia Quintette" and listed all five members by name. In September they appeared at Young's in a benefit for the black theatrical club, the Frogs. A review in the *New York Age* noted that "the members of the Gardenia Quintette showed their deep concern in the success of the entertainment by getting an hour off from Reisenweber's and going post haste to Young's Casino, by taxi, where they pleasingly rendered several vocal numbers. This quintet would attract favorable attention anywhere." By the end of the year the group had changed its name to the Right Quintette. They were billed that way at a Clef Club Concert at Manhattan Casino in November 1912, as well as at a tribute to old-timer Sam Lucas in January 1913.[7]

The quintet was still appearing regularly at Reisenweber's in 1914. A report of a big beefsteak dinner held at the restaurant in February by the Clef Club noted that "the Right Quintette, which is steadily employed at Reisenweber's Café, composed of Messrs. Lightfoot, Tisdale, Thomas, Logan and Adger, sang several songs in their inimitable and pleasing style, and experienced difficulty in getting to another part of the café to resume work." Not showing favorites, the quintet performed the following month with the orchestra from Jim Europe's competing Tempo Club, at a benefit for the Howard Orphanage.[8]

The Right Quintette was well established by the time they recorded four numbers for Columbia in December 1915.[9] The songs all had black themes—Will Marion Cook's "Exhortation," "Rain Song," and "Swing Along," and Stephen Foster's "My Old Kentucky Home." Two of the sides, "Exhortation" and "Rain Song," were ultimately issued. It is not certain whether these songs were a normal part of the group's repertoire, but it is likely that they were, given the polished performances and the special arrangements they used.

The quintet gave a lively, theatrical performance. "Exhortation" opens with an extended dramatic flourish by Adger on the piano, followed by a booming bass (presumably Lightfoot) who sings the principal lyric. The other members of the quintet interject reactions and shouts of encouragement throughout the verse.

> Bass: Remember!
> Tenor: Yes, sir!
> Bass: If a brudder smotes dee . . .
> Tenor: Ahhhh! Uh!
> Bass: On de lef'cheek . . .
> Tenor: Now, what-a ya gwine to do?
> Second Bass: Go on, tell 'im.
> Bass: Turn roun' an' han' him de odder!
> Tenor: Not me, not me.
> Bass: If you kaint 'turn good fu' evil . . .
> Tenor: I cain't, I cain't.
> Bass: Den what's de good o' bein' a brudder?
> Tenor: No good at all.
> Second Tenor: I ain't gwine be no brudder!
> Bass: When de angry passion rises wid-in dee.
> Tenor: What then, what then?
> Bass: Say, "Satan . . ."
> Tenor: What'cha gwine to say?
> Bass: "Go-o-o-o-o! Get thee behind me!" Den stop.
> Tenor: I have stopped.
> Bass: An' count a hundert . . .

Tenors: Aaaaahhh . . .
Bass: Den go on 'bout yo' bus'ness.
Tenor: Dat's me, I goin' now.
Second Tenor: I'm goin'. . . .

"Rain Song" is an even more elaborate production. For nearly the first full minute of the record the quartet members engage in some business about a group of men gathering to talk about the weather. They trade musical lines, as the piano sets up a tense, rhythmic accompaniment, suggesting the anticipation of some coming event.

Tenor: Walk right in, sit a spell, how 'ya feelin' today?
Bass: Jus' moderate, Mr. Simmons, but 'den, I gen'lly feel dat way . . .

Finally they break into Alex Rogers's ingenious lyric, recounting all the signs of rain, with different members taking different verses.

Anytime you hear de chairs an' tables crack,
An' de folks wid rheumatics dey jints is on de rack,
Look out fu' rain, rain, rain!

When de ducks quack loud an' de peacocks cry,
An' de far-off hills seem to be right nigh,
Prepare fu' rain, rain, rain!

These were clever and engaging performances, quite different from what Columbia customers normally found in the catalog. They were released in August 1916, with a photo of the quintet in action (knees bent, arms outstretched, as if their singing was accompanied by a good deal of motion and gesturing). The description read as follows: "The Right Quintette is the best known group of Negro cabaret singers in the East. Their singing of Will Marion Cook's 'Exhortation' and 'Rain Song' is a novelty of novelties. No more harmonious 'Amen' was ever sung than that at the end of 'Exhortation, a Negro Sermon.' In fact, the Right Quintette's harmonies are harmonies that will linger long in memory and give eternal pleasure, to say nothing of decided amusement."[10]

The disc was evidently intended to replace Cook's choral recording of the two songs released the previous year, which was technically deficient. Despite the Right Quintette's popularity, their version was apparently not a particularly good seller either. It remained in the catalog for about four years and was deleted in 1920. They made no others.

The quintet continued to perform in the New York area for several more years. They no longer seem to have been connected with Reisenweber's but were increasingly identified with the Clef Club, performing at the Club's semiannual concert and dance at Manhattan Casino in November 1917. Enthused the *New York Age,* "The vocal hit of the evening was made by the Right Quintette . . . who go big anywhere, anytime." A large photograph of the group in that newspaper showed them all holding instruments (two banjos, bass fiddle, and drums, plus the pianist), so they evidently could do more than sing, although only the piano is heard on the Columbia recordings.[11] There were occasional substitutions. Pianist Leonard Smith replaced Leon Adger at some appearances in 1917 and perhaps permanently in 1918.

In February 1918 they appeared at a Clef Club war benefit and in April at a Club concert at the Academy of Music in Philadelphia. The *New York Age*'s review of the latter event suggests that the principal tenor and bass on the 1916 recordings were probably Tisdale and Lightfoot. "Those 'sure-fire-hit' entertainers the Right Quintet, composed of James W. Loguen, first tenor, Clarence Tisdale, second tenor, James Thomas, first bass, James E. Lightfoot, second bass, and Leonard Smith at the piano—can always be depended on to materially strengthen any bill. There is not a more evenly-balanced aggregation in New York than the Right Quintet, which held the attention of Monday evening's audience from start to finish. The principal solo work was done by Messrs. Tisdale and Lightfoot."[12]

In June they appeared at Aeolian Hall with other Clef Club groups and an orchestra led by Will Marion Cook for a benefit on behalf of the Music School Settlement for Colored People, performing two of the Cook numbers they had recorded in 1916. "What a musical treat it was with the Right Quintette singing 'Swing Along Chillun' and 'Exhortation' to the accompaniment of the [composer's] orchestra!" said the *Age.* Another war benefit and a Manhattan Casino show (where they were on stage for a full hour) followed in late 1918, and in October 1919 they were listed as singing at a "monster benefit" for the heroes of Harlem's 369th Infantry Regiment, which had fought so gallantly in France. Many white stars also appeared, including Eddie Cantor, Van and Schenck, Sophie Tucker, and Fanny Brice.[13]

This is the last engagement that has been located for the quintet. In 1919 James Lightfoot, who was apparently not married, was said to be sharing an apartment with a young Columbia Law School student named Paul Robeson. According to city directories, Lightfoot's address from the 1910s to the 1930s was 115 West 135th Street in Harlem, a black boardinghouse. He worked as a musician and actor in the 1920s and in 1929 played the head waiter and a gambler in the Connie's Inn production of *Hot Chocolates,* the show that introduced the song "Ain't Misbehavin'" (he was also in the choir).[14] He apparently played character roles in a number of Broadway shows in the 1930s and early 1940s; at least we assume the "James Lightfoot" included in several cast lists is ours. His most notable role was that of one of the inhabitants of Catfish Row in the original production of *Porgy and Bess* in 1935; others included supporting roles in *$25 an Hour* (1933), *Sweet River* (1936), *Miss Quiss* (1937), *Natural Man* (1941), and *John Henry* (1941), the latter a short-lived production starring Paul Robeson. After that, Lightfoot, by now in his seventies, dropped out of sight.

Clarence Tisdale also continued to work as a singer. He seemed to be especially interested in recording, as evidenced by the fact that he paid to make personal recordings at Columbia in 1917 and 1919 while still with the Right Quintette. These may have been intended to serve as samples of his work or as "practice discs" to help him improve his craft. The files do not indicate the title recorded in 1917; however, those made in 1919, "Sing Me to Sleep" and "Lullaby from *Jocelyn,*" were quite different from the material he recorded with the quintet. None of these private recordings are known to survive.[15] Tisdale worked in clubs during the 1920s and in 1927 sang at singer/actress Florence Mills's funeral. He appeared for many years with a trio at New York's Le Coq Rouge, originally a speakeasy. He recalled later, "We were supposed to play for just one night, and we had to bring our own piano. We borrowed one of those small ones from a speak that had just closed, tied it on to the back of a taxi, and moved into the Coq Rouge." The customers liked Tisdale's trio, and when prohibition ended the owner kept him on as a regular at his new, legitimate club.

The Tisdale Trio was still there around 1940, by then composed of Tisdale, old-timer Broadway Jones, and a younger pianist named Carroll Boyd. According to a c. 1940 review, "They often sing for a half hour at a stretch. Possibly the secret to their success is the amazing memories of the three singers. 'All a person has to do,' declares Tisdale, 'is ask for a song once, and we sing it the next time he comes in without his asking for it. We have over two hundred customers like that who get their favorite song before they have a chance to request it.' Clarence Tisdale is no youth. If you were to ask him his age, he'd tell you he was born 'the day before yesterday.' He speaks of things that happened thirty years ago and his career takes him back to the earlier successes as a soloist in Europe and Australia."[16]

Clarence Tisdale died on January 1, 1945, at his home on West 138th Street in Harlem, leaving a widow, Peggy. A short obituary in the *New York Times* mentioned that he was a member of the Clef Club and the Negro Actors Guild, and had sung in Australia, England, and France.

James Loguen also remained active, appearing with Lightfoot in *Hot Chocolates* in 1929. According to the 1925 state census he was married (wife's name, Elizabeth) and had a fourteen year-old son. By the end of the 1930s only his wife is listed in the phone book, so he presumably either divorced or died during that decade. Pianist Leon Adger was also married and was listed in city directories until the early 1930s, but nothing is known of him after that. James Mantell Thomas died in 1925.

The Right Quintette disc preserves a talented group of musicians singing Will Marion Cook songs as they were performed in the 1910s. It is a shame they made no other recordings.

PART FIVE

Black Recording Artists, 1916–19

25 Wilbur C. Sweatman: Disrespecting Wilbur

Although he doesn't get much respect from jazz historians today, Wilbur Sweatman was one of the great pioneers of recorded African American music, during the transitional years from ragtime to jazz. Legend has it that he made the first recording of Scott Joplin's "Maple Leaf Rag" on a locally made cylinder around 1903. He made what are arguably the first jazz clarinet recordings in 1916 and what are undeniably some of the first, and most popular, "jass" band records in 1918–19. First and foremost, though, Sweatman was an entertainer, and his highly successful career as a vaudeville novelty performer has for some obscured his musical accomplishments.

Sweatman was born on February 7, 1882, in Brunswick, Missouri. Showing musical aptitude as a youngster, he was taught to play the piano by his sister, then learned the violin and clarinet on his own. He later recalled listening, at age eleven, "to an imported African tribe who were in Excelsior Park in Kansas City playing strange rhythmic instruments." Around the turn of the century, while still a teenager, he embarked on his professional career, first with Prof. Clark Smith's Pickaninny Band of Kansas City, and later with the better-known P. G. Lowery Band, which was touring with the Forepaugh and Sells' Brothers Circus. Cornetist Lowery (c. 1870–1930s) was highly regarded by his contemporaries and toured with some of the top minstrel shows and circuses of the early 1900s. He no doubt opened many doors for the talented young musician. Sweatman played both violin and clarinet with Lowery and on occasion filled in as substitute orchestra leader.[1]

Vaudevillian Tom Fletcher met Sweatman when the latter was with Lowery's band and was sufficiently impressed to devote several pages to him in his 1954 autobiography. In his first-hand account of a visit of the Forepaugh and Sells' Circus to New York City Fletcher says, "In those days, when the circuses played at old Madison Square Garden, there would be a street parade the night before the opening, with bands, animals, actors, clowns, everything except the freaks. The colored band made the parade in New York and the season Sweatman was with the band the crowds that lined the sidewalks started following the band just to hear Sweatman playing his clarinet. Everybody was saying they had never heard anybody play the instrument like that before. Sweatman was the sensation of the parade."[2]

By late 1902 Sweatman had joined a band led by W. C. Handy, which was touring the Midwest with Mahara's Minstrels.[3] His stint with Handy was evidently short (or intermittent), as by late 1902 or early 1903 he had settled in Minneapolis, where he led his own all-black band at the Palace Museum for at least four years. It was early during his stay in Minneapolis that he is said to have made a private cylinder recording of Scott Joplin's famous "Maple Leaf Rag" with a small band for the local Metropolitan Music Store, which may have either sold copies locally or placed them on coin-slot cylinder jukeboxes. No copies of this legendary recording—which may

Jazz connoisseurs will never forgive Wilbur Sweatman for having made his name in vaudeville playing three clarinets at once. (Author's collection)

indeed be only a legend—are known to exist today. Sweatman also went on tours of the Midwest during this period.

Sweatman was ambitious as well as talented, and in 1908 he moved to Chicago hoping to expand his musical horizons. Landing the prestigious position of bandleader at the Grand Theater, he quickly built a reputation as a showy and talented performer, drawing crowds to the theater just to hear his intermission music. A laudatory article in January 1910 pointed out that he was one of a small number of musicians who could lead an orchestra while giving virtuoso performances on his own instrument.

> Mr. Sweatman is one of the "stand-out hits" of the Grand Theater, regardless of who is on the bill. The people pack the house to hear the Grand orchestra and "Sensational Swet" as he is usually called—to hear him play that clarinet. Mr. Sweatman is in a class of four novelties of America as leaders of bands and orchestras. The leader of the orchestra of the old Orpheum Theater in San Francisco led his men with an organ. The leader of the Seventy-second Massachusetts, of Springfield, Mass., leads with a barytone horn. The leader of the orchestra at Paoli Theater, Waterbury, Conn., some years ago, led the orchestra with a trombone. The above accomplishment might not look like anything out of the ordinary to everyday people. But to the educated high-class musician it is next to a marvel to have control of the four above mentioned instruments, [at the same time] that the artist can successfully lead a band or orchestra.

Mr. Sweatman plays four shows and six overtures nightly on the same clarinet. All of this on the unruly B-flat clarinet. He has played five hundred and seventy-six acts in almost two years at the Grand, and has had but one complaint, and that actor in turn made an apology, as [the actor] found that he himself was in the wrong and not the leader.[4]

Sweatman did have his disappointments. The article noted that he had been approached by the famous composer Will Marion Cook to lead the orchestra in a new Williams and Walker show, but that the arrangement had fallen through when George Walker abruptly retired from the stage in 1909. He was later booked to tour Latin America, but that too was aborted when his sponsor, the president of Nicaragua, was overthrown. It was clear, however, that Sweatman had dreams of leading his own first-class black band. The article continued,

> Mr. Sweatman has turned down some very good propositions to travel. He declares he will not go on the road again unless there is a first-class Negro concert band organized, as good as Sousa's Band, which could be easily organized. That music-loving public has no idea how far advanced the colored musician is today in this country. If the Filipino Band [has] turned their heads with astonishment, a real Negro band would place their heads back in shape again. Mr. Sweatman thinks that the Negro musician is about the only professional of the Negro race that has not had a chance to show what he can really do. The first good manager with proper financial backing who will organize a first-class Negro band, regardless of salary, will reap fame and fortune.

A short profile in October 1910 also sang Sweatman's praises and revealed that his wife was working at the Grand. "He has been orchestra leader at the Grand Theatre for two years. His versatility upon the clarinet is due to his original ideas and many people go to the Grand especially to hear 'Sweatman.' He transposes music and plays violin parts of standard overtures. Mr. Sweatman has a charming wife, who is in the box office at the Grand."[5]

A retrospective article in the *Chicago Defender* in 1927, with the perspective of time, asserted that he was playing what would later be called jazz. "He was such a hit with his queer style of playing 'Hot Clarinet' that Broadway [later] went wild about him. People of both races came to hear this three piece orchestra play jazz music, although they didn't call it jazz then. They called it 'hot music.' Sweatman produced the weird, eerie tones on the clarinet that sent thrills through the listener. He was a sensational, rapid, clever manipulator of the clarinet."[6]

Sweatman also appeared at other Chicago theaters, including the Monogram and the Pekin, during his years in that city. By 1911 he had decided to go into vaudeville full-time. Tom Fletcher claimed to have had a hand in persuading Sweatman to take the plunge when he met the clarinetist again in Chicago around 1910. "While laying [over] in Chicago for a week I would meet 'Sweat' after he had finished for the night, and we would sit around and talk. . . . Ragtime was still all the rage and was going strong. I said to Sweat, 'Fellow, I have traveled around a long time and I have never heard anybody play a clarinet the way you play one. Man, you have a novelty. Why don't you get yourself an act just playing the clarinet?' When he revealed to me that he could play two, and even three, clarinets at the same time I declared, 'What are you waiting for?'"[7]

Fletcher wrote that Sweatman got his big break while playing the Crescent, a small black theater in Harlem. Heard by booking agents for the major white vaudeville circuits, he was signed by an agent named Charles Beerbower.[8] Soon he was touring the big Hammerstein and Keith circuits full-time as a solo act, billed as "the Original Ragtime Clarinetist." His specialty was flashy clarinet work, especially on syncopated and ragtime numbers. He worked up a routine in which he played two, and sometimes three, clarinets simultaneously, playing harmony with himself. "His playing of two clarinets got things started," said Fletcher, "and when he played 'The Rosary' in harmony with three clarinets, he took the house."

A review of an Indianapolis appearance in September 1911, accompanied by a photo of him playing two clarinets at once, captured the flavor of his act.

> The treat of the bill was the first appearance of Mr. Wilbur C. Sweatman, the invincible clarionetist. Much had been heard of the great player before he reached these parts, and that he fully came up to all that had been said of him in advance of his coming would be putting the circumstance mildly indeed. Great! Well, yes, the very greatest of them all, and then some. Without a peer, this young man stands out [as] a glorious representation of what the Negro can really accomplish in the field of instrumental music. This line of work is usually shied away [from] by the "brother," and as yet we have been able to produce only a very indifferent representation in this line of stage craft. The brilliant success of this very capable young musician is sure to serve as an impetus to others. . . .
>
> Though somewhat diminutive in stature, Wilbur C. Sweatman has a style and grace of manner in all of his executions that is at once convincing, and the soulfulness of expression that he blends into his tones is something wonderful. His first number was a medley of popular airs and "rags" and had everybody shuffling their pedal extremities before it was half over. The second number was the novelty number of the cast, at which Mr. Sweatman played two clarionets at the same time, rendering that beautiful song "The Rosary." This was followed by a bass clarionet solo "Down in the Deep." He attempted to get away at the conclusion of his rendition of "Temptation Rag," an oddity in music consisting of almost everything. He failed in his attempt, however, and was forced to respond with another encore and close with one of his own compositions called "Cross the Way," which was also a medley of the clean-up variety. Mr. Sweatman is booked solidly for some time and doubtless will remain so, as his act is one of the best of its kind on the stage today.[9]

Sweatman was actively composing by this time, and in September 1911 he copyrighted what was to become his biggest hit, "Down Home Rag." This fast-paced showpiece number could serve as a workout for performers on several instruments and was a highlight of his act. It became a favorite of dancers as social dancing swept America and seems to have first been recorded as accompaniment for dancing the turkey trot or one-step. The first U.S. recording was by the Victor Military Band, released in June 1913, and was coupled with a one-step called "The Horse Trot." Victor referred to the two selections as "lively new compositions—one step and turkey trot—which have been much used of late for dancing these popular new steps."[10] Although Victor's studio brass players were accustomed to more traditional dance and march music, they were consummate professionals and rendered the Sweatman composition with a great deal of verve, if a little stiffly.

Almost simultaneously, "Down Home Rag" was recorded in England by the London Orchestra and released there on the budget Cinch label, a subsidiary of HMV. Additional recordings followed in the United States, with a riotous version by Jim Europe's Society Orchestra (1913), the Van Eps Trio (1914), the Van Eps Banjo Orchestra (1915), and the Six Brown Brothers saxophone sextet (1915). There was also a lively version in England by the Versatile Four, a black combo, in early 1916. Sweatman's ragtime showpiece must have earned him a good deal of money.

Sweatman toured widely as a solo act in the early and mid-1910s, one of the few black performers on the major white vaudeville circuits. At one point he is said to have lived at Scott Joplin's mother's theatrical boardinghouse, where he argued with the egotistical Jelly Roll Morton about who was contributing more to the spread of black music.[11] Sweatman came to know Joplin well and would eventually become the executor of his estate. Around 1913 Sweatman changed his base of operations from Chicago to New York City, establishing a residence at 251 West 143rd Street in Harlem. Appearing at Hammerstein's Victoria Theatre in New York, he played three clarinets simultaneously and was billed as "the Musical Marvel of the Twentieth Century." His circle of acquaintances grew rapidly as he became an important figure in black music. He was active in the Frogs, New York's black theatrical club, appearing at its 1913 summer frolic, among other events.[12]

In December 1916 Sweatman made his first commercial recordings in New York for Emerson, a low-priced label recently established to compete with the majors. The two titles presumably reflected songs he was featuring in vaudeville at the time. "My Hawaiian Sunshine" was a currently popular ballad exploiting the vogue for Hawaii and favored by harmonizing male duets. Van and Schenck were singing it in the Broadway revue *The Century Girl,* and recordings were available by the duos of Albert Campbell and Henry Burr on Victor and Sam Ash and Lewis James on Columbia. Sweatman's short (1:50) instrumental version was loose and lyrical, although the effect is somewhat diluted by the accompaniment of a cornball studio orchestra—pompously called the "Emerson Symphony Orchestra"—which added drum rolls, rickety-tick blocks, and trombone swoops at various points. One modern critic has commented, "[Sweatman's] playing on the 1916 'My Hawaiian Sunshine' shows undoubted improvisation," adding "had it been a setting other than that of the Emerson Symphony Orchestra, it would long ago have been pointed out as an early example of jazz."[13]

The second title recorded for Emerson shows no such compromises. It is Sweatman's "Down Home Rag," and he plays it with gusto and a strong improvisational feel that certainly sounds like early jazz. This time the accompaniment, ostensibly by the "Emerson String Trio," stays discreetly out of the way, as if intimidated by the ferocity of Sweatman's attack. There are swipes and squeals on the clarinet, though without the gimmickry of the early "barnyard jazz" popularized by the Original Dixieland Jazz Band a few months later. As a matter of fact, there are clear similarities between Sweatman's technique and that of clarinetist Larry Shields on the historic ODJB sides recorded by Victor in February 1917. The latter are generally recognized as the "first jazz recordings," but one wonders, who was listening to whom? Sweatman's 1916 Emerson recordings have been vastly underrated in the history of early jazz on record.

Sweatman's Emerson recordings had an odd history. Because the major labels still held patents on the principal recording techniques, would-be competitors had to find ingenious ways to technically differentiate their products; in Emerson's case, this meant recording with a "universal cut," supposedly playable on either lateral- (Victor, Columbia) or vertical-cut (Edison) phonographs. Although Emerson discs do play well on lateral (and modern) phonographs, this may have made some buyers wary of them. They were also small-sized discs. The two Sweatman titles were each issued on six-inch and seven-inch discs, which played for less than two minutes each (the six- and seven-inch versions are similar but different performances). As a final blow, they were issued in March and June 1917, just as the first releases by the ODJB were being launched with enormous publicity by the much bigger Victor label. These hot clarinet solos may have simply been lost in the blaze of publicity about the new "jass band" craze. The six-inch discs were available for only a few months and the seven-inch versions for about two years. All are quite rare today and are seldom reissued.

Sweatman made a test recording of a clarinet solo of his own "Boogie Rag" for Victor on February 28, 1917, just two days after that label's ODJB session, but it was rejected. Seeing which way the musical wind was blowing, he decided to leave the solo clarinet behind and get on the "jass band" train. It was not at all clear what form these new bands would take, however. Rather than imitating the ODJB's lineup of cornet, trombone, clarinet, piano, and drums, Sweatman assembled a band of five saxophonists—two altos, one tenor, one baritone, and one bass—to back him. As it turned out, the ODJB instrumentation would set the pattern for what we know today as a traditional "Dixieland jazz" lineup (they also gave their name to the genre). However, Sweatman's choice was not illogical. Saxophone ensembles were quite popular at the time, and the leading exponents, the Six Brown Brothers, were major stars in vaudeville. Saxophones had a jazz feel and certainly sounded like "new music." They would become intrinsic to the development of jazz after 1920.

Sweatman and his saxophone "Jass Band" quickly landed a contract with New York's Pathé label, which was as eager as he was to cash in on the new music. This was the "Jazz Spring" of 1917. The files of the Pathé company are lost, but it appears that its Sweatman titles were all recorded at one or two sessions in March 1917, within days of the release of Victor's ODJB sides. (The ODJB recordings, made on February 26, were rushed out by Victor in a special mid-March release.)[14]

Musically, the Pathé recordings are a mixed bag. All are dominated by Sweatman's clarinet (he *was* the star), with the saxophones staying well in the background. He improvises, swipes, and slides, giving virtuoso performances. "A Bag of Rags" and "Boogie Rag" are uptempo performances in the style of "Down Home Rag," with a strong improvisational feel. "Joe Turner Blues" (by W. C. Handy) is fast-paced and bluesy, with more fancy fingerwork on Sweatman's part. Apparently

Pathé wanted to make sure he recorded some current hit songs, so Sweatman obliged with Irving Berlin's popular novelty "Dance and Grow Thin" and Jerome Kern's show tune "I Wonder Why" (from *Love o' Mike*), the latter including an interpolation of the monster hit "Poor Butterfly." Even on material such as this Sweatman riffs a bit, but clearly he was more at home with a rag.

Like Emerson, Pathé had to circumvent the major labels' recording patents monopoly and did so with vertical-cut recordings that could be played only on its own (or adapted) phonographs equipped with "sapphire ball" styli. This limited their distribution, although Pathé was a fairly major player in large cities such as New York. Because of this the Sweatman Pathés, released in May and July 1917, seem to have been fairly modest sellers compared to their Victor and Columbia counterparts and are scarce today.

All of the major labels were by now scrambling for credible jazz bands. Columbia sent young talent scout Ralph Peer to New Orleans to look for some, only to have him wire, "I'm coming back. There are no jazz bands in New Orleans."[15] Meanwhile, right in their own New York backyard, Wilbur Sweatman was clearly ready for the recording big-time. Although his touring schedule doubtless made it difficult for him to devote full-time to this aspect of his career, he made test recordings for Columbia in June and August 1917, and by early the following year he had reached agreement with that label to begin regular commercial recording. By this time the instrumentation of jazz bands (and the spelling of the word "jazz") had become more standardized, and Sweatman reconstituted his backup band along accepted lines—clarinet, trumpet, trombone, piano, and drums, sometimes with a tuba added. Personnel were in flux at the time of his first regular Columbia session on March 28, 1918, and the exact lineup at that session is uncertain. The usual sidemen over the next two years were Russell Smith or William Hicks, trumpet, Arthur Reeves, trombone, Dan Parish, piano, Romy Jones, tuba, and Henry Bowser, drums.

Sweatman's Columbia recordings were marketed as "dance music" and the label let him record a wide variety of titles, including commercial blues, some by black composers. The first session consisted of "Regretful Blues" by white composer Cliff Hess and a novelty commenting on the trend, "Everybody's Crazy 'bout the Doggone Blues, but I'm Happy," by black composers Henry Creamer and Turner Layton. Sweatman's distinctive clarinet shared the lead with the trumpet, and trombone and drums were also prominently featured. There were trombone swoops, clarinet squeals, and even a few solo bars for the piano. This was the era of jazz as novelty music, and Columbia clearly wanted a sound resembling the "barnyard jazz" of Victor's best-selling ODJB. Sweatman delivered, with loose, raucous performances that may sound crude today but were part of a musical revolution then. Only the drummer sounds a little stiff. Each tune ended with a little musical signature—a short pause, followed by a few more notes—that would become a Sweatman trademark on record.

Columbia was at the time operating a budget label called Little Wonder, specializing in five-and-a-half-inch, single-sided discs that contained only about a minute and a half of music and sold for a fraction of the price of regular Columbias. Artist names were not shown on the Little Wonder label, but regular Columbia talent was used. Sweatman recorded abbreviated versions of both of his March titles for Little Wonder, possibly at the same session as the regular releases. The little discs are quite scarce today, but the Little Wonder of "Everybody's Crazy" has been located and compared with the regular Columbia, and the performance is virtually identical— just shorter. The band's performance on different takes of the same ten-inch disc was very similar as well, indicating that Sweatman knew how to stick to his arrangement if not the published sheet music.[16]

Columbia must have liked what it heard, as Sweatman was back in the studio three more times to record additional titles before "Regretful Blues" and "Everybody's Crazy" were even issued. Recorded in May were Shelton Brooks's classic "Darktown Strutters' Ball" and Creamer and Layton's "Goodbye Alexander," both medleys with interpolations of current popular songs. The performances are similar to those of March, with growling trombone and squealing clarinet. Sweatman was beginning to yield center stage to his trumpeter and trombonist, while weaving counter melodies around them in classic dixieland style. The repertoire was appropriate to the style, although the bouncy novelty "Oh, Frenchy!" sounds a little out of place interpolated into the middle of "Goodbye Alexander."

Two June sessions brought the even less suitable faux-Indian novelty "Indianola," complete with "tom-tom" motif. Sweatman showed his versatility with wild counterpoint melodies on his clarinet. On the very fast one-step "Oh! You La! La!" both Sweatman and drummer Bowser got a real workout, with the leader doing some of the fancy fingering for which he was famous.

Three takes were normally made of each title, with the best being chosen for release. It is not surprising that the recording engineers had some difficulty obtaining suitable takes of this unusually loud and semi-improvisational music. The acoustic recording horn was unforgiving, recording whatever was placed in front of it at a fixed volume level, in real time. It was impossible to "adjust levels," mike instruments individually, edit, or otherwise use the recording technology to compensate for performance anomalies. The recording files indicate that Columbia engineers did not have undue problems with Sweatman's musicians, although there were occasional lapses. Rejected takes of "Indianola" are noted "clarinet shrill"; one take of "Oh! You La! La!" is marked "too jumbled" (which, for critics, might describe the music generally!). Occasionally the band had difficulties getting its performance exactly right, with notations of "poor start," "poor finish," and "poor rendition" sometimes found. The difficulty of accurately capturing this undisciplined new music with the rigid, primitive technology of 1918 should not be underestimated.

Sweatman's initial Columbia release, "Regretful Blues" and "Everybody's Crazy," was announced in July 1918. The bandleader's first name was misspelled "Wilber" (as it often was at the time), and his aggregation dubbed "Wilber C. Sweatman's Original Jazz Band," a clear nod to the ODJB. The monthly supplement included a picture of him in a white suit, about to play his clarinet, and an enthusiastic description of his first Columbia disc. "The only man who can perform on three clarinets simultaneously, Wilber C. Sweatman, famous as the 'rag-time clarinetist,' originator of jazz playing on that popular instrument and the moving spirit of Sweatman's Original Jazz

Wilbur Sweatman's Jazz Band in action at Columbia in 1918; Sweatman is at the far left. (Columbia supplement, Nov. 1918)

Band, has given Columbia Dance Lists a new shock. Anyone who thinks the limit of jazz music has been reached will guess again after hearing Sweatman's Band."[17]

The record was also released in England, the only Sweatman Columbia to be so honored. "Goodbye Alexander" and "Darktown Strutters' Ball" followed in October, accompanied by a posed and highly stylized picture of the entire six-piece band in action. Sweatman, Smith, and Reeves are crouched down aiming their instruments together in a circle, while Bowser, to the right, attacks his drum set and another band member (possibly Jones) waves excitedly in the rear. Jazz was lively music, the music of youth, and musicians were expected to share in the action. This staged picture would be reprinted several times by Columbia, visually representing the vitality of early jazz. The supplement description continued the theme.

We saw Sweatman and his jazz experts record their dance coupling of the month. There were times we bet ourselves the drummer would never get his stick back from the ceiling in time for the next "drum"—but he did! Our photograph was taken in the Columbia Recording Laboratory and shows the Sweatman jazz experts "in action" and partially explains the "action" to be found in their Columbia dance recordings! The Sweatman crowd are certainly saturated with syncopation. While playing they swing and beat time with their entire anatomy. It is their thorough feeling of the music which enables them to play such rag riots of jazz pyrotechnics as "Good-bye Alexander" and "Darktown Strutters' Ball."[18]

The third disc, from June, was released in November accompanied by the same photograph, and the comment, "Sweatman's Jazz Band knocking the last scrap of common sense out of 'Oh! You La! La!,' and the famous 'Indianola.'"[19]

Sweatman fully justified the company's faith in him. More than 87,000 copies of the first release were shipped by the end of 1918, and 140,000 over its life in the catalog, a bestseller in an era when 50,000 copies shipped constituted a "hit." The next two releases did well, too, with shipment totals in the 75,000–85,000 range. Other jazz bands, including Borbee's Jass Orchestra, W. C. Handy's Memphis Orchestra, the Frisco Jass Band, and Earl Fuller's Famous Jazz Band, had entered the recording fray during 1917–18; there was also something called the Yerkes Jazarimba Orchestra, combining traditional jazz instrumentation with xylophones and marimbas. Fuller even made a recording of Sweatman's trademark "Down Home Rag." However, Sweatman was clearly the leading competitor on record to Victor's mighty ODJB. As one modern writer notes, "of the Negro musicians trying to follow the new jazz-band craze, only Wilbur Sweatman, a clarinetist who had been touring in vaudeville with his ragtime novelties, had much success." Another asserts that "closest in style to the ODJB were perhaps Wilber Sweatman and his Jass Band; an ideal sample for comparison is provided by the two groups' respective Columbia recordings, made one year apart, of 'Darktown Strutters' Ball.'"[20] The two arrangements are quite similar.

Sweatman continued to turn out regular releases for Columbia during 1918 and 1919. Sessions in August, October, and December 1918 produced versions of Al Jolson's big hit, "Rock-a-Bye Your Baby with a Dixie Melody" (from *Sinbad*), "Has Anybody Seen My Corrine?," and four commercial blues: "Those Draftin' Blues," "Dallas Blues," "Ringtail Blues," and "Bluin' the Blues." The last-named was by ODJB pianist Henry Ragas and had been recorded by that band for Victor in June 1918. Again, comparison of the Sweatman and ODJB versions reveals more similarities than differences in their renditions of this bluesy lament, although Sweatman's stiff drummer tends to make his version sound a little more stilted.

Several of the new Sweatman Columbias were very fast performances ("Rock-a-Bye Your Baby," "Those Draftin' Blues," "Dallas Blues"), but all band members had a chance to be featured at least briefly. Sweatman no longer dominated the proceedings. Generally he would weave countermelodies around the trumpet or trombone. An exception is "Has Anybody Seen My Corrine?," in which he takes some extended solos. On some sides, such as "Ringtail Blues," the band has a tighter, more disciplined sound that is a little closer to the modern conception of "Dixieland" than was common in 1917–18.

More anonymous Little Wonders were made during this period. "Dallas Blues" is almost identical to Sweatman's Columbia, but "Has Anybody Seen My Corrine?" sounds much more sedate and lacks the prominent clarinet solos. One is tempted to think it might be by a different band, but perhaps it was simply made at a different Sweatman session.

The band recorded frequently for Columbia in 1919, with seven sessions between January and September. Most of the material was commercial blues or novelties appropriate to the band's now-established Dixieland style. Eddie Green's "A Good

Man Is Hard to Find," Euday Bowman's "Kansas City Blues," and Spencer Williams and Clarence Williams's "I Ain't Gonna Give Nobody None o' This Jelly-Roll" would all become standbys of the jazz repertoire. Sweatman also finally got to record one of his own compositions for Columbia, the lively "That's Got 'Em," which would also be much recorded in years to come. "Slide, Kelly, Slide" was a fast-paced trombone novelty written by Joe Davis and his publishing partner, trombonist George F. Briegel ("Kelly" was a pseudonym used by Davis).[21] There are some nice harmonies between the trumpet, clarinet, and trombone on this side.

Of course Columbia wanted some familiar popular tunes, so Sweatman gave them the bouncy novelty "Ja-Da!" and Jolson's "I'll Say She Does" (from *Sinbad*), the latter interpolating yet another Jolson hit, "N' Everything." The band sounds particularly uncomfortable with the silly "Ja-Da!" incorporating such gimmicks as trombone laughs, the clarinet "talking" to the other instruments, and even bells. Silly, perhaps, but "Ja-Da!" and "I'll Say She Does" turned out to be two of the band's biggest sellers on Columbia. The files indicate that the band had a hard time getting an acceptable take of "Ja-Da!," ultimately succeeding after five tries. The other four attempts were described in the files as "too confused," "out of tune," "wrong tempo for dancing," and "poor tone."

On "I'll Say She Does" and "Lucille," Sweatman varied his sound by adding a quartet of banjo and banjoline players, giving the renditions something of a "Clef Club" sound. "Lucille" in particular has some interesting harmonies. The rhythm provided by the banjos was a welcome relief from the uninspired drumming of Henry Bowser, but they were gone after these two sides. Perhaps realizing that he needed a better rhythm section, Sweatman let the trombone and brass bass propel the band on "Hello, Hello," to good effect.

Several more Little Wonders were recorded during 1919, issued anonymously as by "jazz band." Sweatman later recalled in an interview making Little Wonders for Columbia, but there are no surviving files giving titles, so aural comparison is necessary to identify which ones might be by him. This can be a tricky business. Little Wonder 1091, "A Good Man Is Hard to Find," sounds exactly like Sweatman's Columbia version. However, Little Wonder 1234, "Hello, Hello!" although long assumed to be a Sweatman item, sounds quite different from the Sweatman Columbia of the same title, featuring a banjo among other things. One Sweatman expert now believes that it is actually by the Louisiana Five (which had a regular banjo player), even though that group is not known to have made other Little Wonders.[22] Of particular interest is Little Wonder 1092, "Lonesome Road." The Columbia version of the tune was not issued (a note in the files says "poor rendition"), so the Little Wonder version is the only one we have by the band. Sweatman Columbias continued to be issued regularly through January 1920, although the supplements now tended to list them with minimal comment, simply describing his music with phrases like "sky-hitting syncopations" (December 1918) and "jazzical gyrations" (June 1919).

Some historians have claimed that Sweatman's popularity began to decline in 1919, less than a year after his debut on Columbia. Charters and Kunstadt comment, "For the first few months after end of the war, the jazz craze seemed to be waning.

The slapstick clowning of Earl Fuller and Wilbur Sweatman made it difficult to take jazz seriously."[23] Whatever later critics might think, the record-buying public at the time apparently did not agree. The Columbia files provide month-by-month shipment data for his records, and they indicate that while shipments of his early (1918) recordings dropped off sharply in mid-1919, new releases such as "Ja-Da!", "I'll Say She Does," and "Kansas City Blues" sold well indeed. "Kansas City Blues," in fact, had the largest total of his career, 180,000 copies. On this and the strong-selling "Slide, Kelly, Slide," Sweatman appeared on only one side of the record, the other side in both cases being by a new group called the Louisiana Five. Sales of "Kansas City Blues" were no doubt helped by the Louisiana Five title, "The Alcoholic Blues," an extremely popular novelty song about the onset of Prohibition. Columbia appears to have been right, at least from a commercial viewpoint, when it forced its jazz groups to record well-known popular titles. Victor did the same thing with the Original Dixieland Jazz Band in late 1919, having them record the popular ballad "Margie." Their rendition was rather sedate for such a raucous band, but the song was a monster hit and the record appears to have been their biggest seller ever.[24]

The monthly shipment figures do suggest that Sweatman's records were generally short-term sellers. Most shipped large quantities for their first few months, then dropped off much more sharply than was normal at this time, often to just a few hundred copies per month, perhaps reflecting the ephemeral popularity of his style of early "barnyard jazz." By early 1920 Sweatman's overall sales had dropped precipitously. September 1919 marked Sweatman's last session for Columbia until mid-1920, and January 1920 his last new release on the label for nearly a year.

In June 1920 he was invited back for three more sessions. Seven titles were recorded, but only two of these were issued. Some of the rejected takes had technical problems, being marked "poor balance" or "not up to standard," but in almost all cases at least one acceptable take was obtained. Most appear to have been turned down for issue simply because Sweatman's style of music wasn't selling anymore.

The two titles that were issued, "But" and "Think of Me Little Daddy," were rather restrained by Sweatman standards, but their strong clarinet leads hearkened back to the sound that had originally made him famous. On "Think of Me" Sweatman performed dazzling runs toward the end of the record. There was no doubt who was the star of this band. The disc was released in December 1920, and sales seem to have confirmed the Columbia accountants' worst fears. It had a very healthy press run (nearly 100,000 copies), but nearly all of those were shipped to dealers in advance of release. (Columbia customarily began shipping copies to dealers three months in advance of an official release date, so that copies would be on hand when sales began.) Table 8 gives the month-by-month shipments. Keep in mind that a December 1920 release date meant that copies were placed on sale during the last week of November. Shipments plummeted to almost nothing immediately after this record was put on sale.

Contributing to the falloff was the fact that America was hit by a sharp economic downturn in 1921, sending record sales plummeting generally. Dealers were stuck with large stocks of A2994, which was the last record Sweatman would make for Columbia. Most of his earlier releases remained in the catalog until 1925, when

Table 8. "But" / "Think of Me Little Daddy"
(Columbia A2994)

	Number of Copies Shipped
Aug. 1920	12
Sept. 1920	2,114
Oct. 1920	92,692
Nov. 1920[a]	1,056
Dec. 1920	120
Jan. 1921	453
Feb. 1921	179
Mar. 1921	237
Apr. 1921	178
May 1921	1

a. The record was placed on sale.

acoustic records were deleted en masse to make way for the new electrical record-ings. This was apparently just a way to dispose of unsold stock. A note in the files indicates that manufacturing was suspended on nearly all Sweatman titles on June 19, 1923.

Full-sized, syncopated dance bands like those of Joseph C. Smith, Ben Selvin, and Art Hickman were becoming the rage. Late in 1920 a new band on Victor—Paul Whiteman and His Ambassador Orchestra—scored a mammoth hit with a bouncy tune called "Whispering," which revolutionized the world of recorded dance mu-sic. Whiteman's catchy, highly stylized rendition of the song reportedly went on to sell more than a million copies, dwarfing the sales of such bands as Wilbur Sweatman and the ODJB. Large orchestras with melodic, syncopated arrangements were in, and the noisy little jazz combos of 1917–19 were out, at least with the mass record-buying public.

Sweatman did not lack work, of course, with appearances all over the Northeast. He did not change his style, even though record buyers had moved on to something else. In 1919 he hired veteran jazzman Freddie Keppard for a gig at the Brighton Beach Hotel, supposedly to help teach his younger sideman the real New Orleans style. Sweatman had a good ear for talent. In March 1923, while playing at the Lafayette Theater in Harlem, he hired three young musicians from Washington, D.C., Sonny Greer, Toby Hardwicke, and pianist Edward Kennedy "Duke" Ellington. It was Ellington's first experience in the New York musical world, and in his auto-biography he spoke respectfully of Sweatman, saying, "He was a good musician, and he was in vaudeville because that was where the money was then."[25]

Ellington stayed with Sweatman only briefly, returning to Washington when the clarinetist left on tour. By the summer of 1923 Sweatman was back in New York, playing at the opening of the famous Connie's Inn nightclub in Harlem, with his Original Jazz Kings. One of the sidemen he hired for this gig was a young saxophon-ist named Coleman Hawkins. At some point in the early 1920s he injured his hands so badly that he could not play for a considerable period. That, however, apparently did not prevent him from leading his band. He eventually recovered.[26]

Sweatman, who had been one of the first African Americans to join the American Society of Composers, Authors, and Publishers (ASCAP), in 1917, continued active as a composer and publisher. His "Old Folks Rag" and "That's Got 'Em" had been recorded by a number of bands in the 1910s, and he returned to the recording studio himself from time to time, especially when he had a new song to promote. He now worked for smaller labels. In the fall of 1924 he recorded his new composition, "Battleship Kate," for Gennett and Edison. This was a pleasant little fox trot with a kind of loping rhythm, about a lad and his formidable girlfriend. The Gennett was performed as an instrumental with a seven-piece band dubbed "Wilbur Sweatman and his Acme Syncopaters." Some discographies identify Duke Ellington as the pianist on this session, even though the issued take was made in September, more than a year after Ellington's "brief stay" with Sweatman in March 1923. The piano is well in the background on the recording, which is dominated by the cornets, trombone, and saxophone. Sweatman's clarinet is only briefly heard. A banjo provides the easygoing rhythm.

The Edison version features a similar performance, although, according to an item in *Billboard,* it was made with a ten-piece orchestra dubbed "Wilbur Sweatman's Brownies."[27] Two chirpy male vocalists provide a short vocal duet toward the end ("that's my Battleship Kate!"). It's a cheerful rendition, with a little "Charleston" rhythm thrown in, but again there is little of Sweatman's clarinet. (Perhaps this was the period when his hands were healing.) A note in the Edison files says, "I understand he was quite a hit with Columbia at one time," showing how far out of the mainstream Edison (or perhaps Sweatman) was by 1924. Unfortunately, "Battleship Kate" was not recorded by the major labels. Additional titles recorded for Gennett ("She Loves Me") and Edison ("It Makes No Difference Now") were not issued.

In 1926 Sweatman waxed two clarinet solos for the dime-store Grey Gull label, demonstrating that he was regaining his facility on the instrument after his injury. These were reissued on numerous labels, sometimes under other names. "Poor Papa" was a novelty hit of the day played in a suitably cheerful fashion, while "Get It Now" (also known as "Powder Puff") was an easygoing instrumental on which he could show off his mellow tone, without the fingering pyrotechnics of old. A simple banjo accompaniment accented his performances.

Three more sides were made for the Grey Gull labels in 1929, including two of his own, "Battleship Kate" and "Lead Pipe Blues" (aka "Sweat Blues"). The latter was a mellow, bluesy number featuring Sweatman's trademark squealing clarinet. A trombone and piano provided accompaniment, both being heard in short solos as well. The third number recorded was Charlie Davis's familiar "Jimtown Blues."

In April 1930 Sweatman landed his first session with Victor, consisting of four clarinet solos and highlighting his own material. The songs recorded, with banjo accompaniment, were "Sweat Blues," "Got 'Em Blues," "Breakdown Blues," and— once again—"Battleship Kate." Significantly, these were released in a special "race" series rather than as general issues. They seldom turn up today.

By the end of the 1920s Sweatman was beginning to concentrate more on his publishing activities, although he would still put together a band from time to time. He still kept an eye out for new talent, although they didn't always work out. Drummer Cozy Cole recalled that his first professional job was with the leader in 1929, but that "Sweatman fired the devil out of me because I couldn't play nothin'—I had a beat but I just couldn't read [music]!"[28]

Sweatman's compositions brought him a steady income. The best known by far was "Down Home Rag," which was recorded by such prominent artists as Chick Webb (1935), Harry Roy (1937), Tommy Dorsey (1938), Willie Farmer (1938), Don Redman (1938), and Larry Clinton (1939). A 1937 ASCAP radio directory showed "Down Home Rag" being performed nearly 2,000 times on radio during that year.[29] Other active titles in his catalog included "That's Got 'Em," "Old Folks Rag," "Sweat Blues," and "Boogie Rag."

Dixieland staged a comeback of sorts in the mid-1930s, and in 1935 Sweatman put together an orchestra to record some of the old tunes for Vocalion in an updated setting. Of course his own "Battleship Kate" got featured treatment, with his squealing clarinet showcased in front of what sounded like a small swing band—rather like Benny Goodman on speed. Although the standard discographies list a banjo player in the seven-man lineup, actually a jazz guitarist provides the rhythm.[30] A fairly hot trumpet and trombone were also featured. Gerald "Corky" Williams belted out a raspy vocal about the old girl. The other titles recorded were "Florida Blues," W. C. Handy's "Hooking Cow Blues," and Corky Williams's own "Watcha Gonna Do?" As on Victor, these were treated as "race" releases in the "hot dance" series and were not widely distributed.

Sweatman continued to lead a trio in New York nightclubs, including Paddell's Club, during the 1940s and even into the 1950s. Talent booking, music promotion, and publishing became his main professions as he carefully tended the copyrights of his own songs and those of others, including the estate of Scott Joplin (of which he was executor).[31] Although he couldn't seem to get anyone else to record his beloved "Battleship Kate," he was successful with other titles. By the 1950s his Wilbur Sweatman Music Publishing Company was located at 1674 Broadway, near Times Square in New York, advertising his latest titles in trade newspapers. Among the titles listed, with his comments in parentheses: "Sweet Mania" ("another 'Down Home Rag'"); "Fine, Fine, Fine" ("the chick clicked"); "If the World Is Round, It's Crooked Just the Same" ("so true—so true"); and "Battleship Kate Cha Cha" ("Kate's back with a cha cha beat"). He just wouldn't give up on "Battleship Kate"!

By the mid-1950s Sweatman had been "discovered" by jazz researchers, who fortunately interviewed him about his musical exploits in the early days of the century. An early discography of his recordings by Len Kunstadt and Bob Colton appeared in the specialist magazines *Discophile* in 1955 and *Jazz Journal* in 1958, and an article by the same authors in *Record Research* magazine in 1959 indicated that Sweatman was then working on his autobiography. Unfortunately it was not published and its location today is unknown. Wilbur Sweatman died in New York on March 9, 1961, at the age of seventy-nine, leaving a daughter, Barbara, and a sister, Eva. Obituaries in the *New York Times* and *Variety* treated him as a relic of a time long past, which perhaps he was.

Sales of Sweatman's Recordings

Sales figures for most early labels have long since disappeared, and speculation by modern writers about what sold and what didn't abounds. Clearly Sweatman's Emersons and Pathés had limited distribution. Columbia presents a unique opportunity to gauge the commercial success of certain artists and titles, because files do exist showing month-by-month shipment figures for many of its discs. Shipments are not necessarily the same as sales, of course, and can be misleading in some cases (as in the example given earlier of Sweatman's last Columbia release). By and large, though, the company did not keep shipping records and recording new titles by artists who weren't selling. The overall sales picture is undoubtedly reflected in these figures.

The data in table 9 suggest how brief and intense Sweatman's period of popularity on Columbia was. To ship nearly a million records in a single year (1919) was phenomenal for the period. By way of comparison, two other Columbia artists whose sales have been studied are the Fisk Jubilee Singers, who shipped about 200,000 copies in their peak year on the label (1919), and the extremely popular Broadway star Bert Williams, who reached one million in his peak year (1920). At his height, Wilbur Sweatman was in the same rarefied territory as Williams. Some of Sweatman's releases were substantial sellers. Table 10 gives the total number of copies shipped for individual discs.

Epilogue

What happened to Wilbur Sweatman and his musical legacy? Although he was present at the very birth of jazz and made some arguably historic recordings, jazz historians have not treated him kindly. Leonard Feather asserted in his influential *Encyclopedia of Jazz*, "Sweatman's only relationship to jazz is that in 1922 [*sic*] he was instrumental in bringing Duke Ellington to New York for the first time . . . to work briefly in his elaborate, quasi-symphonic orchestra."[32] Albert McCarthy dismissed him with the curt comment, "what he played was a form of diluted rag-

Table 9. Wilbur Sweatman's Estimated Total Columbia Shipments

	Number of Discs in Catalog	Shipments
1918	6	330,000
1919	12	1,000,000
1920	13	220,000
1921	13	5,000
1922	13	3,000
1923	12	1,500
1924	—	50?[a]
		1,559,550

a. Manufacturing suspended on all.

Table 10. Shipments of Individual Columbia Records by Wilbur Sweatman, 1918–25

	Released	Copies Shipped
"Kansas City Blues" / (Louisiana Five) (A2768)	Oct. 1919	180,300
"Rainy Day Blues" / "Ja-Da" (A2707)	June 1919	144,000
"Regretful Blues" / "Everybody's Crazy" (A2548)	July 1918	140,500
"Slide, Kelly, Slide" / (Louisiana Five) (A2775)	Nov. 1919	137,400
"I'll Say She Does" / "Lucille" (A2752)	Sept. 1919	135,200
"Ringtail Blues" / "Bluin' the Blues" (A2682)	Mar. 1919	124,700
"Hello, Hello" / "I Ain't Gonna Give Nobody" (A2818)	Jan. 1920	115,800
"Has Anybody Seen . . ." / "Dallas Blues" (A2663)	Jan. 1919	115,700
"Rock-a-Bye Your Baby" / "Draftin' Blues" (A2645)	Dec. 1918	98,000
"But" / "Think of Me Little Daddy" (A2994)	Dec. 1920	97,300
"A Good Man" / "That's Got 'Em" (A2721)	July 1919	89,800
"Indianola" / "Oh! You La! La!" (A2611)	Nov. 1918	86,300
"Darktown Strutters" / "Goodbye Alexander" (A2596)	Oct. 1918	76,000

time . . . in any case he was basically a vaudeville entertainer, whose forte was the playing of three clarinets at once."[33] Roger Kinkle, in his much-used *Complete Encyclopedia of Popular Music and Jazz,* described him as "leader of early hot band in cornball style."[34] Sweatman is not even mentioned in Max Harrison, Charles Fox, and Eric Thacker's *The Essential Jazz Records: Ragtime to Swing,* which covers many early artists, and his records were rarely if ever reissued during the LP era (and rarely, so far, in the CD era either).[35]

Part of the problem may be that Sweatman lived in the shadow of the Original Dixieland Jazz Band, which has been widely celebrated as the first band to make a jazz recording. It must have been frustrating for the proud clarinetist to witness the many accolades that the quintet of white kids from New Orleans via Chicago received over the years for launching a musical genre which he had been playing for years. There were numerous ODJB reissues on both 78s and LPs, a major revival of the band in the mid-1930s, mention of them in practically every history of jazz, and a full-scale biography in 1960 (*The Story of the Original Dixieland Jazz Band*).[36] In 1937 the *March of Time* even recreated their historic "first" 1917 recording session for theater audiences across the country. Another factor may be Sweatman's success in vaudeville; jazz cognoscenti (unlike Ellington) simply can't shake that image of a showman playing three clarinets at once.

One other less-recognized reason may be the labels for which Sweatman recorded. Columbia went through bankruptcy and lost most of its early masters, while Emerson and Pathé disappeared entirely. Victor, on the other hand, not only survived as a company but continually mined its earlier catalog for reissues (mostly classical, but sometimes other genres, including ODJB jazz). For those who collect original 78s, Victor pressings often sound better than their Columbia counterparts. Columbias, though well recorded, were pressed in sturdy but noisy material. Sweatman's Columbias sometimes sound muddy not because of the band but because of the pressing.

Sweatman's contemporaries remembered him with awe. Tom Fletcher, who knew him at the turn of the century, later called him a "great jazz player," and described him as follows.

> Sweatman introduced playing the clarinet an octave higher than anyone had previously done, and he produced the same tones and performed the same execution on his clarinet then as one hears today played by our top jazz or swing musicians. Wilbur C. Sweatman was the first musician, white or colored, to introduce that style of clarinet playing. . . . When people talk or write about ragtime and jazz they invariably begin by saying that jazz was started in New Orleans. Actually, Wilbur Sweatman, the first musician to bring that style of playing to the attention of the American public, was playing it and making it popular way back when he joined P. G. Lowery.[37]

Some modern writers have begun to appreciate Sweatman's contributions. One of his leading advocates in recent years has been English historian Mark Berresford, who has written that Sweatman "did much to popularize ragtime and jazz," and that his 1916 Emerson of "Down Home Rag" "clearly shows the move away from ragtime to jazz; it is rhythmically freer and his phrasing presages the direction that jazz was to take in the ensuing decade." Allen Lowe maintains that Sweatman's band was "just beginning to learn the secret jazz art of group/soloist interplay" and had "real bite and swing, [with] significant early attempts at breaks and improvisation." Such views are still outnumbered, however, by the disdainful remarks of critics such as Chris Goddard, who proclaimed, "Listening to Sweatman's records, [his] reputation as a hot player seems hardly justified by comparison with the Original Dixieland Jazz Band. The white musicians play significantly better, their individual voices displaying more imagination while at the same time making more collective sense." Goddard then went on to make the sweeping, and astounding, statement, "The fact that [Sweatman] made such a poor showing at playing jazz is revealing. It suggests that most black musicians, particularly those not from New Orleans, were not playing jazz before 1920."[38]

One wonders if critics who wrote such mumbo-jumbo ever listened to Sweatman's band and the ODJB side by side? Both bands recorded "Darktown Strutters' Ball" and "Bluin' the Blues." Listening to the two versions of each song, it is certainly possible to prefer one over the other, but to call one "jazz" and the other not is absurd.

Hopefully, in years to come, Sweatman's place in the early history of recorded jazz will be more fully recognized. This African American clarinet player made immense contributions to the development and spread of black musical influences in the United States, and his legacy deserves to be preserved and celebrated.

The thriving black musical scene in New York in the 1910s produced a number of less-known entertainers who left their voices on record. One of these was Opal Cooper, a banjo player and vocalist whose career exemplifies the itinerant life of a cabaret musician. Recording as early as 1917, he later became one of the expatriate musicians who brought American jazz to Europe after World War I.

Cooper was born in Cromwell, Kentucky, on February 3, 1889, to Louis and Ellen Cooper, and grew up in Chicago.[1] His father was in the "mechanical business."[2] Nothing further is known of his family or early life, but by the time he was in his late teens he was performing professionally in the Midwest. An item in the December 1910 Indianapolis *Freeman* listed him as a soloist at a Chicago recital featuring classical soprano Anita Patti Brown, commenting that he was "a tenor of excellent timbre." The following year the *Freeman* noted in its Chicago report that "Mr. Opal D. Cooper has made arrangements to travel with a quartet, doing chautauqua work."[3] A later item indicated that he had vocal training at the Chicago Musical College.[4]

Cooper's career soon veered away from concert and recital work. By 1915 he was in New York, appearing in *Darkydom,* a musical staged by black comedians Flournoy Miller and Aubrey Lyles. The show opened at the Lafayette Theatre in Harlem on October 23, 1915, and was an evening of songs combined with an extended sketch from Miller and Lyles's vaudeville act. Cooper performed Will Marion Cook's new song, "Mammy."[5] The show, which was strongly reminiscent of the old Williams and Walker musicals and involved many of the same people, broke little new ground, but at least it gave Cooper the opportunity to work with some of the leading lights of the New York black musical scene, including Cook, conductor James Reese Europe, and producer/critic Lester A. Walton. It had a short run in New York and then went on tour.[6]

The following year saw Cooper in the cast of the *Darktown Follies,* Harlem's version of the *Ziegfeld Follies,* which ran from 1913 to 1916. This time he had several speaking roles, including those of Jim Thomas, Jake, and Ishta, the Temporary Ruler of Somali Land. He sang "Hoola-Boola Love Song" and led the entire company in the grand finale, "Goodbye, Ragtime."[7] (The character "Hoola" was played by Jim Europe's girlfriend, Bessie Simms.)

The association with Jim Europe must have paid off, since by the fall Cooper was appearing with the conductor's troupe. In October 1916 the *New York Age* listed him as a member of the "Europe Double Quintet, the greatest singing and instrumental aggregation on the stage . . . composed of the cleverest colored entertainers known," then appearing at the Lafayette Theatre.[8] Cooper sang tenor and played bandolin; Europe's friend Noble Sissle was also in the group. In December Cooper, Sissle, and Eubie Blake were listed as members of a Europe orchestra that entertained inmates at Sing-Sing Prison in New York.[9]

A CAFÉ DE PARIS 'TURN.'
Clever Coloured Artistes in Popular Duets.
LESLIE HUTCHINSON and OPAL COOPER.

Opal Cooper, at right, with his cabaret partner Leslie Hutchinson in 1927. (Vocalion supplement, Mar. 1927)

In some ways 1917 marked the height of Cooper's career. In a stunning change of direction, he joined the Coloured Players and in April appeared with them in a trio of serious plays by white poet Ridgely Torrence, staged at the Garden Theatre at Madison Square Garden. Cooper starred in the first of the three, the seriocomic *Rider of Dreams,* as Madison Sparrow, a ne'er-do-well black man who unwisely uses his family's savings in an attempt to build a better life. Critics were surprised by Cooper's sensitive performance, as well as that of costar Blanche Deas as his wife, Lucy. "Opal Cooper was the most agreeable surprise of the entire performance," wrote a black newspaper. "Heretofore he attracted favorable attention as a vocalist, this being his first venture in an important speaking role. He was best when telling Lucy Sparrow of his plans to become a businessman and of the visionary schemes that prompted him 'to make his money work for him.' No white actor could modulate his voice with such effectiveness, for the flexibility and religious fervor to produce this singsong effect would be missing."[10]

White critics took notice as well. Heywood Broun, writing in the *New York Tribune,* said "a huge negro delighting in the name of Opal Cooper played the dreamer with fine fervor and humor. Only his dejection seemed a little lacking in sincerity; and indeed, Opal Cooper smiled so broadly after the sixth or seventh encore that it was easy to see he had been having the best sort of time even when he was called upon to sulk." George Jean Nathan, later summing up the season, cited Cooper's performance as one of the ten best of the year. Black critic and historian James Weldon Johnson was even more sweeping in his landmark 1930 book *Black Manhattan,* calling the performances by Cooper and his fellow actors "the most important single event in the entire history of the Negro in the American theatre . . . the beginning of a new era." Johnson maintained that "the stereotypical traditions regarding the Negro's histrionic limitations were smashed. It was the first time anywhere in the United States for Negro actors in the dramatic theatre to command the serious attention of the critics and of the general press and public."[11] *Rider of Dreams* ran for several weeks at the Garrick Theatre, and the Coloured Players reformed for another season in the fall, although it does not appear that Cooper continued with the troupe.

Despite the rave reviews, Cooper returned to music. In April or May 1917, at about the same time he was appearing in *Rider of Dreams,* he made his first known recordings, for the New York–based Pathé label. This is the same label for which Noble Sissle first recorded, and it appears that Cooper and Sissle may have made their recording debuts at the same session.[12]

Two sides by Cooper were issued. "Beans, Beans, Beans" was a comedy number written in 1912 by Chris Smith and Elmer Bowman. A favorite of vaudeville comedians, it was recorded by Eddie Morton for Victor and later Gus Van for Columbia.[13] Cooper gave this tale of marital woe a nice comic delivery, in a half-speaking style strongly reminiscent of Bert Williams.

"Beans, Beans, Beans!"

G'-Good morning, judge, I'm heah again,
Before you and your jurymen.
Now judge, if you'll just give me a little chance I'll explain,
Why I deserted Eva.
Judge, I worked and gave that woman every cent,
To buy the food and pay the house rent,
And her ways really was discontent,
So I thought was best to leave her.
Yessir, 'course she's my lawful wedded wife, that's true,
B'-but Judge, how would you like for your wife to hand to you?

Beans for your breakfast,
Beans for your lunch,
Beans for your suppertime.
Judge, she had boiled beans, stewed beans, soup beans, fried beans,
Beans, rain or shine.
She never had ham, chicken or lamb,
As strange as it may seem.
My home I admired, Judge, but I got so tired,
Of eatin' beans, beans, beans!

The other title was "You're Mamma's Baby," a typical "mammy" song by white songwriter Pete Wendling ("Please promise me, that you'll be . . . your mamma's ba-a-by"). Cooper delivered both songs in a booming tenor voice, with considerable vibrato and clear articulation, as if he was used to making himself heard at the back of a huge theater. There was a strong element of theatricality about his performances. On "Mamma's Baby" he had a real "cry" in his voice, while the comic number "Beans" was delivered in a nervous, conversational tone as if he was acting out the song. The two sides were released in the fall on different discs, backed with a different artist in each case, but had only modest sales.

Cooper and Sissle appear to have auditioned for the larger Columbia label around this time. The Columbia trials file indicates that a test was made c. May 1917 by a tenor duet named "Cooper and Sissle," which presumably means Opal Cooper and Noble Sissle. The title is not known, and nothing was issued.

After Jim Europe and his 15th Regiment Army band left for France at the end of 1917, Cooper most likely continued to perform with other Clef Club aggregations. In a brief interview given many years later he said, "My first musical job was with the Clef Club orchestra in the years 1918–1919" (he probably meant 1917–18). "The band I played with included John Ricks (bass), Harry Williams (cello), Leonard Smith (piano), Noble Sissle, Joe Meyers and myself (banjo), Ralph 'Shrimp' Jones (violin) and Creighton Thompson (drums). I do not remember who were in the other [Clef Club] orchestras, but most of the bands were larger. The dance band craze was on at that time and most of the men were kept very busy."[14] Although Cooper may have been mixing up some facts here, the musicians named were all associated with Jim Europe; some accompanied the bandleader to France and/or recorded with him before or after the war.

Cooper enlisted on September 2, 1918, in New York and was assigned to Will Vodery's 807th Infantry Regiment Band.[15] He sailed for France two days later and was given the rank of sergeant on September 30. He served as the unit's drum major. The following letter from Vodery to Alex Rogers, dated November 22, 1918, and printed in the *New York Age,* reported on the band's success:

> The band has made over good; with a bunch of raw, green material, I have worked it up to the place that I can say I've got a real band. Headquarters has taken us away from the Regiment and attached us to the headquarters as post band of the First Army. Gulfport, Opal Cooper, Eddie Stafford, [Earl] Granstaff, Blackburn with the assistance of about twenty good voices have put on a knock-out show, and seem to please them everywhere. . . . We were commanded to play for the President of France on the 20th at Verdun and he said, in his language, "It is astounding to hear such wonderful music." Well, those babies certainly did play. We have really done our bit and made good.[16]

Another report in the *Age,* in March 1919, indicated that Sergeant Cooper was still with the 1st Army Band, under Second Lieutenant Vodery, in France. The temptations for young troops in liberal France must have been considerable, but Cooper appears to have acquitted himself well. A note in his files from a major, dated December 1918, commended him "for the excellent conduct and wisdom he showed this afternoon when approached by a woman who offered him a bouquet. His manner was dignified and thoroughly in keeping with the excellent opinion I have formed of the band. . . . I appreciate how difficult it was for the drum major to preserve his dignity, and at the same time show a proper courtesy."[17]

Cooper returned to the United States on July 3, 1919, and was given an honorable discharge exactly one week later. He was unmarried, in good health, a hefty six-foot-one, with brown eyes and black hair. He apparently did not take part in any battles (he was not qualified as a marksman or horseman), although he was credited with service in the Meuse-Argonne campaign in October 1918, just as the war was ending. His character was described as "excellent."

Cooper did not remain in the United States for very long. In his own words,

> In January, 1920, I left the U.S.A. for Europe with the Seth Weeks Jazz Band. We opened at the Apollo Theatre, rue de Clichy, Paris, 21st January, 1920, replacing Louis Mitchell's Jazz Kings, who left after a stay of seven months to open at the Alhambra Theatre in Brussels, Belgium. Seth Weeks' Band included Sam Richardson (sax), Roscoe Burnett (sax), Elliott Carpenter (piano), Seth Weeks, Opal Cooper (banjos), Creighton Thompson (drums). In June, 1920, we became The Red Devils, when we broke off with Weeks and went to London (with Richardson, Burnett, Carpenter, Cooper and Thompson).[18]

Author Chris Goddard, interviewing Elliot Carpenter in 1976 for his landmark book, *Jazz Away from Home,* got another view of how Cooper and his cronies came to sail for France, which black musicians regarded as a sort of "promised land." Carpenter explained that he was approached in New York by a Mr. Wickes, who asked if he could get a band together to open a new club in Paris. "Two of the boys, Opal Cooper and Sammy Richardson, had just come back from the war. So I went to them and said, 'Do you guys want to go to France?' And they said, 'My God, yes!' And they started to tell me about the beauties of Paris—what they did and didn't do. They raved, 'Yeah, man, let's go back there!' So I said, 'Hey, wait a minute. I haven't said anything about money.' And they said, 'The Hell with that! Let's just get back to Paris.'"[19]

Carpenter negotiated a salary of $50 per week for each of his musicians, but on arriving in Paris they found that they could easily command several times that. After a few weeks an English agent, learning that they had no contract, offered them an engagement at Rector's in London for $350 per week. In addition, they began playing as the Red Devils in vaudeville at the Coliseum. (The name Red Devils came from the fancy jackets they wore.) Before long they were making $750 per week. Carpenter concluded, "So I said to Sammy Richardson, 'You know, we fell down a well and came up with a roast dinner.'"

None of the musicians spoke French, but that didn't seem to matter. When Carpenter and his boys arrived they couldn't even read the signs, and they were told by some Englishmen that it would take two years to learn the language.

> And Cooper, he was listening, he said, "Didn't take me that long. I could speak to those mademoiselles in two minutes. What the hell. They speak my language . . ."
>
> So when we get to the Gare St. Lazare the man we're going to work for is Mr. Morgan . . . when we got off the train, there's this big, fine-looking brown-skin man. Great big handsome guy. . . . Cooper says, "Yeah man," and he's looking around and he says, "Man, the first place I wanna go is a whorehouse." And I said, "Oh Cooper, for God's sake! Will you get down to business?" And he says, "Well, you're doing the business ain't you? I'm going to the whorehouse."
>
> So [Morgan], he got us into a cab and we heard him speaking French and of course he was a wonder to us. So he takes us uptown, and Cooper says that he's hungry.

So I ask Morgan if we can find a place to eat. And Cooper didn't even get through eating before he's asking Morgan where the nearest sporting house is. And Morgan says, "You boys really are in a hurry!" So on the way over to the hotel he drops Cooper off. Boy, when we saw it, that guy Morgan had a nice place.[20]

Cooper doubled on banjo and vocals with the band, which scored a hit both in Paris and London. Carpenter reported that he had "a tremendous voice." A few weeks after opening at Rector's the band landed a recording session with the largest English label, HMV. On September 1, 1920, as the Red Devils, they recorded four popular songs, "The Crocodile," "My Little Bimbo," "I'll Be Back There Someday," and "If I Forget." According to the files Creighton Thompson handled the vocals. None of these sides were issued.

Europe was a haven for black American musicians at this time, exotic, well paying, and free from the overt racism that was so entrenched in the United States. It is possible that Cooper returned to the United States on occasion during his heady early years performing in Europe. The New York City directory lists him as living on West 131st Street in that city as of November 1920 (as it had in 1917 and 1918); according to his passport application, his "legal domicile" was Chicago, where his father lived. If he did return, his visits must have been brief.

Cooper stayed with the Red Devils throughout 1921 and 1922. Drummer Eddie Gross Bart remembered meeting the band in London in early 1921. "The Red Devils were swell guys—I knew Eli Carpenter and Opal Cooper very well. Sammy Richardson was a very funny guy, and Opal was a fine singer and a tremendous fellow."[21] They were still at Rector's in London in July 1921, although in March of that year Cooper applied for a new passport allowing him to visit France, Italy, Spain, and Belgium as a "performer." In 1922 this was amended to add Egypt. In 1922 the band was appearing at the Accacius Club in Paris, while doubling with Harry Talcus at the Alhambra.[22]

Cooper related that when the Red Devils broke up in January 1923, he continued at the Accacius for the summer of 1923, with Elliot Carpenter (piano), James Shaw (sax), Sammy Richardson (sax), and an unknown drummer. Clifton Webb and the Dolly Sisters were also on the bill. In October 1923 Cooper joined the International Five, replacing banjoist Usher Watts, who had died. The personnel of this group was Nelson Kincaid (sax, clarinet), Louis Vaughan Jones (violin, sax), Palmer Jones (piano), Cooper (banjo), and Harvey White (drums).[23]

In August 1924, Cooper and the International Five appeared in the cast of a new show, *Midnight Shuffle Along,* at the Seymour, a Parisian cabaret. The *Chicago Defender* called it "the first appearance of a real all-colored midnight show in Paris."[24] Cooper continues, "In 1927, Sammy Richardson (sax) took Louis Vaughan Jones' place. I became the leader of the International Five after the death of Palmer Jones in 1928. Then several musicians were added to the band, becoming nine altogether: Jenkins (alto sax), Roscoe Burnett (tenor sax), Green (trumpet), Earl Granstaff (trombone)."[25]

At the same time he was playing with the International Five, Cooper also formed a cabaret act with pianist Leslie Hutchinson, who was then fronting one of the hottest black jazz groups in Paris and London.[26] While appearing at the Café de Paris, the duo recorded four sides for the English Vocalion label in January and February 1927. Under the heading, "Clever Coloured Artistes in Popular Duets," the label's March supplement enthused, "It is by no means easy to discover really original cabaret turns. Here, however, we have something quite unusual and the Café de Paris management are to be congratulated upon their 'find.' Leslie Hutchinson and Opal Cooper are famous in Paris for their attractively individual performances. Both are coloured artists of the first rank, and will be great favorites in London."[27]

Nice photos of the dapper artists were included. Cooper's is one of the few photos of him I have found. The following month's supplement announced the last two sides. "The first performances and first recordings of these gifted Café de Paris artistes have achieved instant popularity—and no wonder. These coloured artistes bring something new and stimulating to the entertainment world; they record exclusively for Vocalion." Reviews in the popular press were generally brief and favorable, although one noted, "I think their style a little too florid, but the items are likely to prove popular."[28]

Four titles were released, "Because I Love You," "Moonlight on the Ganges," "Mamma's Gone Young (Papa's Gone Old)" and "I Wonder What's Become of Joe." Despite the label's enthusiasm, sales were evidently minuscule, and the sides are extraordinarily rare. Hutchinson went on to become a major British recording artist of the 1930s and 1940s, specializing in sophisticated material by songwriters such as Cole Porter and Rodgers and Hart.

Cooper traveled back to the United States periodically, as evidenced by his appearance as a guest with the Fletcher Henderson Orchestra in "A Gay Night in Paris," at the Savoy Ballroom, New York, in October 1930.[29] In fact he may have alternated performing in New York and Europe. A 1934 directory described him as "an international entertainer, better known perhaps in Montmartre, Paris," adding, "He has had a more intimate acquaintance with contemporary celebrities, regardless of nationality, than any other entertainers of his race. He is a member of a world-renowned combination of stars that include (the late) Florence Jones, of Chez Florence, Sammy Richardson, Kid 'Sneeze' Williams, and Elizabeth Welch, who entertained during the winter season in New York and during the summer tourist season in Montmartre."[30]

Cooper himself described his later career as follows. "In 1932 Sidney Bechet (clarinet) played several months with us at Chez Florence, 61 rue Blanche, in Paris. I remained with the International Five until 1934 when the band broke up." Around this time he adopted the name "Ole Cooper" (sometimes written as "Oley"), apparently to sound more French. His repertoire was primarily current popular songs. At some point in the late 1920s or early 1930s he married one Beatrice Lee.[31]

In June 1934 and January 1935, presumably after the disbanding of the International Five, Cooper made four additional recordings as a vocalist for the Gramophone label in France. And fascinating records they are! Three have black themes and two speak of longing for home, a sentiment Cooper might well have felt after fourteen years in Europe. Billed as "Ole Cooper," but singing in English, he was backed by the big jazz-tinged orchestra of Michel Warlop.

"Going Home" is a haunting ballad, sung in the "cry-in-the-voice" crooning style made famous by Bing Crosby in the early 1930s, and not dissimilar from the style Cooper used on "You're Mamma's Baby" back in 1917. It is hard not to imagine an autobiographical twist to this lyric, as Cooper sang of his longing for his "mammy," and home.

> Going back,
> It took me long to find that homeward track,
> I'm mighty happy and my heart is cheering,
> 'cause I'm nearing home.
>
> Guess I'll stay forever near the fireside,
> Make up for the years I . . .
> Spent in roaming,
> Now I'm going home.

"Black Madonna" is a moody love song, full of dark images. The other two sides were "Home to Harlem," whose title speaks for itself, and another lament, the currently popular hit, "Boulevard of Broken Dreams."

Recorded for the full-priced Gramophone label in the depths of the Depression, the two releases had predictably small sales. In fact, none of Cooper's recordings are easily found today. He remarked on this in his later interview: "I made a few song records in France, with HMV, also a few in England, but I do not think you could find any of them."[32]

Cooper remained abroad for a few more years, playing in Bombay, India, in late 1935 and at Melody's Bar in the Rue Fontaine, Paris, until 1939 when war broke out and he returned to the United States. He and Beatrice settled in New York City and for many years thereafter he continued to perform in local bars and taverns, including the Hartsdale Restaurant in Hartsdale, New York, and the Ship Ahoy Café in New Rochelle, New York.[33] In 1949 he married Cora Outten; what became of Beatrice is unknown.

When Cooper was interviewed in the 1960s he said, "At present I work night clubs and cocktail parties. I use a guitar as background to the songs I sing." Judging by his surviving papers his repertoire consisted mostly of new and old popular songs, such as "Lovely to Look At" and "Chickery Chick," although by the late 1950s he was trying to keep current with such material as "Heartbreak Hotel," "Blue Suede Shoes," and "El Paso." He also incorporated comedy numbers in his routine. One was a soldier's parody of "Begin the Beguine" that began, "Then I begin to clean the latrine . . ." He also worked as a cab driver until he was in his eighties.

He kept in touch with some of his old buddies, telling his 1960s interviewer, "I saw Sammy Richardson quite often; he is still in good health. Elliot Carpenter is out in Hollywood where he is in the hospital at present. I have not heard from him recently. Louis Vaughan Jones came back to the U.S.A. to become a professor at Howard University in Washington, D.C. He died last year. After the Red Devils' stage, Creighton Thompson joined a band at the Romance, rue Pigalle in Paris . . . the group later went to Budapest, Constantinople, Venice and Berlin."[34]

Opal Cooper passed away on December 9, 1974, in the Bronx, New York, at the age of eighty-three and was buried in Long Island National Cemetery, Pinelawn, Long Island, New York. Through the generosity of his widow, Cora, his papers are now at the Schomburg Center in New York.[35]

27 Noble Sissle and Eubie Blake

Among African Americans who recorded prior to 1920, two of the best remembered are the team of Noble Sissle and Eubie Blake. In their day they were major stars of vaudeville and the Broadway stage, but probably the chief reason their names live on is the extraordinary success (as a composer) and longevity of Eubie Blake. Blake became a major media celebrity in his eighties and nineties, playing and talking about the ragtime music he loved to a generation far removed from the era in which it was created. He lived to the age of one hundred, and his death in 1983 made national headlines. Sissle and Blake each first recorded in 1917, making them pioneers among black recording artists. Although they would at times have substantial independent careers, their lives were so intertwined that they will be considered together here.

Pianist James Hubert "Eubie" Blake, the older of the two, was born on February 7, 1883, in Baltimore, Maryland.[1] His was a rough upbringing, the kind guaranteed to make a survivor of any lad able to outlast it (ten brothers and sisters all died before reaching adulthood). His father, John, was a stevedore on the Baltimore docks and his mother, Emily, a laundress. Both were former slaves who took the name "Blake" from their former master. Emily in particular was a stern, domineering parent, but her attempts to instill solemnity and religion in fun-loving little Eubie were futile. "Mouse," as he was nicknamed, was constantly getting into trouble with white ruffians in their tough, lower-class East Baltimore neighborhood. "Don't mess with the white folks' business," his father warned him, but it was a difficult admonition to heed. "Mouse" learned to defend himself, one suspects, with the glibness and humor for which he would later become famous; if that didn't work, a sharp right hook to the solar plexus and swift feet would suffice.[2]

Eubie always had an interest in music, and at the age of six persuaded his hard-strapped parents to buy an organ on the installment plan. Emily was determined that it would be used only for godly music and was incensed when she caught her son using it to summon the devil himself into their home. "Take that ragtime out of my house! Take it out!" she would bellow.

So Eubie slipped out and began warming the keyboard wherever he could. His fingers were long and spindly, but strong. At the age of fifteen he landed his first paying job playing at Agnes Sheldon's fancy whorehouse, for lavish tips. When his mother found out she was furious. It was almost the end of a career for Eubie, until the boy showed his father the nearly $100 in earnings that he had stashed under the carpet in his room. John Blake, who made $9 per week ("when it wasn't raining"), paused for a moment, scratched his grizzled chin and murmured, "Well, son . . . I'll have to talk to your mother."

Noble Sissle and Eubie Blake in a frame from their 1923 film short, *Snappy Songs.*

Eubie began composing as a teenager, although it would be a few years before he could get his work published. Some of his early compositions, such as 1899's "Sounds of Africa" (later known as "Charleston Rag"), would be recorded many years later.[3] After about three years at Aggie Sheldon's he traveled for a while with Dr. Frazier's Medicine Show, then found a job at a Baltimore saloon located at Chestnut and Low (where he composed "Corner of Chestnut and Low," also recorded years later). More gigs followed in the early 1900s in assorted Baltimore dives, until in 1907 he was hired to play at the newly opened Goldfield Hotel, built by black boxing champion Joe Gans. Around 1906 or 1907 he began playing summers in Atlantic City, where he met many of the great ragtime pianists of the day. Some, like Willie "the Lion" Smith, James P. Johnson, and Luckeyeth Roberts influenced him greatly, and became close friends. Roberts was instrumental in helping Blake get his first rags published in 1914 ("Chevy Chase" and "Fizz Water").

In 1910 Eubie married Avis Lee of Baltimore, a classical pianist and a schoolmate during Eubie's brief formal education. By 1915, when he turned thirty-two, he had established himself as a good, though minor, piano player working mostly in the Baltimore–Atlantic City area. During the summer of that year he landed a gig with Joe Porter's Serenaders in Baltimore. When the band's vocalist left and was replaced with a new kid from Indianapolis, Eubie made a lifelong friend. The new singer's name was Noble Sissle.

Sissle's upbringing was somewhat more middle class than Blake's, and he certainly had more formal education. He was born on July 10, 1889, in Indianapolis to

Rev. George A. Sissle, a Methodist minister, and Martha Angeline Sissle, a public schoolteacher and temperance advocate. Raised in an educated, proper household, Noble could easily have become a minister like his father. A handsome, gregarious youth, he made friends among both blacks and whites in his social class. When the family moved to Cleveland in 1906 he enrolled in an overwhelmingly white high school but seldom encountered overt discrimination. He was a popular member of the baseball and football teams. On one occasion when he was denied admission to a movie theater with some white friends, they urged him to file a complaint. With the help of the NAACP he won the case and $250 in damages.

Noble was always musically inclined. He sang in his high school glee club, eventually becoming tenor soloist, and in his final year was elected its leader. As early as 1908, while in high school, he had a brief professional engagement singing with Edward Thomas's Male Quartet, playing the chautauqua circuit in the Midwest.[4] When he graduated in 1910 he toured for a time with Hann's Jubilee Singers and Thomas's Jubilee Sextet, traveling as far west as Denver and east to New York.

In the fall of 1913 Sissle resumed his education, enrolling in De Pauw University, then transferred to Butler University in Indianapolis in January 1914. Throughout this period he supported himself with odd jobs entertaining, even organizing his own dance orchestra at the Severin Hotel in Indianapolis in early 1915. It was while there that he got the offer to join Joe Porter's band in Baltimore for the summer and met Eubie Blake.

The suave tenor and the barrelhouse pianist soon found out that each had something the other needed. Eubie had been composing music and needed a lyricist; the educated Sissle dabbled in lyrics. Within a few days they had put together their first song, "It's All Your Fault." Vaudeville headliner Sophie Tucker happened to be playing nearby and Sissle suggested they take it to her. Blake would never have been so forward, but Sissle was "all brass" (in Eubie's words), so off they went, talked their way backstage, and to their surprise the great Sophie Tucker bought the song.[5]

From this point on Sissle and Blake remained close both personally and professionally, even when their careers took them in different directions. In the fall Blake formed the Marcato Band in Baltimore, while Sissle, quitting college, joined Bob Young's sextet across town. Young's band moved to Palm Beach, Florida, for the winter, and Sissle was introduced to New York society in its winter playground. In the spring E. F. Albee brought Young's band to New York for a short engagement, after which Sissle joined one of James Reese Europe's orchestras playing for society functions there. Sissle persuaded Europe to bring his friend Eubie to New York, and the team was reunited.

The summer of 1916 saw the two working both separately and for the first time together, as a piano-vocal duo, at parties held by Europe's exclusive clientele. Sissle, Blake, and Europe—all three smart businessmen, as well as first-rate musicians—became close friends. In the fall Europe accepted a commission as a lieutenant in the Army National Guard with the task of organizing a black regimental band; Sissle enlisted with him and became his right-hand man, with the rank of sergeant (Blake chose not to enlist and was too old to be drafted).

For all three men 1917 was an important year. In the spring Sissle and one of

Europe's comic entertainers, Opal Cooper, began recording for the New York–based Pathé label, possibly at the same session. About a month later, about May 1917, Cooper and Sissle went together to the Columbia Records studio on 38th Street in Manhattan to make a trial recording as a tenor duet. Nothing came of this, but Sissle clearly had a good recording voice and Pathé was interested in further sides.

Over the next four months Sissle made eleven issued sides for Pathé at their studio on 42nd Street. Pathé's files have long since disappeared, and the identity of the accompanying musicians is uncertain, as is the exact number of sessions. The chronology has been reconstructed from master numbers etched faintly in the shellac of issued pressings. There are gaps in the numbering, which may indicate unissued titles or alternate takes of the same titles.

The songs that Sissle recorded during the spring and summer of 1917 were probably chosen by the label. However, the fact that two of them were written by Sissle and Blake, one by Sissle, Blake, and Europe, and another by Europe's friend Will Marion Cook suggests that they were probably part of the repertoire he was using in appearances with Europe's bands at the time. In all of them Sissle comes across as if he is singing on stage—loud, forceful, and with broad inflections that sound as if they might have been accompanied by the exaggerated gestures stage performers then used to "put across" a song to a large theater audience. This would be Sissle's style throughout his career, not at all intimate, but rather forceful, animated, and with crystal-clear diction. Straight out of vaudeville. Unfortunately it was a style shared by many other performers of the period and as a result not terribly distinctive.

Nor was his repertoire. As songwriters, Sissle, Blake, and Europe seemed to be aping every possible Tin Pan Alley cliché in search of a "me-too" hit. Sissle and Blake would not find their "voice" until they wrote their well-crafted Broadway show tunes of the 1920s, such as "I'm Just Wild about Harry" and "Love Will Find a Way." "Good Night, Angeline," which may or may not be a nod toward Sissle's mother, Martha Angeline, was written with Europe. It is a very "white" Tin Pan Alley love song sung at a moderate tempo, full of phrases heard elsewhere: "Leavin' time is grievin' time . . . / Nighttime was made for lovin', / It's the right time for turtle-dovin'."[6]

The accompaniment on this and the other 1917 Pathé sessions sounds like the label's studio band. There has been speculation that Eubie Blake may have been in the orchestra, but if he was he certainly isn't heard. It is unlikely that Pathé would have called in a black pianist to play with its white studio orchestra.

Sissle and Blake's "He's Always Hanging Around" is a choppy, Eddie Cantoresque novelty song about a beau's problems on a date—when you don't have enough money for a taxi, "they're always hanging around"; when you want your little brother to leave you alone, "he's always hanging around." Sissle sings it in the animated Cantor style. Other novelty songs he recorded include "Somebody's Gonna Get You," an upbeat tune about a reluctant girlfriend, and "That's the Kind of a Baby for Me," a cheerful, sarcastic number about a boy with eyes for the rich and pretty divorcée next door. The latter was Eddie Cantor's featured number in the *Ziegfeld Follies of 1917* and appears to have been recorded a few weeks after the show opened in June as Pathé's "cover version" of the song (Cantor himself recorded it for Victor in July, in his first-ever recording).

None of these songs contain any reference to race; indeed, they could have been sung by any one of scores of white tenors then recording for various labels. However, Pathé also featured Sissle on several dialect numbers that speak of Mammy, home, and the dear old Southland. It may seem incredible today that songs about "kinky headed pickaninnies" could have been intended as anything other than demeaning to blacks, but at the time they were regarded as tender lullabies and evocations of a wistful past. Unlike the racist "coon songs" favored by vaudeville shouters, they were thought of as "high class" and sung in concert settings. Many of the melodies are quite lovely. Indeed, Hattie Starr's "Little Alabama Coon" (1893), one of the most famous, was recorded by Metropolitan Opera soprano Mabel Garrison for the prestigious Victor Red Seal classical label.

Sissle recorded these dialect ballads and lullabies concert style, with some feeling and no apparent irony. There was Carrie Jacobs-Bond's pretty "A Little Bit o' Honey" ("You'se my little black baby with a turned up nose"); "Stay in Your Own Back Yard," about a mammy gently telling her little ones not to play with the white children; Sissle and Blake's own "Mammy's Little Choc'late Cullud Chile"; and Starr's famous "Little Alabama Coon," the latter complete with the sounds of a baby crying. "Can't You Heah Me Callin' Caroline" was a southern love song, in dialect ("Lawdy I miss you, Caroline"), though it did not otherwise refer to race. "Mandy Lou" was another southern song, written in 1911 by black composer Will Marion Cook and sung respectfully by Sissle.

Perhaps the strangest of Sissle's 1917 Pathés, and the most unintentionally funny today, was the upbeat "There It Goes Again." Early 1917 was the "Jazz Spring," the time when that wild, cacophonous music first burst upon mainstream America. It had been gestating in the honky-tonks of New Orleans and Chicago, and New Yorkers were introduced to it during the recordbreaking engagement of the Original Dixieland Jass Band at Reisenweber's during the winter. Then, in March, with great fanfare, Victor rushed out the first-ever recording by the ODJB, and it was a runaway bestseller nationwide. Columbia, Edison, Aeolian-Vocalion, and other labels fell all over themselves churning out jass (quickly changed to "jazz") records by various white and black bands, and Tin Pan Alley quickly produced novelty songs about the craze. One of them was "There It Goes Again," about that jazzy music you just can't get out of your head.

Sissle sang the bouncy tune with enthusiasm ("Oh how I love that melody"), as trombones swoop, cornets blare, and the percussionist sounds as if he is banging on pots and pans. Sissle interjects whoops and shouts of "jazz it boys, jazz it!" The frantic accompaniment by an incredibly loose brass band sounds a little like some of the James Europe recordings for Pathé a couple of years later. However, the obvious unfamiliarity of the musicians with this style of music, and the fact that the recording was apparently made at the same time (possibly at the same session) as more standard material, strongly points to the conclusion that this was simply the white Pathé studio orchestra whooping it up.[7] It may not be jazz, but they were certainly having a good time.

Pathé released the Sissle discs between October 1917 and April 1918 in a vertical-cut format playable only on Pathé's "sapphire ball" phonographs. At least one recording, the lullaby "A Little Bit o' Honey," was also leased to other small vertical-cut labels for reissue about the same time. The records appear to have been moderate sellers, probably doing best in the New York area where Sissle and Europe were known.

Pianists were in much less demand for recording than vocalists; the piano simply didn't record very well acoustically. Nevertheless, Eubie Blake also made his first recordings during the summer of 1917, also for Pathé. His friends Sissle and Europe no doubt helped land him the job. Three sides were recorded in August (approximately), billed as by the "Eubie Blake Trio," a piano duo with drums. The identity of the other two musicians is uncertain. Even Eubie himself, interviewed many years later, only dimly remembered the session and was unsure who was playing with him.[8] The drummer may be Europe's star percussionist Buddy Gilmore, and the other pianist Elliot Carpenter, with whom Eubie played piano duets in the Europe band. Blake later recalled that Europe's orchestra always featured two pianos, adding, "This guy, Carpenter, that played the other piano, boy he could play!"[9] The Pathé supplement, although frustratingly vague about names, does suggest that all three musicians in the trio worked closely together outside the studio.

> The Eubie Blake Trio comprises an organization of three extremely clever colored musicians whose talents in entertaining the "400" and ultra-fashionables of N.Y.C. are extremely in favor and much sought after. As exponents of real "jazz" and "ragtime" piano, two of its members are "king Pins." Member number three is the "sassiest" drummer you ever saw. He's a bunch of smiles and nerves, with most dexterous fingers, and when these colored gentlemen begin to play, Oh Lawdy. Well, just hear these two recordings and we will leave the verdict to you. They're simply great. The two selections are happily chosen and afford fine opportunity for display of real "down south" ragging both on the piano and in the drummer. The dance tempo in each is perfection itself.[10]

The three sides have the hollow, tinkly sound characteristic of acoustic piano recordings. All three feature syncopated, slightly raggy pianos accompanied by a busy trap drummer, whose military style does resemble that of Buddy Gilmore and Europe's other drummers. On "Sarah from Sahara," billed as an "oriental fox trot," the drummer is quite prominent, alternating drum rolls with rickety-tick blocks. He is a little less forward on "American Jubilee," a syncopated piano piece with bits of "Yankee Doodle" and "Annie Laurie" thrown in for effect. "Hungarian Rag" is a very fast one-step on which the pianists tear through the melody with runs and other tricks.

A fourth side, made at about the same time and possibly at the same session (judging by its adjacent master number), has long been the subject of speculation as to whether it is a Eubie Blake recording. Titled "Jazzin' Around," it is a piano duo with drums playing a fast one-step that sounds similar to "Hungarian Rag." However, when it was released more than a year later it was credited to Theodore Morse and Abe Frankel, white duo-pianists who made other recordings for Pathé. Though similar in sound to the Blake Trio sides, it is to my ears slightly tighter, more polished, and even a bit gimmicky (the musicians seem to be making squeals and other animal noises toward the end)—just what one might expect from trained white musicians imitating the "black" sound.

It is also uncertain whether Eubie was involved with "Blake's Jazzone Orchestra," which recorded for Pathé about three months later and whose single selection was issued on the reverse side of "Jazzin' Around." A full discussion of this record can be found in the chapter on miscellaneous recordings.

The three Eubie Blake Trio sides were released in May and June 1918 as novelty recordings. "Sarah from Sahara" was in fact paired with a jazzy accordion solo ("Bunch of Blues") by someone named Charles Klass. The records seem to have had a relatively small sale, judging by their rarity today.

While Sissle and Blake were making their first recordings during the summer of 1917, Sergeant Sissle and his boss, Lieutenant Jim Europe, were busy reorganizing the 15th Regiment U.S. Army Band. On July 15 the regiment was called into active service and began training at Camp Whitman, near Poughkeepsie. (Presumably Sissle made his last recordings that summer either before he left or while on leave.) Sissle later described how the band was posted to Fort Dix, New Jersey, to entertain the troops. "The Commanding General of the cantonment made capital use of the band by having it play concerts every evening on a specially constructed platform. This elevation of the band made it possible for the thousands of draftees to come and hear the concerts. Capt. Fish's Company 'K' quartet also added quite a feature to these entertainments. A piano was also placed on the platform with a special enclosure for it. With Lt. Europe playing I would sing a number of popular songs and original compositions that the Lieutenant and I had composed. . . . One of our favorites was that lullaby of Carrie Jacobs-Bond, 'Little Bit o' Honey.'"[11]

In early October the regiment was sent to Spartanburg, South Carolina, for further training. That proved to be a mistake. The citizens of Spartanburg, or some of them at least, were incensed at the idea of northern soldiers—Jews, Puerto Ricans, and especially blacks—moving freely in their midst. The officers did everything they could to keep the situation under control, and the soldiers were under strict orders to avoid "whites only" establishments and to walk away from any insults. Nevertheless, a series of incidents ensued, including one involving Sissle that nearly escalated into a riot.

Sissle had been asked to pick up some New York newspapers from a stand in the lobby of a local hotel, which he had been told was safe to enter. But as he was leaving he was roughly grabbed from behind and his service hat knocked from his head. A gruff voice roared, "Say, nigger, don't you know enough to take your hat off?" A number of white officers and soldiers stood nearby but did nothing. Sissle beat a hasty retreat, but not before his assailant, who proved to be the proprietor, delivered several kicks and insults.

Once Sissle got outside he said nothing, but word spread quickly that a black sergeant had been assaulted. A large crowd of white and black soldiers surrounded the building, demanding an explanation. Lieutenant Europe arrived and told them to stand back while he went inside to find out what had happened. He was met by the same raving bigot, who demanded that he take off *his* hat as well. Despite his imposing stature (he was six feet tall and solidly built), Europe refused to be drawn into a fight; he quietly complied and held the parties apart until the military police arrived. He then spoke to the soldiers outside, urging them to return to camp, which they did.[12]

After two weeks, and more incidents, the War Department abruptly ordered the 15th back north. It finally sailed for France at the end of December, arriving on January 1, 1918. During the following year Sissle worked closely with Lieutenant Europe as the latter led the regimental band in performances throughout France, entertaining the troops, the high command, and the civilian population. Europe's black band was a great novelty and a smashing success, gaining widespread fame for its jazzy performances of songs such as "The Memphis Blues." The French had never heard anything like it, and they immediately fell in love with *le jazz hot*—a love affair that continues to this day.

Not content to merely lead a band behind the lines, Lieutenant Europe requested a combat assignment and was posted to a machine-gun company where, in June, he was caught in a gas attack. While recuperating he wrote some songs with Sissle, including one that would become one of the latter's trademark numbers, "On Patrol in No Man's Land." Sissle continued to sing with the band, and in the fall entered officer training school and was commissioned a second lieutenant.

Sissle and Europe corresponded regularly with Blake, who continued to perform in the New York area. Blake had formed a vaudeville act with Henry "Broadway" Jones, a booming baritone and colorful character who had considerable experience in show business.[13] Together they toured on the Keith circuit. In addition, sometime in mid- to late 1917, Blake had begun making piano rolls, a sideline he would continue for the next four years. The first appears to have been his own "Charleston Rag," for Ampico, followed by a variety of Sissle, Blake, and Europe songs, show tunes, and popular songs for Rhythmodik and Artrio-Angelus during 1917–19. Approximately fourteen rolls were released during this period.[14]

When the 369th U.S. Infantry (the regiment had been renamed) arrived home in early 1919 they were greeting with a heroes' welcome and a huge parade up New York's Fifth Avenue on February 17. They were nicknamed the "Hell Fighters," and for good reason, as the black soldiers had distinguished themselves in several major battles during the war. Lieutenant Jim Europe's "Hell Fighters" Band was one of the stars of that proud day, marching from Midtown to Harlem playing their brand of big band jazz, which had captivated France.

With the men mustering out, Europe set to work booking a triumphal tour of eighteen eastern and midwestern cities, which was to begin in less than a month. Before leaving, however, they held a marathon series of recording sessions for Pathé in which they recorded much of the varied repertoire they would perform on tour. Lieutenant Noble Sissle, billed as the band's "superstar vocalist," was heard on no fewer than ten sides, which are described in detail in the chapter on Europe.

Among Sissle's more notable sides with Europe's band, recorded in March and May 1919, were the rousing "How Ya Gonna Keep 'Em Down on the Farm (After They've Seen Paree)?" the evocative medley "Plantation Echoes," and his showstopper "On Patrol in No Man's Land," which he performed in concert accompanied by sound effects and a light show. He also sang lead with Europe's Singing Serenaders in a lively rendering of the famous gospel number, "Little David Play on Your Harp," including verses that sound more like vaudeville than a traditional spiritual.

> See that sister dressed so fine,
> She ain't got Jesus on-a her mind!
> Little David play on your harp, hallelu'
> Little David play on your harp, hallelu'.[15]

Europe's tour came to a sudden end in Boston on May 9 when he was stabbed by a deranged member of his band. Sissle was in the dressing room with him when the attack occurred, and Europe left the band in his care as he was carried off to the hospital. He died a few hours later. James Reese Europe was a giant figure in the history of black music in America, a pioneer both musically and in his efforts to secure better working conditions for black musicians. He was also central to the careers of Sissle and Blake, and his death left them at a crossroads.

There were attempts to keep Europe's "Hell Fighters" band going, and it continued to perform intermittently during the 1919–20 season. But Sissle and Blake decided to strike out on their own as a vaudeville act billed as "The Dixie Duo." They toured the northeastern United States and Canada, singing both their own songs and some written with Europe. Although Sissle was the singer, Blake would also chime in on some numbers. The finale was Sissle's animated version of "On Patrol in No Man's Land," with Eubie providing the sounds of the bombardment on the piano. At about this time (no one seems sure of the exact date), Sissle married Harriet Toye, a widow.

Both partners resumed their recording careers in 1920. Sissle, as a vocalist, continued to be the most active in the studio. Early in the year he returned to Pathé to cut seven new titles, four of them written by Sissle and Blake. Once again he used a variety of material ranging from peppy novelties to lachrymose ballads, each performed in the forward, clearly enunciated style for which he was known. In fact, "Gee, I'm Glad That I'm from Dixie" is *so* peppy it sounds as if the record has been speeded up. Vertically cut Pathés normally play at 80 rpm (as advertised), but this one sounds as if it may have been recorded at about 76.8. It is possible that Pathé did this deliberately so that on playback at 80 rpm listeners would get a truly energetic performance, but the result makes Sissle sound like a chipmunk.

On this title and "Affectionate Dan" (the "kissingest man what am") Sissle hams it up unmercifully, slurring phrases and interjecting laughs and whoops. The latter title turns into a virtual Al Jolson parody by the end. Sissle and Blake had been using the songs, which they wrote, in their act, and they are good examples of the high-strutting, high-energy vaudeville of the day. In the middle of "Gee, I'm Glad That I'm from Dixie" Sissle goes into a long comic dialogue with an unidentified male (possibly Blake) about their happy childhood days in Dixie. This sort of crosstalk chatter in the middle of a song was sometimes used on record to suggest a stage performance, the most famous example being Al Jolson's "Sister Susie's Sewing Shirts for Soldiers" (1914) in which he stops the song to do a long routine with an imaginary audience.[16]

"Affectionate Dan" and "Gee, I'm Glad That I'm from Dixie" were issued back to back and are our best examples to date of what the Sissle and Blake stage routine must have sounded like. Judging by the master number, "Dan" may have been recorded a year earlier, possibly even at the end of the last Jim Europe band session.[17] It is therefore possible that Sissle may be accompanied on this side by Jim Europe's band, although the subdued backing doesn't sound much like it.

In contrast with these hammy performances, "Gee, I Wish I Had Someone to Rock Me in the Cradle of Love" is a lovesick blues, complete with a mellow saxophone duet in the middle. The lyrics are pretty trite (the singer wants someone to "be my cutie, call me sweet patootie"). "Mammy's Little Sugar Plum" is a ballad along the lines of "Stay in Your Own Backyard," in which a mammy gently tells her "little pickaninny" not to cry; the white childs may be teasin', but "they'll be sorry some sweet day."

Sissle attempted to cash in on the jazz craze with no fewer than three novelty songs using the word in the title—"I'm Just Simply Full of Jazz," "Jazz Babies' Ball," and "Melodious Jazz." These and other faux jazz titles have led some to characterize Sissle as a "jazz singer" during his early career, but he didn't see it that way. Interviewed many years later by biographer Al Rose, the prim and proper Sissle was unequivocal. "'Young man,' he told me politely, 'I was and am a professional entertainer, and I've had a certain success at it for many years. Part of our art lies in being prepared to give the public what it wants. When they wanted ragtime, I sang ragtime.' He turned to go tend to other business, looking back and adding as he left, 'Not that I ever enjoyed it particularly.'"[18]

One wonders if Sissle was simply giving the public "what it wanted" during his next session with Pathé, for which he organized a mixed chorus to sing four spirituals in traditional artistic arrangements. Billed as "Noble Sissle's Southland Singers," it offered the slow laments "Go Down Moses" and "Steal Away to Jesus," and the more upbeat "Year of Jubilee" and "Hallelujah to the Lamb." All were arranged by someone named "Freman," and three of the four featured short solos by Sissle (he does not solo on "Go Down Moses"). Sissle's distinctive voice does not dominate these records, however. They are true choral performances, the only records of this type made by Sissle during his long solo career and quite different from the jazzy "Little David" he recorded with Jim Europe's orchestra.

Eubie Blake also returned to the studio in 1920. In April he provided piano accompaniment for Florence Emory on a Victor test, as she did two Sissle and Blake songs ("Affectionate Dan" and "Gee, I Wish I Had Someone to Rock Me in the Cradle of Love"). Neither was issued. He also participated on some or all of the 1920 Pathé sides by Sissle which have orchestra accompaniment, although exactly which is uncertain.[19] On April 9, 1920, Sissle and Blake made their first duo recording, a test for Victor with two more of their songs ("Goodnight Angeline" and "I'm Simply Full of Jazz"), but these also went unissued.

Finally in July 1920 the popular duo landed a session with the Emerson label, which resulted in their first issued duet recording—Sissle on vocal, accompanied by Blake on piano, just as in their stage act. According to the liner notes to a 1970s LP reissue, prepared with Blake's involvement, "Eubie played a Style B grand piano

NOBLE SISSLE
Famous Colored Vaudeville Headliner
NOW AN EXCLUSIVE EMERSON STAR

Noble Sissle's Sizzling Syncopators, with Eubie Blake at the piano. (Emerson Records ad, *Phonograph and Talking Machine Weekly,* Mar. 16, 1921)

which was situated right under the recording horn and Noble sang directly into the front of the horn. The engineer was in charge of the session, and it was he who requested the team record this popular song."[20] The song, "Broadway Blues," was one of those city-boy-longs-for-home numbers and was a fairly big hit at the time. Among the stars who recorded it were Nora Bayes, Aileen Stanley, Jack Norworth, and Al Bernard. Although the label reads "Blues Character Song" it is hardly that; more notable is Eubie's distinctive piano accompaniment, which alternates a florid introduction with jazzy, syncopated choruses. He complements Sissle's energetic vocal perfectly, and it is obvious why they worked so well together.

Emerson did not issue "Broadway Blues" until early 1921, after the Victor and Columbia versions had begun to sell. In the meantime, during the latter half of 1920, Sissle returned to Pathé for four additional sides, all with orchestra accompaniment. Two of them were to become Sissle and Blake standbys. "Pickaninny Shoes" may sound like a rather bizarre lyric today, but as performed by Sissle this paean by a "darky" to a souvenir of his childhood was a sentimental favorite with audiences.

> When boys would chide me,
> You'd always guide me,
> Safely back home,

Just-a screamin' for dad.
Pickaninny shoes . . .
You saved me many a bruise . . .

Eubie later described how Sissle performed his showstopper. "He stands there on the stage in the amber light, see, and he's got his hands in front of him like he's holdin' a pair of baby shoes in them. Now he got no shoes in his hand, nothin', see, but the audience, they *see* them shoes—he was a great actor—and he sings 'Pickaninny Shoes.' There's no way to follow him. He can't follow *himself*."[21]

The other favorite, somewhat surprisingly, was "Crazy Blues," the song many consider the first true "blues" to become a hit on record, and the song that launched an enormous vogue for black jazz and blues recordings during the 1920s. Written and relentlessly promoted by black composer Perry Bradford ("Mule" to his friends), it was first recorded by a raw blues shouter named Mamie Smith for the Okeh label. It was released in November 1920, and its tremendous success caught everyone by surprise. The song was of course widely covered, and Sissle made no fewer than three versions during 1920–21.

The Pathé folks must have been listening to the best-selling Okeh disc carefully, as Sissle's version has an unusually hot accompaniment—for this label—with sizzling cornet, trombone, and piano work. It almost sounds as if Pathé engaged a real jazz band (there were many around at the time) for the session rather than use its studio orchestra. Unfortunately the identities of the musicians are unknown.

"Great Camp Meetin' Day," written by Sissle with bandmaster Gene Mikell, a close friend from Jim Europe days, is a lively, high-strutting novelty about happy times at an old-fashioned colored revival ("When Deacon Jones begins to walk about / The brothers grab the sisters and begin to shout!"). If nothing else, it demonstrates that black stereotypes were alive and well and making money for everyone, including black performers like Sissle and Blake. Perhaps its most distinguishing feature is a wild drum solo at the end, with Sissle shouting encouragement. "My Vision Girls" is an odd, booming ballad in a minor key, meant to cash in on the vogue for all things oriental.

During the winter of 1920–21 Sissle made additional versions of "Crazy Blues" for two other labels, and they provide a study in contrasts with the Pathé. The Edison version is as sedate and lifeless as the Pathé was hot. The subdued studio orchestra seemed to subdue Sissle as well. Many discographers assume that Eubie Blake was present on virtually all of Sissle's recordings around this time, playing in the orchestra if there was one. But if Eubie attended this session, he must have been asleep in the next room.

The Emerson version of "Crazy Blues" shows a third approach to the song. It is by Sissle and Blake alone, without orchestra, and as such is more intimate than the Pathé or the Edison. Sissle does his moanin' best to Blake's spare, syncopated piano, although the performance does sound a little odd when one is used to hearing this song with a jazz band. Four different takes were issued by Emerson and allied labels. Sissle's performance is similar on various takes that have been heard, although he does throw in different exclamations when Blake takes a short solo toward the end ("Oh play 'em, Mr. Blake, play 'em" on one, "Oh that man plays a wicked tune" on another). These three very different versions of "Crazy Blues" demonstrate Sissle's versatility, although it is the Emerson that is presumably closest to his stage style at the time.

Showmen that they were, Sissle and Blake could clearly see that record buyers preferred the band sound to vocal and piano duets. Paul Whiteman, Ted Lewis, Isham Jones, and other bandleaders were selling millions of records, as were smaller combinations such as the Original Memphis Five and the Original Dixieland Jazz Band. So during the winter of 1920–21 Sissle organized his own six-piece band, dubbed his "Sizzling Syncopators." Eubie, of course, played piano, with other members drawn mostly from the old Jim Europe band (including trumpeter Frank De Broite and drummer Steve Wright, plus trombone, clarinet, and saxophone). With his own backup band Sissle was able to fashion a much more contemporary sound on record than had been possible with the stiff Emerson and Pathé studio orchestras.

The Syncopators were a tight little unit, not so much a jazz band as a novelty orchestra with jazz instrumentation and first-rate musicians who sometimes played in a jazz-influenced style. Despite the sometimes hot playing and imaginative arrangements, the records get little respect from jazz scholars today. I once asked a jazz critic about them, and he snorted, "who needs that shit when you've got Kid Ory on Sunshine?"[22]

Oblivious to the disdain of future pedants, Sissle quickly lined up sessions for the band, recording eight titles for Emerson and Pathé during February and March 1921. All were vocals by Sissle, but the band was prominently featured and there were extended instrumental breaks on most of them. Seven of the eight titles were jazz or blues pieces, including some very interesting material by Sissle and Blake and fellow black composers Clarence Williams, Spencer Williams, and W. C. Handy. Strong trumpet work characterized "Royal Garden Blues," with mutes (like those Paul Whiteman had recently popularized) on the Pathé version. A squealing clarinet, in the Ted Lewis style, was heard on "Boll Weevil Blues" and "Low Down Blues." Blake's piano, while integral to the sound, was not out in front on these recordings, although he does play a nice little passage at the end of Handy's tale of the crook who got away, "Long Gone." On several of the sides the drummer uses blocks for a rickety-tick sound.

Possibly the best of the lot are the band's two readings of "Loveless Love" (aka "Careless Love"), the famous folk blues adapted by Handy into a popular song in 1921. They are possibly the first recording of the tune and certainly preceded its widespread adoption by jazz and blues artists. The two versions recorded by Sissle are a good example of how he could vary his performances. On Pathé the band goes into a long and fascinating instrumental break, with brass harmony that almost sounds like a mariachi band. The Emerson version, on the other hand, has a completely different break with saxophone, clarinet, and those rickety-tick blocks.

All of the initial seven sides by the Syncopators feature interesting arrangements, quite different from what was being heard on most records of the period, and the discs are recommended to modern collectors—if they can find them. The eighth side, "My Mammy's Tears," on the other hand, is a "longing for Mammy" ballad of the type Sissle had sung so many times before. A xylophone is featured. The Syncopators certainly do not sizzle on this one.

Emerson must have seen promise in Sissle's hot new sound, as it offered him an exclusive recording contract, something fairly unusual at this time. A full-page trade advertisement in March 1921 trumpeted that "Noble Sissle Will Hereafter Record Exclusively for Emerson Records" and left no doubt what niche he was expected to fill.

> Oh, yo' Noble Sissle man
> Yo' sure has der stuff
> We'en yo' sings it's simply gran'—
> Cannot get enough.
> Syncopated melody,
> "Broken Time" dat BUBBLES!
> Joyous, happy harmony,
> Takes away mah troubles.
> Puts mah money down to bet,
> Is yo' ain't der bestest yet![23]

A picture showed the band adopting comic poses—clarinet raised, trombone pointing toward the sky, Blake bending over backwards on his piano bench (he looks uncomfortable), and Sissle out in front, hand raised, striking an "Oh, lawdy!" pose. This was clearly supposed to be a "fun" band. The ad went on to claim that Sissle was "the greatest tenor of his race . . . his renditions are typically his own, yet happily natural and spontaneous in their interpretations of the music of his Race." The just-released duets with Blake ("Broadway Blues" and "Crazy Blues") were said to be selling well.

Interestingly, Emerson promised to record Sissle later in a group of spirituals, "in the singing of which he is unexcelled." However, the four early 1920 Pathé sides by the Southland Singers were finally released a month or two after the Emerson announcement, and their lack of success evidently dissuaded Emerson from following suit.

By the time Sissle signed his exclusive contract with Emerson in early 1921 (evidently for a one-year term), he and Blake were already deeply immersed in a project that would result in the biggest hit of their career, as well as a landmark event in the history of black music in America. The seeds had been planted a year earlier when they were performing in a benefit in Philadelphia and first met the vaudeville team of Flournoy Miller and Aubrey Lyles. The two teams were impressed with each others' talents, but nothing much transpired until a few months later when the four men ran into each other again on the streets of New York. Miller began to outline an idea he had to expand one of the Miller and Lyles sketches into a full-length musical comedy. Sissle and Blake had some musical ideas for such a show, and they began to talk.

It was a pipedream, of course. Jim Europe had talked about reviving the black musical theater, which had been practically moribund since the days of Williams and Walker and Cole and Johnson in the early 1900s. Since then Broadway had shown little interest in black talent of any type, aside from old-timer Bert Williams, the token black comedian in the *Ziegfeld Follies*. Moreover, mounting a full production was an expensive, high-stakes gamble, and no one had any money. That *Shuffle Along* came together at all was a miracle or, rather, a series of miracles. First, Sissle, Blake, Miller, and Lyles shopped their idea around and managed to get some marginal financial support from white producer Al Mayer and the Cort theatrical family. Scrounging up discarded sets and costumes from earlier flops, they began rehearsals in Harlem and put together a short out-of-town tryout tour in early 1921. The little company was constantly running out of money, writing checks before there was money in the bank, skipping out on landlords, and borrowing from almost anyone they could.

Finally, after a series of hair-raising close calls, the show opened on May 23, 1921, at Cort's slightly dilapidated 63rd Street Theatre in New York. The book, based on Miller and Lyles's "Mayor of Dixie" routine, concerned shenanigans during a small-town mayoral contest. The slapstick plot was frequently interrupted by dance routines and songs, vaguely (or not at all) related to the story. Eubie Blake led the orchestra from the pit, while Miller, Lyles, and Sissle starred, supported by a talented cast including Gertrude Saunders, Lottie Gee, Roger Matthews, and a bevy of beautiful dancing girls.

Undeterred by adversity, the cast and musicians gave the show everything they had and won over audiences with their sheer energy and enthusiasm. *Variety* called it a "lively entertainment" with an "excellent score"; an influential review in the *New York American* was headlined "'Shuffle Along' Full of Pep and Real Melody." Several hits emerged from the score, including one that has become a standard. "I'm Just Wild about Harry," about one of the scheming candidates for mayor, began life as a pretty waltz, and Blake hated to see it transformed into a fast fox trot. But his partners insisted, and it is in the latter form that we know it today. Just as popular at the time was the first act love duet, "Love Will Find a Way" ("though clouds now are gray"). This was something of a daring inclusion, as a black actor and actress had *never* been permitted to sing a love song to each other in a mainstream show. It was thought unacceptable to white audiences. Sissle later told of being prepared to flee the theater if the audience became unruly during this number, but it didn't happen. The song was a hit.

Other popular numbers included "Bandana Days," "Baltimore Buzz" (shades of Eubie's youth), "In Honeysuckle Time," "Gypsy Blues," "I Am Craving for That Kind of Love," and "If You Haven't Been Vamped by a Brownskin, You Haven't Been Vamped at All." Some of these had originated in Sissle and Blake's vaudeville act, just as much of the comedy had been previously used by Miller and Lyles. But no matter that the score was really a mix of old and new material, it all *seemed* new on Broadway, which hadn't seen a show like this in years. *Shuffle Along* was one of the major hits of the season, running for more than five hundred performances.

During May, June, and July 1921, Sissle and Blake recorded six titles from the original score of *Shuffle Along,* for Emerson and Victor. Some were released under Sissle's name, some under Blake's, and some as by "Sissle and Blake." Both partners participated in all of them.

The first session, for Emerson, took place on about May 3, before the show opened, and featured Sissle on vocal with his Sizzling Syncopators. This was his last session with the band, which was evidently disbanded when he began appearing in *Shuffle Along.* Sissle would not record with his own orchestra again until the late 1920s. A banjo was added for this session, and it dominates the rhythm section; there is little in the way of jazz here. "Baltimore Buzz" was a raggy dance number performed in the show by Sissle and the "Jimtown Jazz Steppers," a chorus line of beautiful girls. Sissle gives it his usual energetic performance, describing the dance and throwing in shouts of encouragement to the band at the end ("Look out—that-a-boy!"). "In Honeysuckle Time" is a cheerful love song to his Emaline ("There'll be no hesitatin', 'cause the preacher will be waitin'"). One imagines him surrounded by chorines twirling parasols as he sings.

Another Emerson session about June 9 produced two sides by Sissle accompanied by Blake on piano. "Love Will Find a Way" was the show's big romantic ballad, a lovely melody with somewhat stilted, operetta-style lyrics. Sissle gave it a heartfelt delivery—not his strong suit as he was primarily a rhythm singer—while Blake ragged a little on the piano behind him. One wonders what John McCormack, Marion Harris, or one of the other first-rate ballad singers of the day might have done with this pretty song. Instead, it was generally treated as an instrumental or included in medleys; few other contemporary vocal versions are known, one by a mysterious tenor named Edwin Dale.[24] "Oriental Blues" was a novelty production number in which Sissle fantasized about going to the "land where oriental maidens dwell," while appropriately costumed dancers swirled around. What that had to do with a mayoral election in a small southern town is an oriental mystery.

While Sissle recorded vocal versions of songs from *Shuffle Along* for Emerson, Eubie Blake—who had costar billing in the show as the orchestra leader and Sissle's onstage accompanist—was approached by Victor, the biggest label of all. The Victor studio was run by first-rate musicians with very high standards who often required many takes to get exactly the performance they wanted. During June and July Eubie made test recordings of piano solos of "Bandana Days," "I'm Just Wild about Harry," "Baltimore Buzz," and the dialect number "Dah's Gwinter Be Er Landslide," and accompanied Broadway Jones in a vocal version of "Baltimore Buzz," but none of these were accepted for issue. Finally, on July 15, he led the full *Shuffle Along* orchestra in two medleys from the show, which were issued on Victor in October.

They were fast, bouncy instrumentals, in more or less strict tempo for dancing. The cornets predominate, with Sissle playing harmony on the violin and banjo and blocks providing a steady rhythm. Though hardly imaginative arrangements, they are clean, crisp recordings and probably sound a lot like the pit orchestra sounded every night at the show. In addition, the "Bandana Days" medley, with its long interpolation of "I'm Just Wild about Harry," gives us the first composer-recording of that famous song. A few days later Blake went to the Emerson studios (he was not exclusive to any label) and recorded two piano solos, "Baltimore Buzz" and his old favorite, "Sounds of Africa" ("Charleston Rag").

Shuffle Along developed into a major hit during the summer and fall of 1921, and several of its songs became quite popular. Sissle and Blake's own recorded versions appear to have sold well, especially Blake's dance-band medleys on the widely distributed Victor label. However the biggest sales went to cover versions by a wide variety of artists (mostly white) on major labels such as Victor, Columbia, and Brunswick. This didn't bother the composers—the fat royalty checks were putting them on easy street for the first time in their lives. Blake later gave credit to Paul Whiteman, the best-selling bandleader in America, for giving "I'm Just Wild about Harry" a major boost. Whiteman's 1922 Victor records of "Harry" and "Gypsy Blues" were huge sellers.

Whiteman was not the only bandleader who helped popularize the tunes from *Shuffle Along*. The list of recordings at the end of this chapter, while undoubtedly incomplete, gives an idea of how widely disseminated the songs were at the time. "Gypsy Blues" was the first to hit big, in the fall and winter of 1921–22, followed by "I'm Just Wild about Harry" almost a year later. There were also a large number of medleys. In all, more than forty recordings of songs from the show have been identified during these two years; "Harry" led with sixteen versions, followed by "Gypsy" with twelve (including medleys).

The huge success of *Shuffle Along* accelerated Sissle and Blake's recording activities. Still under contract to Emerson, Sissle recorded six more sides for the label between July 1921 and January 1922, all accompanied by Blake's syncopated piano. They are all novelties, mostly takes on the current "blues" craze, and all were no doubt featured at one time or another in the spot near the end of the show where Blake jumped up on stage and accompanied Sissle in a few current tunes while the scenery was being changed. Several contain solo breaks by Blake. On "I've Got the Red, White and Blues" he even rags "Home, Sweet Home."

Blake also recorded for Emerson under his own name during this period. Unlike his recordings with Sissle, which were mostly specialty material or songs from their show, the solo dates gave Blake the opportunity to do some of the big pop hits of the day. In September his syncopated piano was heard on "Ma! (He's Making Eyes at Me)" and "Sweet Lady" from the show *Tangerine*. On "Ma!" he plays the familiar melody through a few times, then goes into some imaginative vamps to vary things; on "Sweet Lady" variety is provided by pop singer Irving Kaufman, who comes in part way through with his trademark piercing vocal chorus.

For a February session Blake assembled a dance orchestra to record Rudolf Friml's catchy show tune "Cutie," and a Tin Pan Alley number called "Jimmy, I Love but You." They are cheerfully played fox trots, in the style of the time, with nicely varied arrangements; cornets and saxophones play counterpoint to one another, and a chugging banjo maintains the rhythm. Though pleasant enough, they are indistinguishable from hundreds of dance records of the day. One guesses that Eubie was simply picking up a few extra bucks.

Not that he really needed it. *Shuffle Along* and its songs were bringing Sissle and Blake more money than they had ever seen before. The show ultimately played for 504 performances on Broadway, then went on tour in July 1922. Recording sessions were slipped in around their hectic schedule. Following the expiration of his exclusive contract with Emerson in early 1922, Sissle made two trial recordings for Victor (accompanied, interestingly, by pianists other than Blake), but no issues resulted. In July he teamed with Blake for one last session featuring songs from their hit show, this one for the small Paramount label. One side was a rare vocal version of the dance number "Bandana Days"; after a short chorus, Sissle narrates ("everybody get your partner") as Blake rags on the piano. The other Paramount side was the only contemporary recording of "If You've Never Been Vamped by a Brownskin," a dialect number performed in the show by Miller and Lyles with the chorus girls.

Just prior to the Sissle and Blake session for Paramount, Blake was in the same label's studio accompanying blues singer Alberta Hunter. It is uncertain exactly how many sides he made with her. He is listed as piano accompanist on the label of "I'm Going Away Just to Wear You Off My Mind" and "Jazzin' Baby Blues," but some scholars suggest he may also have led the band that accompanied her on several other sides.[25]

After a season on the road the cast finally took a vacation in the summer of 1923. It was about time. After two solid years of performances the principals needed a rest. As it turned out, the summer break was almost the end of *Shuffle Along*. Trouble had been brewing behind the scenes, as it often does when success is unevenly distributed. Sissle, Blake, Miller, and Lyles were equal partners; together they owned half the show (the producers and a financial "angel" owned the other half, but with an overall gross of nearly $8 million, who was counting?).[26] However, Sissle and Blake had been getting the lion's share of the acclaim, and as songwriters they reaped most of the musical royalties. In addition, they had become recording stars.

When producer George White of *George White's Scandals* offered Miller and Lyles a large amount of money to star in a show of their own, one over which they would have total control, it was too good an offer to resist. At first the proposed show was going to be called *Shuffle Along of 1923,* but Sissle and Blake threatened to sue. The comedians then considered *George White's Black Scandals* (which was thankfully discarded) and finally settled on *Runnin' Wild.* It opened on Broadway on October 29, 1923, and proved a major hit, running for 213 performances. Among its best-known songs were "Old Fashioned Love" and a frenetic dance number that would become a veritable theme song of the 1920s—"The Charleston."[27]

Miller and Lyles took much of the *Shuffle Along* cast with them, leaving Sissle and Blake with the shell of a musical. But *Shuffle Along* still had considerable life in it. It went back on tour in August 1923 and played successfully until January, even as Sissle and Blake began work on a new musical of their own.

Meanwhile, during 1923, the songwriting team continued their activities in other media. They wrote songs for other musicals, including Andre Charlot's *London Calling* and the short-lived *Elsie*. Another series of tests for Victor finally resulted in the first Sissle and Blake vocal-with-piano duet issued on that major label. The tunes, recorded in May, were Billy Baskette's clever "Waitin' for the Evenin' Mail" and "Down-Hearted Blues," a hit for several blues singers. Blake's jaunty piano perfectly complements the Sissle vocals; the singer reciprocates by making approving sounds ("ooo-ooo") during Blake's solo at the end of the latter title.

More trials followed at Victor in August. As successful as Sissle and Blake were in personal appearances, the finicky label evidently had trouble getting exactly the sound or the material it wanted from the duo. Finally, in January 1924, they waxed two titles good enough for issue, although the results were not particularly satisfying. "Sweet Henry (the Pride of Tennessee)" is a takeoff on the "Dapper Dan, Lovin' Sam" syndrome of songs about great lovers, distinguished mostly by Blake's syncopated solo toward the end. "Old Fashioned Love" is a lovely sentimental ballad, the big hit from Miller and Lyles's *Runnin' Wild,* but Sissle gives it his usual shouted performance. The disc does not seem to have sold as well as the previous Victors.

One other project of Sissle and Blake's during 1923 resulted in a historical treasure, literally a picture of them working together on stage. Early in the year they were recruited by inventor Lee DeForest to make one of his pioneering "phonofilms," short sound films of stage performances. Others who did so included Eddie Cantor, Phil Baker, and Weber and Fields. As vaudeville headliners they were paid a substantial amount of money for the privilege—though not as much, Eubie was later to observe, as Eddie Cantor. The resulting film, called *Sissle and Blake's Snappy Songs,* survives and gives a fascinating glimpse of the team at work.[28]

Sissle and Blake appear in formal clothes on a small sound stage in front of a simple drape. Blake is seated at the grand piano and Sissle stands beside him. Since the camera was immobile neither could move very far, which evidently was an imposition on the animated Sissle (at one point he keeps his hand on the piano, presumably so that he doesn't inadvertently get out of camera range while singing). They begin with a bit of chatter, then launch into "Affectionate Dan," one of their trademark numbers. Blake even chimes in on the chorus, something he never did on record. When it ends they move smoothly into a short but lively rendition of "All God's Chillun Got Shoes" to fill out the rest of the time. Blake's spidery fingers dart across the keyboard while Sissle mugs, gestures, flaps his hands as if flying, and even "marches" to the rhythm, all while staying firmly planted on his spot. It is quite a show, communicating, if nothing else, what a high-energy act the pair put on. Unlike so many historic films of the period, this one has not only been preserved but is available on home video.[29]

Sissle and Blake's opulent new show, called *In Bamville,* began previews in Rochester, New York, in March 1924. Renamed *The Chocolate Dandies,* it reached Broadway on September 1, 1924, and ran successfully—if not particularly profitably (due to the high overhead)—until the following May. It was set in a southern plantation town, and more closely resembled a fantasy than the slapstick farce of *Shuffle Along.* The plot revolved around dream sequences and high-jinks at a racetrack. Critic Ashton Stevens wrote, "It is, I felt last night, the fatal influence of the white man that makes the show seem second rate for all its costly costumes and sceneries. There is too much so-called politeness, too much platitudinous refinement and not enough of the racy and the razor-edged. There is, in a word, too much 'art' and not enough Africa. Yes, even in the music of that gifted melodist, Eubie Blake."[30]

Sissle and Blake entered the Victor studios three days before the first tryout to record three of the show's songs, returning in August to rerecord one title and add a fourth. None of these takes were issued. The duo returned again in October and finally, after six takes, produced renditions of "Dixie Moon" and "Manda" that Victor felt were suitable for release. Neither the songs nor the performances were exceptional, and the disc had modest sales. Unfortunately, *Chocolate Dandies* did not produce any hits to equal "Gypsy Blues" or "I'm Just Wild about Harry," even though Blake would later maintain that it was the best score he ever wrote. He was especially proud of "Dixie Moon."[31]

After *The Chocolate Dandies* closed Sissle and Blake returned to vaudeville, where they were always welcome, for the summer of 1925. About this time they picked up some extra change by making two more sides for the Edison company. "Broken Busted Blues" was one of their more gimmicky recordings, with train whistles and Sissle moaning in blues shouter style; Blake takes a nice little bluesy solo. "You Ought to Know," from *Chocolate Dandies,* was a straightforward pop tune, indistinguishable from dozens turned out by white Tin Pan Alley songwriters every year. It is a good illustration of what critic Ashton Stevens was talking about.

The financial failure of *Chocolate Dandies* made the prospect of mounting a new musical especially daunting, so Sissle and Blake chose instead to embark on their first overseas tour. From September 1925 through March 1926 they toured England, Scotland, and France, where they were warmly received.[32] They played some of the leading venues in London, including the Victoria Palace, Coliseum, and Alhambra. They were already known in England from the *Shuffle Along* hits, and several of their U.S. recordings had been released there. While in England they recorded ten sides for the Edison Bell Winner label, including their own material as well as some current pop hits of the day. Among the former were "You Ought to Know" and "A Jockey's Life for Mine" from *Chocolate Dandies,* and the ever-popular "Pickaninny Shoes." Another of their numbers which they recorded, "Why?" was quite successful with English audiences.

While in England the team was commissioned to write songs for *Cochran's Revue of 1926.* Impresario Charles B. Cochran, who had earlier attempted to bring *Shuffle Along* to England, offered them the opportunity to write the entire score for his 1927 revue. But although England was treating Sissle and Blake well professionally, Blake was homesick. They turned down Cochran's offer (Richard Rodgers and Lorenz Hart got the assignment), and Blake persuaded Sissle to return home to resume their vaudeville work there.

In the late summer of 1926 Sissle and Blake recorded for the Okeh label in New York, but the only known title ("Ukulele Lullaby," which they had also recorded in England) was for some reason not released. Busy touring, they did not record again until early 1927, when two further sessions for Okeh produced five issued titles. These were also issued on the affiliated Parlophone label in England for their fans there.

The repertoire was predictable, including one old favorite ("Pickaninny Shoes," evidently their trademark number at the time), a couple of upbeat current pop hits ("'Deed I Do," "Ev'rything's Made for Love"), and a couple of ballads ("Slow River," "Home, Cradle of Happiness"). Sissle seemed to be striving to become a "personality" singer at this time, with bits of chatter and humorous asides in the upbeat numbers and heartfelt crooning in the slow ones. Throughout his career Sissle always tended to reflect current trends rather than putting his own stamp on his material. Here he seems to be aping the new wave of intimate crooners who emerged in the mid-1920s, such as Gene Austin, Tom Waring, and "Whispering" Jack Smith. Blake did the best he could with the rather ordinary Tin Pan Alley material.

Sissle and Blake took another stab at moviemaking during 1927, with two short subjects for the new Vitaphone sound film process. One featured "I Wonder Where My Sweetie Can Be," one of their own compositions which they had recorded in England in late 1925, and the other the currently popular "My Dream of the Big Parade," a dramatic song about World War I veterans, from the film *The Big Parade*. Neither is believed to exist today.

By the early summer of 1927 Sissle was determined to return to England, where the competition was lighter and they had a ready audience. But Blake did not want to go. Despite their success there he did not like the stuffy British atmosphere, preferring the rough-and-tumble of show business in the United States. This difference of opinion led to the biggest fight that Sissle and Blake ever had, and the one that ultimately broke up the act. Sissle walked out, declaring that he would book his own fall tour of the continent, without Blake. There may have been another factor at work as well. Perhaps the two partners, who had been performing essentially the same act for a dozen years, realized that their simple tenor-with-piano act was getting a little stale in the era of elaborate big band stage shows.

Sissle immediately began to experiment with his sound, using new accompanists. On record, at least, he abandoned Sissle and Blake specialty material and began concentrating primarily on popular songs of the day. Between July and September 1927, Sissle recorded ten more sides for Okeh in New York. On most of these he used composer/pianist Rube Bloom, a much quieter, less showy accompanist than Eubie Blake. On the ballad "Here Am I—Broken Hearted" Sissle affects a quaver in his voice, rather like Tom Waring; on "Just Once Again" he hams it up, sniffing and going into falsetto. On the upbeat "Give Me a Night in June" Sissle and Bloom are joined by jazz clarinetist Andy Sannella, who enlivens things considerably. As the clarinet and piano plunge into their solo Sissle throws in exclamations ("hey-hey," "vo-do-de-o-do-do!"), and even urges on his accompanists by name ("Play that thing, Andy," "Listen to Rube spanking them ivories!"). On "Are You Happy?" Sannella switches to steel guitar, changing the sound yet again. On the traditional "Kentucky Babe" Sissle used a string trio consisting of violin, cello, and guitar (he also used the pseudonym "Lee White" on most issues of this title).

All of these discs were issued in England on the Parlophone label for Sissle and Blake's many fans there. The U.S. releases on Okeh did not sell particularly well, and it is possible that the label was recording Sissle primarily for the benefit of its English affiliate. One title, "Who's That Knocking at My Door?" was released only in England.

In the fall of 1927 Sissle embarked on a tour of English music halls with twenty-one-year-old pianist Harry Revel (who later became famous as the composer of such hits as "Did You Ever See a Dream Walking?" and "Goodnight, My Love"). Their act was well received, and Sissle was certain he had made the right choice. From 1927 to 1931 he would be truly an international entertainer, alternating between England, Paris, and Monte Carlo, with only brief trips back to the United States. His wife, Harriet, accompanied him.

Sissle's first solo recordings overseas were for English Parlophone in early 1928, accompanied by "His Own Special Orchestra." This was apparently organized solely for recording purposes and was actually led by Revel and others. In the music halls he continued to perform as a duo with Revel.

Parlophone could not get enough of Sissle, recording more than thirty sides during the remainder of 1928, roughly half of them written by Sissle himself with various partners, frequently Revel. None were released in the United States, and some in fact were British songs not heard in the United States. These are a fascinating group of records and hard to find today. Sissle seems to be trying to project a distinctive personality on record, but his style varies wildly. On "Sunny Skies," "I'm Going Back Home to Old Nebraska," and Will Marion Cook's "I'm Comin' Virginia," he is perilously close to doing an Al Jolson imitation; you expect him to exclaim "Mammy!" at any time. On "Dakota" he's closer to Rudy Vallee's wispy falsetto. On "Good News" he works exceptionally hard to inject personality into his performance, singing the seldom-heard verse and interjecting, "boy when you hear that hot music!" Sissle's exclamations ("hee hee!") and shouts of encouragement to his musicians are heard on many of these sides. Sissle was probably the only bandleader to shout "hee hee!" in the middle of his records. More often than not it worked, as with the hot saxophone break on "Sunny Skies."

True to his billing as the "Ace of Syncopation," Sissle was best on the rhythm numbers, such as "Westwood Bound" (a knockoff of "Alabamy Bound") and "Shout Hallelujah 'Cause I'm Home." Revel's first-rate orchestra, which could really swing, helped as well. The ballads are something else again, ranging from the teary "Since You Have Left Me" to the schmaltzy "Guiding Me Back Home," which comes complete with falsetto and a little recitation ("I never shall forget the day . . ."). "When the Clock Struck 12," a waltz, does have a nice arrangement. Sissle is noticeably unsteady on some of these slower sides, even sliding off-key at times.

Perhaps the strangest pair are two big hits from *Show Boat,* issued back to back. "Ol' Man River" is a real production. The lyrics are somewhat sanitized (the original, controversial introduction, "Niggers all work on the Mississippi," is replaced by "Colored folk work on the Mississippi"), but Sissle gives it a dramatic reading, in the deepest voice he can muster ("Tote that barge! Lift that bale!"). The song is a bit more than he can handle, and he has to drop an octave when it gets out of his narrow range, but he certainly gives it his all. The show's big love ballad, "Why Do I Love You?" on the other hand, has to be heard to be believed. Sissle wavers, falls off-key, and even sings the wrong lyrics, crooning to his girl, "You're a lucky boy, I'm . . . er . . . lucky too!" It is unintentionally hilarious, and it is amazing that Parlophone even issued it. Apparently Sissle had a loyal following that would buy whatever he released and wanted his versions of the pop hits of the day. Ronnie Munro alternated with Revel as director of the orchestra for some of these sessions, but Sissle was always billed as the bandleader, as well as featured vocalist. The old "Sizzling Syncopators" name was revived for some sides, occasionally changed to the "Sissling Syncopators."

During the summer of 1928 Sissle shifted to Paris, where he recruited his own band to play at the exclusive Les Ambassadeurs club on the Champs-Elysées. This band was made up of some of the best black expatriate musicians on the continent, including clarinetist Sidney Bechet. According to some sources composer Cole Porter, whom Sissle had met in Paris, encouraged him to form the band and helped him line up the gig to support it. Other sources indicate that the band was brought from New York by John Ricks.[33]

In the fall Sissle returned to England to play another season in the music halls as a duo with Harry Revel and, later, other accompanists. He resumed recording for Parlophone with a studio orchestra now led by Barry Mills, the repertoire again consisting mostly of pop songs, some written by Sissle himself. Just once, in a November 1928 session, did he return to his older material, waxing "Great Camp Meetin' Day." The song was the subject of an unusual promotion on December 7, 1928, when Sissle led a band and "a large crowd of coloured folk, including many well-known performers," through downtown London with banners flying, singing and pantomiming the song.[34]

Sissle returned to the United States briefly in early 1929 to organize another band of his own, which he brought back to Paris in May. From this time he would no longer appear as a vocalist with piano but was a full-time bandleader. After spending the summer at Les Ambassadeurs the band traveled to England, playing the London Palladium in September, and then to Monte Carlo for the winter. While in England they made a series of recordings for HMV, the biggest label in Britain, in September and October 1929.

The six issued 1929 sides by the "Paris" band (or, as Sissle called it, his "Les Ambassadeurs Orchestra") reveal a dramatically new sound. Although Sissle still sang, increasingly he confined himself to short vocal choruses (and occasional whoops and shouts of encouragement) and let the band take center stage. And what a band it was! He now had some of the best jazzmen available, and he let them shine in hot solos as well as ensemble arrangements. Perhaps the best of the lot was "Kansas City Kitty," a fast novelty that opens with a short and funny scat vocal by Sissle and an unknown male, followed by a series of hot breaks by trumpet, saxophone, trombone, and violin. It even has a bit of "The Charleston" thrown in, and the overall sound is a little like that of the Coon-Sanders Nighthawks, one of the hottest white bands in America.

Other sides recorded for HMV were no less striking. "Camp Meeting Day" is given a big band treatment, quite unlike Sissle's novelty vocal on Pathé in 1920—although he still shouted and laughed ("hee-hee!") to convey the noisy excitement of an old-fashioned black revival meeting. After the last note he interjected a fast "Hallelujah, meetin' adjourned!" In this and in "Miranda" ("a dusky maid of a chocolate shade") it is clear that Sissle was still exploiting black stereotypes in his act, even while mixing in the hot sounds of the jazz age. He was certainly not alone in this, and it was probably what his audience demanded of him.[35]

Sissle's hot new band returned to Les Ambassadeurs for the summer of 1930, shifting to Ciro's in Paris for the fall. They then traveled to England for a few weeks where, in December 1930, they returned to the studio one more time, for English Columbia. There had been considerable turnover in the band, and even though Sissle once again (and for the last time) used the name "Sizzling Syncopators" these were fairly sedate dance-band sides without the hot solos of the HMV sessions. The sudden onset of a worldwide economic depression had tempered the energy and enthusiasm of the 1920s, and much of popular music was at this time becoming calmer and less frenetic. Noble Sissle, as ever, followed the prevailing trends. "Daughter of the Latin Quarter" is a boy-girl novelty in which an unidentified female does a wordless obligato to Sissle's vocal, then engages in a little banter with him in French. "You Can't Get to Heaven That Way" continues the use of mock-black imagery, with a male chorus sarcastically "answering" Sissle's vocal and participating in a long takeoff on "Shout All Over God's Heaven."

Sissle returned to the United States in December 1930, and in February 1931 he played the Palace Theater in New York. That same month he landed the first of two sessions with the Brunswick label. The orchestra lineup was similar to that with which he had recorded in London in December, with one notable exception. Joining on clarinet was Sidney Bechet, one of the all-time greats in the field. By most accounts Bechet had first played with Sissle in Paris during the summer of 1928, but he had not recorded with him until now. These were among Bechet's earlier featured recordings, and as such they are prized by jazz collectors.[36]

On most of the Brunswick sides the band sounds much as it did in London, a big, slick 1930s dance band playing fairly standard arrangements of pop tunes of the day. On "Got the Bench, Got the Park" and "Wha'd Ya Do to Me?" it could be mistaken for any one of a hundred bands then active. "Loveless Love" is a more interesting performance, with a strong rhythm section and nice solos by Bechet and his buddy, trumpeter Tommy Ladnier. Similar solo work is heard on "Basement Blues" and the unissued "In a Cafe on the Road to Calais," which finally saw the light of day on specialist issues many years later.[37] On most sides Sissle makes his vocals short and then gets out of the way so that his talent-filled band can strut its stuff.

After spending one final summer in Paris, Sissle and his band returned to the United States in the fall of 1931, took up residence at New York's Park Central Hotel, and began broadcasting on the CBS radio network. Boosted no doubt by his radio exposure, the Brunswick releases seem to have been reasonably good sellers by the reduced standards of the time. Nevertheless Sissle was very much in the second tier of bandleaders in the big, highly competitive American market. He was billed as the "Colored Rudy Vallee," but he was far behind the *real* Rudy Vallee—and many other big names—in sales and media exposure.[38] And so, in 1932, when he was approached about a revival of Sissle and Blake's great hit *Shuffle Along,* he was willing to listen.

Eubie Blake had taken a somewhat different path after the breakup. He had first partnered with lyricist Henry Creamer to write floor shows. Then, in 1928, he rejoined his former partner Broadway Jones on the Keith-Albee Orpheum circuit in a new, scaled down production of *Shuffle Along,* called *Shuffle Along, Jr.* With a cast of eleven they toured America during the 1928–29 season. Blake and Jones continued in vaudeville during 1929–30, and Blake also contributed songs to the shows *Folies Bergère* and *Hot Rhythm.*

Unlike Sissle, Blake did relatively little recording after the breakup. In December 1929 he made four test recordings for Victor with Broadway Jones, but these were not issued. That is a shame as the titles look interesting, including "House Rent Lizzie," "Dissatisfied Blues," and Fats Waller's "My Fate Is in Your Hands."

Around this time Blake was approached by producer Lew Leslie to write the music for a new revue he had in mind. The book would be by Eubie's old colleague Flournoy Miller and the lyrics by a talented newcomer named Andy Razaf, who was on a hot streak with such recent hits as "Ain't Misbehavin'," "Honeysuckle Rose" and "S'posin'." *Lew Leslie's Blackbirds of 1930,* billed as "Glorifying the American Negro," opened on September 1, 1930, in Brooklyn. In the cast were Miller, Ethel Waters, Buck and Bubbles, Broadway Jones, and Mantan Moreland, among others. Blake's collaboration with Razaf certainly brought him luck, resulting in two big hits, one of which has become an all-time standard. The lovely "Memories of You" was introduced by Minto Cato, a young actress with an exceptionally wide voice range, for whom Blake specifically wrote his soaring melody. "You're Lucky to Me" was the other successful number. Both were recorded by cast member Ethel Waters in a seminal 1930 Columbia recording.[39] After a six-week tour *Blackbirds of 1930* opened on Broadway, where it lasted only sixty-two performances in a very difficult season. However, the score would pay dividends for years to come.

In early 1931, just after Sissle returned to the United States and resumed recording there, Blake, who had been leading the pit orchestra in *Blackbirds,* put together his own band for recording. The first sessions by "Eubie Blake and His Orchestra" were for the small Crown label in New York in March and April 1931. He then had a session at Victor in June, and one final session for Crown in September. Dick Robertson, a popular dance-band vocalist of the day, sang the vocal choruses. The Crown masters were widely reissued, sometimes under other names, on an assortment of low-priced labels. In the late 1930s, when Robertson's fame had eclipsed Blake's, at least one title was reissued as by "Dick Robertson and His Orchestra."

Blake's lineup of musicians was not as stellar as Sissle's, but he had a similar 1930s dance-band sound. Some of the sidemen, such as trombonist Calvin Jones and banjoist Leroy Vanderveer, had worked with him since *Shuffle Along* days, while others (George Rickson, Ben Whittet, Ralph Brown) were drawn from the Johnny Dunn, Charlie Johnson, and Fess Williams orchestras of the 1920s. Most had impeccable jazz credentials, even though they are not listed in the standard jazz biographical dictionaries today.[40] Blake's material consisted largely of current popular songs, such as "Please Don't Talk about Me When I'm Gone," "Little Girl," and the super-cute "Two Little Blue Little Eyes." A few sides stand out, however. There is a wild clarinet solo on "Nobody's Sweetheart" and growling trumpet work on "One More Time." "Blues in My Heart," a Benny Carter song introduced by Fletcher Henderson's Orchestra, is a bluesy lament, while "Thumpin' and Bumpin'" is fast and hot.

Perhaps the most interesting is Blake's version of W. C. Handy's "St. Louis Blues," which was being widely recorded at this time. Once past Robertson's "cute" vocal, it turns into a succession of hot solos by trombone, clarinet, and trumpet. Oddly, Blake himself remained mostly in the background, his piano featured only occasionally and then with rather routine solos.

During the fall of 1931 Blake conducted the pit orchestra for the black musical *Singing the Blues,* which featured a score by Dorothy Fields and Jimmy McHugh.[41] The following year his orchestra was seen in two films aimed at the black market, the feature *Harlem Is Heaven* starring dancer Bill Robinson and the short *Pie Pie Blackbird* with the dancing Nicholas Brothers.

Then there was *Shuffle Along,* the show that refused to die. After the original production in 1921 there had been touring companies, a revival by Miller and Lyles called *Keep Shufflin'* in 1928, and Blake's *Shuffle Along, Jr.* in 1928–29.[42] *Shuffle Along of 1933* reunited Blake, Sissle, and Miller (Lyles died in 1932) in a major restaging of the venerable hit with an entirely new score. Unfortunately the show premiered in December 1932 in the midst of a disastrous Broadway season. It was the absolute depths of the Depression, and few were venturing out for high-price entertainment on the New York stage, surely not such exotic entertainment as the revival of an all-black musical from the 1920s. The show folded after only seventeen performances. It was shortened into a "tab show," a reduced cast production that played moviehouses before the feature film began. This version toured until early 1933, when it too collapsed, leaving the cast stranded in Los Angeles.[43] Among those left unemployed was a young pianist in the show named Nat (King) Cole.

After the demise of *Shuffle Along of 1933* Sissle resumed his bandleading career, appearing at New York's Park Central Hotel and other venues. Later in 1933 he made a Vitaphone film short called *That's the Spirit* with a tap dancer Cora La Redd and a band including trombonist Wilbur De Paris and clarinetist Buster Bailey. Musical numbers included "St. Louis Blues," "Tiger Rag," and "A Shanty in Old Shanty Town."[44]

Though he never reached the first rank of bandleaders in America, Sissle was sufficiently successful to keep his organization together through the rest of the 1930s and into the 1940s. He played hotels and amusement parks, and always employed top-notch black jazz musicians. His "star" instrumentalist was Bechet (who was in and out of the band several times), but he also featured such respected musicians as Wendell Culley, Demas Dean, O'Neil Spencer, Harvey Boone, Chauncey Haughton, and Erskine Butterfield. He gradually turned over vocal duties to Billy Banks and others. While on tour in 1935 he hired a talented teenage singer named Lena Horne.

Sissle recorded intermittently during the 1930s, for Decca and Variety. Many of these recordings have remained available in reissues solely because of the presence of Bechet in the band. They show Sissle's 1930s band to be a highly professional outfit that could play in a variety of styles, from pure "mickey mouse" (as corny bands were called then) to big band swing. The 1934 and 1936 Decca sessions illustrate the band's range. "Under the Creole Moon" is a Latin number, complete with bongos; "Loveless Love" a hard-driving big band version of the old favorite; and "The Old Ark Is Moverin'" a hand-clapping black novelty with Billy Banks rendering the sermon as "Brother Low-Down from Chitlin Switch, Mississippi." The band also recorded slow, sophisticated ballads ("That's What Love Did to Me," with a sexy vocal by eighteen-year-old Lena Horne), fast rhythm numbers ("Polka Dot Rag"), and cornball novelties ("I Wonder Who Made Rhythm"). Sissle featured his star instrumentalists on many of these, with hot solos by trumpet, saxophone, trombone, and especially clarinetist Bechet, who is heard to particular advantage on "Polka Dot Rag."

Some of the songs were cowritten or arranged by Sissle, and several had "black" themes. Times had changed, but there was still a little of the minstrel show in a

Noble Sissle performance. This is what gave the band its personality, and one imagines the preacher's son continuing to wave his hands and interject exclamations during his stage show (he interrupted less now on his records, although he couldn't resist an "ooo-wee!" during "Tain't a Fit Night Out").

In 1937 Sissle was recruited by the independent Variety label to make some new recordings capitalizing on the growing fame of sideman Bechet. These were in fact issued with Bechet's name on the label alongside Sissle's. Four old favorites and two new Bechet numbers were recorded, all of them showcasing the clarinetist. It is a little ironic that the first time either of the coauthors of "I'm Just Wild about Harry" made a full recording of the song it was used as background for a jazz clarinet, sounding not remotely like the saucy love song it was intended to be.[45] Nor did "Bandana Days," an ensemble dance number, make much sense in a big-band swing arrangement. For Bechet's own compositions, "Okey-Doke" and "Characteristic Blues," Sissle used a small combo drawn from the band, dubbed "Noble Sissle's Swingsters," which complemented the clarinetist nicely. On "Characteristic Blues" (cowritten by Sissle) vocalist Billy Banks growls, yodels, and wails to Bechet's wailing clarinet, moaning "I dreamed last night the sky was falling down." Indeed.

Bechet was also featured at a Decca session in February 1938, which would be the Sissle band's last. On these releases Bechet was billed *over* his boss, thusly: "SIDNEY 'POPS' BECHET," and then in smaller letters, "with Noble Sissle's Swingsters."[46] As with the Variety "Swingster" recordings, Bechet was accompanied by a small combo drawn from the Sissle band. Drummer O'Neil Spencer provided the hip vocals, including the drug song "Viper Mad" (this is when drugs were considered strange and exotic). The sound was intimate, much like that of Bechet's own Dixieland combo, "The New Orleans Feetwarmers," with which he recorded during and after his tenure with Sissle. He dominated the recordings with his alternately mellow or hot playing. The sides are prized by jazz enthusiasts and often reissued.

By 1938 Dixieland jazz, played by small combos, was staging a comeback and Bechet decided to take advantage of the trend by leaving Sissle to pursue his own career. With his New Orleans Feetwarmers and other aggregations he made musical history during the remainder of the 1930s and the 1940s. Some of the sides made with Sissle were reissued during the 1940s under Bechet's name.

After Bechet's departure Sissle continued to appear with his band, including a long (1938–42) engagement at Billy Rose's Diamond Horseshoe Club. During the war Sissle and Flournoy Miller staged an updated version of *Shuffle Along* ("the show that would not die") for the USO. In 1945 he returned with his band to the Diamond Horseshoe. He also appeared in a few films made for the black market during the 1940s, among them *Murder with Music* (1941, with singer Bob Howard, featuring the song "I'm a Cute Little Banji from Ubangi"), *Sizzle with Sissle* (1946, with Mabel Lee) and *Howard's House Party* (1947, with Howard).[47]

As the era of the big bands came to a close in the postwar years, so did Sissle's bandleading career. He had been successful at it for nearly twenty years, but now it was time to move on. His band had been more a "show band" than a jazz band per se, but it specialized in rhythm numbers and had certainly made some fine, hot recordings from time to time. Nevertheless it never garnered much respect from the jazz cognoscenti. Longtime *Metronome* writer and cranky critic of the big band era, George T. Simon, gave Sissle this backhanded compliment: "His band seldom projected much rhythmic excitement, though from time to time it featured such diverse jazz soloists as Sidney Bechet and Charlie Parker. . . . What Sissle seemed to want to do more than anything else as a bandleader was to repudiate the stereotype of the Negro musician by showing he could play something other than jazz. In this he was eminently successful."[48] One wonders if Simon had ever listened to "Kansas City Kitty" or "Polka Dot Rag"?

Since the mid-1930s Sissle had been active in various ventures relating to the black community. In 1934 he helped write and produce a pageant depicting the black experience in America, "O, Sing a New Song." In October 1936 he joined six other actors and musicians, including W. C. Handy, in cofounding the Negro Actors Guild, whose goal was to advance the interests of blacks in the theatrical profession. He devoted a great deal of time to this organization, and ultimately became its president.[49] In recognition of his leadership in the community he was elected honorary mayor of Harlem in 1950.

Around 1940 Sissle married his second wife, Ethel; they had two children, Cynthia and Noble Jr. Approaching sixty years of age, in 1949, he might understandably have been thinking of retirement. But then something very surprising happened to one of the songs that he and Eubie had written long ago. It was one of those lightning bolts that sometimes come out of the blue to change one's life in most unexpected ways.

During the 1948 presidential campaign someone on Harry Truman's staff thought it would be a great idea to use that old favorite, "I'm Just Wild about Harry," as the candidate's campaign theme song. The exposure reawakened interest in the song and in its composers. Sissle and Blake had seen each other, off and on, over the years, but now they began to get together more regularly to write new material and to entertain proposals for another revival of—guess what?—*Shuffle Along.*

Blake's career had basically gone into eclipse after the failure of *Shuffle Along of 1933.* He collaborated with a young lyricist named Joshua Milton Reddie on some songs and a show, *Swing It,* which was produced by the WPA in 1937; and with his old friend Andy Razaf, with whom he wrote floor shows, promotional events for commercial sponsors, and, during World War II, the stage piece *Tan Manhattan.*

In 1939 his beloved wife, Avis, died. She had looked after his affairs while Eubie, who was somewhat disorganized, was performing and creating. Without her he was adrift. Finally, in 1945, he married Marion Gant Tyler, a former showgirl who became his second (and final) "life's companion." An excellent administrator, she put his affairs in order and allowed Eubie to go back to doing what he loved best. He chose a surprising course. Now in his sixties, and with tremendous success as a composer behind him, he enrolled in New York University to study the Schillinger system of composition.[50] Always curious, he thought it might help him compose more efficiently. In 1950, at the age of sixty-seven, he graduated with a degree in music.

Sissle and Blake talked over the offers that had come in regarding *Shuffle Along.* Several movie producers were interested, and a London impresario wanted to import the show.[51] But in the end they decided to return to the place where it had all begun, on Broadway. Pearl Bailey was signed to play the lead. Then the "show doctors" went to work, reshaping, recasting, and rewriting until almost nothing was left of the original concept. Instead of high-jinks in a small-town election the plot was now something about black soldiers in World War II Italy. Pearl Bailey quit before the opening, and most of Sissle and Blake's score was thrown out.

Shuffle Along of 1952 opened on May 8, 1952, with Avon Long, Thelma Carpenter, and old Flournoy Miller in leading roles. The critics were devastating; about the only thing they liked were the reprises of original hits "I'm Just Wild about Harry" and "Love Will Find a Way" (the only original songs left in the score). Some even found it offensive. One black critic wrote, "The *Shuffle Along* brand of humor has long since been happily buried—the humor of two shambling comedians murdering the English language and indulging in 'Negroisms' is painfully embarrassing in a much more enlightened 1952."[52] It should be noted that this was a minority view, not mentioned by most white critics. It is debatable how much more enlightened 1952 really was; *Amos 'n' Andy* was running on the CBS Television Network at the time.

The show expired after only four performances and Noble Sissle, sixty-two, and Eubie Blake, sixty-nine, were, it seemed, now truly ready for retirement. Little was heard of them during the decade that followed. Noble Sissle "officially" retired from bandleading in 1960. He then appeared briefly as a disc jockey on New York radio station WMGM and ran a nightclub for a while before retiring to Florida.

Eubie Blake kept going, apparently oblivious to the conventions of aging. Even more remarkable, he kept playing ragtime piano and even made periodic LP recordings for the faithful. His first appears to have been "Maple Leaf Rag," a track recorded in 1951 at the home of author Rudi Blesh and issued on an obscure ten-inch Circle album, *Jamming at Rudi's*.[53] Also in that year RCA Victor issued an extended play mini-album of Blake conducting four songs from the ill-fated *Shuffle Along of 1952*. In 1959, capitalizing on a new vogue for ragtime piano LPs, the 20th Fox label had him record *The Wizard of the Ragtime Piano* with a jazz combo consisting of Buster Bailey (clarinet), Bernard Addison (guitar), Milt Hinton or George Duvivier (bass), and Panama Francis (drums)—plus "participating artist" Noble Sissle on vocals. Eubie chimed in on some cuts, too. This apparently sold well enough to be followed in 1961 by another Fox LP, *Marches I Played on the Old Ragtime Piano,* in which Eubie and a combo tore into such unlikely material as "Stars and Stripes Forever" and "Semper Fidelis." On the last cut he illustrated some of his piano "tricks," accompanied by his own good-natured narration. *Golden Reunion in Ragtime,* on Stereoddities, followed in 1962. On this LP he was reunited with oldtimers Joe Jordan and Charley Thompson, with "Ragtime" Bob Darch as master of ceremonies.

Then came another of those lightning bolts that reorient careers. John Hammond, a powerful and influential producer at Columbia Records, came up with the idea of a retrospective of Blake's long and colorful career. Immaculately produced by the first-rate technicians at Columbia in late 1968 and early 1969, it was issued later that year as a double-LP "souvenir" set titled *The Eighty-Six Years of Eubie Blake.* What a project it was, spanning everything from rags Eubie had written as a teenager ("Charleston Rag") through the great hits from *Shuffle Along* to a new piece, "Blue Rag in 12 Keys." Noble Sissle vocalized on some cuts. The extensive liner notes by historian Robert Kimball brought Eubie's story to many listeners who had previously known him only as a name on records. *The Eighty-Six Years of Eubie Blake* was nominated for a Grammy Award.

The interest stirred by this major-label double LP led to a whole new career for Blake. Big Media began to take notice. Black was now beautiful, and black history was saleable. Here was a piece of *living* black history, who as he neared ninety was as witty and entertaining as ever. Glib, humorous, and still playing well, he was once again in demand as a concert artist, TV performer, lecturer, and general "spark plug of the ragtime revival." America seems to have a fascination with performers who have outlived their contemporaries, and Eubie was the man of the hour. He became a national celebrity, probably more widely known than at any time in his career. He received honorary doctorates from Dartmouth College, the New England Conservatory of Music, Brooklyn College, and Rutgers University, and stories about him appeared in *Time* and *Newsweek*. In 1972 he established his own record company, Eubie Blake Music, operating from his home in Brooklyn. The label ultimately issued nine LPs featuring himself, some old friends (Edith Wilson, Ivan Harold Browning, and, of course, Noble Sissle) and some new protegés (Jim Hession, Mike Lipskin, Terry Waldo). Eubie never forgot his friends. While these LPs were not huge sellers, they must have been eminently satisfying to all involved. Eubie's old piano rolls were also reissued on the Biograph label. He even made some new ones for the still-extant QRS piano-roll company.

Eubie's star rose further in 1973 with the publication of an opulent coffee-table book by Robert Kimball and William Bolcom, titled *Reminiscing with Sissle and Blake.* Containing extensive, well-researched text and gorgeous illustrations, it is a classic of its sometimes maligned genre, the most vivid and entertaining rendering of the team's life story (as well as that of their friend Jim Europe) published up to that time.

Blake was the subject of a French television documentary and in 1974 appeared in an American documentary called *Reminiscing with Sissle and Blake.* Two Sissle and Blake songs were incorporated into the hit all-black revue *Bubbling Brown Sugar,* which opened on Broadway in March 1976 and ran for 766 performances before moving to London. Eubie also had a bit part as a judge in a piano competition in the 1977 Paramount feature film *Scott Joplin.*[54]

Then he was approached about a new musical revue to be based entirely on his music. It was initially to be called *Shuffling Along,* but by the time it reached Broadway in September 1978, the all-singing, all-dancing spectacular had been renamed simply *Eubie!* This last, loose revival of the grand old 1921 show (the last in Eubie's lifetime, at least—we can't guarantee there won't be more) was a substantial hit, running for 439 performances on Broadway and then splitting into touring companies. Featuring Ethel Beatty, Terry Burrell, and the energetic dancing of Gregory Hines and Maurice Hines, it was packed with Eubie's music, from tunes first heard on Pathé discs more than half a century before ("Goodnight Angeline," "Gee I Wish I Had Someone to Rock Me in the Cradle of Love") through the great hits of the 1920s to 1978 ("High Steppin' Days").[55] An original cast album on Warner Brothers records was a substantial seller, and Eubie's score was nominated for a Tony award.

Eubie! was the high point of the 1970s Eubie Blake revival. It was a shame that

Noble Sissle, who had passed away on December 17, 1975, after several years of declining health, was not there to savor it. Eubie certainly was. Seemingly energized by all the attention, he was irrepressible even in his late nineties. I had the pleasure of meeting him in 1977 at a celebration of the one-hundredth anniversary of the phonograph, at Edison's home in West Orange, New Jersey. Eubie was the life of the party (or at least, of his table), cracking jokes, autographing copies of the sheet music for "I'm Just Wild about Harry" (which he thoughtfully provided), and ascending the stage to play the piano, his long, bony fingers as nimble as ever. "It's a shame to take the money from the white folks!" he laughed, with a twinkle in his eye.

Two biographies were published in 1979, one by Lawrence T. Carter and another by Eubie's long-time friend Al Rose. The latter is still in print. Eubie continued to make many media appearances, among them appearances on the 1979 LP *New Orleans Jazz & Heritage Festival* and in the 1980 videocassette *One-Night Stand, A Keyboard Event,* both of which were nominated for Grammy awards. Perhaps the most notable honor was bestowed on October 9, 1981, when he was presented with the Presidential Medal of Freedom by President Ronald Reagan at the White House.[56]

Eubie Blake's 100th birthday, on February 7, 1983, received national attention. However, his beloved Marion had died the year before, and the energy and optimism that had propelled him through the past dozen years drained from him. Suddenly, he was a very old man. Eubie Blake died just five days later, on February 12, ending one of the most remarkable careers in the history of the American popular arts.

SHUFFLE ALONG RECORDINGS, 1921–22 (MEDLEY CONTENTS AND RELEASE DATES ARE IN PARENTHESES)

"Baltimore Buzz"
> Noble Sissle and His Sizzling Syncopators, Emerson 10385 (July 1921)
> Eubie Blake Shuffle Along Orchestra, Victor 18791 (with "In Honeysuckle Time") (Oct. 1921)
> Eubie Blake, piano, Emerson 10434 (with "In Honeysuckle Time") (Oct. 1921)

"Bandana Days"
> Eubie Blake Shuffle Along Orchestra, Victor 18791 (with "I'm Just Wild about Harry") (Oct. 1921)
> The Seven Black Dots, Pathé 20655/Pathé Actuelle 020655 (with "Gypsy Blues") (Dec. 1921)
> James P. Johnson's Harmony Eight, Okeh 4504 (with "Love Will Find a Way") (Mar. 1922)
> Sissle and Blake, Paramount 12002 (Aug. 1922)

"Daddy Won't You Please Come Home"
> Gertrude Saunders with Tim Brymn Black Devils Orchestra, Okeh 8004 (mid-1921)

"Election Day in Jimtown" (comic dialogue)
> Miller and Lyles, Okeh 4766 (Apr. 1923)

"Fourth of July in Jimtown" (comic dialogue)
> Miller and Lyles, Okeh 4766 (Apr. 1923)

"Gypsy Blues"

    Ritz-Carlton Orchestra, Olympic 15121 (Oct. 1921)

    Unidentified orchestra, Little Wonder 1576 (late 1921)

    Ladd's Black Aces, Gennett 4794/Connorized 3030 (Jan. 1922)

    Lanin's Southern Serenaders, Emerson 10467/Regal 9143 (Jan. 1922)

    Julius Lenzberg's Harmonists, Okeh 4461 (Jan. 1922)

    Gene Rodemich Orchestra, Brunswick 2152 (Jan. 1922)

    The Happy Six Orchestra, Columbia A3514 (with "Love Will Find a Way")
        (Feb. 1922)

    Paul Whiteman and His Orchestra, Victor 18839 (Feb. 1922)

    Original Memphis Five, Arto 9140/Bell P-140 (mid-1922)

"If You Haven't Been Vamped by a Brownskin" ("If You've Never . . .")

    Sissle and Blake, Paramount 12002 (Aug. 1922)

"I'm Craving for That Kind of Love"

    Gertrude Saunders with Tim Brymn Black Devils Orchestra, Okeh 8004 (mid-
        1921)

    Sissle and Blake, Emerson 10513? (1922)

"I'm Just Wild about Harry"

    Bar Harbor Society Orchestra, Vocalion 14346 (July 1922)

    Ernest Hussar and His Orchestra, Pathé 20775/PA 020775 (July 1922)

    Bennie Krueger's Orchestra, Brunswick 2272 (July 1922)

    Vincent Lopez Orchestra, Edison 50988 (with "Bandana Days") (Aug. 1922)
    (also issued on Edison cylinder 4604, Oct. 1922)

    Vaughn DeLeath, Gennett 4905 (Sept. 1922)

    Ray Miller Orchestra, Columbia A3640 (Sept. 1922)

    Max Darewski and Stroud Haxton, Zonophone (U.K.) 2292 (Fall 1922)

    Marion Harris with Isham Jones Orchestra, Brunswick 2309 (Oct. 1922)

    Lanin's Southern Serenaders, Banner 1100/Regal 9355 (Oct. 1922)

    Vincent Lopez Hotel Pennsylvania Orchestra, Okeh 4647 (Oct. 1922)

    Paul Whiteman Orchestra, Victor 18938 (Oct. 1922)

    Nathan Glantz and His Orchestra, Emerson 10547 (Nov. 1922)

    Majestic Dance Orchestra, Grey Gull 1124 (late 1922)

    Mitchell's Jazz Kings, Pathé (French) 6565 (late 1922)

    Royal Court Orchestra, Edison Bell Winner (U.K.) 3731 (late 1922)

"In Honeysuckle Time"

    Noble Sissle and Sizzling Syncopators, Emerson 10385 (July 1921)

"Love Will Find a Way"

    Sissle and Blake, Emerson 10396 (Sept. 1921)

    Leroy Smith's Dance Orchestra, Vocalion 14218 (with "Gypsy Blues") (Sept.
        1921)

    Inez Richardson with Fletcher Henderson Orchestra, Black Swan 2023/Para-
        mount 12105 (Fall 1921)

    Selvin's Orchestra, Brunswick 2144 (Dec. 1921)

    The Seven Black Dots, Pathé 20655/PA 020655 (with "In Honeysuckle Time")
        (Dec. 1921)

Charles Harrison, Banner 1011 (1921)

Charles Harrison, Grey Gull 2069 (1922)

Edwin Dale, Columbia A3496 (Jan. 1922)

"Oriental Blues"

Sissle and Blake, Emerson 10396 (Sept. 1921)

"Shuffle Along" medley ("Love Will Find a Way"and "Gypsy Blues")

Harry Raderman Jazz Orchestra, Edison 50866 (Nov. 1921) (also issued on
Edison cylinder 4449, Feb. 1922)

28 Ford T. Dabney: Syncopation over Broadway

One of the most successful black bandleaders and composers of the 1910s was Ford
Dabney. A close associate of Jim Europe, he was a principal composer and conduc-
tor both for dance sensations Vernon and Irene Castle, and for Broadway producer
Florenz Ziegfeld, who featured his orchestra for eight years at his popular *Ziegfeld
Follies* after-theater show, the *Midnight Frolic,* high above Broadway. Dabney was also
one of the most prolific black recording artists of the era, with over fifty sides issued
by 1920, more than any other black artist except for Broadway icon Bert Williams.
Unfortunately they are devilishly hard to find, and as successful as he was, Dabney
is almost completely forgotten today. There are no biographies of him, and only
passing mention in most histories of the era.

Ford Thompson Dabney was born on March 15, 1883, in Washington, D.C., and
raised in a musical atmosphere. Both his father and uncle were professional musicians. The latter, Wendell P. Dabney (1865–1952), went on to achieve considerable
renown as a music educator and author, publishing two widely used instruction
manuals for guitar and mandolin and an interesting-sounding treatise called *Slave
Risings and Race Riots.*[1]

Young Ford attended Armstrong Manual Training School, but preferred music,
which he was taught by his father and private teachers, including Charles Donch,
William Waldecker, and Samuel Fabian. His principal instrument was the piano. By
the age of twenty Dabney had begun his professional career, serving as musical director for a show called *The Czar of Dixie* which opened in Hartford, Connecticut,
on May 30, 1903.[2] In 1904 he accepted an engagement that must have sounded like
a real adventure for a young musician. He agreed to become the official court musician for elderly President Nord Alexis of Haiti and lived in that country for the next
three years. Haiti was (and is) one of the poorest countries in the Western Hemisphere, ruled by iron-fisted dictators who were sometimes overthrown and butch-
ered by their subjects. Voodoo was widely practiced in the hinterlands, and violence
was rampant. Nevertheless the country was admired by blacks in the United States,
since it was black-ruled. Alexis, who seized power in 1902, has been described by one

Ford T. Dabney in later life. (Courtesy of ASCAP)

historian as "a doughty eighty-one year-old warrior with autocratic ideas, whose election was accomplished by mob action and sustained by various assassinations and terrorism." There were constant plots, assassinations, and political turmoil, and Dabney, returning to the United States in 1907, must have been happy to get out alive. The following year his benefactor, President Alexis, was overthrown and run out of the country, a howling mob at his heels.[3]

Compared to that adventure, Dabney's next few years must have seemed calm. He shuttled between Washington, D.C., and New York, establishing a residence in the latter city and hanging out at the Marshall Hotel on West 53rd Street, a favorite gathering spot for musicians.[4] There he met such luminaries of New York's black musical world as Jim Europe, Williams and Walker, and Cole and Johnson. For a time he managed a touring vaudeville act called Ford Dabney's Ginger Girls, with black singer/actresses Effie King and Lottie Gee (Gee went on to become a well-known actress and singer, starring in *Shuffle Along* in the 1920s; she was also Eubie Blake's longtime girlfriend).[5]

Increasingly Dabney devoted his time to composing. Many of his early compositions were rags, including "Oh You Devil" (1909), "The Haytian Rag" (1910, in honor of his recent adventure in that Caribbean nation), "Anoma" (1910), and "Oh You Angel" (1911). "Anoma" is a particularly interesting, delicate piece in rondo format. It later appeared on a piano roll, from which it was picked up by modern ragtime pianists and featured in such collections as *101 Rare Rags.* The word *anoma* is Latin for "without name" or "no name."[6]

Dabney was also active in New York's musical theater, composing the music for a show called *The King's Quest* in 1909.[7] In 1910 he placed the song "That Minor Strain" in the *Ziegfeld Follies,* along with a principal dance number called "The Pensacola Mooch." The former was written in collaboration with Cecil Mack (aka R. C. McPherson), and the latter with Will Marion Cook, showing that by this time Dabney was working with some of the leading writers in New York. Dabney is also said to have written a song called "Porto Rico" that achieved popularity around this time, although some sources credit it to other writers.[8]

Another Dabney-Mack composition published in 1910 attracted relatively little attention at the time but would later become Dabney's most famous and enduring song hit. Originally called "That's Why They Call Me Shine," it was featured by Williams and Walker—perhaps as early as 1907—and the sheet music sported a picture of Walker's glamorous actress wife, Aida Overton Walker. In 1910 Mrs. Walker was using it in the black show *His Honor the Barber,* starring S. H. Dudley and his Smart Set troupe. According to songwriter Perry Bradford, the song was inspired by a real person named "Shine" (possibly "Kid Shine"), a street tough who was a friend of George Walker, and who was caught with Walker in the New York City race riot of August 1900. In his thinly veiled fictional work *Autobiography of an Ex-Coloured Man,* published in 1912, James Weldon Johnson included a character called Shine who was probably based on the same individual.[9] Fourteen years later, in 1924, the song was reissued with revised lyrics by Lew Brown, retitled simply "Shine," and became a major hit.[10]

During 1911 and 1912 Dabney operated two theaters in Washington, the Ford Dabney Theater and the Chelsea (which he bought in October 1911). Assisting him with the management were Louis Mitchell, J. West, and James H. Hudnell. Both live acts and motion pictures were featured, although by December 1911 the Ford Dabney Theater had been converted to a full-time "picture house." He also attempted to organize a vaudeville booking circuit but was apparently unsuccessful. In March 1912 Dabney married Martha J. Gans, the widow of former boxing champion Joe Gans. The *New York Age* reported that "the bride is a member of a well-known family in Baltimore and is regarded as one of the most attractive women in the city. She was graduated from the Baltimore Colored High School in 1900 and taught school there before her marriage to Joe Gans. Since the pugilist's death in August 1910 she has been running the Goldfield Hotel, which was built by the late champion after his defeat of Battling Nelson at Goldfield, Nev."[11]

Even while he was dabbling in talent booking and theater management in Washington, Dabney remained active in New York. He struck up a close friendship with Jim Europe and in 1910 was one of the founding members of Europe's musicians' organization, the Clef Club. Dabney was featured playing his own compositions at several Club concerts beginning in 1910. By the summer of 1913 he had become co-leader and principal pianist of Europe's Society Orchestra, which played for the white elite around New York, as well as for Vernon and Irene Castle. In December 1913, when Europe abruptly resigned from the Clef Club and founded the Tempo Club, Dabney went with him. Europe was named president, Dabney vice-president, and William H. Tyers treasurer.

The years 1913–14 brought major advances in Dabney's career. In December 1913 he recorded for the first time, as one of two pianists in Europe's orchestra at its historic first Victor session. One of the selections recorded at Europe's second session in February 1914 was his own "Castle Walk," cowritten with Europe. Europe and Dabney were collaborating frequently by this time, especially for the Castles, for whom they became virtual "house composers." Securing a publishing contract with Joseph Stern and Company, they wrote many dance numbers for the team, with titles like "Castle Lame Duck" and "The Castle Doggy." Legend has it that they provided the music for one of the most popular dances of the twentieth century, the fox-trot, a dance invented by the Castles. By May 1914 they were turning out so many dance tunes that the publisher started spelling their names backwards ("music by Eporue and Yenbad") to lend variety. One of Dabney's publications was an arrangement of Dvořák's "Humoresque," called "Valse Classique," which was recorded by Prince's Band on Columbia.

The two musicians spent some weekends entertaining at the Castle's Manhasset estate. Irene Castle later recalled, "We always had several weekend guests staying with us and no matter how full a program we had planned for Sunday—all bets were off when Europe and Dabney hove in sight and we would huddle around the piano, enchanted by some new dance number they were in the act of composing for us."[12]

In April 1914 Europe and Dabney traveled to Poughkeepsie, New York, to make piano rolls for the Welte-Mignon company. In the same month their Tempo Club staged a show called "A Night in Tangoland" at Manhattan Casino, which was wildly successful. More than 2,500 persons turned out to see Vernon and Irene Castle dance to music written by Europe and Dabney, and to see Dabney and others conduct their own music.[13]

Dabney sometimes put together his own orchestra, as for a February appearance at the Palace Theatre accompanying Alexander and Logan, who, according to the *New York Age*, were "the hit of the bill." The band members were listed as Messrs. Tyler, Jeter, Gilmore, Joe Myers, and Dabney.[14] Another engagement, the following summer, would be the biggest of his career.

On June 1, 1914, Broadway mogul Florenz Ziegfeld launched an after-theater dance club called the "Danse de Follies" in the roof garden room of the New Amsterdam Theatre, following the main *Ziegfeld Follies* show, to take advantage of the cool summer nights in those days before air conditioning. It was so successful that in January 1915 a full-scale vaudeville show was added between the dance sets, called *Ziegfeld's Midnight Frolic*, entertaining Broadway fun-seekers far into the night. Comedians, jugglers, magicians, singers, and exhibition dancers entertained.[15]

The *Frolic* became one of New York's favorite nightspots in the days before Prohibition. It was open year-round, but there were generally new stage productions twice a year, premiering in the fall and spring (the *Follies* usually premiered in June, and went on tour in the fall). Entertainers in the club were close to (sometimes amid) the audience, giving it a much more intimate atmosphere than the big theater downstairs. *Follies* stars and stars-to-be were featured, including Will Rogers, Eddie Cantor, Bert Williams, Fanny Brice, W. C. Fields, and jazz-dancer "Frisco." Everything was done in the lavish Ziegfeld style, with striking sets by Viennese designer Joseph Urban and dance routines by ace choreographer Ned Wayburn. Of course it wouldn't have been a Ziegfeld show without girls, girls, girls. Ziegfeld had a plate-glass walkway installed above the heads of diners, along which showgirls paraded, their diaphanous dresses blown by tiny fans along the walkway. Favorite attire for showgirls on the main floor was the "balloon" costume, with helium-filled balloons attached to their gowns and headpieces. As they walked around the dance floor the men's cigars and cigarettes invariably burst the balloons. Some of the tables had telephones to phone in requests, and everyone was provided with little wooden hammers to rap the tables when they wanted an encore. After a particularly well-received performance the noise was deafening.

Music was a major part of the entertainment, all the latest tunes plus one-steps, waltzes, fox trots, and tangos for dancing. In order to exploit the new craze for syncopated music, as well as lend an exotic touch, Ziegfeld at one point had a unnamed phonograph company record an authentic Cuban band for him, in Cuba, with the records played back to accompany the dancing of the Dolly Sisters.[16] For live music he booked two orchestras, a white organization and a black band from Jim Europe's Tempo Club.

At first the Tempo Club orchestra was billed as "James Reese Europe's Society Orchestra," but by August it was being identified as "Ford Dabney and His Orchestra," suggesting that Dabney was attracting crowds well enough on his own to dispense with the Europe name. According to two different newspaper reports, Dabney led the seven-piece band, but identifying the members is difficult since only last names were given. It seems likely that the lineup included cornetist G. W. "Cricket" Smith, trombonist Nappy Lee, violinists Allie Ross and William Parquette, drummer Dennis Johnson, and Dabney on piano—in other words, a fairly traditional dance-band instrumentation for the time, with no holdovers from the Palace Theatre lineup.[17] The music was lively and syncopated. An undated review in *Variety* commented that "Dabney's colored orchestra did all the playing, doing it so well that at times the music made them stand up and sway to it while fiddling or blowing."[18]

Ziegfeld was so pleased that he made the syncopated black orchestra a permanent fixture. A 1916 article in the *New York Age* described the atmosphere at the *Midnight Frolic* and the significance of Dabney's engagement there. It was accompanied by a large photo of the leader.

DABNEY'S ORCHESTRA IS MAKING HISTORY
BY LESTER A. WALTON

One of the novel places of amusement on the Gay White Way is *Ziegfeld's Midnight Frolic,* atop the New Amsterdam Theatre, and one of the features of this unusual pleasure resort is Dabney's Syncopated Orchestra. This musical organization enjoys the distinction of being the first colored orchestra to play regularly in a Broadway theatre. And it performs a double duty—furnishes all the music for the soloists, choruses, etc., to sing by, and serves enlivening strains for patrons who desire to indulge in a one-step, fox-trot or a waltz.

Three year ago when the dance craze was at its height, F. Ziegfeld, Jr., who is constantly doing extraordinary things on a large scale in the amusement world, conducted a dancing palace atop the New Amsterdam Theatre, employing two bands—one colored, the other white. He conceived the idea of giving New Yorkers something new in the entertainment line, so he produced *Ziegfeld's Midnight Frolic,* consisting of a two hour show and a dancing program which enables devotees of the terpsichorean art to spend two hours and a half enjoying their favorite form of amusement.

Upon making this radical change Mr. Ziegfeld did the unexpected by discharging the white orchestra and keeping the colored musicians. No one had any idea that a colored orchestra would be installed to accompany the white singers. At the time colored musicians were in great demand as dispensers of dance music, but no one had ever displayed the temerity to put them in a Broadway theatre as the regular house orchestra. But F. Ziegfeld, Jr., is one of the greatest showmen of his time, and has become so because of his daring and originality. He made Bert Williams the star of *Ziegfeld's Follies,* although many of his friends advised him against putting the colored comedian in this big white production. . . .

The experiment of installing a colored orchestra in the *Midnight Frolic* was a big success from the start. Dabney's Syncopated Orchestra has been atop the New Amsterdam Theatre for three years, and along Broadway the colored musicians are accredited with being accomplished and versatile musicians. The orchestra consists of Ford T. Dabney, piano; Allie Ross, violin; William Carroll, violin; William Parquette, mandolin; Charlie Wilson, cello; George Haywood, bass; F. Herrera, flute; Edward [Edgar?] Campbell, clarionet; Crickett Smith, trumpet; Fred Simpson, trombone; and Dennis Johnson, drums.

Ziegfeld's Midnight Frolic is astir when many farmers are about to get up to commence their day's work. It is a haven for amusement lovers who do not care to go home until morning. It is not until 10:30 in the evening, less than half an hour before some theatres close, that the Ziegfeld institution takes on an air of life and activity. Then the patrons dance until midnight. From 12 until 2 o'clock a vaudeville performance, with chorus girls in goodly numbers interspersed on the program at frequent intervals, is given. From 2 until 3 o'clock dancing is in order. Twenty musical numbers are played nightly by Dabney's Syncopated Orchestra for the show alone.

Mr. Ziegfeld proudly refers to the colored musicians as "my boys" and he believes in them because they play with plenty of life and ginger—to use his expression, "plenty of pep." An incident occurred last spring which illustrates the confidence he has in them. Each year when the *Follies* return to New York from their road tour a joint performance and dance are given atop of the New Amsterdam Theatre by the members of the *Follies* and the *Midnight Frolic.* Nathan Franko's Orchestra had been hired to play the musical numbers for the show, and was to alternate with Dabney's Syncopated Orchestra in furnishing the dance music.

Both orchestras were instructed to attend the rehearsal. Franko's orchestra numbered over forty musicians. There were eleven men in the Dabney organization. After the white musicians had played over one of the vocal selections several times,

Mr. Ziegfeld, who was standing nearby, suggested that "my boys" try the number, as he wanted a little more "pep." The eleven musicians, trembling from suppressed excitement, knowing that they were the cynosure of all eyes, nervously took the orchestral arrangements and played as never before. They played as if inspired and sounded more like fifty men than eleven. When they finished there was a big round of applause from onlookers, and Mr. Ziegfeld dryly remarked that "my boys" had better play the number.

A few minutes later the suggestion was again made by Mr. Ziegfeld that "my boys" be permitted to play another number, which they did. The outcome was that the Dabney Syncopated Orchestra was designated to play all the numbers in the show. Franko's Orchestra was retained to alternate with the dance music.

Those familiar with the record made by the colored musicians atop the New Amsterdam Theatre do not wonder why Mr. Ziegfeld has kept them for three years, which is a long life in the theatrical world. The answer is: They make good with a big "G."[19]

Dabney continued to write music, publishing a new rag called "The Georgia Grind" (1915), which was quickly recorded by Victor, Columbia, and Pathé.[20] With Europe he wrote the topical song "At That San Francisco Fair" for the musical *Nobody Home,* which had a successful run on Broadway. (Additional lyrics for the song were contributed by young composer Jerome Kern.) Dabney also remained active in the Tempo Club and was one of the regular conductors at its Manhattan Casino concerts in 1915 and 1916.

By 1917 Ford Dabney was one of the best-known bandleaders in New York. As the revolutionary sounds of jazz filled the air, sparked by the arrival of the Original Dixieland Jass Band at Reisenweber's in January, record companies were scrambling to sign performers who could play the new music. Dabney led a dance band, not a jazz combo, but he played syncopated music at one of the best-known nightclubs in the city. He was approached by the Aeolian-Vocalion company, a maker of quality phonographs and musical instruments that had just begun recording at its new studios on West 43rd Street, stockpiling masters in anticipation of a label launch in early 1918. It had arranged to record several sides by the ODJB, before that quintet was signed exclusively by Victor, and Dabney would add another well-known name to its roster.

Dabney's initial sessions appear to have taken place around August 1917. Indeed, some of the Dabney and ODJB catalog and matrix numbers are so close as to suggest the two bands may have passed each other in the corridor outside the recording studio. Many years later Dabney provided researchers with a "collective band personnel" for his early recordings, consisting of Cricket Smith, cornet, Nappy Lee, trombone, Edgar Campbell, clarinet, Alonzo Williams, saxophone, John Haywood, brass and string bass, Dennis Johnson, drums, and himself on piano. It is obvious from listening to the records that instrumentation changed from side to side. Piccolos and twin cornets (or trumpets) are heard on several sides, and a banjo is heard on some of the later recordings. Dabney himself mentioned that two violins were sometimes used, they being Allie Ross and Bernard "Buttercup" Parker, to which discographer Brian Rust adds a third, Nimrod Jones.

The repertoire was a mix of Tin Pan Alley pop tunes and syncopated novelty songs, some by black composers, and was clearly meant to mirror the kind of material Dabney was playing for dancers at the *Midnight Frolic.* Among the first batch of titles, recorded in August and November 1917, were Shelton Brooks's "Darktown Strutters' Ball," Creamer and Layton's "That's It," "The Jass 'Lazy Blues,'" and the trombone novelty "Sally Trombone." More mainstream (and white) were two tunes from the hit Broadway show *Cheer Up,* "Melody Land" and "Cheer Up, Liza," and Ted Snyder's "Paddle-Addle in Your Little Canoe."

Modern writers generally disdain Dabney's recordings (or overlook them), maintaining that they aren't "jazz." They were never intended to be. This was a syncopated dance band, and most of its recordings are in relatively strict tempo, for dancing. Within those confines Dabney's men play with a certain verve and looseness, occasionally taking liberties with the melodic line, for example, at the end of "Darktown Strutters' Ball," when the clarinet squeals like a siren, and Cricket Smith cuts loose on the cornet. Smith carries the melody on the heavily syncopated "That's It" and the loping, jazzy "Jass 'Lazy Blues,'" while twin slide trombones dominate the fast-paced "Sally Trombone." The drummer, with his syncopated blocks and bells, is kept busy on all these sides, and a piccolo player chimes in on some.

Cricket Smith, whose commanding cornet work is prominent on almost all Dabney recordings, was a veteran of Jim Europe's historic 1913–14 recordings and is regarded as a pioneer jazzman. One modern writer noted that on "Darktown Strutters' Ball," Smith "virtually blazes away from the strict arrangement and injects his own musical temperament into the score."[21] Several of Dabney's other sidemen had respectable careers as well. Dabney's Band may not have been playing what we now consider jazz, but it was certainly jazz-influenced. It was a first-rate dance ensemble, and its recordings exhibit the "pep" that Ziegfeld was so fond of talking about.

Vocalion occasionally used Dabney to accompany its regular vocalists, and in fact on his first (or at least, lowest-numbered) recording Dabney's band backed Arthur Fields on another version of "Darktown Strutters' Ball"—an early, and unusual, example of a white vocalist recording with a black orchestra. Though not the first example of interracial recording, it was progressive for its time.

Another unusual aspect of Dabney's recordings is their length. Vocalion was experimenting in 1917 with close grooving on its records which allowed nearly five minutes of music on a ten-inch disc. The label bragged about this in its 1918 catalog, claiming that "in addition to its superior recording facilities, the Vocalion record is able, through the system of cutting used, to accommodate a selection of music *one-third* longer than the ordinary disc."[22] Dabney's instrumental version of "Darktown Strutters' Ball" runs for four and three-quarters minutes, and "Paddle-Addle" about four and a half. That was fine for dancing, but for listening it results in endless repetitions of the melody, which can be rather monotonous. Also, the prominent use of a tuba for rhythm and the rat-tat-tat drumming make these early sides sound a little like a somewhat raggy military band.

Perhaps recognizing Dabney's talents as a band master, Vocalion had him record a couple of straightforward marches with a real military band in early 1918, billed appropriately as by Dabney's Military Band. "Our Sammies March" and "A Winning

Fight" were spirited affairs with cornets blaring, piccolos twittering, cymbals crashing, and drums in march tempo. The stirring performances may not have been appropriate for dancers at the New Amsterdam Roof Garden (unless they wanted to march around the floor!), but they were appropriate for the patriotic times. They also demonstrated the versatility of Dabney's musicians.

Vocalion announced the debut of its new label in May 1918, and the first list included several Dabney recordings. Sales literature for the label is almost as rare as the records themselves, but the 1918 catalog said of its celebrated artist, "Dabney's Band with *Ziegfeld's Midnight Frolic* attained its initial popularity [with] the exclusive dancing set of New York by supplying the inspiring music originally used by the famous Castles. For the past three years, however, its fascinating syncopations have contributed largely to the success of the *Midnight Frolic*. Several snappy, up-to-the-minute fox trots and one-steps are presented in the first record bulletin, which demonstrate the impossibility of 'sitting out' dances when Dabney's Band plays."

Dabney's connection with Ziegfeld was also promoted on the record labels, most of which read, "Dabney's Band—With Ziegfeld's Midnight Frolic." Although the records were well recorded and well played, they apparently sold in very small quantities judging by their extreme rarity today. There were several reasons for this, none of them having to do with the artist. As a new label, Aeolian-Vocalion had limited distribution, and what it had was primarily through dealers in high-priced phonographs and musical instruments. Its discs were vertically recorded to circumvent the Victor and Columbia lateral-cut patents, which meant they could not be played on phonographs commonly in use. They were full priced ($.75 for the ten-inch and $1.25 for the twelve-inch) and were launched at a time of wartime materiel shortages which may have limited the company's production capacity. No wonder they're hard to find. If the Original Dixieland Jazz Band had remained on Aeolian-Vocalion we might not be talking about them so much today.

Despite these limitations, Vocalion wanted to build up its catalog and had the financial resources to do so. Presumably Dabney and his musicians didn't care how well the records sold as long as they got paid, so over the next two years they made more than fifty recordings for the label. Four titles were recorded in the spring of 1918, besides the two marches previously mentioned. All were Tin Pan Alley songs by white composers, including the enormously popular World War I hit, "Hello Central, Give Me No Man's Land"—a pathetic ballad about a little child who tiptoes to the telephone in the middle of the night to try to telephone her daddy somewhere in France. The song was being sung to great effect by Al Jolson in his hit show *Sinbad*. Listeners to Dabney's instrumental version were spared the lachrymose lyrics: "I want to know why mama starts to weep / When I say, 'now I lay me down to sleep . . .' / Hello central, give me No Man's Land."

Dabney's version was played at strict dance tempo, with no variation, on a twelve-inch disc, which allowed four complete renditions of the verse and chorus. This was obviously meant for dancing, as it is rather repetitive for listening. Also recorded in early 1918 were a full five-minute version of "I'm Sorry I Made You Cry," on the other side of "Hello, Central"; "There's a Lump of Sugar Down in Dixie," another Jolson hit from *Sinbad;* and another trombone novelty, "Slidin' Sid."

Touches of syncopation are heard in all three, particularly "Slidin' Sid," with its ragtime rhythms, drum "shots," and odd little piccolo interjections. Dabney's heavy use of brass and percussion, including prominent tuba and drums, continued to give his records a "military band" sound.

That began to change with four sides recorded in the fall of 1918. "Swinging Along" and "Springtime," two pleasant fox trots written by Gene Buck and David Stamper for the *Midnight Frolic,* sounded unlike anything previously recorded by Dabney. With less prominent tuba, piccolos, and military-style drumming, his band here sounded more like a traditional dance band. "Swinging Along" has interesting minor-key strains, while "Springtime" features a kind of Latin rhythm. Cricket Smith's cornet takes a forceful lead on both sides, although other instruments are heard as well, and the entire band is allowed to go a little wild at the end of "Springtime." It is a shame that these two little gems are not better known. Dabney essayed another one of the numerous commercial blues popular at the time with "Just Blue," by white performer/composers Wheeler Wadsworth and Victor Arden (of the All Star Trio).[23] Cricket Smith again took the lead, his cornet bouncing off a squealing clarinet and swooping trombone, for an appropriately silly performance of what was essentially a novelty song.

The other side recorded at this time was a lively medley of songs from the Feist publishing company ("The Feist All-Hit Medley"), consisting of "Everything Is Peaches Down in Georgia," and the wartime novelties "K-K-K-Katy," about a stuttering soldier, and "Good Morning, Mr. Zip-Zip-Zip!," about those distinctive military buzz-cuts. Although these were instrumentals, one can almost hear the boozy patrons at the New Amsterdam Roof Garden lustily singing along.

> K-k-k-Katy,
> Beautiful Katy,
> You're the only g-g-g-girl that I adore,
> When the m-m-m-moon shines,
> Over the c-c-c-cowshed,
> I'll be waiting at the k-k-k-kitchen door!
>
> Good morning, Mr. Zip-Zip-Zip,
> With your hair cut just as short as mine!

Dabney was back in the studio for more than a dozen new titles during early 1919, most of them mainstream white popular songs and novelties. Patriotism remained a major theme in popular music in the euphoria surrounding the end of the war, and "Mr. Sousa's Yankee Band" was a blatant attempt to cash in on the popularity of bandmaster John Philip Sousa, which was at an all-time high. A collection of faux-Sousa march strains, it was played with appropriate verve and flourishes by Dabney. Interestingly it is not in strict military band tempo but is a one-step. "Old Glory Goes Marching On" was in a similar vein, with a sort of loping march tempo. The biggest war-related hit of the immediate postwar period was the wry novelty, "How Ya Gonna Keep 'Em Down on the Farm (After They've Seen Paree)?" Dabney's medley version, incorporating a couple of other tunes, was delivered with suitable energy, although it is not as fast-paced and raucous as the famous version by Jim Europe's 369th Infantry Regiment ("Hell Fighters") Band, which was recorded at about the same time for Pathé.

Commercial blues continued to be popular, and Dabney recorded several more of these, including "Indigo Blues," "Rainy Day Blues," "Missouri Blues," and a novelty about the craze, "A Foxy Cure for the Blues." Perhaps the most interesting was "Rainy Day Blues," with its changing tempi and odd little harmonies between clarinet and piccolo toward the end. Trombone novelties, with their swoops and barks, remained popular and were represented by the fast-paced "Lassus Trombone" and "Miss Trombone," both by well-known band composer Henry Fillmore. The latter, subtitled "A Slippery Rag," features some furious drumming, presumably by Dennis Johnson.

Yet another change of pace was "Keep Smiling," a sweet, sunny ballad by Rudolf Friml from the smash hit musical *Sometime.* Cricket Smith fairly "crooned" the melody on his cornet in this long, syrupy performance. Vocalion also had Dabney accompany vocalist Arthur Fields on several sides during early 1919, including such drivel as "You Can't Blame the Girlies at All."

Renewed for his sixth season at the *Midnight Frolic,* Dabney continued his heavy recording schedule with Vocalion during the summer and fall of 1919, playing an even wider range of material than before. Among the commercial blues were "Squealing Pig Blues," "Beautiful Ohio Blues," "Slow Drag Blues," "Florida Blues," "Lonesome Blues," "Camp Meeting Blues," and "Blues My Naughty Sweetie Gives to Me." Of those heard by this author, "Camp Meeting Blues" is the most distinctive, with its "war chant" rhythms and pulsing beat. Other interesting titles included Clarence Williams's "I Ain't Gonna Give Nobody None o' This Jelly-Roll," "Frisco's Kitchen Stove Rag (Get the Wood, Burn It Up)," and "The Dancing Deacon," the latter a tribute to Clef Club president Fred "Deacon" Johnson. It is interesting to compare the Dabney version of "The Dancing Deacon" to the one recorded by Dabney's friend and colleague Jim Europe for Pathé, a few months earlier. The instrumentation and performances are quite similar, but Dabney's attack sounds somewhat sharper, due in large part to Cricket Smith's strong cornet. Smith, of course, was Europe's former lead cornet player. Such comparisons illustrate how important it is for historians of early jazz to consider all recordings involving key players of the era, not just those officially admitted into the "jazz canon."

On many of his later sides Dabney experimented with new instrumentation, edging closer to the saxophone and string-dominated dance-band sound that was becoming increasingly popular. Saxophone and banjo, two instruments previously seldom (if ever) heard on Dabney recordings, are prominently featured on "Jelly-Roll" and "Breeze." Twin violins take the lead on the exotic "On the Streets of Cairo," which sounds at times almost like a Victor record by Joseph C. Smith's Orchestra (which was known for its "dancing violins.") On "My Laddie" we finally get to hear Dabney's own piano as a prominent part of the mix, although he never takes a solo. As if to emphasize the "new sound," most of these were labeled as by Dabney's Novelty Orchestra (or Novelty Band), with no mention of the *Midnight Frolic.*

What is missing on these later sides are the raggy rhythms and occasional vamping by the cornet, trombone, or clarinet. The drummer seems to have been sedated as well. On "What's Worth While Getting" Dabney could be leading any one of a hundred bland dance bands of the early 1920s, showing little evidence of his Clef Club roots.

Two final recordings made in February 1920 were "Wedding and Shimmie and Jazz" (aka "The Wedding of the Shimmie and Jazz") and "When My Baby Smiles," the latter an ephemeral pop tune by Irving Berlin not to be confused with the later song "When My Baby Smiles at Me." Despite the interesting titles, both are in strict dance tempo, similar to the late 1919 dance-band sides, and have little to distinguish them.

Vocalion used Dabney to provide accompaniment for vocalists a few more times during his final months with the label. In September 1919 two sides were made with Arthur Fields, and in October, two with Billy Murray. Although these were vocal recordings the band was prominently featured. "Spanking the Baby" begins with an instrumental treatment of the song lasting nearly a minute and a half before Fields comes in with his vocal. The band then interjected suitable sound effects (rattles, baby cries) to illustrate the lyrics. Dabney regularly provided accompaniment for vocalists at the *Midnight Frolic,* so this may have been representative of his work there.

Aeolian-Vocalion converted to lateral recording in January 1920, and Dabney's final three releases were issued in that format, the last of them being announced in March 1920. Shortly thereafter all of his many earlier vertical-cut recordings were deleted, never to be seen again. The three lateral releases, featuring his later dance band, were deleted from the catalog by 1923, marking the end of his five-year tenure with the label.

One modern writer has noted that Dabney's music was "somewhat anachronistic and shows the enormous gap left in black New York musical life by the death of [James] Europe . . . it may not come as a surprise to learn that Ziegfeld dispensed with Dabney's services in 1920, in favor of Art Hickman's Orchestra, with its saxophone section and novel orchestral arrangements."[24] This, of course, ignores the fact that Ziegfeld, who kept relentlessly abreast of (if not ahead of) every new trend in show business, had by then employed Dabney as his principal orchestra leader at the *Midnight Frolic* for six years. Nevertheless, if his records are any indication, by 1920 Dabney was indeed falling behind the current musical trends. Full orchestras like those of Hickman and Paul Whiteman, with saxophone sections, elaborate syncopated arrangements, and less of a brass band sound, were taking over. The small Dixieland units so popular from 1917 to 1919 were also being pushed aside.

Dabney's association with Ziegfeld was not over, however. Hickman, a sensationally successful San Francisco musician whose band had starred in the *Midnight Frolic* for a single week in mid-1919, opened the 1920–21 season as resident bandleader. By November he was gone and Dabney had returned. Max Hoffmann took over the *Midnight Frolic* orchestra in February 1921. Dabney returned once again later that year and continued until the *Frolic* closed permanently in 1922. Evidently the entertainment was getting more and more elaborate, as a photo dated 1920 shows Dabney leading a forty-piece *Frolic* orchestra, with everybody dressed in tuxedos.[25]

Ford Dabney remained an important figure in New York's black musical life after his run at the *Midnight Frolic.* Although he was still in his thirties, he was increasingly associated with the "old guard." His friend and partner Jim Europe had been killed in May 1919. At his funeral, Dabney led "the famous 'Jimmy' Europe Jazz Band" through the streets of Harlem, its members wearing black arm bands and silently carrying their instruments in tribute to their fallen leader.[26] Dabney remained close to Bert Williams, accompanying him in special appearances and contributing the song "You Can't Shake That Shimmie Here" to his act in 1919. But Williams too was of the "old school," and in March 1922 Dabney found himself serving as an honorary pallbearer at the comedian's funeral.

Dabney continued to lead orchestras in appearances in New York and Washington, D.C., during the early 1920s. Some of his Washington concerts are said to have influenced young Duke Ellington, who was just beginning his career in that city. Ellington later called Europe and Dabney two of the "great talents" he followed early in his career.[27] Dabney also made additional recordings. In October 1921 he made two tests for Victor with his "Syncopated Orchestra," consisting of an entirely different lineup of musicians than in his *Midnight Frolic* days. The instrumentation, which included two trumpets, trombone, clarinet, alto saxophone, violin, and drums, suggests that he was trying to adapt to the new sounds of the day. However the tunes, "Dapper Dan" and "Sweet Cookie," were not issued.

He had better luck the following spring with the same orchestra. Three titles were recorded in Paramount's New York studios in March and May of 1922, "Sweet Man o' Mine," "Doo Dah Blues," and "Bugle Call Blues." The most interesting of the three is his own "Bugle Call Blues," which alternated snatches of bugle calls such as "Reveille" and "Taps" with jazz riffs. It is a song with a complicated history. There are, in fact, a number of songs built around army bugle calls, with the device being used as early as 1916 by Eubie Blake and Carey Morgan in a tune called "Bugle Call Rag." In 1922, the same year that Dabney recorded his "Bugle Call Blues," some musicians with Friar's Society Orchestra (later known as the New Orleans Rhythm Kings) came up with their own tune based on bugle calls, which—confusingly—they also called "Bugle Call Blues." By 1923 the title of the latter song had been changed to "Bugle Call Rag." That version, credited to Jack Pettis, Billy Meyers, and Elmer Schoebel, went on to become one of the most recorded songs in all of jazz over the next twenty years, while the Dabney and Blake-Morgan songs disappeared. That is a shame, as Dabney's "Bugle Call Blues" is a catchy number.

All three 1922 Dabney recordings were in the dance-band style popular at the time, with saxophones and banjos prominent on "Doo Dah Blues" and "Sweet Man o' Mine." "Bugle Call Blues" features a strong trumpet lead, believed to be by either Pike Davis or Wesley Johnson, both top-notch jazz session men of the 1920s. Davis is heard on a number of New York and London recordings of the period, including some by Duke Ellington, and played in the pit orchestra for *Lew Leslie's Blackbirds* in 1928; Johnson backed blues vocalists including Ethel Waters and Lucille Hegamin in the early 1920s. Other sidemen on these sessions had notable recording careers as well. Dabney was obviously picking his musicians with care.[28]

Paramount leased its masters freely, and Dabney's 1922 recordings turned up on a number of budget labels, including Puritan, Banner, Famous, Triangle, and National Music Lovers, sometimes issued under pseudonyms (e.g., by the "Master

Melody Makers"). Although well played they were pop tunes of the day and soon faded from sight. They are the last recordings Dabney is known to have made.

In 1923, drawing on his wide contacts, Dabney opened an entertainment bureau. He spent the following years entertaining in Palm Beach, Miami, and Newport, and played several seasons at the Palais Royale in Atlantic City. He also kept writing, scoring his greatest success as a composer in 1923 when he revived his 1910 song "That's Why They Call Me Shine." With slightly revised lyrics by Lew Brown, and retitled simply "Shine," it was first recorded by Herb Wiedoeft and His Orchestra on Brunswick in August 1923. Additional recordings quickly followed by the California Ramblers, the Virginians, and the Original Memphis Five, as well as a vocal version by vaudeville stars Van and Schenck. "Shine" was one of the top sellers of 1924. One modern study estimates that it was a bestseller from June to September 1924, reaching the top ten. It would become Dabney's most profitable copyright by far.[29]

In 1927 Dabney wrote the music for *Rang Tang,* a Broadway musical starring Flournoy Miller and Aubry Lyles, which opened in June. It was a black revue in the style of *Shuffle Along,* with Miller and Lyles grafting some of their old vaudeville routines onto a silly plot about two debt-ridden Harlem barbers who flee their creditors, steal a plane, and fly to Africa (just like Lindbergh!) in search of treasure. Unlike Lindbergh, they find their airplane beginning to disintegrate, with the wings falling off, but they manage to land safely on the Dark Continent where they meet the queen of Sheba, the king of Madagascar, and a Zulu tribe. According to the *Evening World,* "Ford Dabney wrote some music which makes the feet crazy to dance. The lyrics by Jo Trent are bright and rhythmical. . . . Among the numbers which go over the strongest are 'Sambo's Banjo,' 'Jungle Rose,' 'Sweet Evening Breeze,' 'Summer Nights,' 'Zulu Fifth Avenue' and 'Rang Tang,' the latter a new dance number that is certain to be popular in the restaurants and nightclubs." After observing that "first rate dancing is a concomitant of all negro shows," the *New York Times* waxed enthusiastic about the choreography of "Monkeyland," as well as another number in which the entire chorus strummed banjos as they danced. *Variety* thought the plot was pretty threadbare but praised the "tuneful" musical numbers.[30]

Although *Rang Tang* had a successful run of 119 performances and obviously entertained those in the theater, it produced no hit songs. Historian John Graziano, analyzing the song "Jungle Rose," argues that its rhythms are those of a march, and "decidedly old-fashioned." Only by the introduction of some unusual harmonic progressions did Dabney give the song "new life."[31]

As the 1920s gave way to the 1930s Dabney gradually became less active. Few mentions of him are found in the theatrical papers of the day. In 1934 an advertisement for the Columbia film *Social Register* with Colleen Moore noted that special musical material for the movie had been contributed by Ford Dabney. He finally became a member of ASCAP in 1937, and in 1941 he was reported to be a member of the new Crescendo Club, an association of black songwriters.

No doubt Dabney was able to live comfortably on the royalties from his songs, especially "Shine," which had become a much bigger and long-lived hit than anyone could have imagined. It was one of the standards of the jazz and swing repertoire in the 1920s and 1930s, with recorded versions by the Jesse Stafford Orchestra (1928), the Dallas String Band (1929), Boyd Senter (1929), Louis Armstrong (1931), Bing Crosby with the Mills Brothers (1932), Chick Bullock (1932), the Red Nichols Orchestra (1934), Pinky Tomlin (1935), the George Hall Orchestra with Dolly Dawn (1935), Ella Fitzgerald (1936), Django Reinhardt and the Quintette of the Hot Club of France (1936), the Benny Goodman Quartet (1937), and the Jack Teagarden Orchestra (1940), among others. Several of these recordings are considered classics today, especially the versions by Armstrong, Crosby, Fitzgerald, Reinhardt, and Goodman. Goodman featured the song in his famous 1938 Carnegie Hall concert.

"Shine" was heard in movies as early as 1928, when it was sung in a Vitaphone film short by a black quartet called the Pullman Porters. Louis Armstrong used it in his bizarre 1932 short film *Rhapsody in Black and Blue,* and it was interpolated into the feature films *Birth of the Blues* (1941), *Cabin in the Sky* (1943), *The Benny Goodman Story* (1955), and *The Eddy Duchin Story* (1956). It was a major hit on radio in the 1930s, with 3,000 radio plays in 1935 and nearly 6,000 in 1937, according to ASCAP logs.[32]

"Shine" received a new lease on life in early 1948 when a Mercury recording by an energetic newcomer named Frankie Laine became a top-ten hit. Since then the song has been firmly entrenched as a jazz/pop standard, its origins on the streets of New York at the turn of the century long forgotten. Blues-rock guitarist Ry Cooder, in the notes to his 1978 album *Jazz,* commented, "'Shine' has been recorded over the years by nearly everybody, but rarely in its original form." Woody Allen used it in his 1998 jazz tour documentary, *Wild Man Blues.* The cheerful opening verse is likely to be heard for many years to come.

> Just because my hair is curly,
> Just because my teeth are pearly,
> Just because I always wear a smile . . .
> That is why they call me Shine!

Ford T. Dabney passed away on June 21, 1958, at the age of seventy-five. His residence at the time was 318 West 139th Street, in the same Harlem neighborhood he had called home since the early 1910s. He left a widow, Martha (who died in 1961), and a son, Ford Jr. Jim Europe, Bert Williams, and other friends from the heady days of World War I were by now a distant memory, and obituaries in the *New York Times* and *Variety* treated him as a real old-timer, remembered mostly for "Shine," and his association with the Castles and Ziegfeld. A few years before his death he was interviewed by writers from the collector's magazine *Record Research,* but little has been published about him in the years since.[33] Alain Locke, in his influential 1936 book, *The Negro and His Music,* listed Dabney—along with Jim Europe, Will Marion Cook, and W. C. Handy—as one of four musicians who "organized Negro music out of a broken, musically illiterate dialect and made it a national and intellectual music." Dabney's special contribution was that he "revolutionized the Negro dance orchestra."[34] Perhaps it is time to revisit the records he made, and the important role he played in New York's black musical life, in the years just before the "Jazz Age."

29 W. C. Handy

W. C. Handy, "Father of the Blues," is one of the best-known black Americans of the twentieth century and his "St. Louis Blues" is one of its best-known songs. Less well known are the struggles he endured, the important role that records played in popularizing his innovative music during the 1910s, and the story of his own recordings, most of them made between 1917 and 1923.

Handy is one of those lucky musicians who lived long enough to enjoy the fruits of his early accomplishments, as well as the acclaim of later generations. He also wrote an unusually vivid and engaging autobiography, *Father of the Blues* (1941), which has served as the basis of much that has been written about him and, to a large extent, allowed him to define how he would be remembered.[1]

William Christopher Handy was born on November 16, 1873, in Florence, Alabama, the son of ex-slaves. Both his father, Charles, and paternal grandfather, William Wise Handy, were ministers who disapproved of secular music and discouraged him from seeking a musical career. In his autobiography Handy told of buying a guitar with money he had saved, only to have his stern father make him take it back and exchange it for a dictionary. Handy's aptitude for music was unmistakable, however, and Charles did pay for organ lessons in order that his son could learn the proper kind of music. Eventually young W. C. bought a rotary-valve coronet (a kind of trumpet) and practiced on his own. He also studied music at the Florence District School for Negroes.

A lad with a strong independent streak, as well as a certain wanderlust, Handy left home at the age of fifteen to join a small-time minstrel troupe only to have it fail and leave him stranded. He returned to school to finish his education. An excellent student, he easily passed a teaching exam upon graduation and became a teacher in Birmingham, but the pay was so poor he quit and worked for a time in a pipe-works plant before deciding that music was truly his calling.

His first attempt at making a living in music was a disaster. Handy and some friends formed a vocal quartet and hitchhiked to Chicago, hoping to find work at the long-awaited 1892 World's Columbian Exposition, which was being organized to celebrate the 400th anniversary of Columbus's "discovery" of America. When they arrived they found that the fair had been postponed (it would finally open in May 1893); moreover, the country was sliding into a deep economic depression. With employment prospects grim, the quartet disbanded and Handy wandered the Midwest, landing for a time in St. Louis. Penniless, hungry, and literally sleeping in the streets, he later described it as one of the most miserable times of his life, and yet one that affected him greatly. His experiences would find their way into some of his most memorable lyrics. Of the famous opening line of "St. Louis Blues," "I hate to see de evenin' sun go down," he later remarked, "if you ever had to sleep on the cobbles down by the river in St. Louis, you'll understand that complaint."[2]

Eventually Handy settled in Henderson, Kentucky, where he played with a black

When Handy Plays the "Blues"

W. C. Handy's band members refused to have their picture taken, so Columbia commissioned this drawing to accompany his initial releases in 1918. (Columbia supplement, Feb. 1918)

orchestra and learned a great deal about vocal music from Professor Bach, the helpful director of a first-rate German singing society. In August 1896 he received an offer to join Mahara's Mammoth Colored Minstrels, one of the premiere black minstrel troupes then touring the country, as a cornetist.

The next four years provided Handy with a graduate education in show business, as Mahara's Minstrels crisscrossed the United States, Canada, and Mexico. The talented young cornetist was soon promoted to leader of one of the bands traveling with the company, and reports in theatrical journals began to take note of him. The minstrel shows of this era were great theater, and impresarios like Irishman W. A. Mahara knew how to put on a good show for entertainment-starved citizens of small towns. A September 1896 report described the traditional parade through town that preceded the evening performance. "The street parade is in full dress, silk hats and eight silk banners bearing various designs, with six Mexican-dressed drum majors and pickaninny drum corps, six walking gents with white Prince Albert suits and white silk hats, kid gloves and canes, with W. A. Mahara and his St. Bernard dog, Sport, in the lead of the parade."[3]

A year later Handy was marching at the head of one of the bands: "The parade includes two bands, one large band of twenty pieces under the leadership of W. C. Handy, and a pickaninny band of fourteen pieces under Joseph Brink. W. A. Mahara rides in front in a carriage beautifully trimmed, while four buglers ride horseback."[4]

Handy was a popular addition to the troupe. An 1898 report noted that "Mr. Handy has been three seasons with [Mahara's Minstrels] and has become quite popular as a cornet soloist due to the 'soul' which he puts in all he plays." A review in June of the same year said that Mahara had "undoubtedly one of the best bands in the country," while another, in August, said, "Prof. W. C. Handy's clever band of 26 pieces is the feature of the parade and is greeted with cheers by the delighted crowd, which enjoys the patriotic music."[5] He later claimed to have made his first recording during these years, apparently for an Edison dealer in a town he was passing through. The recording was used in a local coin-in-slot jukebox.

> My first experience with a talking machine . . . had been back in Helena, Montana, in 1897. I had made a record with my minstrel band on an old cylinder machine. Funny contraption, that old affair. To hear the recording you had to place two rubber tubes in your ears. Each record began with a spoken announcement much like the radio announcer's lines today. "You will now hear 'Cotton Blossoms' as played by Mahara's Minstrel Band on Edison records." After playing our number each of us was permitted to put the rubber tubes in his ears and thus listen for ourselves. Other music lovers who wished to hear the record had to pay five cents for the privilege.[6]

In July 1898, during a stopover in Henderson, Kentucky, Handy married Elizabeth Price, a local girl he had met there several years earlier. They would have six children, five of whom lived to adulthood.[7]

In early 1900 the troupe sailed to Cuba, where Handy was exposed to Latin rhythms that intrigued him greatly. Much later he would incorporate the music of the *habanera* into the opening strains of the "St. Louis Blues." Elizabeth accompanied him on this and some other trips, but she disliked the travel and uncertainty of an entertainer's life. In addition to the inevitable hardships, life on the road sometimes held real danger, especially in the Deep South. During the 1899–1900 season, while the Minstrels were on their first southern tour in ten years, bandmember Cricket Smith came down with smallpox. The citizens of Tyler, Texas, chased the entire troupe to the outskirts of town, surrounded their railroad car, and threatened to burn it and lynch every member of the company, women included. The performers wisely carried an arsenal of weapons in the railroad car, and an armed standoff ensued for several days, during which more members of the company came down with the disease. Finally the sick actors were able to slip away while Handy's band distracted the townspeople with an impromptu performance at the opposite end of the makeshift compound. Their fate was not as bad as that of Louis Wright, a teenaged member of Handy's band in the late 1890s. In 1902, while traveling with the Georgia Minstrels, Wright insulted a white man in the small town of New Madrid, Missouri, and was lynched by a mob with the complicity of the sheriff. His body was then stuffed in a box and shipped to his mother in Chicago. A vivid account of the incident was published in the Indianapolis *Freeman* and should be required reading for all students of this era.[8]

The rigors of the road, combined with the birth of his first child in June 1900, persuaded Handy to leave Mahara in that year and accept a teaching position at Alabama A&M (Agricultural and Mechanical) College in Normal, Alabama, near Huntsville. He remained there as band master and music teacher for the next two years.[9] Although he was given the opportunity to work as a freelance musician during the summers, the low pay and his ingrained wanderlust led him to rejoin Mahara for a final season in 1902–3. Among his bandmembers was a young clarinetist named Wilbur Sweatman.

In 1903 Handy left Mahara for good and accepted a position as leader of the black Knights of Pythias band in Clarksdale, Mississippi. He was by now an experienced musician, but up to this point he had been playing white music—marches, popular songs, light classics—almost exclusively. Over the next few years, operating out of Clarksdale, Handy and his band traveled throughout the Mississippi delta region, playing affairs of every description in small towns from Clarksdale to Yazoo City. It was here that he first began to notice a new kind of music, a raw, rough-edged style that at first offended his trained ears, but to which he in time became attracted. It was a music of the people—the blues.

Handy, in his autobiography, told two stories about how he was awakened to the music that would secure his fame. In the first, he was nodding off at a train station in Tutwiler, Mississippi, when he encountered a "lean, loose-jointed Negro" scraping the strings of an old guitar with a knife, moaning, "Goin' where the Southern cross' the Dog." The words referred to the intersection of two railroad lines, but it was the plaintive, droning melodic line that struck Handy. Later he was playing a dance in Cleveland, Mississippi, when a patron asked if some local boys might play during the intermission. "They were led by a long-legged chocolate boy and their band consisted of just three pieces, a battered guitar, a mandolin and a worn out bass. . . . They struck up one of those over-and-over strains that seem to have no very clear beginning and certainly no ending at all. The strumming attained a disturbing monotony, but on and on it went, a kind of stuff that has long been associated with cane rows and levee camps. . . . It was not really annoying or unpleasant. Perhaps 'haunting' is a better word." To Handy's astonishment, the scruffy players were showered with coins, earning more for their short set than his own trained orchestra did for the entire engagement. W. C. Handy, scrupulously trained in European music, suddenly saw the light. As he put it, somewhat dramatically, "that night a composer was born, an *American* composer."[10]

Despite this self-reported epiphany, it took Handy several more years to find his muse. He began composing, but one of his first efforts, in 1907, was the stuffy "Roosevelt Triumphal March," in honor of President Theodore Roosevelt, a hero to many blacks. "I didn't have any luck with that number," he later remarked, so he teamed up with a twenty-three-year-old businessman named Harry H. Pace on a southern song called "In the Cotton Fields of Dixie." That one didn't go anywhere either.[11]

Sometime between 1905 and 1908 Handy settled in Memphis, which would be his home for the next ten years. He organized a new band and began booking musicians in and around Memphis. In 1909 he was engaged by the campaign of Edward H. Crump, a white reformer running for mayor of Memphis in a three-way race. The object was to attract the black vote, so Handy composed a campaign song incorporating elements of the strange local music he had heard in his travels around the Delta. The lyrics were not particularly complimentary to the candidate.

Mr. Crump won't 'low no easy riders here,
Mr. Crump won't 'low no easy riders here.
We don't care what Mr. Crump don't 'low,
We gon' to bar'l-house anyhow—
Mr. Crump can go and catch hisself some air![12]

It didn't seem to matter. Crump was elected.

The song was so popular that after the election Handy looked for a way to get it published. Recast as an instrumental (now that Crump was mayor it didn't seem right to keep asking him to "catch hisself some air"), and retitled "The Memphis Blues," it was shopped to a series of publishers, all of whom turned it down as "too complicated" for amateur pianists. Finally, in 1912, Handy paid to have it published by Denver publisher Theron Bennett. When the song didn't seem to sell, Bennett—a songwriter himself—bought Handy's copyright so that he might work on it himself. Bennett commissioned George A. Norton to write some rather insipid lyrics and proceeded to "work" the tune heavily, using his connections in the New York musical world. Still, it took several years before the unusual tune began to catch on.

Because it was so different, professional performances—and recordings—played an important part in the popularization of the new "blues" song. The first two recordings of "The Memphis Blues" were made within days of each other, by the Victor Military Band for Victor (on July 15, 1914) and Prince's Band for Columbia (on July 24). This coup had the fingerprints of Theron Bennett all over it. It was certainly unusual for the two largest labels in America to record a song by an obscure black Memphis composer, virtually at the same time. Another number apparently by Bennett ("One Step Man") was recorded by Columbia at the same time.

Both Victor and Columbia used military-style bands, and the performances were predictably stiff and somewhat formal—not at all what we would today call the "blues." The Victor Military Band used blocks to accentuate the raggy rhythms, while Columbia studio bandleader Charles A. Prince incorporated all sorts of rustic sound effects—slide whistles, roosters crowing, birds twittering, and so on. Although cornball, the Prince version is played with a certain looseness and joie de vivre that makes it rather appealing.

The two instrumental versions were both released in October 1914, with little comment, on lists of new "dance records" catering to the then-current rage for social dancing. The Victor list was recorded under the supervision of dance superstars Vernon and Irene Castle and included one-steps, polkas, waltzes, a new dance called the "fox trot," plus such exotic steps as the "Ta Tao" and the "Lu Lu Fado." Columbia's list was supervised by dance master G. Hepburn Wilson, and included titles by black composers Jim Europe and Ford Dabney. Columbia called Handy's tune a "characteristic Southern shuffle" and titled it "The Memphis Blues, or Mr. Crump." The reference to "Mr. Crump" is interesting, suggesting that Columbia, at least, felt that it was fairly well known by that title. Though neither disc appears to have been a bestseller, both remained in the respective company catalogs for about ten years.

A few months later Victor and Columbia both recorded vocal versions of "The Memphis Blues." Victor's was by Morton Harvey, while Columbia used the "coon duo" Arthur Collins and Byron G. Harlan. Norton's lyrics paid effusive tribute to the still little-known Memphis songwriter.

> I went out a dancin' with a Tennessee dear,
> They had a fellow there named Handy with a band you should hear,
> And while the whi' folks gently swayed,
> All dem darkies played,
> Real . . . harmony.
> I never will forget the tune that Handy called,
> The Memphis Blues . . . Oh them blues!

The lyrics also contained references to religious gatherings and "darky sorrow songs," indicating that white listeners at the time associated the new (to them) blues form with spirituals.

> And when the big bassoon
> Seconds to the trombone's croon . . . croon,
> It moans just like a sinner on revival day, on revival day.
> That melancholy strain, that ever haunting refrain,
> Is like a darkies' sorrow song.
> Here comes the very part
> That wraps a spell around my heart . . .

Before long other recordings appeared—a band version on Edison in 1916, small group instrumental versions on Pathé and Lyric in 1918, and a lively reading by Jim Europe's 369th Infantry "Hell Fighters" Band on Pathé in 1919. As the song began to catch on, Handy was livid, feeling that he had been cheated out of his just rewards. All royalties, of course, were going to Bennett. In his 1941 autobiography Handy could not even bring himself to refer to Bennett by name, calling him "Mr. Z" and using him as an example of a white businessman ripping off an unknowledgeable black composer. However, there are two sides to this story. Handy conceded that Bennett had spent a considerable amount of time and money working on behalf of the song, and that his own fame had been spread by its success. Bennett readily acknowledged Handy as the composer and even had Handy's name worked into the fawning lyrics. Nevertheless, Handy believed that signs of its success were evident early on, and that he had been misled about its potential. He felt that the money that came pouring in should also have been his.

For many years "Memphis Blues," which was registered on September 28, 1912, was thought to be the first published blues song. In fact, it was narrowly preceded by at least two others, "Baby Seals Blues" by Baby Seals (August 3, 1912) and "Dallas Blues" by Hart A. Wand (September 6, 1912). Another song called "I Got the Blues" dates to 1908.[13] "Memphis Blues" was unquestionably the most popular of these, however, and the first to make blues a viable popular music form.

Burned by his experience with "The Memphis Blues," Handy determined to publish his next effort himself, and to that end set up the Pace and Handy Music Company with his sometime-collaborator Harry Pace. In 1913 they published Handy's "Jogo Blues," referring to a jigwalk done by blacks. The song received some attention. Handy claimed that New York bandleader Mike Markel featured it, although neither Markel (who made many recordings between 1917 and 1928) nor anyone else seems to have recorded it as a solo number.[14]

Show business history is littered with stories of composers who lost their biggest hit, but in this case Handy had the last laugh. His next effort would dwarf the success of "Memphis Blues" and everything else he would ever write. At forty years of age, Handy was ready to bring together a lifetime of experiences—sleeping on the cobblestones of St. Louis, overheard phrases of the lovelorn, the melancholy sounds of that guitar picker in Mississippi, even the Latin rhythms he had heard in Cuba—into one special song. Needing to get away from his bustling family, he rented a room in the Beale Street section of Memphis and set to work. As the piano players beat out their rhythms in the saloons down the street, and the pimps paraded in their finery, Handy worked through the night. He even incorporated strains from his failed "Jogo Blues." Learning from past mistakes, he wrote his own lyrics as well. By sun-up, he claimed, the song was essentially done, ready to be orchestrated for his band to play the following evening.

When he finally got home his wife berated him for his absence, but the dancers went wild about the new song he christened "The St. Louis Blues." It was published in September 1914 by Pace and Handy Music Company, but unfortunately took even longer to catch on with the general public than did "The Memphis Blues." More intricate than his earlier numbers, it almost had to be heard rather than played by amateurs. The first recording appears to have been by Prince's Band for Columbia, which took two sessions in November and December 1915 to get it right. This was unusual for the talented and efficient Charles A. Prince, who got most pop tunes down in one or two takes. Once again the brass band treatment is at variance with the way we expect to hear this song, but the "concert" arrangement is not without a certain charm. This time Prince dispensed with the sound effects and was remarkably true to Handy's musical intricacies, including the *habanera* counterpoint under the opening bars, as well as the chant-like quality of certain sections ("Got the St. Louis blues, just as blue as I can be"). Released in March 1916 in a list of dance records, without comment, it seems to have sold only moderately well, although it remained in the catalog until 1924.

The Victor Band included "St. Louis Blues" in a medley with another Handy song ("Joe Turner Blues") in late 1916. By far the most remarkable early version of "The St. Louis Blues," and apparently the first with a vocal, was recorded in England in September 1917 by the black orchestra from London's trendy Ciro's Club, led by Dan Kildare and consisting of expatriates from New York's Clef Club. It featured frantic banjo work by Vance Lowry and Ferdie Allen set against short, enthusiastic vocal interpolations by a deep-voiced baritone (probably Louis Mitchell), and is an extremely energetic performance.

More Handy compositions followed in quick succession, all in the same "blues" style. "Yellow Dog Rag," later renamed "Yellow Dog Blues," was published in 1914, "Hesitating Blues" in 1915, and "Old Miss" in 1916. ("Hesitating Blues" should not be confused with—but often is—"Hesitation Blues" by Smythe, which was published at about the same time.) Handy also adapted an old folk blues in 1915, calling it "Joe Turner Blues." As he explained in his autobiography, this was based on the legend of a Tennessee lawman named Joe Turney who rounded up blacks on trumped-up charges and sold them into forced labor.[15] Two more notable successes followed in 1917, "Beale Street Blues" and "The Hooking Cow Blues."

Handy did not entirely abandon other musical forms. In 1915 he produced "Hail to the Spirit of Freedom March," celebrating heroes of black history. In the same year, on a dare, he turned out a burlesque of Schubert's "Serenade" called "Shoeboot's Serenade."

> Shoeboot Reader was the leader
> Of a colored band.
> Music sweet and grand
> How he sang and played!

Also in 1915 he "assisted" with the music for the first season of the touring revue *Broadway Rastus,* written by and starring Irvin C. Miller.[16]

By 1917 Pace and Handy were making trips to New York City to promote their songs. On one of these visits Pace negotiated a contract for Handy and his band to make some recordings for Columbia. All of the New York labels were looking for bands that could help them cash in on the sudden vogue for jazz, introduced that spring by the phenomenally popular Original Dixieland Jazz Band. Blues and jazz were probably indistinguishable to Columbia executives at the time, and Handy's name was already becoming known through his songs, so the label offered Handy a fee, which, in his words, "seemed to me a fabulous sum to pay twelve men traveling to and from New York for three days' work."[17] Handy accepted but ran into trouble almost immediately. First, he couldn't take his principal band from the Alaskan Roof in Memphis because that engagement was ongoing. Also he was evidently not on the best of terms with many of the musicians who worked for him, and most simply refused to travel with him. When all was said and done he was only able to recruit four musicians from Memphis. He then traveled to Chicago where he picked up seven more, then to New York, where he completed the lineup with clarinetist Nelson Kincaid.

Thus the band that recorded, though billed as "Handy's Orchestra of Memphis," was in fact an amalgam of musicians from three different cities who had never played together. The lineup was Handy, trumpet and leader, Sylvester Bevard, trombone, Wilson Townes, Alex Poole, Charles Harris and Nelson Kincaid, clarinets/saxophones, Edward Alexander, William Tyler and Darnell Howard, violins, Henry Graves, cello, Charles Hillman, piano, Archie Walls, bass, and Jasper Taylor, drums and xylophone. Although Handy recalled making a "dozen records" in three days, the Columbia files indicate that fifteen titles were recorded in four sessions spread over five days in late September 1917. Of the fifteen titles, ten were issued, on five discs.

Handy vividly recalled the bizarre experience of playing for the recording horns in Columbia's "little airtight studios." Most of the musicians perched on stools of varying heights, playing into a series of horns connected to the recording apparatus via acoustical tubing. The clarinetist sat in the corner on a six-foot stool playing into a horn hanging from the ceiling; the saxophonists were on the side with another horn; cornet and trombone played into another in the rear; and the cellist was in another corner with still another horn. The violinists stood up front, directly in front of the main recording horn, in order to maximize their relatively weak sound. "But the poor drummer was a dead goose where the record was concerned," Handy recalled. "While they played as hard as ever in life, the drums and basses could not be recorded in those days."[18] Because of their volume the drums were placed at the rear of the studio, without a separate horn. They can be heard on the finished record, but the sound is faint and thin.

Handy was not entirely satisfied with the results. He was leading what was essentially a "pick-up band," few of whose members were familiar with the awkward process of recording. "To my way of thinking the records were not up to scratch. Our band was capable of better work, but the Columbia people seemed satisfied. They immediately paid us a good part of our money, not even waiting for test pressings to be made." Nevertheless the bandleader proudly noted that the name "Handy" would now be found in the Columbia catalog, between Handel and Haydn![19]

Ever the businessman, Handy used the Columbia sessions to secure additional revenues for his publishing company. Five of the ten issued sides used songs published by Pace and Handy, although only two were actually written by Handy himself—"Ole Miss Rag" and "The Hooking Cow Blues." "Pallet on the Floor," which was interpolated into another number, was credited to Pace and Handy, although it was actually their adaptation of an old folk tune.[20]

Columbia wanted a sound similar to that of Victor's best-selling Original Dixieland Jazz Band, and despite the fact he was leading a much larger orchestra Handy obliged. Many of these sides feature squealing clarinets, swooping trombones, and strong trumpet lines (presumably Handy himself). There are ODJB-type "barnyard" noises on several, and much interweaving of syncopated melodic lines in the Dixieland style. On the one title recorded by both bands ("Livery Stable Blues"), Handy uses virtually the same arrangement heard on the ODJB's Victor made a few months earlier. Overall, Handy's sound differs from that of the ODJB (and of Wilbur Sweatman) in his prominent use of violins, the xylophone, and other instruments. Also, with twelve musicians, his sound is not as sharp and focused as that of the smaller ODJB and Sweatman units. In fact, in some cases the effect is simply chaotic, either because it is a large band trying to play small-unit jazz, or simply for lack of rehearsal. Nevertheless, the individual musicians were good, and under Handy's practiced leadership they produced a loose and raggy sound that at times equaled that of the more established jazz bands.

Columbia appears to have let Handy chose his material, resulting not only in a lot of Pace and Handy songs but also in a predominance of jazz and blues numbers. Two of them, "Fuzzy Wuzzy Rag" and "That Jazz Dance," served as fast-paced showcases for Jasper Taylor's syncopated xylophone. "Fuzzy Wuzzy Rag," credited to Al Morton, is in fact an adaptation of Scott Joplin's "Maple Leaf Rag." "Snaky Blues" has an interesting and varied arrangement. Although Handy's trumpet is prominent, there is also a break for a clarinet duet and another by the violin and 'cello. On a clean copy one can hear the drummer tapping his drumsticks in rhythm behind the strings. "A Bunch of Blues" features a clarinet squealing in classic Sweatman style, propelling the band which plays increasingly hot toward the end.

Handy was not above using ODJB-style musical gimmicks in his arrangements, a notable example being "The Hooking Cow Blues," which incorporates cowbells and other barnyard sounds (the main theme of this tune was later used in Handy's "Aunt Hagar's Blues"). "Livery Stable Blues" contains clarinet "whinnies" and trombone "laughs," much like the classic ODJB Victor recording.

Three of Handy's issued titles were Tin Pan Alley tunes, and in each of those he used the violins to carry the melody. "Sweet Child" is a cheery one-step, worthy of any white Broadway bandleader of the time. "The Old Town Pump" is a relatively bluesy version of a Harry Von Tilzer pop tune. Most bizarre—and out of place—is "Moonlight Blues," a slow waltz played almost exclusively by the violins. It sounds nothing at all like the other nine titles issued. What were they thinking?

Handy recorded three takes of most of the titles, and in almost every case more than one was issued, allowing us to compare different performances of the same song. In the examples I have heard the renditions are virtually identical, leading to the inescapable conclusion that despite the loose and jazzy sound, Handy's musicians were carefully following his prepared arrangements and not improvising.

A month after the September sessions, around October 31, 1917, Handy returned to Columbia to make three test recordings with "Handy's Saxophone Band."[21] Whether these utilized the same personnel as on the issued recordings is not known, but the material was similar ("Lonesome Weary Blues," "Scratchin' the Ground," and "Mamy"). Apparently this was an experiment, as the matrices were numbered in a special trials series and forwarded to A. E. Donovan of the recording department for evaluation. None were issued.

It is surprising, and a bit disappointing, that Handy did not record his own most famous songs at the 1917 sessions. "Memphis Blues," "St. Louis Blues," and "Yellow Dog Blues" were all relatively recent publications, and it would be interesting to hear his early interpretations of them, but he did not record them for Columbia. There are several possible reasons. For one thing, except for "The Memphis Blues" these songs were not particularly well known yet, and Handy may have wanted take advantage of the Columbia opportunity to gain exposure for some of his newer material. Furthermore, Columbia already had versions of "Memphis Blues," "St. Louis Blues," "Joe Turner Blues," "Hesitating Blues," and "Beale Street Blues" in its catalog—all by Prince's Band—and may have wanted something different.

In any event, Columbia had great hopes for Handy's 1917 recordings, which were intended to grab a share of the new market for jazz bands. At this time Victor and Columbia each had one record out by the Original Dixieland Jazz Band. Few other bands had entered the field. It was not until 1918 that Wilbur Sweatman began recording for Columbia, and the ODJB started making additional sides for Victor. Columbia took the unusual step of announcing all ten sides at once, on five consecutively numbered discs, in early January 1918, taking out advertisements in metropolitan newspapers headlined, "The Handy Orchestra's Jazz Dance Blues on Columbia Records."[22] It proclaimed "Handy Week" to draw attention to the new records and promoted them in its catalog supplements for several months thereafter.

New artist announcements were normally accompanied by a photograph and Columbia asked Handy for a picture of his band. He had none. "Sitting for a picture had been one thing in which I'd never been able to interest the band back in Memphis. . . . When the question of photographs arose, they always shrugged their shoulders and began to think of more immediately pressing problems."[23] Apparently the bandmembers in New York didn't want their pictures taken either, so Columbia had one of its artists make a drawing of the band for use in advertising. Curiously, Handy and his musicians (twelve of them) were drawn in full military uniforms, although their instruments were pointed in all directions, jazz-band style.

Promotional copy identified Handy as the leader of a "jazz orchestra," "jazz" and "blues" being at the time considered the same thing. The copy also suggests that Handy had already achieved some degree of national fame as the "originator" of the blues, a musical style which, as interpreted by Tin Pan Alley, was becoming widely popular. Columbia obviously felt that his name would sell records. Under the heading "When Handy Plays the 'Blues,'" the copywriter rhapsodized as follows.

> You do not attempt to describe the music of Handy and his Jazz Orchestra. You dance to it. When the "Livery Stable Blues" is turned over to the tender mercies of a dozen negro musicians equipped with all the instruments of an ordinary orchestra added to a various assortment of barn-yard implements, you find yourself in a maze of melody from which the only escape is to dance.
>
> W. C. Handy is the originator and composer of all the famous "Blues," the most typical, modern truly American dance of the day. Handy's complete orchestra, Handy himself and all his "Blues" is the latest Columbia dance achievement. Ragtime sits ten rows back of the "Blues" when it comes to the "vital spark" of super-syncopation! Remember Handy and his orchestra play *only* for Columbia.
>
> The following "Blues" and jazz dance selections are played by Handy's full orchestra. The entire organization made a special trip from Memphis, "the home of the Blues," to make these unique Columbia records.[24]

The fact that these were considered novelty records for white customers, and quite different from traditional dance records, was evident in the description that accompanied the first individual releases. The primitive musical analysis, and the "us" versus "them" racial overtones, are notable.

> The novelty of the Columbia February Dance List is the initial, exclusive recordings of W. C. Handy and his negro orchestra. A word of explanation is needed regarding the "Blues" originated and played by this famous Southern Orchestra. These dances are not ordinary music. The *tempo* is orthodox but from there all similarity ceases to any music ever heard. The "inside" syncopation, the weird harmonies, unforgettably unique, and the strange use of many of the instruments seem to give us an insight into the real, primal, superstitious, humorous nature of the negro. The Handy records are an absolutely exclusive Columbia novelty—dance records which will make your dance talked about for many a day.[25]

It is interesting that Columbia sought to position the Handy recordings as such a breakthrough when it had been recording his blues compositions with its own studio orchestra for more than three years. However, Charles A. Prince and his military band never sounded like this! Aside from the two discs by the Original Dixieland Jazz Band, and a handful from others, few real jazz records had so far reached the public. Handy's, in early 1918, were among the first, and they appear to have been bestsellers. Production figures for these discs no longer exist, but they are fairly commonly found today, and surviving copies have high stamper numbers in the wax, which suggests a large number of copies pressed. Four of the five remained in the Columbia catalog until the end of the acoustic era in 1925.

Handy's national fame grew steadily. In 1914 producer Salem Tutt Whitney wrote a laudatory piece about him in the *Freeman;* in 1915 the *Crisis* honored him as one of its "Men of the Month"; in 1917 the *Freeman* published another substantial appreciation, with his picture. Nor was Handy exactly shy about self-promotion. In December 1916 he wrote an article entitled "How I Came to Write 'Memphis Blues'" for New York's leading black newspaper, the *New York Age,* which published it with his picture. In it he recounted the same anecdotes he would repeat for the rest of his life, including the story about the guitar player in the train station at Tutwiler (except here the setting was changed to "a plantation in Mississippi") and the one about the intermission musicians who had made more money than his band.[26]

Though based in Memphis, Handy had been traveling to New York for a number of years to promote his songs, sometimes with his band. An April 1917 newspaper item reported that Handy and his musicians were in New York entertaining vaudeville offers.[27] In his autobiography he talked of meeting Clef Club founder Jim Europe, Ziegfeld arranger Will Vodery, and Ziegfeld bandleader Ford Dabney, who took him to *Ziegfeld's Midnight Frolic,* where he met the great showman himself. When they were introduced, Florenz Ziegfeld's first words were, "I'll forgive you!" It seems the producer liked "The Memphis Blues" so much he had had his bands play it incessantly at his lavish parties.

Handy had lived in the south all his life, and Memphis had been his home during his period of greatest creativity, but New York was the center of the publishing and recording industries in America. In addition to business, Handy had other reasons to consider relocating. He had been booking bands in the Memphis area for nearly ten years, and the stress of that profession was beginning to wear him down. His musicians were a fractious bunch, constantly giving him grief, as shown by the refusal of most of them to accompany him to New York for the Columbia sessions. At one point he bought uniforms for his men including caps emblazoned with his name; some of the men cut the name "Handy" out of their caps and substituted another.[28] Reading between the lines of his autobiography, it appears that Handy was not particularly easy to get along with, perhaps because of his strong ego. He wanted to concentrate on writing and publishing. First he moved to Chicago, and then, in mid-1918, to New York.

The timing of the move was auspicious. Jazz (or jass, as it was first called) was the hottest new trend in popular music, and along with it there was a demand for blues—or, at least, for songs with "blues" in the title. Handy was the composer of the most famous blues published to date ("The Memphis Blues"), and he arrived in New York like a conquering hero. Pace and Handy Music Company set up shop in the Gaiety Building at 1547 Broadway. Harry H. Pace was president, Handy's brother, Charles, was vice-president, and Handy himself took the title of secretary-treasurer. White pianist J. Russel Robinson was hired as professional manager.[29]

Almost immediately the firm scored two hits. A catchy tune by teenager Eddie Green called "A Good Man Is Hard to Find" was widely recorded and went on to sell 500,000 copies of the sheet music. Almost simultaneously a character number by Clarence A. Stout called "O Death Where Is Thy Sting?" was picked up by Bert Williams for the *Ziegfeld Midnight Frolic* and recorded by him in August 1918. Pace and Handy was off to a strong start in New York, quickly adding staff and expanding its quarters. The company became known for "Negro music."

Of course the jewels of the Pace and Handy catalog were Handy's own blues, which he promoted relentlessly. Unlike the old-line publishers, who still thought primarily in terms of sheet music, Handy realized early on that there was significant money to be made from recordings of songs for which he held the copyright. As a result he put heavy emphasis on placing his songs with the record companies. An interesting contrast can be drawn between the treatment of recording in his memoirs and in those of Tin Pan Alley giants Edward B. Marks and Isidore Witmark. Handy talks repeatedly about how he sought recordings of his songs, while Marks and Witmark rarely refer to them. Witmark wrote that his firm (M. Witmark and Sons) did not establish a department to coordinate with the record and piano-roll companies until 1920—and he thought that he was the first major publisher to do so.[30] Handy had recognized the value of recordings long before this.

Handy's interest in recording was no doubt born of necessity, because he did not have the large sheet-music distribution networks of his bigger rivals. It may also have stemmed in part from the fact that his new type of music, the blues, was less familiar, and perhaps harder for the average amateur to play, than normal Tin Pan Alley tunes. Indeed, this was one of the reasons he had so much difficultly getting "Memphis Blues" published in the first place. In the hands of professionals, however, its appeal was undeniable. People would buy the records, dance to it, and grow to like it. Florenz Ziegfeld had his bands play it whenever possible. This was music almost made to be exploited through live performance and recordings.

In his autobiography, Handy described a trip to New York to secure recordings of one of his songs. "It was difficult to get 'Joe Turner [Blues]' recorded. I came to New York for that purpose and while walking down Broadway I met my old friend Wilbur Sweatman—a killer-diller and jazz pioneer. He invited me home with him, and his wife Nettie prepared a lovely dinner. While dining she turned on the phonograph and lo and behold it played 'Joe Turner Blues,' which Sweatman had recorded not only on the Pathe but Emerson records also."[31] This was presumably in mid-1917, as the Sweatman recording for Pathé was made in April of that year. The Emerson, which was actually by the Emerson Military Band, was recorded at about the same time.

Recordings of Handy's own songs increased markedly after he relocated to New York in 1918, fueled by (and no doubt fueling) the booming interest in "blues" songs. Table 11 gives a count, by year, of the number of records of Handy compositions that have been traced, not including interpolations. A full list of the records is given at the end of this chapter.

In 1914 just two recordings of Handy songs were released, and in 1915 two more, all versions of "The Memphis Blues." In 1916 there were six new recordings, includ-

Table 11. Recordings of Handy Songs, by Year Released

	1914	1915	1916	1917	1918	1919	1920	Total
Memphis Blues	2	2	1		2	1		8
St. Louis Blues			1		1	8	3	13
Yellow Dog Blues						2	5	7
Joe Turner Blues			1	4				5
Hesitating Blues			2			2	1	5
Shoeboot's Serenade			1					1
Ole Miss					1	2		3
Beale Street Blues				2	1	2	3	8
Hooking Cow Blues					1			1
	2	2	6	6	6	17	12	51

Note: This lists original releases, not reissues, but in some cases it is unclear whether a release was new or a reissue from another label. For example, Empire and Arrow drew masters from Pathé, releasing them under disguised names.

ing the first version of "St. Louis Blues," and even his little musical joke "Shoeboot's Serenade." In 1917 there were six more, including four of "Joe Turner Blues" and two of the new "Beale Street Blues."

By 1917 a significant change was taking place in the way Handy's songs were being performed, at least on record. The first recordings had been mostly formal dance versions by military bands or novelty vocals by studio artists such as Collins and Harlan. The first sign of change was Earl Fuller's 1917 jazz band version of "Beale Street Blues." Fuller's band was patterned after the Original Dixieland Jazz Band, with Harry Raderman on trombone and Ted Lewis (later a famous bandleader in his own right) on clarinet. Wilbur Sweatman's 1917 Pathé of "Joe Turner Blues," with its squealing clarinet backed by a saxophone band, gave that song a jazz-oriented treatment as well. The following year saw the release of Handy's own jazz-styled Columbia recordings, as well as a syncopated saxophone version of "The Memphis Blues" by F. Wheeler Wadsworth, accompanied by Victor Arden on piano.

Nineteen-nineteen was Handy's first full year in New York and his breakthrough year on record. No fewer than seventeen recordings of his songs were released, eight of them versions of the suddenly popular "St. Louis Blues." Among Handy's boosters was Jim Europe, who in a marathon series of sessions for Pathé in early 1919 with his 369th Regiment "Hell Fighters" Band recorded jazzy big-band versions of "Memphis Blues," "St. Louis Blues" and "Hesitating Blues." Saxophonist Wheeler Wadsworth continued to feature Handy songs, both with his dance orchestra and with a new group called the All Star Trio, consisting of himself, pianist Victor Arden, and xylophonist George Hamilton Green. Green played the xylophone in a heavily syncopated style, and the Trio's version of "St. Louis Blues" has an ingratiating rhythm that showed how adaptable the song really was.

Numerous vocalists began using Handy's songs in their acts. Sophie Tucker featured "St. Louis Blues" in vaudeville, and Gilda Gray did the shimmy to it in her 1919 Winter Garden debut.[32] On record perhaps its biggest fan was Al Bernard, a young vaudevillian from New Orleans who styled himself "the Boy from Dixie." Bernard recorded four vocal versions of "St. Louis Blues" between early 1919 and early 1920, including short recitations on some of them. On Aeolian-Vocalion he was accompanied by the Novelty Five, which featured a hot xylophonist who sounds a lot like (and probably was) George Hamilton Green of the All Star Trio. Bernard later made additional recordings of "St. Louis Blues" and became so identified with it that Victor picked him to sing the vocal chorus on its version by the Original Dixieland Jazz Band in 1921, which sold more than 200,000 copies. Handy liked the handsome young singer with a southern drawl and in his autobiography acknowledged Bernard's help in launching "The St. Louis Blues" on its remarkable career.[33]

Probably Handy's biggest hit of 1919, however, was "Yellow Dog Rag," written in 1914 but not recorded until five years later. Victor and Columbia made versions that they decided not to issue, and an early 1919 Pathé by Wheeler Wadsworth's Novelty Dance Orchestra drew little attention. Then in December 1919 Victor issued an unusual arrangement of the song by Joseph C. Smith's dance orchestra. The gimmick was the sound of a man laughing at appropriate interludes, immediately answered by Harry Raderman's laughing trombone. The record was a bestseller, and Raderman went on to use basically the same arrangement (and laughing trombone) on other labels, including a version with his own orchestra on Edison. Retitled "Yellow Dog Blues," it was for a time one of Handy's most popular songs.

Twelve more recordings of Handy songs followed in 1920, including a well-regarded vocal version of "The St. Louis Blues" by Marion Harris on Columbia (she would later record several other Handy songs), and five new versions of "The Yellow Dog Blues." Several bands recorded medleys of Handy songs.

In all, between 1914 and 1920, at least fifty-one recordings of Handy-composed songs were released, providing a substantial stream of revenue to Pace and Handy. In his autobiography the composer spoke glowingly about the money he made from recordings. While he was still in Memphis his brother Charles called him one day, breathless, to tell that they had received a check from Victor for royalties on Earl Fuller's recording of "Beale Street Blues." Expecting at most a couple hundred dollars, Handy ventured that this one was maybe for, say, $300? "Up," said Charles. $400? $500? "Here I commenced to gulp," said Handy. The check turned out to be for $1,857, more than he had ever seen in one place, and dwarfing the few dollars per night he was making playing one-night stands with his band. Soon other checks began to come in, $3,827 from Columbia, $1,000 from Emerson. A couple of years later, he reported with pride, he received a single check from Victor for $7,000 for royalties on "Yellow Dog Blues."[34] Some recording executives told him he was making too much money.

Pace and Handy Music soon had to move to larger quarters and increase its staff, which at one point numbered twenty-five. It began advertising regularly in the musical trade papers. Fletcher Henderson was hired as staff pianist, and William Grant Still (later an eminent classical composer) as an arranger. Handy himself was also in demand, fronting bands in special appearances throughout the metropolitan area. It is unclear whether he had a regular band at this time; it seems more likely that he simply put one together when required. During 1919 he led a big Clef Club orchestra in concerts at the Brooklyn Academy of Music ("50 Joy Whooping Sultans of High Speed Syncopation"), the Manhattan Casino ("Real Blues, Jazzy and Classics"), and elsewhere. In the fall of 1919 he embarked on a tour of the region with Bryant and Handy's Memphis Blues Band ("chain your feet down!").[35]

Handy appears to have had one recording session at this time, around September 1919 for the independent Lyric label. The titles, announced in the November 1919 *Talking Machine World,* were mouth-watering: four of his most famous songs, none of which he had recorded before. They were "Beale Street Blues," "Joe Turner Blues," "Hesitating Blues," and "Yellow Dog Blues," all by Handy's Memphis Blues Band, which at the time may have included famed jazz cornetist Johnny Dunn. Based on the *Talking Machine World* announcement these records have been included in many discographies, but it appears that they were never issued. No copies have ever been found, and the release numbers were quickly reassigned to other (non-Handy) recordings. Lyric sales literature of the period lists the latter recordings and none by Handy. The mix-up may have been caused by the fact that Lyric was converting from vertical to lateral recording at this time. Perhaps the Handys were recorded vertically and had to be pulled at the last minute.[36]

Handy continued to compose. An attempt at a topical song during World War I ("The Kaiser's Got the Blues") went nowhere, but the rhythmic "Long Gone (from Bowling Green)," adapted from a folk blues, achieved some popularity in 1920. The words were by Chris Smith.

From 1918 to 1920 Pace and Handy's business was thriving, but just as fast as good times had come, they were suddenly gone. A drought in new hits, plus a general economic recession in 1921, conspired to collapse the firm's revenues and drive it to the edge of bankruptcy. Handy laid off employees and worked long hours trying to keep the business afloat. Adding to his troubles was a split with Harry Pace, who withdrew from active involvement in the firm in order to set up his own record label, Black Swan Records, in early 1921 (Handy was not involved). Pace and Handy Music was reorganized as Handy Brothers' Music. As bills continued to mount Handy was forced to sell his house on 139th Street. As if this was not enough, his eyesight, which had always been problematic, began to fail. In late 1921 he went blind.

After a period of severe depression, things gradually began to improve. Friends rallied round, and treatment by a specialist slowly restored his sight. But it was a long, hard road. Between 1922 and 1924 Handy was forced to sell off many of his best copyrights to avoid bankruptcy. Some of these he would buy back when things improved. Handy also had to endure attacks on his reputation. As early as 1917 the respected writer James Weldon Johnson had called into question his authorship of "The Memphis Blues," saying it was really just a folk song that "like Topsy, just grew." In 1922 noted musicologist Henry Krehbiel joined the chorus, saying that "Memphis Blues" really came from a Memphis "bawdy house," and that is was "a vulgar type of music" (Krehbiel promoted the more "serious" types of African American music, such as spirituals). Handy was wounded by these attacks, as documented by his correspondence at the time. In the long run he would prevail, although there would always be questions raised about the originality of his compositions. That is ironic, since he freely acknowledged the folk origins of many of his strains.[37]

Two new songs published in 1921 caught on, easing his financial burdens. Neither was entirely original. "Loveless Love" was based on the old folk tune "Careless

Love," which Handy had first heard in the 1890s. It was, he said later, "too beautiful a melody to be lost." As soon as it was ready Handy taught it to blues singer Alberta Hunter for her cabaret act, and "it made a bull's eye."[38] Another folk song was fashioned into "Aunt Hagar's Children Blues," also known as "Aunt Hagar's Blues" (the striking opening strain had already been used in 1917's "Hooking Cow Blues"). The unusual title was a reference to the biblical story of Abraham, Sarah, and Sarah's black handmaiden Hagar, from which blacks sometimes referred to themselves as Hagar's children. A year later "Aunt Hagar's Blues" was interpolated into the revue *Put and Take* as a vocal number, with words by Tim Brymn. It became a favorite of jazz bands, with notable recordings by the Virginians (1923), Ted Lewis (1923), and King Oliver (1928).

Lewis, it should be noted, was a major promoter of Handy songs, recording "St. Louis Blues," "Memphis Blues," "Beale Street Blues," and "Aunt Hagar's Blues" all within the space of a few months in 1922–23. He rerecorded them electrically during the late 1920s, using top-rank jazz sidemen and producing records now considered to be jazz classics.

In January 1922 Handy returned to the recording studio, probably to earn some money to ease his financial woes. With his Memphis Blues Band he recorded two medleys for Paramount built around the Handy classics "St. Louis Blues" and "Yellow Dog Blues," neither of which he had recorded before (at least not for release). They are fascinating performances but, one suspects, bore little resemblance to the way he would have performed the songs in Memphis a few years earlier. "St. Louis Blues" gets a full 1920s dance-band treatment with an elaborate, multilayered arrangement. It opens with a commanding trumpet figure (by Handy himself?), followed by various instruments taking solos and playing counterpoint to one another. Latin rhythms weave in and out. Toward the end a clarinet introduces "Ole Miss Blues," which gets a similar treatment. The whole effect is that of a large orchestra playing a complex, rhythmic arrangement worthy of Ferdie Grofe, the classically-trained arranger for Paul Whiteman's concert orchestra. This is 1920s big-band dance music and, while toe-tapping, it is hardly "the blues." "Yellow Dog Blues," a medley with "Hesitating Blues" and "Beale Street Blues," has a similarly showy big orchestra arrangement, with a great deal going on musically during its three-plus minutes.

On one hand it is unfortunate that Handy did not record his most famous songs earlier, so that we could hear his original conception of them. Here he seems to be adapting to the times, just as he had at his 1917 Columbia sessions when he mimicked the raucous sound of the then-popular Original Dixieland Jazz Band. It is even possible that because of his serious health problems during early 1922 these sessions were not under his control.[39] He does not mention them in his memoirs. Paramount sometimes appears to have brought in outside arrangers to "dress up" the sound of its celebrity bands, and it may have done so here.[40] The recordings do suggest, however, that unlike some of his contemporaries Handy did not stand still musically. While his inspiration was rooted in the blues idiom, he wrote songs that were deceptively complex and adaptable to all sorts of treatments. He also seems to have been partial to intricate, musically literate (yet jazz-oriented) arrangements. Years later he commented that elaborate concert arrangements of his songs "sounded to me like a farmer plowing in evening dress."[41] Ironically the same could be said of some of his own recordings.

At about the same time Handy's orchestra accompanied daughter Katherine, an aspiring singer, on a vocal version of "Loveless Love." Although released on Paramount, the master is in a different numerical series and may have originated elsewhere.

In March Paramount recorded two more tunes by the Handy band. The more interesting was George W. Thomas's "Muscle Shoals Blues," an ingratiating, repetitive melody in Handy's own style, which was frequently recorded by jazz and blues singers and bands in the 1920s. Here Handy used a much simpler arrangement, treating the song gently with clarinet counterpoint and various jazz riffs, but taking care not to overwhelm its light, rhythmic charm. "She's a Mean Job" was a more typical dance tune of the day, performed with a saxophone lead and strong banjo accompaniment.

Handy's four Paramount sides were released on two discs in mid-1922 to moderate sales. Paramount was a Wisconsin-based independent label without the massive distribution of Victor or Columbia and would become known primarily for its blues and jazz recordings. The Handy recordings ultimately achieved good distribution, however, because the company leased its masters to a plethora of department store and budget labels. Handy's Paramount masters have been found on Banner, Belvedere, Black Swan, Claxtonola, Davega, Famous, National, Puritan, Regal, and Triangle, and may be on other independent labels as well.

In the wake of the Paramount sessions, and the departure of Harry Pace to start a record label, Handy decided to get into the record business himself. On August 29, 1922, he filed incorporation papers for the Handy Record Company, with a capitalization of $25,000 and himself, eldest daughter Lucille, and three associates as directors. Little is known of this venture, which apparently folded before issuing any records. Experts believe that several masters may have been recorded by the company and subsequently released on other labels including Paramount, Black Swan, and Grey Gull. The artists are believed to be Katherine Handy (possibly the source of the Paramount side noted above) and an unidentified orchestra.[42]

Meanwhile negotiations were underway with Okeh, a larger label, which resulted in a long series of sessions between January and August 1923. Okeh issued a total of fourteen sides by Handy during 1923 and 1924, plus at least three others on which he backed blues singer Sara Martin. Handy was still struggling with his eyesight at this time, and he recalled in his memoirs, "I found something to do to keep myself busy, in this way forgetting my condition. R. S. Peer and Fred Hager of the Okeh Company engaged me to make records with a band under my name. Although I couldn't see the notes I did have definite ideas of how the arrangements should be made and interpreted."[43]

On Okeh Handy used a smaller band and arrangements more in line with those of the small-unit jazz bands of the day rather than the elaborate Whiteman-esque productions heard on Paramount. Unfortunately there were better bands already plying this trade, among them Victor's best-selling Virginians (made up of top sidemen from the Whiteman band) and Columbia's Georgians. The Handy Okehs are pleasant enough, but in the main not terribly distinctive. No commanding soloists are heard, at least none that equal cornetist Henry Busse and clarinetist Ross Gorman of the Virginians or trumpeter Frank Guarente of the Georgians.

Handy's 1923 Okeh of "St. Louis Blues" takes yet another approach to his most famous song. It is somewhat slower than his 1922 Paramount and not as full of musical tricks; basically, it is a straightforward reading. The jazz feeling is there, with the clarinet periodically weaving countermelodies around the other instruments, but a long piano solo gives it a more formal tone.

Other Handy compositions recorded for Okeh included "Memphis Blues," "Ole Miss Blues," "Sundown Blues," and "Darktown Reveille." The famous "Memphis Blues" is done at a rather slow, loping tempo, emphasizing its insistent rhythm. Trumpet and violin get featured spots. The violinist is also showcased on "Ole Miss Blues," along with a swooping trombonist. The arrangement is somewhat similar to the 1917 Columbia. "Sundown Blues" and "Darktown Reveille" were both 1923 publications that Handy was pushing at the time, though neither achieved much currency. "Darktown Reveille" was said on the label to be "adapted from W. C. Handy's famous 'Bugle Blues,'" but the origin of the latter is unclear. Much like Eubie Blake's "Bugle Call Rag" (1916) and Ford Dabney's "Bugle Call Blues" (1922), it featured Army bugle calls interspersed with jazz riffs. The most famous song of this type, and the one favored by jazz bands for years to come, was the Pettis-Meyers-Schoebel "Bugle Call Rag," recorded in 1922 and published in 1923.

Other songs recorded by Handy in 1923 came from a variety of composers, many of them black. All were in the jazz and blues tradition. "Louisville Blues" is a swinging, jazzy tune that steps right along, propelled by banjo, drums, and drummer's blocks. In the upbeat "My Pillow and Me," by Tim Brymn, Chris Smith, and Clarence Williams, the saxophone and clarinet "talk" to each other (are they the "pillow" and "me"?), while trombone and piano are also featured. Other numbers were more in the "low down blues" style being popularized by such singers as Bessie Smith and Sara Martin. "Down Hearted Blues" was, in fact, one of Bessie Smith's early hits, recorded by her for Columbia in February 1923 and also popularized by co-composer Alberta Hunter. "Gulf Coast Blues" was another Bessie Smith number. "Mama's Got the Blues" by Sara Martin and Clarence Williams features long bluesy saxophone and piano solos. Perhaps the most famous blues of this style recorded during these sessions was "Farewell Blues." More than fifty versions of this song are listed in the standard discographical reference, *Jazz Records,* including early recordings by the Virginians, the Georgians, and Isham Jones's Orchestra. Handy gives it a bluesy, moderate-tempo rendition, not unlike the famous Ted Lewis version of 1929.

Handy's 1923 Okehs, though they did not set the musical world on fire, contain some good jazz ensemble performances and it is a shame that they so quickly passed out of print. They were not strong sellers, and all had been deleted from the catalog by 1928. They are rarely found and even more rarely reissued.

Why were these Handy recordings not bigger sellers? A clue may be found in a comparison of Handy's Okeh recording of his own "Aunt Hagar's Blues" with the Victor version by the Virginians released a month earlier.[44] The Virginians' version, building on a strong rhythm foundation by banjoist Mike Pingitore, is full of musical surprises, including wah-wah cornet, clever little piano figures, cymbal crashes, and powerful trumpet work. It is so slick and commercial that scholars may argue whether it is really jazz, but it was apparently a very big seller, judging by the number of copies found today. The Handy reading is calmer and more predictable. Cornet, clarinet, and saxophone get short solos, and a xylophone is prominently featured. It is a perfectly good, jazz-oriented rendition, but no soloists stand out, and one can see why it did not attract the same attention as the Virginians' record.

Although he would not record again himself for many years, Handy continued to promote the career of his blues-singer daughter, Katherine. In addition to accompanying her on Paramount in 1922, he backed her on a Victor trial recording on June 29, 1923. The title was none other than "St. Louis Blues," which would make this a very interesting piece of Handy family history. Unfortunately Victor did not offer her a contract, and the trial was not issued. Katherine's career never really took off, although she recorded one side with Fletcher Henderson in 1932. She worked in the music business, at one time serving as secretary to Irving Mills, and wrote a regular column for the *Chicago Defender*. She also sang on radio.[45] Handy's daughter Lucille also had a minor career in show business.

By the mid-1920s Handy had decided to concentrate exclusively on publishing. In 1924 he became a member of the American Society of Composers, Authors and Publishers (ASCAP) and in 1926 published his first book, *Blues: An Anthology,* containing many of his adaptations and the stories of the songs' origins. One of the earliest serious blues collections, the book grew out of a series of interviews with Handy conducted in 1925 by Edward Abbe Niles, a Wall Street lawyer whose hobby was the study of American folk and popular music. Niles would become one of Handy's closest friends and protectors in the years to come. Handy was also becoming increasingly interested in spirituals, writing new arrangements of such songs as "Steal Away to Jesus" (1925), "Let Us Cheer the Weary Traveler" (1927), "I've Heard of a City Called Heaven" (1928), and "Go Down, Moses" (1930). In January 1929 Paramount recorded two of Handy's sacred songs, "Aframerican Hymn" and "Let Us Cheer the Weary Traveler," with a chorus called Handy's Sacred Singers. It is not known what connection, if any, Handy had with this group.

Handy continued to compose, but few paid attention to his recent work. Instead his fame was spread by the enormous popularity of his early classics. Defying the odds of popular music, an ephemeral business if ever there was one, those early songs became increasingly popular over time, infusing themselves into America's musical fabric. They were heard everywhere, on record, on radio, and in live performances. In 1926 *George White's Scandals* built a lavish stage production around "the birth of the blues," highlighting "The Memphis Blues" and "The St. Louis Blues." Lew Leslie's *Rhapsody in Black* (1931) also featured Handy's music.[46]

Although "Memphis Blues," "Beale Street Blues," and other Handy songs remained popular, "St. Louis Blues" was beginning to move out in front, rising to the level of one of the most popular songs in American musical history. The Broadway show *Blackbirds of 1928* featured a big choral production of the song. A two-reel mini–feature film called *St. Louis Blues* appeared in 1929. This was Bessie Smith's only film appearance, and the credits also listed James P. Johnson, the Hall Johnson

Choir, and Handy himself as musical director. The film was retitled *Best of the Blues* in 1939. "St. Louis Blues" was featured in at least a dozen other short films in the late 1920s and early 1930s.[47] Recordings also proliferated, some with alternate titles to make them seem fresher ("The New St. Louis Blues," "Newest St. Louis Blues," and so on). The royalties rolled in, sometimes from unexpected sources. The song was so popular that crooner Rudy Vallee included an anemic version on one of his early Victor releases, in 1930. The flip side of the record, an old warhorse called "The University of Maine Stein Song," unexpectedly became the biggest hit of Vallee's career, carrying Handy's good old "St. Louis Blues" along with it. Handy may not have thought much of Vallee's garish version of his masterpiece, complete with its affected black pronunciation ("if I'se feelin' tomorrow just like I feels today"), but he didn't complain. As he put it, the Vallee record "sold from here to Rio, from Rio to Bali."[48]

Handy himself was becoming a musical celebrity. In 1928 he was invited to produce a mammoth historical survey of black music at Carnegie Hall, beginning with the slave era and moving forward in time to the present day. Among those on the program were Fats Waller and soloist Minnie Brown. Backed by Wall Street investor Robert Clairmont, the concert included everything from folk to symphonic music and started a vogue for historical surveys of black culture.

Scholars began to take notice. In 1930 Handy was given featured treatment in Isaac Goldberg's influential book, *Tin Pan Alley,* which included his biography and quoted his 1926 book *Blues: An Anthology.* Memphis dedicated a "W. C. Handy Square," just off Beale Street. Much in demand for personal appearances, Handy even toured around 1933–34 with a "Memory Lane" old-timers revue, organized by Joe Laurie Jr. With him on the tour were an eighty-nine-year-old dancer who had performed in Lincoln's time, and an actress who had gotten her start in *The Black Crook.*[49] Handy, at age sixty, might be forgiven if he was beginning to feel like a public monument.

Known for promoting black music of all kinds, Handy in 1933 served as a consultant to the Chicago World's Fair, and in 1935 he published a monograph called *Negro Authors and Composers of the United States.* In 1937 he became treasurer of the newly organized Negro Actors Guild in New York City, and in 1938 published another book, *W. C. Handy's Collection of Negro Spirituals.* He had earlier maintained that spirituals did more for the Negro's emancipation than all the guns of the Civil War.[50]

In 1938 his place in American music was recognized in a unique manner when the Library of Congress invited him to record some songs and reminiscences of his youth for posterity. The recordings, supervised by folklorist Alan Lomax, were made in Washington, D.C., on May 9, 1938, and had Handy singing, playing the guitar, and describing such songs as "I Walked All the Way from East St. Louis," "I Got No More Home Than a Dog," "Joe Turner," and "Careless Love," as well as describing scenes such as "Sounding the Lead on the Ohio River."

In 1939 he was honored at the New York World's Fair as a leading contributor to American culture and served as a consultant to both the New York and San Francisco World's Fairs. With J. Rosamond Johnson and Harry T. Burleigh he arranged an all-black program of music called "From Symphony to Swing," which took place on October 2, 1939, as part of ASCAP's Silver Jubilee week of musical celebrations at Carnegie Hall.

The popularity of "St. Louis Blues" seemed to know no end. Hundreds of recorded versions were made. More than 130 versions are listed in the leading discography of pre–World War II jazz, and that doesn't begin to count the many popular versions such as the one by Rudy Vallee. Overall, "St. Louis Blues" is believed to be one of the two or three most recorded songs of the first half of the twentieth century. It was also heard incessantly on radio. ASCAP logs indicate that it received an astonishing 11,000 performances on radio in 1935 and 16,500 in 1937, more than many hit songs of the day.[51] Hollywood jumped on the bandwagon with a 1939 Dorothy Lamour feature film called *St. Louis Blues.* According to one reviewer, this musical comedy about a Broadway showgirl (Lamour) who runs away to perform on a Missouri riverboat was "mostly an excuse to stage W. C. Handy's title masterpiece and the many other songs."[52] In March 1938 Handy was lauded on Robert Ripley's nationally broadcast radio show *Believe It or Not* as "Father of the Blues."

This kind of celebrity was bound to stir jealousies in the jazz world, and in 1938 Handy found himself the target of a vicious public attack by another jazz pioneer. Handy must have been distressed when he picked up a copy of the August 1938 *Down Beat,* a widely read national musical magazine and saw the front-page headline, "'W. C. Handy Is a Liar!' Says Jelly Roll" (*Down Beat* was known for its provocative headlines). Inside was a long, rambling letter from pianist Jelly Roll Morton, who claimed that he created jazz in the year 1902 and further asserted that Handy had stolen just about everything he said he wrote. "St. Louis Blues" was said to be the creation of Handy's guitarist, Guy Williams. While he was at it, Morton also attacked Paul Whiteman, Duke Ellington, and others. Morton, who had one of the legendary egos in the history of jazz, modestly signed his missive "Originator of Jazz and Stomps, World's Greatest Hot Tune Writer." Handy fired back in the next month's issue, refuting Morton point by point, and calling his letter the "act of a crazy man."[53] The world seemed to agree, and the episode simply added to Morton's reputation as an angry, vituperative man whose undeniable talent was sometimes overshadowed by his disagreeable personality.

On the crest of all this notoriety Handy was induced to make a few commercial records for the newly launched Varsity label, operated by independent producer and record industry wheeler-dealer Eli Oberstein. On December 26, 1939, the day after Christmas, he cut four of his own songs with backing by six of New York's top jazz sidemen. Five were drawn from the Louis Armstrong band-pianist and arranger Luis Russell, trombonist J. C. Higginbotham, bassist Pops Foster, tenor sax man Bingie Madison, and drummer Big Sid Catlett. Rounding out the band was freelance clarinetist Edmond Hall. All were veterans of some of the most highly regarded jazz bands of the 1930s. With first-rate talent like that, the recordings should be of interest to jazz aficionados today.

The four sides were all done in a low-key, smooth jazz style that showed Handy once again adapting to the style of the time. "St. Louis Blues" and "Beale Street Blues" featured his own trumpet, played in a rather restrained fashion, while his experienced sidemen provided a lightly swinging accompaniment. Tango rhythms were introduced in both numbers, and Higginbotham, Hall, and Russell all took solos. On "Loveless Love" and "'Way Down South Where the Blues Begin" (written in 1932) Handy sang(!) in a light, shaky baritone. He was no vocalist, though his earnestness did lend a certain charm to the numbers. His wavering tones were a little out of place on some of the more dramatic lyrics ("and in the wreckage of desire"), but the extremely smooth accompaniment kept the proceedings from degenerating into an amateur hall performance. There were short and sweet tenor saxophone solos on both of the vocal sides.

The Varsity label lasted only about a year, although Oberstein reissued "St. Louis Blues" on his Elite and Philharmonic labels between 1941 and 1943. Later the four Handy masters were sold to publisher Joe Davis, who reissued two of them in 1946 on his Davis label in a 78-rpm album called *Rare Records, Volume 1.* None of these releases had very wide distribution, and they are moderately rare today.[54]

The early 1940s brought still more honors. In June 1940 NBC broadcast an all-Handy program of music, and in September of the same year the composer appeared at the big ASCAP Festival of American Music held at Treasure Island in San Francisco. More than 66,000 attended.[55] In 1941 his autobiography, *Father of the Blues,* was published by Macmillan, a major New York publishing house. Extremely well written, it was as much the story of black American music as it was of Handy, and it has become a standard reference in the field, remaining in print to the present day. Handy also continued to publish musical collections, including *Unsung Americans Sung* (1944), consisting primarily of light classical pieces and tributes to famous black Americans, and *Treasury of Blues* (1949), a revision of his 1926 collection.

Despite the activity and honors, the early 1940s were difficult years personally. His beloved wife, Elizabeth, had died in 1937, after thirty-nine years of marriage. His eyesight had been failing badly, and a 1943 fall from a subway platform left him completely blind. Yet his energy and enthusiasm for life were unquenchable. A letter to publisher and old friend Joe Davis in March 1948 summarized his outlook at the time. After plugging one of his less-known songs, he concluded, "You know, we used to get around together and have dinner occasionally—most of the time at your expense. By being seventy-four years old and so blind that I cannot see what the chicks look like, I have saved so much money, and it would be a pleasure if you would tell me when and where we can dine together at my expense. R.S.V.P. . . . Your friend, W. C. Handy."[56]

Handy continued to make public appearances. He was a periodic guest at Billy Rose's Diamond Horseshoe Club, including an appearance at the 1948 New Year's Eve show, with Noble Sissle leading the orchestra. Eubie Blake biographer Al Rose met him there, describing him as "blind [and] full of dignity." Another major tribute was his seventy-eighth birthday party at the Waldorf Astoria Hotel, on November 16, 1951, where he introduced his latest endeavor, the Foundation for the Blind. A little blind girl sang, "I Am Blind But I Still Can See."[57] During the 1950s Handy appeared on TV on the *Ed Sullivan Show* and Edward R. Murrow's *Person to Person.*

The continuing interest in Handy led to a final recording project in 1952. He was approached by independent producer G. Robert Vincent, best known as the founder of the Armed Forces's V-Disc label during the 1940s and a specialist in spoken-word

An American icon: W. C. Handy in later life. (Author's collection)

recordings. Vincent induced him to commit his reminiscences to tape, in a more extensive series of sessions than the one held by the Library of Congress in 1938. He wanted Handy to talk about his famous songs, and Handy was more than willing to oblige. Most of the recordings were made at Handy's comfortable little home in Yonkers, New York, a New York City suburb. He sang and reminisced about his life in his gentle, kindly voice. He spoke of his early years and awakening to the blues music of the south; the story of "The Memphis Blues"; and the stories of many of his other songs. On some tracks he played trumpet or guitar, and on some he was accompanied by his long-time associate Dr. Charles L. Cooke on piano. "St. Louis Blues" was performed in two parts, first the story and a solo performance by Handy, accompanying himself on guitar, then a larger production with his daughter Katherine Handy Lewis accompanied by Cooke and the New York Choral Ensemble.

It was a slick production, integrating spoken interludes and music, performed in a variety of settings, and occupying both sides of a twelve-inch LP. Although the LP is interesting listening and historically important, it appears to have had limited circulation. Vincent issued it in June 1952 on his Audio Archives label, under the title *Father of the Blues,* with an illustrated gate-fold cover containing pictures of W. C. Handy at various ages, Katherine Handy, Dr. Cooke, and Vincent himself at the controls of his portable recording equipment. It was an elaborate project for an independent label in the early LP era. By late 1953 Audio Archives had changed its name to Heritage, and in early 1954 the album was renumbered and retitled *Blues*

Revisited. It seems to have remained available under the latter name until 1958.[58] A higher profile presentation of Handy's music on record was the Columbia LP *Louis Armstrong Plays W. C. Handy,* recorded in 1954 with Handy's involvement. The composer was said to be flattered and moved by this tribute from one of the greatest living jazzmen.

On January 1, 1954, at the age of eighty, Handy married his second wife, Irma Louise Logan. Although confined to a wheelchair during the last three years of his life, he continued to make public appearances, including an eighty-fourth birthday celebration at the Waldorf Astoria Hotel in 1957, which drew eight hundred people. W. C. Handy died on March 28, 1958, in New York, of pneumonia.

The Handy legend has remained strong in the years since his death. Just a few months after he died a big-screen biography loosely based on his life was released by Paramount, called *St. Louis Blues* (of course). The cast included an interesting assortment of musicians. Starring as the adult Handy was Nat "King" Cole; the young Handy was played by future rock star Billy Preston, then age eleven. Also in the cast were Eartha Kitt (as Gogo, a speakeasy singer who inspired him), Cab Calloway, Ella Fitzgerald, Mahalia Jackson, Pearl Bailey, and Ruby Dee. Filmed in black and white, the movie is infrequently shown today.

Plays incorporating Handy's music have included *The Weary Blues* (1966), *Down on Beale Street* (1973) and *Black and Blue* (1989). The latter had a long run on Broadway.[59] Handy's legacy has been recognized in other diverse ways. In 1969 he was honored with a U.S. postage stamp, which described him as "Father of the Blues." In 1967 a new National Hockey League team in St. Louis was named the St. Louis Blues. According to the team's official history, "The selection of the team's name was an easy one for owner Sid Salomon, Jr. 'The name of the team has to be the Blues,' exclaimed Salomon, after being awarded the new franchise. 'It's part of the city where W. C. Handy composed his famed song while thinking of his girl one morning.'"[60]

Handy has become a sort of patron saint to the jazz and blues world, even though it is common knowledge that he didn't "invent" the blues, nor did he write in the classic blues style. The year 1980 saw the establishment of the Blues Foundation, a non-profit organization headquartered in Memphis that presents the annual "Handy Awards" to leading performers in the field, based on balloting by fans worldwide. A weeklong W. C. Handy Music Festival was launched in 1982 at the University of North Alabama at Florence, Alabama (Handy's hometown) and continues annually to the present day. Guest artists over the years have included Dizzy Gillespie, Nancy Wilson, Little Milton, Billy Taylor, and Charlie Byrd.

Perhaps the most famous summary of his contribution was by Isaac Goldberg, in his classic book *Tin Pan Alley,* who wrote, "Handy, the Father of the Blues, is not the inventor of the genre; he is its Moses, not its Jehovah. It was he who, first of musicians, codified the new spirit in African music and sent it forth upon its conquest of the North."[61]

Considering W. C. Handy's renown, and his acknowledged importance to American music, it is surprising that his own recordings of his most famous songs are so little known and seldom reissued. They represent an essential part of the biography of one of the most famous figures in African American cultural history.

RECORDINGS OF W. C. HANDY SONGS, 1914–20 (MEDLEY CONTENTS AND
RELEASE DATES ARE IN PARENTHESES)

"Memphis Blues" (pub. 1912)—*see also* "Joe Turner Blues"

 Victor Military Band, Victor 17619 (Oct. 1914)

 Prince's Band, Columbia A5591 (Oct. 1914)

 Morton Harvey, Victor 17657 (Jan. 1915)

 Collins and Harlan, Columbia A1721 (July 1915)

 National Promenade Band, Edison 2881 and 50349 (May 1916)

 Wadsworth and Arden, Pathé 20378 (July 1918)

 Bennett Brothers, Lyric 4146 [or 4152?] (Aug. 1918)

 Jim Europe band, Pathé 22085 (c. June 1919)

"Jogo Blues" (1913)—*see* "Beale St. Blues"

"St. Louis Blues" (1914)—*see also* "Joe Turner Blues"

 Prince's Band, Columbia A5772 (Mar. 1916)

 Ciro's Club Coon Orchestra, Columbia (U.K.) 699 (c. Mar. 1918)

 Wadsworth's Novelty Dance Orchestra, Pathé 22038/Empire 31104 (Mar. 1919)

 All Star Trio, Okeh 1142 (Apr. 1919)

 Al Bernard, Emerson 7477 and 9163 (May 1919)

 Ernest Hare, Gennett 4513 (May 1919)

 All Star Trio, Edison 3741 and 50523 (May 1919)

 Jim Europe Band, Pathé 22087 (c. June 1919)

 Al Bernard, accompanied by the Novelty Five, Aeolian-Vocalion 12148 (July 1919)

 Al Bernard, Lyric 5152 (Oct. 1919)

 All Star Trio, Lyric 4208 (Feb. 1920)

 Al Bernard, Edison 50620 and 3930 (Mar. 1920)

 Marion Harris, Columbia A2944 (Sept. 1920)

"Yellow Dog Blues" (1914)

Ben Kelly Jass Band, Victor (1918, not released)

 Wadsworth's Novelty Dance Orchestra, Pathé 22038/Empire 31107 (Mar. 1919)

 Art Hickman's Orchestra (with "Joe Turner Blues"), Columbia (1919, not released)

 Jos. C. Smith Orchestra (with "Hooking Cow Blues"), Victor 18618 (Dec. 1919)

 Bal Taberin Jazz Orchestra, Lyric 4212 (Feb. 1920)

 Paul Biese and His Novelty Orchestra, Aeolian-Vocalion 14007 (Feb. 1920)

 Paul Biese and His Novelty Orchestra, Okeh 4061 (Mar. 1920)

 Selvin's Novelty Orchestra (with "A Good Man Is Hard to Find"), Emerson 10133 (May 1920)

 Harry Raderman's Jazz Orchestra, Edison 3991 and 50650 (June 1920)

"Joe Turner Blues" (1915)—*see also* "Yellow Dog Blues"

 Victor Band (with "St. Louis Blues"), Victor 18174 (Dec. 1916)

 Prince's Band (with "Yellow Dog Rag"), Columbia A5854 (Jan. 1917)

 Emerson Military Band (with "Down by the Chattahoochee River"), Emerson 7145 (Mar. 1917)

Rogers' Band, Par-O-Ket 105 (June 1917)
Wilbur Sweatman's Jazz Band (with "Memphis Blues"), Pathé 20167 (July 1917)
"Hesitating Blues" (1915)
Prince's Band, Columbia A5772 (Mar. 1916)
Arthur Collins, Emerson 751 (Aug. 1916)
Jim Europe Orchestra, Pathé 22086 (c. June 1919)
Adele Rowland, Columbia A2769 (Oct. 1919)
Art Hickman's Orchestra (with "Beale St. Blues"), Columbia A2813 (Feb. 1920)
"Shoeboot's Serenade" (1915)
Morton Harvey, accompanied by Malvin Franklin, piano, Emerson 729 (1916)
"Ole Miss" (1916)
Handy's Orchestra of Memphis, Columbia A2420 (Feb. 1918)
New Orleans Jazz Band, Okeh 1156 (Apr. 1919)
Wadsworth's Novelty Dance Orchestra, Pathé 22206/Empire 507 (Dec. 1919)
"Beale Street Blues" (1917)—*see also* "Hesitating Blues"
Prince's Band (with "Jogo Blues"), Columbia A2327 (Oct. 1917)
Earl Fuller's Famous Jazz Band, Victor 18369 (Nov. 1917)
Wadsworth's Novelty Orchestra, Pathé 20441 (Nov. 1918)
Davies Trio, Empire 6268 (Jan. 1919)
Futurist Jazz Band, Arrow 504 (Feb. 1920)
Al Bernard, Edison 50536 and 3784 (July 1919)
All Star Trio, Lyric 4209 (Feb. 1920)
Gilt-Edge Four, Grey Gull H-1007/L-1014 (1920)
"Hooking Cow Blues" (1917)—*see also* "Yellow Dog Blues"
Handy's Orchestra of Memphis, Columbia A2420 (Feb. 1918)

This list includes original issues only. Some minor label releases may remain untraced. Sources include the trade paper *Talking Machine World,* original records and catalogs in the author's collection, and various modern discographies.

30   Roland Hayes

Of all the fields of music and art in the early 1900s, none was so thoroughly closed to black Americans as that of classical music. Blacks could succeed in popular music and theater. Comedy was open to them, as was, to a certain extent, poetry and literature. They could sing their spirituals. But the classical concert stage was the exclusive province of America's white elite.

In 1905 Sylvester Russell, a budding tenor as well as a talented and successful writer, abandoned his concert career after years of struggle, stating ruefully, "there is no financial future for a colored male classical singer in America, no matter how great he may be."[1]

Into this hostile environment came an ambitious young man from a farm in Georgia, with no money, no sponsors, and little education. What he had, however, was undeniable talent and extreme determination. He would need them both, as

An advertisement for Roland Hayes's self-produced recordings, 1918. (Boston Symphony Orchestra program; courtesy of Boston Symphony Orchestra Archives)

during the 1910s and 1920s, by sheer force of will, he single-handedly broke the "color line" in classical concert music, opening the door for many to follow.

Roland Hayes was born on June 3, 1887, to Fanny and William Hayes, ex-slaves who were barely scratching out a living on their poor farm near Curryville, Georgia. The sixth of seven children, he had to work to help his parents make ends meet, although their determination that their children would have a better life than they had allowed him to get at least a grade-school education. When his father died about 1897 Roland went to work full-time to help pay off the family's debts. Around 1900 the family moved to Chattanooga. For the next few years he worked at a foundry and at odd jobs.

Hayes began to take singing lessons while in his teens, although his mother thought it was a waste of time. Hayes's love of European classical vocal music was awakened when his teacher, Arthur Calhoun, played him some recordings by Enrico Caruso. The beautiful, controlled voice that came pouring out of the acoustic phonograph made him realize the beauty of singing as a finished art, and he decided that he would one day become such a singer himself. He wasn't interested in popular music, the usual venue for black entertainers, and doesn't seem to have paid much attention to it, although he couldn't necessarily avoid it. On one occasion he was supposed to assist Professor Calhoun at a performance in a nearby town, and Calhoun was unavoidably detained. The expectant audience insisted that the young man perform himself, which he did, running through all the "simple songs" he knew. Finally he was reduced to making up songs. He recalled in his biography, "I invented a story about a preacher and a bear," then went on to describe the exact lyrics of the immensely popular hit "The Preacher and the Bear."[2] He thought that he might have picked up the "outline of the story" at a minstrel show. He obviously had no idea that he was singing from memory one of the most popular songs of the day.

In 1905 Hayes left Chattanooga intending to enroll in Calhoun's alma mater, Oberlin College. He got as far as Nashville when his money ran out, so he looked around for a way to get into that city's Fisk University instead. With no money and only a grade-school education, it seemed impossible. However, once the director of the music department, Jennie Robinson, heard him sing she took him under her wing and secured for him some menial employment so that he could enter the school on probation. For the next four years Hayes studied at one of the south's premiere schools for blacks, under the tutelage of Miss Robinson, an extremely stern and demanding taskmaster. He spent much time with the famous Fisk Jubilee Singers, who were not actually sponsored by the school at that time but were rather a sort of extracurricular activity. With fellow student Leon P. O'Hara and two others he also organized his own Apollo Quartet, which appeared at local churches.[3]

Just as he was about to reach his goal of a college degree, fate struck a devastating blow. In 1910, the end of his fourth year, after exams and before commencement, Miss Robinson called him aside and announced that he was being expelled from the university! She refused to give any reason, demanding that he return all study materials and leave immediately. Confused, angry, and distraught, Hayes appealed to another professor, and to the president of Fisk, but to no avail. He never learned the reason for his dismissal (he said), except that he had evidently disappointed Miss Robinson in some way. Her vehement opposition to spiritual singing may have played a role. Subsequently he would discover that she had been secretly paying his tuition during his years at Fisk, when he thought he had been paying his own way.

Though devastated, Hayes was not broken. This unexpected and seemingly inexplicable blow was probably good training for the even greater challenges he would face in the future as he sought acceptance in the hostile world of classical music. The director of the Jubilee Singers, John Wesley Work II, who was not a member of the music department and not subject to Miss Robinson's wishes, allowed him to sing at commencement. Miss Robinson walked out of the ceremony.

The following year Work offered him the opportunity to join the world-famous Singers on tour in Boston, an offer that he eagerly accepted. This led directly to Hayes's first encounter with recording. A quartet from the Singers had recorded several discs for Victor in 1909 and early 1911 which became bestsellers, and they were now engaged by the Edison Phonograph Company to make a series of cylinders. Work himself was first tenor, and he chose Hayes as his second tenor, Hayes's friend Leon P. O'Hara as first bass, and Charles Wesley as second bass.

Nine selections were recorded in New York City during the last week of December 1911. All were spirituals from the Singers' familiar repertoire, such as "Roll Jordan Roll," "Little David," and "Swing Low, Sweet Chariot." The performances were dominated by Work's strong lead tenor, leaving little opportunity for the other members of the quartet to stand out. Although Hayes is not individually audible on the cylinders—at least not on those I have heard—he was named and pictured in Edison promotional literature. The quartet must have remained in (or returned to) New York City, since a test disc recording was made for Edison in February 1912.

Hayes may also have been involved with some recordings made in New York for Columbia at about the same time, by a mystery group called the Apollo Jubilee Quartette. This group, whose members were not identified on the label or in promotional literature, recorded four familiar spirituals from the Fisk repertoire, using the same arrangements as the Fisks. The recordings were made on February 26 and 27, 1912, just days after the last Edison session. It will be recalled that the name "Apollo Quartet" was used by Hayes at Fisk. However, there is no direct evidence of his connection with the Columbia recordings.

Even before the Edison sessions Hayes had decided to settle in Boston, a liberal northern city that had a strong tradition in the arts and where, he thought, a black man might have a chance. Declining to return to Nashville with the Fisk Singers, he secured a job as a messenger for the John Hancock Insurance Company in early 1912. Hayes, O'Hara, and two college friends formed a quartet of their own which performed at small venues in the Northeast. Determined to perfect his art, Hayes began studying with a music teacher named Arthur J. Hubbard, "a rough Yankee giant who both terrified and attracted me." Initially Hubbard told him to come to his home for tutoring, so as not to antagonize the white students at his downtown Boston studio. He also booked his young student at recitals in surrounding towns to give him experience, although he sometimes encountered resistance to a black man performing serious music. Once Hayes overheard his teacher when a local church called to say they were declining to engage Hayes. Hubbard roared at the representative over the phone about their lack of Christianity. The church backed down and thereafter engaged Hayes every Easter for as long as he remained in Boston.[4] Good luck trying *that* tactic in Georgia!

Almost immediately after he settled in Boston Hayes returned to Chattanooga, packed up his beloved mother (whom he called "Angel Mo'"), and brought her to Boston to live with him in his apartment in the Roxbury district. A simple woman, Fanny Hayes insisted on continuing to work as a domestic to help pay the bills. Her purpose in life now, it seemed, was to tend to her talented son and make sure that when success came his way he didn't get a swelled head.

On November 11, 1912, Hayes gave his first formal recital at Jordan Hall in Boston. He would appear there many times in the years that followed, as well as at other venues up and down the East Coast. On one of these, on January 13, 1913, he appeared with baritone and composer Harry T. Burleigh at a Jordan Hall memorial concert for Samuel Coleridge-Taylor, the noted black composer who had died a few months earlier.[5] Burleigh would become a close friend, using his influence to further Hayes's budding career. Hayes returned the favor by using Burleigh's art songs at his recitals. Hayes's repertoire at this time consisted largely of European art songs and arias, with a few similar compositions by black American composers mixed in.

Later, when he began to incorporate spirituals into his programs, Burleigh's arrangements were copiously used.

Slowly, Hayes began to attract notice. In 1914 he was chosen to sing, along with Burleigh, on a Booker T. Washington lecture tour, which opened doors to more contacts among influential blacks in the arts. About this time he also formed the Hayes Trio with tenor/pianist William Lawrence and baritone William Richardson, which performed in the Boston area. As news of his achievements reached Fisk, Hayes received a letter from his estranged sponsor Jennie Robinson offering to "bury the hatchet." Hayes went to Fisk to sing "Elijah," with Burleigh, with Miss Robinson's approval, bringing some closure to one of the more unpleasant episodes in his life. They became friends and years later, when she died, she left him all of her teaching notes. Judging by the tone of his 1942 biography, the proud Hayes never completely forgave her, however.[6]

Hayes made his New York debut on January 28, 1915, at a recital staged by noted orchestra leader Walter Craig. Also making her New York debut on the program was rising young soprano Anita Patti Brown. Some sources credit Minnie Brown, the companion of New York musical figure Daisy Tapley, with introducing Hayes to his first New York audience, but that is unconfirmed. Three months later the young tenor sang at a Carnegie Hall benefit concert for the Music School Settlement, and that summer he toured the Pennsylvania chautauqua circuit with Lawrence and Richardson. At about this time he quit his job at John Hancock, deciding, as one article put it, to "burn all his bridges behind him and roam henceforth in the fair fields of music alone."[7]

That Hayes did not restrict himself exclusively to classical fare is documented by a report that in early 1916 he was singing "Mammy," a new song by Lester Walton and Will Marion Cook (not to be confused with the Al Jolson hit of a few years later, although Jolson apparently sang this one as well). In May Hayes appeared at a music festival at Hampton Institute in Virginia, directed by R. Nathaniel Dett, and in the fall he began running regular advertisements in the *Crisis,* the publication of the National Association for the Advancement of Colored People, advertising his availability. A review of an appearance in Cleveland in May 1917, sponsored by the local chapter of the NAACP, compared him to the white Welsh tenor Evan Williams. He also made several appearances in 1917 in the New York area and in Canada, with Daisy Tapley as his accompanist.

Hayes felt that he was ready to make his solo debut in a major concert hall but was frustrated because no one would sponsor the project. Time and time again he was told that while blacks might work around the fringes of classical music, and put on recitals for their "own people" in churches and similar venues, there was simply no place for a black artist in a major concert hall playing to a white audience. It would never happen. It was not so much that there was a "glass ceiling" in classical music; there was a large, obvious, and explicit wall, and he had reached it.

He was not easily deterred. Finding no one willing to sponsor, or even manage the venture, Hayes rented Boston's Symphony Hall with $400 of his own money. He was then obliged to print tickets, compile a mailing list of three thousand names, and solicit attendees himself. As word of his daring project spread through the corridors of the John Hancock Company, friends and former coworkers pitched in and helped. "I sold eight hundred dollars' worth of tickets in that way," he later recalled, "and had so many patrons and patronesses that it cost me a fortune to print their names in the program."[8]

Despite dire predictions, the concert, on November 15, 1917, was a huge success. From John Hancock, "everybody from the President to the smallest office boy turned out."[9] The hall was filled to capacity, and seven hundred people were reported to have been turned away. The program consisted of Schubert *Lieder,* arias by Mozart and Tchaikovsky, and spirituals arranged by Burleigh. The musical establishment was taken aback but was still not willing to admit him to the top rank of concert performers.

For one thing, no record company would touch him. Classical recordings in those days carried a great deal of prestige. They were segregated into special series by the major companies, were generally premium priced, and often came with custom labels. Victor had a veritable caste system that separated artists by label color. Those of the very highest rank appeared on discs with a red label ("Red Seal"), while those of lesser attainments got a blue or purple label. At the bottom of the ladder were the poor souls consigned to the popular black label series. At Victor, Columbia, and Edison, the classical catalogs were their flagship lines. To admit a black man into those hallowed precincts was unthinkable.

This state of affairs brought periodic complaints in the black press. In January 1916 the *Chicago Defender* editorialized that at Christmas its readers had "paid to hear Tetrazzini, Caruso. But how many of our race ever asked for a record of Mme. Anita Patti Brown, Mr. Roland Hayes, Miss Hazel Harrison, Miss Maude J. Roberts, Mr. Joseph Douglas[s]?" The following October the same newspaper said that the record companies wanted to know how many phonographs were owned by blacks so that they might gauge the market. It asked readers who owned a talking machine to send in their names and addresses so that the *Defender* could pressure the record companies to better serve blacks. Nothing came of this, however.[10]

Hayes was certainly familiar with these complaints and had no doubt been asked many times himself when his art might become available on record. If a disembodied voice on a phonograph record could inspire a young black boy in the backwoods of Georgia, as Caruso's records had inspired him so many years ago, what might the recorded voice of the first black concert tenor do to inspire others of his race? The problem was how to get the records made and distributed, how to get past the wall of indifference thrown up by the large, white-controlled record companies.

In the wake of his Symphony Hall triumph, Hayes, typically, decided to tackle the problem head on. He would make and sell the records himself. On the face of it, it was an impossible and foolhardy plan, but of course that didn't stop him. In late 1917 he began making inquiries of the major record companies about the possibility of paying to have some records made, which he could then sell himself. Neither Victor nor Edison did much work of this type, but Columbia responded promptly. The company had long conducted a profitable sideline business making "personal" records for private individuals—generally churches, social organizations, companies wishing to promote their goods, or well-heeled ordinary citizens who wanted to record a souvenir for their relatives. In 1915 Columbia had established a special department for this purpose and had sales literature and price schedules available.

The full story of Roland Hayes's private recordings of 1917–18, and indeed the details of Columbia's personal recording operation, have never before been made public. Thanks to correspondence found in Hayes's personal files, now at the Detroit Public Library, we have the first clear picture of how these historic recordings—the first ever by a black concert tenor—were made.[11]

It was an expensive endeavor. The manager of Columbia's Personal Record Department, A. E. Donovan, responded to Hayes's inquiry as follows.

Replying to your inquiry of recent date, I take pleasure in advising that the Personal Record Department of the Columbia Graphophone Company is now equipped to make disc talking machine records for anyone who may desire to have them; these records play upon Columbia Graphonolas or upon any standard disc talking machine.

This record manufacture is a most delicate process and requires infinite care; on this account we are compelled to charge $50 for making a 10 inch matrix and $75 for a 12 inch matrix—in either case delivering three single disc records. Additional 10 inch records are $1 each and 12 inch records $1.50 each. If a large number of records are ordered, however, a reduction in the price per record can be made.

A 10 inch record consumes about 3¼ minutes of time and a 12 inch record about 4¼ minutes of time; from this you can get some idea as to how much matter can be recorded on records of each size.

The prices quoted herein include piano accompaniment, if desired, without extra charge; if orchestra accompaniment is required we must add to the prices quoted the cost of the orchestra and leader and this will vary with the number of men employed in the orchestra. There is also an additional charge if several voices are to be recorded—for instance, trio, quartette or chorus.

All personal records are made only in the recording laboratory of the Company, #102 West 38th Street, New York City, and only by appointment made several days in advance.

We have already made a large number of personal records and they are without exception entirely satisfactory. "It's just as easy as telephoning"—tells the whole story in a nutshell—even a little child can make a satisfactory record.

If there is any other information which you would like to have, I hope that you will write and I will be very glad to give it to you. Hoping that you will find it possible to have a a record made through the Personal Record Department and assuring you of our desire to assist you in every way, I am,

Very truly yours,
(A. E. Donovan)[12]

Attached were price schedules outlining the costs of recording and of additional copies of the four principal types of pressings (ten-inch single or double face, twelve-inch single or double). Fifty dollars was the bare minimum for recording a solo voice accompanied by piano, on a single-faced ten-inch disc. Higher charges applied for recording two or three voices or instruments ($60), four to eight ($75), or more than eight ($100). That was on a single-face ten-inch disc. Higher fees applied for double-faced and the longer twelve-inch discs, up to $300 for a chorus or orchestra on double-faced twelve-inch. To that, of course, had to be added the cost of the musicians.

Columbia's fees were high, but there was some logic behind them. Donovan was not exaggerating when he said that recording was "a most delicate process and requires infinite care." In the acoustic recording era all recordings were made "live," and the sound of various voices or instruments had to be funneled by horns to a single recording stylus, which cut into a wax master. Balancing the sounds of multiple voices or instruments to achieve adequate playback was a difficult and time-consuming process. There was no editing and no volume control. Columbia's technicians were among the best in the business, and its own studio musicians were familiar with the nuances of recording, but with amateurs in front of the horn it must at times have been an excruciating process.

Columbia provided three copies of the finished disc for the base price. Hayes, of course, needed more, because he intended to sell them. Columbia had no objection to that, but the cost of copies was high. For a single-sided ten-inch disc, the fee was one dollar each for the first 50, $0.75 each for the next 50, $0.60 each for the next 150, and $0.50 each for quantities over 250.[13] Taking into account all costs, recording as well as pressings, it was obvious that Hayes would have to spend several hundred dollars up-front before he could begin to see any return. In 1917, for a private individual, that was a substantial amount of money.

Hayes might have secured a better rate from one of the smaller record companies then starting up, such as Emerson, Gennett, or Paramount. However, Victor and Columbia held the all-important patents for lateral-cut recording, the type that would play on most phonographs. The vertical-cut discs produced by most of the smaller companies at this time could only be played on specially equipped machines. If Hayes wanted to reach the largest possible audience, he had to use Columbia. He would also have to figure out how to market the records on his own.

He engaged a black entrepreneur named George W. Broome, who had wide contacts in the world of black concert music and the arts, to be his sales manager.[14] Once associated with Will Marion Cook's *Clorindy* theatrical company, Broome had staged concerts and produced documentary motion pictures about black educational institutions. They made arrangements for Hayes's first session at the Columbia laboratories in New York, which was held on or about December 21, 1917. The selection chosen was Harry T. Burleigh's arrangement of "Swing Low, Sweet Chariot," accompanied by piano, on a single-faced ten-inch disc.

It was an impressive performance of one of the most popular spirituals then in the repertoire. Hayes gave it a quiet and sensitive reading, with understated accompaniment by an unidentified pianist (probably Lawrence Brown, a young man who had arrived in Boston from Charleston in 1917 and become Hayes's regular accompanist). The recording quality was quite good. Commercial versions of the song were available by the Fisk University Jubilee Quartet on Victor and Columbia, as well as by the Tuskegee Institute Singers, but never had it been recorded in a solo version by an African American. Hayes was probably counting on a well-known and popular title to launch his recording venture.

Early in 1918 Hayes left Boston with Lawrence Brown on a self-arranged transcontinental tour. In due course copies of his record arrived, bearing the Columbia Graphophone Company "Personal Record" label ("Specially Made for Roland W. Hayes"). For a time Hayes left the promotion of his record in the hands of Broome and his mother. According to his biography, "my best salesman was my mother, who sold a good many records to members of her church."[15] His marketing efforts were wider than that, however. He placed ads in Boston Symphony Orchestra programs and, in May 1918, began advertising in the *Crisis,* the national magazine of the NAACP. His advertisement contained an explicit appeal to racial pride.

RECORDS OF NEGRO ARTISTS

Do you own a phonograph of any make and have you tried to purchase records which would bring to your home the singing and playing of the best Negro artists? Of course you were offered records of popular airs and popular music and possibly a few records of quartet songs by Negro singers. But that wasn't what you wanted. You wanted to bring to your home and to your family and to your friends the voice of the individual Negro singer or the playing of the individual Negro performer who would take high rank among the invisible makers of music and singers of song whom the phonograph has brought to cheer your spare moments after the grind of the day's work is done.

At last this is possible. Roland W. Hayes, the acknowledged leading singer of the Negro race, has brought out his first record and he has plans for many others in the very near future. Nothing else could so well introduce the series as the favorite and plaintive Negro melody, "Swing Low, Sweet Chariot." The record sells for $1.50 and can be used on any machine using disc records.[16]

Readers were urged to contact Hayes at 130 Boylston Street in Boston, where he had obtained space at the A. J. Jackson and Co. piano store, from which he also booked his personal appearances.

Response to the initial disc was evidently good enough to encourage Hayes to make more records after he returned from the West Coast. On May 4, 1918, he recorded three more titles. Seeking to vary his repertoire on record as he did at his concerts, these were art songs and an aria rather than spirituals. One was "Twilight," a short (1:55) and very tender art song by Katherine A. Glen. Another was "I Hear You Calling Me" by Charles Marshall, an art song made famous by John McCormack in a hugely popular Victor recording first released in 1910.[17] Hayes's rendition of the latter was not up to his standards and was not released; he remade the title several months later.

The third title was the most ambitious he had undertaken thus far. It was the aria "Vesti la giubba" from Leoncavallo's opera *I Pagliacci,* with full orchestra accompaniment. This was a fairly recent piece, the opera having made its debut in the 1890s. The aria was a bravura selection strongly identified with Enrico Caruso, whose recording (originally made in 1902) practically set the standard for Golden Age singing. Caruso's version was an enormous seller. Victor later claimed that it was the company's only pre-1920 recording to sell more than a million copies. It may well have been one of the Caruso recordings that inspired Hayes as a young farm boy in the early 1900s.

Hayes gave a powerful performance, reaching all the high notes and rattling the rafters (though not blasting) with his fortissimo. His intensity was as evident as his tenderness on quieter numbers such as "Twilight." He was, truthfully, no Caruso, though he seemed to be trying to sound as much like him as possible. If nothing else, the first three issued discs were testimony to Hayes's extraordinary range. His selections also showed that he was not afraid to choose pieces strongly identified with and inevitably inviting comparison with established white artists—Caruso's "Vesti," McCormack's "I Hear You Calling Me," the Fisks' "Swing Low." Perhaps that was the point.

Four discs were advertised in the June 1918 issue of the *Crisis,* including "I Hear You Calling Me," which was apparently withdrawn after the ad was placed. Despite the added cost of recording "Vesti la giubba" (which the label called simply "Arioso from Pagliacci"), all were initially priced at the same $1.50. Later prices were adjusted to range from $1 to $2 per disc.

Close on the heels of his second session, Hayes returned on May 25 to record two twelve-inch selections with orchestra, the spiritual "Steal Away to Jesus" and the aria "Una furtiva lagrima" from Donizetti's *L'Elisir d'Amore.* Two additional selections were recorded at about this time, although exact dates are unknown. "A Spirit Flower" was an art song with piano accompaniment advertised just once and possibly not issued (no copies are known to exist).[18] The aria "Solenne in quest'ora" from Verdi's *La Forza del Destino* was an even more ambitious undertaking than "Vesti la giubba," being a duet with baritone Dr. Sumner Wormley with orchestra accompaniment, on a twelve-inch disc. This must have been the most costly of all Hayes's Columbias to record, but for some reason it was not listed in his regular advertisements in the *Crisis.* Lasting almost four-and-a-half minutes, it is a creditable performance but may have suffered by comparison with the celebrity version by Caruso and Antonio Scotti on Victor.

Hayes was back at Columbia once again on June 15 to record a final spiritual, Burleigh's arrangement of "By an' By," with piano accompaniment. Here he displayed the same combination of intensity and tenderness evident on his earlier spiritual recordings. He might imitate the great white singers in the operatic arena, but none—at least at this time—could approach him in the solo singing of spirituals.

This was the last of Hayes's known personal recordings at Columbia, except for a successful remake of "I Hear You Calling Me" in December. The latter half of 1918 seems to have been occupied with aggressive marketing of the eight or nine discs he had made.[19] They were sold at his concerts, and national advertising continued in the *Crisis.* Without the marketing apparatus of the established record companies, he was obliged to sell the records by mail from his office at 130 Boylston Street and through a network of agents he recruited across the country. Ordinary record stores, most of which were aligned with one or more of the major labels, apparently would not stock his "independent" discs.

The recruiting of agents was a time-consuming endeavor, as evidenced by the contracts and correspondence located among his surviving papers. In the fall of 1918 Hayes began listing his agents in his *Crisis* ad (while soliciting more), eventually reaching a total of forty-five names in twenty-five states and the District of Columbia.[20] Among them were his colleague Dr. C. Sumner Wormley of Washington, D.C., and the Pace and Handy Music Company in New York City. Most, however, were private individuals, lovers of the arts, who agreed to play copies for their friends and attempt to arrange private sales. This was a very personalized operation!

The correspondence illustrates what a difficult task it was to conduct this type of one-on-one marketing. The most frequent complaint was the high price of the records and the fact that they were all single-faced. Ordinary store-stock Columbias in 1918 sold for $0.85 for ten-inch, and $1.25 for twelve-inch (although celebrity selections could cost more), and virtually all were double-faced. Hayes's offerings ranged in price from $1.00 to $2.00 for a single-faced disc. Another barrier to sales was the deadly influenza epidemic that swept the country in the winter of 1918–19. Typical was a letter from an agent in Jacksonville, Florida.

> My Dear Mr. Broome,
> I have been out of the city for a week or ten days and I have just taken up the work with the records. I have had a few people to listen to them and they are very much pleased with the beautiful voice of Mr. Hayes. But I think the price of [the] records a bit high, on account of the short selections and only one side of the disc used. You will notice that most Columbia records are double records. I think it will help the sale of the records in the future if they are double. I regret that you did not send Marshall's sentimental song "I Hear You Calling Me." I think it will sell fast down here. I do not think I can make a report this month since I am just beginning. The epidemic of influenza is on here and I cannot get into the homes as I wish, but hope to make things hum next month. . . . Hoping to hear from you soon, I am,
>
> J. M. Robinson, Jr.

Another lady wrote that her entire city was under quarantine because of the flu.

Hayes could not do much about the flu or about the price of the records. He wrote repeatedly of his frustration regarding the latter, in an almost plaintive tone, in his response to Mr. Robinson.

> Dear Mr. Robinson:
> Your favor of Oct. 10th at hand and contents duly noted. In replying I wish to say that I thank you from my heart for your suggestion of double disc records, but my friend please let me inform you of some things which I know you have not thought of. First, that there isn't a Phonograph Company in the U.S. that is willing to make classic records for Negroes; they will, and do, make ragtime and Jubilee singers records, but they refuse absolutely to make standard art songs and operatic numbers for colored artists.
> Therefore it is up to the artist to make his or her own records and put them out at their own personal expense, which expense I assure you is very great.
> We as a race, I regret to say, must suffer this treatment or do what we can to offset it. I have done and am doing what I can in that direction. Every record I put out costs me so much that were I to put out double disc records I should

have to charge at least $3.00 per record, and at that I should make almost no profit at all, as I am now doing on these. With me it is a sacrifice, but I am willing to make it that my people may hear and become acquainted with the best, which I a humble artist of the race can give them. As an agent I wish you would explain this to your purchasers, and help them to understand as I am sure you now do. . . .

Sincerely yours,
Roland Hayes

Hayes was correct about the costs. Working from the Columbia price schedule, the average cost to have one hundred single-sided ten-inch discs pressed was $0.875 per disc. A press run of 500 worked out to $0.61 each. To that, of course, had to be added the cost of recording and marketing, which we will estimate at $0.20 per record. According to his standard contract agents received a discount of 20 percent. That meant that on a $1.00 record Hayes was receiving only $0.80, and it was costing him about the same amount.[21]

A scribbled note by Hayes that "it costs me 60 [cents] for every record made" gives us a clue as to how many copies of these records may have been pressed. If he was referring to the average price, that would be equivalent to about 500 ten-inch copies. If he meant the marginal price of each additional copy, it would be between 100 and 250. In any event, the number pressed seems to have been in the hundreds, not thousands, which would explain why these records are so rare today.

With Hayes back in Boston by the middle of 1918, and sales of his records evidently not going well, it was inevitable that there would be friction with his sales manager. About September he severed his relationship with George Broome and took over management of the enterprise himself, changing its mailing address to his home at 3 Warwick Street in Roxbury. To save money he continued to use his old stationery and contract forms, crossing out Broome's name and substituting his own.

Advertisements for the records continued in the *Crisis* until July 1919, at which point only four titles were still listed. Perhaps as he sold out of the original press runs of the others he simply did not reorder. In terms of spreading his music far and wide the venture had been a failure. In terms of preserving his art at this critical juncture, just before his emergence on to the world stage, it has been a godsend to historians.

Hayes had one more, little-known brush with recording shortly after his 1917–18 private recordings. According to a notebook of "voice trials" located at the Edison National Historic Site in New Jersey, in February 1919 Hayes was considered for recording by the Edison company. It is unclear whether he auditioned in person or company personnel simply reviewed one of his records. In either case, the reaction was chilly. The notation, in Thomas Edison's own hand, was "Roland W. Hayes, colored tenor—Can't see any value in this voice."[22]

On January 30, 1919, Hayes appeared in recital at Aeolian Hall in New York, accompanied by Harry T. Burleigh on piano. Included on the program were four of Burleigh's arrangements of spirituals and two of his art songs.[23] Soon thereafter Hayes set off on another tour of the United States. Because of racial disturbances in the East he remained in California for most of the year. He returned to the East Coast in the fall with a new goal in mind.

It was axiomatic that to reach the upper echelons of the concert world a singer must have studied in Europe. Even more desirable was to have established one's reputation there. Hayes, of course, had done neither, so he began saving money to finance an extended trip, embarking on an intense round of concerts and recitals in the East. In one of the defining moments of his career, he approached William H. Brennan, a friend and manager of the Boston Symphony, for help in advancing to the top rank of concert singers. Looking at the black man, Brennan said without rancor, "it will never happen here." Hayes was determined to prove him wrong.

After a busy winter, including one concert in Washington, D.C., that netted the phenomenal sum of $1,100, he sailed for England on April 23, 1920, with his accompanist Lawrence Brown. Hayes's plan was to study and concertize in Europe, then travel on to Africa to study the origins of Negro folk music, "gathering the threads which led to its development in Africa, which will enable him to trace its progress to the present time."[24] Arriving in London he was immediately taken in by members of the city's tight-knit black community, including Dusi Mohammed Ali and Amanda Aldridge. He began studying with George Henschel. His first concert, at Aeolian Hall in London, received good reviews, but it was slow going for the next year. Although he performed regularly, the venues were small and the income smaller. By the spring of 1921 he could barely make ends meet and was seriously thinking of giving up.

In April 1921 his managers, Messrs. Ibbs and Tillett, determined that he was ready for a larger-scale concert at prestigious Wigmore Hall. They advanced the reservation money themselves, since Hayes didn't have any. Then Hayes came down with pneumonia. On the night of the concert he was barely able to stand; but he sang as if it was his final concert (which it might have been). Then, miraculously, after the intermission, his fever disappeared. The reviews were excellent. The next day he received word that he had been commanded to perform at Buckingham Palace for King George and Queen Mary ("I fainted dead away"). One month later he sang for the great soprano Dame Nellie Melba, who on hearing him rushed up to him with outstretched arms.

With royal recognition and Melba's patronage, doors swung open everywhere. The next two and a half years were a whirlwind of triumphs across Europe—Paris, Vienna, Budapest, Prague, Leipzig, Munich, the Hague, Amsterdam, Madrid, Copenhagen. In France he met Frederick Delius and Gabriel Fauré.

There were also offers from recording companies. In 1921 he was approached by HMV and recorded five spirituals as a test. He was then offered a contract but, feeling the terms were "ungenerous," turned it down. "I went to the manufacturer's office to recover the matrixes, which somebody handed to me, together with a pair of metal shears and an inferential nod. Although I had not felt exactly satisfied with my disembodied voice, I had taken some secret pleasure in listening to it, and I hated to cut up the recordings without hearing them again. But I accepted the scissors, sliced the metal discs neatly in half, and went away."[25]

More successful were negotiations in 1923 with the English Vocalion label, which recorded six spirituals by Hayes, all accompanied by Lawrence Brown. Although he featured European art music in his concerts, it was his spirituals that record companies wanted. The recordings were apparently made at two sessions early in the year, although exact dates are not known. Four were arrangements by Harry T. Burleigh, "Go Down Moses," "By an' By," "Deep River," and "Swing Low, Sweet Chariot." Two of these titles had also been recorded by Hayes in 1917–18 ("Swing Low" and "By an' By"). The vocal performances were quite similar, as were the accompaniments, lending credence to the theory that Lawrence Brown accompanied Hayes on both. "Steal Away" was arranged by Brown, and "Sit Down" by Hayes himself.

On the affirmative "Go Down Moses" Hayes was commanding, delivering his ultimatum to "ol' Pharaoh" in no uncertain terms ("Let my people go!"). Most of the selections were quieter and more contemplative, however, and Hayes sang them appropriately, with the quiet intensity for which he had become famous. They are remarkable recordings, although they have been somewhat upstaged by the more dramatic readings by basso Paul Robeson for Victor in the mid- and late 1920s.

All six sides were released in England during 1923. Four of them were also released by Vocalion in the United States in January 1924. The U.S. releases appear to have sold rather well, remaining in the catalog for nearly ten years, despite the fact that they were acoustically recorded and electrical recording rendered most acoustic discs obsolete in 1925. They are fairly frequently found today.

In late 1923 Hayes returned to the United States to resume his career there (he had made a short visit during the winter of 1922–23 to visit his ailing mother, who died soon thereafter). His studies in Africa would have to wait. His stature was boosted immeasurably by his European triumphs. He had sung for the king of England and been embraced by Melba! William Brennan, who had told him that he could never reach the top ranks of his craft in the United States, changed his mind and agreed to manage his concert tours, which he did for the next fifteen years.

Hayes was welcomed home with a triumphal tour, including a November 1923 appearance with the Boston Symphony conducted by Pierre Monteux—believed to be the first time a black singer had appeared with a major orchestra. This was followed by a spectacularly successful December 1923 concert at New York's Town Hall, which created an uproar and brought him dramatically to the attention of the American public. He also appeared at Carnegie Hall.

The 1920s and 1930s were the years of Roland Hayes's greatest fame. He was internationally known, touring for part of each year in the United States and the remainder in Europe. In 1925 he sang for Queen Mother Maria Christina of Spain and in 1927 made his Italian debut. In early 1928 he gave ten concerts in Russia as a guest of the State but was unimpressed by the Communists (who wanted to portray him as a liberator of the oppressed). The honors were many, including in 1924 the coveted Spingarn Medal, awarded by the NAACP for exceptional achievement by an African American. In 1932 he received an honorary doctorate of music from Fisk University, in the presence of Jennie Robinson. He also received honorary degrees from a number of other institutions. He became, as he had hoped, an inspiration and a role model to a new generation of talented black artists who followed him on to the concert stage, among them Paul Robeson, Marian Anderson, and Dorothy Maynor.

At the top of his craft, he was performing sixty to eighty concerts per year, earning $2,000 to $4,000 for each. He bought a villa outside Paris. The French liked him so much they installed a sculpture of him singing "Steal Away" in the Salles Gaveua, an art gallery in Paris. He also bought a farm in Georgia, which he named "Angel Mo'" in memory of his beloved mother.

Although he lost heavily in the 1929 Wall Street crash Hayes retained enough money and property to continue living the life of an international concert star. After two final seasons of transcontinental touring in 1931 and 1932, he decided in mid-life to go into semi-retirement, singing only when he wanted to. Settling at Angel Mo' farm in Georgia, he opened a school for young singers. Redneck neighbors caused problems when they learned that he was allowing white pupils to live on the premises.

Through all these years he had remained single, devoted to his mother, and to his art. In September 1932, at age 45, he married his cousin Alzada, and two years later they had a daughter, Africa (later spelled Afrika). In the 1960s Afrika would become a professional singer and teach in the Boston school system.

During sixteen years of fame and accomplishment Hayes issued no recordings. The reasons are not clear and are not mentioned in his biography. It certainly could not have been the same reasons that kept him out of the recording studio at the start of his career. Now many black artists were recording, and some, like Robeson and Anderson, to great acclaim. More likely the record companies saw in Hayes a good, but not exceptional, seller and would not meet his price. As HMV learned in 1921, the proud tenor would rather cut the matrices in two than agree to a contract he did not feel was fair.

In 1935 he did record three rather esoteric titles for RCA Victor at Symphony Hall in Boston, "Auch kleine dinge," "Trocknet nicht," and "Let Me Shine." The reason they were not issued is not known, but one writer has said that it was because of background noises, including the sound of a fire engine passing the theater. Victor certainly could have obtained additional takes if it wished, but perhaps felt the market for such fare would be limited. Test pressings exist.[26]

A more productive engagement was with Columbia in 1939. Between September 29 and November 15 of that year he had five sessions at the company's studios, recording eighteen titles, many more than once. Just as in his concerts, the repertoire was primarily art songs with a few spirituals mixed in. On most sides he was accompanied by pianist Reginald Boardman, although a few were sung a capella. From these sessions Columbia culled ten sides that were packaged in a 78-rpm album entitled *A Song Recital by Roland Hayes*. It was released in January 1940 with rather plain packaging, in the Columbia Masterworks series, as album set M-393.

The selections were well recorded and Hayes was in fine voice, but the album seems to have had limited sales. Perhaps it was because the repertoire was, again, esoteric. Hayes sang selections by Monteverdi, Galuppi, Bononcini, Beethoven, Massenet, Bach, and Quilter (with text by Shakespeare), plus a thirteenth-century French chanson. Of the ten selections, only two were spirituals, and neither was terribly familiar: "Crucifixion (He Never Said a Mumberlin' Word)" and "'Roun' 'Bout de Mountain." Nevertheless the set remained in the Columbia catalog for about ten years, along with a short, glowing description of his career and achievements.

In February 1940 two additional sides from the 1939 sessions were released on a single twelve-inch disc. These were spirituals, sung with the restraint for which Hayes was famous. On "Hear de Lambs a Cryin'" and "Plenty Good Room" (on one side of the disc) he was accompanied by Boardman's tasteful piano, but on "Were You There" (on the other) he sang a capella. The latter was a striking, intimate performance, with Hayes's ethereal tenor alternately soft and soaring. It is an exceptionally "live" recording (in original pressings), with an eerie intensity that is enough to make the hairs on the back of one's neck stand on end.

Hayes returned to Columbia on February 20, 1941, and April 7, 1942, to record eleven more titles, but this time the art songs went unissued. Only four sides from the first date were released (others have since appeared on CD), a mix of spirituals and folksongs. May 1941 saw the release of "Lit'l Boy" and "I Want to Go Home" / "You're Tired, Chile." Columbia announced this curiously, with a small drawing of an angel in blackface and the words, "Roland Hayes, like Lotte Lehmann, is one of the very greatest vocal artists of our day; and when it comes to singing the music of his own race he is incomparable."[27]

Almost a year later, in January 1942, two unusual and intriguing sides appeared on another disc which, if nothing else, demonstrated the range of Hayes's musical interests. "Xango" was an African religious chant of the Makumba, as arranged by Villa-Lobos, delivered with an ominous, insistent rhythm. "Micheu Banjo" ("Mister Banjo") was a catchy, syncopated Louisiana Creole folksong about a fancy dude. Both the 1941 and 1942 discs stayed in the catalog for many years.

Hayes's biography, *Angel Mo' and Her Son, Roland Hayes,* by MacKinley Helm, was published in 1942 by Little, Brown and Company of Boston. It was an adequate retelling of the artist's remarkable career to that point, although sometimes frustratingly vague as to dates and places and quite definitely from his point of view (it was written in the first person, like an autobiography). Hayes's frustration at the racial barriers placed in his path, and his overwhelming love for his angelic late mother, shine through. One day, hopefully, the objective and thoroughly researched third-person biography he deserves will be published.

During the early war years Hayes traveled to Britain to sing for the citizens of that blitzed nation. He was now in his fifties and his voice could not be expected to be quite what it was thirty years earlier, but his technique showed no sign of lessening. A *New York Times* review of a 1946 Carnegie Hall concert noted that "his voice is long past its prime, but his art is at its zenith. This is not to say that the voice has lost its beauty—once in a while there is a flash of liquid gold."[28]

In December 1947 and January 1948 he made some private recordings, utilizing the services of the Telavix Corporation in Boston. At least eight titles were recorded, primarily spirituals but including a few art songs (e.g., Schubert's "Der Jungling an der Quelle"). Only two appear to have been issued, on a single twelve-inch disc bearing his own custom Angel-Mo' label. They were "Lit'l Boy," a favorite at his concerts, on which he was accompanied by Reginald Boardman, and "Were You There," performed a capella as on his haunting 1939 Columbia. A copy in my collection plays at 78 rpm but is pressed in vinyl, like an LP. The Angel-Mo' disc had very limited distribution, perhaps at only one store in Boston, and is unknown to most collectors.[29]

In 1948 Hayes published a book of his arrangements of spirituals, titled *My Songs: AfroAmerican Religious Folk Songs*. In 1950 he was appointed to the music faculty of Boston University.

Hayes resumed recording on a larger scale during the 1950s, producing several LPs. In 1953 he recorded *A Roland Hayes Recital* at Telavix which was issued on the small A-440 label (later renamed Heritage). Once again Reginald Boardman was his accompanist. This led to a contract with the larger Vanguard label, which in 1954 commissioned an ambitious double-LP set called *Six Centuries of Song*. As suggested by the title, the repertoire ranged from the work of fourteenth-century French poet and composer Guillaume de Machaut to African American spirituals, as well as oddities such as the aforementioned "Xango." Another Vanguard LP followed in 1955, *The Life of Christ in Folksongs,* and a third in 1956, *My Songs.*

Despite his advancing age Hayes continued to perform, touring England, Holland, and Denmark in 1954. In 1955 he began an association with Boston record collector and audio engineer Stephen Fassett, who recorded many of his concerts during the next twelve years. A few selections from these tapes were released on CD in the 1990s.[30]

A major concert was staged at Carnegie Hall in 1962 to benefit black colleges. In the mid-1960s Hayes sometimes appeared with his daughter, Afrika, a soprano. Roland Hayes gave his last concert in 1973 at the age of eighty-five, at the Longly School of Music in Cambridge, Massachusetts. He was singing the familiar "Lit'l Boy" but when he reached the middle verse, he forgot the words. His longtime accompanist Reginald Boardman tried to call the words to him, but Hayes could not hear. Then Afrika whispered them to him, and he smiled and went on with the lyric: "Lit'l boy, how old are you?" It was time to retire.[31]

Roland Hayes passed away on January 1, 1977, in Boston, at the age of eighty-nine.[32] He had spent his long life opening doors, and breaking down the barriers that lesser-minded people placed in his path and the paths of others of his race. His historic 1917–18 Columbias, the first recordings of concert music by an African American, are a landmark in the history of music in the United States.

31   The Four Harmony Kings

Male quartets specializing in close harmony were quite popular at the turn of the twentieth century. Today we think of this style of singing as "barbershop," but there were many variations at the time and almost every type of music was performed by quartets. African Americans were well represented in the field. As one early study commented, "Pick up four colored boys or young men anywhere and the chances are ninety out of a hundred that you have a quartet. Let one of them sing the melody and the others will naturally find the parts. Indeed it may be said that all male Negro youth of the United States is divided into quartets."[1]

By the 1920s the vogue for popular quartets was beginning to subside, but that is when one particular black quartet achieved its greatest fame. The Four Harmony Kings, an outgrowth of a gospel group, hit the big time in the Broadway musical *Shuffle Along* in 1921, and enjoyed a long career thereafter, performing in Europe and America. They also recorded for several labels.

Little is known about the early life of the group's founder, William A. Hann, other than that he was born about 1881.[2] A basso profundo, he was by the early 1910s touring the Midwest on a chautauqua circuit managed by Edward Thomas. Based on the scraps of information that can be found, it appears that he originally sang with a group called the Midland Jubilee Singers, which later became known as Hann's Jubilee Singers. This was the group that gave a young Indianapolis boy named Noble Sissle his first professional experience around 1911 or 1912. Sissle recalled that the group traveled from Denver to New York City. An undated photo of the group shows five men and two women.[3]

In May 1914 Hann was listed as "an operatic bass" appearing in "An Evening with Negro Composers" at Quinn Chapel in Chicago. By the following winter he was touring again with Hann's Jubilee Singers on the West Coast. In January 1915 the *Los Angeles Tribune* carried this item about the group, noting the presence of not only Hann and his wife, but of future concert star Florence Cole-Talbert and her husband:

> Formerly known as the Midland Jubilee Singers, traveling under the direction of the Midland Lyceum Bureau, Des Moines, Iowa, this company was repeated for seven successive seasons on the Midland Chautauqua circuit and set a record unparalleled, it is said, by any jubilee company under one management. This group of singers consists of seven highly cultured musicians—Mrs. Florence Cole-Talbert, soprano; Miss Mamie Morrison, contralto; Mrs. W. A. Hann, second soprano; W. H. Berry, tenor; George R. Gardner, tenor soloist; W. A. Hann, bass; W. P. Talbert, pianist and celloist. All of these singers possess voices of extraordinary quality.[4]

Sometime during the next two years Hann organized the Four Harmony Kings, in which he would sing bass, as an offshoot of his Jubilee Singers. Recruited to be first tenor was a young man named Ivan Harold Browning. Browning was born on February 20, 1891, in Brenham, Texas, and as a teenager had appeared as a soloist in concerts in that state, singing spirituals and classics. He had moved with his family to California in 1911, where he married Maurine Moss (in 1913) and sang with the California Jubilee Singers and the Exposition Four, which performed at the 1915 San Francisco World's Fair.[5]

For second tenor, Hann chose William Howard Berry from his jubilee chorus. Berry was born in Kansas City and had attended Wilberforce Academy and Oberlin Conservatory before joining Hann.[6] The baritone was Charles Exodus Drayton, another experienced performer who had toured with the Chaflin University Quartette and the Transcontinental Southland Jubilee Quartet, which was described as "a quartet of mixed voices, each [of whom also] played instruments of various kinds."[7]

The elegant Four Harmony Kings during an English engagement. (*Performer* magazine, June 19, 1929; courtesy of Arthur Badrock)

Exactly when the Four Harmony Kings began performing under that name has not been determined. One source indicates that they were appearing in vaudeville as early as 1915; others speculate 1916. Their first performances appear to have been in and around Chicago. By 1918 they were beginning to attract national attention, with the *New York Age* listing their vaudeville itinerary as they criss-crossed the country.[8]

In April 1919, while they were appearing in Chicago, they met James Reese Europe, who gave them their first opportunity to record. Europe was a bandleader and war hero just back from France, who was touring with a big stage show featuring his 369th Infantry "Hell Fighters" Band. Europe is remembered today as a pioneer in the transition to jazz, but his show presented a wide variety of musical entertainment including sentimental songs, novelty numbers, classical pieces, and spirituals, as well as "hot" numbers by the band. He hired the Harmony Kings as his resident quartet, supplementing an existing sextet, the Singing Serenaders.[9]

Europe had recorded for Pathé before leaving New York in March and was scheduled for one additional session in early May just before the tour concluded. Pathé gave him a great deal of latitude regarding repertoire, and when the session took place in New York, on May 7 or 8, he chose six selections by the band and two by his new quartet, which for recording purposes Pathé dubbed "Lieut. Jim Europe's Four Harmony Kings."

The two titles chosen for the Harmony Kings were both unaccompanied spirituals. "Swing Low, Sweet Chariot" uses a different text and melody than is commonly heard today. It is sung slowly and reverently, with a tenor prominently featured, and the rest of the quartet harmonizing. "One More Ribber to Cross" is performed similarly, with much emphasis on group harmonics. The bass (Hann) is prominently heard, at times singing lines in counterpoint to the others. The records reveal a well-rehearsed group whose emphasis is on ensemble sound rather than serving as a showcase for any one member.

The Harmony Kings continued with Europe to Boston, for one last out-of-town concert on May 9 before a scheduled finale in New York City on May 10. But in a shocking turn of events, Europe was attacked and stabbed by a mentally unbalanced drummer on the evening of May 9. Three of the Harmony Kings—Browning, Berry, and Drayton—were in the room when the attack occurred. Europe's wound at first seemed superficial, but within hours he was dead. His colleagues, and indeed the entire black community, were in shock. A huge funeral was held in New York City on May 13.

Europe's May recordings were released posthumously, most of them during the summer of 1919. For some reason the spirituals by the Harmony Kings were held until February 1920, when they were released on a single disc. Like the rest of the Europe titles, they had been recorded using Pathé's vertical-cut technology and could be played only on its own (or specially adapted) phonographs. By 1920 the entire industry—including Pathé—was converting to lateral-cut recordings, which could be played on ordinary phonographs. Thus the Harmony Kings' Pathés were issued in a format that was already obsolete when they went on sale and, as a result, had limited distribution. They were reissued in lateral format in 1923.

After their short stint with the Jim Europe troupe, the Harmony Kings resumed touring on their own. During July 1919 they appeared with the Red Devils Band in New York, and for the rest of the year they played throughout the East, with appearances in Boston, Philadelphia, and Jersey City, among other places.

Their next major break came in September 1921 when they were approached to join the hit musical *Shuffle Along,* which was then in its fourth month on Broadway. The score for the show was written by Noble Sissle and Eubie Blake, and Sissle had known Hann for about ten years, since his days with Hann's Jubilee Singers. More recently they had worked together on the Jim Europe tour (Sissle was Europe's close friend and second-in-command). Very likely it was Hann's relationship with Sissle that helped secure the offer to join the show.

Shuffle Along had debuted in May 1921 with a group called the Palm Beach Four as its resident quartet. Evidently their work was not entirely satisfactory, and in September they were replaced by the Four Harmony Kings, who were an immediate hit. A review in December 1921 raved, "The Four Harmony Kings score one of the biggest hits in *Shuffle Along* and literally stop the show in the second act." A later review added, "In the second act the singing of the Four Harmony Kings created a great sensation. They gave a number of selections in the style of the old minstrel days and were recalled so often that their turn was about doubled in length."[10]

In addition to providing musical interludes, members of the Harmony Kings assumed roles in the cast. The most important went to first tenor Ivan Harold Browning, who took over the role of the romantic lead opposite leading lady Lottie Gee. Together they sang "Love Will Find a Way," the show's big romantic duet and a major hit. The fact that two black actors sang a love song—something rarely if ever seen before on stage—was one of the breakthrough aspects of the show. The show's other big hit, and the one better remembered today, was "I'm Just Wild about Harry," which was about Browning's character, Harry Walton.

The Harmony Kings recorded for two different labels around the time they joined *Shuffle Along,* and at least one of the titles recorded was from the show. The files for both labels have long since disappeared, and exact recording dates are not known. The only discographies to venture a guess as to when the records were made place them in July and August 1921, which would have been before the quartet joined *Shuffle Along* in September.[11] The recording dates are highly uncertain and could easily have been in September.

Whenever the records were made, they show a group that lived up to its name, emphasizing meticulous harmonizing in a style that was in some ways more appropriate to a period twenty years earlier. Perhaps that was the point. For its predominantly white audiences, *Shuffle Along* was a nostalgic journey back to an earlier and gentler era—and one with less turbulent black-white relations. The smooth harmonizing of the Harmony Kings fit this nostalgic theme perfectly.

Three titles were recorded for the Black Swan label. "Ain't It a Shame" is a rhythmic spiritual, in which the narrator lectures a group of backsliders, then suddenly turns the "moral" on its head.

Tenor: Ain't it a shame to steal on Sunday, ain't it a shame,
Quartet: Ain't it a shame?
   Ain't it a shame to steal on Sunday,
   Ain't it a shame, ain't it a shame?
   Ain't it a shame to steal on Sunday,
   When you got Monday, Tuesday, Wednesday, Thursday, Friday, Saturday . . . ooh,
   Ain't it a shame?

Toward the end of the record the singing stops and a deep-voiced elder (Hann) begins to lecture the congregation about sinning on Sunday. Loudly interrupted, he abruptly announces, "the last stanza," and the quartet finishes the song. Throughout, tenor and quartet alternate in a modified call-and-response pattern.

"Goodnight Angeline" is a melodious but rather clichéd southern love song by Sissle and Blake, introduced by them in vaudeville and interpolated into *Shuffle Along.* After a brief piano introduction, the Harmony Kings sing sweetly and unaccompanied, as if serenading crinoline-clad southern belles in a blossom-strewn Georgia lane. Again, the tenor begins the verse and the quartet answers in harmony. The Harmony Kings recorded at least one additional title for Black Swan at the same time, which was not issued until 1922. It was the sentimental number, "Love's Old Sweet Song," rendered with straightforward harmonies, and is quite rare. In addition, Ivan Browning recorded two solo numbers for the label shortly after the quartet's 1921 session, "Christians Awake" and "My Task." Other titles may have been recorded for Black Swan but not issued, as matrix numbers adjacent to these remain unidentified.

At about the same time the Harmony Kings recorded two sentimental songs for Emerson. One was the old barbershop warhorse "Sweet Adeline," which would seem to have been perfect for them. It is, however, an unexceptional rendition. The other was the gentle lullaby, "Doan You Cry, Ma Honey," sung with their characteristic attention to careful harmonizing. These recordings of popular material are certainly practiced and smooth, although they do not necessarily live up to the rave reviews that the quartet received for its live appearances. Perhaps it was their stage presence that made them so special. Judging by both reviews and photos, they put on a class act, wearing tuxedos and sporting top hats and canes.[12] This elegant appearance would be the group's trademark for the rest of its history.

The first two Black Swan titles were issued in late 1921, while the Emersons were released in January 1922. Neither record seems to have been a particularly large seller, although both companies leased their masters to other labels so some of these titles can be found on Paramount, Grey Gull, and Symphonola, among others.

While their records may not have attracted great attention, the Harmony Kings continued to draw positive reviews in *Shuffle Along,* which continued its New York run until July of 1922. In June 1922 Hann had to leave due to illness and was replaced for a short period by twenty-four year-old Columbia law student Paul Robeson. Some sources have taken this to mean Robeson recorded with the Harmony Kings, but this does not appear to be the case. Robeson was a dramatic basso who would begin recording spirituals for Victor in 1925 and soon thereafter become an international stage, film, and singing star. He was well known to the *Shuffle Along* principals. In the fall of 1922 he attended a Harlem party with Sissle and Blake, Will Hann, and Ivan Browning, among others. According to Sissle, Robeson later felt that his stint in *Shuffle Along* was the beginning of his professional singing career.[13]

During the winter of 1923–24 the Harmony Kings stayed with *Shuffle Along* as it toured the United States and Canada. Reviews continued to be good both for the quartet and its individual members. From Pittsburgh, "I. H. Browning and W. A. Hann, with his melodious rich bass, contribute no little portion to the success of *Shuffle Along*"; from Columbus, "When I heard that wonderful basso voice of Prof. William Hann it reminded me of our old jubilee days."[14]

In March 1924 previews began for a new Sissle and Blake show called *In Bamville,* which was renamed *The Chocolate Dandies* when it reached Broadway in the fall. The plot of this lavish production centered around a horserace, which was simulated on stage by real horses on a treadmill. The Harmony Kings appeared in the show, and three of its members also had acting roles. Browning was again the romantic lead who got the girl (Lottie Gee), while Hann played a plantation owner and sang "The Sons of Old Black Joe" with a chorus. Baritone George Jones Jr., who had by this time replaced Charles Drayton in the Harmony Kings' lineup, had a smaller role as a bookmaker.[15] Exactly when Jones joined the quartet is uncertain; he may have been with them in *Shuffle Along* as well. He had some prior recording experience, having recorded a tribute to Bert Williams for Black Swan in early 1922.

In the fall of 1924, during the run of *Chocolate Dandies,* the Harmony Kings recorded two spirituals for the Vocalion label. One of these is interesting as an early recording of "When the Saints Come Marching In," later famous as a Dixieland band favorite but at this time still a religious song. The song was copyrighted in 1896 by J. M. Black, and subsequently used in revival meetings. Legend has it that it was played at funerals in New Orleans from around the turn of the century, in slow, dirge-like tempo on the way to the cemetery, then in fast tempo after the burial.[16] It seems to have first been recorded in November 1923 in a sober rendition by the Paramount Jubilee Singers, followed by other versions, including that of the Harmony Kings, in 1924–25. More recordings followed in the late 1920s, including a country version by the McCravy Brothers (1927), by which time it was better known as "When the Saints Go Marching In." The song became firmly entrenched in oral tradition, as evidenced by its frequent appearance in Library of Congress field recordings of the 1930s and 1940s. It entered the jazz repertoire with Louis Armstrong's 1938 Decca version and has been a Dixieland favorite ever since.

The Harmony Kings' rendition is done in a stately tempo, rather like "When the Roll Is Called Up Yonder" (which it resembles), but with the famous "echo" lines.

> Tenor: When the saints . . .
> Quartet: When the saints . . .
> Tenor: Come marching in . . .
> Quartet: Come marching in . . .

Also at the c. November Vocalion session the quartet recorded "My Lord's Gonna Move This Wicked Race," a rhythmic spiritual performed with multipart harmony. Both titles were with organ accompaniment.

After *Chocolate Dandies* closed in May 1925 the Harmony Kings returned to vaudeville. But a split was brewing within the group. After four years of featured billing in two highly successful stage shows, there were evidently differences about the quartet's future. There may have been friction between Hann and Browning, who had become the "star" of the group. In any event, in November 1925 Hann and baritone George Jones left and formed a new quartet called Hann's Emperors of Song (later changed to Hann's Emperors of Harmony), while Browning and Berry retained the name Four Harmony Kings.

Hann, no longer a "king" but now an "emperor," recruited Farley B. Graden as his new first tenor and Edward Caldwell as second tenor. Initially they remained in the United States, playing the Cotton Club and winning second place in a Harmony Contest for quartets held in the Wanamaker Auditorium in New York. Fifteen quartets from the top shows in New York (including *No, No, Nanette, Rose Marie,* and *The Student Prince*) competed. Hann's Emperors was one of two black quartets participating.[17]

In January 1926 the Emperors recorded two selections at the Edison studios in New York, "My Lord's Gonna Move This Wicked Race" and "What Band Is This?" According to the Edison files Hann, as manager, was paid $75 for the session. The first title was the same arrangement that the Harmony Kings had used on its 1924 Vocalion recording, although Hann seems to have made his bass part more prominent in the 1926 version. "What Band" was a "counting" song, counting the number of angels in that Sunday morning band (by the end of the song it was up to fifty). Edison quickly issued "My Lord" on a Blue Amberol cylinder in May 1926, but the disc release, containing both selections, had to wait until October 1927. By that time Edison was only a minor factor in the record business, and sales of both cylinder and disc were small.

In August 1927 Hann's Emperors sailed to Australia, where they were warmly received. They continued the Harmony Kings tradition of elegance with silk top hats and tuxedos. Caldwell wrote letters back to the United States reporting on their progress, several of which were published in the *Chicago Defender,* which occasionally confused them with the Four Harmony Kings. A November 1927 item reported that "the [Australian] newspapers laud them up to the sun. They really have impressed and have been given long-term contracts that will keep them across the Pacific for some time to come. They are vocal specialists in the rendering of the exquisite melodies of Stephen C. Foster, the yodeling songs of the Alpinists, the Race spirituals and the modern syncopated numbers that have revolutionized the music world. They divide their time between Sydney and Brisbane, Australia." Their itinerary also included appearances in Newcastle, Haymarket, Melbourne, Geelong, Perth, and Enmore, and broadcasts on radio station 3 LO.[18]

Another Australian newspaper said, "Tivoli patrons during the last couple of days have waxed enthusiastic at the singing of these colored songsters. Their chanting negro spirituals, yodeling songs, lullabies and syncopated ditties are a delight to the musical ear. Their understanding of the finer points of harmony, their intonation, which renders their 'pianissimo' passages a triumph of voice control, and their sympathetic interpretation of each number are the chief characteristics which contribute to the success of their act."[19]

No doubt there was some promotional hype here, but the length of their stay does suggest that the tour was a success. Billed as "Four Unbleached Americans," they remained for the better part of a year, returning to the United States in May 1928. In August 1928 they appeared in Los Angeles and in 1929 toured New England. Also in 1929 they are believed to have made a Fox Movietone short film, although no details are known. A tour of England was planned for the fall of 1929 but may not have materialized. The last notices of the group in U.S. black newspapers were around that time. Hann's death in San Jose, California, in December 1930 seems to have spelled the end of this group.[20]

Meanwhile, the reconstituted Four Harmony Kings went on to an even more extensive touring and recording career. Browning, the new manager, recruited Charles Drayton, a former Harmony King, as baritone, and John S. Crabbe, a former member of the Williams Singers, as bass. On November 24, 1925, they sailed for England, where they were booked for three weeks at London's Coliseum Theatre. Traveling with them were Maurine Browning and Mrs. Crabbe. After the London engagement they moved on to Dublin, where, according to one report, the city "[went] wild over these American race artists, exponents of deep harmony singing." Initial reports suggested that the Harmony Kings planned to stay in Europe for a few months and then return to the United States, but their success was so great that they remained permanently. Like Hann's group they dressed elegantly, with tuxedos, top hats and canes, and offered a varied repertoire. A later review noted, "Their reception on Monday night was great and deafening applause was given every number. They had to acknowledge the plaudits again and again. Their repertoire appears to be inexhaustible and its variety is amazing. Coupled with their musical ability they have a striking stage presence and are faultlessly dressed in the latest Saville Row creations. Compared with them the dandy Colored man of old time fame is a mere slouch."[21]

Browning quickly struck a deal with the Edison Bell Winner label to record some of the group's most popular and characteristic "black" numbers. The arrangements were credited to Browning, Drayton, and occasionally Berry. The group's label billing, pointedly, would be the Original Four Harmony Kings.

Four titles were recorded in January or February, "Jesus Moves in de Middle ob de Air," "Little David, Play on Your Harp," "Long Ago Lullaby," and "Ain't It a Shame?" The first two were rendered reverently, while "Long Ago Lullaby" (which is actually "Doan Ya Cry, Ma Honey" with interpolations) was sung quite tenderly, lingering on the harmonies, with a dramatic ending. The comic "Ain't It a Shame" was done with a loping rhythm, and interjected comments, but not the spoken interlude of the U.S. version. In all of these songs there were frequent interjections or asides of encouragement, evidently a Harmony Kings trademark. Curiously, all of the group's 1926 recordings were accompanied by banjo, strummed softly in the background, providing rhythm.

Six more titles were recorded in March and April in a similar style. Perhaps the most unusual was "A Calliope Yodel," a stage piece in which the quartet imitated a calliope's alternating high and low notes, and yodeled ("Then he climbed so high, nearly reached the sky"). Alpine yodeling specialties were popular novelty fare with stage quartets, showing off their versatility and precision, but were seldom recorded. "Dis Wicked Race" was the group's familiar "My Lord's Gonna Move This Wicked Race," while "Heabben" was the traditional "Gonna Walk All Over God's Heaven." "Joshua Fought the Battle of Jericho" was the most syncopated side of the lot, with quartet members swapping lines and solos leading to harmonized responses. A similar approach was used on "De Gospel Train" ("Get on board, little children, there's room for many a' more") and "Rolling and Rocker Dem in His Arms" ("I'm goin' home to glory!").

The Edison Bell Winner titles were varied, including comic songs, spirituals, and a yodel, but none were the type of popular material the group had recorded during its run in *Shuffle Along*. It must have been entertaining to watch these elegantly attired black men in tuxedos doing "Joshua Fought the Battle of Jericho," the comic "Ain't It a Shame," and imitating a calliope.

The Edison Bell Winner titles were released on five discs between March and July 1926, as the Harmony Kings toured the United Kingdom. The trade paper *Sound Wave* reviewed "Rolling and Rocker Dem" and "Joshua Fought the Battle," calling them "two pleasing spirituals or sacred numbers," and adding, "the quaint English used by the Negro may raise a smile and the banjo may seem hardly the instrument for the purpose, but there is no gainsaying the fervour and the simple faith expressed in these representative examples. The Original Four Harmony Kings sing with expression, and their voices blend harmoniously."[22]

The records seem to have been only modest sellers as they are rare today. The group's success in the music halls was unabated, however, changing their plans to return to the United States. In the spring of 1926 the *Chicago Defender* reported, "For the past [season] the Harmony Kings have been abroad, and they don't know when

America will see them again. Their sojourn on the Continent has been a tremendous success—royalty has been entertained by these music masters, and they are much sought after by everyone. . . . They open at the Plaza, one of London's magnificent picture houses, April 12, the first time Race artists have ever played this house."[23]

The unidentified writer, who evidently was connected with the group at one time, then reminisced about their background.

> I feel very proud of the Four Harmony Kings because I know their history. Overriding many obstructions that threatened to break up the unit, they have succeeded in going over the top, carrying the banner of success for the Race. I had the honor of arranging and compiling the opening ensemble that they are until today using. It was about seven years ago [sic] that they started out working in what we in show business call "The Dumps," in and around Chicago. Hitting right away the boys jumped to New York, where you must register and get the stamp [of approval] before you amount to anything in the show business. Well, the Harmony Kings hit, were sewed up with *Shuffle Along,* stayed with them until the finish and then sailed across the pond, where they are today idolized by thousands.

Ivan Browning sent periodic letters to the *Defender* and eventually began writing an occasional column for the paper on black artists in Europe called "Across the Pond." The quartet continued to tour, although strict British labor laws made it necessary for them to periodically move to the Continent to avoid long, unbroken stays in England. They were offered parts in West End stage productions but turned them down because the money was better in variety (the British equivalent of vaudeville). Other engagements included private parties for wealthy Americans and radio broadcasts. The singers liked the atmosphere in Britain, where racial discrimination was not as rampant as it was in the United States. Ivan Browning's daughter Haroldine was born there in 1926 and spent her childhood years in England, being educated at a private girls' school in London.[24]

A delightful Paris review from 1927, translated into English in the *Chicago Defender,* illustrates how black entertainers were viewed as a novelty by European audiences.

> The Harmony Kings are all four decapitated by their stiff white collars. All four faultlessly dressed in beige trousers, white bosoms and black coats. They sing things which we do not understand but which in their intact mystery are delicious. They have marvelous voices extraordinarily modulated which roll forth and vibrate in an incomparable art. We get the impression of unexpected music, far away harmony. We think on closing our eyes we hear the singing of sirens. It is appealing and profoundly touching. We feel ourselves gliding toward a languidness and moments of undecided inactivity. In truth these Harmony Kings are unique artists and it is agreed that we thank the [British] Empire for revealing them to us.[25]

In February 1929 the Harmony Kings returned to the recording studio for the English Dominion label. The records indicate that the quartet had made a major change in direction and was now performing pop songs with light, rhythmic arrangements. Accompaniment was by a lightly swinging piano, sometimes augmented by percussion. These records sound a lot like those of the Revelers, a best-selling white quartet in the United States with a similar "pop" sound. There were no more spirituals, although the emphasis was still on harmony.

"Shout Hallelujah! 'Cause I'm Home" was a jaunty, and rather silly, pop song that had also been recorded by Noble Sissle.

> Run up the steps, knock at the door,
> Down on my knees, kissing the floor,
> Shout hallelujah 'cause I'm home, home, never to roam!
> Take off my coat, take off my hat,
> Wind up the clock, throw out the cat,
> Shout hallelujah 'cause I'm home, back home.

"Beautiful" featured a long, syncopated piano solo and 1920s-style vamping by the quartet ("do-do-do-de-oo!"), while "Dixie Dawn," a longing-for-home number, incorporated a long quotation from "Old Folks at Home" and the lines "so peaceful and happy, it's heaven to me." "When Eliza Rolls Her Eyes" was an obscure tune by pop songwriters Gus Kahn and Harry Warren, with several syncopated piano interludes. It is not known who the pianist was on these records, although as of late 1929 the quartet's stage pianist was Cyril Birmingham (by 1932 it was Frank Parker).[26] The Dominion records were released in March and May 1929 but were available for only about a year, as the company went out of business in 1930.

As far as is known the Harmony Kings did not return to the United States for any length of time, which makes all the more mysterious certain 1929 entries in the recording ledgers of the Gennett label. According to the ledgers, four songs were recorded in Richmond, Indiana, on October 9, 1929, by an unaccompanied vocal group called the "Four Harmony Kings." The titles ("Let's Go Down in Jordan," "The Queen Street Rag," "You Got to Know How to Love," and "He's Got His Eyes on Me") do not look much like those of "our" Harmony Kings, but given the group's varied repertoire, it is hard to tell. None of the Gennett recordings were issued, and the masters were marked "destroyed," so we may never know whether this was the Browning (or possibly the Hann) quartet, or someone else entirely.

In May 1931 it was announced that the Four Harmony Kings would return to the United States for an American tour the following season, but this apparently did not take place.[27] Browning did return to the United States around May 1932 due to the death of his father, and Drayton led the group in his absence. By this time John Crabbe had been replaced by George Dosher as the group's bass. Dosher, billed as "the American Negro Bass," had recorded for the Piccadilly label in 1929.

In June 1933 lead tenor Browning quit the Harmony Kings. Little is known of the group's history after this. According to researcher Ray Funk they struggled on as a trio, now consisting of Berry, Drayton, and Dosher. They were under increasing pressure from the British authorities, who made it as difficult as possible for foreign entertainers to make a living in England. In 1940 the group was stranded in Brussels at the time of the German invasion, and only after several months were they able to leave and return to the United States. Berry died in 1942, but the other members have not been traced.[28]

That, as far as we know, was the end of the original Four Harmony Kings. In 1938 the name was used for a black gospel group formed by tenor Claude Jeter, in West Virginia. In 1942 Jeter changed the name of his group to the Swan Silvertones, and under that name it became one of the best-known gospel groups of the 1950s and 1960s.

Meanwhile, Ivan Harold Browning went on to further success. After a trip to New York in mid-1933, he returned to London where he formed a vaudeville team with Bob Williams, a pianist, composer and former accompanist for Mae West. During 1933–34 Williams and Browning appeared in clubs, broadcast on the BBC, and made recordings for Parlophone.

By late 1934 Williams and Browning had broken up and Browning again visited New York, where he met Henry Starr, a pianist of mixed Afro-American and Mexican parentage. They formed a new duo, which debuted at New York's Cotton Club and then moved to London in early 1935. Browning and Starr had a busy and successful career for the rest of the 1930s, playing posh clubs and theaters across Europe. One of their major engagements was at the Bal Taberin Revue in Paris in 1936, for which they also wrote songs. In 1935 the team recorded for the English Regal-Zonophone label, including such disparate titles as "Lovely to Look At" and "When the First Pickaninny Was Born." They made further recordings in 1939. Shortly after the outbreak of World War II they moved back to the United States. Browning settled in Los Angeles with his family and began pursuing an acting career, "portraying," as one source delicately put it, "Negro stereotypes."[29] He had small parts in a number of movies and TV shows, including the films *Mr. Peabody and the Mermaid* (1948) and *Sunrise at Campobello* (1960) and the 1950s TV series *Amos 'n Andy*. He also gave concerts at area schools and churches, specializing in what he called "Sermons in Song."

In the spring of 1971, during a Eubie Blake concert in Los Angeles, Blake recognized his old friend Browning in the audience and asked him if he would come up and sing. That fall the two old troupers made an LP together, which was issued on Blake's own Eubie Blake Music label, as its first issue. Another LP followed in 1972. A review of the first album in *Stereo Review* enthused, "By God, these granddaddies sure whip the young folks. . . . I wish I had been around when Eubie and Ivan Harold were in their prime; it must have been a grand time."[30] Indeed it was. Ivan Harold Browning passed away on May 20, 1978, in Los Angeles, at the age of eighty-seven.

The original Four Harmony Kings had a substantial career from the 1910s to the 1930s, appeared in musical comedy, and were pioneer recording artists with a repertoire ranging from spirituals to popular song. Arguably, they were the most prominent black quartet of their era, possibly the most popular prior to the debut of the Mills Brothers. "Deep harmony" was their specialty. How many other black quartets of the era would attempt "Sweet Adeline"?

32 Broome Special Phonograph Records

One of the more exciting recent developments in the study of early black recordings is the discovery of the first black-owned and -operated record label. That label was long assumed to be Black Swan Records, founded in 1921 by Harry H. Pace, the publishing partner of W. C. Handy, which made its name in the field of jazz and blues.[1]

Nearly two years earlier, however, a black entrepreneur in Medford, Massachusetts, launched a label dedicated to black concert music, which he sold by mail. Fewer than a dozen sides were issued, but what remarkable records they were! The few artists on Broome Special Phonograph Records were among the most famous and important black concert figures of the era. For three of them, these were their only commercial records. Broome records are little known and exceedingly rare, but they are vital sound documents of black cultural history.

Broome was founded by a man who devoted much of his career to the advancement of black culture. Information about the life of George Wellington Broome is sketchy. He was born in Brooklyn, New York, most likely on April 8, 1868, although various sources indicate that the year might have been as early as 1866 or as late as 1871.[2] According to his death certificate his father, George Broome, was born in England and his mother, Louise Brooks, in Washington, D.C. Early in his life Broome lived in New York, Washington, D.C., and Boston.

An alumni publication of Howard University indicates that he attended medical school there from 1894 to 1896, but he apparently did not become a doctor.[3] Instead he was attracted to the New York musical and theatrical world, where in April 1897 he helped arrange a benefit concert at Carnegie Hall for the Pickford Sanitarium for Consumptive Negroes. A letter survives from Harry T. Burleigh to Booker T. Washington in which Burleigh introduced Broome to the great educator and solicited the latter's help in making the concert a success.[4] Soon thereafter Broome became associated with Will Marion Cook as manager of Cook's pioneering black musical, *Clorindy; or, The Origin of the Cakewalk,* although it is not clear whether this was during the original 1898 run or for a 1900 touring company. In February 1900 he was reported to be the American representative and agent for O. M. McAdoo's Australian musical and vaudeville enterprises.[5] Broome's office at this time was on 29th Street in New York City, although he lived in Newark, New Jersey. Around 1900 he married; he and his wife, Mary, would have a son named Charles.

After a few years trying to get a foothold in New York's competitive theatrical world, Broome moved his family to Medford, Massachusetts, where his occupation was variously listed as porter, laborer, and waiter. His first listing in the Medford city directory was in 1907, and he would remain in that city for the rest of his life. He apparently worked in some capacity for the government, while continuing to dabble in various theatrical and educational enterprises. In 1910 the *New York Age* reported that he had formed the Broome Exhibition Company to produce documentary films of black colleges. His purpose was to show "the progress of the Negro along industrial lines by means of moving pictures," and he was said to be exhibiting films of Tuskegee Institute at the Crescent Theatre in Boston and Carnegie Hall in New York. "Among the well known institutions to be given consideration in the future will be Hampton, Fisk and Shaw."[6] There is no indication whether additional films were made.

In the 1910 census Broome claimed that he was thirty-nine (perhaps optimistic) and gave his profession as "producer, moving pictures" (which no doubt sounded better than "porter"). He was living at 23 Clayton Avenue in Medford with his wife, Mary E. Broome (age 38), and sister-in-law Fannie M. Ellis (age 24). He owned his own home. City directories show Broome living at this address from 1907 until at least the late 1920s. Mary Broome died on April 6, 1918, at about the time her husband became involved in a new enterprise with a young tenor named Roland Hayes.

Hayes, a Southerner, had come to Boston in 1911 with the Fisk Jubilee Singers and decided to stay. His goal was to become a successful concert tenor, a field that was traditionally closed to blacks. Despite the many obstacles placed in his way by white America, he succeeded in building a substantial reputation during the 1910s as a singer of operatic arias, art songs, and spirituals. A self-arranged concert at Boston's Symphony Hall in November 1917 was a huge success, and in its wake he tackled another field closed to black concert artists: recording. Since no record company would engage him, he decided to make his own records and sell them by mail. They would be the first commercial recordings of a black concert artist ever issued.

Hayes named George Broome to serve as his sales manager. He presumably knew Broome through the latter's long involvement in the black concert world; for example, they both knew Harry T. Burleigh, Broome since the 1890s and Hayes since the early 1910s. Hayes's first selection, "Swing Low, Sweet Chariot," was recorded at the Columbia Graphophone Company studios in New York in December 1917. He then left on a winter concert tour. Exactly when Broome began working for him is not certain, but Broome's signature has been found on contracts dating from July 1918, and since his name is printed on both contracts and stationery it is likely that he was involved from the start.

An office was established at the A. J. Jackson piano store at 130 Boylston Street, Boston, and advertising for the first disc, "Swing Low," appeared in May 1918. Additional recordings were made during May and June and placed on sale almost immediately. Since stores would not stock them, much of Broome's time was spent placing advertising in Boston Symphony Orchestra programs and in the *Crisis* (the magazine of the NAACP), and lining up agents in cities across the country. These were generally individuals supportive of Hayes's work, who agreed to demonstrate the records for acquaintances and attempt to sell them copies. Records were also sold directly by mail.

It was a cumbersome way to sell records, and sales evidently did not go as well as Hayes had hoped. Due to the high cost of recording and securing pressings from Columbia, his margins were extremely low. Around September Hayes fired Broome and took over the operation himself, changing its address to his own home. The parting must have been abrupt, as Broome's name appears in an October 1918 advertisement in the *Crisis,* but correspondence dating from the same month bears

Hayes's signature and the statement that "Mr. Broome is no longer in my employ." The ad was presumably submitted weeks earlier.

It is not known what caused the falling-out between Hayes and Broome, but the tenor had a reputation for being rather rigid in his views. Hayes did not mention Broome by name in his biography, *Angel Mo' and Her Son, Roland Hayes* (1942), saying merely that he had engaged "a sales manager."[7] But then Hayes did not mention a lot of people with whom he was involved over the years.

The experience with recording apparently gave Broome the idea to start his own mail-order record company. He hoped to learn from Hayes's mistakes. Columbia had charged the tenor so much for pressings that it was almost impossible for him to make a profit. At the same time he received many complaints because he sold only single-faced records, yet charged premium prices for them. Columbia operated its Personal Recording Service as a vanity business, not a custom pressing operation priced to allow others to get into the business.

It is not known at what studio Broome did his recording, or who pressed his records, but it was almost certainly not Columbia. Columbia routinely assigned a Columbia matrix number to records made in its studios and entered details of the session in its files. Broome recordings show no such number in the wax and are not mentioned in the Columbia files.

Where, then? There is circumstantial evidence that Broome may have struck a deal with Gennett, an Indiana-based independent label that had entered the record business in 1917. A pressing has been found that bears a Broome recording on one side (mislabeled) and an English-derived Gennett master on the other.[8] This type of mixup would logically have occurred at a Gennett pressing plant. Broomes were laterally recorded, and Gennett was one of the first independent labels to switch to lateral recording, in early 1919. The first Broomes are believed to have been recorded at about that time, and they were recorded in New York City, where Gennett operated a studio.[9]

There are some problems with a Gennett connection. Broome pressings do not look much like Gennett pressings of the 1919–20 period. The latter have a raised ridge on the outer rim to prevent the needle from skidding off, while Broome pressings have no such ridge. (However, some early Gennetts also lack this ridge.) Further, the handwritten matrix number engraved in the wax of early Gennetts seem to be in different handwriting than those in the wax on Broomes.

Whoever Broome engaged to do his recording and pressing, it is obvious that he was able to cut a better deal than Hayes had secured, in part because his timing was good. Immediately after World War I the patent monopoly of the two biggest recordmakers—Victor and Columbia—began to break down. Independent labels were entering the field and daring to produce lateral-cut records, playable on all phonographs, in defiance of the majors' patents. Gennett was one of the first to do so and was promptly sued by Victor for patent violation. Victor eventually lost the case. In the meantime the floodgates opened for scores of independent labels. Hayes had been forced to deal with Columbia to obtain lateral pressings, but because he entered the business a year later, as these events were unfolding, Broome was no doubt able to strike a much more favorable deal with a smaller label.

The first Broome recording sessions appear to have taken place in New York during the summer or early fall of 1919. Like Hayes, Broome wanted to promote black concert artists, and he used his connections in the field to line up some impressive talent. Moreover his artists had not recorded elsewhere because of the prejudice of the white companies against black classical artists. Broome had the field virtually to himself.

Broome's first issued recording was a real coup. The eminent composer and baritone Harry T. Burleigh, one of the leading figures in the black musical world, agreed to record for his old friend. According to an item in the September 1919 issue of the *Crisis*, "'Go Down, Moses,' one of the finest of the Negro Spirituals arranged by H. T. Burleigh, and sung by the composer, is announced as the first of a number of phonograph records to be presented by this distinguished musician."[10]

Splendidly recorded, it is a powerful performance of the famous spiritual by the singer who is said to have influenced Dvořák at the precise time the great composer was both urging America to recognize its black music heritage and reflecting spiritual themes in his own "New World" Symphony. It was the only commercial recording Burleigh would make during his long life (1866–1949). Other Burleigh titles planned for Broome apparently did not materialize, but Burleigh apparently was willing to advise Broome and was present for at least one of his later sessions.

Burleigh arrangements were used by young baritone Edward H. Boatner, a protegé of Roland Hayes, when he recorded "Sometimes I Feel Like a Motherless Child" and "I Don't Feel No Ways Tired" for Broome. Burleigh was present at the session, and it is even possible that he was the piano accompanist.[11]

Other artists recorded by Broome were sopranos Florence Cole-Talbert and Antionette Garnes, violinist/composer Clarence Cameron White, and pianist/composer R. Nathaniel Dett, the latter two playing their own compositions. All of these

The record that was not supposed to exist: Harry T. Burleigh's only commercial recording, on the black-run Broome label (1919). (Author's collection)

individuals were important figures in early twentieth-century black concert music, and none of them recorded very widely elsewhere.

Broome's former associate, Roland Hayes, did not record for him, although this may not have been due to any personal animosity. The initial Broome recordings seem to have been made in mid-1919, while Hayes was on the West Coast. Late in the year the tenor returned for a few months of whirlwind touring and concerts, then in April 1920 sailed for Europe, where he would remain for three and a half years. He may simply not have been available.

There is evidence that not all of the recordings made by Broome were released, leading to speculation that test pressings of unreleased material might exist. Boatner later recalled recording three Burleigh arrangements for Broome, but only two were issued.[12] The peculiar Broome matrix numbering system offers clues as to how many recordings each artist made. Most labels assigned matrix numbers sequentially, at the time of recording. This number appeared in the wax, often followed by two numbers separated by dashes, representing the take and the stamper (the metal part from which the pressing was made). For example, on most labels "34-2-2" would mean matrix number 34, take two, stamper two.

George Broome did it differently. First he assigned a number to each artist. Each selection by that artist was then represented by a dash and a number, and each take by a second dash and number after that. In Broome's numbering scheme, "34-2-2" meant Florence Cole-Talbert ("34"), selection number two (first "-2"), take two (second "-2"). The second number in the sequence tells us how many selections had been recorded by the artist up to that time. Table 12 lists the five known Broome artists, with the artist numbers and numbers that have been found for each. Thus for Cole-Talbert and Boatner, at least, there is the strong suggestion that at least one other selection must have been recorded but not released.

Broome's peculiar numbering system presents another mystery. Why did he number his artists 34, 35, 45, 77, 85, and 86? It is extremely unlikely that he recorded eighty-six artists, and only issued six of them.

Broome Special Phonograph Records were announced in the fall of 1919. In October an item in the *Crisis* reported that "George W. Broome of Medford, Mass., is manufacturing a series of phonograph records by Negro artists. 'Go Down, Moses' by Harry T. Burleigh and 'Villanelle' sung by Mme. Florence Cole-Talbert [were] announced in September."[13] In January 1920 Broome began advertising in the *Cri-*

Table 12. Broome Matrix Numbers

	Selections	
	Issued	Not Issued?
Florence Cole-Talbert	34-2, 34-3	34-1
Harry T. Burleigh	45-1	
Edward Boatner	85-2, 85-3	85-1
R. Nathaniel Dett	86-1, 86-2	
Clarence C. White	35-4	
Antionette Garnes	77-1	

sis. Curiously the ad listed three single selections, apparently single-faced discs, priced at $1.25 each plus $0.25 for "mailing, packing and insurance." This was roughly the same price as the Hayes discs. The records were said to be "now ready and on sale" by mail order and could be ordered from 23 Clayton Avenue, Medford, Mass., which was George Broome's home. There was no mention of agents, as Hayes had, or of availability in stores.[14] These early single-faced Broomes are believed to have had white labels with blue lettering.

In late 1920 Broome brought out another selection. The November 1920 issue of the *Crisis* reported, "The Columbia Graphophone Company is making a reproduction of the address on the Atlanta Exposition made by the late Booker T. Washington."[15] This was, in fact, a private recording made by the great statesman and educator at the Columbia studios in 1908, recreating the famous speech he had delivered at the Atlanta Exposition in 1895 in which he laid out his program for the advancement of the race. It was the speech that made him a national figure and was widely admired by both blacks and progressive whites. In December Broome advertised this disc under the heading, "An Appreciated Christmas Gift." Copies that have been found are single-faced and bear a Broome "Brown Seal" label, pasted over a standard Columbia Personal label. The price for this memento was $1.50.

Broome's margins may have been higher than Hayes's, but sales seem to have been infinitesimal, even less than for the Hayes recordings. All are extremely rare today. In December 1920 a Broome ad advised that "another set of records [is] coming out next month—write for circular." This may have marked the introduction of lower-priced double-faced Broome discs, using the same masters. This more "common" type—relatively speaking—of Broome record used a numbering system that ran from 51 to 55. The labels bear the legend "Brown Seal Records" and are indeed light brown with black print. The price is given as $1.00 and the manufacturer as "Geo. W. Broome, Medford, Mass." Tantalizingly, advertisements offered not only the aforementioned circular but an "illustrated catalog." No copies of this literature have been found.

George Broome continued selling records for several years, at least on a small scale, from his home in Medford. The 1923 *Talking Machine World Trade Directory* contains the following entry for the label: "Broome Special Phonograph Records. Est. 1920. 23 Clayton Ave., Medford. Geo. W. Broome, sole owner and manager. Manufactures 'Brown Seal' lateral cut records. Made by Negro artists exclusively. Markets its products by mail."

The record label was evidently a sideline. George Broome is listed in the 1920 census as a laborer for the government and in the 1920 Medford city directory as a "waiter." The census shows him as a widower living with his sister-in-law Fannie M. Ellis and three boarders. The 1920 city directory contains the first listing for his son, Charles E. Broome, who was living nearby with his wife Jennie.

George Broome and his son soon embarked on a new and more lucrative business. The 1924 city directory indicates that the elder Broome had by then become proprietor of the Shawmut Press, a printing establishment at 454 Main Street. Charles's occupation is given as "printer." The firm also advertised in the directory, offering "printing of every description." This would be George Broome's occupation for the rest of his life.

George W. Broome died in Medford on April 1, 1941, of heart disease, at the age of seventy-four, and was buried in Oak Grove Cemetery. He was survived by his son, Charles, and his sister-in-law, Fannie Ellis. An obituary in the local paper indicated that he had been a resident of Medford for forty-five years and had run the Shawmut Press in South Medford for twenty. It added that he "was very well known and highly thought of in that section [of town]. He was active even in his last years managing his business and directly supervising the printing establishment up to a few weeks before his death."[16]

Broome Special Phonograph Records were for years forgotten, unknown even to specialists in recording history. Only recently has information about the label come to light. It has been rumored that members of the Broome family were still living in the Medford area in the 1990s, but efforts to contact them were to no avail. As for the records, one collector recalled seeing "hundreds" of them in a black music store in South Philadelphia in the mid-1950s.[17] The store and the collector are now gone, but hopefully the records survive—somewhere. Due to their unusual content, they are extremely important sound documents and deserve to be preserved and reissued.

33 Edward H. Boatner

George W. Broome's Broome label preserved the artistry of several black musicians who were pioneers in introducing African Americans to the world of concert music during the first half of the twentieth century. One of these, Edward Hammond Boatner, was best known as a composer, arranger, and choral director. He was twenty years old and just embarking on his career when he recorded for Broome in 1919.

Boatner was born on November 13, 1898, in New Orleans to Dr. Daniel Webster Boatner, a well-educated Methodist minister who moved his family several times during Edward's childhood as he assumed new positions.[1] The surname was derived from the slave owners who had owned Edward's grandparents. Musically inclined, young Edward was fascinated by the spirituals he heard at his father's prayer meetings and began collecting them at an early age. Nevertheless he was initially denied music lessons by his stern father, who wanted him to become a minister. Dr. Boatner eventually relented, and by the time Edward graduated from high school in Kansas City, Kansas, in 1916, he was giving recitals locally as a baritone.

It was at one of these recitals that he was heard by tenor Roland Hayes, who advised him to go to Boston to seek further training. Hayes was a hero to many young blacks aspiring to careers in the previously all-white world of concert music, and his encouragement fired young Boatner's enthusiasm. His father would have none of it, so he was forced to work for months to save the money to go to Boston on his own.

Boatner arrived in Boston in 1917 with, as he later recalled, five dollars in his pocket. Taking odd jobs to support himself, he introduced himself to everyone who would listen, and tracked down Hayes, who helped him make further contacts. By 1918 he was giving piano lessons, and in that year he published his first arrangement of a spiritual, "Give Me Jesus."

Boston had a thriving black cultural community, and it was not long before Boatner crossed paths with George W. Broome, an arts entrepreneur who in 1918 was managing Roland Hayes's private recording venture. The following year Broome launched his own mail-order label, Broome Special Phonograph Records, dedicated to advancing the cause of black concert music. He was particularly anxious to record the spiritual arrangements of Harry T. Burleigh, which were gaining considerable currency in the white concert world through performances by John McCormack and others. Burleigh himself consented to record one of these ("Go Down, Moses"), and Broome recruited Boatner to record some others.

The young baritone traveled to New York City, probably during the summer of 1919, where he made at least three recordings for Broome. Burleigh was present at the sessions to ensure that the performances met his high standards.[2] Two titles are known. "Sometimes I Feel Like a Motherless Child" is sung very slowly and deliberately by Boatner, in a deep and resonant baritone. "I Don't Feel No Ways Tired" is in moderate tempo but, like "Motherless Child," is performed more with dignity and respect than with emotion. Both have an unobtrusive piano accompaniment, possibly by Burleigh himself. Given the circumstances under which the recordings were made, these somewhat dry, dignified performances presumably reflect the way Burleigh wanted his arrangements to be heard.

The Boatner recordings were probably released in single-faced format in late 1919 or early 1920, when Broome began advertising in the *Crisis,* although they are not specifically listed in Broome ads. When the label began producing double-faced "Brown Seal Records" around 1921, they appeared in that format, backed with recordings by Burleigh and pianist R. Nathaniel Dett. Interestingly, artist credit on the label was given as "Edward H. S. Boatner," indicating that he was using a second middle name in addition to the "Hammond" cited in biographies. Due to Broome's limited distribution none of the records sold very well. They were obscure even then, let alone now.

Following this brief encounter with recording (he is not known to have ever recorded again) Boatner went on to a distinguished career as a performer and teacher. He continued his education and in 1921 won a one-year scholarship to the Boston Conservatory of Music. He won a prize in a state vocal contest in 1922 and shortly thereafter embarked with pianist Dett on a concert tour. He also taught, one of his early students being Josephine Baker, at the time (1921) a chorus girl in *Shuffle Along.* Another was singer/dancer/actor Clifton Webb.

Around this time Boatner married Claudine Wicks, a singer in a Chicago choir. Their child, Edward Jr., was born in Chicago in February 1924. The boy was adopted by a family named Stitt at age seven and raised in Saginaw, Michigan. In 1925 Boatner was appointed director of the National Baptist Convention Choir in Chicago, and moved to that city, serving as the choir's director until 1933. He also served as choir director at area churches and continued teaching. Boatner continued his studies in Chicago, and in 1932 finally received his bachelor's degree in music from the Chicago College of Music.

During the 1930s he taught music at Samuel Houston College in Austin, Texas (1933–35), and Wiley College, Marshall, Texas (1936–37). A second son, Clifford, and a daughter, Adelaide, were born to his second wife, Adelaide, who raised them after she separated from Boatner. He had another daughter, Sarah, by his third wife, Julia.

Boatner relocated to New York City in the late 1930s and opened the Edward Boatner Studio, which he operated for the rest of his life, first in Brooklyn and later in Manhattan. Among his celebrity students were singer Libby Holman and Metropolitan Opera tenor George Shirley. He may have been associated with *The Nat "King" Cole Show* on NBC-TV in 1956; at least, that program featured a chorus called "The Boataneers."[3] He was for many years director of music at Brooklyn's Concord Baptist Church.

The decades from the 1940s to the 1970s saw a surge in his music publishing activities. This included numerous arrangements of spirituals, many published by his own Hammond Music Company, and original songs for choruses. In the 1960s he turned to larger works, including "Freedom Suite" (1964), a musical portrayal of African Americans from slavery to the civil rights era. "The Life of Christ" (1971) depicted Christ's thirty-three years on earth through dramatic readings, dance, and twenty-five spirituals. Unpublished works from the 1960s include the musical comedy "Julius Sees Her in Rome, Georgia" and an opera, "Troubled in Mind (Forbidden Love)." Most of these are preserved with his papers at the Schomburg Center in Harlem. Among his collections were *30 Afro-American Choral Spirituals* (1964) and *The Story of the Spirituals: 30 Spirituals and Their Origins* (1973).

An intensely religious man, Boatner devoted much of his life to sacred music. Of his "Life of Christ" he said in 1971, "I'm hoping that the work will do much to persuade thousands that have drifted away from the church and from Christianity to come back."[4] Teaching was also a vital part of his life, especially helping those less fortunate than himself, and he continued teaching into his eighties. In a 1979 interview he remarked, "You know, I'm 81, but I don't feel that old. I give more than 85 lessons a week, to interested children, youth and adults . . . because of the lack of financial support, many gifted young people and children must suffer defeat and are not able to continue a career."[5]

Edward Boatner died in New York on June 16, 1981, at the age of eighty-two. Three of his four children also had musical careers. Clifford became a concert pianist, and Adelaide was a contralto who appeared in productions of *Jamaica* and *Show Boat*. Best known, however, was eldest son Edward. Attracted to jazz, in the early 1940s he became a disciple of bop pioneer Charlie Parker, and under the name Sonny Stitt went on to an forty-year career as a top ranked jazz tenor saxophonist, making many recordings. He died in 1982.

Although Edward Boatner never achieved the fame of some who are included in this book, he made many contributions to the world of music during his long and productive life. His first love was the spiritual, and his recording of two of those songs in his younger days are a suitable testimonial.

34 Harry T. Burleigh

Harry T. Burleigh was perhaps the most prominent figure in the world of black concert music in America during the early twentieth century. He is known today primarily for his arrangements of Negro spirituals, which are still used, but he was also a composer of art songs and, in his day, a baritone of considerable renown. He is also remembered for his contribution to one of the defining moments in American music. It was Burleigh who, as a student at the National Conservatory of Music in the 1890s, introduced the visiting Bohemian composer Antonin Dvořák to the spiritual, inspiring the composer to urge his American colleagues to look to African American music rather than to European models as the basis for a uniquely American music. This prescient call was the basis for much that was to transpire musically during the following century. Dvořák himself reflected spiritual themes in his own greatest work, the "New World" Symphony.

It was long believed that the man who influenced Dvořák, and who shaped our modern conception of the spiritual, never recorded. His modern biographer, Anne Key Simpson, declared flatly, "Burleigh's own voice was never recorded."[1] As we shall see, this is not the case.

Henry Thacker Burleigh was born just after the close of the Civil War, on December 2, 1866, in Erie, Pennsylvania. His parents were free-born, but his grandfather, Hamilton Waters, who lived with them, was a former slave. Waters, who had been partially blinded as a young man, apparently when he attempted to learn to read, influenced young Harry greatly. It was from him that the lad heard stories of the Old South and learned the plantation melodies that would become such an important part of his life.[2]

Burleigh was musically inclined and as a youth sang in local choirs. His father (who died in 1873) had been a servant at the home of Elizabeth Russell, a wealthy white woman who sponsored recitals and arranged the visits of notable concert artists to Erie. She took young Harry under her wing and exposed him to fine music.

By 1882, sixteen year-old Harry, an Episcopalian, was singing in three church choirs, at St. Paul's Episcopal Church, the First Presbyterian Church, and the Reform Jewish Temple. In religion, at least, music knew no bounds. In 1887 he graduated from Erie High School and for the next few years worked as a stenographer, while pursuing music on the side. His musical endeavors, while they may not have paid much, did attract attention. The first known item about him in a national newspaper was in the Indianapolis *Freeman* in October 1891, which noted that he had been expected to join the Fisk Jubilee Singers, but that the First Presbyterian Church had raised his salary in order to retain him.[3]

Despite the efforts of the church to keep him, in his mid-twenties Burleigh realized that he would have to leave Erie to further his career. In January 1892 he set out for New York City and with some difficulty secured a scholarship at the National Conservatory of Music, a liberal institution founded in 1866 by Jeanette Thurber for

Harry T. Burleigh. (Courtesy of Steven Richman)

the education of musically gifted students, whatever their social status. During the next few years he made many important acquaintances within New York's large cultural community. His reputation as a baritone singer of exceptional skill grew.

Perhaps his most historically significant meeting was with the world famous composer Antonín Dvořák, who arrived in the fall of 1892 to become the conservatory's new director. Dvořák was fascinated with folk musics of all types and had incorporated folk themes of his native Bohemia into his work. The young student from Erie introduced him to the black "folk music" of America, singing for him the songs he had learned as a child. Although Burleigh was not technically Dvořák's student (the composer taught only the most advanced classes), the director invited Burleigh to his home to sing and discuss the songs. He listened intently, interrupting with questions such as, "Is that really the way the slaves sang it?" As Burleigh later recalled, Dvořák "saturated himself with the spirit of these old tunes" and asked hundreds of questions about Negro life, demonstrating the importance of knowing the cultural context from which they sprang.[4]

In addition to his duties at the conservatory, Dvořák was busy working on a symphony. Burleigh transcribed the manuscripts for this new work, which incorporated elements of the spirituals that he had sung for the composer in his study. When it debuted in New York in December 1893, Dvořák's "New World" Symphony was an immediate sensation, and it has remained a staple of the symphonic repertoire ever since. Along with public statements by the composer, it opened the eyes of many in America to the value of the music of black Americans.

Within months of his enrollment Burleigh was making appearances as a singer in the New York area, often sharing the stage with leading black artists. In September 1892 he appeared in Washington, D.C., with Sissieretta Jones (the "Black Patti"), and in August 1893 he sang at the World's Columbian Exposition in Chicago, on Colored American Day. During the summer of 1893 he was a vocalist with Victor Herbert's orchestra at white resorts outside New York. In early 1894 he applied for the position of soloist at the autocratic St. George's Church in New York City, a church that would never have let a black man share a pew with its wealthy white parishioners. In the auditions the singers stood behind a screen so that their appearance would not be a factor in the final selection. Burleigh was the only black among sixty applicants, and when he was selected, and revealed to be black, there was consternation in the congregation. However the pastor, Dr. William S. Rainsford, and influential parishioners including J. Pierpont Morgan stood by him and eventually "the troubled waters settled down."[5] Burleigh would remain with the church for a remarkable fifty-two years.

Burleigh's recital career and his position at St. George's gave him some financial stability, but of course he was limited to the rather small world of black concert music. There was far more money to be made in popular music, and for a time in the late 1890s he flirted with the theater, where blacks were beginning to have a major impact. He appeared for a month or so with Sissieretta Jones's Black Patti Troubadours—a high-class vaudeville touring show—and in September 1898 he directed the orchestra for the Bert Williams–George Walker show, *Senegambian Carnival.* His consummate musicianship won him the job, but Burleigh had a streak of showmanship in him as well. One evening the comedian who was supposed to sing the show's big hit "Who Dat Say Chicken in Dis Crowd?" failed to appear. "Harry vamped once, twice, thrice, then went into the song from the pit amid hearty applause." When the actor still did not appear, Burleigh "gave the baton to the first violinist, went back stage, donned an old coat and hat, and with cane in hand, appeared before the proscenium singing this ribald song."[6]

Burleigh later fondly recalled his vaudeville days, saying they were "great fun, but that was not for me."[7] He continued to frequent the Marshall Hotel on West 53rd Street, a gathering spot for black actors and musicians, where close friends nicknamed him "Burly Harry." Professionally, however, he turned his attention exclusively to concert music. He probably realized that involvement in the popular theater could compromise his position at St. George's, as well as any standing he might achieve in the classical world. This was also a period when he was beginning to settle down in his personal life. In 1898 he married Louise Alston, a poet and actress. Their only son, Alston Burleigh, was born in August 1899.

In 1900 he became the first black soloist at Temple Emanu-El, one of the wealthiest Jewish congregations in New York City. He would remain there for twenty-five years, alternating with his duties at St. George's.

In addition to appearing at prestigious but low-paying black recitals, Burleigh began composing. Despite his closeness to Dvořák, the leading champion of incorporating black themes into serious American music, Burleigh would for the next twenty years write primarily in the European art song tradition. His first three songs, published in 1898, were "If You But Knew," "Life," and "A Birthday Song." Probably his most popular art song, published in 1903, was "Jean," a musical setting of a sentimental poem by Frank L. Stanton. As he would later recall, this sweet song "somehow or another 'caught on' immediately" and became one of his most enduring successes, featured by concert singers both black and white. It has not a trace of African American influences.

> Jean, my Jean, with the eyes of light,
> And the beautiful, soft brown hair,
> Do you know that I'm longing for you tonight,
> For your lips, for the clasp of your hand so white,
> And the sound of your voice so dear?[8]

Burleigh published numerous other art songs during the following years, many of which gradually found favor on the white recital circuit. Among the more popular were "Mammy's L'il Baby" (1903), "Just My Love and I" and "O Perfect Love" (1904), "Tide" (1905), "Through Love's Eternity" and "Perhaps" (1906), "Mother o' Mine" (1914), "Just You" and "The Grey Wolf" (1915), "In the Wood of Finvara" (1916), and "Little Mother of Mine" (1917). He also composed a setting of Stanton's poem "Just A-Wearying for You," although the 1901 version by Carrie Jacobs-Bond is better remembered today. In addition to this lily-white repertoire he edited a collection of "Southern songs," including some by Stephen Foster, called *Negro Minstrel Melodies* (1909), and composed a series of piano sketches called *From the Southland* (1910). He also wrote some choral arrangements of spirituals. However, his best work in that field was yet to come.

Burleigh met Booker T. Washington in the 1890s and around 1900 was invited to join the great educator on his summer fundraising tours as a soloist. For approximately fifteen years he toured with Washington, singing spirituals and other southern songs to raise money for Tuskegee Institute. So closely associated with these tours did he become that in 1905 the *Freeman* published an account that was at once laudatory and a bit sarcastic. "Harry T. Burleigh, the New York baritone with an Erie accent in his voice, who has been on tour with the Booker T. Washington lectures but more recently with [Samuel] Coleridge-Taylor, the composer, must have been good company to keep Taylor posted on some of his interviews. Taylor's Philadelphia interview was quite an improvement on his Washington talk. . . . I shouldn't wonder myself but what Burleigh might possibly snort a little now since he has been dining on a Washington-Taylor bill of fare at [an expensive] $2.50 per meal."[9]

In the summers of 1908 and 1909 Burleigh visited Great Britain, where he sang for the king and queen. He also was associated with Will Marion Cook's Marion School of Music, which operated briefly in New York in 1909–10. The *Freeman*, admittedly not an unbiased source, called him "King of baritones and a great society favorite and entertainer of New York City."[10]

Burleigh's art songs were being used by an increasing number of white recitalists. Ernestine Schumann-Heink, to whom he dedicated "Mammy's L'il Baby" in 1903, was one of the first. By the 1910s such prominent artists as John McCormack, Vernon Stiles, Reinald Werrenrath, Pasquale Amato, Dan Beddoe, Paul Althouse,

Lucrezia Bori, Grace La Rue, Andres de Segurola, and Charles Harrison were programming them, as were black artists Roland Hayes and Anita Patti Brown.

"Jean" appeared on a piano roll as early as 1905. The first known recording of a Burleigh song, however, was Evan Williams's version of that song, recorded first in England in 1906 and then in the U.S. in 1912 for the prestigious Victor Red Seal label.[11] Williams was one of Victor's more prominent artists, and the supplement announcing the release indicated that he had been using the song in recitals. It also suggested that Burleigh was "well known" to Victor's white record buyers. There was no attempt to conceal his race. "This effective song—a setting of some favorite verses by the 'Atlanta Poet'—was written by the well-known negro composer, Henry Thacker Burleigh. It is one of Mr. Williams's favorite concert numbers, its rather pathetic tone affording the tenor a fine opportunity for some expressive singing."[12] Sales figures are not known for early Victor records, although this one seems reasonably successful, remaining in the catalog for ten years.

Several more recordings of Burleigh art songs appeared during the next few years. Columbia's announcement of "Jean" by baritone Albert Wiederhold in September 1915 said, "Everyone knows 'Jean.' Everyone should hear Albert Wiederhold's interpretation of this song. Particularly beautiful is the pathos brought out in the ritardando of the finale."[13] Other versions included Paul Althouse on Pathé (1918) and Edith MacDonald on Edison (1920).

"Just You," published in 1915, was recorded at least five times during the following two years, by Maggie Teyte on Columbia, Herbert Witherspoon and Frieda Hempel on Victor, Paul Althouse on Pathé, and Hubert Eisdell on English Columbia. Columbia called it "as sweet an andante cantabile as ever written." Victor noted that "the natural pathos of the melody is emphasized by the touching use of minor harmonies in a major key, furnishing just the background of mingled emotions aroused by the singer's art."[14]

Burleigh's fame was growing. The November 1916 Victor supplement, announcing Witherspoon's version of "Just You," included a short biography of him, carefully noting that he was "of the Negro race." The story of his influence on Dvořák was recounted and his recent songwriting activities enumerated. The January 1917 supplement added that he had "written many charming songs, notwithstanding his activity as a church and concert singer in New York, where high gifts and unassuming simplicity have won him many friends."

Burleigh's setting of another Frank L. Stanton poem, "Since Molly Went Away" (1907), was recorded by Emilio De Gogorza for Victor in late 1916. The composer was again mentioned in the announcement, although it was clear he was viewed as being in a special class, a black composer writing "white" art music. "We all know how things change when 'Molly' goes away. On this tender theme H. T. Burleigh has spun a touching thread of melody which De Gogorza sings with becoming sympathy. H. T. Burleigh has the fine tunefulness and rhythmic feeling so frequently met with among the best of the Negro composers."[15]

One of Burleigh's most popular numbers in 1916 was "The Young Warrior," a martial setting of a poem by James Weldon Johnson about a soldier's farewell to his mother.

Mother, shed no mournful tears,
But gird me on my sword,
And give no utt'rance to thy fears,
But bless me with thy word.

Introduced by tenor Pasquale Amato at an Italian war benefit at the Biltmore Hotel in New York in February 1916, it was an immediate sensation. It was translated into Italian as "Il giovane guerriero" and became a favorite song of Italian soldiers during World War I. The irony of an Italian marching song being written by two black Americans was duly noted but did not seem to harm its popularity. The only known period recording was made in Italy in 1918 by an obscure tenor named Luigi Simonetta. He rendered the song fervently, accompanied by blaring trumpets and military drums, an appropriate performance for a song about a young man marching off to war.

Probably the most famous recording of any Burleigh art song was John McCormack's version of the treacly "Little Mother of Mine," released in 1918. McCormack was immensely popular. His concerts were held in large auditoriums and were often sold out. He was also one of the most popular recording artists of the early 1900s, and his Victor records cumulatively sold in the millions. McCormack had been featuring Burleigh songs in his concerts since at least 1914, among them "Her Eyes Twin Pools" (which he called one of his "Ten Favorite American Songs" and which was dedicated to him), "Jean," "One Year," "Mother o' Mine," and "Will I Wake." He adopted "Little Mother of Mine" immediately upon its publication in 1917 and sang it—often as an encore—at all his concerts. The story is told of one spectacular evening when he sang it at New York's Hippodrome stadium to a packed audience, including one thousand people seated on the stage behind the singer. "At the close of the song the audience rose in an ovation and Mr. McCormack insisted that Burleigh, who sat near him, should go forward with him to acknowledge the applause. Burleigh, smiling modestly, declined the honor. 'You went, of course?' he was asked. 'I couldn't. I couldn't. But he sang it wonderfully.'"[16]

The lyrics, by an obscure poet named Walter H. Brown, could hardly have been more sentimental.

Sometimes in the hush of the evening hour,
When shadows creep from the west,
I think of the twilight songs you sang,
And the boy you lull'd to rest.
The wee little boy with the tousled head,
That long, long ago was thine;
I wonder if sometimes you think of that boy,
O little mother of mine!

The announcement of the recording was one of the features of the July 1918 Victor supplement. Alongside a full-page picture of McCormack, his wife, and their two small children in a homey family scene, the florid copy tied the song to the singer's own childhood. "Perhaps John McCormack was thinking of the little home in Athlone, where his childhood days were spent, when he made this record . . . warm and tender, the melody ebbs and flows as the memories surge back, and the wonder arises in the heart of the singer as he thinks of the mother who so often cuddled him to sleep in the soft haven of her enfolding arms; and as the last high note sinks softly into silence one cannot help feeling that the song is a genuine tribute, a genuine expression of the man's own secret thoughts. The song is worthy of John McCormack."[17]

McCormack excelled at this kind of sentimentality. His pure tenor glided effortlessly between tender reverie and powerful crescendos, and his rendition is affecting even today. A full orchestra, complete with harp, provided a very classy accompaniment. It is no wonder that he brought the house down with the song in encores, and his recording of it must have produced more than a few moist eyes in parlors across America.

By the mid-1910s Burleigh was established as a respected, albeit second-tier, composer of high-class, often sentimental, art songs. In 1915 *Musical America* asked twenty-seven noted concert artists to list their ten favorite American songs. Six listed songs by Burleigh, and ten others performed Burleigh songs at various times.[18] Still, Burleigh was clearly not in the same league as Edward MacDowell or Charles Wakefield Cadman, and was often referred to as if he was in a special category—"the Negro composer." Besides composing, his busy professional life consisted of his engagements at St. George's and Temple Emanu-El, recitals, and, beginning in 1913, a position as an editor at the prestigious music publishing firm of G. Ricordi and Company. In 1914 he was one of only two blacks among the 170 composers invited to become founding members of the American Society of Composers, Authors, and Publishers (ASCAP). In the same year eleven of his choral arrangements of spirituals were included in critic Henry Krehbiel's influential book, *Afro-American Folksongs*.[19]

Burleigh took his career to a new level with his popularization of solo arrangements for spirituals. He had been singing spirituals on his summer fundraising tours with Booker T. Washington, and he provided solo arrangements to his friend Kitty Cheatham, a remarkable woman who did much to spread interest in and understanding of African American music. A daughter of the southern white aristocracy, Cheatham toured widely in the early 1900s presenting lecture/recitals on various folk musics, including spirituals. At some concerts she was accompanied by Burleigh himself.[20] Cheatham recorded some of these songs as early as 1910.

Until the mid-1910s, however, most published arrangements of spirituals were for choral ensembles, and they were most frequently sung that way by groups such as the Fisk Jubilee Singers and the Tuskegee Institute Singers. In 1916 Burleigh published an arrangement of "Deep River" for solo voice, dedicating it to Mary Jordan, the contralto soloist at Temple Emanu-El who was an active recitalist and "ardent champion of American musical independence."[21] To everyone's surprise this arrangement took off like wildfire, adopted by singer after singer. It was the hit of the 1916–17 recital season, its emotional power and intensity adding a new dimension to audience appreciation of the venerable song. One study has documented thirty-four nationally and internationally known white singers who used the arrangement during the 1916–17 season alone.[22] Its success was much discussed in the musical press.

Burleigh immediately set to work composing solo settings for other spirituals, including such favorites as "By an' By," "Go Down Moses," "Swing Low, Sweet Chariot," and "Nobody Knows de Trouble I've Seen." They too were widely adopted. Among the major artists who used Burleigh's arrangements during the 1916–18 period were Frances Alda, Paul Althouse, Marian Anderson, Dan Beddoe, Sophia Braslau, Royal Dadmun, Alma Gluck, Frieda Hempel, Percy Hemus, Louise Homer, Theo Karle, John McCormack, Nellie Melba, Christine Miller, Reed Miller, Alice Nielsen, Oscar Seagle, Marcella Sembrich, and President Wilson's musically inclined daughter, Margaret Woodrow Wilson.

Many of these soloists initially incorporated one or two of Burleigh's spiritual arrangements into their programs or used one as an encore. A turning point came in May 1917, when Oscar Seagle, a major promoter of Burleigh's work, programmed an entire set of them. The world-famous soprano Nellie Melba did the same thing, first using them as encores, then programming a full set. A few artists stopped using Burleigh's work when they realized that he was black. The vast majority, however, were well aware of his race and celebrated it. Art, they felt, should be color-blind. Some used their influence to help Burleigh personally. One often repeated story involved John McCormack, who berated a hotel manager when he learned that Burleigh, who had come to visit him, had been forced to use the freight elevator because he was black.[23]

The success of Burleigh's solo arrangements led to a new wave of recordings of his work. The first seems to have been Oscar Seagle's recording of "Deep River," made for Columbia in December 1916. It was announced in the March 1917 supplement, accompanied by photos of both Seagle and Burleigh. The description reflected the distance white readers felt from black religious music, and to some extent their feeling of superiority to it (its "child simplicity"). "Oscar Seagle has greatly enriched his Columbia repertoire by an intensely dramatic rendering of Burleigh's 'Deep River.' Mr. Seagle has expressed himself regarding this song spiritual as 'true art.' Certainly no other composition of Burleigh's has developed more beautifully the child simplicity of negro melody. There is sincerity and pathos in Seagle's interpretation, a record of which both the composer and singer may well be proud."[24]

Additional recordings of "Deep River" followed in 1917–18, by Kathleen Howard on Pathé and Marion Green on Lyric. Seagle recorded two more Burleigh arrangements in November 1917, "I Don't Feel No Ways Tired" and "Nobody Knows de Trouble I've Seen," which were released on two sides of a single Columbia disc in March 1918. Burleigh's picture was again published, and this time the description celebrated his legend, although it reserved for the young white baritone the ability to properly interpret the "subtle traits of this Negro music." "Many years ago a young negro boy stood outside of a window in the snow for two hours listening to the great Joseffy play. Music was in the soul of that boy, and as Harry Burleigh grew to manhood he gave to all the world many unique and remarkably musical songs. Burleigh's arrangement of negro spirituals are without an equal. Oscar Seagle has been giving untold pleasure singing these spirituals in recent concerts. Seagle is a master of the elusive, subtle traits of this negro music."[25] Recordings of Burleigh arrangements of "By an' By" and "Swing Low, Sweet Chariot" followed in 1918, by Reed Miller for the Edison label.

Black artists were largely ignored in this rush to perform and record Burleigh's spiritual arrangements. Roland Hayes and others included them in their concerts, but the white-run record companies had no interest in recording black concert artists. Hayes's frustration with this situation led him in late 1917 to pay to make some records of his own, which he sold by mail from his home city of Boston. They included two popular Burleigh arrangements, "Swing Low, Sweet Chariot" and "Bye an' Bye," and are most likely the first recordings of Burleigh's work by a black artist.

A year later Hayes's one-time associate George W. Broome, a black arts entrepreneur, launched Broome Special Phonograph Records, which was dedicated to recording black concert performers. Naturally he wanted some spirituals, and he approached Burleigh himself about recording them. By all accounts Burleigh did not like recording, feeling that it did not do justice to his voice. His grandson, Harry Burleigh II, recalled that in later years, at least, Burleigh was very opposed to recording, saying records were "what you hear on a Victrola . . . not adequate." He did not keep any in the house.[26] However, George Broome was a very persuasive man. He and Burleigh had known each other for at least twenty years, and he prevailed on the busy composer to help him record this most important part of the black heritage. The result was announced in the September 1919 issue of the *Crisis:* "'Go Down, Moses,' one of the finest of the Negro Spirituals arranged by H. T. Burleigh, and sung by the composer, is announced as the first of a number of phonograph records to be presented by this distinguished musician."[27]

Despite the suggestion that several recordings by Burleigh would be forthcoming, only this one was issued. If others were made, they were not released. "Go Down, Moses" appears to have been recorded by Burleigh in New York City, at the Gennett label studios, in the summer of 1919. Burleigh sang the old spiritual with power and passion, although there is a hint of uncertainty in his voice, perhaps due to the unfamiliar process of singing into a large, forbidding recording horn. There is a competent piano accompaniment, possibly by Burleigh himself. Burleigh's grandson, who heard this recording years later, commented, "I never heard any record that sounded like he sounded."[28] Burleigh was fifty-two years old when the record was made, perhaps a little past his prime, but still actively performing and well regarded for his vocal abilities. The recording itself was well made for the acoustic era, and surviving copies are clear and crisp. This may not be precisely the voice that Dvořák heard twenty-five years earlier, but it is as close as we are going to get.

Broome released the Burleigh recording as a single-faced disc in September 1919 and began advertising it in the *Crisis* in January 1920 along with other Broome records. Later it appeared on one side of a double-faced release. Although George Broome continued to operate his mail-order label until at least 1923, sales on all Broome titles were extremely limited.

While Burleigh made no further records for Broome (and, so far as is known, never mentioned the one he had made), he did attend a Broome recording session by young baritone Edward Boatner, at which Boatner recorded at least three more of his arrangements, including "Sometimes I Feel Like a Motherless Child" and "I Don't Feel No Ways Tired." Given Burleigh's presence in the studio, it can be assumed that these performances met with his approval. They are very straightforward, unornamented renditions, delivered with feeling and true to the letter of Burleigh's arrangements.

With the great success of his spiritual arrangements, Burleigh virtually stopped performing art songs and turned to lecture/recitals on spirituals. He wrote many more arrangements, with Ricordi issuing four dozen of them between 1917 and 1924. Their popularity stoked the ongoing debate about the "authenticity" of these old religious songs. Some, like Roland Hayes, felt they were of African origin, while others, including influential white critics Richard Wallaschek and W. J. Henderson, claimed they were merely the result of black slaves hearing and appropriating European songs. Wallaschek called "these negro songs very much overrated," while Henderson said, "the negroes have received a great deal of glory to which they are not entitled." Others, including Henry Krehbiel, felt that spirituals were "original and native products" of American soil. Burleigh, at one point, suggested that they might be of Hebrew origin.[29]

Whatever their origins, Burleigh's arrangements of them were his ticket to immortality. Long after his sentimental art songs had faded from memory, the spirituals would be sung and remembered. Numerous recordings ensued in the 1920s and later, including versions by Roland Hayes, Mabel Garrison, Marian Anderson, Clara Butt, Nelson Eddy, Jascha Heifetz, Ezio Pinza, Sherrill Milnes, and the Boston Pops Orchestra, among others. In 1925 a young baritone named Paul Robeson created a whole new vogue for spirituals with his intense, best-selling solo recordings on Victor. Robeson at first favored Burleigh's arrangements, although he later substituted arrangements by himself and with his accompanist, Lawrence Brown. So popular were Burleigh's arrangements that there was some backlash, including complaints that they were too sophisticated, and not sufficiently "authentic" (that word again).[30] But they would prevail.

In June 1917 Burleigh was honored with the third annual Spingarn Medal, the NAACP's award for achievement by an African American. In 1919 St. George's celebrated his twenty-fifth anniversary with the church, and in 1920 he received an honorary doctorate of music from Howard University.

In 1921 Burleigh ventured into the recording studio again, this time providing piano accompaniment on an private Emerson record by baritone J. C. H. Beaumont. The selection was "His Word Is Love," a religious poem by Englishman Fred G. Bowles that Burleigh had set to music in 1914. Beaumont gave a somewhat unsteady rendition of the song, although Burleigh's accompaniment was fine; the recording revealed him to be an excellent, sensitive accompanist. One writer has suggested that the singer might in fact be Burleigh, incognito, but comparison with the 1919 Broome proves that this is not the case.[31] The label does explicitly state, "piano accompaniment by the composer" [Burleigh]. The single-faced disc was apparently made for private purposes and was not released commercially. Burleigh also made at least one piano roll for QRS in 1921 or 1922. The example that has been found (no. 80912) contains short versions of two spirituals, "I Want to Be Ready" and "Go Down Moses."[32]

Burleigh continued to be active throughout the 1920s, widely lauded as having given new life to the venerable spirituals and earning for them respect as "art." He railed against jazzed-up versions of the beloved old songs and seems to have been particularly incensed by a popular hit during the summer of 1922 called "Dear Old Southland." This was nothing more than a set of sentimental lyrics set to the music of "Deep River," but it became a bestseller and was widely recorded by pop vocalists and dance orchestras. Paul Whiteman's fox-trot version on Victor featured Latin rhythms, some hot trumpet work, and interpolated strains from "Sometimes I Feel Like a Motherless Child," "Nobody Knows the Trouble I See," and Stephen Foster's "Old Folks at Home." The recording by Rudy Wiedoeft's Californians on Vocalion was an even bigger grab-bag of southern cliches, interpolating pieces of "My Old Kentucky Home," "Old Folks at Home," "Sometimes I Feel Like a Motherless Child," "Kingdom Coming (The Year of Jubilo)," "Goin' Home" (from Dvořák's "New World" Symphony), "Old Black Joe," and "Dixie," all to the sound of a frantically strumming banjo. The irony was that this popular adaptation was by two black songwriters, Henry Creamer and Turner Layton.

In a lengthy November 1922 letter, published in several newspapers, Burleigh expressed his disgust in no uncertain terms.

> The growing tendency of some of our musicians to utilize the melodies of our Spirituals for fox trots, dance numbers and semi-sentimental songs is, I feel, a serious menace to the artistic standing and development of the race. These melodies are our prized possession . . . they are the only legacy of slavery days that we can be proud of; our one, priceless contribution to the vast musical product of the United States. . . .
>
> [D]elinquent musicians contemptuously disregard these traditions for personal, commercial gain. Their use of the melodies debases the pure meaning of the tunes, converting and perverting them into tawdry dance measures or maudlin popular songs. Their work is meretricious, sacrilegious and wantonly destructive . . . because some of us have endeavored never to sink the high standard of our art nor commercialize the sacred heritage of our people's songs but rather to revere and exalt it as a vital proof of the Negro's spiritual ascendancy over oppression and humiliation, we feel deeply that the wilful, persistent, superficial distortion of our folk songs is shockingly reprehensible.
>
> Have these men sufficient race pride to forgo the cheap success and the easy money? Have they sufficient racial pride to refuse to prostitute the inherent religious beauty of our Spirituals? Can we not convince them that it is all in bad taste; that it is like polluting a great, free fountain of pure melody?[33]

Burleigh conceded that "these melodies are public property and there is no real means of protecting them except through race pride." His indignation had little effect, as adaptations of one kind or another continued. Future generations danced to versions of "Deep River" as diverse as Duke Ellington's moody reading (1933), Benny Goodman's lightly swinging version (1935), and Tommy Dorsey's super-fast jitterbugger's delight (1941). Ironically, Burleigh himself had been criticized for "adapting" the choral spirituals of earlier years to the solo performance style, which also changed their basic nature. It could be argued that the dance-band versions were often respectful of the underlying melodies and did not always "jazz" them unduly.

The beauty of the "Deep River" melody is certainly evident in the Paul Whiteman version of "Dear Old Southland," for example. Such adaptations may have help spread awareness of the music, making it easier for Paul Robeson to achieve such widespread success with his "straight" versions a few years later. Burleigh, however, was a purist who wasn't interested in such compromises—or, in fact, in popular music of any type. It wasn't that he disliked it; for the most part he simply ignored it.

Burleigh remained busy throughout the 1920s, giving fewer recitals now, but publishing and occasionally appearing on radio. He resigned from Temple Emanu-El in 1925, after a quarter-century there. In 1929 he provided the arrangements for *Old Song Hymnal,* a collection by Dorothy S. Bolton. In the 1930s, as he passed through his sixties and into his seventies, he was less active, although he still made appearances and sang regularly at St. George's. He was a strong supporter of Marian Anderson, the black contralto who became world-famous and broke racial barriers on the concert stage. In 1939, along with W. C. Handy and J. Rosamond Johnson, he arranged an all-black program called "From Symphony to Swing" as part of the ASCAP Silver Jubilee celebration. In 1941 he became the first black to be elected to the board of directors of ASCAP.

His long tenure at St. George's was his anchor, and in February 1944 the church celebrated his fiftieth anniversary as its principal soloist. At age seventy-seven, his voice was obviously not the deep, rich instrument it once had been, but the parishioners did not seem to care. He was by now an icon, a living legend. He dressed the part, too, dapper in his suit and vest. *Cue* described him as a "chunky, voluble little man . . . incredibly nimble. Neatly groomed, he carries a cane and wears spats."[34]

G. Schirmer, Inc., a local music store that also issued its own recordings, arranged to record the 1944 service as a memento for parishioners. Burleigh signed a letter waiving his rights to royalties from the sale of these recordings, which were presumably the last he ever made. According to biographer Jean Snyder, "these may have been the recordings Burleigh was particularly concerned should not be available publicly, since his voice was well past its prime."[35] They were not commercially issued, and indeed no copies have been located by this writer or by either of his biographers. Since they were made available only to members of the congregation, copies may survive among someone's heirlooms. However, they would not represent the voice that introduced Dvořák to the spiritual a half century earlier.

Even after his fiftieth anniversary, St. George's did not want to let Burleigh go. He sang there for two more years, increasingly anxious to retire. In 1946, when he finally did retire, he commented, "do you want me to go till I drop?"[36] A year later his son, Alston, moved him into a convalescent home in Amityville, Long Island, where he continued to sing spirituals for visitors. His health deteriorating, he was later moved to a facility in Stamford, Connecticut, where he died on September 12, 1949, at the age of eighty-two. His funeral at St. George's was attended by two thousand people. Honorary pallbearers included Noble Sissle, Eubie Blake, W. C. Handy, and Clarence Cameron White.

Harry T. Burleigh was an important figure in the black concert world in the early 1900s. His art songs, while of high quality, are largely forgotten, but his arrangements of spirituals set the standard by which all others are judged. His influence on

Dvořák, and more generally the place of African American music in America's cultural life, is enough to secure his legacy. Thanks to an enterprising colleague, George Broome, his voice survives as well, ready to inspire us as it did another generation.

RECORDINGS OF HARRY T. BURLEIGH SONGS AND ARRANGEMENTS, 1912–20 (RELEASE DATES ARE IN PARENTHESES)

"Jean" (Stanton-Burleigh) (1903)
 Evan Williams, Gramaphone (U.K.) 3-2425 (1906)
 Nellie Melba, HMV (U.K.) unissued (1910)
 Evan Williams, Victor 64280 (Dec. 1912)
 Albert Weiderhold, Columbia A1779 (Sept. 1915)
 Paul Althouse, Pathé 27012 (July 1918)
"Since Molly Went Away" (Stanton-Burleigh) (1907)
 Emilio De Gogorza, Victor 64624 (Feb. 1917)
"The Young Warrior" (J. W. Johnson-Burleigh) (1915)
 Luigi Simonetta, Pathé (Italian) 13066 (1918) (as "Il giovane guerriero")
"Just You" (Miller-Burleigh) (1915)
 Maggie Teyte, Columbia A1957 (May 1916)
 Herbert Witherspoon, Victor 64535 (Nov. 1916)
 Frieda Hempel, Victor 87261 (Jan. 1917)
 Paul Althouse, Pathé 27005 (Dec. 1917)
 Hubert Eisdell, Columbia (U.K.) D1370 (1917)
"Little Mother of Mine" (Brown-Burleigh) (1917)
 Charles W. Harrison, Columbia A2446 (Feb. 1918)
 Lewis James, Pathé 20323 (May 1918)
 John McCormack, Victor 64778 (July 1918)
 Theo Karle, Brunswick 13001 (Apr. 1920)
"Deep River" (1917)
 Oscar Seagle, Columbia A2165 (Mar. 1917)
 Kathleen Howard, Pathé 27504 (Jan. 1918)
 Marion Green, bar., Lyric 6130 (June 1918)
"I Don't Feel No Ways Tired" (1917)
 Oscar Seagle, Columbia A2469 (Mar. 1918)
 Edward H. S. Boatner, Broome (1919)
"Nobody Knows the Trouble I've Seen" (1917)
 Oscar Seagle, Columbia A2469 (Mar. 1918)
"By an' By" (1917)
 Roland Hayes, Columbia 91012 (1918)
 Reed Miller, Edison 3538/Edison 80487 (Sept. 1918)
"Swing Low, Sweet Chariot" (1917)
 Roland Hayes, Columbia 62050 (1918)
"Go Down Moses" (1917)
 Reed Miller, Edison 3574/Edison 80487 (Oct. 1918)
 Harry T. Burleigh, Broome (Sept. 1919)
"Sometimes I Feel Like a Motherless Child" (1918)
 Edward H. S. Boatner, Broome (1919)

35 Florence Cole-Talbert

One of the first wave of African American women to achieve success in the twenti-eth-century concert hall was Florence Cole-Talbert, a young soprano from Detroit who was active from the mid-1910s to 1930. Many of her fellow vocalists and instru-mentalists were never recorded due to the reluctance of the record companies at the time to record black "classical" artists. Cole-Talbert was fortunate to record for three different labels between 1919 and 1924.

She was born on June 17, 1890, in Detroit, to a musical family.[1] Her mother had at one time sung with the Fisk Jubilee Singers. Florence studied piano and at age twelve was accompanying her mother in recitals. Around 1910 the family moved to Los Angeles where she continued her education at the College of Southern Cali-fornia. Leaving college during her senior year, Cole went on tour with Hann's Jubi-lee Singers, run by W. A. Hann, later the founder of the Four Harmony Kings, and at about the same time married Wendell P. Talbert, a pianist and 'cellist in Hann's troupe. The marriage was short-lived. They separated in 1915, although she kept his name for professional purposes. "Wen" Talbert went on to a career as a jazz pianist and bandleader, appearing on record in the 1920s with blues singers Rosa Henderson and Lethia Hill and making some unissued recordings of his own for Vocalion and Gennett.[2]

Cole-Talbert was still with Hann in 1915, but by 1916 she had begun to make solo appearances. In June of that year she graduated from Chicago Musical College with honors.[3] During the following months she appeared in concert in Chicago, Detroit, and Los Angeles, and in April 1918 made her New York recital debut at Aeolian Hall. Among her recital partners during this period was New York musical maven Daisy Tapley.

In 1919 Cole-Talbert was approached by George W. Broome to record for his new Broome Special Phonograph label, which had been established specifically to dis-seminate the work of black concert artists. At least three titles were recorded, prob-ably at the Gennett studios in New York City during the summer. Two were even-tually issued, the spiritual "Nobody Knows de Trouble I've Seen" in an arrangement by Clarence Cameron White, and the art song "Villanelle" by Dell'Acqua, sung in French. The recordings reveal a pleasant soprano of considerable range. "Nobody Knows" is sung slowly and tenderly, more with recital-hall artistry than with deep feeling, ending on a high, sustained note. "Villanelle" is a vocal showpiece for so-pranos, full of runs and trills, and Cole-Talbert used it to demonstrate her flawless technical ability. The label on the latter indicated piano accompaniment by Wil-liam Leonard King; he presumably accompanied her on the other sides as well.

"Villanelle" was issued with the first group of Broome single-faced discs in Sep-tember 1919.[4] It is not known exactly when "Nobody Knows" was issued, but both were on sale in double-face format by 1921. Broome records were sold by mail from the owner's home in Boston, and distribution was limited.

An item in the *Crisis* for November 1919 gave Cole-Talbert's address as Detroit and reported that she had begun her first tour of the southern states in September. The next few years were spent touring and giving recitals to favorable notice (an item in the *Los Angeles Times,* reproduced in her advertising, stated, "she has one of the best voices that God has given her race").[5]

A curious rumor persists that she recorded several popular songs for the Paramount label in late 1920 and early 1921 under the pseudonym "Flo Bert."[6] The repertoire certainly doesn't sound like her, consisting of titles such as "Don't Take Away Those Blues," "What'cha Gonna Do When There Ain't No Jazz," and "Sweet Mamma, Papa's Getting Mad." There was a white vaudevillian by the name "Flo Bert" at the time, and the singer could be her. The origin of the rumor is unknown.

What is known is that in 1921 Cole-Talbert recorded for the new Black Swan label, established by publisher Harry Pace to feature both popular and classical black artists. For prestige purposes Pace was anxious to build up his classical catalog, and to that end he engaged sopranos Cole-Talbert, Antoinette Garnes, and Hattie King Reavis, and violinist Kemper Harreld for a special "Red Label" series—a clear nod to Victor's prestigious "Red Seal" records. Cole-Talbert recorded at least four titles. "The Bell Song" from the opera *Lakme,* "The Kiss" by Arditi, and "The Last Rose of Summer" by Balfe, all with orchestra accompaniment, were issued in March 1922 on two discs, one single-faced and one double-faced. A fourth title, "Wondrous Morn," was announced but apparently not released. A general catalog issued in May contained a picture of Mme. Cole-Talbert, looking glamorous in her jewels and gown.[7]

While Cole-Talbert may have brought a certain amount of prestige to the new label (and it to her), sales of such repertoire was limited, especially since the country was in a major economic recession. Even blues records, the mainstay of the Black Swan catalog, were hard hit. By mid-1923 Black Swan had ceased recording and leased its masters to Paramount, which many months later reissued two of the Cole-Talbert sides, briefly, on its own label.

In 1924 she recorded two new titles for Paramount, "Swiss Echo Song" by Eckert and "Homing" by del Riego, which seem to have been issued around April or May of that year. The 1924 Paramount catalog included her picture and the following description: "Paramount is proud to offer you records by the celebrated soprano, Florence Cole-Talbert. She is the premier concert star of the Race, and is known to millions from Coast to Coast because of her concert tours of the United States. These records are undoubtedly the highest type of Race music sold today."[8]

Cole-Talbert's performing career culminated in the late 1920s with a nearly three-year stay in Europe, during which she studied with several eminent teachers, concertized, and sang the title role in the opera *Aida* at the Teatro Comunale, Cosenza, Italy. She returned to the United States in the fall of 1927. After three more seasons of recitals, she married Dr. Benjamin F. McCleave and ceased touring in 1930, accepting a teaching position at Bishop College, Marshall, Texas.

For the rest of her career Cole-Talbert taught at southern colleges, including Tuskegee and Fisk. She remained active in the National Association of Negro Musicians, of which in 1919 she had been a charter member. She died in Memphis on April 3, 1961, at the age of seventy.

Florence Cole-Talbert did not achieve the fame of such later black female artists as Marian Anderson and Leontyne Price, but her success in the 1910s and 1920s helped pave the way for their triumphs. Her recordings preserve a voice that was an important factor in gaining entree for African Americans into the modern concert hall.

36 R. Nathaniel Dett

One of the most eminent black musical figures of the early 1900s was pianist, composer, and academic Robert Nathaniel Dett. Best known as a choral conductor and composer of piano pieces, he spent much of his life advocating the preservation of black folk music, both in its original form and by incorporating it into newly composed art music. Many of his own refined works reflected African American themes. Unfortunately the demands of making a living and supporting his family, which left limited time for creative endeavors, may have prevented him from reaching even greater heights.

Dett was a Canadian, born in Drummondville, Ontario, on October 11, 1882.[1] His mother was a cultural leader in the community and encouraged young Robert's musical tendencies. When the family moved across the nearby border into Niagara Falls, New York, in 1893, Dett continued his musical education and soon began playing piano at hotels and churches in the resort area. He also worked as a bellhop at the Cataract Hotel and at other jobs. His first composition, a piano piece called "After the Cake Walk," was published in 1900.

Dett's ability to improvise at the keyboard attracted the attention of hotel patrons, and a wealthy banker from Cleveland offered to support his further study at Oberlin Conservatory in Ohio. Dett enrolled in 1903 and was the first black to complete the five-year program in music, receiving a bachelor's degree in 1908. He then taught at Lane College in Jackson, Tennessee (1908–11), and Lincoln Institute in Jefferson, Missouri (1911–13). He was profoundly affected by his first extended exposure to the American south.

During these early teaching years Dett began to write and compose, finding time when he could in his busy teaching schedule. A collection of poems, *The Album of a Heart,* was published in 1911; while at Lane he completed his first piano suite, *Magnolia.* The latter brought him to the attention of the QRS piano-roll company in Chicago, which invited him to record selections from the suite in 1912. This was a highly unusual honor. Most piano rolls were made by white studio pianists or, occasionally, by well-known white concert artists. Dett's are believed to be the first commercial rolls ever made by a black pianist. He recorded five selections from *Magnolia Suite* on QRS rolls: "Mammy," "The Place Where the Rainbow Ends," "Magnolia," "Deserted Cabin," and "My Lady Love." The four that have been heard reveal a thoughtful artist, playing in a neoclassical style not particularly reflective of black influences.[2]

While the QRS rolls are of interest, there is some debate about the authenticity of piano rolls as sonic documents, due to the fact that they could be easily altered

R. Nathaniel Dett in the 1920s. (Author's collection)

and did not necessarily reflect the dynamic range intended by the performer. Nevertheless, these early examples of Dett's work are historically significant and worthy of preservation.

In 1913, through the influence of black arts patron E. Azalia Hackley, Dett was appointed to the faculty at prestigious Hampton Institute in Virginia, a post he would hold for the next eighteen years. Under his leadership the Hampton Institute Choir developed a national and, eventually, an international reputation. He did much for the university, establishing a Musical Art Society in 1919 and a full-fledged music department in 1928. He also wrote and composed when he could, lectured widely, and became known as a leader in black academic music circles in the United States.

Dett's wider reputation was based on his piano works and choral arrangements. In 1913 he published a second piano suite, *In the Bottoms,* which included a catchy little number called "Juba Dance" that became popular. One modern writer has called it "one of the best evocations of black folk dance in the classical literature."[3] Dett himself described it as follows: "This is probably the most characteristic number of the suite, as it portrays more of the social life of the people. 'Juba' is the stamping on the ground with the foot and following it with two staccato pats of the hands in two-four time. At least one-third of the dancers keep time in this way while the others dance. Sometimes all will combine together in order to urge on a solo dancer to more frantic (and at the same time more fantastic) endeavors. The orchestra usually consists of a single fiddler perched high on a box or table, who, forgetful of self in the rather hilarious excitement of the hour, does the impossible in the way of double-stopping and bowing."[4]

Dett continued to compose and appear in recitals during the mid- and late 1910s. His choral arrangement of the spiritual "Listen to the Lambs" (1914) was widely adopted, and his appearances at the All Colored Composers concerts in Chicago from 1914–16 were well received. He also spoke out on musical issues, including an article entitled "Negro Music of the Present," which appeared in the *New York Age* in 1918.[5] In December 1916 he married pianist Helen Elise Smith, cofounder of the prestigious Martin-Smith School of Music in New York City. During the 1919–20 academic year he took a leave of absence from Hampton to study at Harvard University in Boston, where he won a prize for his essay, "The Emancipation of Negro Music."

In 1919 or possibly 1920 Dett was approached by George W. Broome, the Boston-based black promoter, to record some of his piano selections for his Broome Special Phonograph label. It is not known exactly when or where the recordings were made, but other Broome recordings are believed to have been made in New York during the summer and fall of 1919. It is likely that Dett recorded while he was living in Boston, where he would have come into contact with Broome.

Two records were eventually issued. These are the only commercial records that Dett ever made, and they provide an insight into his intentions and piano style. "Mammy" from *Magnolia Suite* is played very slowly and dreamily, as in a reverie. There is a slightly faster section in the middle of the piece, treated lightly, almost playfully, but the effect is clearly nostalgic. The performance is similar to that on the 1912 piano roll, but played slower and with more feeling.

"Barcarolle" from *In the Bottoms* is played at moderate tempo, again with a light, playful touch, including a wistful melody line in the upper register. Neither performance seems to offer much in the way of African American influences, suggesting instead a kind of proper Victorian (though not maudlin) sentimentality. Dett's Chopinesque style may seem a little strange for someone who built his reputation promoting black folk music. Nor was his style particularly showy, at least in these performances. Rather than trying to dazzle with his piano technique, Dett let the music weave its own emotional spell.

The first Broome releases were single-faced and were placed on sale in the fall of 1919; however, the Dett recordings were not included in Broome advertisements of that period. The only known copies surviving today are double-faced releases, which are believed to have been introduced about 1921. Broome records were sold at least until 1923, but copies are extremely rare today.

Other artists began to record Dett's work in the early 1920s. A major supporter was the eccentric Australian-born pianist-composer Percy Grainger, who was particularly fond of "Juba Dance" and played it at his concerts. He recorded it for Columbia in February 1920, on a twelve-inch disc together with Brahms's "Valse in A-Flat." Columbia had little to say about the selection when it was released in June, observing only that "'Juba Dance' is full to overflowing with the spirit of the buoyant composer-pianist [Grainger]."[6]

Grainger also played "Juba Dance" for a Duo-Art reproducing piano roll in the early 1920s. Reproducing rolls provided much more tone and texture than ordinary player piano rolls. Duo-Art called it "a clever, lively, engrossing novelty that is sure to win great popularity . . . a capitally written piece of music."[7]

Dett's compositions were not as widely recorded as those of his contemporary Harry T. Burleigh or as those of numerous black popular songwriters. During the 1920s "Juba Dance" was performed by pianists David Pesetzki on Vocalion (1924) and Gruen Roycroft on Roycroft (1927–28), as well as by the Victor Symphony Orchestra (1928). In the latter recording, made for the Victor Educational Catalog, conductor Rosario Bourdon led a thirty-five-piece orchestra in a very elaborate arrangement, complete with flutes, 'cellos, rumbling drums, and phalanxes of violins.

Hardly the sound one would expect accompanying black dancers "in the bottoms," unless they had a symphony orchestra lurking behind the bushes.

In 1924 Reinald Werrenrath recorded Dett's arrangement of "Follow Me" for Victor, which called it a modern spiritual. It was backed with "Goin' Home," a pseudospiritual based on themes from Dvořák's "New World" Symphony. Of the Dett selection, Victor said, "[It] is by a prominent American Negro composer, is highly dramatic in style, and makes extraordinary demands even upon Werrenrath's rich and powerful baritone voice; an unexpected head tone and a prolonged closing note of almost terrific power and grandeur appear in it."[8]

Dett's arrangements of other spirituals also attracted some attention, especially from black artists. "Somebody's Knockin' at Your Door" and "I'm So Glad That Trouble Don't Last Alway" were recorded by Mme. Fairfax-Hurd on Paramount in 1923, while "I'm So Glad" was covered by Hattie King Reavis on Black Swan (1923) and Carroll Clark on Columbia (1924). Dett may have attended some of these sessions.[9]

Dett slowly added to his body of work during the 1920s. In 1921 he published a new piano suite, *The Chariot Jubilee,* based on the old spiritual "Swing Low, Sweet Chariot." This was followed in 1928 by *The Cinnamon Grove.* His 1927 collection, *Religious Folk-Songs of the Negro as Sung at Hampton Institute,* was published by the university.

Dett had been a primary mover in the founding of the National Association of Negro Musicians (NANM) in 1919, and from 1924 to 1926 he served as the organization's third president. In 1925 he became a member of ASCAP. During the same period he received honorary doctorates from Howard University (1924) and Oberlin (1926). Much of his time was spent touring with the Hampton Choir, which traveled to Europe in early 1930 in the wake of the highly successful Fisk Jubilee Singers tours, and was the first mixed group to sing at Salzburg Cathedral. While there the choir made two short films for Pathé. The Hampton Choir also performed at the White House for Presidents Herbert Hoover and Franklin D. Roosevelt.

In 1931 Dett was abruptly dismissed from Hampton Institute after eighteen years of service, apparently the victim of faculty jealousies and an unsympathetic new president. Though a severe blow, its effect was not entirely negative. Hampton had not been very supportive of his creative work, giving him a heavy workload and allowing little time for composition or writing (which he did mostly in the "wee small hours," as he put it). He received a paid leave for the 1931–32 academic year, which allowed him to spend the year studying at the Eastman School of Music. Even after he achieved success as a composer, Dett never stopped studying. He received a master's degree in music from Eastman in 1932 at the age of fifty. In 1929, he had studied with Nadia Boulanger at the American Conservatory in France.

Dett then opened a studio in Rochester, New York, and led a choir that broadcast occasionally over the NBC radio network. Major works in the 1930s included the four-volume *Dett Collection of Negro Spirituals* (1936) and the oratorio *The Ordering of Moses* (1937). From 1937 to 1942 he returned to teaching at small colleges in Texas and North Carolina.

Despite his intensity and academic seriousness, Dett did have a sense of humor, as evidenced in his wry poem, "The Rubinstein Staccato Etude."

Staccato! Staccato!
Leggier agitato.
    In and out does the melody twist;
Unique proposition,
In this composition.
    Alas! For the player who hasn't the wrist![10]

In 1943 Dett accepted a position as musical advisor to the United Service Organization (USO), in support of the war effort, and was sent to Battle Creek, Michigan, to work with a Women's Army Corps chorus. He died there on October 2, 1943, of a heart attack quite possibly brought on by overwork, just short of his sixty-first birthday.

R. Nathaniel Dett was one of the most influential black academics of his time, although his work is not frequently performed today. He is remembered mostly in specialist circles. An scholarly biography, *Follow Me: The Life and Music of R. Nathaniel Dett* by Anne Key Simpson, was published in 1993. He is also remembered at Howard, where several facilities are named after him, and at a number of black schools across the United States. Seeking to draw attention to him, and to raise consciousness about black music in the country of his birth, Canadian choral director Brainerd Blyden-Taylor founded the Nathaniel Dett Chorale in Toronto in 1998. Dett's recordings of his own work, long out of print, are an important part of his legacy.

37 Clarence Cameron White

Black concert music and recitals during the early 1900s constituted a small but growing field, separate and segregated from the much larger white concert world. It had its own "stars," among them tenor Roland Hayes, baritone Harry T. Burleigh, pianist R. Nathaniel Dett, and a bevy of black sopranos, including E. Azalia Hackley, Anita Patti Brown, and Florence Cole-Talbert. Probably the two most prominent violinists were Joseph Douglass, a grandson of fiery abolitionist Frederick Douglass, and Clarence Cameron White.[1]

White was born in Clarksville, Tennessee, on August 10, 1880, to James and Jennie White.[2] His father, a doctor, died when he was young and the family moved first to Oberlin, then to Chattanooga, and finally around 1890 to Washington, D.C. He studied music as a child, playing violin at age eight, and as a youth in Washington attracted the attention of such notables as Joseph Douglass and Will Marion Cook. In his memoirs White tells how, at age eleven or so, he went with great anticipation to a concert by violin virtuoso Cook. Cook's appearance was preceded by a lengthy and boring recital by several of his students, and by the time he appeared young White had fallen fast asleep in his mother's arms. He was awakened only by the applause following Cook's performance and was so upset at having missed it that "I burst out crying and made such a fuss that my mother had to hustle me out of the concert and home I went in disgrace." All was not lost, however. "This rather unusual 'carrying on' at the concert prompted Cook to inquire who the little boy was, and when he discovered the cause of my great disappointment he came to see my parents and offered to give me violin lessons during the coming summer vacation. Every lesson was one of pure joy and it was during this period that I definitely made up my mind to be a violinist."[3]

In 1894–95 White attended Howard University in Washington, playing in a community orchestra. In 1895, at the age of fifteen, he played his own composition at a local recital. His musical aptitude was by this time quite evident, and from 1896 to 1901 he attended Oberlin Conservatory in Ohio, graduating with a degree in music. He had already begun to give professional recitals, and notices of them, along with his picture, appeared as early as 1897 in the national black newspaper, the *Freeman*.[4] Nevertheless, the months following his graduation from Oberlin were difficult. A teaching job in Pittsburgh fell through, and finding steady work as a black classical violinist was hard. "This was a dark period," he later wrote. "There seemed to be no opening unless I joined a dance orchestra and somehow that didn't appeal to me."[5]

Around 1902 he returned to Washington and taught in the public schools while struggling to further his desired musical career. Influential friends, including Harry T. Burleigh and Paul Laurence Dunbar, helped. He continued to concertize, earning the nickname "The Bronze Kubelik" (after Czech virtuoso Jan Kubelik, who was the same age).[6] During 1902–3 he wrote extensively on violin technique for *Negro Music Journal,* and in 1903 he helped Harriet Gibbs Marshall found the Washington Conservatory of Music, whose string department he headed from 1903 to 1907.

In April 1905 he married Beatrice Warrick, a talented pianist who accompanied him at recitals. Another woman who entered his life at about this time would have an even more profound effect on his artistic career. That was the formidable E. Azalia Hackley, a soprano who had made it her life's work to encourage and promote the careers of young black concert artists. In late 1905 White appeared at a farewell concert for Mme. Hackley prior to her departure for Europe, then followed her to London to study during the summer of 1906. He returned to Europe from 1908 to 1910 for further study on a scholarship raised by Hackley. Among those with whom he studied was Samuel Coleridge-Taylor, the famous black composer, who inspired White to compose.

Back in the United States in 1910 White resumed a very active program of touring and concertizing throughout the United States, including a long tour of the south and west. Notices of his recitals appeared frequently in the black press. In 1911 he relocated to Boston, arguably the black cultural capital of America, where he opened a studio.[7] There he began composing in earnest, at first primarily small pieces in the salon style of the period, later with works incorporating black folk idioms. He was also active in promoting black music and the musical education of African Americans, and in 1916 he circulated a letter proposing the establishment of a national association of black musicians for this purpose. The proposal came to fruition with the organization of the National Association of Negro Musicians (NANM) in Chicago in 1919. He served as the association's second president (1922–24). The NANM continues to function to the present day.

The years 1919–21 were quite productive for White. Spirituals had recently come into vogue due to the work of Burleigh and others, and there was a gold rush among composers to publish new and improved arrangements. White published three popular collections of spirituals arranged for violin, *Bandanna Sketches, Cabin Memories,* and *From the Cottonfields.*

White had long been dismayed by the almost total lack of records by black concert artists. In 1915 he wrote to the Victor Talking Machine Company, urging them to consider making such recordings. The reply from the company gives us a fascinating insight into the thinking of the white-run industry at this time. It also helps answer the frequently asked question why the large companies did not even consider recording for blacks until the explosion in small-label blues records in the early 1920s made it painfully obvious that a large market was waiting.

September 25, 1915
Mr. C. C. White
802 Tremont Street
Boston, Mass.
Dear Sir:

We have your favor of recent date, suggesting the making of a series of records by singers of the negro race. Our experience has taught us that our customers judge records entirely by the way they sound to them, and care nothing at all about the race of the singer. We do not believe that records by negro singers would appeal to our negro customers except to the few, like yourself, who would be enthusiastic on the subject.

A somewhat parallel case may be found in our college records. Members of the various colleges are very gratified to see their songs in the Victor Catalogue, and we receive many letters urging us to list this or that college song. When they are listed, however, very few of the alumni or the college body ever acquire them. We have quite a number of records by negro singers—Tuskegee, Fisk Jubilee and by Mr. Myers—but we do not believe that a very large proportion of these records are to be found in negro homes.

Thanking you for your letter, and regretting that we cannot consider a series of records such as you suggest, we are

Very truly yours,
VICTOR RECORDING LABORATORY

Note that Victor neatly avoided the fact that ethnic records, made for and marketed to specific subsegments of the immigrant population, were a lucrative business, and that the few black artists they had recorded (the Tuskegees and Fisks) played primarily to white audiences. It may well have been that blacks playing white classical music would have found little favor, but blacks playing for blacks—well, the enormous sales of blues records in the 1920s proved there was an audience for that.

If Victor would not consider recording such artists, others would. Around 1919 White was approached by George W. Broome, a Boston-based arts entrepreneur, to record for his new Broome Special Phonograph label. Broome, a former business associate of Roland Hayes, had established the label specifically to make records by black concert artists. Information about the label is extremely limited, and it is not known exactly when White recorded, although circumstantial evidence points to the summer of 1919. The titles selected were "Lament" and "Cradle Song," both his own compositions. Of these only "Lament," from *Bandanna Sketches,* has been heard by the author, and it is indeed just that, a rather doleful performance with none of the technical fireworks often heard from a Fritz Kreisler or Jascha Heifetz. It may be unfair to judge White's abilities by this single example, as his repertoire was varied and his critical notices quite good. Piano accompaniment was by William Leonard King. The first Broome records were released in single-faced format in the fall of 1919, and White's "Cradle Song" was among the first three advertised. Later both titles were released on double-faced discs. Copies are extremely rare today.

White had better luck promoting his music to white artists. Fritz Kreisler, perhaps the greatest living violinist, was particularly taken with his arrangement of "Nobody Knows the Trouble I've Seen" from *Bandanna Sketches* and featured it frequently at his concerts.[8] Kreisler, who was one of Victor's best-selling classical artists, recorded White's arrangement in 1919. This is the first known recording of a White composition by a major artist, and White was extremely proud of it. It was cited repeatedly in his reminiscences and concert literature, while his own recordings (for Broome) were never mentioned. It was almost as if black composer/performers, relentlessly denied access to recordings and the larger concert world themselves, felt vindicated when white artists accepted and performed their work.

When Victor released the disc in November 1919, it paid more attention to the song than to White, saying "Fritz Kreisler has seized upon a plain negro melody and made of its simple and sincere measures this memorable record. The melody is slow, almost mournful in its tenderness. Half the time the violin makes its own harmony, the 'double-stopping' of two strings going into the deeper tones of the instrument. But the melody rises again, far above, to a high harmonic note that disappears like the last note of a bird that flies too high for human ear to follow."[9]

White's arrangement was also recorded by soprano Florence Cole-Talbert on Broome, and violinists Marie Dawson Morrell on Vocalion (1921) and Albert Spaulding on Brunswick (1925). According to White's memoirs it was likely his biggest selling sheet music, selling more than ten thousand copies over the next ten years.[10]

White continued to tour for a few more years from his base in Boston, then in 1924 moved to academia, accepting the position of director of music at West Virginia State College, a small black college near Charleston. There he worked with the men's glee club, which on February 21, 1927, recorded eight spirituals in Brunswick's New York studios as the West Virginia Collegiate Institute Glee Club. The repertoire was standard, including "I'm So Glad Trouble Don't Last Alway," "Ezekiel Saw de Wheel," and "Walk in Jerusalem Just Like John." Although the twenty-voice chorus was directed by White, and all of the arrangements were credited to him, his name did not appear in the catalog. Evidently Brunswick did not think it would mean much to the mass market. Six of the eight sides were released in the United States during 1927 and 1928, and several also appeared on Brunswick's export label.

Also while at West Virginia State White published the collection, *Forty Negro Spirituals,* which had a substantial circulation, further exploiting the interest in spirituals. He was also becoming increasingly interested in Haitian music, due in part to the influence of fellow faculty member John Matheus. In 1928 Matheus and White visited Haiti to study its folk customs, resulting in a play by Matheus (*Tambour*) and the inspiration for a folk opera by White. White left West Virginia State in 1930 but continued work on the opera, which was completed in 1931. Titled *Ouanga* (roughly, "voodoo charm"), it was based on the story of the slave Dessalines who led the revolt for Haiti's independence in the early 1800s and became its first emperor. *Ouanga* was first performed in Chicago in 1932 and has had various performances since then.

In 1932 White was appointed director of music at Hampton Institute, succeeding his friend R. Nathaniel Dett. During this time he received an honorary doctorate of music from Wilberforce. He resigned in 1935 when Hampton discontinued its music program and moved back to Boston, where he opened a studio and resumed some touring.

His beloved wife Beatrice died in 1942, whereupon White, now in his sixties, moved to New York City. There he met another talented and successful woman, Pura Belpre, whom he married in December 1943. Belpre was the first Puerto Rican librarian in the New York City Public Library system and spent much of her life working on outreach and education for the city's Puerto Rican community. She wrote several children's books and pushed through programs at the library for children and minorities. She also helped the aging White, who was by now something of a legend in the black cultural community, achieve performances for many of his earlier works. *Ouanga,* for example, had its first full-scale stage production in South Bend, Indiana, in 1949, followed by performances at the Philadelphia Academy of Music (1950), Carnegie Hall (1956), and the Metropolitan Opera (1956).

Clarence Cameron White died in New York City on June 30, 1960, of cancer, at the age of seventy-nine. He was an inspiration for many young black concert artists during the early years of the century, through his performances, his body of work, and the institutions he touched, including West Virginia State, Hampton, and the NANM. Although he was an infrequent visitor to the recording studio, his few discs for Broome and Brunswick are an essential part of his story.

PART SIX

Other Early Recordings

38 Miscellaneous Recordings

In a field ignored as long as that of early black recording artists, it is inevitable that there would be oddities, lost recordings, and more than a few mysteries. I am not certain whether all of the following recordings—or even some of the artists—actually existed. We explore their stories in the hope that future research will turn up more information.

This chapter examines pre-1920 black recordings that were made for noncommercial purposes (or very limited distribution), unissued recordings, rumored but unconfirmed recordings, records by artists whose identity is uncertain, records by artists sometimes misidentified as black, and miscellaneous records.

Custom and Noncommercial Records

As noted in the introduction, a number of blacks—mostly unnamed—made cylinders for exhibition purposes during 1888 and 1889. These were generally single copies made by phonograph owners for use in their demonstrations (cylinder phonographs doubled as recording machines, so private recordings were common). Although such recordings were in a sense "commercial," since people paid to hear them played, they were not made in multiple copies for sale. This type of custom recording continued on a small scale throughout the 1890s, and occasionally blacks were mentioned as taking part. Early examples are cited in the introduction; some of the more interesting later cases will be described here.

In September 1890 the Kentucky Phonograph Company reported that it was specializing "almost exclusively [in the] Negro business—plantation dialogues, with banjo solos interspersed, and scenes on the levees." One particularly vivid picture of black life—or, at least, whites' image of it—was called "Row at a Negro Ball," "in which you hear the fiddle and the banjo, listen to the conversation of the guests, witness the progress of a quarrel over a dusky belle, and finally hear threats, accompanied by the drawing of 'razzers' and a pistol shot, with the subsequent flight from the police. . . . Real darkies are used for the darkey scenes."[1]

The following year the Ohio Phonograph Company disclosed at a convention that it had hired "an old Kentucky nigger" to sing "a number of banjo songs, and that cylinder was put on a machine in our arcade, and it was announced as an old-time-darkey-before-the-war banjo song sung by a plantation darkey. I think the receipts from that machine ran about $4.75 to the day. It went way ahead of some of the [popular] Marine Band receipts."[2]

Among the lost celebrity recordings of the 1890s are cylinders by the **Black Patti Troubadours,** a troupe led by the famous soprano Sissieretta Jones, who was known as the "Black Patti." Mme. Jones (1869–1933) was one of the most influential of all early black concert artists but is believed to have never recorded. A short item in the *Freeman* in December 1897 reported that "The Black Patti Troubadours does a land office business with the Edison Phonograph agents who realize the value of first-class selections."[3] Just what this means is unclear. Neither Jones nor her troupe made any commercially issued Edison cylinders, so most likely this refers to cylinders made by a local dealer in a town in which the troupe was appearing. No examples have been found.

A more specific reference, of considerable interest to jazz historians, regards cylinders made in 1898 by clarinetist **Lorenzo Tio Sr.** while on tour with the **Oliver Scott Colored Minstrels.** The Tios, "Creoles of color," were one of the most famous musical families of New Orleans. Both Lorenzo (1867–1908) and his older brother Louis "Papa" Tio (1862–1922) taught and performed there. Among their students were such future notables as Sidney Bechet and George and Achille Baquet. Lorenzo's son, Lorenzo Jr., would become a noted jazz clarinetist in the 1920s, recording with Armand Piron's New Orleans Orchestra, Jelly Roll Morton, Clarence Williams, and others.[4]

Lorenzo Sr. joined the Oliver Scott Minstrel company for a single season in 1898, and shortly thereafter, while passing through Iowa, several members of the company evidently made some cylinder records. The sum total of our knowledge of the incident is from the August 20, 1898, *Freeman:* "The Oliver Scott Famous Orchestra, under the baton of Frank M. Hailstock, Jr., still retains its place on the list of hits. Mr. Hailstock has completed arrangements with the Hall Phonographic Co. of Sioux City Iowa to insert among their records the Cuban dance 'Trocha,' Mr. Simpson's trombone solo 'Battle Cry of Freedom,' Mr. Lorenzo Tio's clarionet solo 'Sonambula' and sketches of Victor Herbert's comic opera 'The Wizard of the Nile.'"

Hailstock was a young violinist just beginning his career; he had toured with *South before the War* in 1894–95 and the Al G. Field Colored Minstrels in 1895. In 1897 he composed some of the earliest songs "in rag-time," including "On the Suaunee" and "Zambo's Frolic on the Swanee." He joined the Scott company when it was spun off from the Al G. Field troupe. Hailstock's career was cut short when he contracted pneumonia during the following winter. He died in February 1899 at the age of 23.[5] Trombonist Fred Simpson was formerly with Mahara's Minstrels.[6]

While it would be interesting to hear these black recordings from 1898, judging by the titles they would probably not give much evidence of early ragtime or nascent jazz. The musicians were playing the kind of generic popular repertoire that white patrons wanted to hear. The cylinders were apparently made by a local phonograph dealer (the Hall Phonographic Company) as the troupe passed through town, either for use on local coin-in-slot jukeboxes, or to sell as souvenirs. Quantities would have been extremely limited, and none has survived.

Other references in the *Freeman* and elsewhere document numerous local recordings by black musicians. In 1892 an item on the Greenbaugh and Mallory Brothers Minstrels noted that "George Bailey, the favorite colored trombone soloist, can be heard in Edison's phonograph." In the same issue, a report from Oswego, Kansas, said "Billy Johnson's latest topical song, 'Until After the World's Fair Is Over' and Tom Brown's recitation 'It's All Right Kase Dad Live There' can be heard in Edison's electric phonograph."[7] These are undoubtedly cylinders made by local Edison dealers. W. C. Handy recalled making a cylinder with his minstrel band in

Helena, Montana, in 1897. Clarinetist Wilbur Sweatman claimed to have made a cylinder of "The Maple Leaf Rag" with his band for a music store in Minneapolis around 1903. Amateurs also recorded in this manner. A June 1897 item in the *Freeman* reported on a music festival at the black Bethel Church, Indianapolis, saying that "the principal solos and choruses of the 3rd annual music festival will be taken on cylinders for the [Columbia] Graphophone."[8]

One custom recording of considerable historic significance that does survive is **Booker T. Washington**'s 1895 Atlanta Exposition speech, delivered by the great educator himself. The full story of Booker T. Washington (1856–1915) is too well documented to bear repeating here, but some background will be helpful in understanding the recording. Born a slave, Washington was an industrious youth who believed strongly that the best way for blacks to improve their lot was through their own hard work. He managed to get into Hampton Institute, graduating at the top of his class, then taught for a few years, until being invited to head the new Tuskegee Normal and Industrial Institute in Alabama. From the time Tuskegee opened its doors in 1881 until his death in 1915, Washington devoted all of his considerable intelligence and energies into building it into a great school.

He also had a message to bring to the black and white citizens of America, which was as controversial in its day as it is now. Washington argued that Negroes should apply themselves first to learning the tools of business and agriculture so that they could support themselves and gain economic power, and that whites should help them do this. Political rights and social equality would follow once they had economic power, not the other way around. To achieve this goal their education should stress practical skills, not theoretical concerns.

These views appealed to many poor blacks who felt that votes and seats in Congress meant little if they could not put bread on their tables. Washington put his energies where his mouth was and built a college that did indeed provide the tools that helped thousands of blacks improve their economic lot. It was also at the forefront of agricultural research, developing new and better ways for southern farmers to maximize the use of their land. The southern white establishment liked his message as well, since it minimized social agitation and left their power structure essentially in place. Blacks could till their lands and save their money, but stay out of the legislatures and remain socially separate.

Many black leaders and northern liberal whites were strongly opposed to Washington's message for just these reasons. They felt that without full legal equality, southern whites would always find a way to thwart the advancement of blacks. Social and political equality was a *right,* something they deserved to see in their lifetimes, not some distant—and perhaps illusory—goal. As for education, blacks were entitled to the same intellectual pursuits as whites, and the same opportunity for a liberal, not just a trade, education. To prove themselves equal they had to excel in every type of pursuit, including arts and literature. Booker T. Washington was to them a dangerous accommodationist who would set back the common goal of black equality. His critics did not want a war of attrition, they wanted a glorious battle, and they wanted it now.

During the 1880s and early 1890s Washington concentrated on building his school and slowly gained a national reputation. The undisputed spokesman for American blacks was Frederick Douglass (1817–95), a fiery orator who had escaped from slavery in the 1830s and been one of the leaders in the Northern abolitionist movement before the Civil War. A commanding presence, devoted to achieving equality for his race, he dominated the stage during the decades that followed the war.

When Douglass died in February 1895 the Negro press lamented the prospect of a vacuum in black leadership. Seven months later, on September 18, 1895, Washington delivered an address at the opening of the Cotton States Exposition in Atlanta, Georgia, a large industrial fair designed to demonstrate the economic progress of the South. It was a turning point in his career and one of the most important single addresses in black history, as it concisely laid out his beliefs and helped set the black agenda for years to come. It also secured for Washington the role of the leading national spokesman for African Americans.

The eloquent twenty-minute address walked a fine line, seeking to avoid threatening his white southern audience while quietly asserting the rights of blacks. Most of all, Washington urged his white listeners to support his crusade to raise black living standards by showing them that it was in their own self-interest to do so. The early black emphasis on political rights had been a mistake, he said. "A seat in Congress or the state legislature was more sought than real estate or industrial skill." Southern whites and blacks must not look outside (i.e., to the north) for solutions to their problems, but to themselves and to each other. His recurring theme was "Cast down your bucket where you are." To southern whites, he said,

> Cast down your bucket among these people who have, without strikes and labor wars, tilled your fields, cleared your forests, builded your railroads and cities, and brought forth treasures from the bowels of the earth, and helped make possible this magnificent representation of the progress of the South. Casting down your bucket among my people, helping and encouraging them as you are doing [at this Exposition], and to education of head, hand and heart, you will find that they will buy your surplus land, make blossom the waste places in your fields, and run your factories. While doing this, you can be sure in the future, as in the past, that you and your families will be surrounded by the most patient, faithful, law-abiding and unresentful people that the world has seen . . . in all things that are purely social we can be as separate as the fingers, yet one as the hand in all things essential to mutual progress.[9]

The reaction to the speech, with its sweeping vision and its emphasis on conciliation in a racially troubled time, was nothing short of sensational. Washington was suddenly in great demand for speaking engagements, and donations poured in for his beloved Tuskegee. Northern politicians took notice, with Grover Cleveland praising the speech. His counsel was sought, and in 1901 he was invited to dine at the White House with Theodore Roosevelt. As unexceptional as that event might seem today, a black man dining with the President was revolutionary at the time, and it outraged racial conservatives in the south.

In 1900 Washington helped found the National Negro Business League, dedicated to advancing the commercial interests of the race. In the same year he published the first of two autobiographies, *Up from Slavery,* in which he recounted his own inspirational rise from poverty, set forth his theories for the advancement of blacks, and reprinted in full the "Atlanta Address." It was a bestseller and highly influential in shaping the debate over black goals.

During the following decade Washington was at the height of his power and influence. Presidents sought his counsel, and few major decisions regarding race were made without his input. Business leaders supported his goals, and his words were reprinted in newspapers across America. Despite the complaints of some, he was the "Voice of the Negro in America." Washington guarded his power and influence jealously. An intensely political man, he schemed against his opponents and supported (sometimes covertly) his allies. The "Tuskegee Machine" was much talked about in leadership circles, and to oppose it was dangerous.

In 1908, during this period of maximum influence, Washington recorded portions of his historic Atlanta address. The recording was made at the studios of the Columbia Phonograph Company on December 5, 1908. One account states that it was made in Chicago, although this is not confirmed.[10]

Washington recorded about one-third of the speech, including the opening paragraphs, and the line "Cast down your bucket among these people who have, without strikes and labor wars, tilled your fields, cleared your forests, builded your railroads and cities, and brought forth treasures from the bowels of the earth." His delivery was deliberate rather than passionate, firm but hardly rabble-rousing. Washington, it appears, swayed his listeners by the calm power of his reasoning rather than by the force of his style.

This was not a commercial record, but rather a personal recording which Washington (or someone associated with him) paid to have made. The label on a surviving copy that was pressed some years later reads "specially made for E. Davidson Washington" (Washington's son).[11] It may have been sold at fundraising appearances, or it could have been made strictly for the family as a memento. It did not appear in Columbia catalogs and was evidently pressed in small quantities. Copies are quite rare today.

By 1910 Washington's leadership role in the black movement was under serious attack. As early as 1903 northern intellectual W. E. B. Du Bois had launched a broadside against his views in his influential book *The Souls of Black Folk.* Du Bois later founded the Niagara Movement (1905), and was instrumental in the establishment of the biracial National Association for the Advancement of Colored People (1909); both of these organizations served as rallying points for opposition to Washington's accommodationist views. Many then, and now, were unaware that Washington had also taken action behind the scenes to more directly combat racism by the use of political pressure and lawsuits.

Washington lost considerable clout with the white political establishment with the election in 1912 of Democrat Woodrow Wilson, who as president was far less friendly to black goals than his Republican predecessors. Washington nevertheless remained a formidable and venerated figure on the national stage until his death in 1915, at the age of fifty-nine, reportedly from overwork.

His 1908 recording received additional distribution in 1920 when a quantity was pressed with the Columbia Personal label, presumably at the request of the Washington family. Some of these were sold to black label owner George W. Broome, who pasted his own Broome Special Phonograph label over the Columbia label and sold them as well. Advertisements for the Broome version appeared in the *Crisis*.[12] It was the only known recording of his voice, and thus the only aural link we have to one of the most famous and influential leaders in African American history.

Unissued Recordings

A number of black artists made records prior to 1920 that were not issued. Since record companies rarely retain unissued material, most of these are now lost.

Unless a test pressing turns up, we are unlikely to ever hear the noted violinist **Joseph H. Douglass** (1871–1935), who made tests for Victor on August 28, 1914. Douglass was the grandson of the great abolitionist Frederick Douglass, who also played the violin, and who encouraged young Joseph and arranged for him to take music lessons. Joseph studied at the New England Conservatory from 1889 to 1891 and then began playing professionally in the Washington, D.C., area, where his family lived. For the next forty years he gave recitals and toured widely throughout the United States. He was billed as "the most talented violinist of the race"—although the equally famous Clarence Cameron White might have contested that title.[13]

Douglass was in his forties and at the height of his career when he was approached by Victor in 1914 to make some test recordings. According to the files two titles were recorded, "Auld Lang Syne" and "Old Folks at Home"—a rather uninspired choice of repertoire—accompanied by pianist Helen Dammond. They were not issued, and he is not known to have ever recorded again.

Soprano **Anita Patti Brown** (c. 1870–1950) was a prominent recitalist from the 1900s to the 1920s. Little is known about her early life, other than that she was born Patsy Dean in Georgia.[14] Showing an early aptitude for music, she sang in various church choirs and about 1900 moved to Chicago to further her studies. There she met and married Arthur A. Brown, a choral director who supported her interest in music. After making her Chicago debut at the Chicago Opera House in 1903, Brown toured so extensively throughout the United States, Caribbean, and South America that she was dubbed by the black press "the globe-trotting prima donna." Another nickname was "The Bronze Tetrazzini," after the world-famous soprano. Her professional name morphed from Patsy Dean to Mme. Patti Dean Brown to Mme. Patti Brown to Mme. Anita Patti Brown.[15] The "Patti," evidently, was meant to be evocative of the great soprano Adelina Patti, a star since the 1870s.

Brown put on a glamorous show, with beautiful gowns that she changed several times during a performance, and black newspapers treated her as their version of the celebrated prima donnas of the white concert world. In later years she dabbled in beauty products, running ads for perfumes and skin-care products.

In June 1916, while touring in the East, she made at least one test recording for Victor in New York. According to the files this was an unidentified aria from the opera *Mignon,* accompanied by pianist "E. King" (presumably Victor staff musician Edward King). The record was not issued, although it was mentioned in the *New York*

Age, which reported that while in New York she had made "a number of records" for the label.[16] This may have been in error, as the files indicate only one title.

Four years later, in April 1920, Mme. Brown paid to have a private recording made by Columbia. The files show this to be a twelve-inch single-faced record, made on April 14 by "Mrs. A. A. Brown" of Chicago and approved for pressings on the Columbia personal label. The selection was the soprano showpiece "Villanelle" by Dell'Acqua. Brown sold copies by mail, mentioning it in her skin-care products advertisements in black newspapers such as the *Chicago Defender* and the *Crisis.* The record was also mentioned in the November 1920 *American Musician* as being played at one of her concerts.[17] Brown continued to concertize during the 1920s. During the 1930s she operated a vocal studio in Chicago. She died on December 28, 1950.

Jazz pianist and composer **Charles Luckeyeth "Luckey" Roberts** (1887–1968) flirted with the recording studio several times during his long career. Born in Philadelphia, he was in show business from childhood, playing piano and appearing as a youthful dancer and acrobat.[18] He first worked in the nightclubs of Philadelphia, then around 1910 moved to New York, establishing himself as one of the leading ragtime pianists in Harlem. A small man (four feet ten inches tall), with extraordinary dexterity and infectious enthusiasm, he quickly became a favorite of the black New York musical scene.

In 1913 Roberts published two very popular ragtime pieces, "Junk Man Rag" and "Pork and Beans," which were recorded by a number of white artists, as well as by Trinidadian pianist Lionel Belasco in 1914 and 1915. For the next six years (1913–19) Roberts was musical director of *The Smart Set,* one of the most popular black touring shows. It was during this period, in 1916, that he apparently visited both the Victor and Columbia studios to make test recordings.

The Victor tests are not noted in surviving company files; however, a laudatory item in the June 24, 1916, *Freeman* said that "Charles 'Lucky' Roberts is the most sensational and one of the most popular piano players in the country. . . . He has the distinction of being the only 'ragtime' pianist who has succeeded in making an acceptable record for the Victor machine." No titles were given.

The Columbia session is better documented. According to the files, on October 26, 1916, Roberts recorded two piano solos, "Shoo Fly" and "Shy and Sly," both his own compositions, published in 1915 and 1916 respectively. Additional takes of "Shy and Sly" were made on December 27. Columbia must have been interested since there were two sessions and one take of each song was initially marked "OK" for issue. However, neither was released. The reason was contained in a mysterious letter from Columbia executive E. N. Burns, dated June 12, 1917, and referenced in the files, which has since disappeared. No doubt the reason had to do with the fact that the piano was notoriously hard to record well at this time, and piano solos did not sell well. Oddly, two takes of "Shy and Sly" were marked "unsuitable to artist," despite the fact that Roberts was playing his own composition. The 1916 Luckey Roberts recordings would be quite interesting as examples of early black ragtime piano, if test pressings should ever turn up.

In 1923 Roberts began making piano rolls for QRS, and in 1924 he played piano accompaniment for two routines by actor-friends Eddie Hunter and Alex Rogers on

Victor, "Bootleggers' Ball" and "I'm Done." These were half-talking, half-singing routines written by Rogers and Roberts, and they sound like a recreation of black vaudeville of the period. Roberts provided a light, unobtrusive piano accompaniment, for which he received label credit. In announcing the release, the Victor supplement said, "Song and story combine in describing a violent public event and a domestic tragedy of the sulky sort. The songs are in half-spoken style, very distinct, with piano accompaniment."[19]

In 1927 Hunter and Rogers returned to Victor and recorded five more sketches coauthored by Rogers and Roberts. Roberts again provided piano accompaniment, but none of the sides were issued. Far more successful was the work Roberts did that year for white comedians George Moran and Charles E. Mack, who had a blackface act in *Earl Carroll's Vanities.* Early in the year Moran and Mack recorded their "Two Black Crows" routine, a dialogue between two lazy blacks, for Columbia. It was a mammoth hit. Columbia immediately called them back for more, yielding additional sketches in a similar vein—"Two Black Crows Parts 3 and 4," "Two Black Crows Parts 5 and 6," and so on. On each of these records they were accompanied by piano, with different pianists sitting in on the various sessions. Luckey Roberts was among the pianists used and can be heard on certain takes of "Two Black Crows" parts three, four, and seven.[20] These records were huge sellers, but no one would have known it was him, since he did not receive label credit.

Rogers and Roberts's connection with Moran and Mack allowed them to place one of their own routines, "Our Child" (a comic ode to a couple's new baby), with Charles Mack, who recorded it as a solo for Columbia. This time Roberts was credited on the label as providing piano accompaniment, an indication that his name was well enough known to sell records, at least in the opinion of Columbia executives.

On all of these comic records by Moran and Mack (and Mack alone) the piano was used as background, giving Roberts little opportunity to show his abilities as a pianist. By the late 1920s he had moved beyond ragtime and, along with James P. Johnson and Willie "the Lion" Smith, pioneered the Harlem stride piano style, an essential element in the transition from ragtime to jazz piano. He continued to perform as a soloist and bandleader, staging large concerts of his work at Carnegie Hall in 1939 and at New York's Town Hall in 1941. He also continued to compose and in 1941 adapted one of his more difficult early rags, "Ripples of the Nile," into a slow and dreamy popular song called "Moonlight Cocktail," which became a major hit for the Glenn Miller Orchestra.

Oddly, despite all of this musical activity, there were no commercial recordings of Roberts's own solo piano playing until 1946, when the small Circle label issued a 78-rpm album of him playing some of his own most famous rags. A dozen years later, at the age of seventy, he cut an LP called *Harlem Piano Solos* on the independent Good Time Jazz label. Luckey Roberts passed away on February 5, 1968, in New York City.

Pianist, composer and publisher **Clarence Williams** (1893–1965) was one of the movers and shakers in the world of jazz during the 1920s.[21] He is said to have made more than seven hundred recordings in the 1920s and 1930s, many with his Blue Five combo which included (at various times) such jazz greats as Louis Armstrong, Sidney Bechet, and Don Redman. He was also one of the first African Americans to become an important figure in the business of jazz, managing artists and bands, and co-composing and publishing such standards as "Sugar Blues," "Baby, Won't You Please Come Home," and "Royal Garden Blues." Although not as well remembered today as some of the artists who worked for him (Armstrong, Bechet, King Oliver, et al.), he is cited and sometimes eulogized in practically every history of jazz. Williams is usually thought to have first recorded in 1921, but recent research indicates that he may have made some unissued recordings as part of his song-plugging activities five years earlier, in 1916.[22]

Williams was born in a small town in Louisiana and moved to New Orleans when he was a child. There the young prodigy soaked up the exciting influences of that most musical of American cities. A born hustler, he was managing cabarets and bands by the time he was twenty. In 1914 he met a talented young violinist named Armand J. Piron, with whom he formed a songwriting partnership, and in 1915 they incorporated their own publishing company. Among their early collaborations were "I Can Beat You Doing What You're Doing Me" and "Brown Skin (Who You For?)," which they promoted relentlessly during the winter of 1915–16. Years later New Orleans old-timer Lemon Nash told researchers about the origins of "Brown Skin," saying, "I'm going to tell you the life of this song. The girls used to pass on Rampart Street; the guys would ask, 'Hey, brownskin, you who for?' Sometimes, one of the girls, she might say, 'I'm for you, baby.' . . . Another girl might pass, they'd say, 'Hey, brownskin, who you for?' She'd say, 'I'm for your daddy when your mother ain't home.' So Clarence Williams took it right from that. He started writing and he wrote that song, 'Brown Skin, Who You For?'"[23]

In February 1916 the *Freeman* reported that Estella White was singing "I Can Beat You Doing Me" and Williams's wife, Georgia Davis, was singing "Brown Skin" at Williams's cabaret. Both songs were featured at the annual police minstrel show, where patrolman Paul R. Monau sang "Brown Skin," took seven encores, and stopped the show. A few weeks later "Brown Skin" was the hit of the Mardi Gras, which was held that year in early March. "The whole town is 'Brown Skin' crazy, and all the whites and blacks are praising this latest hit," said one report.[24] No doubt the energetic Williams planted many of these stories, but it is clear that "Brown Skin" was off to a strong start.

Early in 1916 Williams and Piron interested Columbia in making a recording of their local hit. This is where the story gets both interesting and confusing. The national record companies, based in New York, were always on the lookout for material and would sometimes record regional hits if their local dealers could assure them of enough orders to make the recording worthwhile. Williams and Piron had close relationships with several stores and may well have enlisted their aid in persuading Columbia to record their songs. In an interview years later Williams recalled that Columbia "sent a representative down and they recorded it on a dictaphone and sent it up to New York. And a band recorded it there and the next thing I knew, I got this check [for $1,600]."[25]

The band Williams was referring to was Prince's Band, led by Columbia studio conductor Charles A. Prince. Prince, a talented arranger and conductor, usually worked from sheet music, but he may have wanted to get a sense of the performance style that was making this somewhat unusual number such a hit in New Orleans. "Blues" numbers were new to white New York studio musicians, who were trained in a European brass band style of playing. The Dictaphone (manufactured by Columbia) was a cylinder phonograph intended for business dictation, and a field recording made on it would have been for reference purposes only, not for release.

Complicating the story, the *Freeman* on March 11, 1916, carried the following report, probably fed to it by Williams. "Clarence Williams and Armand J. Piron are having great success with their two latest song hits, 'Brown Skin' and 'I Can Beat You Doing What You Are Doing Me.' Mr. Williams and wife, Mrs. George Darrs Williams [*sic*], have their voices on the Columbia record together in their song 'Brown Skin.' Mr. Williams plays the piano and Mr. Piron assisted with the violin. Mrs. G. Williams sang 'I Can Beat You Doing What You're Doing Me' alone. Her voice took fine. . . . The records will be on sale in two weeks' time."[26]

The date these recordings were made is not specified but was probably during the preceding month, as the *Freeman* was regularly reporting on Williams's activities at this time. There are two possibilities as to what these vocal recordings might be: disc recordings (either regular issues by Columbia or personal recordings to be sold by Williams himself), or the Dictaphone "reference" cylinders mentioned previously.

The first possibility is unlikely. It is hard to imagine that Williams and Davis made disc records in New Orleans. Field recording was rarely done at this time because it involved the shipment of bulky recording equipment and normally attracted considerable attention. Williams, Davis, and Piron might have traveled to New York to make the records, but there is no indication that they did so and no indication of such recordings in the Columbia files.[27] Nor were any such records later advertised for sale, either by them or by Columbia.

Despite the fact that the article says the records would be "on sale" shortly, I believe that the article is a garbled reference to the Dictaphone cylinders made by the Columbia representative. Either Williams or the *Freeman* may have misunderstood and thought it was Williams's own version that would be placed on sale, rather than a New York recording by Prince's Band. It is highly unlikely that such reference recordings would survive today.

What has survived is the recording of "Brown Skin" by Prince's Band made on February 14, 1916. Advance copies were rushed to New Orleans, and a Columbia advertisement appeared in the April 7, 1916, issue of the *Times Picayune* promoting it and indicating that it was available at five local stores. In addition to "Brown Skin," four other recent twelve-inch dance records by Prince's Band were listed, including W. C. Handy's "Memphis Blues."[28]

Upon its national release in June, the Columbia supplement referred to "Brown Skin" as "the hit of the South."[29] Although it had only modest sales nationally (about 9,000 copies shipped over the next three years, according to the files), it apparently did well in New Orleans. The May 20, 1916, *Freeman* carried the following awkwardly worded item, reporting on a recent appearance by Williams and Piron at New Orleans's big Maison Blanche department store to promote the record.

Maison Blanche, the first to [stock] the popular song hit "Brown Skin" on records to fit any instrument using same. Without a doubt, you will have to crown these two gentlemen for their talent. A song for the people of color that has made such an impression on the white people even more than on the ebony humble populace, and all day long the people of every nationality crowded the third floor of the largest store of the city to purchase records of the popular song, for it is a hit. Let's see if it was. The receipts of the day: sold 976 records for graphophone, 210 music rolls for electric pianos, 41 orchestrations, 200 music rolls for the organ syndicate of New Orleans, by Dugans Co.

976 records, $1 each	$ 976.00
41 orchestrations, 60 cents each	24.60
210 music rolls, 75 cents each	150.00
200 music rolls, $1 each (half deposit)	150.00
Total	$1,300.60

It must be going some for one day's work, and one day's triumph for Messrs. Williams & Piron, who seemed at their best at the piano and violin, playing and singing this composition all day at the big store. Get it, for it is on sale any way you want it, for the price address Maison Blanche, New Orleans, La.

Some explanation is in order. The phrase "fit any instrument" was used at the time to denote lateral-cut recordings, which could be played on widely available Victor and Columbia phonographs, as opposed to vertical-cut recordings which could be played only on specially equipped machines. "Graphophone" was the Columbia trade name for its products. Music rolls for electric pianos doubtless meant ordinary player piano rolls, while "music rolls for the organ syndicate" probably meant rolls for street organs (this song must have been heard everywhere in New Orleans). The origin of the piano rolls is undetermined. They could have been locally made, as there were hundreds of companies producing rolls at this time. "Orchestrations" were sheet music.

It is notable that more than 10 percent of the total copies of "Brown Skin" that Columbia ultimately shipped were sold in this one store on a single day. Williams emphasized that the song appealed to white as well as to black customers, as he was well aware that the white market was where the money was and wanted readers—and potential customers—to perceive his songs as "crossover hits."

The newspaper report was clearly a promotional piece planted by Williams and Piron, but it does indicate how popular the number was in New Orleans at the time—and the important part the Prince recording played in that popularity. Williams's report that he received an initial $1,600 royalty check from Columbia also suggests its success, although the amount is a little surprising. Publishers generally received two cents per side as a mechanical royalty, which would not add up to Williams's figures. Since he was speaking many years later, it is possible he may have been remembering amounts received later for this or other songs.

Victor followed suit with its own recording of "Brown Skin" by the Victor Military Band, released in February 1917. Victor's announcement wryly noted that "'Brown Skin' has a few special surprises in the way of cow bells and rattles that will keep you guessing," and indeed it is a novelty treatment with blocks, bells, and other rhythmic noises.[30] Neither the Columbia or Victor versions can be considered indicative of how "Brown Skin" sounded when played by black musicians in the south, but it is how white America first heard this type of music.

The Williams and Piron partnership lasted only a few years. The ambitious Williams soon opened an office in Chicago and in 1921 he moved to New York. Piron didn't want to leave New Orleans, so Williams partnered with another songwriter, Spencer Williams (no relation), with whom he wrote "Royal Garden Blues" and other hits. In 1921 he made his first commercial recordings, a series of vocals for Okeh including "Brown Skin (Who You For)," as a duet with blues singer Daisy Martin. However he became better known as a composer/publisher, a bandleader (with his Blue Five), and a piano accompanist for many blues singers, including his new wife, Eva Taylor. From 1923 to 1928 Williams was manager of Okeh's race music series and a major player in New York's black music business. He got many black artists into the studio, including Bessie Smith and his old friend Armand Piron. He continued to record and publish during the 1930s and 1940s, but as the craze for 1920s blues died down his career cooled off somewhat. He and Eva appeared on radio, and he continued to plug his songs.

Clarence Williams sold his song catalog to Decca Records in 1943 and went into semi-retirement, operating a record store in Harlem. He died in Queens on November 6, 1965.

Henry Creamer (1879–1930) and **J. Turner Layton** (1894–1978) were a very successful black songwriting and vaudeville team who made a test recording in 1918.[31] Creamer was born in Virginia but raised in New York, and gravitated toward the theater around 1900, at first as an usher and program-seller, and later as a stage manager and eccentric dancer. A talented wordsmith, he began to write lyrics around 1906, at first with the more established Tom Lemonier. During the next ten years he scored a number of minor hits with various partners. His first love was the theater, and his songs were heard in shows starring Bert Williams, Marie Cahill, and others.

Creamer was in the midst of a dry spell when he met young pianist Turner Layton in 1916. Fifteen years Creamer's junior, Layton was the son of a conservatory-trained educator who was the longtime director of music for the Washington, D.C., public schools. Layton had not published anything before he met Creamer, but his head was full of melodies with a youthful insouciance that was missing from the music of Creamer's previous collaborators. It was the meeting of an old pro and a young turk, and it worked beautifully. Before long they had placed numbers in the Broadway revue *Follow Me* and in the *Ziegfeld Follies,* where Bert Williams featured two of their songs. It was a song in a failed show called *So Long, Letty,* though, that became their signature tune. "After You've Gone" was interpolated into *So Long, Letty* while it was on the road in 1917 but was not published until 1918.

Creamer and Layton appeared on stage together in vaudeville, and it was just prior to the first burst of success for "After You've Gone" that they entered the Columbia recording studios to make a trial recording, on or about April 18, 1918. The title of the duet they recorded is not given, but it is tempting to think that it may have been a creator recording of the new number, "After You've Gone." The contact address given for them in the files was Broadway Music, which was their publisher at the time. The test was sent to A. E. Donovan, a Columbia recording executive who passed on the black duo. This may have made sense for Columbia economically, but it left history a little bit poorer.

Donovan must have liked the duo's new song, however, because just eleven days later, on April 29, "After You've Gone" was recorded by regular Columbia artists Albert Campbell and Henry Burr. It was the first recording issued of the famous song, and it can hardly be a coincidence that Columbia chose to record it as a duet, the way Creamer and Layton no doubt performed it. Almost all subsequent renditions were solos. According to one study the song became widely popular that fall and was a bestseller from September 1918 through January 1919.[32] The Campbell and Burr recording was released in September, just in time to catch this wave, and seems to have sold well. It was a rather dreary performance, however, sung more as a "coon" novelty than as a love song. The song was much better served by a slower rendition by torch singer Marion Harris on Victor, released in January 1919. Creamer's lyric is a lament by a lovelorn woman, not two bachelors standing by a piano harmonizing!

The song's fame was spread further by its inclusion in an exceptionally cheerful one-step dance medley by Joseph C. Smith's orchestra on Victor, released in early 1919 and a bestseller. Smith's dancing violins showed just how versatile the melody could be and no doubt served as an inspiration to later instrumentalists who preferred to use the song as a swinging, upbeat number. "After You've Gone" was on its way to becoming a pop classic. Notable later versions include those by Ruth Etting (1927), Sophie Tucker (1927), Louis Armstrong (1932), and the Benny Goodman Trio (1935). It would be fascinating to hear how Creamer and Layton originally envisioned the song. However, few Columbia trial recordings survive, so we'll probably never know.

Creamer and Layton went on to compose more hits, including "Dear Old Southland" (based—much to the disgust of traditionalists—on the old spiritual "Deep River"), "Strut Miss Lizzie," and the perennial "Way Down Yonder in New Orleans." They also recorded for the Paramount and Black Swan labels. The partnership broke up in 1923 during financial difficulties of the Broadway show *Strut Miss Lizzie* (the song was a hit, the show was not).

Layton then teamed with singer Clarence "Tandy" Johnstone, and that duo became a favorite in high-class cabarets. They left for England in 1924 and performed (and recorded) there for eleven years, before breaking up in 1935 due to a romantic scandal involving Johnstone and a married woman. Layton then continued as a solo act until the 1950s. He died in England in 1978. Creamer teamed with other composers, and in 1926 produced another all-time classic, "If I Could Be With You One Hour Tonight" (with James P. Johnson). He died in New York City in 1930, at the age of fifty-one.

An interesting recording, if it could ever be found, would be the test made for Victor on December 2, 1918, by the **Creole Jass Band.** The identity of the band is not known for certain, but it is believed to be Bill Johnson's pioneering Creole Jazz Band, with Johnson himself on string bass. Johnson (1872–c. 1960s) was a New Orleans bandleader who began playing guitar at the age of fifteen, then switched to string bass around 1900.[33] He organized the Original Creole Band around 1910 and from 1913 to 1917 toured with it across the United States. This has been described as the first black dance band to make transcontinental tours, and in the mid-teens it was one of the first New Orleans bands to spread the gospel of "jass" to New York. Among its personnel, at various times, were George Baquet, Freddie Keppard, and Dink Johnson.

After 1917 the band was led for various periods by Keppard, while Johnson led other bands and played as a sideman in King Oliver's Creole Jazz Band. He recorded two sides for Brunswick in 1929 (as "Bill Johnson's Louisiana Jug Band") with vocal by Frankie "Half Pint" Jaxon. The 1918 Victor test, whoever it was by, was a title called "Tack 'Em Down." Since it was not issued and no test pressings survive, more than that we cannot know.

Another successful black songwriter who made an unreleased recording prior to 1920 was **Shelton Brooks** (1886–1975). Born in Ontario, Canada, the son of a minister, he moved to the United States as a child and in his teens found work as a theater and café pianist in Detroit.[34] By the age of twenty Brooks was in Chicago, playing in clubs and gaining some local vaudeville fame as a Bert Williams imitator. His first published song, in 1909, failed to catch on, and his publisher turned down his second effort—a number called "Some of These Days."

Another publisher reluctantly issued it, and Brooks worked hard to get it performed, sneaking it in front of vaudeville headliner Sophie Tucker through the connivance of Tucker's maid. Sophie loved it, added it to her act, and made it her own, singing it incessantly for the next fifty years. Some plug!

"Some of These Days" was unusual for its time, relying not so much on cute lyrics or novelty imagery as on the honest emotions of a jilted lover ("Some of these days, you're gonna miss me honey / Some of these days, you'll feel so lonely"). The protagonist, in fact, could have been either black or white, although the assumption at the time was that she was black.

Tucker recorded the song on an Edison cylinder in 1911 and on other labels thereafter. It became a major hit and established Brooks as a songwriter. However, he remained a performing artist with writing only as a sideline. Perhaps he knew how uncertain either profession could be, so he kept his hand in both. He also refused to leave his adopted hometown of Chicago for the bright lights of New York City, the capital of the entertainment world. Neither of these decisions seemed to crimp his success, and over the next few years he produced several major hits. His catchy melodies and slangy, streetwise lyrics were perfect for a generation just emerging from the strait-laced Victorian era into the hedonistic dancing teens and the Roaring Twenties. Among his hits were "I Wonder Where My Easy Rider's Gone" (1913), "Walkin' the Dog" (a very popular dance tune of 1916), and towering above them all, the irresistibly syncopated "Darktown Strutters' Ball" (1917)—"I'll be down to get you in a taxi, honey / You better be ready 'bout half past eight!"

Brooks did not finally move to New York until 1922, but on or about November 1, 1918, he entered the Columbia studios in that city to record an unidentified title for the company's "trials" series. The purpose of the recording is not clear; it may have been a vanity recording paid for by Brooks himself or a test by Columbia to see if he had commercial recording potential. The fact that it was noted "professional department" suggests the latter. His contact address was given as 69 Cumberland Street, Jamaica, Long Island, a nearby suburb.[35]

Columbia did not bite, and record buyers had to wait three more years to hear him on record. From 1921 to 1926 Brooks recorded a long series of discs for Okeh, mostly elaborate comic sketches complete with a supporting cast. Sample titles included "Darktown Court Room," "Murder in the First Degree," and "Then I'll Go in That Lion's Cage." He also recorded a few vocals, including duets with blues singer Sara Martin, but, oddly, no renditions of his own most famous songs.

During the 1920s Brooks played leading roles in Lew Leslie's *Plantation Revue* (1922) and *Dixie to Broadway* (1924), and toured Europe with Leslie's *Blackbirds of 1926.* In all of these he costarred with the beautiful and talented Florence Mills, whose sudden death in 1927 seems to have ended his heyday on the stage. Thereafter Brooks appeared in smaller shows and in clubs, and later on radio and in a few films. In the 1940s he was a regular in Ken Murray's *Blackouts,* a salute to burlesque that ran for years in Los Angeles (where Brooks had moved) and New York. Eventually he became a Grand Old Man of Show Business, and as late as 1972 (at the age of eighty-five) he was featured on the television special *Johnny Carson Presents the Sun City Scandals '72,* an hour of music and comedy by show-business veterans. Shelton Brooks died in Los Angeles on September 6, 1975.

Scholars interested in native musics were among the first to grasp the research value of Thomas Edison's phonograph. A machine that could "bottle any sound" could capture unfamiliar music in a way that standard musical notation could not. As early as 1890 ethnomusicologists with portable equipment were recording Native Americans, and it was inevitable that black "folk music" would also be studied in this way. One of the most famous of these early projects was the recording of student quartets at **Hampton Institute** in Virginia in the mid-1910s.

Hampton, founded in 1868, was one of several southern black institutions of higher education set up by Northerners in the aftermath of the Civil War (others included Fisk, Tuskegee, and Howard). Following the lead of Fisk, it fielded its first student troupe of jubilee singers in 1873 to raise money. While not as fabulously successful as the pioneering Fisk Singers, the Hampton group nevertheless brought a considerable amount of money to the struggling institution, and it quickly became a fixture in the school's operation, first as a chorus, and after 1875 as a quartet. It drew from the numerous musical groups that were active on the Hampton campus.

Between 1915 and 1917 Hampton was visited by Natalie Curtis Burlin (1875–1921), an ethnomusicologist known for her transcriptions of Native American music.[36] At Hampton she recorded two student quartets, the "First Quartet" and the "Big Quartet," on a cylinder phonograph singing a wide range of spirituals, work, and play songs. Among the former were "Every Time I Feel the Spirit," "Go Down, Moses," and "Listen to the Lambs." She then painstakingly transcribed the music into standard notation and two years later published the results in a four-volume work called *Hampton Series Negro Folk-Songs* (1918–19).

Even though she recorded her source material at a black college, whose music director at the time was the eminent composer R. Nathaniel Dett, Burlin saw her work as capturing black folk music in a relatively primitive state. With all the zeal of a white missionary, she said of her black subjects, "That they can sing extemporaneously in harmonies that not only approach real art but that touch one's very soul seems a proof that, though this is still a child-race, the long path of human evolution and advance stretches before it in endless promise."[37] Some of these cylinders survive and, although cracked and deteriorating, they provide a fascinating glimpse into another place and time.

Field recordings of both solo and ensemble singers were made at Hampton in 1925 by one Milton Metfessel. Quartets and other ensembles from the college were recorded by the Archive of Folk Song at the Library of Congress between 1935 and 1942 as part of the Library's wide-ranging program to preserve American folk music. The Hampton Institute Quartet finally made some commercial recordings around the same time, in 1939 for Musicraft and in 1941 for Victor. These were issued in 78-rpm albums of spirituals by the two labels.[38]

Rumored Recordings

Inevitably there are "rumored" recordings, recordings of early black artists which may or may not have ever existed—but which we surely wish did. No doubt the most famous of these recording chimeras is the legendary **Buddy Bolden** cylinder. Bolden (1877–1931), a cornetist of awesome power, is often regarded as the father of jazz.[39] Born in New Orleans, he began playing professionally as a teenager in the mid-1890s and from about 1895 to 1905 led one of the most popular bands in the city. They played everything from waltzes to spirituals, but it was for his improvised "hot blues" that he became best known. According to legend, his horn was so powerful it could be heard for miles around the parks in which he played, drawing crowds to hear him. Among his signature tunes were "Make Me a Pallet on the Floor," "Bucket's Got a Hole in It," and "Buddy Bolden's Blues" (aka "Funky Butt").

Bolden lived as loud and fast as he played, and around 1906 he began suffering from temporary bouts of insanity, probably brought on by syphilis. In 1907 he was committed to a mental hospital, where he spent the rest of his life. He made no commercial recordings, but his trombone player, Willy Cornish, insisted in a 1939 interview that the band had made at least one cylinder recording for an unidentified "white company." That would have to have been no later than 1898, when Cornish left the band to serve in the Spanish-American War. The song was apparently a march or other standard piece, rather than a blues or stomp, but it would be interesting nevertheless to hear an 1890s recording by the "father of jazz."

Was there really such a record? The legend seems to have originated in a 1957 *Saturday Review* article by Charles Edward Smith, the jazz researcher who had interviewed Cornish in 1939.[40] According to Smith, Cornish was old and sick (he died the following year) but nevertheless lucid and quite certain about the recording session, in which he had participated. He could not remember the date or the title, but he directed Smith to a person who he thought might have a copy. That individual said the cylinders she had possessed—whatever they were—were "old and just sitting there" and had been thrown out a year or two earlier. According to this version, jazz history wound up in the New Orleans city dump.

Smith seemed rather boastful about his research accomplishments, and it is possible that he embellished the story in some details. However, old-time New Orleans musicians George Baquet, Alphonse Picou, and Bob Lyons also claimed to have recorded with Bolden, perhaps at a slightly later date (c. 1906).[41] Baquet remembered recording a corny version of "Turkey in the Straw," which unfortunately also makes this an unlikely candidate for "lost jazz classic."

What was the "white record company"? There was a white-owned record company operating in New Orleans from about 1891 to 1893 (the Louisiana Phonograph Company), but not thereafter, and it seems unlikely that any of the national labels headquartered in the Northeast would have sent a recording team to the city at the turn of the century for recordings such as these. There is no indication in their files that they did so. If Bolden really did record it was probably a custom recording for a local dealer using one of the omnipresent cylinder machines of the day, most of which could record as well as play back. Few copies would have been made, and it is unlikely any would survive. More's the shame, we may never get to hear the father of jazz play "Turkey in the Straw."

Other unconfirmed black recordings are just as questionable. In the late 1890s the phonograph trade paper *Phonoscope* listed new releases by title, sometimes with a name following. Usually this meant the artist, but sometimes it was the composer, or a stage personality currently featuring the song. For example the January–February 1897 issue listed a new cylinder of the great hit "All Coons Look Alike to Me" followed by the name **Ernest Hogan**. Hogan (1865–1909) was perhaps the biggest black stage star of the day but is not known to have ever recorded. A recording by him would be historically important. He was the composer of "All Coons Look Alike to Me" and featured it in his act, so the notation could mean anything. Nearby in the same list is the title "Mammy's Little Pickaninny Boy" followed by the name **Bert Williams.** His first recording? Williams wrote the song with George Walker, and was no doubt singing it in vaudeville, so again the entry could mean artist, composer, or performer. Neither of these titles turns up by its creator in any known record catalogs or company documents of the period.

Another rumored early black recording is that of **James MacNeal,** a prominent New Orleans cornetist in the 1890s.[42] MacNeal (c. 1876–1945), whose name is sometimes given as MacNeil, played in two of the city's top black bands in the mid-1890s, the John Robichaux Orchestra and the Onward Brass Band. The Onward Band was said by some to be the best marching band in the city. During the summer of 1898 he was one of about a dozen members of that band to enlist in a black Army band being recruited to go to Cuba to serve in the Spanish-American War. The military band became known as the Ninth Volunteer Infantry Immunes Band (the regiment was dubbed the "Immunes" because black men were supposed to be immune to diseases such as malaria or yellow fever, a notion that proved to be spectacularly untrue when the unit reached Cuba and many of its soldiers died of those diseases).

MacNeal was appointed leader of the band, eventually becoming a second lieutenant. After nine months' service in Cuba the band returned to the United States via New York in late April 1899. According to some accounts it marched down Fifth Avenue in a victory parade, but others state that it was excluded from the celebrations and mustered out quietly because of a well-deserved reputation for hellraising gained while in Cuba.

Samuel B. Charters and Leonard Kunstadt, in their *Jazz: A History of the New York Scene,* note that "a cylinder recording of a cornet solo was made in New York about this time by 'James McNeil,' and it has been suggested that this is the same New Orleans musician who was leading the Ninth Immunes Band." Unfortunately they give no details about the recording, and the name "James McNeil" is not found in the catalogs of any of the major New York record companies of the period. Cylinders were easy to make, however, and there were many small companies operating. Even Edison and Columbia did not list all of their releases in their catalogs. So the existence of such a cylinder is possible, although it probably would have had limited distribution.

Whether the cornetist on that cylinder is the black "James MacNeal" of the Immunes Band is another matter. Did some enterprising local company record the leader of the visiting New Orleans marching band, which was just back from the Spanish-American War? Until more can be learned about the Charters-Kunstadt cylinder, we have only a rumor.

A rumor has floated around the blues world for years that **Gus "Banjo Joe" Cannon** recorded as early as 1898. This would be highly significant as it would make him the first folk blues artist to record, in fact, the *only* one prior to the 1920s. Cannon (1883–1979) was born on a plantation in Mississippi, the son of a former slave, and as a child fashioned his first homemade banjo from a frying pan and raccoon skin.[43] By his early teens he was playing at local parties, and in 1898 he ran away from home to work in various parts of the south, both as a musician and at nonmusical jobs. Exactly what he was playing at this time would be very interesting to hear. The roots of the blues are tangled, to say the least, and by the time real Delta blues made it on to record in the 1920s it is hard to imagine what resemblance they bore to their progenitors. According to one liner-note writer, "[Cannon's] beginning parallels the beginnings of the blues itself and his roots dip deeply into this pre-blues body of Negro folk music."[44]

I have been unable to determine where the legend of Cannon's early recording began; perhaps it came from Cannon himself, who lived a long life and was much interviewed by researchers in his later years. It has taken some bizarre forms. According to the eminent black scholar Eileen Southern, in her *Biographical Dictionary of Afro-American and African Musicians* (1982), "In 1901 he made a cylinder recording at Belzoni, Mississippi, for the Victor Talking Machine Company—thereby becoming the first bluesman to record." This is, of course, impossible. Victor made discs, not cylinders, and the company was not founded until 1901. It was hardly in a position to send its bulky and primitive disc-recording equipment out for field recordings. There is no indication in Victor's files that it did field recording of this type at the time.

Southern qualified her statement somewhat in the 1983 edition of her book *The Music of Black Americans,* saying that Cannon reputedly made such a record but "no proof of it is extant."[45] Meanwhile, blues researcher Sheldon Harris, in *Blues Who's Who* (1979), told readers that Cannon "reportedly recorded banjo solos [for the] Victor (cylinder) or Columbia (disc) labels, Belzoni, MS, early 1900s." As noted, Victor made discs, not cylinders, and there is no indication in either company's files that either was doing any field recording in the south at this time or that either recorded Cannon.

Most likely, Cannon (or someone else) was referring to some type of local cylinder recording, perhaps by a dealer, and confusing the "record company" with a name he had seen on a phonograph—or with the companies he recorded for many years later. There is no indication that any such cylinders survive today.

Cannon played in blues bands and medicine shows for the next twenty-five years while working at odd jobs to supplement his income. In the late 1920s he formed Cannon's Jug Stompers, a jug band, and recorded commercially, first for Paramount and later for Victor and Brunswick. Between 1927 and 1930 he made more than thirty sides, many of which are considered classics today. During the 1930s and 1940s he continued a hand-to-mouth existence, playing blues and working at other jobs, sometimes singing for tips. He was "rediscovered" during the folk boom of the 1950s, making an album for Folkways in 1956.

Cannon's real "rediscovery" came in 1963 when an old song of his, "Walk Right In," was recorded by a white group, the Rooftop Singers, and became a major pop hit. The Singers thought it was a folksong and were unaware that the writer was a down-on-his-luck elderly black man eking out a living in the railroad yards of Memphis.[46] In the glow of this latest rediscovery, Cannon was brought into the studio to record another album (for Stax) and appeared in filmed and television documentaries about the blues. He continued active until his late eighties and died in 1979 at the age of ninety-six.

Identity Uncertain

One of the enduring mysteries in the field of early black recordings is the identity of **Blake's Jazzone Orchestra,** which recorded one title for Pathé in late 1917. The record, Overstreet's "The Jazz Dance," was held for a full year before finally being released in November 1918. In announcing it the Pathé supplement said, tersely, "Blake's Jazzone Orchestra, a colored organization, is a New York sensation." That short statement has set off years of speculation among jazz experts as to the identity of these musicians.

The record itself is a fast-paced, fairly tight reading of the jazz standard, in the noisy, Original Dixieland Jazz Band–influenced style of the time. A strong cornet (or two?) dominates the rendition, with trombone, clarinet, saxophone, violin and drums (using blocks) also heard.

An obvious guess is that "Blake" is pianist Eubie Blake, leading a pick-up band of local New York musicians. Eubie had recorded several titles for Pathé just a few weeks earlier and was quite active in the New York area at this time. However, this does not sound like anything else he ever recorded, and no piano is audible. Eubie was frequently interviewed by researchers in later years, but he never mentioned this record. Nevertheless several major discographers, including Bruyninckx, Lord, and Berresford, confidently attribute it to him.[47]

Another theory is that it is an out-of-town band, led by someone else entirely. Charters and Kunstadt asserted that "another Negro group from the South [that] was recorded [was] Blake's Jazzone Orchestra, playing out of Richmond." Jazz discographer Brian Rust, who first believed the record was by Eubie Blake, later subscribed to the "out-of-town" theory, stating that the Jazzone Orchestra was "at first thought to have been a band led by Eubie Blake, [but] is now known to have come from Virginia." Pursuing this theory, another researcher has suggested that the leader may be Enoch W. Blake, a cornetist and bandleader who appeared around this time with the Rabbit Foot Minstrels, and the Silas Green and Florida Blossom companies.[48]

Many discographers have the unfortunate habit of making definitive statements with no evidence, and with no sources indicated, and this has been the case with "Blake's Jazzone Orchestra." None of the forgoing discographers offers any basis for his claims. Moreover several of them copy information from each other, perpetuating mistakes. Both the Bruyninckx and Lord volumes cite an incorrect matrix number and recording date for this record.

No mention of the orchestra has been found by this author in period sources (some "New York sensation"). The mystery will endure until someone finds documentation. In the meantime, we have the sound of that commanding cornetist, whoever he was, on a very interesting black recording made during the very first year of recorded jazz.

Even less can be deduced about the identity of the **Memphis Pickaninny Band,** which also recorded one side for Pathé in 1917. The song, "Some Jazz Blues," was recorded about June 1917, at the very start of the "jazz boom." It cannot even be certain that this is a black orchestra, as Pathé said nothing substantive about them and no mention of them has been found in the contemporary black press. However, the name and the performance style, as well as the fact that Pathé was recording black musicians around this time, suggest that it may have been.

Brian Rust describes the recording as a "small brass band with percussion"; researcher George Blacker, writing in *Record Research* magazine, was less kind, calling it "a hilariously corny brass band item of no jazz value."[49] It is, in fact, a fast-tempo, clearly jazz-influenced recording, and rather remarkable for the middle of 1917. Trumpets (two?), trombones, and clarinets dominate the sound, with some rather frantic drumming and numerous sound effects—slide whistles, a washboard(?), and blocks, among other things—corny by today's standards perhaps, but progressive at the time. The intention seems to have been to recreate the "barnyard" sound used to such great effect by the Original Dixieland Jazz Band in its initial Victor release just a few weeks earlier. Not as loose as the ODJB, the band sounds as if it could be composed of practiced brass band musicians—perhaps even the Pathé studio band—trying to imitate the syncopated music that had suddenly become popular during the preceding winter. It certainly doesn't sound like children ("pickaninnies").

Pathé released "Some Jazz Blues" as one of a group of standard dance records in December 1917, saying merely, "special attention is directed to the fox trot 'Some Jazz Blues' played by the Memphis Pickaninny Band. It's simply wonderful!"[50] On the other side of the disc was a much more stiffly played one-step ("He's Just Like You") by the Pathé Dance Orchestra. Pathé leased its masters to minor labels, and "Some Jazz Blues" was also released on Crescent, Empire, Schubert, and possibly others. All of these labels used the vertical-cut technology, and distribution was much smaller than for releases on Victor and Columbia.

Whoever these musicians were, they left us a lively recording that reflects the musical experimentation going on during the summer of 1917, at the moment recorded jazz was being born. To dismiss it as of "no jazz interest" misses entirely the sounds of this musical evolution.

Misidentified as Black

Finally we turn to a number of early artists who are sometimes thought to have been black, but either probably or definitely were not. The **Brilliant Quartette** was a popular act in vaudeville in the 1890s and one of the first quartets to record. Early in the decade they made many cylinders for the New York Phonograph Company (1890–93) and Columbia (1891–95), later switching to discs for Berliner (1896–99). Much of their repertoire was black material, such as "Hear Dem Bells," "Blind Tom" ("Negro camp-meeting shout"), "Haul the Woodpile Down," and "Keep Hammering in My Soul." That, combined with a lack of information about their personnel, led researcher Leonard Kunstadt, among others, to speculate that they might be black.

Despite their popularity, no picture of the quartet is known to exist. However there are many reviews of their appearances in theatrical journals of the 1890s. As of 1890 the lineup was C. O. Marsh, T. H. Rapp, F. Mitchell, and H. Wrille (or Willie).[51] Ten years later the spring 1900 Berliner Gramophone Company catalog listed a similar lineup—Marsh, Rapp, Miller, and Marion. The quartet appeared at the top white vaudeville theaters, including Tony Pastor's and Keith's Union Square Theater in New York, as well as in mixed-race shows such as George C. Thompson's *Our Southern Home* in 1894.[52] No reference to them ever suggested that they were other than white. Reviews of black acts in white journals of this period almost always specified race.

The quartet's repertoire was actually quite varied, including not only the spirituals and comic black songs mentioned earlier (which many white quartets sang), but also songs like "Remember Poor Mother at Home," "The Irish Queen," "German Medley," and "Nearer My God to Thee." A particularly interesting title is "Fight for Home and Honor," in memory of the July 1892 Homestead, Pennsylvania, strike in which many strikers were killed. Examples of the quartet's recordings that have been heard by the author contain no distinctive mannerisms that would suggest they were black.[53] Most persuasively, an obituary for Charles O. Marsh (c. 1859–1938), identifies him as both "a member of the old Brilliant Quartet" and a nephew of George Thatcher, one of the white minstrel moguls of the 1880s.[54] Barring new evidence, this would seem to prove conclusively that this pioneering quartet was white.

Sometimes racial mistakes spring from poorly worded original sources. **Charles A. Asbury,** a singer and banjo player of the 1890s, recorded a lot of black-themed material which was popular at the time. He is found on cylinders made by the New Jersey Phonograph Company and by Columbia from c. 1892–1897.[55] Both the 1892 New Jersey catalog and the September–October 1894 *Edison Phonographic News* called him "the popular colored banjoist and comedian." However, New Jersey's 1894 catalog published his picture and he is not black; the copy said that his songs were in "the good old plantation negro style." His picture also appears in the December 1892 issue of the *Phonogram,* an industry trade paper.

George Graham was another popular recording artist of the 1890s who is sometimes thought to be black because of his repertoire. Graham was said to be a patent medicine salesman who was "discovered" on a Washington, D.C., sidewalk, where he was hawking his wares. His fast-talking monologues first appeared on Berliner in 1895 and proved quite popular. He later recorded for Columbia and Zonophone. His last traced recordings were Victor and Columbia discs made in 1903.[56] Some of his routines had black themes ("Colored Preacher," "Negro Funeral Sermon"), but many did not. His picture in the April 1897 Berliner catalog establishes that he was white.

S. H. Dudley is a particularly confusing case, because there were two well-known show business figures by that name at the turn of the century, one white and one black. The S. H. Dudley (1864–1947) who recorded was a white baritone. Born Samuel Holland Rous, he began singing professionally in his teens and adopted the name S. H. Dudley early in his career.[57] Drawn to opera, he sang minor roles with the Boston Ideal Opera Company, Grand English Opera Company, and Tavary Grand English Opera Company in the 1880s and early 1890s. He began recording about 1894, and for the next decade or so was an extremely familiar name on record, first on cylinders and later on discs, on many labels. His recording repertoire was almost entirely popular songs, including the then popular "coon songs." He also presided over minstrel routines. By 1903 he had begun to scale back his recording activities in favor of executive responsibilities at Victor, where he was in charge of popular recording. He also edited Victor's catalogs and supplements and was the author of the *Victor Book of the Opera,* for which he sometimes received credit under his real name, Samuel Holland Rous. He retired from Victor in 1919.

The black S. H. Dudley (1872–1940), a comedian, apparently never recorded, which is our loss as he was one of the most popular black performers of his day. Born Sherman Houston Dudley, he broke into show business in the mid-1890s, playing mostly on the black circuits. Thus he came to prominence perhaps a decade after Rous began using the name. In 1898 he was with P. T. Wright's Nashville Students, and the following year was billed as an "up and coming young comedian" with the *Hot Time in Old Dixie* touring company.[58] He toured with McCabe and Young's Minstrels and Richards and Pringle's Georgia Minstrels, gradually achieving star billing. In 1904 he took over the leading role with the Smart Set Company, where he starred in the comedies *His Honor, the Barber* and *Dr. Beans from Boston.* As a performer he was best known for his act with a live mule named Patrick. Dudley made theatrical history in 1913 when he retired from performing and organized the first black-run vaudeville circuit, which evolved into the Theater Owners Booking Association (TOBA), with which he remained associated for many years.

One of the more bizarre citations in the early black press involved the popular white team of **Dave Montgomery** (1870–1917) and **Fred Stone** (1873–1959). These two small-time comedians teamed up in 1895, working in blackface and appearing together for the first time at Boston's Keith Theater. Working their way quickly up the vaudeville ranks, they soon achieved the status of headliners. It was during this initial burst of fame in 1897 that the *Freeman,* a leading black newspaper, and a generally reliable source on the black entertainment world, ran the following curious item: "It is not generally known that Montgomery, of the team of Montgomery & Stone, is a colored man."[59]

What prompted this strange assertion, early in their career, is not known. Montgomery and Stone went on to become one of the most famous vaudeville and musical comedy partnerships of all time, starring in a series of hit Broadway shows including *The Wizard of Oz* (1903), *The Red Mill* (1906), and *The Old Town* (1909). They recorded several sides for Victor in 1911. After Montgomery's death in 1917 Stone continued as a single, appearing in stage and film productions until the 1950s. There was never again any suggestion that his beloved partner had been black. Did the *Freeman* know something we don't?

Miscellaneous

Some might nominate the **Original New Orleans Jazz Band** for inclusion in a survey of early black groups on the strength of one of its members. This band, which recorded for Okeh in November 1918 and Gennett and Paramount in 1919–20, was led by white pianist (and later comedian) Jimmy Durante and mixed music and comedy. Jimmy later cracked, "In some bands in those days the cornet player played the melody, in some others the clarinet player played the melody. In our band, nobody played the melody."[60]

Durante's band was composed mostly of white musicians. The clarinetist, however, was a "Creole of color" named Achille Baquet. Baquet was the brother of George Baquet, clarinetist with Freddie Keppard's Creole Band, but was so light-skinned that the other bandmembers reportedly did not even know that he was black.

Although this is a survey of recording artists, mention should be made of a number of black pianists who made commercial piano rolls prior to 1920. Player pianos were first marketed in the late 1890s, but most rolls were not created by pianists. Instead the holes representing the notes were punched in the paper by technicians working from scores. Even hand-played rolls, which originated around 1910, were frequently altered by having additional holes (notes) added to "augment" the pianist's performance. Except for premium-priced "reproducing rolls," which came later, most piano rolls had a narrow dynamic range and could not reproduce the artist's loud and soft passages. So for a variety of reasons some rolls are a curiosity rather than a reliable documentation of a pianist's intentions. Table 13 lists black pianists who are believed to have made hand-played rolls prior to 1920. Also shown is the year they began and the companies they worked for. This is a tentative list, and further research is urgently needed.

Table 13. Black Pianists Who Made Hand-Played Rolls

1912	R. Nathaniel Dett, QRS[a]
1912	Blind Boone, QRS
1912	Fred M. Bryan
1914	James Reese Europe, Welte-Mignon[a]
1914	Ford T. Dabney, Welte-Mignon[a]
1915	Clarence M. Jones, Wurlitzer Pianola, Rolla-Artis[a]
1916	Scott Joplin, Uni-Record, Connorized
1917	Eubie Blake, Ampico, Rhythmodik, Artrio-Angelus[a]
1917	"F. Morton" (Jelly Roll Morton?)[a]
1917	James P. Johnson[a]
1919	Luckey Roberts, Vocalstyle[a]

a. The artist also made phonograph records.

APPENDIX: CARIBBEAN AND SOUTH AMERICAN RECORDINGS

Dick Spottswood

It is interesting to speculate what sorts of music would have been captured on early records if Thomas Edison had built his laboratories in—say—North Carolina, Alabama, or Texas, where rich indigenous preindustrialized music traditions thrived, black, white, and otherwise. Instead, sound recording was invented in West Orange, New Jersey, a suburb of New York City, where music publishing became a thriving business after the Civil War. Music became a commodifiable product of Tin Pan Alley on the one hand and of the classical/art establishment on the other. New copyrightable New York music was a major component of sound recordings from 1889, when music cylinders were first produced for coin-operated salon phonographs, to the 1920s. When the record industry belatedly discovered that black and white regional and traditional styles of music from other parts of America could produce profits, mountain music, cowboy songs, jazz, and the blues became available on records.

Abroad, as the phonograph industry was gearing up at the end of the nineteenth century, English and European entrepreneurs quickly set out to create markets throughout Europe and Asia. Portable equipment and sound technicians traveled to urban centers throughout the continents to capture local and regional music, correctly assuming that, if familiar music was available, consumers would buy phonographs and records. The process ensured that an impressive body of folk, classical, religious, and popular music from many locales was captured. Some of those recordings survive today, giving us invaluable glimpses into the kaleidoscopic world of music a century and more ago.

When American record-makers wanted to sell their products beyond U.S. borders, they quickly came to terms with the popular local, regional, and folk styles of other nations in this hemisphere, including the artistry of black and creole music-makers. Fortunately they did so in abundance, though relatively few of the early discs and cylinders they produced survive today. Examples of Cuban *danzones,* Brazilian *chôros,* and Trinidadian *paseos* from the 1900s and 1910s have been reissued, allowing us to enjoy African American music from the other Americas. But, as we trace our own music history, we stare at old photos of North American black music-makers, desperately wishing for surviving sounds to accompany the fading images—sounds from the early records that were never made.

With Tin Pan Alley providing the hits, and capable singers and musicians performing them, New York record products reflected enough popular taste of the time that no one thought of capturing and distributing regional music from other parts of the country. It wasn't until 1920 that blues singer Mamie Smith demonstrated that there was a separate and identifiable audience for recorded African American music. Three years later, a surprise hit record by Atlanta's Fiddlin' John Carson showed that a comparable audience existed for southern white rural music. By then, enterprising record-makers learned that they could work profitably in locales remote from New York and find appealing songs and styles unique to particular places.

The early industry did supply appropriate music to the foreign-born audience. New York had no shortage of immigrants from many lands, and language variety was reflected in foreign-language catalogs after 1905. European products were available for reissue here, supplemented by examples of popular local immigrant talent. Among diverse genres, there were Greek songs from Ottoman Turkey, romantic Neapolitan melodies, klezmer dances from Eastern Europe, Spanish-language music, and Arabic popular songs imported from Cairo and Damascus.

In the early days, records were expected to do little more than keep standard material available, supplementing it with soundprint equivalents of published sheet music. New York–created products sufficed to supply a broad-based market that demanded little else; consequently, Victor, Columbia, and Edison were in less of a hurry than their counterparts in Europe to explore remote recording sites. Occasional journeys were made to record presidential candidates' speeches or other isolated events. Other exceptions to the rule included Edison recordings of Cantonese opera from San Francisco in 1902 and Columbia recordings of Polish and Bohemian titles from Chicago in 1915. But there were no general field-recording sorties in North America before the 1920s, when excursions to cities like Buffalo, Atlanta, Chicago, St. Louis, Los Angeles, Dallas, and other remote locales for the specific purpose of recording regional music became a frequent and profitable activity.

Fortunately, early cylinder phonographs could create records as well as reproduce them. Several early anthropologists, ethnomusicologists, and folklorists made use of the phonograph to record Native American and other music, beginning with expeditions to Maine and Arizona by the Smithsonian's Jesse Walter Fewkes in 1890. The Chicago World's Fair in 1893 offered another opportunity to record "exotic" music, and to show off the phonograph that, to many, seemed as exotic as the performers. Benjamin Ives Gilman's records of Turkish, Sundanese, and Kwakiutl music were the first in those genres to be made anywhere. Such recordings have to be listened to patiently, but they do offer fascinating glimpses of what lay beyond New York—way beyond. Closer to home, ragtime historian Rudi Blesh has noted that pioneering black pianists Johnny Seymour and Plunk Henry were also in Chicago in 1893. If only Gilman had captured some of their music too . . .

Though record-makers lacked the imagination to capture and market varieties of their own national music, they were less reluctant to explore possibilities in Mexico, Cuba, and parts of Central and South America. Columbia (1903), Edison (1904), and Victor (1905) made the first over-the-border records in Mexico City, returning regularly until the country's revolution began in 1910.[1]

If American record companies were slow to venture out of New York, their operatives soon made up for lost time. Taking to the high seas in 1903, Columbia made its way to China and Japan, while in 1905 Victor technicians recorded in China, Honolulu, and Buenos Aires. Victor's subsidiary company Zonophone went to Buenos Aires and to Havana, where non-U.S. African Americans were recorded for the first time.[2] Little detailed documentation survives from Columbia's early days, but a handful of single-sided Columbia discs from Buenos Aires may also date from 1905.[3] That company appears to have visited Havana in 1906 as well; surviving records from these pioneering expeditions provide examples of rewarding and compelling music.

Much remains to be learned about Argentina's first recordings. They did feature tango, a genre that evolved in the 1880s and 1890s as local *payadores,* or troubadours, emerged from rural areas and urban dives to attract broad new audiences. Chief among them was Gabino Ezeyza (or Ezeiza, 1858–1916), who wrote and sang urban tangos, composing over five hundred songs during a long career. He was tango's first star, preceding Carlos Gardel by a generation. At least one of his recordings survives, a single-sided Columbia ("Cosmopolismo," 55098).

Cuba

Cuba proved a fertile field for black music. More than eighty sides were made by cornetist Pablo Valenzuela and his orchestra for Zonophone in 1905.[4] The group produced forty cylinders for Edison the following year.[5] Valenzuela (1859–1926) was an outstanding soloist who assumed leadership of a long-standing ensemble following the death of his trombonist brother Raimundo (1848–1905), who had joined Juan de Díos Alfonso's orchestra in 1864, becoming director when the leader died.

Pablo Valenzuela's recordings span the years 1905 to 1919. They allow us to hear the work of an exceptional musician born nearly two decades before the legendary New Orleans cornetist Buddy Bolden. His works were normally in the form of the *danzón,* a form credited to one Miguel Faílde (d. 1921), who introduced it in 1879. Typically, a danzón opens with a melody that recurs between successive themes in a simplified rondo format, such as ABACAD. Tunes from opera, popular songs, and other sources would often appear as secondary danzón themes.

Valenzuela was one of three prominent African-Cuban cornetists whose groups recorded prolifically between 1905 and 1920. Felipe Valdés founded an ensemble in 1899 that recorded for Columbia in 1906. His discography approached 350 titles over the years. Enrique Peña (1881–1922) founded a group in 1903 that soon included several prominent musicians. One of them, Félix González (1877–1967), played the *figle* (ophicleide), a nineteenth-century serpentine military horn that was all but obsolete before the days of record-making. But González played it with pride, becoming a leader and record-maker in his own right in 1915. He remained musically active in Havana until his death. His clarinetists, José Urfé (1879–1957) and José Belén Puig, were talented composers who later became bandleaders themselves.

The Valenzuela, Valdés, and Peña danzón groups produced several hundred records before 1910 for Victor, Zonophone, Columbia and Edison. Their groups are called *orquestas típicas,* a term designating bands who play music that is "down home" or old-fashioned. In addition to each leader's cornet, their ensembles included one or two clarinets and violins, a trombone, brass or bowed bass, and *timbales* (kettle drums). Except for the last, the típica instrumentation wasn't unlike those in old photographs of New Orleans dance bands, though we can only guess at the similarities and differences between early Cuba and Louisiana music without contemporary recordings of the latter. The Cuban records document a rough-and-ready folk band style, best suited for large dance halls or outdoor pavilions. The music isn't jazz, though the performances can and do swing—in a way that wouldn't be matched on records from North America for years to come.

Race was a factor in Cuban music and it worked in an unusual way. Segregation patterns of the time placed white performers on stage in concert halls and Havana's celebrated Teatro Alhambra. African-descended musicians played for performers in the Alhambra pit, their art valued at a lower level. The situation evolved somewhat after 1910, with the development of a style called *orquesta francesa* (later *charanga*), which replaced some of the típica brass front line with violins and flutes and the inclusion of a piano. Charangas included white musicians, and the music became more polite.

Parenthetically, the first charanga on record was the Sexteto Torroella (Edison, 1906) led by pianist Antonio (Papaíto) Torroella, with two violins, flute, and string bass. But no Torroella cylinders have been found, and no more charangas were recorded until the mid-teens.

Charanga/francesa evolved into music with a sophisticated lighter touch in the hands of leaders like flautists Octavio (Tata) Alfonso and Juan Francisco (Tata) Pereira (1874–1933), whose orchestras recorded after 1915. Antonio María Romeu (1876–1955) was a white pianist whose charanga played and recorded his popular danzones from 1915 until his death. He was a major musician and composer, and an influence on black and white musicians alike.

Other black Cuban bandleaders making records before 1920 included Domingo Corbacho and pianist Tomás Corman (1895–1957). Típica pioneers Peña, Valdés, Valenzuela, and González continued to release records in quantity during those days; Valdés and González both recorded as late as 1929.

Puntos guajiros were rural songs that appeared on several hundred records between 1906 and the mid-1920s. Many were topical pieces that documented historical and current events at home and abroad. Other subjects included amorous strife, and political and social controversy. The punto singer's role as musical editorialist derived from the West African *griot* tradition and had its counterpart in Puerto Rico's *plena* and Trinidad's calypso. Some puntos were openly critical of the Cuban government and of the United States, which occupied Cuba from 1898 to 1901 and 1906 to 1908.

Punto singers composed verses in the old Spanish *décima* format and usually accompanied themselves with a *laúd* (twelve-stringed descendant of the Arabic *ut*) or *bandurría,* a smaller instrument resembling a twelve-string mandolin. A *claves* player can often be heard as well. Two performers account for most early punto records, Antonio Morejón and Martín Silveira. From catalog photos, Silveira was black and

Morejón white. Morejón was first to record (Edison, 1906) and made no records after 1910. Silveira produced close to 150 titles for Victor and Columbia between 1907 and 1924. Two prolific punto singers whose racial origins are unknown are Juan Pagés (Victor, 1916–27) and Miguel Puertas Salgado (Victor, Columbia, 1919–ca. 1923).

Son, the central style of Cuban music in the twentieth century, emerged from Oriente province to achieve popularity in Havana in the 1910s and 1920s, largely through the appearances and recordings of the Sexteto Habanero and Sexteto Nacional. Those and other sextetos blended harmony vocals with guitar, *tres* (smaller version of the guitar, using six strings in three courses) string bass, *bongós, maracas,* and claves. Musicians who would be central to the growth of son and sexteto in 1920s included Guillermo Castillo (guitar), Gerardo Martínez (claves), Carlos Godínez (tres), Felipe Neri Cabrera (maracas), and Ricardo Martínez (director). Some of them were members of the Cuarteto Oriental, recording for Columbia early in 1917, in a style then called *son santiaguero.*

Next, the Sexteto Habanero Godínez recorded six sides for Victor in Havana on February 8, 1918. The group didn't record again until 1925, when a new batch of Victor releases became popular, inspiring a number of imitators. Among the 1918 members was *trovador* Manuel Corona. María Teresa Vera and Alfredo Boloña became members (respectively) of the Sexteto Occidente and Sexteto Boloña in the mid-1920s. Godínez himself was a permanent member of the Sexteto Habanero. One further group, Son Santiaguero, recorded a handful of Columbia sides in November 1920.

Finally, there were many romantic singers, or *trovadores,* who performed in cafés and other intimate venues, often in pairs and usually to their own guitar accompaniments. Surviving photos show roughly equal numbers of white and black faces. Afro-Cubans who found their way onto records in the 1900s and 1910s included Manuel Corona, Juan Cruz, Juan de la Cruz, Sindo Garay, Bienvenido León, Higinio Rodríguez, Miguel Zaballa, and Floro Zorrilla. María Teresa Vera (1895–1965) stood out in the field. She was a remarkable performer, whose aggressive voice and guitar were instantly recognizable. Her first recordings for Victor in 1914 were duets with her long-time partner, Rafael Zequeira, who died in 1924. She recorded around 125 titles before 1920, mostly for Columbia. She was a member of the Sexteto Habanero Godínez (Victor, 1918) and her own Sexteto Occidente (Columbia, 1926).

Puerto Rico

Though Puerto Rico became a permanent U.S. territory after the Spanish-American War, the island commanded only sporadic interest as an early record market. Columbia paid a visit to San Juan in 1910, primarily to record *danzas* by the Orquesta Cocolía and Orquesta M. Tizol. The latter was directed by Manuel Tizol (1876–1940), an older cousin of Juan Tizol (1900–1984), a member of Duke Ellington's trombone section for many years. Manuel later led an Orquesta Azul that recorded for Victor in San Juan on January 10, 1917, and the Banda Municipal de San Juan that made records the following day. Whether young Juan played on any of these records is not known.

Victor recorded a variety of ensembles in San Juan from January 10 to 13, 1917. The roster included a danza ensemble led by G. Arguinzoni, the twenty-four-piece Banda del Regimiento de Puerto Rico, the Orquesta Hernández, led by the famous composer (and later Harlem music retailer) Rafael Hernández (1892–1965), the (string) Trio Germán Hernández (no known relation), cancionero-guitarist Francisco Quiñones, and even a group of singing schoolgirls (Canciones Escolares). Each of the Hernández groups recorded some Cuba-style danzones; other music captured on this brief visit seems to have been more formal.

Puerto Rico's permanent territorial status encouraged emigration, and New York became home to many of the island's best musicians in the 1920s, including Rafael Hernández, Pedro Flores, Canario, Rafael González Levy, and Pedro Marcano.

Trinidad

Despite the later popularity of calypso, few examples survive from the early years. The island's most prolific early record-makers were bandleaders George (Lovey) Baillie (d. 1937) and Lionel Belasco (ca. 1882–1967). Both led string ensembles whose repertoires consisted primarily of paseos, waltzes, and an occasional tango. Lovey's Band was first to record. Its fourteen members sailed from Trinidad to New York on May 7, 1912, for a summer tour of the American northeast. On June 20 Lovey made eight titles for Victor and appeared in the Columbia studios on June 26, 28, and July 1 (and possibly other dates) for at least seventeen further titles. Columbia created a special catalog series (L 1—) especially for Lovey.

A Victor recording team traveled to Port-of-Spain two years later to record an interesting (though small) array of local talent. Lionel Belasco's group included fiddler Cyril Monrose and guitarist Gerald Clark—or musicians who sound very much like them. Both would appear on Belasco records in the 1920s and then become prominent ensemble leaders in their own right. Victor recorded Belasco's Band (Banda Belasco) on seven dates between September 3 and 14, 1914. Belasco recorded four piano solos on September 16, a waltz, paseo, and two rags: Luckey Roberts's "Junk Man Rag" and Scott Joplin's "Maple Leaf Rag." Sadly, these first recordings of piano rags by a black performer were not released, and the masters have not survived. But there was a consolation prize: "Junk Man" was remade in 1915 and released on Victor 67685.

Belasco's forty-nine recorded titles were complemented by chants from the Koran recorded by S. M. Akberali and a series of waltzes by the Orquesta Venezolano de Chargo. More interesting were the first recorded calypsos, by the noted Iron Duke, or Julian White Rose (Henry Julian), whose releases were credited simply as J. Resigna. Julian had been leader of the prominent White Rose carnival band at the turn of the century. Only one of his records has been recovered, "Iron Duke in the Land" (Victor 67362). It is classic calypso, boasting of Julian's charisma, prowess, and ambitious vocabulary. Just as fascinating were two titles by Jules Sims, calypso calindas (stick-fighting songs) in Creole French, or patois. No more Trinidad calypsonians would be recorded until 1927, when Wilmoth Houdini began his long career. No further records would be made in Trinidad until 1937.

Lovey recorded again for Columbia from July 31, 1914, through at least August 5. It is not clear if he recorded in Port-of-Spain or New York, since no documents survive except for the records themselves. But there were many new titles, enough that a local Columbia retailer could subsequently advertise that "you have 38 [Lovey] records to choose from." No other Trinidad artists recorded for Columbia, though two mysterious groups, Orquesta Típica de Trinidad and Estudiantina Criolla (or one group using both credits), recorded about fifty titles between them. Their specialty was waltzes, and they recorded no material of particular relevance to Trinidad.

Victor next encountered Lionel Belasco in 1915 when he came to New York to seek his fortune. Many 1914 band titles had been passed over for release, and Belasco remade several as piano solos in August–September 1915, rerecording most of them once or twice. Beginning in December 1916, he recorded ensemble pieces again with groups of available New York musicians. The Victor sessions continued through May 1920, producing around twenty-five records of Trinidadian and South American instrumental music.

Brazil

A 1910 Victor catalog advertised 175 ten-inch single-side records, "made in Rio Janeiro." These appeared in a 98700–98874 series (with fifteen more in a twelve-inch 99700 series). The listings and a handful of surviving examples suggest that most if not all of the records were by romantic troubadours, military bands, and possibly some salon music. Many songs were in the early *lundu* and *modinha* genres developed in the eighteenth century. How much of this music was performed by black or creole artists remains to be learned. More titles were added to Victor's 1911 catalog; most are by baritone Mario Pinheiro, who came to New York for several lengthy sessions between June 24 and July 7, 1910.

Columbia's first Brazilian records were made around 1908, probably in Rio de Janeiro. The company recorded a number of *chôros,* regional tunes derived from nineteenth-century polkas, waltzes, schottisches, and other popular European dances. Chôros are small multistrain suites, reminiscent of the danzón in Cuba and ragtime in North America; all three were African American genres developed in the last quarter of the nineteenth century. Several chôro ensembles, including Grupo Lulu Cavaquinho, Grupo Larangeira, and Grupo Chiquinha Gonzaga, performed as trios with flute, *violâo* (guitar), and *cavaquinho,* a four- (steel) stringed rhythm instrument related to the ukulele. This instrumentation had been current since the 1870s and may not have survived into the electrical recording era. Others, like Grupo Honorio and Grupo Luiz de Souza, were small wind ensembles. The Grupo Bahianinho was a mandolin-guitar duet.

It is worth noting that a Brazilian ballroom dance, the *maxixe,* was a brief, unsuccessful rival to the Argentine tango in 1913–14. Bandleader James Reese Europe recorded a maxixe/tango pairing for Victor in 1913 at the behest of Irene and Vernon Castle, who were promoting both dances in North America.

Other Areas

Broader areas of early record-making in South America have yet to be comprehensively documented. The Edison Company never traveled beyond Havana and Mexico City and did no out-of-country recording after 1910. Victor and Columbia were preparing to cover significant parts of the hemisphere by then; occasional traces of their activities in the 1910s survive, though not enough to create a complete historical document. It is a story worth pursuing. Along with it will come more valuable examples of early black and creole musical artistry. Early recordings exist in private and institutional collections that undoubtedly could and will supplement this account. I look forward to the time when more of them will surface, allowing our knowledge and appreciation of this fascinating area to increase.

NOTES

Introduction

1. For a somewhat similar discussion of ethnic influences in the early film industry, see Neal Gabler, *An Empire of Their Own: How the Jews Invented Hollywood* (New York: Crown, 1988).

2. Compare, for example, Cook's evocations of the black experience in "Swing Along" and "Rain Song" with Sissle and Blake's formulaic Tin Pan Alley tunes such as "Good Night, Angeline" and "Love Will Find a Way." Blake on his own wrote more distinctive material. See their respective chapters.

3. Experts are still debating which surviving recording is the earliest. See "A Dialogue on 'The Oldest Playable Recording,'" *ARSC Journal* 33, no. 1 (Spring 2002): 77–84.

4. Tim Brooks, "Columbia Records in the 1890s: Founding the Record Industry," *ARSC Journal* 10, no. 1 (1978): 3–36.

5. "It Speaks for Itself," *Kansas City Times*, Jan. 8, 1889; "A Machine That Talks," *Albany Argus*, July 24, 1889; "A Wonderful Exhibition," *Albany Times*, July 24, 1889. These clippings were located in the files of the Edison National Historic Site, West Orange, N.J., by the researcher Patrick Feaster.

6. National Phonograph Association, *Proceedings of the Second Annual Convention of Local Phonograph Companies of the United States,* 66.

7. The case for the Bohees has been advanced by Rainer Lotz in "The Bohee Brothers," in Lotz, *Black People,* 35–50. See also Peter Burgis, "Archibald Quest," *Hillandale News,* no. 173 (Apr. 1990): 4. Burgis has located an 1890 advertisement for an Archibald demonstration that includes a recording of a "banjo solo by Bohee Brothers" (*Daily Telegraph* [Launceston, Tasmania], Nov. 13, 1890, cited in Burgis's letter to the author, Nov. 1, 1999). It is possible that Archibald had the cylinder shipped to him, or that the Bohees recorded in Australia, which they apparently visited (one such trip is reported in *Freeman* [Indianapolis], Dec. 19, 1891). No mention of such a cylinder has been located in England, and no further recordings by either brother are known until 1898. With all this uncertainty, we can only say the Bohees probably recorded somewhere prior to November 1890.

8. Tim Brooks, "Early Recordings of Songs from *Florodora:* Tell Me, Pretty Maiden . . . Who Are You?—A Discographical Mystery," *ARSC Journal* 31, no. 1 (Spring 2000): 51–69.

9. Noncommercial field recordings by ethnomusicologists have fared somewhat better. Institutions such as the Archives of Traditional Music at Indiana University and projects such as "Save Our Sounds" (a cooperative venture of the Library of Congress and Smithsonian Institution) work to preserve such material.

10. A recording is here defined as a discrete title on an originating label, issued on disc or cylinder. It does not include reissues, or rerecordings of the same title by the same artist, a common practice in the 1890s.

11. Tim Brooks, "The Artifacts of Recording History: Creators, Users, Losers, Keepers," *ARSC Journal* 11, no. 1 (1979): 18–28; Brooks, "An Appeal to Collectors and Archives," *ARSC Journal* 28, no. 2 (Fall 1997): 196–97.

Chapter 1: The Early Years

1. We cannot, of course, know exactly what was said on that morning in New York Criminal Court, but the foregoing scene, reconstructed from surviving evidence, is believed to be a reasonable representation.

2. Gaisberg, *The Music Goes Round,* 8, 42.

3. Jim Walsh, "Favorite Pioneer Recording Artists: George Washington Johnson," *Hobbies,* Sept. 1944, 27.

4. Jim Walsh, "Favorite Pioneer Recording Artists: In Justice to George Washington Johnson," *Hobbies,* Jan. 1971, 37–39, 50, 91, Feb. 1971, 37, 39–40, 50, 92.

5. See John Calvert, "Regional News: Midlands Group," *Hillandale News,* Feb. 1989, 166; "Mystery Artists," *In the Groove,* Apr. 1989, 12; "Mystery Artists," *In the Groove,* May 1989, 16; Peter Adamson, liner notes to *Emile Berliner's Gramophone, The Earliest Discs,* Symposium 1058 (CD), 1989. Despite being advised of their errors, none of these authors seemed interested in acknowledging their mistakes. The flurry of erroneous statements about Johnson in 1989 led me to write about the situation in my column in the *ARSC Journal,* under the heading "Lies That Will Not Die." This became the first of a "Lies That Will Not Die" series about persistent historical misstatements in articles about recording history. This particular rumor about Johnson seems to have been less frequently repeated since then. See Tim Brooks, "Current Bibliography," *ARSC Journal* 20, no. 2 (Fall 1989): 224–25.

6. Some scholars have even concluded that blacks may not have recorded prior to 1900. See, for example, Susan M. Leonard, "An Introduction to Black Participation in the Early Recording Era, 1890–1920," *Annual Review of Jazz Studies,* no. 4 (1989): 42.

7. No birthdate has been found in any article or official document, including his death certificate. Newspaper articles at the time of his arrest (Oct. 13, 1899) stated that he was then fifty-two; at the inquest, October 17, 1899, he was said to be fifty-three. If these are to be taken literally, Johnson would have to have been born between October 13 and 17, 1846. However an article in the *New York Herald,* Dec. 21, 1899, 6, stated that even Johnson himself did not know exactly how old he was. As for the place of birth, an error-laden obituary in the *New York Age* (Feb. 5, 1914) stated that he was born in "Havana County, Va." There is no such place, but this could be a corruption of Fluvanna County. His mother's slave name ("Ann Pretty") may be a corruption of Priddy, the name of a family in Fluvanna County, and it is possible that Johnson was born there and brought to Wheatland as an infant. In any event, it is clear from many other sources that he was in Wheatland from an early age.

8. Samuel Johnson, his father, is listed in the "Free Inhabitants" census roster for 1850 rather than in the separate Slave Census; however, county court records indicate that Samuel Johnson was not freed until 1853. The census-taker could have been in error, not an uncommon occurrence. (This also assumes these two "Samuel Johnsons" were the same, which they probably were, given the match in age and location.) Many articles about George W. Johnson in later years stated that he had been born a slave.

9. "Record of Free Negroes," Loudoun County, Va., 155, Loudoun County Court House, Leesburg, Va. This is an original ledger of court actions taken between 1844 and 1861 in Loudoun County regarding slaves.

10. Johnson's mother's name is given as Druanna on the 1860 census roster, and "Ann Pretty" on his death certificate. Presumably these are the same person.

11. Loudoun County Property Transactions, book 5E, 195. The property is located near the north fork of the Catoctin Creek on the Berlin Turnpike (present-day Route 287),

about a mile north of the junction with Route 9. It was still an operating farm when I visited it in 1990.

12. The Moore family was composed of the following: George L. Moore (1808-82), father; Ann Amanda Russell Moore (1814-94), mother, and their children Sarah (1835-?), Elizabeth (1837-?), Henry (1839-64), William (1843-?), Samuel L. (1845-1927), Jonathan (1848-c. 1925), Charles (1859-59), Alice (1851-1919), Lulu (1853-1925) and Rosalie (1855-1926). Dates based on William Arthur Owen, "George Lewis and Some of His Descendants," *Genealogies of Virginia Families* 3 (1982): 394, and various newspaper obituaries located by Jane Sullivan of the Thomas Balch Library. Despite considerable effort I have not been able to locate a Moore family historian or trace Samuel Moore's descendants to the present day. Samuel's grandson, William H. Moore Jr., died in Delaware in December 1993.

13. John Divine, letter to the author, Jan. 16, 1990.

14. Free Inhabitants, 1850 and 1860, and Slave Census, 1860, both in Loudoun County, U.S. Census. See also Loudoun County Lists of Tithables and Personal Property, 1860.

15. *New York Herald,* Dec. 13, 1899, 14.

16. George is listed as literate in the 1870 census. For information on laws against teaching slaves in prewar Virginia to read and write, see Poland, *From Frontier to Suburbia,* 132. Johnson's obituary in the *New York Age,* Feb. 5, 1914, claimed that he was "educated in Lynn, Mass.," even though all other evidence places him in Loudoun County until the mid-1870s. This could be an error (the obituary had several), or perhaps Johnson traveled to Massachusetts at some point.

17. Data for Loudoun from Poland, *From Frontier to Suburbia,* 65, 132; for the United States from the *Encyclopedia Britannica* (1965 ed.), 22:764.

18. Poland, *From Frontier to Suburbia,* 158-61.

19. Ibid., 132.

20. Free Inhabitants, 1860, Loudoun County, U.S. Census.

21. Poland, *From Frontier to Suburbia,* 171.

22. Ibid., 176.

23. Voting list for referendum on secession, May 23, 1861, cited by John Devine in letter to the author, Dec. 27, 1989. See also Poland, *From Frontier to Suburbia,* 177-80, for a description of the sequence of events.

24. Poland, *From Frontier to Suburbia,* 191-92.

25. Ibid., 186.

26. Bull, *Soldiering,* 26.

27. Obituary, *New York Age,* Feb. 5, 1914.

28. *Phonogram,* Nov. 1900, 14. The death certificate, filed Jan. 28, 1914, stated that he had been a resident of the city for thirty-seven years.

29. *New York Herald,* Oct. 13, 1899, 14.

30. *Phonogram,* Nov. 1900, 14-15.

31. For a concise chronology of this era, see Koenigsberg, *Edison Cylinder Records,* xiii.

32. *New York Sun,* quoted in *New York Age,* Nov. 29, 1980; reprinted in Abbott and Seroff, *Out of Sight,* 103-4. *Trow's New York City Directory,* a valuable annual book listing residents of New York with street address and occupation, gave Johnson's occupation as "musician." There is an additional listing in 1878 for a "G. W. Johnson, music," at 464 Eighth Avenue, but I doubt this is our subject. This was a more upscale address, and the entire block was white as of the 1880 census. *Trow's* listed several dozen other citizens named "George Johnson" or "George W. Johnson" between 1870 and 1890, but none were musicians or could otherwise be identified as ours.

33. *New York Herald,* Dec. 21, 1899, 6.

34. *New York Tribune,* Oct. 13, 1899, 14.

35. *New York Times,* Oct. 13, 1899, 7.

Chapter 2: Talking Machines!

1. National Phonograph Association, *Proceedings of the 1890 Convention of Local Phonograph Companies,* 163, and *Proceedings of the Second Annual Convention of Local Phonograph Companies,* 118.

2. Victor H. Emerson, "The Making of a Disc Record," *Columbia Record,* Sept. 1907 (unpaged). Emerson gave the date rather precisely as "seventeen years ago," so these events presumably took place in 1890, a date that matches other evidence. The New Jersey Phonograph Company was founded in 1889, but did not get "fairly under way" in the musical slot-machine business until the fall of 1890. The following scene with Emerson and Johnson is based on Emerson's article, plus other evidence of where Johnson plied his trade, customs of the time, the phonographs then in use, and so on.

3. "The Whistling Coon," © 1878 by Sam Devere, in *Daly Brothers K.H.K. South Carolina Cloe Songster,* no. 13 (1878): 38; and in *Oh, Dem Golden Slippers Songster,* no. 57 (1879): 53; both cited in Meade, Spottswood, and Meade, *Country Music Sources,* 474. Copies of both these songsters are located in the Library of Congress, which kindly provided photocopies. "The Whistling Coon," words and music by Sam Devere, © 1888 by Wm. A. Pond; only the words were reprinted in *Delaney's Song Book,* no. 4 (1893): 18. The text here has been altered slightly to match the way Johnson generally sang it, at least on his later recordings (he also frequently substituted "head" for "cranium"). A fourth verse was contained in sheet music entitled "The Happy Whistling Coon" (music by Sam Raeburn, words by Sam Devere, © 1889 by Oliver Ditson Co., Boston), in which Devere's lyrics were set to an odd but interesting minor-key tune.

> No matter what comes, you'll always find him jolly,
> You may put him out to sea on a log . . .
> But he'll roll up his eyes, and kick up his heels,
> And laugh like a fat bull-dog . . .
> He will dance when the rain comes down in a flood,
> He will shuffle by the light of the moon . . .
> He's a flat footed, double toed, lively son of Ham,
> And he's happy when he whistles this tune . . .
> (*Whistles chorus*)

4. Koenigsberg, in *Edison Cylinder Records,* xvii, quotes prices for Edison musical cylinders at this time as being in the $0.75–$2.00 range. The number of cylinders that could be recorded per "round" has been the subject of speculation, but apparently varied in the three-to-five range. An interesting interview with an unnamed recording expert in the Jan.–Feb. 1895 issue of the extremely rare *Edison Phonographic News* (p. 67), a publication of the Ohio Phonograph Co., reads in part, "It is somewhat difficult to say how many good vocal records can be taken at one time, whether one or five horns should be used on a singer, because this depends on the quality of the singer's voice, and upon the conditions of the voice on the day in question, and strange as it may seem, upon certain external questions such as atmosphere, etc. Using five horns some days I will not get more than two good records, and another day as high as four." On average, this expert said he got three to four saleable cylinders per round. Bands yielded more.

5. According to the National Phonograph Association, *Proceedings of the Second Annual Convention of Local Phonograph Companies,* 58, New Jersey was "fairly underway" in the coin-slot business by October or November 1890. *Phonogram* (June 1891, 6) commented on the number of plays possible from a single cylinder.

6. New York Phonograph Company Journal no. 2 and Cash Book no. 3, Edison National Historic Site.

7. There appears to have been an agreement between the local companies not to steal each other's star talent, although it was often breached. In one notable case, in 1893, the

Columbia Phonograph Company obtained an injunction to prevent outsiders from bringing recording equipment to Washington to record its biggest seller, the U.S. Marine Band. See Tim Brooks, "Columbia Records in the 1890s: Founding the Record Industry," *ARSC Journal* 10, no. 1 (1978): 19.

8. Newspaper clippings in the files of the Edison National Historic Site document studio activity there as early as 1888. See also Koenigsberg, *Edison Cylinder Records,* 111, 134; Brooks, "Columbia Records in the 1890s," 6–7; and "Charles Marshall, New York City," *Phonogram,* Mar. 1891, 63. The Metropolitan Phonograph Company (New York City) was closely allied with the New York Phonograph Company (which covered the rest of the state), and was absorbed by the latter company in June 1890.

9. *Phonogram,* Jan. 1891, 23.

10. *Phonogram,* Mar. 1891, 78, and May 1891, 116.

11. "The Laughing Song," © 1894 by George W. Johnson, Ko-La'r Music, 302 W. 36th St., New York. Lyrics transcribed from original recordings.

12. Rare handbill in the author's collection advertising the *Inspector;* Brown, *A History of the New York Stage,* 381; Witmark and Goldberg, *From Ragtime to Swingtime,* 84; *New York Sun* quoted in *New York Age,* Nov. 29, 1890, reprinted in Abbott and Seroff, *Out of Sight,* 103–4.

13. Koenigsberg, *Edison Cylinder Records,* 130.

14. The U.S. Marine Band version of "The Whistling Coon" was listed from November 1890 until June 1891, but AtLee's stayed in the catalog from December 1890 until March 1895. AtLee's version of "The Laughing Song" was listed from June 1892 until September 1894. Weaver's "Whistling Coon" is found in the September 1894 catalog. Other versions are difficult to trace due to the extreme scarcity of surviving catalogs from this period.

15. Fields and Fields, *From the Bowery to Broadway,* 81.

16. *New York Clipper,* Jan. 31, 1891, 742.

17. "From a Phonograph Exhibitor," *Phonogram,* July 1892, 162–63. The sequence of quotes has been rearranged slightly for purposes of clarity.

18. "Famous Record-Makers and Their Work," *Phonogram,* Dec. 1892, 279–80. The pictures were supplied by the New Jersey Co., though not all of the artists were theirs.

19. "Unique Entertainment at a Typographical Society's Banquet," *Phonogram,* Feb. 1893, 332.

20. New Jersey Phonograph Co. advertisement, *Phonogram,* Mar.–Apr. 1893, 346.

21. *Catalogue of Standard New Jersey Records,* Mar. 1, 1894, 14, reproduced in Walsh, "Favorite Pioneer Recording Artists: In Justice to George Washington Johnson," Jan. 1971, 38.

22. *Phonoscope,* Feb. 1898, 10; *New York Herald,* Dec. 21, 1899; U.S. Department of Commerce, *Historical Statistics of the United States,* 165, 167.

23. Walsh, "Favorite Pioneer Recording Artists: In Justice to George Washington Johnson," Jan. 1971, 91, quoting from an unspecified late 1906 issue of the *Music Trades Review.*

24. The New York figures are $52.00 for thirteen sessions in 1890, $86.00 for twenty-three sessions in 1891, and $37.50 for eight sessions in 1892. In 1893, the year New York closed its recording operation, he received an additional $10.00 for two sessions in May and June. Data from recently discovered journals and cash books at the Edison National Historic Site.

25. Duplicate cylinders, generally made by attaching a playback machine to a recording machine by means of acoustical tubing or a mechanical pantograph device, were the bane of the industry in the 1890s. They were nearly always fainter and less clear than originals, and companies such as New Jersey took pains to assure their exhibitor customers that *they* supplied only originals. (Some companies openly advertised duplicates at a lower price.) The fact that the controversy was so vociferous and continuing indicates that the practice was more widespread than anyone wanted to admit, however.

26. *Catalogue and (New Jersey) Records for Use on the Phonograph,* Newark, N.J., 1892. The only known surviving copy originally belonged to Len Spencer and is marked "sent as marked, October 7, 1892." It is now at the Library of Congress.

27. The origins of minstrel recordings needs to be more thoroughly researched, but it appears that such records appeared as early as 1891. See Koenigsberg, *Edison Cylinder Records,* 141, 151.

28. *Catalogue of Standard New Jersey Records,* Mar. 1, 1894, 17.

29. Ibid., 17–18.

30. Transcribed from a version made slightly later (c. 1897), with orchestra accompaniment.

31. Transcribed from Columbia 13004 (cylinder) and 644 (seven-inch disc).

32. Raymond R. Wile, "Berliner Sales Figures," *ARSC Journal* 11, nos. 2–3 (1979): 140–41.

33. D. E. Boswell Co., *Dealers in High Grade Original Records for the Phonograph and Graphophone,* catalog, Chicago, c. 1895, 35.; unidentified (U.S. Phonograph Co.?) catalog, c. 1895, 84. Both catalogs contain the same text and picture, differing only in the quantity cited.

34. "Mr. Leonard Spencer," *Phonoscope,* Nov. 1896, 14.

35. "New and Selected Records" and "Practical Phonograph Points," *Edison Phonographic News,* 1, no. 3 (Sept.–Oct. 1894): 42, 47, rare copy provided by Allen Koenigsberg.

36. Undated flyer, "The Very Latest Up-To-Date Songs. High Grade Records for Phonographs and Graphophones at Popular Prices." Identified by Koenigsberg as from Reed and Dawson, New York, issued in early 1897, judging by the content.

37. The Stoppa cylinder is listed in *Phonoscope,* Nov. 1896, and in an early 1897 U.S. Phonograph Co. catalog, in which his first name is spelled as shown (rather than the normal "Giuseppe"). "Karl August" is listed in Spottswood, *Ethnic Music on Records,* 2709. A copy at the Library of Congress has been auditioned and is the Johnson song.

38. Various sets of verses have been located for "Good Bye, Liza Jane." See *DeMarsan's Singer's Journal,* no. 86 (c. 1871), and *Delaney's Song Book,* no. 13 (1896): 25, as well as the original sheet music published by Lee and Walker, Philadelphia, © 1871 (copy at the Library of Congress). "The Laughing Coon" most closely resembles the 1896 verses in *Delaney.* The melody is very close to that of the 1871 sheet music. An entirely different "Laughing Coon," words by George Cooper, music by Joseph P. Skelly, was published in 1891. Oddly enough, the lyrics of that song are a bit reminiscent of Sam Devere's "The Whistling Coon."

39. Transcribed from original cylinders and discs. Slightly different, but no less offensive, lyrics were used by other singers in some later versions.

40. See Brooks, "Columbia Records in the 1890s," 26–27, for details and a list of the artists involved.

41. "Gallery of Talent Employed for Making Records," *Phonoscope,* July 1898, 12.

42. *New York Evening Telegram,* Oct. 13, 1899, 3.

43. Cited in Walsh, "Favorite Pioneer Recording Artists: In Justice to George Washington Johnson," Feb. 1971, 40. Johnson's two American recordings were also listed (with their U.S. numbers) in the Feb. 22, 1899, English list, of which this author has an unidentified reprint.

44. *Societe des Micro-Phonographes Bennini, Rouleaux enregistres,* catalog no. 11, June 1901, 50.

45. Statement by Officer William F. Boyle of the Thirty-first Precinct, dated Nov. 16, 1899. Boyle was not called as a witness.

46. Statement by Officer Boyle at the inquest, Oct. 17, 1899.

47. Statements by James Morton, Nov. 16, 1899, and Oct. 17, 1899 (inquest).

48. Statements by Hattie Thomas, Nov. 16, 1899; statements by Herbert Small at inquest, Oct. 17, 1899.

49. Statement by Lena Small at inquest, Oct. 17, 1899.

50. Statements by Officer Boyle, who arrested Johnson, at inquest, Oct. 17, 1899, and on Nov. 16, 1899. *Phonoscope,* Feb. 1898, 10.

51. Statement by Herbert Small, Nov. 16, 1899.

52. Emerson, "The Making of a Disc Record," *Columbia Salesman,* Oct. 1907.

53. *New York Sun,* Dec. 22, 1899.

54. Emerson, "The Making of a Disc Record."

55. Obituary for Emanuel M. Friend, *New York Times,* Nov. 2, 1904, 9.

56. *New York Times,* Dec. 20, 1899.

Chapter 3: The Trial of George W. Johnson

1. Obituary for Joseph E. Newburger, *New York Times,* July 20, 1931, 17.

2. Obituary for Edward Hymes, *New York Times,* May 15, 1938, sec. 2, p. 6. Hymes's son, Edward Jr., was also a successful attorney and a championship bridge player.

3. *The People, etc. v. George W. Johnson,* Court of General Sessions of the Peace, City and County of New York, Part IV, New York, November 20, etc., 1899. The transcript was located in the Special Collections Department, John Jay College of Criminal Justice, New York, N.Y.

4. Statement by Herbert Small at inquest, Oct. 17, 1899.

5. Statement by Hattie Thomas, Nov. 16, 1899.

6. Johnson's signature appears on the receipt for these items, when they were returned to him after the trial. It is the same signature that appears on the 1898 Columbia "exclusive artists" ad, which should lay to rest the speculation in Walsh ("Favorite Pioneer Recording Artists: In Justice to George Washington Johnson," Feb. 1971, 37) that Johnson's name might have been signed for him by someone else.

7. *New York Sun,* Dec. 22, 1899.

8. *New York Times,* Dec. 22, 1899.

9. *Cleveland Gazette,* Dec. 30, 1899. It was this clipping, located by researcher Doug Seroff, that led me to the trial transcript and all it led to.

10. *New York Herald,* Dec. 21, 1899.

11. Ibid.

12. *Phonoscope,* May 1900, 8.

13. Transcribed from a variety of period recordings, which differ only slightly. On Columbia, the sketch was titled "Coon Wedding in Southern Georgia."

14. Johnson also recorded the title for Victor, but it was not released.

15. Gaisberg, *The Music Goes Round,* 41. Gaisberg consistently misspells Shepard's name as "Sheppard."

16. *Talking Machine News* (London), Apr. 1, 1907, quoted in Walsh, "Favorite Pioneer Recording Artists: In Justice to George Washington Johnson," Jan. 1971, 37–38.

17. Victor 52000, later reissued on double-sided no. 17232.

18. Edison Cash Payment books for the dates indicated, Edison National Historic Site.

19. Fred Rabenstein, former Edison paymaster, letter to Jim Walsh, quoted in Walsh, "Favorite Pioneer Recording Artists: In Justice to George Washington Johnson," Jan. 1971, 50.

20. *Columbia Record,* May 1906.

21. *Columbia Record,* Aug. 1907.

22. *Music Trades Review,* undated (but late 1906), quoted in Walsh, "Favorite Pioneer Recording Artists: In Justice to George Washington Johnson," Jan. 1971, 91. Walsh quotes the identical article from *Talking Machine News,* Dec. 1, 1906, in his article, "Favorite Pioneer Recording Artists: George Washington Johnson," 27.

23. Although Rabenstein does not state this explicitly, it is inferred from the fact that when Johnson died he was living at a Harlem address; that no one claimed his body; and

that Spencer's daughter Ethel, who as a child later spent time at her father's office, did not remember seeing Johnson there (Walsh, "Leonard Garfield Spencer, as His Daughter Ethel Lovingly Recalls Him," *Hobbies*, Aug. 1958, 32).

24. Walsh, "Favorite Pioneer Recording Artists: In Justice to George Washington Johnson," Jan. 1971, 50.

25. *Freeman,* May 6, 1905.

26. *New York Age,* Feb. 5, 1914.

27. Obituaries: "V. H. Emerson Dies; Phonograph Head," *New York Times,* June 23, 1926; *Variety,* June 30, 1926; *Talking Machine World,* July 15, 1926, 40.

28. John Divine, letter to the author, Leesburg, Va., Jan. 1990. Divine, as a small boy, knew Moore. The quote is from a sermon delivered at the fiftieth anniversary of the reorganization of the Waterford Baptist Church, in 1926, and was kindly supplied by Divine.

29. The following is an excerpt, as transcribed from Edison Diamond Disc 50745. The cast refers to each other by their real names in the text; the personnel are also confirmed by Walsh in "A Directory of Pioneer Recording Groups," *Hobbies,* Oct. 1962, 33.

30. Meeker's "Laughing Song" was issued on Blue Amberol cylinder 3427 and Diamond Disc 50745 (1921); "The Whistling Coon" was on Blue Amberol 3466 and Diamond Disc 50478 (1919).

31. See Brown, *Folk Songs from North Carolina,* 510, where it appears as "The Happy Coon."

32. *Phono-Cylinders, Volume 2,* compiled by George A. Blacker, Folkways FS 3887; *The World's First Entertainment Recordings, 1889–1896,* Mark 56 #859 (which assigns inaccurate dates to the recordings); *Emile Berliner's Gramophone, The Earliest Discs,* Symposium 1058 (CD).

Chapter 4: The Unique Quartette

1. The Unique Trio, which performed a sketch called "Uncle Jasper's Reception," was composed of George Vance, J. H. Graham, and James Gray (later replaced by Sam Burnell). None of these names turn up in connection with Moore's Unique Quartette in later years, and there is no suggestion that the trio is black. See *New York Clipper,* Sept. 22, 1883, 442; Mar. 1, 1884, 850; and May 31, 1884, 170.

2. *New York Clipper,* Oct. 11 and Dec. 13, 1890.

3. *Phonogram,* Nov.–Dec. 1891, 240–41.

4. *Phonogram,* Mar. 1891, 63.

5. New York Phonograph Company Journal no. 2 and Cash Books, located at the Edison National Historic Site.

6. *New York Clipper,* Mar. 7, 1891.

7. *New York Clipper,* Apr. 25, 1891.

8. *New York Clipper,* Apr. 8 and 29, Aug. 5, and Oct. 14, 1893; Feb. 17, Apr. 14, and May 5, 1894; and Nov. 14, 1896. In later years it was identified with Mark Murphy, who may or may not be the same as Con T. Murphy.

9. Transcribed from the cylinder by the author.

10. Allen Lowe, notes to *American Pop: An Audio History,* West Hill WH-1017 (CD), 1:13.

11. *Wehman's Collection of Songs,* no. 16.

12. *New York Clipper,* Dec. 30, 1893, and Jan. 13, 1894.

13. *New York Clipper,* Dec. 8, 1894, and Jan. 12, 1895.

14. *New York Clipper,* Apr. 20, May 18, June 27, Oct. 5, and Dec. 7, 1895.

15. The cylinders have been dated, approximately, by their physical characteristics. They are brown wax with thick, flat ends and no markings, and play at a slow speed, all characteristics of the mid- to late 1890s.

16. *Delaney's Song Book,* no. 12 (1896): 9.

17. *Freeman,* Oct. 10, 1896, and Mar. 19 and 26, 1898.

18. *Freeman,* Aug. 6 and Oct. 1, 1898.

19. *Freeman,* Feb. 18, 1899.

20. *New York Clipper,* Aug. 24, 1894; Sampson, *The Ghost Walks,* 225; *Variety,* Oct. 3, 1914; Samuel Baker, death certificate, Sept. 21, 1914, City of New York.

21. Sampson, *The Ghost Walks,* 196, 318, 474.

22. Ibid., 298.

23. Ibid., 76, 77, 84, 148, 190, 218, 303, 326, 359, 413; Woll, *Dictionary of the Black Theatre,* 156, 171. See also references in the *New York Clipper* and *Freeman.* "W. A. Dixon" was listed with A. G. Allen's troupe in the April 16 and July 2, 1910, *Freeman;* however later cast lists cite a "Jim Dixon," so perhaps this was somebody else.

24. Sampson, *The Ghost Walks,* 51, 54, 97, 130, 219, 251–53, 271, 275, 278, 285, 457; Marks, *They All Sang,* 92.

25. Sampson, *The Ghost Walks,* 254; *Freeman,* Jan. 15, 1910.

Chapter 5: Louis "Bebe" Vasnier

1. Bolden (1877–1931) came into his prime after the Louisiana Phonograph Company's period of greatest activity. By 1893–94 the company was already winding down, while the teenage Bolden was still studying music. He formed his first band in the mid-1890s and his peak years were 1895–1905. See Southern, *Biographical Dictionary of Afro-American and African Musicians,* 40.

2. Dan Weisman, "The Louisiana Phonograph Company," *Jazz Archivist* 4, no. 2 (Dec. 1989): 1–5. Weisman provided valuable leads on Vasnier's early life; however, his observations on phonograph history are less reliable, e.g., his repeated claim that Vasnier was "probably . . . the first black recording artist in the world" (2).

3. "Organization and Progress of the Phonograph Companies of the United States," *Phonogram,* Nov.–Dec. 1891, 244–45.

4. *Phonogram,* Apr. 1891, 85, and Dec. 1891, 243. Clarkson died on March 25, 1891.

5. *Phonogram,* Nov.–Dec. 1891, 243–44, and Jan. 1892, 9.

6. "Now, the Phonograph," *New Orleans Sunday States,* Jan. 25, 1891, 8. The text has been slightly edited for clarity.

7. "The Perfected Phonograph," *New Orleans Daily States,* Jan. 27, 1891, 2.

8. Weisman, "Louisiana Phonograph Company," 1.

9. *Phonogram,* June–July 1891, 138, and Jan. 1892, 9.

10. Reported by collector Rick Wilkins.

11. U.S. Census, 1900 (St. Louis, Missouri). Vasnier's name is found in various sources as "Vassier," "Vaseiner," "Vannier," etc.

12. *New Orleans City Directory* (L. Soards and Co.) for 1880, 1881, 1884, 1885.

13. *New Orleans Weekly Pelican,* Feb. 5 and 19, 1887.

14. "The Louisiana Phonograph Company, Limited," *Phonogram,* Jan. 1892, 10–11.

15. "Phono Chat," *Phonogram,* Jan. 1892, 29.

16. Advertisement, *Phonogram,* Apr.–May 1892, vii.

17. *Phonogram,* July 1892, 149.

18. Despite the poor condition of the cylinder, the English collector John S. Dales deserves considerable thanks for giving it to the author for taping. A copy of the tape, such as it is, has been deposited with the Rodgers and Hammerstein Archive of Recorded Sound at the New York Public Library.

19. William Bryant, interview with author.

20. Compare, for example, "Coon Wedding in Southern Georgia" as lampooned by various white quartets in the early 1900s.

21. "Queries," *Phonogram,* July 1892, 174.

22. "Rock Dat Ship in de Morning," William J. Scanlan, © 1880, T. B. Harms and Co., reprinted in *Delaney's Song Book,* no. 1 (1892): 9.

23. "Good Bye, Susan Jane," reprinted in *Delaney's Song Book,* no. 6 (1894): 23.

24. Advertisement, *Phonogram,* Aug.–Sept. 1892, iv.

25. *Phonogram,* Nov. 1892, 261.

26. "Phono Chat," *Phonogram,* Jan. 1893, 310.

27. "Phono Chat," *Phonogram,* Feb. 1893, 340; "From the Crescent City," *Phonogram,* Mar.–Apr. 1893, 398.

28. National Phonograph Association, *Proceedings of the Fourth Annual Convention of the National Phonograph Association of the United States,* Chicago, Sept. 20–22, 1893, copy located at the New York Public Library.

29. *Freeman,* July 23, 1898.

30. *New Orleans City Directory,* various editions, 1881–96. Vasnier lived with his parents until they died in the early 1890s, remaining in the house (at 147 St. Anthony) until 1895. *Gould's St. Louis Directory,* 1898, 1899, 1901.

Chapter 6: The Standard Quartette and *South before the War*

1. *Freeman,* Mar. 9, 1895.

2. *New York Clipper,* Aug. 15, 1891.

3. New York Phonograph Company Cash Book, Edison National Historic Site.

4. Fletcher, *One Hundred Years of the Negro in Show Business,* 91; *New York Clipper,* Jan. 6, 1894. Abbott and Seroff, *Out of Sight,* 360–68, contains the best history of the early days of *South before the War.*

5. Handwritten ms., unsigned and undated, but believed to have been composed by Harry Martell in the early or mid-1890s, located with *South before the War* Papers, a small collection of papers and musical scores from the show, at the Historical Sound Recordings Archive, Yale University, New Haven, Conn.

6. *Freeman,* Apr. 23, 1910.

7. Odell, *Annals of the New York Stage,* 15:33.

8. *New York Clipper,* Apr. 1, 1893.

9. *New York Clipper,* Jan. 6, 1894.

10. *New York Clipper,* Dec. 9, 1893, and Mar. 3, 1894.

11. Transcription by Tim Brooks with Lynn Abbott, Bill Bryant, and Doug Seroff. Some parts of the cylinder are quite faint, so this should be considered a "best guess" at what is being sung. The only accessible copy of this cylinder is a tape made several years ago by its owner at the time. There seems to be cross-talk during parts of the verse, which may be quartet members interjecting comments or simply noise on the poorly made audiotape.

12. *New York Clipper,* Sept. 22, 1894.

13. *Edison Phonographic News* 1, no. 5 (Jan.–Feb. 1895): 67; 1, no. 6 (Mar.–Apr. 1895), 91. Photocopies of the only known specimens of this rare publication published by the Ohio Phonograph Co. were kindly provided to the author by Allen Koenigsberg.

14. *Freeman,* Mar. 9, 1895.

15. *New York Clipper,* May 4 and July 6, 1895; *Freeman,* May 11, 1895.

16. Zonophone Quartette, "Every Day'll Be Sunday Bye and Bye," Zonophone 567 (c. 1906).

17. *New York Clipper,* Nov. 30, 1895.

18. *New York Clipper,* Apr. 29, 1899.

19. Peterson, *A Century of Musicals in Black and White,* 262.

20. *Freeman,* May 11, 1900, and Feb. 14, 1903.

21. *Freeman,* Nov. 5, 1898, and Feb. 11, 1899.

22. *Freeman,* Feb. 22, 1902, and Mar. 7, 1903.

23. *Freeman,* Jan. 8, 1898.

24. Different sources give Scott's date of death as April 26 (*Freeman,* May 1, 1897) or April 29 (Sampson, *The Ghost Walks,* 128).

25. Sampson, *The Ghost Walks,* 170, 254, 398, 413; *New York Clipper,* Apr. 1, 1893, Jan. 27, 1894, Aug. 24, 1895, and Aug. 22, 1896; *Freeman,* Dec. 24, 1898, and Feb. 11, 1899.

26. A short biography of Jenkins appears in Sampson, *Blacks in Blackface,* 379. Other references include *Freeman,* Feb. 11 and Mar. 11, 1899; and Peterson, *A Century of Musicals in Black and White,* 288, 309.

27. *Freeman,* Dec. 6, 1902.

Chapter 7: The Kentucky Jubilee Singers

1. Odell, *Annals of the New York Stage,* vol. 10.

2. Ibid., 10:350, 353, 12:538.

3. *Freeman,* Aug. 8, 1891.

4. Koenigsberg, *Edison Cylinder Records,* 122–27, lists the 1889 recordings. Other versions include Columbia Orchestra, Columbia 15028 (cylinder, 1897) and Columbia 616 (disc, c. 1902); Prince's Orchestra, Oxford 38631 (1913); Prince's Band, Columbia A5696 (1915); Issler's Orchestra, New Jersey cylinder (c. 1894–96); Leeds Orchestra, Leeds 4174 (c. 1904).

5. The best history of Forbes Randolph's Kentucky Jubilee Singers is written by Ray Funk, "Three Afro-American Singing Groups," in *Under the Imperial Carpet,* ed. Lotz and Pegg, 157–63.

Chapter 8: Bert Williams and George Walker

1. The best source of information on Bert Williams's personal life and theatrical career (though not on his music and recordings) is Smith, *Bert Williams.*

2. "Mammy's Pickaninny Boy," words and music by Williams and Walker, © 1896, M. Witmark and Sons, reprinted in *Delaney's Song Book,* no. 16 (1897). It is cited in some sources, including *Phonoscope,* as "Mammy's Little Pickaninny Boy."

3. "New Records for Talking Machines," *Phonoscope,* Jan.–Feb. 1897, 16. It has been suggested that the entry merely means the title was associated with Williams, not that it was recorded by him. However the facts that he did do business with Stern, that they were recording theatrical celebrities at this time, and that the same *Phonoscope* list (and only that list) contains several other titles recorded by Stern, suggests to this writer that it is probably a genuine Williams recording.

4. Marks, *They All Sang,* 103.

5. *Freeman,* Oct. 30 and Nov. 20, 1897.

6. Different sources give different accounts of exactly what happened that terrible night. The most authoritative, quoted here, seems to be a story in the *New York Journal,* reprinted in *Freeman,* Sept. 1, 1900 (a slightly garbled version is transcribed in Sampson, *The Ghost Walks,* 221–22). Johnson, in *Black Manhattan,* 126–27, writes that the mob deliberately targeted black celebrities, that Walker had a "narrow escape" and that Hogan hid in the theater. Charters, *Nobody,* 54–55, claims that it was Hogan who was beaten and Walker who hid. As usual she gives no source for her account, although she includes a short quote from the *Dramatic Mirror* indicating that both Hogan and Walker were among the "victims of the mob." There was extensive and generally even-handed coverage of the riot in the *New York Times* (Aug. 16–18, 1900), but no mention of Hogan or Walker.

7. Review signed by "Roma," *Freeman,* Dec. 14, 1901.

8. Smith, *Bert Williams,* 47.

9. Victor Talking Machine Co. catalog, Feb. 1902, 43.

10. For an explanation of this complicated changeover see Fagan and Moran, *The Encyclopedic Discography of Victor Recordings, Pre-Matrix Series,* xviii.

11. "My Little Zulu Babe" (counted here once) was recorded both as a solo and as a duet. An additional title, "If You Love Your Baby, Make Dem Goo-Goo Eyes," was not released.

12. "Where Was Moses When the Light Went Out," by Vincent P. Bryan and Harry Von Tilzer, © 1901, reprinted in *Delaney's Song Book,* no. 29 (1902): 16.

13. "When It's All Going Out and Nothing Coming In," by Williams and Walker, © 1902, reprinted in *Delaney's Song Book* no. 33 (c. 1902): 8. The text here is as sung by Bert Williams on Victor 994.

14. Gardner, *Popular Songs of the Twentieth Century,* 1:149.

15. The word Williams used is not completely clear—it could be "bucka-man" or even "buffer-man"—but it is undoubtedly related to "buckra," old Negro slang for the white man. The term was fairly well established; it appeared years later in the libretto of *Porgy and Bess.*

16. Fagan and Moran, *The Encyclopedic Discography of Victor Recordings, Pre-Matrix Series,* 81.

17. *New York World,* Feb. 19, 1903, 3.

18. *Era* (London), June 27, 1903.

19. Bert A. Williams, "The Comic Side of Trouble," *American Magazine* 85 (Jan. 1918): 35. The complete text of this important article is reprinted in Sampson, *Blacks in Blackface,* 87–91.

20. *Freeman,* Dec. 9, 1905.

21. Versions of "Nobody" by Collins were Victor 4391 (released Aug. 1905), Edison 9084 (Sept. 1905), Columbia cylinder 32800 (Oct. 1905), and Columbia disc 3264 (Nov. 1905). The only one of these for which an exact recording date is known is the Victor, which was recorded on May 22, 1905. Since the Edison and Columbia release dates are later, it is assumed that their recording dates were later as well.

22. "Nobody," words by Alex Rogers, music by Bert Williams, Attucks Music, © 1905. There are numerous other verses to this song; many are contained in the original sheet music as reprinted in Charosh and Fremont, eds., *More Favorite Songs of the Nineties,* 215–19. See also *Delaney's Song Book,* no. 42 (1905). The text here is as sung by Williams on his 1906 disc recording.

23. Williams, "The Comic Side of Trouble," 34.

24. "Columbia Records for July," *Columbia Record,* July 1906, 3.

25. "Columbia Records for October," *Columbia Record,* Oct. 1906, 10.

26. *Columbia Record,* Aug. 1906, 6 (disc) and Nov. 1906, 2 (cylinder). Each month Columbia cited a half-dozen cylinders and a half-dozen discs issued during the previous month as "last month's best sellers." "Nobody" was the only Williams title to appear on these lists in 1906.

27. "Columbia Records for December," *Columbia Record,* Dec. 1906, 6.

28. The name of the musical was originally *Mrs. Wilson, That's All;* it changed to *Mrs. Wilson-Andrews* two weeks after opening. *Columbia Record,* Jan. 1907, indicated that "He's a Cousin of Mine" was written for this show; however, Bordman, *American Musical Theatre,* 222, says that it was previously interpolated into a Marie Cahill show, *Marrying Mary,* which opened on Aug. 27, 1906. Fletcher, in his memoirs *One Hundred Years of the Negro in Show Business,* 147, says that the song was written for Cahill.

29. "Columbia Records for January," *Columbia Record,* Jan. 1907, 6.

30. "Columbia Records for February," *Columbia Record,* Feb. 1907, 5.

31. Albert Williams, Quindaro, Kansas, to Bert Williams and George Walker, Oct. 16, 1907, published in *Variety,* Dec. 14, 1907, 30. Williams and Walker's reply, dated October 18, was printed in the same issue.

32. "Coon Songs Must Go," *Freeman,* Jan. 2, 1909.

33. *Freeman,* Oct. 6, 1906.

34. "Williams Alone Next Season," *Variety,* May 22, 1909, 5.

35. "New Acts—Bert Williams," *Variety,* May 22, 1909, 15. The song "That's a-Plenty"

mentioned in this review was by Creamer and Williams and should not be confused with the jazz standard of the same name by Lew Pollock (1914).

36. Quoted in Charters, *Nobody,* 115.No source is given.

37. Rogers, *World's Great Men of Color,* 379–80.

38. Charters, *Nobody,* 115–16.

39. Ashton Stevens, review, *Chicago Examiner,* Sept. 17, 1910.

40. *New York Herald,* June 21, 1910, 12.

41. Booker T. Washington, "The Greatest Comedian the Negro Race Has," *American Magazine* 70 (Sept. 1910): 601–4.

42. Ewen, *American Popular Songs,* 448.

43. "Bert Williams the World Famous Comedian Now Makes Records Exclusively for the Columbia," Columbia Records supplement, Nov. 1910, 6.

44. Lynn Abbott, "'Play That Barbershop Chord': A Case for the African-American Origin of Barbershop Harmony," *American Music* 10, no. 3 (Fall 1992): 312.

45. "Follies of 1911 Here," *New York Tribune,* June 27, 1911, 7.

46. *New York World,* June 27, 1911, 4; *New York Post,* June 27, 1911, 9.

47. The correct title is "Woodman, Woodman, Spare That Tree." However the label reads simply "Woodman, Spare That Tree," which has sometimes led writers to confuse it with the famous early American song of that name by George Pope Morris and Henry Russell (1837).

48. Those making comparisons should be aware that the take reissued on the CD *Music from the New York Stage,* vol. 2 (Pearl GEMM CDS 9053-5), which is labeled "take two," is actually take eight.

49. Columbia Records supplement, May 1913, 6.

50. *Columbia Double Disc Records,* May 1914 (full catalog), 442.

51. *New York Herald,* June 2, 1914, 9.

52. Smith, *Bert Williams,* 173.

53. Columbia Records supplement, Mar. 1916, 9.

54. Smith, *Bert Williams,* 144.

55. Klotman, *Frame by Frame,* 177.

56. Rowland, *Bert Williams,* 150.

57. Ragan, *Who's Who in Hollywood,* 1818.

58. *Variety,* Feb. 9, 1917, 18, and Aug. 27, 1917, 24.

59. Columbia Records supplement, Feb. 1918, 13.

60. *New York Age,* July 20, 1918, 6.

61. "The Argentines, The Portuguese, and the Greeks" by Carey Morgan and Arthur Swanstrom, as recorded by Nora Bayes on Columbia A2980 (1920).

62. Bordman, *American Musical Theatre,* 341–42.

63. "The Moon Shines on the Moonshine," by Francis DeWitt and Robert Hood Bowers, © 1920, as sung by Bert Williams on Columbia A2849.

64. "I'm Sorry I Ain't Got It, You Could Have It if I Had It Blues," by Sam M. Lewis, Joe Young, and Ted Snyder, © 1919, as sung by Bert Williams on Columbia A2877.

65. Bordman, *American Musical Theatre,* 354.

66. "I Want to Know Where Tosti Went When He Said 'Good-Bye,'" by Chris Smith, as recorded by Bert Williams on Columbia A3305.

67. Columbia Records supplement, Feb. 1921, 5.

68. Smith, *Bert Williams,* 209–12.

69. "'Tain't No Disgrace to Run When You're Skeered," words by Jas. Burris, music by Ernest Hogan and Chris Smith, © 1903, reprinted in *Delaney's Song Book,* no. 39 (1903): 19.

70. Columbia Records supplement, Feb. 1922, 8.

71. Allison Gray, "A Ghostly Knock That Spoiled an Expensive Record," *American Magazine,* May 1922, reprinted in *New Amberola Graphic,* no. 57 (Summer 1986): 13–15.

72. Smith, *Bert Williams,* 220.

73. Ed Sullivan, *Detroit Free Press,* Jan. 29, 1935.

74. Columbia Records supplement, June 1922, 11.

75. U.S. Census of Manufactures, various volumes.

76. "So Long Bert" by George P. Jones, Jr., Black Swan 2056, released in June 1922.

77. For more on this subject see Allan Sutton, "Bert Williams' Imitators," *Victrola and 78 Journal,* no. 5 (Summer 1995): 19–21, updated on <http://www.mainspringpress.com>.

78. "Save a Little Dram for Me" by Duke Rogers, Edison cylinder 4565 (released Aug. 1922) and Edison disc 50976 (Nov. 1922). The master was recorded in July 1921, before Williams's death. Nothing is known about "Duke Rogers." Some have speculated that the singer may be Williams himself, incognito, but a photo at the Edison archives proves that he was white.

79. American Society of Composers, Authors, and Publishers, *Program Listings: 1937.*

80. By Phil Harris: "Constantly," Victor 22855; "Nobody," Vocalion 3430; "Woodman, Spare That Tree," Vocalion 3466; "Constantly," Vocalion 3583. The 1941 reissue was Okeh 6325.

81. "Darktown Poker Club," ARA 116; "Darktown Poker Club" / "Woodman, Spare That Tree," RCA Victor 20-2075; "Darktown" was then recoupled with Harris's signature song, "That's What I Like about the South," on RCA Victor 20-2471. The 78-rpm album set, *On the Record* (RCA Victor P-199), was also issued in a truncated 45-rpm format (WP-199). Both "Darktown" and "Woodman" were available on 45-rpm singles in the early 1950s.

82. Walsh, "Bert Williams, a Thwarted Genius," *Hobbies,* Nov. 1950, 19.

83. Ibid., 21.

84. Stephen Holden, "Black Musicals Have Cause to Sing," *New York Times,* Mar. 7, 1986; Mike McIntyre, "Backstage," *Washington Post,* Mar. 11, 1986; Alvin Klein, "Striking Theater Piece Emerges at Crossroads," *New York Times,* Feb. 15, 1987; and Alvin Klein, "Williams and Walker: Cakewalk and Slapstick," *New York Times,* Mar. 17, 1991. The show was first called *Nobody: An Evening with Bert Williams.*

85. Rowland, *Bert Williams,* 128.

86. Williams, "The Comic Side of Trouble," 34.

87. Ibid., 61.

Chapter 9: Cousins and DeMoss

1. *Freeman,* Oct. 15, Nov. 5, and Nov. 19, 1898, Feb. 25, 1899.

2. *Freeman,* Feb. 25, Mar. 11, 18, and 25, 1899.

3. *Freeman,* Dec. 3, 1898.

4. The two, both of which have been located, were numbered in a 3000 series which appears to have been introduced in 1897. All other known recordings in the series date from 1897 or 1898. See Charosh, *Berliner Gramophone Records,* 82. Since the youthful Cousins seems to have begun his stage career about 1898, and Berliner also recorded his acquaintance Thomas Craig in that year, I think 1898 is more likely.

5. The reissue on Document DOCD-5216 omits the spoken title "Poor Mourner," and the text was also misheard by the writer of the liner notes, leading him to state that the record opened with the words "A song by Cousins & DeMoss."

6. Sampson, *The Ghost Walks,* 190, 256, 298; *Freeman,* June 10, 1905.

Chapter 10: Thomas Craig

1. *Freeman,* July 3 and Aug. 28, 1897.

2. Charosh, *Berliner Gramophone Records,* 75–76.

3. *Freeman,* Feb. 22 and Mar. 18, 1899.

4. *New York Clipper,* Oct. 28, 1899; *Freeman,* Dec. 9, 1899, and Nov. 3, 1900.

Chapter 11: The Dinwiddie Quartet

Special thanks to Lynn Abbott, who provided numerous clippings regarding the Dinwiddie Quartet and Sterling Rex (letter to the author, Dec. 8, 1994).

1. Browder and Lunsford, *An Economic and Social Survey of Dinwiddie County.*
2. See W. Rollo Wilson, "Ernest Hogan: A Pioneer in Musical Comedy," *Louisiana Weekly,* Mar. 2, 1929, which claims "hundreds of thousands of dollars" were raised. The figure is suspect; see "Over $5,000 Raised for Dinwiddie School," *New York Age,* Sept. 13, 1917.
3. *Freeman,* May 18, 1901.
4. Sylvester Russell, "Smart Set in 'Enchantment,'" *Freeman,* Nov. 1, 1902. This and many other *Freeman* references are reprinted in Sampson, *The Ghost Walks,* albeit with numerous errors in dates and spellings.
5. Ibid.
6. "'Smart Set' Captivates Philadelphia," *Freeman,* Nov. 8, 1902.
7. George A. Moonoogian, "This Was Number One," *Goldmine,* June 1979, 33.
8. Lyrics transcribed from Victor 1714; they also appear in Richard K. Spottswood, liner notes to *Religious Music, Congregational and Ceremonial,* LC LBC-1 (LP), and Moonoogian, "This Was Number One."
9. Sampson, *The Ghost Walks,* 285; *Freeman,* Mar. 21, 1903.
10. Wilson, "Ernest Hogan."
11. *Freeman,* Aug. 19, 1905; the 1910 census indicated that Rex and Guigesse had been married for about five years.
12. *Freeman,* Oct. 16 and Nov. 20, 1909.
13. *New York Age,* Oct. 6, 1910.
14. *Freeman,* Aug. 8, 1914; *Philadelphia Tribune,* Mar. 30, Apr. 6, and Apr. 13, 1912, and Feb. 5, 1916.
15. Rex is last listed in the 1938 Philadelphia telephone book. No listing is found in the 1939 edition or scattered issues thereafter, but unfortunately no obituary has been located so an exact date of death is not known. Ray Funk in his liner notes to *The Earliest Negro Vocal Quartets* (Document DOCD 5061) says that "there are many notices in the *Philadelphia Inquirer* to support the assertion that lead singer Sterling Rex went on to a prominent concert career," but Funk, when contacted, was not able to supply specific citations.
16. The Aug. 19, 1905, issue of *Freeman* lists Thomas as from Philadelphia; however his death certificate (1925) says that at that time he had been a resident of New York City for twenty-five years. All documents give his place of birth as merely "U.S."

Chapter 12: Carroll Clark

1. Denver, Colorado, 1900 U.S. Census. "Records Racial Melodies as Sung by Members of the Race," *Chicago Defender,* June 4, 1921, 6.
2. Denver City Directories, 1890 to 1911, and U.S. Census, 1900. Evaline is not found in directories prior to 1890, but there are entries for Charles Clark and William Clark—who may or may not be the same as the Charles and William who later lived with her—in the early and mid-1880s. By the early 1900s Charles and William were living at other addresses in Denver.
3. M. Marguerite Davenport, *Azalia: The Life of Mme. E. Azalia Hackley* (Boston: Chapman and Grimes, 1947); "E. Azalia Hackley," in Jessie Carney Smith, ed., *Notable Black American Women* (Detroit: Gale, 1991), 429–34; Lisa Pertillar Brevard, *A Biography of E. Azalia Smith Hackley (1867–1922), African-American Singer and Social Activist* (New York: Edward Mellen Press, 2001).
4. Lester A. Walton, "Music and the Stage," *New York Age,* Oct. 29, 1908.

5. *Philadelphia Inquirer,* Oct. 22, 1908, 4; *Philadelphia Public Ledger,* Oct. 23, 1908, 4.

6. Sheet music for this and many of the following songs may be found at <http://scriptorium.lib.duke.edu/sheetmusic>.

7. *New York Age,* Feb. 26, 1914, 1. The reference is to baritone "C. C. Clark," presumably our subject. Other early issues of the *Age* in which recital notices are found include Mar. 3 and Apr. 28, 1910, and Nov. 30, 1911.

8. *New York Age,* Nov. 30, 1911.

9. Jas Obrecht, "African American Recording Pioneers," *Victrola and 78 Journal,* no. 4 (Spring 1995): 13; Southern, *The Music of Black Americans,* 284. It is possible that Obrecht, who gives no sources, is confusing the Settlement for Colored with the similarly named Music Settlement School, or its successor the Martin-Smith School, in which case Clark might have been there at a later date.

10. *Talking Machine World,* July 1911.

11. Columbia catalog, Nov. 1913, 100.

12. *Crisis,* May 1918.

13. "Black Swan Records," *Chicago Defender,* May 7, 1921, 8; *Chicago Defender,* Apr. 29, 1922, quoted in Thygesen, Berresford, and Shor, *Black Swan,* 10.

14. "Records Racial Melodies as Sung by Members of the Race."

15. *Crisis,* July 1921, 140.

16. *Crisis,* Sept. 1921, 236.

17. Thygesen, Berresford, and Shor, *Black Swan,* 7.

18. Allen, *Hendersonia,* 576.

19. Ibid., 576. The speculation was based on an item in *Billboard,* Sept. 16, 1933, about an entertainer named Carroll Clark of Piggott, Arkansas, who was killed in a truck accident in Tennessee. According to sources in Piggott, that Carroll Clark was white, was born in 1906, and was buried in the Piggott cemetery (correspondence with Gay Johnson, Piggott Library, and Camilla Cox, Piggott Genealogy Society, Sept. 1993).

20. Just to rule out a few, he is not the Carroll C. Clark listed in the Denver City Directory in 1910–11; according to the 1910 Census, that one was white and born c. 1893. He is also not the C. [Clarence] Carroll Clark listed in many New York City directories who was rector of the Chapel of the Comforter in New York City from 1911 to 1950; that was a white Episcopal minister whose dates are 1875–1973. Presumably he is not the actor "Carroll Clark" who played one of the residents of Catfish Row in the original Broadway production of *Porgy and Bess* in 1935 and appeared in Thornton Wilder's *The Skin of Our Teeth* in 1942.

Chapter 13: Charley Case

The most comprehensive prior article about Case was Jim Walsh, "Charley Case," in *Hobbies* magazine, May through Aug. 1979. Walsh based his article principally on newspaper clippings in the Charley Case folder in the Theater Collection of the New York Public Library, and the same source has been used here, augmented by new research in the Lockport, N.Y., area and elsewhere. My thanks to the genealogist Rick D. Huff for his assistance. Clippings from *Lockport Daily Journal* and most unidentified local clippings are located in the Bio Files at the Niagara County, N.Y., Historian's Office.

1. Case himself said that he was born in Lockport, both in interviews (e.g., "New York Always Beckoned," *New York Telegraph,* Dec. 5, 1909) and on his 1909 recording "Experiences in the Show Business." However at least one story ("Charlie Case's Start," *Pittsburgh Post,* Apr. 1, 1909) claimed that he was born in nearby Buffalo and raised in Lockport. His parents' full names are on his death certificate (certificate no. 33478, 1916, New York City Dept. of Health, Borough of Manhattan).

2. "Charley Case Was Best Monologuist of Day," clipping from an unidentified (modern) Lockport area newspaper. The incident with the reporter occurred in 1905.

3. William E. Sage, "Charlie Case as a Trouper," *Cleveland Leader,* Dec. 12, 1912.

4. "New York Always Beckoned."

5. *Lockport Daily Journal,* Mar. 16, 1888, 3.

6. Sage, "Charlie Case as a Trouper"; "Case Takes Well in East," *Lockport Journal,* Oct. 20, 1904; "Charlie Case, Famous Comedian, Shot Accidently in New York," *Lockport Journal*(?), Nov. 27, 1916.

7. *New York Clipper,* July 28, 1894; Odell, *Annals of the New York Stage,* 15:688, 719.

8. *New York Clipper,* Aug. 17, 1895, at Keith's in New York.

9. *New York Telegraph,* Apr. 4, 1913; *Los Angeles Examiner,* July 26, 1914; unidentified newspaper, May 27, 1906, clipping in New York Public Library.

10. Review of act at Alhambra, *Variety,* Oct. 17, 1908.

11. "Charlie Case Tells Story of a String," *Cincinnati Commercial,* Apr. 11, 1909; "Charlie Case's String," unidentified Chicago newspaper, Nov. 4, 1906, clipping in New York Public Library.

12. Spaeth, *A History of Popular Music in America,* 302.

13. This and the following are quoted in Walsh, "Charley Case," June 1979, 36.

14. "Case Scoring High," *Lockport Journal,* Aug. 27, 1903; *Lockport Union-Sun,* Aug. 7, 1903, 1.

15. "Joseph Clarke in Town," *Lockport Journal,* Aug. 24, 1903.

16. *Indianapolis Star,* Dec. 19, 1906.

17. "An Expensive Meerschaum," unidentified clipping; "Charlie Case and His Hobby," *Morning Illustrated,* n.d., clipping in New York Public Library.

18. As of the year 2000, both the street and the houses were still there, and Case's own residence was for sale. Clarence O. Lewis, "Lockport Stories Recall Great Singer, Comedian," unidentified local newspaper, n.d.; "Charley Case's Retirement," *New York Mirror,* Dec. 21, 1907; "Charlie Case's Book," *Lockport Journal*(?), Oct. 15, 1904. Charley Case, *Charley Case's Father* (Lockport, N.Y.: Case Publishing, 1903).

19. "Charley Case's Retirement."

20. *New York Telegraph,* Nov. 1, 1908.

21. *Boston Traveler,* July 15, 1909.

22. Transcribed by the author from Victor 16328.

23. Transcribed by the author from Victor 16547.

24. Transcribed by the author from Victor 16354.

25. "Well Balanced Orpheum Bill," *Spokane Review,* c. 1909.

26. Walsh, "Charley Case," May 1979, 35.

27. *Victor Records of Historic and Personal Interest* (Victor Talking Machine Company, Apr. 1927).

28. "Charlie Case and His Hobby."

29. "Fifth Avenue," *New York Mirror,* Jan. 23, 1909.

30. *New York Telegraph,* Jan. 25, 1914.

31. "New York Always Beckoned."

32. Karl S. Brong, "Lockport Legends: 'Barn Painting' Costs $300 Offer," unidentified local newspaper, n.d.

33. *Cleveland Leader,* Nov. 6, 1910.

34. *Duluth Herald,* May 1, 1912.

35. *Los Angeles Examiner,* July 26, 1914.

36. "Charles Case Is Victim of Accidental Shooting while Cleaning Revolver," unidentified newspaper (probably *New York Telegraph*), Nov. 28, 1916.

37. "Wife Dies at News That Charles Case, Actor, Is Killed," *New York American,* Nov. 28, 1916.

38. "Charlie Case," obituary, *Variety,* Dec. 1, 1916.

39. Walsh, "Charley Case," Aug. 1979, 35.

40. Walsh, "Charley Case," May 1979, 35. Walsh's source may have been the Broadway author and habitué Joe Laurie Jr.

41. Lester A. Walton, "Charlie Case," *New York Age,* Nov. 30, 1916.

42. Laurie, *Vaudeville,* 174; Walsh, "Charley Case," May 1979, 36.

43. Reported in "Recalls Popularity of Charlie Case on Stage of Vaudeville," unidentified Lockport-area newspaper, Jan. 8, 1932.

44. See, for example, Gracyk, *The Encyclopedia of Popular American Recording Pioneers,* 61; Slide, *The Encyclopedia of Vaudeville,* 49; Rust and Debus, *The Complete Entertainment Discography,* 145; Ed Manning, notes to *American Vaudeville and Variety,* vol. 2, Rococo 4009 (LP).

45. "Opened a Restaurant," *Lockport Journal,* Oct. 23, 1903.

46. "Charlie Case's Start," *Pittsburgh Post,* Apr. 1, 1909.

47. The Dalhart recordings were issued on Harmony 729-H and affiliated labels.

Chapter 14: The Fisk Jubilee Singers and the Popularization of Spirituals

1. The quote originally appeared in the *New York Herald,* May 25, 1893, cited in Southern, *The Music of Black Americans,* 265, among many other places.

2. Important sources on the Singers' early history include Ward, *Dark Midnight When I Rise;* Anderson, "The Fisk Jubilee Singers"; and Lovell, *Black Song.* Doug Seroff's excellent "The Fisk Jubilee Singers in Britain," in *Under the Imperial Carpet,* ed. Lotz and Pegg, 42–54, focuses on the British tours in the 1870s. The few sources dealing with recordings are problematic. Dixon, Godrich, and Rye, *Blues and Gospel Records, 1890–1943,* is the standard reference. Turner, *Dictionary of Afro-American Performers,* was a pioneering early attempt at a discography, unfortunately with many errors. The entry in Marco, ed., *Encyclopedia of Recorded Sound in the United States,* is filled with mistakes—almost every factual statement is incorrect; and Jim Walsh, "A Directory of Pioneer Recording Groups," in *Hobbies,* Oct. 1962, 33–34, is the source of a number of erroneous statements reprinted elsewhere regarding the Singers' recording history.

3. Allen, Ware, and Garrison, *Slave Songs of the United States.*

4. Lovell, *Black Song,* 400.

5. Epstein, *Sinful Tunes and Spirituals,* 290.

6. J. B. T. Marsh, *The Story of the Jubilee Singers, with Their Songs* (London: Hodder and Stoughton, 1877, 1903), 175, quoted in Shaw, *Black Popular Music in America,* 3.

7. Lovell, *Black Song,* 407; Epstein, *Sinful Tunes and Spirituals,* 340; Dena J. Epstein, "Black Spirituals: Their Emergence into Public Knowledge," *Black Music Research Journal* 10, no. 1 (Spring 1990): 58–64. The latter article discusses the early history and influence of the Fisks.

8. *Freeman,* July 28, 1900.

9. Du Bois, *The Souls of Black Folk,* 267.

10. *Freeman,* June 29, 1901.

11. Invincible Quartette, "Characteristic Negro Medley," Edison 8115 (cylinder), Columbia 31792 (cylinder), Columbia 890 (disc), all released in 1902. The title remained in the catalog for many years, turning up on other labels as well.

12. See, for example, listings in Brooks, *Columbia Master Book Discography,* vol. 1; Fagan and Moran, *The Encyclopedic Discography of Victor Recordings, Pre-Matrix Series.* Some labels gave the routine the slightly more dignified name "Negro Wedding in Southern Georgia."

13. *New Jubilee Songs as Sung by the Fisk Jubilee Singers* (1901); Frederick J. Work, *Folk Songs of the American Negro* (Nashville: Work Brothers and Hart Co., 1907); John W. Work, *Folk Songs of the American Negro* (Nashville: Fisk University Press, 1915).

14. It is beyond the scope of this chapter to plunge into the raging debate about "authenticity," or the manner in which spirituals changed over time. For more on those subjects the reader is referred to Jon Cruz, *Culture on the Margins: The Black Spiritual and the Rise of American Cultural Interpretation* (Princeton, N.J.: Princeton University Press, 1999); Paul Gilroy, *The Black Atlantic: Modernity and Double Consciousness* (Cambridge, Mass.: Harvard University Press, 1993); Paul Gilroy, "Sounds Authentic: Black Music, Ethnicity, and the Challenge of a Changing Same," *Black Music Research Journal* 2, no. 2 (Fall 1991): 111–36; Ronald M. Radano, "Soul Texts and the Blackness of Folk," *Modernism/Modernity* 2, no. 1 (Jan. 1995); Ronald M. Radano, "Denoting Difference: The Writing of the Slave Spirituals," *Critical Inquiry* 22, no. 3 (Spring 1996). A search of the Internet will turn up many other sources.

15. Victor Talking Machine Co., *Alphabetical List of Records,* Mar. 1910 (a dealer booklet that consolidated all domestic releases in alphabetical order).

16. There is a large body of literature on Dunbar, whose work has passed in and out of favor over the years. For a relatively even-handed summary of his career and critical reaction to his prose and poetry see Draper, ed., *Black Literature Criticism;* and Robyn V. Young, ed., *Poetry Criticism* (Detroit: Gale, 1992).

17. "When Malindy Sings," first published in *Majors and Minors* (Toledo, Ohio: Hadley and Hadley, 1895). For a modern reprint see Jay Martin and Gossie H. Hudson, eds., *The Paul Laurence Dunbar Reader* (New York: Dodd, Mead, 1975), 299–301.

18. Victor records supplement, Feb. 1910, 7.

19. Ibid., Mar. 1910, 6.

20. Ibid., Oct. 1911, 5.

21. Ibid., June 1911, 10.

22. Ibid., July 1911, 9.

23. No listings are found in the 1913 or 1919 catalogs of His Master's Voice, Victor's affiliated label in England.

24. Lovell, *Black Song,* 416.

25. Thomas A. Edison, Inc., "Edison Records by the Fisk Jubilee Quartet," promotional flyer, dated 1912, Form 2161.

26. The 1911 cylinders are extremely rare; of the nine issued I have heard five (originally issued as Edison 979, 980, 982, 985, and 986).

27. Thomas A. Edison, Inc., "Edison Records by the Fisk Jubilee Quartet."

28. "Fisk Jubilee Records," *Edison Phonograph Monthly,* Mar. 1912, 6.

29. Ibid.

30. Rust and Brooks, *The Columbia Master Book Discography,* vol. 4; Rust and Debus, *The Complete Entertainment Discography,* 148–50.

31. *Columbus Evening Dispatch,* n.d., quoted in Fisk Jubilee Singers promotional booklet, Spring 1916, 7–8, Fisk University archives.

32. Columbia Records supplement, Jan. 1916, 14.

33. Ibid., Feb. 1916, 17.

34. Ibid., June 1916, 12.

35. Ibid., Jan. 1917, 15.

36. Recording notebook, Edison National Historic Site, which also indicates titles recorded and a review (not necessarily recording) date of July 10, 1916.

37. Snyder, "Harry T. Burleigh and the Creative Expression of Bi-Musicality," 298.

38. Doug Seroff, review of Turner, *Dictionary of African-American Performers,* in *Antique Phonograph Monthly* 11, no. 2 (1993): 11.

39. *Columbia Record,* Mar. 1909, 13, 15. This presumably included a back shelf in practically every general store in America.

40. William Robyn (an exclusive Victor artist from 1920 to 1923), quoted in Tim Brooks, "Willie Robyn: A Recording Artist in the 1920s," *ARSC Journal* 23, no. 1 (1992): 48.

41. "Criticism," in *Encyclopedia of Recorded Sound in the United States,* ed. Marco, 154; Tim Brooks, "A Survey of Record Collectors' Societies," *ARSC Journal* 16, no. 3 (1984): 18. In 1935 *Phonograph Monthly Review* was renamed *American Record Guide.*

42. Author's estimate based on figures in the U.S. Census of Manufactures, 1909, 1914, 1919, and 1921; and annual production figures of Victor, the dominant manufacturer, in B. L. Aldridge, *The Victor Talking Machine Company* (New York: RCA Sales Corporation, 1964), appendix 4, 109. The Aldridge monograph has been reprinted in Fagan and Moran, *The Encyclopedic Discography of Victor Recordings, Pre-Matrix Series.*

43. U.S. Department of Commerce, *Historical Statistics of the United States,* 41.

44. Millard, *America on Record,* chap. 2; Thomas A. Edison interviewed by Clarence Axman in *The Music Trades,* c. 1907, reprinted in *Edison Phonograph Monthly,* Feb. 1907, 14.

45. See, for example, advertisements for Roland Hayes's first, personal recordings (*Crisis,* May 1918, 43, and June 1918, 97) and articles about the formation of Black Swan records (*Chicago Defender,* May 7, 1921, 8, and June 4, 1921, 6).

46. Simpson, *Hard Trials,* 82–83, 309, 350.

47. Francis Rogers, "Songs the Soldiers Like," *Music Courier,* Oct. 3, 1918.

48. "Swing Low, Sweet Chariot" by Mabel Garrison, Victrola 64969 (1921); "Swing Low, Sweet Chariot" by Nellie Melba, Victrola 6733 (1927).

49. "Negro Spirituals" by Vincent Lopez and His Orchestra, Okeh 40175 (1924). The medley includes "Go Down Moses," "Nobody Knows de Trouble I've Seen," "Oh Peter," "I Want to Go to Heaven When I Die," "It's Me O Lord" and "Deep River."

50. Dixon, Godrich, and Rye, *Blues and Gospel Records, 1890–1943.*

51. The exception is Columbia A3370, which is unspecified. However this too sounds like a male quartet.

52. Columbia Records supplement, June 1920, 3.

53. See, for example, Marco, ed., *Encyclopedia of Recorded Sound in the United States,* 262; and Dixon and Godrich, *Blues and Gospel Records, 1902–1943,* 690. The error has been corrected in the fourth edition of the latter volume.

54. Edison Re-Creations (disc) supplement, May 1922. Also, a picture of the Southern 4 in the files of the Edison National Historic Site does not depict known members of the Fisk Singers.

55. See Dixon and Godrich, *Blues and Gospel Records, 1902–1943,* for the erroneous information; and Dixon, Godrich, and Rye, *Blues and Gospel Records, 1890–1943,* for a correction. The label of the 1920s issue of Victor 16453 identifies the members of the Bethel Quartet by name and specifies the director to be Rev. T. H. Wiseman.

56. Unsigned review, *Phonograph Monthly Review* 1, no. 1 (Oct. 1926): 41.

57. Doug Seroff, correspondence with author, 1997; Louise Davis, interview reported by Seroff, Feb. 8, 1989, in *Gospel Arts Day—Nashville,* brochure, June 18, 1989, 16.

58. Edison Blue Amberol stock cards, Edison National Historic Site.

59. *New York Times,* Jan. 28, 1925, 8; Feb. 5, 1925, 3; and Apr. 24, 1925, 21. The controversy is summarized in Low and Clift, eds., *Encyclopedia of Black America,* 388.

60. Dixon, Godrich, and Rye, *Blues and Gospel Records, 1890–1943,* 261, states that the 1935 discs are in the collection of the Museum of Broadcasting in New York City and that the 1940 discs are either there or at the Country Music Foundation in Nashville. Contents of the 1935 discs are unknown.

61. Sutton and Nauck, *American Record Labels and Companies,* 179. From pressing codes in the shellac we know that the discs were pressed by RCA in 1946.

62. Doug Seroff, "Mrs. James A. Myers, 1989 Gospel Arts Day Honoree: A Life Devoted to the Spiritual," *Gospel Arts Day—Nashville,* June 18, 1989.

63. Matthew W. Kennedy entry in *Who's Who in America,* 49th ed., 1:1983. The entry indicates that Kennedy directed the Singers from 1957 to 1968, 1971 to 1973, and 1975 to

1986. He also taught at Fisk for various periods between 1947 and 1986, and during the 1970s served as chairman of the music department.

64. Dixon and Goodrich, *Blues and Gospel Records, 1902–1943,* 235.

Chapter 15: Polk Miller and His Old South Quartette

1. Microfilms of Miller's scrapbooks are at the Country Music Foundation Library and Media Center in Nashville; the originals are part of the historical collection of the Valentine Historical Museum in Richmond, Virginia. Researchers Ray Funk and Doug Seroff deserve considerable credit for locating these scrapbooks and persuading their owners to allow them to be preserved in this way. Contents of the scrapbooks are extensively quoted by Seroff in two articles on Miller, both titled "Polk Miller and the Old South Quartette," the first appearing in *JEMF Quarterly* 18, nos. 67–68 (Fall–Winter 1982): 147–50; and the second in *78 Quarterly* 1, no. 3 (1988): 27–41. One other important article about Miller that is frequently cited is Jim Walsh, "Polk Miller and His Old South Quartet," *Hobbies,* Jan. 1960, 34–37.

2. Quote from Mrs. Garland C. Chewning in a letter to Walsh, printed in Seroff, "Polk Miller" (1988), 37.

3. Unidentified Richmond newspaper, Aug. 1892, cited in Seroff, "Polk Miller" (1988).

4. For a detailed discussion of this phenomenon, and a meticulous reconstruction of the evidence that does exist, see Epstein, *Sinful Tunes and Spirituals.*

5. "Polk Miller Dies of Heart Failure at Bon Air Home," *Richmond Times-Dispatch,* Oct. 21, 1913.

6. Withers Miller, unpublished biography of Polk Miller, quoted in Walsh, "Polk Miller and His Old South Quartet."

7. According to several sources, including Withers Miller's account, it was 1871. The modern Web site of Sergeant's Pet Products, the firm that grew out of his business, states that it was in 1868, but this may refer to his first employment as a druggist by Powhatan Dupuy.

8. "Polk Miller, Banjo Player," unidentified Richmond newspaper, c. Aug. 1892, quoted in Seroff, "Polk Miller" (1988).

9. "Twain and Polk Miller," *Cincinnati Commercial Gazette,* c. Oct. 14, 1894, cited in Seroff, "Polk Miller" (1988) and quoted in numerous Miller flyers. Seroff gives the date as Feb. 27, 1894; Odell, *Annals of the New York Stage,* 15:762, confirms that Mark Twain and James Whitcomb Riley read from their own works at the Garden on Feb. 26 and 27, 1894.

10. "Polk Miller and Negro Prejudice," *Richmond Journal,* Jan. 4, 1912.

11. From a retrospective article in the *Richmond Times,* Sept. 24, 1927.

12. Original advertising material in the Polk Miller scrapbooks.

13. Seroff, "Polk Miller" (1988), 31; Harris quotes from a personal communication to Miller in "Polk Miller: Stories, Sketches, Song," promotional flyer, author's collection.

14. *New York Dramatic Mirror,* Apr. 9, 1898, 20.

15. "Polk Miller's Funeral Here," *Richmond News-Leader,* Oct. 21, 1913.

16. *New York Clipper,* Sept. 22, 1894.

17. "Abandons Show Biz," *Richmond Journal,* Jan. 3, 1912.

18. Brochure from Polk Miller scrapbooks, c. 1910, emphasis in the original.

19. "Polk Miller—Stories, Sketches, Songs," c. 1910 brochure, photocopy in author's collection.

20. W. W. Landrum, Pastor, Second Baptist Church, Richmond, Va., letter dated Feb. 7, 1894, in promotional flyer, "The New Genius of the South," photocopy in author's collection.

21. Ibid.

22. Ibid.

23. *Edison Phonograph Monthly,* Jan. 1910, 19.

24. *New Phonogram,* June 1911, quoted in Walsh, "Polk Miller and His Old South Quartet."

25. "The Bonnie Blue Flag," by Harry Macarthy, "the Arkansas Comedian," as sung at his "Presentation Concerts" (New Orleans: A. E. Blackmar and Bro., © 1861). Sheet music and lyrics for this best-selling song may be found on numerous Internet sites. A majority of early printings did say "property," although some replaced this with "liberty." See, for example, <http://www.pdmusic.org> and <http://levysheetmusic.mse.jhu.edu>.

26. *Edison Phonograph Monthly,* Mar. 1910, 18.

27. Ibid., May 1914, 67.

28. *Richmond Planet,* Mar. 5, 1910.

29. *Richmond Journal,* Jan. 3, 1912.

30. "Polk Miller and Negro Prejudice."

31. "Polk Miller's Funeral Here."

32. "Polk Miller Dies of Heart Failure at Bon Air Home."

33. Walsh, "Polk Miller and His Old South Quartet."

34. QRS flyer pictured in Seroff, "Polk Miller" (1988).

35. Ibid., 40.

36. Polk Miller, *Dogs: Their Ailments and How to Treat Them,* rev. ed. (Richmond, Va.: Whittet and Shepperson, 1903). As this is a revised edition, the book may have originally been published earlier.

37. Sergeant's Web site is <http://www.sergeants.com/>.

38. "Polk Miller's Funeral Here."

Chapter 16: Jack Johnson

1. Johnson claimed a number of colorful adventures in his early life which have been called into question by some biographers. Randy Roberts, in *Papa Jack,* is particularly skeptical, discounting almost everything Johnson said he did. Unfortunately, some of Roberts's "evidence" is rather flimsy. For example he cites city directories and census reports as proving Johnson stayed in Galveston, apparently unaware that such sources routinely listed people by their home location even when they were "temporarily" traveling. He also claims that Johnson's real name was "Arthur John Johnson," although the evidence for that is questionable. Roberts did, however, have access to FBI files relating to Johnson's later legal troubles, which makes his account of those years valuable. Other sources used here with caution include Johnson's autobiography, *Jack Johnson Is a Dandy,* Farr, *Black Champion,* and deCoy, *Jack Johnson.* DeCoy knew Johnson in his later years, and based much of his book on personal conversations with the champ. However it is a very biased account, portraying Johnson virtually as a saint.

2. deCoy, *Jack Johnson,* 21.

3. Ibid., 24.

4. Roberts, *Papa Jack,* discounts Johnson's first three claimed marriages, saying that he merely lived with the women and did not marry them. Even if true, they may have been common-law wives.

5. Sampson, *The Ghost Walks,* 319.

6. Roberts, *Papa Jack,* 68.

7. Review, *Variety,* Apr. 3, 1909, quoted in Sampson, *The Ghost Walks,* 462.

8. *Freeman,* Nov. 20, 1909; Riis, *Just before Jazz,* 122; Sampson, *The Ghost Walks,* 510–11 (review of Lowery and Morgan's Mighty Minstrels, Mar. 26, 1910).

9. Two ads from competing companies, each claiming "exclusive" pictures from Johnson's camp, appear in *Moving Picture World,* June 4, 1910, 967.

10. *Freeman,* July 16, 1910.

11. *New York Times,* July 5, 1910, 1–4.

12. *Moving Picture World,* July 23, 1910.

13. American Cinephone advertisement, *Moving Picture World,* Aug. 13, 1910, 394.

14. *New York Times,* July 5, 1910, 1–2. Sullivan covered the fight for the *Times.*

15. *New York Times,* July 4, 1910, 14.

16. This and the following passages were transcribed by the author from the original disks.

17. "Mr. Johnson Talks," *Moving Picture World,* Aug. 20, 1910.

18. *New York Age,* July 14, 1910.

19. *New York Age,* Nov. 10, 1910; Smith, *Bert Williams,* 138–39.

20. deCoy, *Jack Johnson,* 135.

21. Ibid., 155.

22. E. S. Stansfield, "More Edison Bell Enterprise—Jack Johnson Makes Records," *Talking Machine News,* July (for Aug.), 1914.

23. "Jack Johnson Makes Records," *Sound Wave,* Aug. 1914.

24. Charters and Kunstadt, *Jazz,* 166–67.

25. Ragan, *Who's Who in Hollywood,* 1:831.

26. Ajax advertisement, *Phonograph and Talking Machine Weekly,* undated but c. May 17, 1924.

27. deCoy, *Jack Johnson,* 298–99.

28. Sampson, *Blacks in Blackface,* 7; Fletcher, *One Hundred Years of the Negro in Show Business,* 205, 313; "Times Ain't Like They Used to Be" (videotape, Yazoo 512; the tape contains three takes of the band playing "Tiger Rag"). Farr, *Black Champion,* 6, mentions another Johnson memoir called *Mes Combats,* published in Paris, but this has not been traced.

29. deCoy, *Jack Johnson,* 306–7.

Chapter 17: Daisy Tapley

1. Black women had recorded in Europe prior to Tapley (e.g., Belle Davis in London in 1902).

2. This and much of the following personal detail is drawn from the following obituaries: "Beloved Harlem Musician Laid to Rest," *Amsterdam* (New York) *News,* Feb. 11, 1925, 1; "Miss Daisy Tapley, Singer and Musician, Buried at Sag Harbor," *New York Age,* Feb. 11, 1925, 10; "Miss Daisy Tapley Dies in New York," *Chicago Defender,* Feb. 14, 1925, 1; "Mrs. Tapley Passes Away," *Pittsburgh Courier,* Feb. 14, 1925, 17; G. E. Taylor, "Broadway Turns Out for Daisy Tapley," *Baltimore African-American,* Feb. 14, 1925, 4; and *Crisis,* Nov. 1925, 20. See also her death certificate, no. 3873, Feb. 5, 1925, New York City. A short and not altogether accurate biography of Tapley appears in Turner, *Dictionary of Afro-American Performers,* 369–70.

3. A. N. Fields, "Early Chicagoans Achieve Stardom on the Stage," *Chicago Defender,* Feb. 11, 1933.

4. Although the date and place of their marriage has not been positively established, as early as June 13, 1903, the *Freeman* contained a short note sending regards to "Mr. and Mrs. Green Tapley" in Chicago.

5. None of the three was in the principal casts of these shows, but Daisy has been found in cast lists for *Abyssinia* and *Mr. Lode of Koal,* and G. Henri Tapley and Minnie Brown in reviews of all three shows. It is only uncertain whether Daisy was in *Bandanna Land.* See Sampson, *Blacks in Blackface,* 137, 263, and *The Ghost Walks,* 354, 377, 454, 483; see also Mantle, *Best Plays of 1899–1909,* 557; and Woll, *Dictionary of the Black Theatre,* 13.

6. "Miss Daisy Tapley Dies in New York."

7. The 1915 *Trow's City Directory* for New York shows Daisy living at 165 West 136th St. (occupation, music teacher) while Green Tapley was at 142 West 131st St. (occupation, musician). In 1913 Green was even closer, living at 48 West 136th.

8. June 1915 New York State Census; 1920 U.S. Census.

9. *New York Age,* Jan. 19, 1918.

10. *New York Age,* Feb. 11, 1925, 10.

11. *Baltimore African-American,* Feb. 14, 1925, 4.

12. *New York Age,* Feb. 11, 1925, 10.

Chapter 18: Apollo Jubilee Quartette

1. Columbia Records supplement, Aug. 1912, 6.

2. According to Victor file data supplied by William R. Moran, Victor's "Apollo Quartet" (note the absence of the modifier "Jubilee" in the name) recorded the old, and very white, sentimental song "When the Corn Is Waving, Annie Dear" (1860), on March 3, 1911. It was issued on Victor 16858, backed with the "darky song" "Lindy," sung by the white contralto Marguerite Dunlap. No other titles by the Apollo Quartet are found in the Victor files until 1916–17, when it made four unissued trial recordings ("Eternity," "At Dawning," "Long Long Ago," and "The Drum"), which do not suggest a black quartet either. The names of the singers are not given in the files, and the June 1911 announcement of Victor 16858 says virtually nothing about them.

3. See advertisement in *Nashville Globe,* Jan. 28, 1910, for a performance at the Spruce Street Baptist Church, Feb. 14, 1910, reproduced in Doug Seroff, "Nashville's 'Golden Age' of Jubilee Singing," in the brochure *Gospel Arts Day—Nashville,* June 19, 1988. Also in Hayes's 1910 Apollo Quartet were second tenor J. C. Olden and basso N. H. Patton.

Chapter 19: Edward Sterling Wright and the Poetry of Paul Laurence Dunbar

1. "Edward Sterling Wright," *Edison Phonograph Monthly,* Dec. 1913, 9. The same bio appeared on slips enclosed with Wright's Edison cylinders. One of these slips is reprinted in Dethlefson, *Edison Blue Amberol Recordings,* 2:475.

2. Death certificate no. 284, Jan. 16, 1922, New York City, Borough of Queens.

3. Robert Fleming, Emerson College Archives, letter to the author, July 14, 2000. A Samuel Edward Wright from Brooklyn, New York, born c. 1873, attended from 1896 to 1898, but this is probably not the same person. In addition to being several years older, his father's name is given in school records as Samuel.

4. "Design of the College," *Emerson College Catalog, 1890–91.*

5. *Trow's New York City Directory, Borough of Manhattan,* 1913.

6. *Freeman,* Mar. 11, 1911.

7. "Paul Laurence Dunbar," in *Black Literature Criticism,* ed. Draper, 623.

8. Edison release list for February 1914, reproduced in Dethlefson, *Edison Blue Amberol Recordings, 1912–1914,* 110.

9. "Tree Hears Negro in Part of Othello," *New York Times,* Apr. 3, 1916, 11.

10. Lucien H. White, "Edward Sterling Wright in *Othello*—Premieres with All-Negro Cast," *New York Age,* Apr. 27, 1916.

11. "A Darktown Othello," *New York Telegraph,* May 13, 1916.

12. "Negro Players Give 'Othello,'" *New York Telegraph,* May 16, 1916.

13. "Negro Players Give 'Othello,'" *Philadelphia Public Ledger,* c. Mar. 22, 1916; "Negro Players Give 'Othello' at Walnut," *Philadelphia North American,* May 22, 1916; "'Othello' in Odd Guise," *Philadelphia Telegraph,* May 22, 1916.

14. His obituary mentions a production at the Lafayette "two years ago" (see "Wright Buried," *Chicago Defender,* Jan. 28, 1922). Woll also mentions a 1919 production at the Lafayette in his *Dictionary of the Black Theatre,* 203. However no mention of such a production has been found in the Lafayette's regular advertising in the *New York Age* during 1919.

15. "Wright Buried."

Chapter 20: James Reese Europe

1. The Europe family consisted of Henry (1847–99), Lorraine (c. 1849–1937), and their children Minnie (1868–1920s), Ida (1870–1920s), John (1875–1932), James (1880–1919), and Mary (1885–1947). Note that most of the family members were not particularly long-lived and that Lorraine outlived four of her five children. Dates from Badger, *A Life in Ragtime.*

2. Sampson, *The Ghost Walks,* 330–31.

3. Ibid., 416.

4. Ibid., 440.

5. *New York Age,* Oct. 6, 1910.

6. Quoted in Rose, *Eubie Blake,* 59–60. Quotes have been rearranged somewhat for clarity.

7. Sissle, "Memoirs of Lieutenant 'Jim' Europe," 22–23.

8. Badger, *A Life in Ragtime,* 71. Much of the following information on Europe's personal life comes from this source.

9. A number of native bands and "orquestas" recorded in the Caribbean in the early 1900s.

10. All of these titles seem to have appeared on labels at one time or another.

11. Castle House Orchestra titles are listed in the Victor monthly supplements for May and July 1914, which specify that the orchestra was led by McKee and supervised by Castle. Additional McKee recordings can be found in numerous Victor catalogs from the mid-1910s through the early 1920s. His picture appears in the November 1914 supplement.

12. "Three Modern Dances," printed Mar. 23, 1914, also "Victor Records for Dancing," printed Feb. 18, 1916 (print codes are on the back cover), copies in author's collection.

13. Columbia Records supplement, July 1914, 5.

14. Victor record supplement, Apr. 1914, 5.

15. Prince's Band, Columbia A5562 and A5589; National Promenade Band, Edison cylinder 2407 and disc 50191.

16. Introductory flyer titled "New Victor Records of the Latest Dance Music: Tangos, Maxixe and Trots by Europe's Society Orchestra," undated but probably from February 1914, reprinted in Kimball and Bolcom, *Reminiscing with Sissle and Blake,* 60.

17. *New York Age,* Apr. 16, 1914.

18. Lucien H. White, "An Enjoyable Program," *New York Age,* Nov. 20, 1913.

19. "'Jim' Europe Out," *New York Age,* Jan. 1, 1914.

20. Badger, *A Life in Ragtime,* 88.

21. Lester A. Walton, "Theatrical Comment," *New York Age,* Jan. 14, 1914.

22. "Negro's Place in Music," *New York Evening Post,* Mar. 13, 1914, reprinted in Kimball and Bolcom, *Reminiscing with Sissle and Blake,* 60–61.

23. "Europe on Race's Music," *New York Age,* Nov. 26, 1914, quoting from an article in the previous Sunday's edition of the *New York Tribune.*

24. Badger, *A Life in Ragtime,* 115–17.

25. *New York Age,* May 11, 1916. Many of the names in the article were misspelled; they have been conformed here to commonly accepted spellings.

26. *Chicago Defender,* Feb. 22, 1919, 11.

27. Badger, *A Life in Ragtime,* 180.

28. By Val Trainor and Harry De Costa, M. Witmark and Sons (1918); also known as "He Draws No Color Line." See Cohen-Stratyner, ed., *Popular Music, 1900–1919,* 388.

29. *New York Age,* Feb. 22, 1919, 1.

30. *Talking Machine World,* Feb. 15, 1919, 112. Andrews, who had won praise helping organize the army's Motor Transport Division and who had risen to the rank of lieutenant colonel, joined Pathé in early 1919 in charge of advertising and sales promotion.

31. Badger, *A Life in Ragtime,* 237, estimates that as many as twenty-two may have recorded, though this surely would have taxed the acoustic recording equipment then in use. A picture of Europe's band in the Fifth Avenue parade shows about ninety musicians (*Talking Machine World,* Apr. 15, 1919, 153), and eighty or more were advertised as participating in his concerts.

32. This analysis is necessarily somewhat speculative. It is based in part on my interviews with the singer William Robyn, who recorded for both labels around this time and who spoke frequently of the "perfectionism" and high musical standards of Victor's recording managers compared to those of other labels, including Pathé. Tim Brooks, "Willie Robyn: A Recording Artist in the 1920s," *ARSC Journal* 23, no. 1 (Spring 1992): 35–59, and no. 2 (Fall 1992): 178–227.

33. Among the others were Prince's Band in 1916 and Ciro's Club Coon Orchestra (also a relatively hot performance) in England in 1917.

34. Lawrence Gushee, liner notes for *Steppin' on the Gas: Rags to Jazz, 1913–1927,* New World NW 269 (1977).

35. The full text can be found in Kimball and Bolcom, *Reminiscing with Sissle and Blake,* 78.

36. Badger, *A Life in Ragtime,* 207.

37. *Talking Machine World,* Apr. 15, 1919, 153.

38. "Exhortation," words by Alex Rogers, music by Will Marion Cook, © 1912.

39. "Sissle and Blake's Shuffle Along," New World NW 260 (1976). The notes speculate that the song may have been sung by Sissle and Blake in their constantly changing vaudeville spot within the 1921 show.

40. *Talking Machine World,* Apr. 15, 1919, 142.

41. Sissle, "Memoirs of Lieutenant 'Jim' Europe," 199.

42. *New York Sun,* Mar. 17, 1919, quoted in Badger, *A Life in Ragtime,* 206.

43. Badger, *A Life in Ragtime,* 208.

44. *Phonograph and Talking Machine Weekly,* Apr. 30, 1919, 32. The article, which reads like (and probably was) a Pathé press release, is quoted in Kimball and Bolcom, *Reminiscing with Sissle and Blake,* 248.

45. The "popular supplement" containing Europe's first Pathé discs has not been located, however the April release is confirmed by news items in *Talking Machine World,* Apr. 15, 1919, 153; *Music Trades,* Apr. 26, 1919; and the aforementioned *Phonograph and Talking Machine Weekly* article.

46. *Talking Machine World,* Apr. 15, 1919, 153.

47. "Like Europe's Jazz Band Records," *Talking Machine World,* May 15, 1919, 14.

48. *Talking Machine World,* May 15, 1919, 73, and June 15, 1919, 80–81.

49. Pathé advertisement, *Talking Machine World,* June 15, 1919, 81, quoting from the publication *Work.*

50. I am indebted to Reid Badger for reconstructing the Europe band's itinerary; Badger, letter to the author, Nov. 28, 1994.

51. The dedication is reported in the *New York Age,* May 27, 1915. The entertainer Tom Fletcher related that Johnson was given his nickname by Jim Europe's brother John, because Johnson sang the old song "The Preacher and the Bear," "just like a Deacon." See Fletcher, *One Hundred Years of the Negro in Show Business,* 265.

52. Longstanding rumors that "The Missouri Waltz" was written by a black man are apparently false; see Galen Wilkes, "The Graveyard Waltz: A Portrait of Lee Edgar 'Jelly' Settle," *Ragtime Ephemeralist* 1, no. 2 (1999): 170–202, for the detailed story of the song's tangled history.

53. *New York Age,* May 10, 1919.

54. Sissle, "Memoirs of Lieutenant 'Jim' Europe," 223–36, contains the best eyewitness account of the events in Boston, including the attack in Europe's dressing room. Badger,

A Life in Ragtime, 214–17, uses both this source and newspaper reports to assemble a clear and concise summary of the tragedy. The following quotes are from Sissle.

55. "Herbert Wright Sentenced from Ten to Fifteen Years," *New York Age*, June 14, 1919, 1. Wright was paroled in 1927 after serving eight years of his sentence (*New York Times*, Apr. 1, 1927).

56. Badger, *A Life in Ragtime*, 218.

57. "Lieut. Europe's Funeral," *New York Times*, May 14, 1919.

58. *New York Herald*, May 16, 1919, part 2, p. 6.

59. At least, this is the first time Europe is mentioned as the subject of a story in the *New York Times* index.

60. Badger, *A Life in Ragtime*, 223.

61. *Talking Machine World*, May 15, 1919, 14, 73, 107, 154.

62. Pathé Records monthly supplement, Oct. 1919, author's collection.

63. *Crisis*, July 1919, 162. The ad also indicates that Europe recorded its "Dancing Deacon," "Hesitating Blues," and "St. Louis Blues," all of which were issued.

64. Perry Bradford, *Born with the Blues* (New York: Oak Publications, 1965), quoted in *Storyville* magazine in letters from Ernest Virgo (*Storyville*, no. 157 [Mar. 1994]: 14) and Mark Berresford (*Storyville*, no. 161 [Mar. 1995]: 183).

65. Goddard, *Jazz Away from Home*, contains nice summaries of some of these careers.

66. Badger, *A Life in Ragtime*, 226.

67. Ibid., 231–34.

68. *James Reese Europe Featuring Noble Sissle*, IAJRC CD 1012; *Lieut. Jim Europe's 369th U.S. Infantry "Hell Fighters" Band: The Complete Recordings*, Memphis Archives MA 7020; *The Earliest Negro Vocal Groups*, vol. 2, *1893–1922*, Document DOCD-5288.

69. Badger, *A Life in Ragtime*, 228.

70. Rose, *Eubie Blake*, 60–61.

71. Handy, *Father of the Blues*, 228–29.

Chapter 21: Will Marion Cook and the Afro-American Folk Song Singers

1. Southern, *Biographical Dictionary of Afro-American and African Musicians*, 81–82; and Southern's entry "Will Marion Cook" in *New Grove Dictionary of American Music*, ed. Hitchcock and Sadie, 489–90.

2. Johnson, *Along This Way*, quoted in Woll, *Black Musical Theatre*, 6.

3. Ibid., 175.

4. Sylvester Russell columns, *New York Age*, Nov. 19, 1902, and May 2, 1903.

5. Sampson, *Blacks in Blackface*, 81.

6. Fletcher, *One Hundred Years of the Negro in Show Business*, 260; Rose, *Eubie Blake*, 43. Sissle, "Memoirs of Lieutenant 'Jim' Europe," 22, says that Cook conducted the numbers but this is disputed by Fletcher (who was there) as well as Rose.

7. Advertising flyer, Mercer Cook Papers, Box 157-8, folder 25, Manuscript Division, Moorland-Spingarn Research Center, Howard University.

8. "Negroes Give a Concert," *New York Times*, Mar. 12, 1914, 3.

9. "Negroes Perform Their Own Music," *Musical America*, Mar. 21, 1914, 37.

10. The Columbia file date of Thursday, March 12, is not a recording date per se, but rather the date the wax master was shipped to the factory for processing, which is usually the same. It is possible that the session was held a day or two earlier, although it is unlikely that the chorus recorded on the day of its Carnegie Hall appearance (March 11).

11. Will Marion Cook, "Will Marion Cook on Negro Music," *New York Age*, Sept. 21, 1918.

12. Advertisement, *New York Age*, Feb. 1, 1919.

13. *New York Age*, Mar. 22, 1919.

14. Ellington, *Music Is My Mistress,* 97.

15. Sampson, *Blacks in Blackface,* 271.

16. Will Marion Cook, "Spirituals and Jazz" (letter to the editor), *New York Times,* Dec. 26, 1926.

Chapter 22: Dan Kildare and Joan Sawyer's Persian Garden Orchestra

An earlier version of this chapter, by Howard Rye and Tim Brooks, appeared in Laurie Wright, ed., *Storyville 1996–97,* a collection of articles on early jazz recordings. Rye, who is one of the world's leading writers on early jazz and blues, did the research on Kildare's years in England, and I am most grateful to be able to make use of his meticulous research here.

1. Last Will and Testament of Dan Kildare, dated June 19, 1920, which gives his name as "(Daniel) Nathaniel Augustus Kildare," suggesting that the "Daniel" was adopted after his birth; U.S. Passport Applications nos. 53457 and 53458, filed Mar. 23, 1915; Jeffrey P. Green, "The Negro Renaissance and England," in *Black Music in the Harlem Rensaissance,* ed. Floyd, 155.

2. New York State Census, 1915 (which states that Kildare had been in the United States for twenty years); *Freeman,* July 28 and Nov. 3, 1900, and Aug. 17, 1901; Fletcher, *One Hundred Years of the Negro in Show Business,* 67, 264.

3. Charters and Kunstadt, *Jazz,* 26, 29.

4. Ibid., 39.

5. "The Clef Club a Royal Host," *New York Age,* Feb. 19, 1914.

6. Lucien H. White, "Clef Club Triumph," *New York Age,* June 11, 1914. Following Europe's departure the *Age* seemed partial to the Clef Club, giving it considerably more coverage than it gave the Tempo Club. It was never derogatory toward Europe's new organization, however.

7. *New York Age,* Oct. 29, 1914.

8. Much of the following account is based on clippings in the Joan Sawyer file at the Theater Collection of the New York Public Library. Birth information is from the Toronto (Canada) marriage register, Oct. 27, 1902. Her parents are listed there as Frank Morrison and Ida Roberts Morrison, and her age is given as twenty-two. Archives of Toronto, York County, Div. of Toronto, MS-932, Reel 106, no. 003112.

9. Toronto marriage register, 1902; Sawyer, twenty-three, was born in St. Louis and described as a "traveler."

10. *Variety,* Feb. 20, 1914; *New York Age,* Feb. 26, 1914; *Brooklyn Eagle,* Apr. 21, 1914; *Philadelphia Telegraph,* May 20, 1914; *Philadelphia Telegram,* May 20, 1914; *Boston Globe,* May 26, 1914; *Variety,* June 26, 1914; *New York Review,* Oct. 3 and 10, 1914 (the last two clippings state that Kildare had played for her during the previous season and was returning for the fall season).

11. *New York Dramatic Mirror,* July 1, 1914; *Variety,* May 29, 1914; *Boston Globe,* May 26, 1914.

12. *Talking Machine World,* June 15, 1914, 32, 39; Report to Gramophone Co. Music Committee, July 1915, which, however, was off slightly as to the year, stating that Kildare had recorded in the United States in 1913 (information provided by Brian Rust).

13. Lester A. Walton, "A Delicate Situation," *New York Age,* Nov. 12, 1914.

14. *New York Age,* Dec. 3, 1914.

15. *New York Age,* Feb. 8 and June 7, 1917.

16. *Philadelphia Public Ledger,* Mar. 2, 1915; *Rochester Union and Advertiser,* Mar. 9, 1915.

17. *New York Age,* Feb. 4 and Mar. 11, 1915.

18. This personnel is from the *Megantic* passenger list, with ages from passport documents. The March 25, 1915, issue of the *New York Age* reported that the group (minus

Ricks) sailed the preceding Tuesday (March 23); however, *Lloyd's List* for March 29 confirms an actual departure date of March 27. There are some minor discrepancies in the passenger list. Mitchell's first name is given as George, but the person referred to is almost certainly Louis. Ricks's first name is given by Charters and Kunstadt in *Jazz* as George but appears on departure and arrival documents as John.

19. "Ciro's," *Town Topics,* Mar. 27, 1915, 3; "Our Belgian Fund, Ciro's Restaurant Club," *Daily Telegraph,* Apr. 19, 1915, 11; "Ciro's in London," *Era* (London), Apr. 21, 1915, 17; "A Gourmet's Club," *Times* (London), Dec. 15, 1916, 5; "Round and About," *Town Topics,* Apr. 24, 1915, 2; unknown "English columnist," quoted by Marvel Cooke in *Amsterdam* (New York) *News,* Mar. 2, 1940, 15.

20. "The Letters of Eve," *Tatler,* no. 796 (Sept. 27, 1916): 388.

21. Ibid., no. 727 (June 2, 1915): 252.

22. *Times,* July 26, 1916, 3; *Daily Telegraph,* July 26, 1916, 11; *Tatler,* no. 788 (Aug. 2, 1916): 134–35, the latter with a photo spread.

23. "Clef Club Notes," *New York Age,* Apr. 29, 1915; Lester A. Walton, "Bojangles Wins Harlem," *New York Age,* May 6, 1915.

24. *New York Age,* Sept. 16, 1915, 1. The death certificate states that he died on September 11 of "bullet wound in brain, self-inflicted with a magazine pistol. Accidental."

25. Seth Jones had returned to the United States in May 1916, along with Meyers and Ricks. The date of his return to Britain has not yet been traced.

26. *Sound Wave* 10, no. 10 (Oct. 1916): 374.

27. Review of Columbia 662, *Sound Wave* 11, no. 6 (June 1917): 204; review of Columbia 669, *Talking Machine News* 9, no. 265 (July 1917): 268.

28. Howard Rye and Tim Brooks, "Visiting Firemen 16: Dan Kildare," in *Storyville 1996–97,* ed. Wright, 42.

29. Prosecution of Ciro's Club—Supplying liquor after Magistrate's order (MEPO3, MEPO3/251), Clubs file, Correspondence and Papers, Special Series, 1830–1974, Office of the Commissioner, Metropolitan Police, London. Subsequent quotations from Metropolitan Police filing are also from this file. These documents were unearthed by Howard Rye during his extensive research.

30. "A Raid at Ciro's," *Times,* Nov. 10, 1916, 4; "The Letters of Eve," *Tatler,* no. 802 (Nov. 8, 1916): 164.

31. "Ciro's Struck Off the Register," *Times,* Dec. 21, 1916, 4; *Times,* Jan. 19, 1917, 29.

32. "The Letters of Eve," *Tatler,* no. 816 (Feb. 14, 1917): 194.

33. *Hansard,* Feb. 27, 1917, col. 1836; Mar. 5, 1917, col. 21; Mar. 12, 1917, col. 714; Ciro's Club program (undated), Metropolitan Police File.

34. "Ciro's Out of Bounds," *Times,* Mar. 14, 1917, 7; "The Letters of Eve," *Tatler,* no. 821 (Mar. 21, 1917): 355; "The New Ciro's," *Times,* May 24, 1917, 3.

35. However a picture in a 1956 article shows seven men (Len Gutteridge, "The First Man to Bring Jazz to Britain," *Melody Maker,* July 14, 1956, 6, reprinted in McCarthy, *The Dance Band Era,* 12). The personnel of the Seven Spades is anything but certain. See Rye and Brooks, "Visiting Firemen," 46, for details.

36. *Encore,* Nov. 29, 1917, 6; "The Shoreditch Empire," *Stage,* Nov. 29, 1917, 18.

37. "Shoots Self and Women," *Variety,* July 2, 1920.

38. "Genuine Jazz on Columbia," *Sound Wave* 13, no. 8 (Aug. 1919): 358; Brian Rust, letter to the author, July 1993.

39. *Dancing Times,* Oct. 1919, 31; "Small Talk," *Sketch,* Oct. 1, 1919, 8; "Letters of Eve," *Tatler,* no. 955 (Oct. 15, 1919): 66.

40. "A Night at Ciro's," *Sketch,* Nov. 26, 1919; "New Stories of the Triple Crime," *Evening Standard,* June 22, 1920, 6; "Triple Tragedy of Jealousy," *The People,* June 27, 1920, 4; *Chicago Defender,* Mar. 6, 1920.

41. "Shoots Self and Women"; Last Will and Testament of Mary Rose Frances Kildare, Feb. 21, 1919.

42. Bertin Depestre Salnave, "The Bertin Depestre Salnave Story, as told to Bertrand Demeusy," translated from the French by Howard Rye, *Storyville,* no. 78 (Aug.–Sept. 1978): 211.

43. This account was assembled from a number of sources, including "Shooting Affray in London," *Times,* June 22, 1920, 13; "Fourfold Crime by Jazz Musician," *Daily Express,* June 22, 1920, 1; "Two Women Shot Dead," *Daily Mail,* June 22, 1920, 7; "Double Murder and Felo De Se," *Morning Advertiser,* June 24, 1920, 6; "Three Shot Dead," *News of the World,* June 27, 1920, 5; coroner's inquest (Certified Copy of an Entry of Death, no. 202, June 21, 1920, Registration District: St. Marylebone, Death in the Sub-District of All Souls in the County of London), as reported in Rye and Brooks, "Visiting Firemen."

44. Last Will and Testament of Dan Kildare.

45. "Dan Kildare Kills Three and Commits Suicide," *New York Age,* June 26, 1920, 1; "Shoots Self and Women"; *Billboard,* July 3, 1920, 92.

46. "Three Shot Dead."

47. "Miss Gilder Helps Campaign of Antis," *New York Times,* Aug. 24, 1915.

Chapter 23: The Tuskegee Institute Singers

1. From the Tuskegee University Choir Web site, Sept. 24, 2000, <http://www.tuskegee.edu/Global/category.asp?C=36046>.

2. Harlan, ed., *Booker T. Washington Papers,* 5:592, quoted in Snyder, "Harry T. Burleigh," 292–93.

3. Turner, *Dictionary of Afro-American Performers,* 373; Doug Seroff, letter to the author, Jan. 5, 1993.

4. There is some uncertainty about the location. Dixon, Godrich, and Rye, *Blues and Gospel Records, 1890–1943,* 936, gives the location as New York. The original recording ledger sheets at Victor specify no location, and that usually means the recordings were made at Victor's Camden headquarters.

5. New Victor Records (supplement), Jan. 1915, 10. The substance of this little essay was reprinted in the general catalog each year from 1918 until 1925.

6. New Victor Records (supplement), Feb. 1915, 7.

7. Notes to *Tuskegee Institute Singers/Quartet,* Document DOCD-5549 (CD); Dixon, Godrich, and Rye, *Blues and Gospel Records, 1890–1943.*

8. Turner, *Dictionary of Afro-American Performers,* 373.

9. New Victor Records supplement, Apr. 1917, 21.

10. Turner, *Dictionary of Afro-American Performers,* 373.

11. Lovell, *Black Song,* 418.

12. Southern, *Biographical Dictionary of Afro-American and African Musicians,* 98–99.

13. Turner, *Dictionary of Afro-American Performers,* 373; Gart, *ARLD;* Seroff letter; *Schwann* catalog, Sept. 1955 (the LP was Westminster 18080, later renumbered 9633).

Chapter 24: The Right Quintette

1. *Freeman,* Dec. 25, 1897. Lightfoot gave his age to New York and federal census-takers in 1915, 1920, and 1925 as "40," meaning he was born in 1875, 1880, or 1885, depending on which you believe. Given that census entries are self-reported and notoriously unreliable and that the *Freeman* article is earlier (when he would be less likely to be fudging) and cites an exact year, I assume that it is correct. No birth or death certificate has been located.

2. *New York Clipper,* July 13, 1895; *Freeman,* Nov. 6, 1897. Many references to Lightfoot's tenure with the Canadian Jubilee Singers are found in the *New York Clipper* and *Freeman* during the 1890s. See also Sampson, *The Ghost Walks,* 135.

3. *Freeman,* Sept. 16, 1899; Sampson, *The Ghost Walks,* 189.

4. Date and location of birth from obituary, *New York Times,* Jan. 2, 1945, and death certificate (Death Certificate no. 168, Jan. 1, 1945, New York City, Borough of Manhattan). Fletcher, *One Hundred Years of the Negro in Show Business,* 236, lists Tisdale as one of the "great performers" who appeared in the Williams and Walker casts, but does not specify when. This association has not been confirmed.

5. *Evening Post* (Wellington, New Zealand), Jan. 21, 1905, quoted in Sampson, *The Ghost Walks,* 335.

6. *New York Age,* Jan. 14, 1909.

7. *New York Age,* July 10, Sept. 5, and Nov. 7, 1912, and Jan. 26, 1913.

8. *New York Age,* Feb. 15 and Mar. 28, 1914.

9. The recording files are somewhat confused on the date of this session, indicating in one place that the masters were recorded on December 28 and in another that they were shipped to the factory for processing on December 24. I have assumed that the earlier date is correct.

10. Columbia Records supplement, Aug. 1916, 15.

11. *New York Age,* Nov. 15 and 29, 1917.

12. *New York Age,* Apr. 27, 1918.

13. *New York Age,* June 1, Nov. 2, and Nov. 16, 1918, and Oct. 11, 1919.

14. Duberman, *Paul Robeson;* Sampson, *Blacks in Blackface,* 223–25.

15. The 1917 private recording (matrix 62036) was made on December 8; Tisdale's address is given as 2283 7th Avenue. The 1919 recordings (matrices 91050 and 91051) were made on January 11, with his address shown as 38 West 131st Street. A second take of the first title was made on April 12, 1919, so Tisdale was obviously trying to get it right.

16. "Tisdale Trio Tells Secret," unidentified newspaper clipping, c. 1940.

Chapter 25: Wilbur C. Sweatman

1. Len Kunstadt and Bob Colton, "Daddy of the Clarinet: Wilbur Sweatman," *Record Research* no. 4 (Sept.–Oct. 1959): 3; *Freeman,* May 10, 1902. For a short biography of Lowery see Southern, *Biographical Dictionary of Afro-American and African Musicians,* 250.

2. Fletcher, *One Hundred Years of the Negro in Show Business,* 149.

3. Sampson, *The Ghost Walks,* 277.

4. Simpson Johnson, "Wilbur C. Sweatman," *Freeman,* Jan. 29, 1910, 5. The article was accompanied by a picture of Sweatman holding a (single) clarinet.

5. *Freeman,* Oct. 8, 1910, 5.

6. *Chicago Defender,* Feb. 5, 1927, 6.

7. Southern, *Biographical Dictionary of Afro-American and African Musicians,* 365; Kenney, *Chicago Jazz,* 8; Fletcher, *One Hundred Years of the Negro in Show Business,* 151.

8. Fletcher spells the agent's name "Bebaur." An advertisement for Sweatman's act in the *New York Star,* March 1, 1913, says "Director, Charles Beerbower, Management, Jo Paige Smith."

9. "Acts of the Week at the Crown Garden, Indianapolis—Wilbur C. Sweatman—Musical," *Freeman,* Sept. 30, 1911, 5.

10. Victor Records release, June 1913, 4.

11. Kunstadt and Colton, "Daddy of the Clarinet"; Charters and Kunstadt, *Jazz,* 235. Neither of these gives the specific years when Sweatman and Morton lived under the same roof.

12. Smith, *Bert Williams,* 168.

13. Bastin, *Never Sell a Copyright,* 4.

14. The exact date the ODJB recording was placed on sale is unclear. The print code on the Victor announcement flyer ("3-7-17") has been interpreted by some as a release date, but this merely establishes when the flyer was printed. The records were probably shipped to stores throughout March.

15. Brunn, *The Story of the Original Dixieland Jazz Band,* 107. Some modern researchers question this story, which seems to have originated with ODJB leader Nick LaRocca, a not-always-reliable source. Lawrence Gushee, correspondence with author, February 2001.

16. Takes four and seven of "Hello Hello" (A2818) have been compared and are virtually identical.

17. Columbia Records supplement, July 1918, 4.

18. Ibid., Oct. 1918, 8.

19. Ibid., Nov. 1918, 8.

20. Charters and Kunstadt, *Jazz,* 78; Ivan Deputier, notes to *Jazz Tribune no. 70: The Complete Original Dixieland Jazz Band,* Black and White/RCA ND 90026 (French CD).

21. Bastin, *Never Sell a Copyright,* 4.

22. Brooks, ed., *Little Wonder Records,* 50; Mark Berresford, correspondence with author, Feb. 9, 1995.

23. Charters and Kunstadt, *Jazz,* 122.

24. There are no sales figures surviving for individual Victor releases; however, based on the number of copies found today, the ODJB's "Margie" is a good candidate for their all-time bestseller.

25. Ellington, *Music Is My Mistress,* 36.

26. Allen, *Hendersonia,* 62–63, 251; Fletcher, *One Hundred Years of the Negro in Show Business,* 153.

27. *Billboard,* Nov. 15, 1924.

28. Simon, *Simon Says,* 447.

29. American Society of Composers, Authors, and Publishers, *ASCAP Program Listings, 1937.* Note that this total may count each station separately when a tune is performed on a network.

30. This was confirmed aurally and by the recording files.

31. Southern, *Biographical Dictionary of Afro-American and African Musicians,* 365; <http://www.redhotjazz.com>; Gracyk, *Encyclopedia of Popular American Recording Pioneers,* 356.

32. Feather, *The Encyclopedia of Jazz,* 434–35.

33. McCarthy, *The Dance Band Era,* 10.

34. Kinkle, *The Complete Encyclopedia of Popular Music and Jazz, 1900–1950,* 1830.

35. Max Harrison, Charles Fox, and Eric Thacker, *The Essential Jazz Records, Volume 1: Ragtime to Swing* (Westport, Conn.: Greenwood Press, 1984). I have not been able to locate any microgroove reissues of Sweatman's recordings.

36. Brunn, *The Story of the Original Dixieland Jazz Band.*

37. Fletcher, *One Hundred Years of the Negro in Show Business,* 152.

38. Mark Berresford, notes to *Ragtime to Jazz 1, 1912–1919,* Timeless CBC 1-035 (CD); Lowe, *That Devilin' Tune,* 48; Goddard, *Jazz Away from Home,* 26–27.

Chapter 26: Opal D. Cooper

1. Cooper's personal and professional papers are in the Manuscript Division (Sc MG 599), Schomburg Center for Research in Black Culture, New York City (hereafter Cooper Papers). Biographical information is drawn from that source and others obtained by the author, including Cooper's 1919 army discharge papers, a passport application filed in Paris, France, on March 8, 1921, a Social Security application dated 1940, and the New York City death index. Some sources give his place of birth as the nonexistent "Cromwell, Ohio," but that appears to be a misreading of the fact that Cromwell, Kentucky, is located in that state's Ohio County.

2. Passport application, 1921.

3. *Freeman,* Dec. 31, 1910, and Sept. 30, 1911, 1. The first item refers to a "Mr. Opal Cool,"

but I have assumed that it is the same person (misspellings were quite common in the press of the day).

4. "Merry Melody Makers Create Rage with Ragtime at Rector's," *Dancing World,* Sept. 1920, quoted in Edward S. Walker, "A New Look at the S.S.O.," *Storyville,* no. 51 (Feb.–Mar. 1974): 96.

5. Sampson, *Blacks in Blackface,* 191.

6. Riis, *Just before Jazz,* 182–83, contains the best description of the show.

7. Sampson, *Blacks in Blackface,* 188–90.

8. *New York Age,* Oct. 19, 1916.

9. *New York Age,* Dec. 7, 1916.

10. Lester A. Walton, "Negro Actors Make Debut in Drama at Garden Theatre; Given Most Cordial Welcome," *New York Age,* Apr. 12, 1917, 1.

11. Heywood Broun, "Negro Players Score Success in Interesting Bill of Short Plays," *New York Tribune,* Mar. 14, 1917; Johnson, *Black Manhattan,* 175.

12. This is suggested by the fact that their initial Pathé recordings have adjacent matrix numbers—66295 for Sissle and 66296 for Cooper.

13. Eddie Morton, Victor 17108 (1912); Gus Van, Columbia A2629 (1918); *Storyville,* no. 158 (June 1994): 48–49 reprints a variation of the lyrics.

14. "Musical Career of Opal Cooper, as Told to Bertrand Demeusy," *Record Research,* no. 90 (May 1968): 4 (hereafter Demeusy interview). This is believed to be the only published interview with Cooper. It is not specified when or where the interview took place, but a copy of the original typescript, obtained by this author, is dated Aug. 16, 1966, which may be the date of the interview. There are some differences between the typescript and the article published in *Record Research,* and portions of both are quoted here.

15. This and the following military information is drawn from Cooper's enlistment record, discharge papers, and other military files, as provided to the author by the U.S. Department of Veterans Affairs, Hartford, Conn., Regional Office, Aug. 8, 1994.

16. *New York Age,* Dec. 21, 1918.

17. *New York Age,* Mar. 8, 1919; memorandum from Major Allen Potts, Dec. 15, 1918, Cooper Papers.

18. Demeusy interview. Weeks's name is spelled "Week" in the interview, but Heier and Lotz, eds., *The Banjo on Record,* and other sources confirm that it should have an *s.* Heier and Lotz also give a short biography of the African American bandleader, who recorded mandolin solos as early as 1900 in England.

19. Interview with Elliot Carpenter in Los Angeles, June 1976, reprinted in Goddard, *Jazz Away from Home,* 19–20.

20. Ibid., 299.

21. Mark Berresford, "From New York to London—Eddie Gross Bart's Story," *Storyville,* no. 102 (Aug.–Sept. 1982): 213.

22. Passport application, 1921, with extension issued at Alexandria, Egypt, Apr. 4, 1922; Len Kunstadt, "Panorama of Jazz Events," *Record Research,* no. 15 (Oct.–Nov. 1957): 11 (item dated July 9, 1921); *Record Research,* no. 18 (July–Aug. 1958): 24 (dated 1922). Though unsourced, these citations are in fact from the *Chicago Defender.*

23. Demeusy interview.

24. *Chicago Defender,* Aug. 2, 1924, 6, quoted in "Can't We Talk It Over?" *Storyville,* no. 78 (Aug.–Sept. 1978): 205.

25. Demeusy interview.

26. Richard C. Lynch, "Mabel Mercer, Hutch and Elisabeth Welch," *Kastlemusick Monthly Bulletin* (Aug. 1980): 12.

27. Vocalion (UK) supplement, Mar. 1927.

28. Vocalion (UK) supplement, Apr. 1927; W. S. H., "New Records for the Gramophone," *Sheffield Independent,* Feb. 25, 1927, Cooper Papers.

29. *Amsterdam* (New York) *News,* Sept. 24, 1930, 8, quoted in Allen, *Hendersonia,* 262. Sammy Richardson also appeared.

30. Nancy Cunard, "Musical and Theatrical Negro Stars," in *Negro,* ed. Cunard, 189.

31. Demeusy interview. Cooper married Lee at some point prior to Oct. 1931, when he registered with the French authorities in Paris (Cooper Papers); they were still married in 1940, after he returned to America.

32. Demeusy interview.

33. Opal Cooper, application for social security number, Mar. 11, 1940, Cooper Papers.

34. Demeusy interview.

35. Military records and New York City death index. Due to rigid New York City regulations prohibiting the release of death certificates to anyone but immediate family for forty-five years, cause of death and information on relations at death are not accessible at this time.

Chapter 27: Noble Sissle and Eubie Blake

1. Recent research based on census and Social Security records indicates that contrary to everything he told the public in later years, Blake's actual date of birth may have been Feb. 7, 1887. More research needs to be done on this. See Peter Hanley, "Eubie Blake: Everybody's Just Wild about Eubie," published in 2003 on the Web site <http://www.doctorjazz.freeserve.co.uk>.

2. Unless noted otherwise, biographical details of Sissle's and Blake's early lives are from Kimball and Bolcom, *Reminiscing with Sissle and Blake,* and Rose, *Eubie Blake.*

3. Blake later claimed that he had written the piece as a teenager around 1899 and that it was given the name "Sounds of Africa" by Will Marion Cook. It was later retitled "Charleston Rag." See Rose, *Eubie Blake,* 42, 172.

4. News item dated Aug. 15, 1908, from an unidentified source, quoted in Sampson, *The Ghost Walks,* 436. The item lists Sissle as tenor, with W. H. Talbert, tenor and pianist, Chas. W. Boyd, baritone and reader, and E. S. Reese, bass and manager. The quartet was under the management of the Chicago Lyceum Bureau.

5. Rose, *Eubie Blake,* 55. The song was published by the Maryland Music Publishing Company, but the sheet music is quite rare as the song died after Sophie Tucker left town. See David Jasen, "Eubie at One Hundred," *Storyville,* no. 105 (Feb.–Mar. 1983): 86.

6. "Good Night, Angeline," by Noble Sissle, James Reese Europe, and Eubie Blake, as sung by Sissle on Pathé 20226.

7. Pathé's musicians were not unfamiliar with syncopated music; the Pathé Dance Orchestra made early recordings of rags and blues in 1915–16.

8. Kimball and Bolcom, *Reminiscing with Sissle and Blake,* 248.

9. Rose, *Eubie Blake,* 59.

10. Pathé supplement, 1918, quoted in Kimball and Bolcom, *Reminiscing with Sissle and Blake,* 248.

11. Sissle, "Memoirs of Lieutenant 'Jim' Europe," 76–77.

12. Ibid, 79–83.

13. Rose, *Eubie Blake,* 61.

14. The best "Rollography" is by the piano roll expert Mike Montgomery and was published in Rose, *Eubie Blake,* 189–95.

15. "Little David Play on Your Harp" by Lieut. Noble Sissle with Lieut. Jim Europe's Singing Serenaders, Pathé 22084.

16. "Sister Susie's Sewing Shirts for Soldiers" by Al Jolson, Columbia A-1671.

17. Europe's May 1919 session, at which Sissle sang vocals, covered master numbers 67666–71; the master number for "Dan" is 67675.

18. Rose, *Eubie Blake,* 104.

19. In a letter to his wife Avis, dated Sept. 29, 1920, Blake writes of accompanying Sissle on an unidentified Pathé record. Kimball and Bolcom, *Reminiscing with Sissle and Blake,* 82.

20. David A. Jasen, notes to *Sissle and Blake: Early Rare Recordings,* vol. 1, Eubie Blake Music EBM-4. Jasen dates the session as taking place in September 1920.

21. Rose, *Eubie Blake,* 70. Blake related a similar story in Kimball and Bolcom, *Reminiscing with Sissle and Blake,* 80.

22. Verbatim response from a well-known jazz critic, who shall remain nameless, at the annual conference of the Association for Recorded Sound Collections, Kansas City, Missouri, May 1996. The records referred to are rare West Coast releases by the legendary jazzman Edward "Kid" Ory on the tiny Sunshine and Nordskog labels in 1922.

23. Advertisement in *Phonograph and Talking Machine Weekly,* Mar. 16, 1921.

24. "Edwin Dale" was apparently a pseudonym. According to Sutton, *Guide to Pseudonyms on American Records,* 34, the singer is actually the Metropolitan Opera tenor Charles Hackett. However, the classical music expert Lawrence Holdridge identifies the voice as that of the concert tenor Tandy Mackenzie, an identification that is also suggested by the Columbia files.

25. Dixon, Godrich, and Rye, *Blues and Gospel Records, 1890–1943,* 412–13.

26. Rose, *Eubie Blake,* 82.

27. Woll, *Dictionary of the Black Theatre,* 141.

28. Kimball and Bolcom, *Reminiscing with Sissle and Blake,* 138. Some film historians believe that Sissle and Blake may have made a second DeForest film, but this has not been traced.

29. "The Library of Congress and Smithsonian Video Present The African-American Cinema II: *The Scar of Shame* (1926), with the early sound short *Sissle and Blake* (1923)," Library of Congress Video Collection, vol. 5, eighty-minute VHS (Washington, D.C., 1993).

30. *Chicago Herald and Examiner,* Mar. 31, 1924, quoted in Kimball and Bolcom, *Reminiscing with Sissle and Blake,* 180.

31. Kimball and Bolcom, *Reminiscing with Sissle and Blake,* 181.

32. A detailed account of Sissle and Blake's 1925–26 tour, and of Noble Sissle's British appearances from 1927 to 1930, is in Howard Rye, "Visiting Firemen No. 7: Eubie Blake and Noble Sissle," *Storyville,* no. 105 (Feb.–Mar. 1983): 88–95.

33. Kimball and Bolcom, *Reminiscing with Sissle and Blake,* 203, which claims Porter met Sissle in 1928 and helped him recruit the clarinetist Sidney Bechet for the band in that year. However Bechet does not appear to have recorded with Sissle until 1931. *New York Age,* Sept. 15, 1928.

34. *Stage,* Dec. 13 and 20, 1928.

35. "Miranda" was unrelated to Sissle's earlier song "Mirandy," which he had written with Blake and Europe, and owed more to Williams and Walker's cheery 1901 show tune "Good Morning, Carrie." "Carrie" opens with "Good mornin' Carrie, how'ya do this mornin'?"; "Mirandy's" similarly upbeat chorus begins "Good evenin' Miranda, how'ya feelin' this evenin'?"

36. *New York Times,* Feb. 16, 1931, 16; Feather, *The Encyclopedia of Jazz,* 131; Rye, "Visiting Firemen No. 7," 91. Bechet had been heard on record as early as 1923, accompanying the blues singer Rosetta Crawford.

37. See "The Chronological Sidney Bechet, 1923–1936" (Classics 583).

38. Rose, *Eubie Blake,* 103.

39. Columbia 2288-D.

40. At least not in Feather, *The Encyclopedia of Jazz,* or in Kinkle, *The Complete Encyclopedia of Popular Music and Jazz, 1900–1950,* which list most top rank artists.

41. Review, *New York Times,* Sept. 17, 1931; Sampson, *Blacks in Blackface,* 309–10.

42. Woll, *Black Musical Theatre,* 94, 95, 233.

43. Bordman, *American Musical Theatre,* 481.

44. Meeker, *Jazz in the Movies,* entry no. 1991.

45. Blake had included it in a medley in the 1920s.

46. This layout appears on original copies of Decca 7429 and 3521, author's collection.

47. Meeker, *Jazz in the Movies,* see under those titles.

48. Simon, *The Big Bands,* 500.

49. Kimball and Bolcom, *Reminiscing with Sissle and Blake,* 225; Frank Kelly, "Where Are They Now?" *Record Research,* no. 91 (July 1968): 2; Handy, *Father of the Blues,* 249–51.

50. Rose, *Eubie Blake,* 122.

51. Kimball and Bolcom, *Reminiscing with Sissle and Blake,* 232.

52. Miles Jefferson in *Phylon,* quoted in Woll, *Dictionary of the Black Theatre,* 150.

53. Rudi Blesh, *Combo USA* (Philadelphia: Chilton, 1971), quoted in Kimball and Bolcom, *Reminiscing with Sissle and Blake,* 252.

54. Southern, *Biographical Dictionary of Afro-American and African Musicians,* 37 (the 1974 film was originally made for television, but then shown in theaters instead); Woll, *Dictionary of the Black Theatre,* 35–36: Maltin, *Leonard Maltin's Movie and Video Guide,* 1223.

55. Woll, *Dictionary of the Black Theatre,* 59–60.

56. Kaplan, ed., *The Complete Book of Major U.S. Show Business Awards,* 385, 398; Jasen, "Eubie at One Hundred," 87–88.

Chapter 28: Ford T. Dabney

1. A short biography of Wendell Dabney can be found in Southern, *Biographical Dictionary of Afro-American and African Musicians,* 92. See also Lovell, *Black Song,* 178.

2. *Freeman,* May 9, 1903.

3. Rotberg, *Haiti,* 99. A vivid portrait of the violent reign of Nord Alexis can be found in Heinl and Heinl, *Written in Blood,* chap. 10, "Plots and Revolutions." After a period of extreme violence Haiti was occupied in 1915 by U.S. Marines, who remained in control until 1934.

4. *Trow's New York City Directory* for 1908 gives his address as 102 West 53rd Street. The Marshall was at 127–29 West 53rd. Fletcher, *One Hundred Years of the Negro in Show Business,* 251.

5. Southern, *Biographical Dictionary of Afro-American and African Musicians,* 91. King and Gee evidently continued the act for a number of years after their association with Dabney; see review in *Freeman,* Aug. 1, 1914, 6.

6. An analysis of "Anoma" by the ragtime expert Bill Edwards appeared on the Web site <http://www.perfessorbill.com>, together with Edwards's performance of the piece.

7. Southern, *Biographical Dictionary of Afro-American and African Musicians,* 92.

8. "Porto Rico" is credited to Dabney in American Society of Composers, Authors, and Publishers, *ASCAP Biographical Dictionary,* which ought to be authoritative, and it was also credited to him in a 1910 review of the *Smart Set* (*Freeman,* Sept. 17, 1910). However, Riis, *Just before Jazz,* 144, reproduces the music and credits it to Cecil Mack and J. T. Brymn.

9. Review of *The Smart Set* in Washington in *Freeman,* Sept. 17, 1910; Peterson, *A Century of Musicals in Black and White,* 171–72; Woll, *Dictionary of the Black Theatre,* 77–78; Thomas L. Morgan, "Cecil Mack (R. C. McPherson)," <http://www.jass.com>; Don Rouse, "Musicians from D.C.—Ford Dabney," *Tailgate Ramblings,* Sept. 1987, 9.

10. The original sheet music appears in David Jasen, ed., *Thirty-five Song Hits by Great Black Songwriters* (Mineola, N.Y.: Dover, 1998).

11. *Freeman,* June 10, Aug. 12, Oct. 21, and Dec. 2, 1911; *New York Age,* Oct. 12, 1911, and Mar. 21, 1912.

12. Irene Castle McLaughlin, "Jim Europe, a Reminiscence," *Opportunity,* Mar. 1930, 91.

13. *New York Age,* Mar. 19 and Apr. 16, 1914; Badger, *A Life in Ragtime,* 102.

14. *New York Age,* Feb. 26, 1914.

15. The best history of the *Midnight Frolic* that I have located is in Ziegfeld and Ziegfeld, *The Ziegfeld Touch,* 62–71. I have also consulted reviews of and advertisements for the *Frolic* appearing in the *New York Times* from 1914 to 1920.

16. *New York Age,* Nov. 8, 1917, 6.

17. Those listed were Messrs. Ross, Gibson, Parquette, Lee, Scott, Smith, and Dennis Johnson. *Freeman,* July 18, 1914, 5, and Aug. 22, 1914, 4; *New York Age,* Aug. 13, 1914.

18. Charters and Kunstadt, *Jazz,* 57.

19. *New York Age,* Dec. 21, 1916.

20. "Georgia Grind" was recorded by Prince's Band on Columbia, the Pathé Dance Orchestra on Pathé, and "Signor Grinderino" (street organ) on Victor, all in 1915.

21. "RC and LK" (Robert Colton and Leonard Kunstadt), "Ford Dabney Discography," *Record Research,* no. 2 (Apr. 1955): 7–8.

22. *The New Aeolian-Vocalion Records* (New York: Aeolian Company, 1918), 3.

23. Wadsworth and Arden's All Star Trio (piano, xylophone, and saxophone) recorded "Just Blue" for Victor, Columbia, Edison, and Okeh around the same time.

24. Berresford, notes to *Ragtime to Jazz 1.*

25. Ziegfeld and Ziegfeld, *The Ziegfeld Touch,* 62, 289. See also Bruce Vermazen, "Art Hickman and His Orchestra," in Gracyk, *The Encyclopedia of Popular American Recording Pioneers, 1895–1925,* 168–70.

26. Badger, *A Life in Ragtime,* 218.

27. Ellington, *Music Is My Mistress.*

28. Rust, *Jazz Records, 1897–1942,* artist index.

29. Gardner, *Popular Songs of the Twentieth Century,* 195. "Shine" is also mentioned in a bestsellers' roundup in *Variety,* July 16, 1924, 30.

30. *New York Evening World,* July 13, 1927; *New York Times,* July 13, 1927, sec. 20, p. 1; *Variety,* Jan. 18, 1928, 50. See also entries in Woll, *Dictionary of the Black Theatre,* 133; Peterson, *A Century of Musicals in Black and White,* 287; and Bordman, *American Musical Theatre,* 426.

31. John Graziano, "Black Musical Theater and the Harlem Renaissance Movement," in *Black Music in the Harlem Renaissance,* ed. Floyd, 101.

32. American Society of Composers, Authors, and Publishers, *ASCAP Program Listings,* 1935 and 1937. Note that these totals may count each station separately when a tune is performed on a network.

33. *New York Times,* June 23, 1958; *Variety,* June 25, 1958; Colton and Kunstadt, "Ford Dabney Discography," 7–8.

34. Alain Locke, *The Negro and His Music* (1936), quoted in Samuel Floyd Jr., "Music in the Harlem Renaissance: An Overview," in *Black Music in the Harlem Renaissance,* ed. Floyd, 6–7.

Chapter 29: W. C. Handy

1. An interesting analysis by Hurwitt in "W. C. Handy as Music Publisher," 432–33, suggests that the most lyrical portions of the manuscript may not be by Handy, but rather were ghostwritten for him by Arna Bontemps.

2. Handy, *Father of the Blues,* 121.

3. Unidentified report of performance in Belvidere, Ill., Sept. 6, 1896, quoted in Sampson, *The Ghost Walks,* 110.

4. Unidentified report of performance in Joliet, Ill., Aug. 22, 1897, quoted in Sampson, *The Ghost Walks,* 133.

5. *Freeman,* Feb. 4, 1898 (with a picture of the young Handy), June 18, 1898; unidentified report dated Aug. 22, 1898, in Sampson, *The Ghost Walks,* 156.

6. Handy, *Father of the Blues,* 173.

7. They were, in order, Lucille, Katherine, William C. Jr., Florence (died in infancy), Elizabeth, and Wyer.

8. *Freeman,* Mar. 15, 1902, reprinted in Sampson, *The Ghost Walks,* 246–48. Wright was twenty-two at the time.

9. *Freeman,* Sept. 15, 1900, and May 25, 1901.

10. Handy, *Father of the Blues,* 73–74, 76–77.

11. W. C. Handy, interviewed on "W. C. Handy: Father of the Blues," Audio Archives A-1200 (LP), © 1952. Hurwitt, "W. C. Handy as Music Publisher," 17, suggests that these songs may not have actually been published, or if they were, not widely distributed.

12. Handy, *Father of the Blues,* 93.

13. Hurwitt, "W. C. Handy as Music Publisher," 479.

14. Handy, *Father of the Blues,* 117. "Jogo Blues" was interpolated into a 1917 recording of "Beale Street Blues" by Prince's Band on Columbia A2327.

15. Handy, *Father of the Blues,* 145–47. "Joe Turner Blues" is discussed in detail in Archie Green, *Only a Miner: Studies in Recorded Coal-Mining Songs* (Urbana: University of Illinois Press, 1972).

16. Peterson, *A Century of Musicals in Black and White,* 57.

17. Handy, *Father of the Blues,* 131.

18. Ibid., 173–74.

19. Ibid., 126.

20. The five issued titles published by Pace and Handy were "Fuzzy Wuzzy Rag," "The Snaky Blues," "Ole Miss Rag," "The Hooking Cow Blues," and "Sweet Child" (including "Pallet on the Floor"). In addition, three unissued titles were from the firm: "Preparedness Blues," "Coburn Blues," and "I'm So Glad My Daddy's Coming Home" (in "Those Drafting Blues" medley).

21. A news item in the Nov. 4, 1917, issue of *Billboard,* datelined October 26, noted that Handy and his musicians had already returned to Memphis. However Handy might not have returned with his band, the *Billboard* report could be in error, and the October 31 recording date is approximate. Given the repertoire and Handy's recent dealings with Columbia, I think it is extremely likely that "Handy's Saxophone Band" was in fact led by W. C. (*Billboard* reference supplied by Lawrence Gushee).

22. *New York Times,* Jan. 2, 1918, 8.

23. Handy, *Father of the Blues,* 174.

24. Columbia supplement, Feb. 1918, inside front and back covers.

25. Ibid., 10.

26. Salem Tutt Whitney, "Seen and Heard While Passing," *Freeman,* Sept. 26, 1914; "Have You Ever Heard the Blues?" *Crisis* 11, no. 1 (Nov. 1915): 15–16; "Handy Music Composer," *Freeman,* Dec. 22, 1917; *New York Age,* Dec. 7, 1916.

27. *New York Age,* Apr. 5, 1917.

28. Handy, *Father of the Blues,* 175.

29. Ibid., 193.

30. Witmark and Goldberg, *From Ragtime to Swingtime,* 382; Marks, *They All Sang.*

31. Handy, *Father of the Blues,* 147.

32. Ewen, *American Popular Songs,* 338.

33. W. C. Handy, "I Would Not Play Jazz If I Could," *Down Beat,* Sept. 1938, 5; Handy, *Father of the Blues,* 196.

34. Handy, *Father of the Blues,* 132–35, 198.

35. Charters and Kunstadt, *Jazz,* 74–75; advertisements, *New York Age,* Nov. 19, 1919, and surrounding issues.

36. The "New Releases" section of *Talking Machine World,* Nov. 1919, listed Lyric 4211 and 4212 as by Handy's Memphis Blues Band. The January and February 1920 issues

corrected this to assign the same numbers to the Bal Taberin Jazz Orchestra, as did Lyric's own sales literature (Bulletin no. 16). I have both of the Bal Taberin releases, and they are clearly not by Handy, even though one contains a Handy title ("Yellow Dog Blues"). The Bal Taberin was a nightclub whose orchestra recorded a number of times.

37. Hurwitt, "W. C. Handy as Music Publisher," 298–314, 246–49.

38. Handy, *Father of the Blues*, 148–49.

39. Handy mentioned in an April 1922 letter that he had been suffering from a "partial loss of eye sight" (it may have been more serious than that) for the previous seven months. Hurwitt, "W. C. Handy as Music Publisher," 249.

40. A similar situation occurs with Charles A. Prince, who switched to Paramount after more than twenty years as the principal studio band leader at Columbia. His "Way Down Yonder in New Orleans" on Paramount 20188, recorded in December 1922, is slick and strongly jazz-oriented, quite unlike anything he ever recorded on Columbia. He was known for such a conservative, old-fashioned style that some experts question whether the Paramounts are even by him. It is perhaps not coincidental that Handy also sounds much different on Paramount than on any other label.

41. Handy, *Father of the Blues*, 218.

42. Hurwitt, "W. C. Handy as Music Publisher," 259–60; *Talking Machine World,* Sept. 15, 1922; *Chicago Defender,* Oct. 7, 1922; Walter C. Allen, "The Handy Record Company," *Storyville,* no. 4 (Apr. 1966): 14–15. Allen lists eight issued masters, all with some connection to Handy, and all numbered in an otherwise unknown "100" master series, which may have been recorded for the venture.

43. Handy, *Father of the Blues*, 206.

44. "Aunt Hagar's Blues" by the Virginians, Victor 19021.

45. Allen, *Hendersonia,* 61, 178, 578; Sies, *Encyclopedia of American Radio, 1920–1960,* 248; Sampson, *Blacks in Blackface,* 415.

46. Peterson, *A Century of Musicals in Black and White,* 143, 291.

47. Hurwitt, "W. C. Handy as Music Publisher," 373.

48. "St. Louis Blues" by Rudy Vallee, Victor 22321; Handy, *Father of the Blues,* 222.

49. Handy, *Father of the Blues,* 242–49, 252–53.

50. Lovell, *Black Song,* 583.

51. Rust, *Jazz Records,* 1952; American Society of Composers, Authors, and Publishers, *ASCAP Program Listings,* 1935 and 1937. Note that ASCAP's totals may count each station separately when a tune is performed on a network. The biggest hits of 1937 ("That Old Feeling," "September in the Rain") had performance counts in the 30,000–40,000 range, but many top ten songs were much lower than that.

52. Moses, *American Movie Classics,* 453.

53. Jelly Roll Morton, "I Created Jazz in 1902, Not W. C. Handy," *Down Beat,* Aug. 1938, 3, 31; Jelly Roll Morton, "Jelly Roll Says He Was First to Play Jazz," *Down Beat,* Sept. 1938, 4; Handy, "I Would Not Play Jazz If I Could," 5. The Handy response contains some interesting figures on record sales, quoted to prove his points.

54. Bastin, *Never Sell a Copyright,* 161–62.

55. Handy, *Father of the Blues,* 282.

56. Bastin, *Never Sell a Copyright,* 184.

57. Rose, *Eubie Blake,* 104; Fletcher, *One Hundred Years of the Negro in Show Business,* 223.

58. "W. C. Handy: Father of the Blues," Audio Archives A-1200, first appeared in *The Long Playing Record* (predecessor of the *Schwann* Catalog) in June 1952. By November 1953 the label name had been changed to Heritage, at first retaining the Audio Archives release number. By January 1954, however, the album was being listed as "Blues Revisited" and the number was given as Heritage H-0052. Its last traced listing in Schwann was in the June 1958 issue; however, it was later reissued on specialist labels such as DRG and Mark56.

59. Peterson, *A Century of Musicals in Black and White,* 34, 114, 375.

60. "St. Louis Blues Team History," at the team's Web site, <http://www.stlouisblues.com>.

61. Goldberg, *Tin Pan Alley,* 241.

Chapter 30: Roland Hayes

1. *Freeman,* July 15, 1905. Russell later gained a substantial reputation as a pioneer black theater critic for the *Freeman* and *Chicago Defender.* For a concise biography see Southern, *Biographical Dictionary of Afro-American and African Musicians,* 328.

2. Helm, *Angel Mo',* 80. Although written by Helm, Hayes's biography is in the first person, as if narrated by its subject. "The Preacher and the Bear" by Joe Arzonia was a very popular song, introduced in 1904 and widely recorded.

3. Advertisement in *Nashville Globe,* Jan. 28, 1910, for a performance at the Spruce Street Baptist Church, Feb. 14, 1910, reproduced in Doug Seroff, "Nashville's 'Golden Age' of Jubilee Singing," in *Gospel Arts Day—Nashville,* June 19, 1988 (brochure). Also in the 1910 Apollo Quartet were the second tenor J. C. Olden and the basso N. H. Patton.

4. Helm, *Angel Mo',* 98, 103.

5. Rawn Spearman, "Vocal Concert Music in the Harlem Renaissance," in *Black Music in the Harlem Renaissance,* ed. Floyd, 49; Simpson, *Hard Trials,* 57.

6. Helm, *Angel Mo',* 108–9.

7. *New York Age,* Jan. 28, 1915; Handy, *Father of the Blues,* 213; Badger, *A Life in Ragtime,* 126; Helm, *Angel Mo',* 110; Henry Gideon, "Roland Hayes, Gifted Negro Tenor, 'Got Start' in an Iron Foundry," *Musical America,* undated clipping, c. 1918, 36.

8. Helm, *Angel Mo',* 111–12.

9. Gideon, "Roland Hayes," 36.

10. *Chicago Defender,* Jan. 1916, and Oct. 14, 1916, 4, cited in Dixon and Godrich, *Recording the Blues,* 9.

11. For a brief explanation of the venture, see "Columbia Records, 1901–1934: A History," in Brooks, *The Columbia Master Book Discography,* 1:15–16. Thanks are due to Agatha Kalkanis, manager of the Music and Performing Arts Department, Detroit Public Library, who searched the unsorted Hayes papers and located the correspondence regarding the tenor's recordings, and to Kurtz Myers, who first suggested that I contact the library. Kalkanis, correspondence with the author, May 23, Aug. 4, and Aug. 10, 1994.

12. A. E. Donovan, manager, Personal Record Department, Columbia Graphophone Company, undated (c. 1917) form letter, Roland Hayes Collection, Detroit Public Library.

13. Donovan's price chart only goes up to a maximum of five hundred copies. It is not clear whether the $0.50 rate applied over five hundred, or if special arrangements could be made for even larger quantities. It is possible that Columbia would not press more than five hundred copies, but given the frequency with which some personal recordings are found (e.g., those by the Swedish evangelist Rev. J. A. Hultman of Worcester, Mass.), and Columbia's general approach to business, it is likely that if greater quantities were needed they would "make a deal"—or sign the artist themselves.

14. It is not certain exactly when Broome began managing sales of Hayes's recordings, although it would seem logical that the tenor would have engaged him before leaving on his cross-country tour in early 1918. Broome's signature appears on a contract dated July 18, 1918, and his name is printed on both the contract form and on Hayes's stationary, which probably date to the early days of the enterprise.

15. Helm, *Angel Mo',* 114, 166.

16. Advertisement, *Crisis,* May 1918, 43.

17. John McCormack, "I Hear You Calling Me," Victrola 64120. Words by Harold Harford (aka Harold Lake), music by Charles Marshall. The song was first recorded by McCormack in March 1910, and went on to become perhaps his biggest all-time seller. Johnston, *Count John McCormack Discography,* 11.

18. "A Spirit Flower," by Campbell-Tipton, was advertised in the June 1918 issue of the *Crisis,* 97, but not thereafter.

19. Nine titles have been identified; however, it is uncertain whether "A Spirit Flower" was ever sold. Hayes eventually began numbering his discs in his ads, but only reached number seven (omitting, for some reason, "Solenne quest'ora," copies of which have been found).

20. According to an ad in the May 1919 issue of the *Crisis,* he had agents in Alabama, California, Connecticut, Delaware, the District of Columbia, Florida, Georgia, Illinois, Indiana, Kentucky, Maryland, Massachusetts, Michigan, Mississippi, Missouri, New Jersey, New York, Ohio, Oklahoma, Oregon, Pennsylvania, Rhode Island, South Carolina, Texas, Virginia, and West Virginia.

21. The $0.20 per disc recording and marketing figure is speculative, but conservative. The minimum studio recording charge was $50.00 for a solo voice with piano, which amortized over five hundred discs would be $0.10 per disc. Marketing would include office expense and advertising. Other charges would include travel, payment to the pianist, and so on.

22. Edison Laboratory Notebook 17-10-04.2 (Voice Trials), sheet dated Feb. 13, 1919, Edison National Historic Site.

23. *New York Age,* Feb. 8, 1919.

24. "Roland Hayes, Tenor, Soon to Leave for Europe," *Master Musician,* Mar. 1920, 4.

25. Helm, *Angel Mo',* 167–69, places this event in 1923, but the Vocalion records Hayes made in that year were issued. The reference was evidently to 1921, and HMV. Another version of the story, reported in a 1955 article by a friend of Hayes, was that "the matrixes were given to Mr. Hayes who smashed them over his knee, in front of the company officials and his agent." Arthur E. Knight, "Roland Hayes," *Record Collector* 10, no. 2 (July 1955): 42.

26. Knight, "Roland Hayes," 42–43.

27. Columbia Masterworks announcement, June 1941.

28. Quoted in Robert C. Hayden, notes to the CD *The Art of Roland Hayes,* Smithsonian RD-041 (1990), 12.

29. Knight, "Roland Hayes," 43.

30. Hayden, *The Art of Roland Hayes.*

31. Ibid., 12.

32. Many sources give the date as Dec. 31, 1976, but this is apparently incorrect. Patricia Turner reports that she checked with Massachusetts General Hospital, which confirmed the date as January 1 (Turner, *Dictionary of Afro-American Performers,* 201). More recent sources, such as *Grove* and the immaculately researched CD notes by Hayden, have adopted the January 1 date. The error may have stemmed from Hayes's obituary in the *New York Times,* which was published in the January 2, 1977, issue, datelined January 1, and somewhat confusingly reported that Hayes "died yesterday."

Chapter 31: The Four Harmony Kings

I am indebted to Ray Funk, a leading researcher on black musical groups, for providing clippings and information about the Four Harmony Kings. Funk has written about the group in "Three Afro-American Singing Groups," in *Under the Imperial Carpet,* ed. Lotz and Pegg, 150–55. Additional information appears in Arthur Badrock, "Ivan Harold Browning: A Small Tribute," *Talking Machine Review* 101 (1999): 3120–23.

1. James Weldon Johnson and J. Rosamond Johnson, *The Books of American Negro Spirituals* (New York: Viking Press, 1926), quoted in Allen, *Hendersonia,* 16.

2. Ray Funk, correspondence with the author. Hann's obituary appears in *Amsterdam*

(New York) *News,* Dec. 3, 1930. His name is sometimes spelled "Hahn." Some modern sources give his middle initial as *H* rather than *A,* but this appears to be an error.

3. Kimball and Bolcom, *Reminiscing with Sissle and Blake,* 32–33. An undated photo of Hann's Jubilee Singers appears on page 35.

4. *Chicago Defender,* Jan. 2, 1915, 6.

5. Turner, *Dictionary of Afro-American Performers,* 78–79. Turner drew her information in part from interviews with Browning's daughter, Haroldine Browning Brewington. See also Stanley O. Williford, "In Memoriam: Ivan Harold Browning: A Trouper to the End," *Los Angeles Times,* June 4, 1978, 71.

6. Funk, "Three Afro-American Singing Groups," 152. Allen, *Hendersonia,* 577, gives Berry's date of birth as c. 1900, but this seems unlikely as it would have made him fourteen or fifteen at the time he joined Hann. More likely he was in his early twenties.

7. *Chicago Defender,* June 1914, quoted in Funk, "Three Afro-American Singing Groups," 153. Badrock speculates that William D. Burns may have been the first baritone, replaced at a later date by Drayton.

8. "Four Harmony Kings," *Chicago Defender,* May 3, 1926, sec. 1, p. 8. Funk, "Three Afro-American Singing Groups," 150; Southern, *Biographical Dictionary of Afro-American and African Musicians,* 137. For listings of the group's vaudeville appearances see the *New York Age,* Oct. 19, 1918, and following issues.

9. Badger, *A Life in Ragtime,* 207. Badger lists the classical tenor Roland Hayes as a member of the Harmony Kings, which is clearly an error and is apparently a misreading of the fact that Hayes was in the room with three of the Kings when Europe was attacked in Boston a few days later.

10. *Chicago Defender,* Dec. 10, 1921, 6, and Sept. 8, 1923, 6.

11. Dixon, Godrich, and Rye, *Blues and Gospel Records, 1890–1943,* 296; Allen, *Hendersonia,* 22. Both sources wisely preface their dates with "c." or "about." These sources are generally consistent with the matrix dating in Rust, *Jazz Records,* and may in fact have derived their dating from Rust. It is also possible that the Harmony Kings joined *Shuffle Along* somewhat earlier than September, as stated in Funk, "Three Afro-American Singing Groups," 150. As one might deduce, nothing is entirely certain.

12. See their photo in the May 1923 Black Swan catalog, reproduced (poorly) in Thygesen, Berresford, and Shor, *Black Swan,* 62.

13. Some sources say that Hann left because of his own illness, others that it was because of the illness of his mother. See Kimball and Bolcom, *Reminiscing with Sissle and Blake,* 116; Duberman, *Paul Robeson;* Allen, *Hendersonia,* 16.

14. Unidentified Pittsburgh newspaper, quoted in "Shuffle a Show," *Chicago Defender,* Sept. 15, 1923, 6; Howard C. Washington, "Howard Writes," *Chicago Defender,* Dec. 15, 1923, 7.

15. Sampson, *Blacks in Blackface,* 181, 235. Most articles and discographies list Drayton as the baritone during the run of *Shuffle Along,* but Funk says it was Jones. No original references have been found to resolve this discrepancy.

16. An excellent history of "When the Saints Come Marching In" can be found in Fuld, *The Book of World Famous Music,* 641–42.

17. "Win Place in Wanamaker Harmony Contest," *New Orleans Herald,* Dec. 5, 1925, 6.

18. "Four Harmony Kings," *Chicago Defender,* Nov. 12, 1927, sec. 2, p. 12. Itinerary compiled by the Australian researcher Gary Le Gallant.

19. *Brisbane Courier,* Sept. 21, 1927.

20. *Amsterdam* (New York) *News,* Dec. 3, 1930.

21. "Four Harmony Kings," *Chicago Defender,* Jan. 30, 1926, sec. 1, p. 7; "Harmony Kings Grow in Favor of Public," *London Daily Echo,* reprinted in *Chicago Defender,* Aug. 17, 1929, sec. 1, p. 9.

22. *Sound Wave,* July 1926, quoted in Badrock, "Ivan Harold Browning."

23. "Four Harmony Kings," *Chicago Defender,* May 3, 1926, sec. 1, p. 8.

24. *Chicago Defender,* Sept. 15, 1928, sec. 1, p. 12, and June 5, 1926, sec. 1, p. 8; Badrock, "Ivan Harold Browning," 3121.

25. *Daily Midi* (Paris ed.), reprinted in *Chicago Defender,* Aug. 6, 1927, 9.

26. Badrock, "Ivan Harold Browning," 3121.

27. *Chicago Defender,* May 30, 1931, 27.

28. Funk, "Three Afro-American Singing Groups," 154–55.

29. Carl Seltzer, notes to *Eubie Blake Featuring Ivan Harold Browning,* EBM-1 (1971).

30. "J.V.," review of *Eubie Blake Featuring Ivan Harold Browning,* EBM-1 (LP), *Stereo Review,* June 1972, 105.

Chapter 32: Broome Special Phonograph Records

1. The first modern references to Broome are believed to be in Turner, *Dictionary of Afro-American Performers,* 59, and Tim Brooks, "Broome: The First Black Record Label?" *New Amberola Graphic,* no. 78 (Oct. 1991): 15–16. I am indebted to Turner for leads that aided my research.

2. The only source to give a specific date (Apr. 8, 1868) is his entry in D. S. Lamb, *Howard University Medical Department: Historical, Biographical, and Statistical Souvenir* (1900), 236 (in *Black Biography: 1790–1950 Microforms*). Broome's death certificate and obituary give his age then as seventy-four, which would backdate to 1866–67 (death certificate for George W. Broome, no. 186, Apr. 1, 1941, City of Medford, Middlesex County, Commonwealth of Massachusetts; "G. W. Broome, Shawmut Press Head, Is Dead," *Medford Daily Mercury,* Apr. 2, 1941, 1). The age he gave to the 1910 and 1920 U.S. census-takers would backdate to 1871. A search of Brooklyn, N.Y., birth records for the period has failed to produce a birth certificate.

3. Lamb, *Howard University Medical Department,* 236. Inquiries to Howard University have failed to locate records of Broome's years at the medical school. Nesta H. Bernard, director, Howard University Department of Alumni Affairs, letter to the author, Apr. 14, 1994.

4. Burleigh, handwritten letter to Washington, dated Apr. 18, 1897, provided by Burleigh's biographer Jean Snyder, Feb. 8, 1994.

5. *Freeman,* Feb. 3, 1900. Lamb, in 1900, also reported that Broome was "connected with the Clorindy company."

6. *New York Age,* Jan. 20 and 27, 1910.

7. Helm, *Angel Mo',* 166.

8. The pressing has "Villanelle" by Florence Cole-Talbert on one side (mislabeled as "Cradle Song" by Clarence Cameron White, another Broome title) and "So Near the Kingdom" by Robert Carr and Ethel Toms on the other. The latter, by two white singers, is an English matrix issued in the United States on Gennett 9080 in 1920 (collection of Martin Bryan).

9. Sutton and Nauck, *American Record Labels and Companies,* 86–87. Edward Pritchard, "The Music Master," foreword to *Thirty Afro-American Choral Spirituals, SATB* (New York: Hammond Music, 1964), 5, states that Boatner's Broome recordings were made in New York City in 1918. This book was published by Boatner himself, so the information presumably came from him; the date, however, is probably in error. The first news item stating that Broome had begun making records, and the first advertisements for them, appeared in *Crisis* in the fall of 1919; in addition, Broome's are laterally recorded, and independent labels did not begin converting to that technology until 1919. George Broome himself was occupied managing Roland Hayes's enterprise in 1918.

10. *Crisis,* Sept. 1919, 253.

11. Pritchard, "The Music Master," 5.

12. Boatner claimed in a 1979 letter to Turner that he had made three recordings of Burleigh arrangements for Broome. Turner, letter to the author, July 5, 1991; see also Turner, *Dictionary of Afro-American Performers,* 59.

13. *Crisis,* Oct. 1919, 307.

14. This advertisement appeared, unchanged, in *Crisis* for January, March, April, and May 1920.

15. *Crisis,* Nov. 1920, 37.

16. "G. W. Broome, Shawmut Press Head, Is Dead." The statement that Broome had been a resident of Medford for forty-five years was obviously incorrect, since census records and city directories place him in Newark, New Jersey, at the turn of the century.

17. Don Wetzell, "Broome Records: A Follow-Up," *New Amberola Graphic* 79 (Jan. 1992): 10. Wetzell, who is now deceased, revisited the store in the 1970s, but the records were gone. He returned again in 1991, attempting to locate the owners, but found that the store had closed as well. A nearby AME church and a black newspaper office held some promise for further information, but he was not able to follow up at the time.

Chapter 33: Edward H. Boatner

1. These and most other biographical details are from Gisele Glover, "The Life and Career of Edward Boatner and Inventory of the Boatner Papers at the Schomburg Center," *American Music Research Center Journal* 8–9 (1998–99): 89–106. Glover drew much of her material from the Boatner Collection at the Schomburg Center in New York, including an interview with the composer recorded in 1972. Additional biographical references include Claghorn, *Biographical Dictionary of American Music,* 56–57; Southern, *Biographical Dictionary of Afro-American and African Musicians,* 39; Southern, *The Music of Black Americans,* 418; American Society of Composers, Authors, and Publishers, *ASCAP Biographical Dictionary,* 47; and Turner, *Dictionary of Afro-American Performers,* 45–49.

2. Pritchard, "The Music Master," 5.

3. Brooks and Marsh, *The Complete Directory to Prime Time Network and Cable TV Shows,* 716.

4. Thomas A. Johnson, "Spirituals, Reflecting New Attitude, Regain Popularity," *New York Times,* Sept. 30, 1971, 49.

5. Earl Calloway, "CMA Honors Noted Black Composer," *Chicago Defender,* Jan. 27, 1979, "Accent" sec., p. 1.

Chapter 34: Harry T. Burleigh

1. Simpson, *Hard Trials,* 402.

2. Snyder, "Harry T. Burleigh," 11–12. This is an excellent and detailed analysis of Burleigh's life, music, and musical influences.

3. *Freeman,* Oct. 17, 1891.

4. Snyder, "Harry T. Burleigh," 302.

5. Johnson, *Black Manhattan,* 117.

6. Unidentified 1944 interview with Burleigh, quoted in Snyder, "Harry T. Burleigh," 245. *Senegambian Carnival* was the road-company version of the pioneering musical *Clorindy, the Origin of the Cakewalk,* which was produced on Broadway during the summer of 1898. According to Peterson, *A Century of Musicals in Black and White,* 306, Burleigh led the orchestra at the start of the tour, in Boston from September 5 to 7, but was later replaced by the show's composer, Will Marion Cook. Burleigh may have stayed with the production longer than that, however, as his departure from the company was not noted in the *Freeman* until Jan. 28, 1899.

7. Snyder, "Harry T. Burleigh," 246.

8. "Jean" (1903), words by Frank L. Stanton, music by Harry T. Burleigh, reprinted in Snyder, "Harry T. Burleigh," 140–42.

9. Sylvester Russell, "Stage Notes and Shop Talk," *Freeman,* Jan. 28, 1905.

10. *Freeman,* Mar. 17, 1906.

11. "Jean," on Aeolian 65025 (a piano roll intended for voice accompaniment), is listed in *Catalog of Music for the Pianola and Pianola Piano* (New York: Aeolian Company, 1905), 273.

12. "New Victor Records," Dec. 1912, 15.

13. "Columbia Records," Sept. 1915, 8.

14. "Columbia Records for May 1916," 3; "New Victor Records for January 1917," 8.

15. "New Victor Records," Feb. 1917, 5.

16. Bullock, *In Spite of Handicaps,* 41; Hammond, *In the Vanguard of a Race,* 129.

17. "New Victor Records," July 1918, 7.

18. Snyder, "Harry T. Burleigh," 206–7.

19. Simpson, *Hard Trials,* 385.

20. Ibid., 76; Snyder, "Harry T. Burleigh," 293–97.

21. *Musical America* 20 (July 24, 1916): 6.

22. Snyder, "Harry T. Burleigh," 323.

23. Simpson, *Hard Trials,* 82.

24. "Columbia Records," Mar. 1917, 10.

25. "Columbia Records," Mar. 1918, 16.

26. Harry T. Burleigh II (born 1923), telephone interview with the author, June 5, 1994 (hereafter Burleigh interview). Burleigh's godson, James C. Hall (born 1932), also recalled that Burleigh did not own a phonograph (Simpson, *Hard Trials,* 192).

27. *Crisis,* Sept. 1919, 253.

28. Burleigh interview.

29. For a full discussion of "the Origin-of-African-Music Controversy," see Snyder, "Harry T. Burleigh," 214–30.

30. Ibid., 369–75.

31. Turner, *Dictionary of Afro-American Performers,* 88.

32. Mike Montgomery, letter to the author, Dec. 20, 2001.

33. *Musical Courier,* Nov. 23, 1922, 21.

34. Simpson, *Hard Trials,* 138.

35. Snyder, "Harry T. Burleigh," 104.

36. Simpson, *Hard Trials,* 150.

Chapter 35: Florence Cole-Talbert

1. Biographical details from Turner, *Dictionary of Afro-American Performers,* 112–14, and Southern, *Biographical Dictionary of Afro-American and African Musicians,* 367–68.

2. See listings in Rust, *Jazz Records,* and Dixon, Godrich, and Rye, *Blues and Gospel Records, 1890–1943.* Talbert also conducted the 372nd Infantry Glee Club on V-Disc 249 during World War II.

3. *New York Age,* June 1, 1916, reported on her appearance at a musical festival held at Hampton Institute.

4. *Crisis,* Oct. 1919, 307.

5. *Crisis,* Jan. 1920, 159.

6. Dixon, Godrich, and Rye, *Blues and Gospel Records, 1890–1943,* 54.

7. "The Pace Phonograph Company," *Negro Musician* (published by the National Association of Negro Musicians), July 1921, 8; Thygesen, Berresford, and Shor, *Black Swan,* 58.

8. Vreede, *Paramount 12000/13000 Series,* unpaged but opposite listing for 12151.

Chapter 36: R. Nathaniel Dett

1. Principal sources for biographical details are Simpson, *Follow Me;* Southern, *Biographical Dictionary of Afro-American and African Musicians,* 184–85; and Turner, *Dictionary of Afro-American Performers,* 144–53.

2. Telephone interview with the piano-roll expert Michael Montgomery, May 26, 2001. QRS also recorded the well-known black pianist "Blind" Boone (1864–1927) in 1912, but the serial numbers on Dett's rolls (80184–96) are lower than those on Boone's (which are in the 80200s), suggesting that Dett recorded earlier in the year. Montgomery has located three of the four rolls, and a CD reissue has been discussed. The Dett rolls are listed in "QRS Player Rolls, 1920," 58, catalog in author's collection.

3. Clark Bustard, "Robert Nathaniel Dett," *Richmond Times-Dispatch,* Feb. 1, 2001.

4. Quoted in *Library of Duo-Art Music Rolls* (New York: Aeolian Company, 1924), 81.

5. *New York Age,* July 13, 1918.

6. Columbia Records supplement, June 1920, 7.

7. *Library of Duo-Art Music Rolls,* 81.

8. Victor Records supplement, Nov. 1, 1924, 6.

9. Simpson, *Follow Me,* 133, mentions a visit by Dett to Black Swan in the "mid-1920s."

10. Originally published in *The Album of a Heart* (1911), reprinted in Johnson, ed., *The Book of American Negro Poetry.*

Chapter 37: Clarence Cameron White

1. A good overview of this period is in Southern, *The Music of Black Americans,* 277–83.

2. White's personal and professional papers, including several self-prepared biographical sketches, are in the Manuscript Division (Sc Micro R-2474), Schomburg Center for Research in Black Culture, New York (hereafter White Papers). Biographical information is drawn from that source and from Southern, *Biographical Dictionary of Afro-American and African Musicians,* 398–400; and Turner, *Dictionary of Afro-American Performers,* 383–91. Turner gives White's year of birth as 1879, but all other sources cite 1880.

3. "Biographical Sketch of Clarence Cameron White" (c. 1933), White Papers.

4. *Freeman,* Dec. 11 and 18, 1897, and Jan. 1, 1898.

5. "Biographical Sketch of Clarence Cameron White."

6. *Freeman,* Jan. 20, 1906.

7. Most sources, including Southern, give the year of his move to Boston as 1910. However, an item in the June 10, 1911, issue of the *Freeman* datelined Washington, D.C., stated that "Mr. Clarence Cameron White, the celebrated violinist, is in the city [Washington] with his family after a long and successful tour of the West. Mr. White contemplates moving his family to Boston, where he will locate in the early Fall."

8. *New York Age,* Nov. 29, 1919.

9. Victor records supplement, Nov. 1919, 7.

10. "Biographical Sketch of Clarence Cameron White." White's papers also contain a 1922 statement of earnings from Edison for "Nobody Knows," but the recording is not identified and has not been traced. The only recording of the song in the Edison catalog at this time (no. 80482) was an arrangement by J. Rosamond Johnson.

Chapter 38: Miscellaneous Recordings

1. Rene Bache, "Do Monkeys Have Speech?" *Brooklyn Times,* Sept. 21, 1890, in Thomas E. Jeffrey, ed., *Thomas A. Edison Papers: A Selective Microfilm Edition* (Frederick, Md.: University Publications of America, 1985) (reference provided by Patrick Feaster).

2. National Phonograph Association, *Proceedings of the Second Annual Convention of Local Phonograph Companies,* 63, 65.

3. *Freeman,* Dec. 25, 1897. A badly garbled version of this item appears in Sampson, *The Ghost Walks,* 139.

4. A concise history of the Tio family can be found in Charles E. Kinzer, "The Tios of New Orleans and Their Pedagogical Influence on the Early Jazz Clarinet Style," *Black*

Music Research Journal 16, no. 2 (Fall 1996): 279–302. See also Southern, *Biographical Dictionary of Afro-American and African Musicians,* 376.

5. Hailstock's obituary appeared in *Freeman,* Mar. 4, 1899.

6. *Freeman,* Nov. 6 and 27, 1897, and Oct. 14, 1893.

7. *Freeman,* Oct. 1, 1892.

8. *Freeman,* June 19, 1897.

9. Washington, *Up from Slavery* (New York: Doubleday, 1901), chap. 14.

10. Rust, *Discography of Historical Records on Cylinders and 78s,* 295. Columbia did not maintain a studio in Chicago at this time, but did occasionally record with portable equipment.

11. A copy inspected by the author bears the name "Columbia Graphophone Company," and so must have been pressed in 1913 (when that corporate name was adopted) or later. Ernest Davidson Washington was born in the late 1880s and would have been about twenty when the record was made.

12. *Crisis,* Nov. 1920, 37, and Dec. 1920, 92 (advertisement).

13. Southern, *Biographical Dictionary of Afro-American and African Musicians,* 114.

14. Ibid., 49–50; Turner, *Dictionary of Afro-American Performers,* 60–61.

15. See *Freeman,* Jan. 23, May 5, Oct. 29, and Dec. 3, 1904, and Dec. 25, 1909 (among others) for her evolving name.

16. *New York Age,* July 13, 1916.

17. *Chicago Defender,* undated c. late 1920, cited in Turner, *Dictionary of Afro-American Performers,* 61; *Crisis,* Nov. 1920, 37; *American Musician,* Nov. 1920, 18.

18. Southern, *Biographical Dictionary of Afro-American and African Musicians,* 322; Jasen and Tichenor, *Rags and Ragtime,* 187–88; Southern, *Music of Black Americans,* 388–89; Feather, *The Encyclopedia of Jazz,* 398–99. Some sources give Roberts's year of birth as 1895, although this seems a little late given his pre-1910 activities.

19. Victor supplement, Feb. 15, 1924.

20. Rust, *The Columbia Master Book Discography,* vol. 3. Rust errs in failing to show that part three, take six, and part four, take three, both by Roberts, were issued (Columbia 1094-D, in author's collection).

21. Southern, *Biographical Dictionary of Afro-American and African Musicians,* 403–4; Jasen and Jones, *Spreadin' Rhythm Around,* 278–307; Charters and Kunstadt, *Jazz,* 224–230.

22. My thanks to Lynn Abbott and Doug Seroff, premiere researchers of the early black press, for pointing me to press accounts of this matter in the *Freeman* during our correspondence in 1992–93. In turn I was privileged to provide them with information from the Columbia files that augmented the story. Lynn summarized the research in his excellent article "'Brown Skin, Who You For?', Another Look at Clarence Williams's Early Career," in *Jazz Archivist* 8, nos. 1–2 (Dec. 1993): 1–15. Further information is in Lynn Abbott and Doug Seroff, "Brown Skin (Who You Really For?)," *Jazz Archivist* 15 (2001): 10–16.

23. The New Orleans entertainer Lemon Nash, as interviewed by Richard B. Allen and Marjorie T. Zander, Sept. 28, 1960, Hogan Jazz Archive, cited in Abbott, "Brown Skin, Who You For?" 6.

24. *Freeman,* Feb. 5 and 19, and Mar. 18, 1916.

25. Shapiro and Hentoff, eds., *Hear Me Talkin' to Ya,* 57.

26. *Freeman,* Mar. 11, 1916.

27. Two caveats: there is a handwritten notation on the back of the file card for Prince's version of "Brown Skin" (Columbia A5797) which reads "On 'Brown Skin'—Clarence Williams, piano, (wife) Georgia Davis, vocal, Mr. —— Piron, violin." However there is no vocal on the issued recording, nor any audible piano or violin. Such notes are highly unusual in the Columbia files of this period, and this one does not appear to be contemporaneous with the original card. It is my belief that it was added later—probably much

later—by some misguided researcher who had seen the story in the *Freeman* (an interesting example of contamination of original sources by later users). Second, it cannot be proven conclusively that the Williamses and Piron did *not* make a personal recording at Columbia. Many of the personal recording cards for this period are missing. However that they would have to have traveled to New York to do so and that no such recording seems to have been subsequently sold or mentioned makes this unlikely.

28. Reprinted in Abbott, "'Brown Skin, Who You For?'" 8.

29. Columbia supplement, June 1916, 6.

30. Victor supplement, Feb. 1917, 13.

31. The best biographical sketch of the team is in Jasen and Jones, *Spreadin' Rhythm Around,* 360–72.

32. Gardner, *Popular Songs of the Twentieth Century,* 1:183. Gardner's carefully researched popularity rankings show "After You've Gone" rising to number seven during late November 1918, in other words, a moderately big hit.

33. Southern, *Music of Black Americans,* 213.

34. Southern, *Biographical Dictionary of Afro-American and African Musicians,* 48–49; Jasen and Jones, *Spreadin' Rhythm Around,* 145–51.

35. It should be noted that the handwritten name on the recording card is spelled "Sheldon Brooks," so this could be someone else. Spelling errors were common in the files, and the reference to "professional dept." suggests that it was the singer/composer.

36. "Natalie Curtis Burlin at the Hampton Institute," *Resound* 1, no. 2 (Apr. 1982), Archives of Traditional Music, Indiana University; Anthony Seeger and Louise S. Spear, ed., *Early Field Recordings: A Catalog of Cylinder Collections at the Indiana University Archives of Traditional Music* (Bloomington: Indiana University Press, 1987), 32, 68; Simpson, *Follow Me,* 288–90; Turner, *Dictionary of Afro-American Performers,* 188–90.

37. "Negro Folk Songs Recorded," *Talking Machine World,* Mar. 15, 1919, 26.

38. Details on all of these recordings can be found in Dixon, Godrich, and Rye, *Blues and Gospel Records, 1890–1943,* 341–42.

39. Bolden is profiled in many sources, including Southern, *Biographical Dictionary of Afro-American and African Musicians,* 40.

40. Charles Edward Smith, "The Bolden Cylinder," *Saturday Review of Literature,* Mar. 16, 1957, 34–35.

41. Engelbert Wengel, "Again, the Bolden Cylinder," *New Orleans Music,* Dec. 1994, 11–12 (which cites Al Rose, *I Remember Jazz,* as its source).

42. Charters and Kunstadt, *Jazz,* 53. A more thoroughly researched account of the band in which MacNeal served is found in John McCusker, "The Onward Brass Band and the Spanish American War," *Jazz Archivist* 13 (1998–99): 24–35. McCusker corrects several aspects of the Charters-Kunstadt account.

43. Biographical information from Harris, *Blues Who's Who,* 106; and Southern, *Biographical Dictionary of Afro-American and African Musicians,* 63.

44. Steve LaVere, Adelphi album AD-1009-S, quoted in Harris, *Blues Who's Who.*

45. Southern, *Music of Black Americans,* 304.

46. Norm Cohen, correspondence with the author, Feb. 2, 2002.

47. Bruyninckx, *Fifty Years of Recorded Jazz* (1960s), and subsequent editions including *Eighty-five Years of Recorded Jazz* (2001); Lord, *The Jazz Discography;* Berresford, notes to *Ragtime to Jazz 1.* That Eubie Blake did not mention making the record is not conclusive, as he was often vague about his early recording activities.

48. Charters and Kunstadt, *Jazz,* 76–77; Rust, *Jazz Records, 1897–1942;* Doug Seroff, letter to the author, Dec. 9, 1996.

49. Rust, *Jazz Records, 1897–1942,* 1045; George Blacker, "Crescent Pathé Tie In? Preliminary Research," *Record Research,* no. 102 (Nov. 1969): 4.

50. Pathé Double-Disc Records supplement, Dec. 1917.

51. *New York Clipper,* Nov. 29 and Dec. 20, 1890.

52. *New York Clipper,* Apr. 28, 1894. Also in this show was Jessie Oliver from the *South before the War* company.

53. "Remember Poor Mother at Home," Berliner 859 (1896); "I'se Gwine Back to Dixie," Berliner 0658 (1899).

54. *Variety,* Sept. 14, 1938.

55. Tim Brooks, "A Directory to Columbia Recording Artists of the 1890s," *ARSC Journal* 11, nos. 2–3 (1979): 105.

56. Ibid., 112.

57. Gracyk, *Encyclopedia of Popular American Recording Pioneers, 1895–1925,* 98–101.

58. Sampson, *The Ghost Walks,* 191.

59. *Freeman,* Aug. 28, 1897.

60. Charters and Kunstadt, *Jazz,* 80. The band also recorded as Jimmy Durante's Jazz Band and the Whiteway Jazz Band.

Appendix

Among the sources consulted for this appendix are Diaz Ayala, *Discografia de la Musica Cubana, 1898 a 1925,* vol. 1; Pekka Gronow, "The Record Industry Comes to the Orient," *Ethnomusicology* 25, no. 2 (1981): 251–84; and John F. Perkins, Alan Kelly, and John Ward, "On Gramophone Company Matrix Numbers," *Record Collector* 23, nos. 3–4 (May 1976): 51–90.

1. "Spanish Records: Mexican Specialties," *Columbia Record,* Jan. 1904, 2; "Installing a Record Plant in Mexico," *Edison Phonograph Monthly,* June 1904, 4.

2. The International Zonophone Co. (a U.S.-based firm active in Europe) recorded in Rio de Janiero and Buenos Aires in 1902–3, before the Zonophone name was taken over by Victor in the United States and Gramophone and Typewriter Co. in Europe in 1903. Bayly and Kinnear, *The Zon-O-Phone Record,* 1–36.

3. Brooks, *Columbia Master Book Discography,* 1:427.

4. *Catalogo de Discos Zon-O-Fono* (Universal Talking Machine Mfg. Co., May 1906), 22.

5. "Making Records in Cuba," *Edison Phonograph Monthly,* Apr. 1906, 10.

SELECT CD DISCOGRAPHY

In the course of my research I compiled discographies of all the artists in this book, with full details on their issued and unissued recordings. Unfortunately these lengthy listings would fill another book, so for this volume a brief summary of CD reissues, some of which I am proud to have contributed to, will have to suffice. The emphasis is on reissues of recordings from the cylinder and 78-rpm era (a few artists such as Eubie Blake and Roland Hayes continued to record into the LP era). Some of these CDs are themselves now out of print, but it should be possible to obtain most of them from dealers in new or used records. It is worth the search to hear the voices and sounds of African American culture nearly one hundred years ago. It is a shame that more of this heritage is not currently available. (An asterisk indicates that the full CD title is at the end of the discography.)

The Internet is an excellent source for tracking down these recordings, as well as original 78s and LPs. A list of Web sites for some of the labels is at the end; others may be found by using your favorite search engine. Note that most labels reissuing early African American recordings are specialist and/or located overseas, a consequence of both the disinterest shown by the major labels and the oppressive copyright laws in the United States.

Chapters 1–3: George W. Johnson

Emile Berliner's Gramophone: The Earliest Discs, Symposium 1058 ("The Laughing Song")
Brown Wax Cylinder Phonograph Recordings: 1898, Sage ("The Laughing Song")
The 1890s, Vol. 1: Wipe Him Off the Land, Archeophone 9004 ("The Whistling Coon," "The Laughing Song")

Chapter 4: The Unique Quartette

Earliest Negro Vocal Groups, Vol. 2, Document DOCD 5288 ("Mamma's Black Baby Boy")
*American Pop, West Hill WH-1017 ("Mama's Black Baby Boy")
Too Late, Too Late, Vol. 8, Document DOCD 5574 ("Who Broke the Lock")

Chapter 5: Louis "Bebe" Vasnier

Too Late, Too Late, Vol. 4, Document DOCD 5321 ("Brudder Rasmus")

Chapter 6: The Standard Quartette

The Earliest Negro Vocal Quartets, Document DOCD 5061 ("Keep Movin'")
Earliest Negro Vocal Groups, Vol. 2, Document DOCD 5288 ("Every Day'll Be Sunday")
Brown Wax Cylinder Phonograph Recordings: 1895–1897, Sage ("Poor Mourner")

Chapter 7: The Kentucky Jubilee Singers

No recordings by this group are even known to exist, much less be reissued.

Chapter 8: Bert Williams and George Walker

Music from the New York Stage, Vols. 1–4, Pearl GEMM CDS 9050-61 (19 titles)
Bert Williams: The Remaining Titles, Document DOCD 5661 (24 titles)
Bert Williams: His Final Releases, 1919–1922, Archeophone 5002 (24 titles)
Bert Williams: The Middle Years, 1910–1918, Archeophone 5003 (26 titles)
Nobody and Other Songs, Smithsonian Folkways RF602 (14 titles)
*American Pop, West Hill WH-1017 ("Nobody"—1906 version)
This Is Art Deco, Columbia CK-57111 ("Nobody"—1913 version)
Star Spangled Rhythm, Smithsonian Collection 111 ("Nobody"—version?)
1913: Come and See the Big Parade, Archeophone 9005 ("Woodman, Spare That Tree")
Jazz/Some Beginnings, Smithsonian Folkways RF031 ("You Can't Get Away from It")
A Tribute to Black Entertainers, Columbia/Legacy C2K 52454 ("The Moon Shines on the
    Moonshine")
Music of Prohibition, Sony 65326 ("The Moon Shines on the Moonshine")
Pop Music, The Early Years 1890–1950, Columbia/Epic/Legacy J2K 65788 ("The Moon
    Shines on the Moonshine") (CD also included in set *Sony Music 100 Years: Soundtrack
    for a Century*, Columbia 65750)
1920: Even Water's Getting Weaker, Archeophone 9001 ("Moon Shines on the Moon-
    shine")
*Rhapsodies in Black, Rhino 79874 ("Brother Low Down")
Voices of Black America, Naxos NA224812 (four monologues)

Chapter 9: Cousins and DeMoss

Too Late, Too Late, Vol. 2, Document DOCD 5216 ("Poor Mourner")
*American Pop, West Hill WH-1017 ("Poor Mourner")

Chapter 10: Thomas Craig

No known reissues.

Chapter 11: The Dinwiddie Quartet

The Earliest Negro Vocal Quartets, Document DOCD 5061 (5 titles)
Earliest Negro Vocal Groups, Vol. 2, Document DOCD 5288 ("My Way Is Cloudy")

Chapter 12: Carroll Clark

*American Pop, West Hill WH-1017 ("De Little Old Log Cabin in De Lane")

Chapter 13: Charley Case

Voices of Black America, Naxos NA224812 (three titles)
*Before Radio, Archeophone 1002 ("How Mother Made the Soup")

Chapter 14: The Fisk Jubilee Singers

Fisk Jubilee Singers: In Chronological Order, Vols. 1–3, Document DOCD 5533-35 (seventy-three titles, 1909-40)
The Earliest Negro Vocal Groups, Vol. 5, Document DOCD 5613 (fourteen titles, 1911–26)
Voices of Black America, Naxos NA224812 (four readings by Rev. J. A. Myers)
Folk, Gospel, and Blues: Will the Circle Be Unbroken, Columbia/Legacy 65804 ("Ezekiel Saw de Wheel") (CD also included in set *Sony Music 100 Years: Soundtrack for a Century,* Columbia 65750)
*Every Tone a Testimony, Smithsonian/Folkways 47003 ("There's a Great Camp Meeting")

Chapter 15: Polk Miller and His Old South Quartette

The Earliest Negro Vocal Quartets, Document DOCD 5061 (seven titles from 1909, and seven from 1928)
Two Minute Wax Cylinder Recordings: Popular Songs, Sage ("Jerusalem Mournin'")
*American Pop, West Hill WH-1017 ("Oysters and Wine"—1928 version)

Chapter 16: Jack Johnson

No known reissues.

Chapter 17: Daisy Tapley

No known reissues.

Chapter 18: Apollo Jubilee Quartette

The Earliest Negro Vocal Quartets, Document DOCD 5061 (two titles)

Chapter 19: Edward Sterling Wright

Voices of Black America, Naxos NA224812 (two excerpts)

Chapter 20: James Reese Europe

James Reese Europe Featuring Noble Sissle, IAJRC CD 1012 (twenty-four Pathé titles, 1919)
Jim Europe's 369th Hell Fighters Band, Memphis Archives MA7020 (twenty-four Pathé titles, 1919)
Ragtime to Jazz 1, 1912–1919, Timeless CBC 1-035 ("Too Much Mustard," "Down Home Rag," 1913)
Anthology of Jazz Drumming, Vol. 1: 1904–1928, Masters of Jazz 804 ("Castle House Rag," 1913)
I'll Dance Till de Sun Breaks Through, Saydisc SDL-336 ("Castle Walk," 1913)
Jazz/Some Beginnings, Smithsonian Folkways RF031 ("Down Home Rag," 1913)
Kings of Ragtime, Gold Collection 4013 ("Down Home Rag," 1913)
Ragtime, Vol. 1, Jazz Archives 159052 ("Too Much Mustard," "Russian Rag")
*American Pop, West Hill WH-1017 ("Down Home Rag," "Memphis Blues")
Ken Burns Jazz: The Story of America's Music, Columbia/Legacy 61432 ("Memphis Blues," 1919)
Earliest Negro Vocal Groups, Vol. 2, Document DOCD 5288 (four titles by Singing Serenaders, 1919)

Chapter 21: Will Marion Cook

Earliest Negro Vocal Groups, Vol. 2, Document DOCD 5288 ("Swing Along," "Rain Song")
*Introduction to Ethel Waters, Best of Jazz 4013 ("I'm Coming Virginia")
Ethel Waters 1926–1929, Classics 688 ("I'm Coming Virginia")

Chapter 22: Dan Kildare

The Earliest Black String Bands, Vols. 1–2, Document DOCD 5622-23 (twenty-nine titles)
Too Late, Too Late, Vol. 12, Document DOCD 5659 ("Boy of Mine," "Clef Club March")
The Original Dixieland Jazz Band in England, JazzTime 252 716-2 ("St. Louis Blues," "Hindustan")
From Ragtime to Jazz, Vol. 3, Timeless CBC 1-070 ("Never Let Your Right Hand Know")

Chapter 23: The Tuskegee Institute Singers

Tuskegee Institute Singers/Quartet, Document DOCD 5549 (twenty titles, 1914–27)
Church Choirs, Vocal Groups and Preachers, Document DOCD 5616 (two 1927 titles)

Chapter 24: The Right Quintette

Earliest Negro Vocal Groups, Vol. 2, Document DOCD 5288 (two titles)

Chapter 25: Wilbur C. Sweatman

Ragtime to Jazz I: 1912–1919, Timeless CBC 1-035 (four titles, 1916–18)
Ragtime, Vol. 1, Jazz Archives 159052 ("Down Home Rag," "Dallas Blues," 1916–18)
Rhapsodies in Black: Music and Words from the Harlem Renaissance, Rhino 79874 ("Indianola," 1918)
Preservation Jazz, Music Club 50159 ("Darktown Strutters' Ball," 1918)
Ragtime to Jazz 2: 1916–1922, Timeless CBC 1-045 ("Good Man Is Hard to Find," "Lonesome Road," 1919)
Gennett Records Greatest Hits, Vol. II, Starr-Gennett Foundation ("Battleship Kate," 1924)

Chapter 26: Opal Cooper

No known reissues.

Chapter 27: Noble Sissle and Eubie Blake

Sissle

Black Vocal Groups, Vol. 10, Document DOCD 5632 (Sissle's Southland Singers, 1919)
Black Jazz in Europe, 1926–1930, JazzTime 252 714-2 (nine English titles, 1920s)
A Tribute to Black Entertainers, Columbia/Legacy C2K 52454 ("Camp Meeting Day," 1929)
Harlem Comes to London, DRG 8444 ("Camp Meeting Day," 1929)
Jazz Violin: 1926/1942, Jazz Archives 158002 ("Kansas City Kitty," 1929)
Anthology of Big Band Swing (1930–1955), GRP GRD-2-629 ("Polka Dot Rag")
Ken Burns Jazz: The Story of America's Music, Columbia/Legacy 61432 ("Dear Old Southland," 1937 unissued Variety recording)
Best of AFRS Jubilee, Vol. 9, Rst 1009 ("Skater's Waltz," "Sunday, Monday or Always," "Hey Lawdy Mama," "Blues in the Night," 1940s)

BLAKE

Ragtime, Vol. 1, Jazz Archives 159052 ("Jazzing Around," 1917)
From Ragtime to Jazz, Vol. 3, Timeless CBC 1-070 ("Hungarian Rag," 1917)
Ragtime to Jazz 2: 1916–1922, Timeless CBC 1-045 ("Sounds of Africa," 1921)
*Rhapsodies in Black, Rhino 79874 ("Sounds of Africa")
Kings of Ragtime, Gold Collection 4013 ("Baltimore Buzz," 1921)
Female Blues Singers, Vol. 6: E/F/G, Document 5510 (acc. Miss Frankie, 1920s)
Thumpin' and Bumpin', Frog 11 (1931 Victor sides)
(There are also numerous reissues from Eubie's second career from the 1950s to the 1970s, and several CDs of his early piano rolls.)

SISSLE AND BLAKE MIXED

*American Pop, West Hill WH-1017 (Sissle and Blake: "Love Will Find a Way"; Blake: "Sounds of Africa")
Star Spangled Rhythm, Smithsonian Collection 111 (Sissle and Blake: "Love Will Find a Way," 1921)
Note: Numerous Sidney Bechet and Lena Horne reissues contain sides made with the Noble Sissle Orchestra in the 1930s. Following are a few examples.
Sidney Bechet, 1924–1938, ABC Records 838 032-2 (seven titles with Bechet)
Sidney Bechet: 1923–1936, Classics 583 (sixteen titles with Bechet, Horne)
Lena Horne: L'Art Vocal, Vol. 11: 1936–1941, France Telecom/Cedar 11 (two titles)
The Fabulous Lena Horne, ASV/Living Era 5238 (two titles)

Chapter 28: Ford T. Dabney

From Ragtime to Jazz, Vol. 3, Timeless CBC 1-070 ("That's It," "Jass Lazy Blues," 1917)
Jazz/Some Beginnings, Smithsonian Folkways RF031 ("Round the Corner," 1919)
Ragtime to Jazz I: 1912–1919, Timeless CBC 1-035 ("Slow Drag Blues," 1919)

Chapter 29: W. C. Handy

W. C. Handy's Memphis Blues Band, Memphis Archives MA7006 (sixteen titles, 1917–23)
They All Play the Maple Leaf Rag, Archive CD-1600 ("Fuzzy Wuzzy Rag," 1917)
Ragtime, Vol. 1, Jazz Archives 159052 ("Fuzzy Wuzzy Rag," 1917)
Sara Martin in Chronological Order: Vol. 1, Document 5395 (1923)
Sara Martin, The Famous Moanin' Mama, Challenge 79028 (1923)
Jazzin' the Blues, RST/Document 1515 (four Varsity titles, 1939)
Carousel of American Music, Music and Arts CD 971 (1940 live appearance)
Chamber Music Society of Lower Basin Street, Storyville 3005 (1940 broadcast)
NBC's Chamber Music Society of Lower Basin Street, Harlequin 60 (1940 broadcast)

Chapter 30: Roland Hayes

The Art of Roland Hayes, Smithsonian RD 041 (twenty-three titles from 1939–67)
*Brother Can You Spare a Dime, Pearl Flapper 9484 (ten Columbia titles, 1940s)

Chapter 31: The Four Harmony Kings

Earliest Negro Vocal Groups, Vol. 2, Document DOCD 5288 (two titles, 1919)
Pace Jubilee Singers, Vol. 1, Document DOCD 5617 (six titles, 1921–24)

Chapter 33: Edward H. Boatner

No known reissues.

Chapter 34: Harry T. Burleigh

Dvořák Discoveries, Music and Arts CD 926 ("Go Down Moses," 1919)

Chapter 35: Florence Cole-Talbert

No known reissues.

Chapter 36: R. Nathaniel Dett

No known reissues.

Chapter 37: Clarence Cameron White

No known reissues.

Chapter 38: Miscellaneous Recordings

Jazz/Some Beginnings, Smithsonian Folkways RF031 (Luckey Roberts: "I'm Done," 1924)
Ragtime to Jazz I: 1912–1919, Timeless CBC 1-035 (Blake's Jazzone Orchestra: "The Jazz Dance," 1917)
From Ragtime to Jazz, Vol. 3, Timeless CBC 1-070 (Original New Orleans Jazz Band: "Ja-Da," 1918)
Every Tone a Testimony, Smithsonian/Folkways 47003 (Booker T. Washington)
Voices of Black America, Naxos NA224812 (Booker T. Washington)

Appendix

CUBA

Early Music of the North Caribbean, 1916–1920, Harlequin HQ CD 67 (two 1918 tracks by the Sexteto Habanero)
The Music of Cuba, 1909–1951, Columbia Legacy CK 62234 (two pre-1920 tracks by Felipe Valdés, Floro y Zorilla)
Hot Music from Cuba, 1907–1936, Harlequin HQ CD 23 (7 pre-1920 tracks by Felipe Valdés, Pablo Valenzuela, Enrique Peña, Terceto "Nano," etc.)

TRINIDAD

Trinidad 1912–1941, Harlequin HQ CD 16 (two 1912 tracks by Lovey's Band and a 1915 piano solo by Lionel Belasco)
Trinidad Loves to Play Carnival 1914–1939, Matchbox MBCD 302-2 (one 1914 track by Jules Sims, sung in Creole patois)
Calypso Pioneers 1912–1937, Rounder CD 1039 (Lovey, Belasco, Julian White Rose)

BRAZIL

Portuguese String Music 1908–1931, Heritage HT CD 05 (Grup Bahianinho, Grupo Larangeira, Grupo Lulu Cavaquinho)

Full CD Titles

American Pop: An Audio History—From Minstrel to Mojo, West Hill WH-1017
Before Radio: Comedy, Drama and Sound Sketches, 1897–1923, Archeophone 1002
Brother Can You Spare a Dime: The Roots of American Song, Pearl Flapper 9484
Every Tone a Testimony: An African American Aural History, Smithsonian/Folkways 47003
Introduction to Ethel Waters: Her Best Recordings, 1921–1940, Best of Jazz 4013
Rhapsodies in Black: Music and Words from the Harlem Renaissance, Rhino 79874

Web Sites

Archeophone: <http://www.archeophone.com>
Document (U.K.): <http://www.document-records.co.uk>
IAJRC: <http://www.geocities.com/IAJRC>
Music and Arts: <http://www.musicandarts.com>
Sage: <http://www.tinfoil.com>
Smithsonian-Folkways: <http://www.folkways.si.edu>
Timeless (Netherlands): <http://www.timeless-records.com>
West Hill Audio Archives (Canada). <http://www.musicandarts.com/wh1017-2.html>.

BIBLIOGRAPHY

Abbott, Lynn, and Doug Seroff. *Out of Sight: The Rise of African-American Popular Music, 1889–1895*. Jackson: University Press of Mississippi, 2003.

Allen, Walter C. *Hendersonia: The Music of Fletcher Henderson and His Musicians*. Highland Park, N.J.: By the author, 1973.

Allen, William Francis, Charles Pickard Ware, and Lucy McKim Garrison. *Slave Songs of the United States*. New York: A. Simpson, 1867.

American Society of Composers, Authors, and Publishers. *ASCAP Biographical Dictionary*. 4th ed. New York: R. R. Bowker, 1980.

———. *Program Listings, 1935*. New York: ASCAP, n.d.

———. *Program Listings, 1937*. New York: ASCAP, n.d.

Anderson, Toni Passmore. "The Fisk Jubilee Singers: Performing Ambassadors for the Survival of an American Treasure, 1871–1878." Ph.D. diss., Georgia State University, Atlanta, 1997.

Annand, Major H. H. *Block Catalogue of the Cylinder Records Issued by the U.S. Phonograph Company, 1890–1896*. Hillingdon, England: By the author, 1970.

———. *The Complete Catalog of the U.S. Everlasting Indestructible Cylinders, 1908–1913*. London: City of London Phonograph and Gramophone Society, 1966.

Badger, Reid. *A Life in Ragtime: A Biography of James Reese Europe*. New York: Oxford University Press, 1995.

Barlow, William. *Looking Up at Down: The Emergence of Blues Culture*. Philadelphia: Temple University Press, 1989.

Bastin, Bruce. *Never Sell a Copyright: Joe Davis and His Role in the New York Music Scene, 1916–1978*. Chigwell, England: Storyville Publications, 1990.

Bayly, Ernie, and Michael Kinnear, *The Zon-O-Phone Record*. Heidelberg, Australia: Michael S. Kinnear, 2001.

Berliner Records in the Library of Congress. Washington, D.C.: Library of Congress, n.d.

Bordman, Gerald. *American Musical Theatre: A Chronicle*. New York: Oxford University Press, 1978.

Brooks, Tim. *The Columbia Master Book Discography*. Vol. 1. Westport, Conn.: Greenwood Press, 1999.

———, ed. *Little Wonder Records: A History and Discography*. St. Johnsbury, Vt.: New Amberola Phonograph Co., 1999.

Brooks, Tim, and Earle Marsh. *The Complete Directory to Prime Time Network and Cable TV Shows, 1946–Present*. 7th ed. New York: Ballantine Books, 1999.

Browder, Walter, and Linwood Lunsford. *An Economic and Social Survey of Dinwiddie County*. Charlottesville: University of Virginia Press, 1937.

Brown, Frank C. *Folk Ballads from North Carolina*. Vol. 2 of *The Frank C. Brown Collection of North Carolina Folklore*. Durham, N.C.: Duke University Press, 1952.

———. *Folk Songs from North Carolina*. Vol. 3 of *The Frank C. Brown Collection of North Carolina Folklore*. Durham, N.C.: Duke University Press, 1952.

Brown, T. Allston. *A History of the New York Stage*. 1903. New York: Benjamin Blom, 1964.

Brunn, H. O. *The Story of the Original Dixieland Jazz Band*. Baton Rouge: Louisiana State University Press, 1960.

Bruyninckx, Walter. *Eighty-five Years of Recorded Jazz*. Mechelen, Belgium: By the author, 2001.

———. *Fifty Years of Recorded Jazz*. Belgium: By the author, 1960s.

Bryan, Martin, and William R. Bryant. *Oxford and Silvertone Records*. St. Johnsbury, Vt.: New Amberola Phonograph Co., 1975.

Bull, Rice C. *Soldiering: The Civil War Diary of Rice C. Bull, 123rd New York Volunteer Infantry*. Edited by K. Jack Bauer. San Rafael, Calif.: Presidio Press, 1977.

Bullock, Ralph W. *In Spite of Handicaps*. New York: Association Press, 1927.

Charosh, Paul. *Berliner Gramophone Records*. Westport, Conn.: Greenwood Press, 1995.

Charosh, Paul, and Robert A. Fremont, eds. *More Favorite Songs of the Nineties*. New York: Dover Publications, 1975.

Charters, Ann. *Nobody: The Story of Bert Williams*. New York: Macmillan, 1970.

Charters, Samuel B., and Leonard Kunstadt. *Jazz: A History of the New York Scene*. 1962. New York: Da Capo, 1981.

Claghorn, Charles Eugene. *Biographical Dictionary of American Music*. West Nyack, N.Y.: Parker Publishing Co., 1973.

Cohen-Stratyner, Barbara, ed. *Popular Music, 1900–1919*. Detroit: Gale Research, 1988.

Cunard, Nancy, ed. *Negro: An Anthology*. 1934. New York: Frederick Ungar, 1970.

Cuney-Hare, Maude. *Negro Musicians and Their Music*. Washington, D.C.: Associated Publishers, 1936.

deCoy, Robert H. *Jack Johnson: The Big Black Fire*. 1969. Los Angeles: Holloway House, 1991.

Dethlefson, Ron. *Edison Blue Amberol Recordings, 1912–1914*. New York: APM Press, 1980.

———. *Edison Blue Amberol Recordings, 1915–1929*. Vol. 2. New York: APM Press, 1981.

Diaz Ayala, Cristobal. *Discografia de la Musica Cubana, 1898 a 1925*. Vol. 1. San Juan: Fundacion Musicala, 1994.

Dixon, Robert M. W., and John Godrich. *Blues and Gospel Records, 1902–1943*. 3d ed. Chigwell, England: Storyville, 1982.

———. *Recording the Blues*. New York: Stein and Day, 1970.

Dixon, Robert M. W., John Godrich, and Howard Rye. *Blues and Gospel Records, 1890–1943*. 4th ed. New York: Oxford University Press, 1997.

Draper, James P., ed. *Black Literature Criticism*. Detroit: Gale Research, 1992.

Du Bois, W. E. B. *The Souls of Black Folk*. 1903. New York: Signet Classics, 1995.

Duberman, Martin Bauml. *Paul Robeson*. New York: Knopf, 1988.

Ellington, Duke. *Music Is My Mistress*. New York: Doubleday, 1973.

Epstein, Dena J. *Sinful Tunes and Spirituals: Black Folk Music to the Civil War*. Urbana: University of Illinois Press, 1977.

Ewen, David. *American Popular Songs*. New York: Random House, 1966.

Fagan, Ted, and William R. Moran. *The Encyclopedic Discography of Victor Recordings, Matrix Series 1 through 4999*. Westport, Conn.: Greenwood Press, 1986.

———. *The Encyclopedic Discography of Victor Recordings, Pre-Matrix Series*. Westport, Conn.: Greenwood Press, 1983.

Farr, Finis. *Black Champion: The Life and Times of Jack Johnson*. 1965. Greenwich, Conn.: Fawcett, 1969.

Feather, Leonard. *The Encyclopedia of Jazz*. New ed. New York: Bonanza Books, 1962.

Fields, Armond, and L. Marc Fields. *From the Bowery to Broadway: Lew Fields and the Roots of American Popular Theater*. New York: Oxford University Press, 1993.

Fletcher, Tom. *One Hundred Years of the Negro in Show Business*. 1954. New York: Da Capo Press, 1984.

Floyd, Samuel A., Jr., ed. *Black Music in the Harlem Renaissance*. Westport, Conn.: Greenwood Press, 1990.

Fuld, James J. *The Book of World Famous Music, Classical, Popular, and Folk*. 4th ed. New York: Dover Publications, 1995.

Gaisberg, F. W. *The Music Goes Round*. New York: Macmillan, 1942.

Gardner, Edward Foote. *Popular Songs of the Twentieth Century*. Vol. 1, *1900–1949*. St. Paul, Minn.: Paragon House, 2000.

Gart, Galen. *ARLD: The American Record Label Directory and Dating Guide, 1940–1959*. Milford, N.H.: Big Nickel Productions, 1989.

Gilmore, Al-Tony. *Bad Nigger! The National Impact of Jack Johnson*. Port Washington, N.Y.: Kennikat Press, 1975.

Goddard, Chris. *Jazz Away from Home*. London: Paddington Press, 1979.

Goldberg, Isaac. *Tin Pan Alley: A Chronicle of American Popular Music*. 1930. New York: Frederick Ungar, 1961.

Gracyk, Tim. *The Encyclopedia of Popular American Recording Pioneers, 1895–1925*. Granite Bay, Calif.: Victrola and 78 Journal Press, 1999.

Hammond, L. H. *In the Vanguard of a Race*. New York: Council for Women for Home Missions and Missionary Movement of the U.S. and Canada, 1922.

Handy, W. C. *Father of the Blues: An Autobiography*. 1941. New York: Da Capo Press, 1991.

Harlan, Louis R., ed. *The Booker T. Washington Papers*. 13 vols. Urbana: University of Illinois Press, 1976.

Harris, Sheldon. *Blues Who's Who*. New Rochelle, N.Y.: Arlington House Publishers, 1979.

Heier, Uli, and Rainer E. Lotz, eds. *The Banjo on Record: A Bio-Discography*. Westport, Conn.: Greenwood Press, 1993.

Heinl, Robert Debs, and Nancy Gordon Heinl. *Written in Blood: The Story of the Haitian People, 1492–1971*. New York: Houghton Mifflin, 1978.

Helm, MacKinley. *Angel Mo' and Her Son, Roland Hayes*. Boston: Little, Brown, 1943.

Hicks, John D. *The American Nation*. 3d ed. New York: Houghton Mifflin, 1955.

Hitchcock, H. Wiley, and Stanley Sadie, eds. *New Grove Dictionary of American Music*. New York: Macmillan, 1986.

Hurwitt, Elliott S. "W. C. Handy as Music Publisher: Career and Reputation." Ph.D. diss., City University of New York, 2000.

Jasen, David A. *Tin Pan Alley*. New York: Donald I. Fine, 1988.

Jasen, David A., and Gene Jones. *Spreadin' Rhythm Around: Black Popular Songwriters, 1880–1930*. New York: Schirmer Books, 1998.

Jasen, David A., and Trebor Jay Tichenor. *Rags and Ragtime: A Musical History*. New York: Seabury Press, 1978.

Johnson, Jack. *Jack Johnson Is a Dandy: An Autobiography*. 1927. New York: Chelsea House, 1969.

Johnson, James Weldon. *Along This Way: The Autobiography of James Weldon Johnson*. New York: Viking Penguin, 1933.

———. *Black Manhattan*. 1930. New York: Da Capo Press, 1991.

———, ed. *The Book of American Negro Poetry*. New York: Harcourt, Brace, 1922.

Johnston, Brian Fawcett. *Count John McCormack Discography*. Bournemouth, England: Talking Machine Review, 1988.

Kaplan, Mike, ed. *The Complete Book of Major U.S. Show Business Awards*. New York: Garland, 1985.

Kenney, William Howland. *Chicago Jazz: A Cultural History, 1904–1930*. New York: Oxford University Press, 1993.

Kimball, Robert, and William Bolcom. *Reminiscing with Sissle and Blake*. New York: Viking Press, 1973.

Kinkle, Roger D. *The Complete Encyclopedia of Popular Music and Jazz, 1900–1950*. New Rochelle, N.Y.: Arlington House, 1974.

Klotman, Phyllis Rauch. *Frame by Frame: A Black Filmography.* Bloomington: Indiana University Press, 1970.

Koenigsberg, Allen. *Edison Cylinder Records, 1889–1912.* 2d ed. Brooklyn, N.Y.: APM Press, 1987.

Laurie, Joe, Jr. *Vaudeville: From the Honky Tonks to the Palace.* New York: Henry Holt, 1953.

Lord, Tom. *The Jazz Discography.* 26 vols. Redwood, N.Y.: Cadence Jazz Books, 1992–2002.

Lotz, Rainer E. *Black People: Entertainers of African Descent in Europe and Germany.* Bonn: Birgit Lotz Verlag, 1997.

Lotz, Rainer E., and Ian Pegg, eds. *Under the Imperial Carpet: Essays in Black History, 1780–1950.* Crawley, England: Rabbit Press, 1986.

Lovell, John, Jr. *Black Song: The Forge and the Flame.* 1972. New York: Paragon House, 1986.

Low, W. Augustus, and Virgil A. Clift, eds. *Encyclopedia of Black America.* 1981. New York: Da Capo Press, n.d.

Lowe, Allen. *That Devilin' Tune.* Berkeley, Calif.: Music and Arts Programs of America, 2001.

Malnig, Julie. *Dancing till Dawn: A Century of Exhibition Ballroom Dance.* Westport, Conn.: Greenwood Press, 1992.

Maltin, Leonard. *Leonard Maltin's Movie and Video Guide.* New York: Signet, 2000.

Mantle, Burns. *The Best Plays of 1899–1909.* New York: Dodd, Mead and Co., 1944.

Marco, Guy A., ed. *Encyclopedia of Recorded Sound in the United States.* New York: Garland, 1993.

Marks, Edward B. *They All Sang: From Tony Pastor to Rudy Vallee.* New York: Viking Press, 1934.

McCarthy, Albert. *The Dance Band Era.* Philadelphia: Chilton, 1971.

Meade, Guthrie T., Jr., with Dick Spottswood and Douglas S. Meade. *Country Music Sources: A Biblio-Discography of Commerically Recorded Traditional Music.* Chapel Hill, N.C.: University of North Carolina Press, 2002.

Meeker, David. *Jazz in the Movies: A Guide to Jazz Musicians, 1917–1977.* London: Talisman Books, 1977.

Millard, Andre. *America on Record: A History of Recorded Sound.* New York: Cambridge University Press, 1995.

Moogk, Edward B. *Roll Back the Years: History of Canadian Recorded Sound and Its Legacy.* Ottawa: National Library of Canada, 1975.

Moses, Robert, ed. *American Movie Classics: Classic Movie Companion.* New York: Hyperion, 1999.

Murrells, Joseph. *Million Selling Records from the 1900s to the 1980s.* New York: Arco Publishing, 1984.

Nathan, Hans. *Dan Emmett and the Rise of Early Negro Minstrelsy.* Norman: University of Oklahoma Press, 1962.

National Phonograph Association. *Proceedings of the 1890 Convention of Local Phonograph Companies.* 1890. Nashville: Country Music Foundation Press, 1974.

———. *Proceedings of the Second Annual Convention of Local Phonograph Companies of the United States.* New York, 1891.

———. *Proceedings of the Third Annual Convention of Local Phonograph Companies of the United States.* Chicago, 1892.

———. *Proceedings of the Fourth Annual Convention of Local Phonograph Companies of the United States.* Chicago, 1893.

Odell, George C. D. *Annals of the New York Stage.* 15 vols. New York: Columbia University Press, 1927–49.

Oliver, Paul, ed. *Black Music in Britain: Essays on the Afro-American Contribution to Popular Music.* Milton Keynes, England: Open University Press, 1990.

Peterson, Bernard L., Jr. *A Century of Musicals in Black and White.* Westport, Conn.: Greenwood Press, 1993.

Poland, Charles Preston, Jr. *From Frontier to Suburbia.* Marceline, Mo.: Walsworth, 1976.

Ragan, David. *Who's Who in Hollywood.* New York: Facts on File, 1992.

Riis, Thomas L. *Just Before Jazz: Black Musical Theater in New York, 1890 to 1915.* Washington, D.C.: Smithsonian Institution Press, 1989.

Roberts, Randy. *Papa Jack: Jack Johnson and the Era of White Hopes.* New York: Free Press, 1983.

Rogers, Joel A. *World's Great Men of Color.* Vol. 2. New York: Macmillan, 1972.

Rose, Al. *Eubie Blake.* New York: Schirmer Books, 1979.

Rotberg, Robert I. *Haiti: The Politics of Squalor.* New York: Houghton Mifflin, 1971.

Rowland, Mabel. *Bert Williams: Son of Laughter.* 1923. Westport, Conn.: Negro Universities Press, 1969.

Rust, Brian. *Discography of Historical Records on Cylinders and 78s.* Westport, Conn.: Greenwood Press, 1979.

———. *Jazz Records, 1897–1942.* 4th ed. New Rochelle, N.Y.: Arlington House, 1978.

Rust, Brian, and Tim Brooks. *The Columbia Master Book Discography.* 4 vols. Westport, Conn.: Greenwood Press, 1999.

Rust, Brian, and Allen G. Debus. *The Complete Entertainment Discography.* 2d ed. New York: Da Capo Press, 1989.

Sampson, Henry T. *Blacks in Blackface.* Metuchen, N.J.: Scarecrow Press, 1980.

———. *The Ghost Walks: A Chronological History of Blacks in Show Business, 1865–1910.* Metuchen, N.J.: Scarecrow Press, 1988.

Shapiro, Nat, and Nat Hentoff, eds. *Hear Me Talkin' to Ya: The Story of Jazz as Told by the Men Who Made It.* 1955. New York: Dover Publications, 1966.

Shaw, Arnold. *Black Popular Music in America.* New York: Schirmer Books, 1986.

Sies, Luther F. *Encyclopedia of American Radio, 1920-1960.* Jefferson, N.C.: McFarland and Co., 2000.

Simon, George T. *The Big Bands.* New York: Macmillan, 1967.

———. *Simon Says: The Sights and Sounds of the Swing Era, 1935-1955.* New Rochelle, N.Y.: Arlington House, 1971.

Simpson, Anne Key. *Follow Me: The Life and Music of R. Nathaniel Dett.* Metuchen, N.J.: Scarecrow Press, 1993.

———. *Hard Trials: The Life and Music of Harry T. Burleigh.* Metuchen, N.J.: Scarecrow Press, 1990.

Sissle, Noble Lee. "Memoirs of Lieutenant 'Jim' Europe." TS, 1942. Copies may be found in the Manuscript Division, Library of Congress, under NAACP Records, Group 2, Box J72, and at the Schomburg Center for Research in Black Culture in New York City.

Slide, Anthony. *The Encyclopedia of Vaudeville.* Westport, Conn.: Greenwood Press, 1994.

Smith, Eric Ledell. *Bert Williams: A Biography of the Pioneer Black Comedian.* Jefferson, N.C.: McFarland and Co., 1992.

Snyder, Jean Elizabeth. "Harry T. Burleigh and the Creative Expression of Bi-Musicality: A Study of an African-American Composer and the American Art Song." Ph.D. diss., University of Pittsburgh, 1992.

Southern, Eileen. *Biographical Dictionary of Afro-American and African Musicians.* Westport, Conn.: Greenwood Press, 1982.

———. *The Music of Black Americans.* 2d ed. New York: W. W. Norton, 1983.

Spaeth, Sigmund. *A History of Popular Music in America.* New York: Random House, 1948.

Spottswood, Richard K. *Ethnic Music on Records.* Urbana: University of Illinois Press, 1990.

Sutton, Allan. *A Guide to Pseudonyms on American Records, 1892–1942.* Westport, Conn.: Greenwood Press, 1993.

Sutton, Allan, and Kurt Nauck. *American Record Labels and Companies: An Encyclopedia.* Denver: Mainspring Press, 2000.

Thygesen, Helge, Mark Berresford, and Russ Shor. *Black Swan: The Record Label of the Harlem Renaissance.* Nottingham, England: VJM Publications, 1996.

Toll, Robert C. *Blacking Up: The Minstrel Show in Nineteenth-Century America.* New York: Oxford University Press, 1974.

Trow's New York City Directory, Borough of Manhattan (annual), 1878 and 1900–1914.

Turner, Patricia. *Dictionary of Afro-American Performers: 78 RPM and Cylinder Recordings of Opera, Choral Music, and Songs c. 1900–1949.* New York: Garland, 1990.

U.S. Department of Commerce, Bureau of the Census. *Historical Statistics of the United States, Colonial Times to 1970.* New York: Kraus International, 1989.

Vreede, Max E. *Paramount 12000/13000 Series.* London: Storyville Publications, 1971.

Ward, Andrew. *Dark Midnight When I Rise: The Story of the Jubilee Singers Who Introduced the World to the Music of Black America.* New York: Farrar, Straus, and Giroux, 2000.

Who's Who in America. 49th ed. New Providence, N.J.: Marquis Who's Who, 1994.

Witmark, Isidore, and Isaac Goldberg. *From Ragtime to Swingtime.* New York: Lee Furman, 1939.

Woll, Allen. *Black Musical Theatre: From Coontown to Dreamgirls.* 1989. New York: Da Capo Press, n.d.

——. *Dictionary of the Black Theatre.* Westport, Conn.: Greenwood Press, 1983.

Wright, Laurie, ed. *Storyville 1996–97.* Chigwell, England: L. Wright, 1997.

Ziegfeld, Richard, and Paulette Ziegfeld. *The Ziegfeld Touch: The Life and Times of Florenz Ziegfeld, Jr.* New York: Harry N. Abrams, 1993.

INDEX

American Cinephone Company, New York City, 242, 244, 245
American Conservatory, France, 491
American Graphophone Company, 90
"American Jubilee," 368
American label, 59, 60, 195
American Missionary Association, 192
American Musician, 505
American Place Theater, New York, 147
American Quartet, 59
American Society of Composers, Authors and Publishers (ASCAP), 349–50, 408, 409, 429, 431, 432, 479, 491; Silver Jubilee celebration, 484
Amos 'n Andy, 391, 463
Ampico, piano rolls for, 370
"And Then I Laughed," 62
Anderson, Marian, 450, 480, 482, 484
Andrews, Barrett, 280, 555 n. 30
Androcles and the Lion, 129
Angel-Mo' label, 451
"Annie Laurie," 96, 99, 368
"Anoma," 396
Apollo Jubilee Quartette, 202, 258–59, 320, 439
Apollo (Male) Quartet, 259
Apollo Male Trio and Quartet, 259
Apollo Quartet of Boston, 259
Apollo Quartet, 259, 439
Apollo Theatre, Paris, 359
Apollo Trio, 259
ARA label, 146
"Arabian Nights," 283
Arabic music, 524
Arcades, 86, 91, 98. *See also* Phonographs, coin-slot
Archibald, Douglas, 6
Archive of Folk Song, Library of Congress, 514
Archives of Traditional Music, Indiana University, 531 n. 9
Arcola, Va., 24
Arden, Victor, 404, 423
Arditi, Luigi, 487
"Are You from Dixie?", 286
"Are You Happy?", 383
Aretino label, 166
Argentina, recording in, 524
"Argentines, the Portuguese, and the Greeks, The," 133
Argonne Forest, 278
Arguinzoni, G., 528
Arias, 439, 441, 444, 465
"Arkansas Traveler," 63, 219
Arlington National Military Cemetery, 289
"Armorer's Song, The," 328
Armstrong, Gen. Samuel, 320
Armstrong, Louis, 137, 145, 409, 458, 506, 511; band, 431; *Louis Armstrong Plays W. C. Handy,* 434
Armstrong Manual Training School, 395
Art songs, 168, 169, 439, 447, 449, 451, 465, 476
Arthur Godfrey and His Friends, 327
Artrio-Angelus, piano rolls for, 370
Arzonia, Joe, 570 n. 2
As the World Rolls On, 251
Asbury, Charles A., 519–20
Ash, Sam, 341
"Asleep in the Deep," 310
Asquith, Lord, 308
Association for Recorded Sound Collections, 215, 565 n. 22
"At That San Francisco Fair," 401
Atlanta Exposition, 322, 469, 501, 502, 503
Atlantic City, N.J., 364
Atlantic Monthly, 193
AtLee, John Y., 33, 40, 61, 87
"Auch kleine dinge," 450
Audio Archives label, 433
"Auld Lang Syne," 231
"Aunt Hagar's Blues," 419, 426, 428
Austin, Gene, 382
Austin, Mary, 238
Australia, 104, 251, 329, 332
Automatic music machines. *See* phonographs, coin-slot
Avery, Dan, and Charles Hart, 81, 150, 152, 328
Ayers, Prof. Brown, 85

"Baby," 507
"Baby Seals Blues," 415
"Baby's Lullaby," 165, 166
Bach, Johann Sebastian, 450
Bach, Professor, 411
Bachman, Fred, *61*
Badger, Reid, 270, 274, 282; *A Life in Ragtime,* 291
"Bag of Rags, A," 342
Bailey, Al, 300
Bailey, Buster, 388, 391
Bailey, George, 500
Bailey, Pearl, 391, 434
Baillie, George (Lovey), 528
Baker, Josephine, 471
Baker, Phil, 381
Baker, Samuel G., 76, 79, 80
Bal Taberin Jazz Orchestra, 435
Bal Taberin Revue, 463
Balfe, William Michael, 487
Ball, Ernest R., 169
Ball, Rosa, 150
"Baltimore Buzz," 377, 378, 393
Baltimore Colored High School, 397
"Band of Gideon," 109, 211

Black Swan label, 145, 168, 169, 170, 171, 425, 427, 456, 457, 464, 487, 491, 511
Black Thunderbolt, 251
Black, J. M., 457
Blacker, George, 518
Blackface, 106, 123, 128, 132, 147, 175, 178, 180, 185, 218, 219, 520
Blacklock, William, 305
Blake, Avis Lee, 364, 390
Blake, Emily, 363
Blake, Enoch W., 518
Blake, James Hubert "Eubie," 7, 269–70, 277, 280, 283, 284, 287, 290, 355, 363–95, *364, 373,* 396, 407, 428, 455, 456, 463, 484, 517, 518, 522; death of, 393; *Eubie!,* 392; Eubie Blake Music, 392; Eubie Blake Trio, 368, 369; and His Orchestra, 387, 393; income, 380
Blake, John, 363
Blake, Marion Gant Tyler, 390, 393
Blake's Jazzone Orchestra, 369, 517–18
Bland, Jim, 298
Blesh, Rudi, 391, 524
"Blind Tom," 519
Blinn, Holbrook, 277
Bloom, Rube, 383
"Blow, Gabriel, Blow," 104
"Blue and the Gray, The," 58
Blue Five, 506, 510
"Blue Rag in 12 Keys," 391
"Blue Suede Shoes," 362
Blues and Gospel Records, 214, 324
Blues Foundation, 434
"Blues in My Heart," 387
Blues music, 7, 136, 140, 168, 211, 231, 281, 464, 516–17, 523; shouters, 137, 140, 374. *See also specific artists; specific songs*
"Blues My Naughty Sweetie Gives to Me," 405
Blues Revisited (LP), 433–34
"Bluin' the Blues," 346, 353, 354
Blumenberg, Milton W., 242
Blyden-Taylor, Brainerd, 492
BMG label (successor to Berliner and Victor), 10
Boardinghouses, for blacks, 102, 341
Boardman, Reginald, 450, 451
Boatner, Adelaide (daughter), 472
Boatner, Adelaide (wife), 472
Boatner, Claudine Wicks, 471
Boatner, Clifford, 472
Boatner, Dr. Daniel Webster, 470
Boatner, Edward Hammond, 467, 468, 470–72, 481–82, 485; *30 Afro-American Choral Spirituals,* 472; *The Story of the Spirituals: 30 Spirituals and Their Origins,* 472; Studio, 472
Boatner, Edward, Jr., 471

Boatner, Julia, 472
Boatner, Sarah, 472
"Bode of Education" (sketch), 102
Bohee Brothers (James and George), 6
"Bohunkus and Josephus," 231
Bolcom, William, 291, 392
Bolden, Buddy, 83, 514, 525, 539 n. 1
"Boll Weevil Blues," 375
Boloña, Alfredo, 527
Bolton, Dorothy S., *Old Song Hymnal,* 484
"Bon Bon Buddy," 121
"Bonnie Blue Flag, The," 219, 222, 224, 228
Bononcini, Giovanni, 450
Bontemps, Arna, 567 n. 1
"Boogie Rag," 342, 351
Booker, Col. Tom, 229
Booking agencies, 63, 301
Boone, Blind, 522, 576 n. 2
Boone, Harvey, 388
"Bootleggers' Ball," 506
Borbee's Jass Orchestra, 346
Bordman, Gerald, 138
Bori, Lucrezia, 477
"Borrow from Me," 126
Bostic, Arthur, *212*
Boston, 237, 273, 439, shows in, 108, 112, 151, 221, 286, 438, 455, 493
Boston Conservatory of Music, 471
Boston Ideal Opera Company, 520
Boston Pops Orchestra, 482
Boston Symphony Orchestra, 444, 448, 449, 465
Boston University, 452
Boulanger, Nadia, 491
"Boulanger's Patrol," 26
"Boulevard of Broken Dreams," 362
Bourdon, Rosario, 490
Bowles, Fred G., 482
Bowman, Elias, 277
Bowman, Elmer, 357
Bowman, Euday, 347
Bowser, Henry, 343, 344, 345, 347
Boyd, Carroll, 333
Boyd, Charles W., 564 n. 4
Boyd, Julian P., 71
Boyle, William, 46, 48, 55
Bradford, Perry, 290, 374, 397
Bradley, Will, 299
Brady, Pat, monologues, 87
Brahms, Johannes, 490
Braslau, Sophia, 480
Brazil, 529
"Breakdown Blues," 350, 351
Breckenridge, John C., 22
"Bregeiro (Rio Brazilian Maxixe)," 304, 306
Brennan, William, 449
Brice, Fanny, 123, 131, 132, 332, 399
Briegel, George F., 347

Butterfield, Erskine, 388
"By the Waters of Minnetonka," 170
"Bye and Bye" / "By an' By," 209, 445, 449, 480, 481, 485
Byrd, Charlie, 434

Cabrera, Felipe Neri, 527
Cabin in the Sky, 409
Cadman, Charles Wakefield, 479
Café de Paris, 360, 361
Cahill, Marie, 118, 510
Cairo, Egypt, music from, 524
Cakewalks, 43, 93, 94, 106, 107, 108, 113, 240, 273
Caldwell, Edward, 458, 459
Calhoun, Arthur, 437
California Jubilee Singers, 453
California Ramblers, 408
Call-and-response, 78, 79, 97, 99, 156, 196, 231, 283, 323, 456
"Calliope Yodel, A," 460
Calloway, Cab, 434
Calypso, 526, 528
Camden, N.J., recording in, 323
Cameron-Falconet, Mrs., 246, 247, 252
"Camp Meeting," 258
"Camp Meeting Blues," 405
Camp Mills, Long Island, 278
Camp Whitman, Poughkeepsie, N.Y., 278, 369
"Camp-Ground Jubilee," 77
Campbell, Albert, *61*, 511; and Henry Burr, 341
Campbell, Edgar, 271, 400, 401
"Can't You Heah Me Callin' Caroline," 367
Canada, 302; Jack Johnson in, 247; tours in, 328, 371, 411, 440
Canadian Jubilee Singers, 327, 328, 560 n. 2
Canario, 528
Canciones Escolares, 528
Cannibal King, The, 294
Cannon's Jug Stompers, 517
Cannon, Gus "Banjo Joe," 516–17
Cantor, Eddie, 135, 137, 138, 142, 283, 306, 332, 366, 381, 399; *As I Remember Them*, 132
"Careless Love," 426, 430
Carnegie, Andrew, 322
Carnegie Hall, 275, 291, 294, 326; concerts at, 191, 257, 270, 409, 430, 431, 440, 449, 451, 452, 464, 465, 496, 506
Carnes, Fred G., 104; *Songs of the Kentucky Jubilee Singers*, 103
Carolina Jubilee Singers, 103
Carpenter, Elliot, 359, 360, 362, 368
Carpenter, Judge George A., 251
Carpenter, Thelma, 391
Carr, Robert, 573 n. 8

Carranza, Pres. Venustiano, 250
Carroll, William, 400
"Carry Me Back," 94
"Carry Me Back to Old Virginny," 215, 219
"Carry Me Back to Tennessee," ("Ellie Rhee"), 165, 172
Carson ("Cayson"), J., 79
Carson, Billy, 78
Carson, Fiddlin' John, 524
Carson, J. E., 76
Carter, Benny, 299, 387
Carter, Katie, 94
Carter, Lawrence T., 393
Caruso, Enrico, 8, 138, 169, 171, 437, 441, 444–45
Carver, George Washington, 322, 325
"Carving the Duck," 60
Case, Catherine (Kate) Martin, 173, 174, 190
Case, Charles M. (Charley), 3, 66, 172–91, *179, 181, 186;* death of, 187–88
Case, Charley, Jr., 174, 191
Case, Charlotte Bush, 174, 188
Case, Florence, 191
Case, Moses, 173, 174, 190
Case, William B., 174, 191
Case, William M., 191
"Casey at the Bat," 180
Casino Girl, The, 293
Casino Theatre, New York, 257, 293
Castillo, Guillermo, 527
Castle, Vernon and Irene, 4, 7, 270–71, 272, 273, 274, 275, 277, 288, 302, 303, 304, 320, 395, 397, 398, 403, 409, 414, 529
"Castle Doggy, The," 398
Castle House Orchestra, 273
"Castle House Rag," 272, 274
"Castle Polka," 273
"Castle Walk," 272, 273, 274, 398
"Castle's Lame Duck," 272, 276, 398
"Castles in Europe, The," 272
Castles in the Air Band, 277
Catlett, Big Sid, 431
Cato, Minto, 387
CBS radio, Sissle on, 386
CDs, 9, 10
Central America, recording in, 524
Century Girl, The, 341
Chaflin University Quartette, 453
Chalmers, Donald, 70
Chanson, 450
Chantecler, 123
Chappelle, Pat, Rabbit Foot Company, 81
"Characteristic Blues," 389
"Characteristic Negro Medley, A," 195
"Charity ob de Heart," 87
Charleston, S.C., 443
"Charleston, The," 299, 380, 385
"Charleston Rag," 364, 370, 378, 391

Fletcher, Tom, 302, 337, 339–40, 354; *One Hundred Years of the Negro in Show Business,* 300
Florence, Ala., 410, 434
Florence District School for Negroes, 410
Flores, Pedro, 528
Florida Blossom company, 518
"Florida Blues," 351, 405
Florodora, 8
Flowers, Madam ("The Bronze Melba"), 300
Foley, Red, 146
Folies Bergère, 247, 386
Folk music, 448, 517, 523; Louisiana Creole, 451
Folk Songs of the American Negro, 195
Folkways, 71, 214, 517
Follow Me, 510
"Follow Me," 491
"For All Eternity," 169
For His Mother's Sake, 251
Forepaugh and Sells' Brothers Circus, 337
Fort Dix, N.J., 369
Fort Sumter, S.C., 22, 217
Fort Worth, Tex., 277
Forza del Destino, 445
Foster, Lemuel L., 202, 204
Foster, Pops, 431
Foster, Stephen C., 28, 151, 159, 164, 165, 167, 197, 219, 330, 459, 476, 483
Foster, William, 131
Four Harmony Kings, 7, 284, 287, 290, 291, 452–63, *454,* 486
Four Hundred, 275
4th French Army, 278
"Fourth of July in Jimtown," 393
Fox, Eddie, 43, 146
Fox film company, 102
Fox Movietone short film, 459
Fox trot, 273, 277, 290, 350, 398, 399, 414, 518
"Fox Trot," 274, 289
"Foxy Cure for the Blues, A," 405
Francis, Panama, 391
Frankel, Abe, 368
Franklin, Malvin, 436
Franko, Nathan, Orchestra, 400
Frazer, Johnella, 204
Frazier, Dr., Medicine Show, 364
"Freedom Suite," 472
Freeman (Indianapolis), 66, 82, 90, 98, 101, 103, 120, 148, 155, 195, 207, 240, 268, 355, 412, 421, 473, 476, 493, 499, 500, 501, 505, 507, 508, 521
Freiberg, Mr., 210
Friar's Society Orchestra, 407
Friend, Emanuel M., 49, 50
Friml, Rudolf, 379, 405

"Frisco," 399
Frisco Jass Band, 280, 346
"Frisco's Kitchen Stove Rag (Get the Wood, Burn It Up)," 405
Frogs theatrical club, 121, 128, 268, 269, 329, 351; *Frog Frolics,* 270
"From Symphony to Swing," 484
Fugitive Slave Act, 20
Fuller, Earl, 280, 346, 348, 423, 424; Famous Jazz Band, 436
Funk, Ray, 462
Futurist Jazz Band, 436
"Fuzzy Wuzzy Rag," 419, 568 n. 20

"Gabie," 82
"Gabriel's Trumpet," 157
Gaisberg, Fred, 62, 70; *The Music Goes Round,* 16
Galerie Charles, III, 307
Galuppi, Baldassare, 450
Galveston, Tex., 237
Gans, Joe, 364, 397
Garay, Sindo, 527
Gardel, Carlos, 524
Garden Theatre, Madison Square Garden, 356
Gardenia Quintette, 329–30
Gardner, George R., 453
Garfield, Pres. James A., 36
Garnes, Antoinette, 487
Garrick Theatre, 357
Garrison, Mabel, 207, 367, 482
Gaskin, George J., 66
Gavotte, 273
"Gay Night in Paris, A," 361
"Gee, I Wish I Had Someone to Rock Me in the Cradle of Love," 372, 392
"Gee, I'm Glad That I'm from Dixie," 371, 372
Gee, Lottie, 377, 396, 455, 457
Geelong, tours in, 459
Gennett label, 204, 209, 349, 443, 462, 466, 481, 486, 521
"Gentle Annie," 165, 166
George V, 298, 448
George White's Scandals, 299, 380, 429
"Georgia Grind, The," 401
Georgia Minstrels, 78, 412
Georgia Phonograph Company, 84
Georgians, 427, 428
"German Medley," 519
"Get It Now," 350
"Get Up," 137, 139, 143
"Ghost of a Coon, The," 108
Gibbs, L., 282
Gideon, Melville, 313
Gilder, Jeanette, 302–3, 319
Gillespie, Dizzy, 434

Gillett, Gov. James N., 241
Gilman, Benjamin Ives, 524
Gilmore, Buddy, 150, 270, 271, 272, 277,
    290, 306, 368
Gilmore, Patrick S., 193
Gilpin, Charles, 140
Gilson, Lottie, 107
Gilt-Edge Four, 436
"Give Me a Night in June," 383
"Give Me Jesus," 471
"Give Way Jordan," 211
Glees, 75
Glen, Katherine A., 444
Glenmore, 18, 20, 24, 69
Glover, J. R., 101
Gluck, Alma, 480
"Go Down Moses," 193, 194, 323, 324, 372,
    429, 449, 467, 471, 480, 481, 482, 485,
    513, 550 n. 49
"Go Tell All the Coons I'm Gone," 219
Goat Alley, 266, 267
Gobel, George, 191
Goddard, Chris, 354; *Jazz Away from Home,*
    359
Godínez, Carlos, 527
Godoy, Señorita Maria, *61*
"Goin' Home," 483
"Goin' to Shout All Over God's Heaven,"
    202, 203, 205, 209, 210, 211, 213, 258,
    283, 325, 327, 386
"Going Back to Ole Virginny," 219
"Going Home," 362
Going Up, 315
Gold Bug, The, 106
Goldberg, Isaac, *Tin Pan Alley,* 430, 434
Golden, Billy, and Joe Hughes, 184
Golden Gate Quartet, 213
"Golden Slippers," 196
Goldfield Hotel, 364, 397
Goldwyn film company, 102
"Gonna Walk All Over God's Heaven,"
    460
González, Félix, 525, 526
"Good Bye, Liza Jane," 43, 536 n. 38
"Good Bye, Susan Jane," 89
"Good Man Is Hard to Find, A," 346–47,
    353, 422
"Good Morning, Carrie," 111, 565 n. 35
"Good Morning, Mr. Zip-Zip-Zip!," 404
"Good News, the Chariot's Coming," 203,
    323, 326
"Good News," 384
"Good Night, Angeline," 366, 372, 392,
    456, 531 n. 2
"Good Ole Georgie" ("Good Old Georgia"),
    151
Good Time Jazz label, 506
"Good-Bye (Addio)," 138

"Goodbye Alexander," 344, 345, 353
"Goodbye, Ragtime," 355
Goodman, Benny, 299, 351, 483, 511; Quar-
    tet, 409; *The Benny Goodman Story,* 409
"Goodnight, My Love," 383
Goose Creek, Va., 19
Gorman, J. W., Alabama Troubadours, 300
Gorman, Ross, 428
Gospel music, 463
"Got 'Em Blues," 350
"Got the Bench, Got the Park," 386
Gotham Music Company (later Gotham-
    Attucks), 294
Graden, Farley B., 458
Grady, Lottie, 131
Grafton Galleries, 312
Graham, George, 520
Graham, J. H., 538 n. 1
Grainger, Percy, 490
Grainger, Porter, 252
Grammy award, 392, 393
Gramophone and Typewriter Company,
    113
Gramophone label, 62, 361, 362
Gramophone, 206
Grand English Opera Company, 520
Grand Marches, 273
Grand Opera House: Boston, 265; New
    York, 32
Grand Rapids, Mich., 255
Grand Theater, Chicago, 338
Granstaff, Earl, 358, 360
Grant, Gen. Ulysses S., 23
Grape Lawn, Va., 216
Grappelly, Stephane, 299
Graves, Henry, 417
Graves, Randall, 222, 223
Gray, Gilda, 423
Gray, James, 538 n. 1
Graziano, John, 408
"Great Camp Meetin' Day," 374, 385
"Great Camp Meeting," 200, 205, 211
Great Day, 299
"Great Day," 299
Greek music, 524
Green, Eddie, 346, 422
Green, George Hamilton, 423, 424
Green, Jeffrey, 300
Green, Marion, 480, 485
Green, Silas, company, 518
Green Pastures, 159
Greenbaugh and Mallory Brothers Min-
    strels, 500
Greenfield, Elizabeth Taylor (the Black
    Swan), 168, 192
Greer, Sonny, 349
Grey Gull label, 350, 427, 457
"Grey Wolf, The," 476

Griot, 526
Grofe, Ferdie, 426
Grupo Bahianinho, 529
Grupo Chiquinha Gonzaga, 529
Grupo Honorio, 529
Grupo Larangeira, 529
Grupo Luiz de Souza, 529
Grupo Lulu Cavaquinho, 529
Guarente, Frank, 428
Guarini, W., 61
"Guiding Me Back Home," 384
"Gulf Coast Blues," 428
Gushee, Lawrence, 282
Guy and Rex, 158
"Gwine Back to Dixie," 219
"Gypsy Blues," 377, 379, 381, 393, 394, 395

Hackett, Charles, 565 n. 24
Hackley, Edwin, 161
Hackley, Mme. E. Azalia, 161, 489, 492, 493
Hager, Fred, 61, 427
"Hail Jerusalem," 195
"Hail to the Spirit of Freedom March," 417
Hailstock, Frank M., Jr., 500
Hairston, Jester, 291
Haiti, 395–96
Half and Half, 273
Hall, Edmond, 431, 432
Hall, George, Orchestra with Dolly Dawn, 409
Hall Johnson Choir, 429–30
Hall Phonographic Co., 500
"Hallelujah to the Lamb," 195, 372
Hallett, Mays and Hunter, 63
Hallett, Wilson, 63
"Hambone Medley," 80
Hamilton, Ontario, 158, 327
Hammerstein circuit, 340
Hammerstein's Victoria Theatre (New York), 115, 125, 189, 275, 341
Hammond Music Co., 472
Hammond, John, 391
Hampton Institute, 161, 209, 257, 320, 440, 465, 489, 496, 501, 513–14; Choir, 491; Hampton Colored Students, 103; Quartet, 514; Singers, 194
Hampton Series Negro Folk-Songs, 513
Hampton, Pete, 7
Hanby, B. R., 163
"Hand Down That Robe," 77
"Hand of Fate, The," 63
Handy, Charles, 410, 421
Handy, Elizabeth Price, 412, 432
Handy, Irma Louise Logan, 434
Handy, Lucille, 427, 429
Handy, W. C. (William Christopher), 3, 4, 7, 277, 281, 284, 290, 291–92, 315, 337, 342, 351, 375, 387, 390, 409, 410–36, 411,

433, 484, 500; Blues: An Anthology, 429; death of, 434; Father of the Blues, 410, 432; first recording, 412; Memphis Orchestra, 346; Music Festival, 434; Negro Authors and Composers of the United States, 430; Treasury of Blues, 432; Unsung Americans Sung, 432; W. C. Handy's Collection of Negro Spirituals, 430
Handy, William Wise, 410
Handy Brothers' Music, 425
Handy Record Company, 427
Handy's Orchestra of Memphis, 417, 436
Handy's Saxophone Band, 419
Hann, Mrs. W. A., 453
Hann, William A., 453, 455, 456, 457, 458, 459, 462, 486
Hanna, Mark, 230
Hann's Emperors of Harmony, 458
Hann's Emperors of Song, 458, 459
Hann's Jubilee Singers, 365, 453, 455, 486
"Hans and Gretchen," 63
"Happy Coon," 538 n. 31
Happy Six Orchestra, 394
"Happy Whistling Coon," 534 n. 3
Harbach, Otto, and Rudolf Friml, 311
"Hard Times," 130
Hardwicke, Toby, 349
Hare, Ernest, 435
Harkins and Barbour, 151
Harlan, Byron G., 61, 164, 415; and Frank C. Stanley, 184
Harlem Is Heaven, 387
Harmony label, 166, 214
Harney, Ben, 147
Harpers Ferry, W.Va., 21, 23
Harper's Weekly, 261
Harreld, Kemper, 487
Harrigan's Park Theatre, 32
Harrington, Ham Tree, 145
Harris, Charles, 417
Harris, J. Everett, 202, 204
Harris, Joel Chandler (Uncle Remus), 219, 221
Harris, Marion, 378, 394, 424, 435, 511
Harris, Phil, 146
Harris, Sheldon, 517
Harrison, Charles, 395, 477, 485
Harrison, Fox, and Thacker, The Essential Jazz Records: Ragtime to Swing, 353
Harrison, Hazel, 326, 441
Harrison, James F., and Harry Anthony, 255
Harrison, Pres. Benjamin, 25, 267
Harrison, Richard B., 161
Hart, Annie, 107
Hart, Lorenz, 382
Hartford, Conn., 395
Hartsdale Restaurant, Hartsdale, N.Y., 362

Koster and Bial's, 106, 107
Krehbiel, Henry, 425, 482; *Afro-American Folksongs,* 479
Kreisler, Fritz, 495
Krueger, Bennie, Orchestra, 394
Ku Klux Klan, 24
Kubelik, Jan, 493
Kunstadt, Len, 347, 351, 516, 519
Kwakiutl music, 524

La Musique, 210
La Redd, Cora, 388
La Rue, Grace, 477
Labels, and copyright law, 10. *See also specific labels*
Ladd's Black Aces, 394
Ladnier, Tommy, 386
Lafayette Theatre, Harlem, 172, 265, 266, 349, 355
Laine, Frankie, 409
Lakme, 487
Lambert label, 114
Lambs theatrical club, 121, 268
"Lament," 494
Lamour, Dorothy, 431
Lampkins, Oswald, *212*
Lanchmere, Lo La, 95
Lane College, Jackson, Tenn., 488
Lanin's Southern Serenaders, 394
Lardner, Ring, 132
Larkins, Jolly John, 150, 267
Larsen, Jens, 63
Lasky film company, 102
"Lassus Trombone," 405
"Last Farewell, The," 77
"Last Rose of Summer, The," 487
Lateral-cut format, 200, 203, 290, 342, 403, 406, 443, 455, 466, 509
Latin America, 339
Lattimore, George W., 297, 298
Lauder, Harry, 209
"Laughing Coon, The," 43; by Cal Stewart, 60
"Laughing Darkey, The," 36
Laughing Husband, The, 272
"Laughing Medley, The," 59
"Laughing Policeman, The," 71
"Laughing Song" (Polk Miller), 223, 228, 231
"Laughing Song, The" (George W. Johnson), 8, 17, 30, 31, 32, 33, 34, 35, 36, 38, 39, 40, 41, 45, 58, 59, 62, 63, 64, 65, 66, 71; by Cal Stewart, 60
"Laughs You Have Met," 63
Laurie, Joe, Jr., 430; *Vaudeville,* 190, 191
Lawrence, William, 440
Layton, Turner, 134, 207, 343, 344, 402, 483, 510–11

Le Coq Rouge, New York, 333
"Lead Pipe Blues," 350
Leavenworth penitentiary, Kansas, 251
Lee, Ann, 24
Lee, Col. Robert E., 22
Lee, Mabel, 389
Lee, Matthew, 24
Lee, Nappy, 399, 401
Lee, T., 282
"Lee Family, The," 131
Leeds Orchestra, 541 n. 4
Leesburg, Va., *16*, 21, 69
Lehmann, Lotte, 451
Lemaire, George, 135, 137, 138
Lemonier, Tom, 510
Lenzberg, Julius, Harmonists, 394
León, Bienvenido, 527
Leonard, Eddie, 185
Leonard, Larry. *See* Spencer, Len
Leoncavallo, Ruggiero, 444
LeRoy, New York, 173
Les Ambassadeurs, Paris, 384, 385
Les Ambassadeurs Orchestra, 385
Leslie, Amy, 177
Leslie, Lew, 145, 386, 387, 407, 429; *Blackbirds,* 387, 407, 429, 513; *Plantation Revue,* 513
"Let It Alone," 115, 118, 119
"Let Me Shine," 450
"Let Us Cheer the Weary Traveler," 429
"Let's Go Down in Jordan," 462
Levy, Rafael González, 528
Lewis, Katherine Handy, 427, 429, 433
Lewis, Ted, 375, 423, 426, 428
Liebling, Emil, 255
"Life," 475
"Life of Christ, The," 472
Lightfoot, James Escort, 120, 158, 159, 327–30, 332
Lightfoot, Mrs. A. A., 328
Lightfoot, Mrs. E., 328
"Lilly Dale," 165
Lincoln, Abraham, 22, 217
Lincoln Institute, Jefferson, Mo., 488
"Lincoln's Speech at Gettysburg," 63
"Lindy," 554 n. 2
Lipp, L. W., *61*
Lipskin, Mike, 392
"Listen to the Lambs," 489, 513
"Listen to the Mocking Bird," 27, 85
Literary League of Greater New York, 166
"Lit'l Boy," 451, 452
"Little Alabama Coon," 367
"Little Annie Rooney," 27
"Little Bit o' Honey, A," 367, 369
"Little Black Lamb," 164
"Little Brown Jug," 43
"Little Christmas Basket," 263

"Little David Play on Your Harp," 196, 199, 200, 203, 205, 209, 213, 258, 283, 371, 439, 460
"Little Girl," 387
"Little Log Cabin in de Lane," 219
Little Milton, 434
"Little Mother of Mine," 476, 478, 485
"Little Old Log Cabin in De Lane." *See* "De Little Old Log Cabin in De Lane"
Little Wonder label, 59, 343–44, 346, 347
"Live a-Humble," 323, 326
Liverpool, Lethia, 82
"Livery Stable Blues," 419, 420
Locke, Alain, *The Negro and His Music,* 409
Lockport, N.Y., 173, 177, 178, 190; *Daily Journal,* 175, 178
Loguen, Elizabeth, 333
Loguen, James W., 329, 332, 333
Lomax, Alan, 430
London, 185–87, 246, 250, 255, 307
London, Jack, 239, 240
London Calling, 380
London Orchestra, 341
London Times, 308, 313, 318
"Lonesome Alimony Blues," 143
"Lonesome Blues," 405
"Lonesome Road," 347
"Lonesome Weary Blues," 419
Long, Avon, 146, 391
"Long Ago Lullaby," 460
Long Beach Quartette, 301
"Long Gone (from Bowling Green)," 375, 425
Long Island City, N.Y., 231, 266
Long Island National Cemetery, Pinelawn, Long Island, 363
Longly School of Music, Cambridge, Mass., 452
Lopez, Vincent, 207; Orchestra, 394, 550 n. 49
Lord, Tom, 518
Los Angeles Times, 487
Los Angeles Tribune, 453
Lotz, Rainer, *Black People: Entertainers of African Descent in Europe and Germany,* 7
Loudin, Frederick J., 194
Loudoun County, Va., 17, 18, 20, 23
Louis, Joe, 253
"Louis and Lena at Luna Park," 63
Louisiana Five, 280, 347, 348, 353
Louisiana Phonograph and Kinetoscope Agency, 90
Louisiana Phonograph Company (New Orleans), 6, 58, 83, 84, 86, 87–88, 515
Louisville, Ky., 97, 329
"Louisville Blues," 428
Love o' Mike, 343

"Love Will Find a Way," 366, 377, 378, 391, 393, 394, 395, 455, 531 n. 2
Love's Law, 319
"Love's Old Sweet Song," 96, 456
"Loveless Love," 375, 386, 388, 425, 427, 432
Lovell, John, 327
"Lovely to Look At," 362, 463
Lovey's Band, 528
"Low Down Blues," 375
Lowe, Allen, 354
Lowery, P. G., Band, 337, 354
Lowry, Vance, 307, 309, 310, 314, 316, 416
Lozier, Burt, 79
Lu Lu Fado (dance), 273, 414
Lucas, Sam, 300, 330
Lucia Sextette, 328
"Lucille," 347, 353
Lucky Coon, A, 108, 293
Ludlow, Lucy, 317
"Lullaby from *Jocelyn,*" 332
Lundu, 529
Lyles, Aubrey, 355, 376, 408. *See also* Miller, Flournoy, and Aubrey Lyles
Lynas, Joe, 277
Lynching, 132, 412
Lyons, Bob, 515
Lyric label, 415, 425, 480
Lyric Theater, Philadelphia, 304

"Ma Curly Headed Baby," 168
"Ma! (He's Making Eyes at Me)," 379
MacDonald, Edith, 477
Macdonough, Harry, *61,* 324
MacDowell, Edward, 479
Machaut, Guillaume de, 452
Mack, Cecil. *See* McPherson, R. C.
Mack, Charles E. *See* Moran, George, and Charles Mack
Mackenzie, Tandy, 565 n. 24
MacNeal, James, 515–16
Macon, Uncle Dave, 222
Macon County, Ala., 320
Madiera, A. D., *61*
Madison, Bingie, 431
Madison Square Garden, 218, 337
Magley, Irene, 315
"Magnolia," 488
Magnolia Blossoms, 212–13
"Magnolia Tree, The," 6
Mahara, W. A., 411; Mammoth Colored Minstrels, 102, 337, 411, 412, 500
Mahoney, Jere, *61*
"Maid of the Mill," 77
Mainer, J. E., 146
Majestic Theatre, New York, 115, 117
Majestic Dance Orchestra, 394

New Amsterdam Musical Association, 269

New Amsterdam Theatre, New York, 132, 398, 399, 400, roof garden, 403, 404

New England, tours in, 459

New England Conservatory of Music, 392, 503

New Jersey Phonograph Company, 26, 27, 29, 30, 31, 33, 34, 35, 36, 39, 40; recording for, 78. *See also* U.S. Phonograph Company

New Jubilee Songs as Sung by the Fisk Jubilee Singers, 195

"New Laughing Song, or 'So Do I,' The," 41

New Orleans, 241, 343, 353. *See also* Louisiana Phonograph Company; Vasnier, Louis "Bebe"

New Orleans Feetwarmers, 389

New Orleans Jazz and Heritage Festival, 393

New Orleans Jazz Band, 436

New Orleans Jubilee Singers, 100

New Orleans Minstrels, 82

New Orleans Rhythm Kings, 407

"New St. Louis Blues, The," 430

"New World" Symphony, 467, 473, 474, 483, 491

New York Age, 67, 120, 161, 164, 188–89, 204, 207, 230, 242, 244, 246, 257, 261, 265, 269, 274, 275, 277, 294, 297, 301, 302, 305, 306, 308, 329, 331, 332, 355, 358, 397, 398, 399, 454, 464, 489, 505

New York American, 188, 240, 377

New York Choral Ensemble, 433

New York Clipper, 75, 76

New York Colored Theatrical Club, 78, 98

New York Cylinders, 40, 78

New York Dramatic Mirror, 219

New York Evening Telegram, 49

New York Herald, 49, 57, 123

New York Journal, 49

New York Phonograph Company, 30, 31, 32, 33, 35, 75–76, 92, 93; bankruptcy, 33; recording for, 148, 519

New York Post, 126, 275

New York Sun, 48, 49, 57, 284

New York Syncopated Orchestra, 297, 298

New York Telegraph, 188, 265

New York Times, 49, 57, 142, 242, 289, 295, 299, 319, 333, 351, 408, 409, 451

New York Tribune, 49, 191, 276, 356

New York University, 390

New York World, 49, 57, 126

New York World's Fair, 430

New Zealand, 329

Newburger, Judge Joseph E., 15, 49, 53, 55, 56, 57

Newcastle, tours in, 459

"Newest St. Louis Blues," 430

Newport, R.I., 270, 408

Newsome, Billy. *See* Clark, Carroll

Newsweek, 392

Newton, Marguerite, *61*

Niagara County, N.Y., 174

Niagara Falls, N.Y., 488

Niagara Movement, 503

Nicaragua, 339

Nicholas Brothers, 387

Nichols, Red, Orchestra, 409

Nielsen, Alice, 480

"Night Alarm, The," 41

"Night in Tangoland, A" (show), 398

Niles, Edward Abbe, 429

"Ninety Days from Broadway" (sketch), 138

"Ninety-nine bottles of beer on the wall," 137

Ninth Volunteer Infantry Immunes Band, 515–16

Niscan (or Nixon), James, 17, 18

"No Hiding Place Down Here," 231

"No Place Like Home," 132

No, No, Nanette, 458

"Nobody," 66, 111, 117, 122, 124, 129, 135, 136, 138, 142, 143–44, 145, 146; by Arthur Collins, 542 n. 21; lyrics, 116; recording of, 115, 117, 119, 127, 128. *See also* Williams, Bert

Nobody Home, 401

"Nobody Knows de Trouble I See," 170, 294, 325, 480, 483, 485, 486, 495, 550 n. 49

"Nobody Never Let Me in on Nothin'," 145

"Nobody's Sweetheart," 387

Noll, Albert, 161

Nora Bayes Theatre, New York, 297

Norfolk Jubilee Quartet, 209

Normal, Ala., 412

Norris, Josephine, 150

North American Phonograph Company, 26, 30, 32, 35, 76, 83, 85; bankruptcy, 90; collapse of, 39; and phonograph as toy, 84

Norton, George A., 414

Norworth, Jack, 373

"Not Lately," 141, 142, 143

Novelty Five, 424, 436

"Now Take Thy Rest," 289

Nugent, Richard Henri, 297

"O Death Where Is Thy Sting?," 133, 136, 145, 422

"O Lord What a Morning," 171

"O Perfect Love," 476

"O Promise Me," 98

"O, Sing a New Song," 390

Oak and Ivy, 261

O'Bannon, Horatio, 209

Oberlin College, 438

Rogers, Will, 132, 172, 191, 399
Rogers' Band, 436
"Roll, Jordan, Roll," 104, 193, 194, 197, 208, 211, 283, 324, 327, 439
"Rolling and Rocker Dem in His Arms," 460
Romeu, Antonio María, 526
"Rondo Capriccioso," 294
Rooftop Singers, 517
Rooney, Andy, 1
"Roosevelt Triumphal March," 413
Roosevelt, Pres. Franklin D., 326, 491
Roosevelt, Pres. Theodore, 322, 413, 502
"Rosary, The," 340
Rose, Al, 372, 393, 432
Rose, Billy, Diamond Horseshoe Club, 389, 432
Ross, Allie, 399, 400, 401; Orchestra, 172
Rose Marie, 458
Rothafel, Samuel "Roxy," 326
"Roun' 'Bout de Mountain," 451
"Row at a Negro Ball," 499
Rowland, Adele, 436
Roxbury, Mass., 447
Roy, Harry, 351
Royal Air Corps, 277
Royal Court Orchestra, 394
"Royal Garden Blues," 375, 510
Roycroft, Gruen, 490
Roycroft, recording for, 490
"Run, Nigger, Run," 219
"Runnin' Down the Title Holder," 251
Runnin' Wild, 380
Rusco and Holland's Big Minstrel Festival, 81, 328
Russell, Elizabeth, 473
Russell, Luis, 431, 432
Russell, Sylvester, 66, 82, 155, 294, 436
Russia, 247, 250, 449
"Russian Love Song," 101
"Russian Rag," 282, 284
Rust, Brian, 316, 401, 518
Rutgers University, 392
Ryder, Noah, *196,* 198
Rye, Howard, 312, 313, 318

"S'posin'," 387
Sag Harbor, Long Island, N.Y., 258
Salgado, Miguel Puertas, 527
Salles Gaveua, 450
"Sally Trombone," 402
Salomon, Sid, Jr., 434
Salvain, Sam, 188
Salzburg Cathedral, 491
"Sambo's Banjo," 408
"Samuel," 130
Samuel Houston College, 472
San Francisco, 103, 105, 241; World's Fair, 430, 453

Sannella, Andy, 383
Sapphire ball styli, 343, 367
"Sarah from Sahara," 368, 369
Saturday Review, 514
Saulles, Bianca de, 319
Saulles, Jack de, 319
Saunders, Gertrude, 377, 393, 394
"Save a Little Dram for Me," 137, 138, 143, 145
Savino, Dominic, 284
Savoy Ballroom, New York, 361
Sawyer, Alvah, 302
Sawyer, Joan, 4, 7, 273, 274, 299–320, *303,* 319–20; Persian Garden Orchestra, 274, 299, 319–20. *See also* Kildare, Dan
"Say Bo, Give Me Them Two Bits," 96
"Scandalize My Name," 202
Scanlan, William J., 89
"Scene in Reno, A" (sketch), 123, 246
Schillinger system of composition, 390
Schirmer, S., Inc., 484
Schoebel, Elmer, 407
Scholl, Nick, *61*
Schomburg Center, New York, 363, 472
Schottisches, 87, 273, 529
Schreiber, Belle, 239, 240, 246
Schubert, Franz, 451; *Lieder,* 441
Schubert label, 519
Schumann-Heink, Ernestine, 476
Scotland, tours in, 382
Scott Joplin, 392
Scott, Oliver, Colored Minstrels, 500
Scott, Rufus L., 92, 94, 98, 101
Scotti, Antonio, 445
Scranton, Pa., 66
"Scratchin' the Ground," 419
Seagle, Oscar, 207, 480, 485
Seals, Baby, 415
Sears, Roebuck, 166
Seconds Out, 247, 250
Segregation, 2, 88, 268
Segurola, Andres de, 477
Selig, William, 132
Selig film company, 241
"Selika," 103
Selika, Marie, 103
Sellers, H. Lee, 83, 84–85
Sellers, Robert H., 83, 84, 90
Selvin, Ben, 349; Novelty Orchestra, 394, 435
Selznick film company, 102
Sembrich, Marcella, 207, 480
"Semper Fidelis," 391
Senegambian Carnival, A, 108, 293, 475, 574 n. 6. *See also* Walker, George; Williams, Bert; Williams and Walker
Senter, Boyd, 409
"Serenade" (Schubert), 417

Waltzes, 87, 273, 306, 399, 414, 514, 529
Wanamaker, John, Jr., 289
Wanamakers, 267; Auditorium, 458
Wand, Hart A., 415
Ward and West Minstrels, 175
Warfield, William, 291
Waring, Fred, Pennsylvanians, 213
Waring, Tom, 382, 383
Warlop, Michel, 361
Warner Brothers Records, 392
"Warning to Boys, A," 176–77, 186, 191
"Warning to Girls, A," 176–77, 191
Warren, Harry, 462
Washington, Booker T., 7, 123, 150, 239, 260, 291, 320–22, 323, 324, 440, 464, 469, 476, 479, 501–4; death of, 325
Washington, D.C., 22, 23, 100, 267, 277, 292, 395, 446
Washington, E. Davidson, 503
Washington Conservatory of Music, 294, 493
"Washington Post March," 27
Washingtonian (Leesburg, Va.,), 19
Washington's Metropolitan A.M.E. Church, 294
Watch Your Step, 277
"Watcha Gonna Do?", 351
Waterford, Va., 21, 23
"Watermelon Party," 223
"Watermelon Song, The," 221, 231
Waters, Ethel, 171, 298, 387, 407; and Her Singing Orchestra, 298
Waters, Hamilton, 473
Watson, George P., 58, 61
Watters, George, 301, 307, 309
Watts, Usher, 360
"Way Down South Where the Blues Begin," 432
"Way Down Yonder in New Orleans," 511, 569 n. 40
"Way Down Yonder in the Cornfield," 99
Wayburn, Ned, 399
Weary Blues, The (play), 434
Weaver, A. C., 33
Weavers, the, 191
Webb, Chick, 351
Webb, Clifton, 360, 471
Weber, Joe, and Lew Fields, 381
"Wedding and Shimmie and Jazz" ("The Wedding of the Shimmie and Jazz"), 406
Weekly Pelican, 86
Weeks, E., 307
Weeks, Seth, 307, 359
Weems, Ted, 150
Weir, Felix, 288
Weissner, George, 53–54
Welch, Elizabeth, 361
"We'll Anchor Bye-and-Bye," 157

"We'll Cross de Ribber ob Jordan," 103
Wells, H. G., 241
Welte-Mignon Company, Poughkeepsie, N.Y., 274, 398
Wendling, Pete, 357
"Were You There?", 171, 208, 211, 214, 451
Werrenrath, Reinald, 324, 476, 491
Wesley, Charles, 200, 438
West, J., 397
West, Mae, 463
West End, New Orleans resort, 86
West Virginia, 320; State College, 495
Westminster, duke of, 308
"Westwood Bound," 384
"Wha'd Ya Do to Me?", 386
Whallen, John, 93
"What a Time," 222
"What Band Is This?", 458
"What Do You Want to Make Those Eyes at Me For?", 314
"What'cha Gonna Do When There Ain't No Jazz," 487
"What's Worth While Getting," 406
Wheatland, Va., 17, 23
Whelan, Albert, 63
"When Alexander Takes His Ragtime Band to France," 278
"When de Corn Pone's Hot," 231, 263
"When Eliza Rolls Her Eyes," 462
"When I Return," 133, 136
"(When It's) All Going Out and Nothing Coming In," 111, 112, 113, 116
"When Malindy Sings," 197, 202, 208
"When My Baby Smiles," 406
"When My Baby Smiles at Me," 406
"When the Bees Make Honey (Down in Sunny Alabam')," 284
"When the Clock Struck 12," 384
"When the Corn is Waving, Annie Dear," 259, 554 n. 2
"When the First Pickaninny Was Born," 463
"When the Good Lord Makes a Record of a Hero's Deed, He Draws No Color Line," 278
"When the Mists Have Rolled Away," 99
"When the Roll Is Called Up Yonder," 458
"When the Saints Go Marching In," 457, 458
"When Uncle Joe Steps into France," 278
"When You're a Long, Long Way from Home," 306
"Where Did Robinson Crusoe Go with Friday on Saturday Night?", 314
"Where Was Moses When the Light Went Out?", 110
"Whispering," 349
Whistling. *See* Johnson, George W.

TIM BROOKS is an executive in the television industry who leads a double life researching and writing about early recordings. His professional biography can be found in *Who's Who in America*. He is a past president of the Association for Recorded Sound Collections and has contributed to the *ARSC Journal* and other record research publications for more than thirty years. He is the author of *Little Wonder Records: A History and Discography* and coauthor of the four-volume *Columbia Master Book Discography*, both ARSC Award winners, as well as coauthor of the bestselling *Complete Directory to Prime Time Network and Cable TV Shows*, an American Book Award winner that is now in its eighth edition.

DICK SPOTTSWOOD, a freelance author, broadcaster, and record producer, has published articles and reviews in numerous journals, including *Bluegrass Unlimited*. He is the editor and annotator of the fifteen-record set *Folk Music in America*, produced with the Library of Congress, and the author of the seven-volume *Ethnic Music on Records: A Discography of Ethnic Recordings Produced in the United States, 1893–1942*.

"My Song Is My Weapon": People's Songs, American Communism, and the Politics of
   Culture, 1930–50   *Robbie Lieberman*

Chosen Voices: The Story of the American Cantorate   *Mark Slobin*

Theodore Thomas: America's Conductor and Builder of Orchestras, 1835–1905
   Ezra Schabas

"The Whorehouse Bells Were Ringing" and Other Songs Cowboys Sing   *Guy Logsdon*

Crazeology: The Autobiography of a Chicago Jazzman   *Bud Freeman,
   as Told to Robert Wolf*

Discoursing Sweet Music: Brass Bands and Community Life in Turn-of-the-
   Century Pennsylvania   *Kenneth Kreitner*

Mormonism and Music: A History   *Michael Hicks*

Voices of the Jazz Age: Profiles of Eight Vintage Jazzmen   *Chip Deffaa*

Pickin' on Peachtree: A History of Country Music in Atlanta, Georgia
   Wayne W. Daniel

Bitter Music: Collected Journals, Essays, Introductions, and Librettos   *Harry Partch;
   edited by Thomas McGeary*

Ethnic Music on Records: A Discography of Ethnic Recordings Produced in the
   United States, 1893 to 1942   *Richard K. Spottswood*

Downhome Blues Lyrics: An Anthology from the Post-World War II Era
   Jeff Todd Titon

Ellington: The Early Years   *Mark Tucker*

Chicago Soul   *Robert Pruter*

That Half-Barbaric Twang: The Banjo in American Popular Culture   *Karen Linn*

Hot Man: The Life of Art Hodes   *Art Hodes and Chadwick Hansen*

The Erotic Muse: American Bawdy Songs (2d ed.)   *Ed Cray*

Barrio Rhythm: Mexican American Music in Los Angeles   *Steven Loza*

The Creation of Jazz: Music, Race, and Culture in Urban America   *Burton W. Peretti*

Charles Martin Loeffler: A Life Apart in Music   *Ellen Knight*

Club Date Musicians: Playing the New York Party Circuit   *Bruce A. MacLeod*

Opera on the Road: Traveling Opera Troupes in the United States, 1825–60
   Katherine K. Preston

The Stonemans: An Appalachian Family and the Music That Shaped Their Lives
   Ivan M. Tribe

Transforming Tradition: Folk Music Revivals Examined   *Edited by Neil V. Rosenberg*

The Crooked Stovepipe: Athapaskan Fiddle Music and Square Dancing in Northeast
   Alaska and Northwest Canada   *Craig Mishler*

Traveling the High Way Home: Ralph Stanley and the World of Traditional
   Bluegrass Music   *John Wright*

Carl Ruggles: Composer, Painter, and Storyteller   *Marilyn Ziffrin*

Never without a Song: The Years and Songs of Jennie Devlin, 1865–1952
   Katharine D. Newman

The Hank Snow Story   *Hank Snow, with Jack Ownbey and Bob Burris*

Milton Brown and the Founding of Western Swing   *Cary Ginell, with special assistance
   from Roy Lee Brown*

Santiago de Murcia's "Códice Saldívar No. 4": A Treasury of Secular Guitar Music
   from Baroque Mexico   *Craig H. Russell*

The Sound of the Dove: Singing in Appalachian Primitive Baptist Churches
   Beverly Bush Patterson

My Lord, What a Morning: An Autobiography *Marian Anderson*
Marian Anderson: A Singer's Journey *Allan Keiler*
Charles Ives Remembered: An Oral History *Vivian Perlis*
Henry Cowell, Bohemian *Michael Hicks*
Rap Music and Street Consciousness *Cheryl L. Keyes*
Louis Prima *Garry Boulard*
Marian McPartland's Jazz World: All in Good Time *Marian McPartland*
Robert Johnson: Lost and Found *Barry Lee Pearson and Bill McCulloch*
Bound for America: Three British Composers *Nicholas Temperley*
Lost Sounds: Blacks and the Birth of the Recording Industry, 1890–1919 *Tim Brooks*

The University of Illinois Press
is a founding member of the
Association of American University Presses.

Composed in 9/13 ITC Stone Serif
with Gill Sans and ITC Stone Sans display
by Jim Proefrock
at the University of Illinois Press
Designed by Paula Newcomb
Manufactured by Edwards Brothers, Inc.

University of Illinois Press
1325 South Oak Street
Champaign, IL 61820-6903
www.press.uillinois.edu